Transport and Tourism

Themes in Tourism

Series Editor: Professor Stephen J. Page, *Scottish Enterprise Forth Valley Chair in Tourism, Department of Marketing, University of Stirling, Stirling, Scotland FK9 4LA.*

The Themes in Tourism Series is an upper level series of texts written by established academics in the field of tourism studies and provides a comprehensive introduction to each area of study. The series develops both theoretical and conceptual issues and a range of case studies to illustrate key principles and arguments related to the development, organisation and management of tourism in different contexts. All the authors introduce a range of global examples to develop an international dimension to their books and an extensive bibliography is complemented by further reading and questions for discussion at the end of each chapter.

Books published in the Themes in Tourism Series

S.J. Page *Transport and Tourism, third edition*

C.M. Hall *Tourism Planning, second edition*

S.J. Page and R.K. Dowling *Ecotourism*

R. Scheyvens *Tourism for Development*

S.J. Page and C.M. Hall *Managing Urban Tourism*

D.J. Timothy and S.W. Boyd *Heritage Tourism*

Transport and Tourism
Global Perspectives

THIRD EDITION

Stephen J. Page

PEARSON
Prentice
Hall

Harlow, England • London • New York • Boston • San Francisco • Toronto • Sydney • Singapore • Hong Kong
Tokyo • Seoul • Taipei • New Delhi • Cape Town • Madrid • Mexico City • Amsterdam • Munich • Paris • Milan

Pearson Education Limited
Edinburgh Gate
Harlow
Essex CM20 2JE
England

and Associated Companies throughout the world

Visit us on the World Wide Web at:
www.pearsoned.co.uk

First published 1999
Second edition published 2005
Third edition published 2009

ISBN 978-0-273-71970-0

British Library Cataloguing-in-Publication Data
A catalogue record for this book is available from the British Library

Library of Congress Cataloging-in-Publication Data
A catalog record for this book is available from the Library of Congress

10 9 8 7 6 5 4 3 2 1
11 10 09

Typeset in *10 pt Sabon* by *73*
Printed and bound by Ashford Colour Press, Gosport

The publisher's policy is to use paper manufactured from sustainable forests.

Contents

List of figures

List of plates

List of tables

Preface to third edition

The development of tourism studies as a legitimate area of academic study in the 1980s and 1990s saw a growing literature appearing in specialist journals, an expanding range of textbooks and more specialist research monographs and edited books. As with any subject, its intellectual development is not simply measured in terms of the volume of material published. The effect such literature has on the way in which students and educators are encouraged to think about the subject and pursue new avenues of research is one way of gauging the impact of such studies. The methodological and philosophical debates encapsulated in studies such as Lew et al. (2004), *A Companion of Tourism*, highlight many of the problems associated with tourism research as well as new research agendas in the 1990s and progress in these areas by 2004. In each case, particularly the failure to link multidisciplinary research together to develop a more holistic understanding of tourism, tourists and their impact, remains a fundamental weakness. This is still the case in transport and tourism at the time of writing. This book is by no means a response to the call for a more explicit methodological concern in tourism research: it is an attempt to highlight how disciplinary research on tourism and transport can be integrated to provide a clearer understanding of the interface and relationship between tourism and transport, with a focus on how to manage some of these interactions and the wider implications resulting from processes such as globalisation. This is a major re-evaluation of an earlier text by the author, first published almost 15 years ago as *Transport for Tourism*, in 1994 as the initial book in the Routledge (and then Cengage Learning) Tourism and Hospitality Management Series and its subsequent revision in 1999 and 2005 as *Transport and Tourism* as a much more substantive assessment of the interface between transport and tourism.

One consistent problem from which *Transport for Tourism* suffered was a lack of space to deal with issues associated with the transport and tourism interface. Despite the demand for the text, the limited space meant that key themes such as infrastructure development, transport planning and a greater emphasis on management issues (e.g. marketing) were omitted. In contrast, the first edition in 1999 of *Transport and Tourism* developed a more rounded student text that has a wider appeal to undergraduate and postgraduate students and subsequently was translated into Japanese and Portuguese. In broad terms the initial framework developed in the first edition of *Transport for Tourism* was initially retained and expanded, and new chapters added.

In this third edition of *Transport and Tourism* the underlying model from the second edition has been retained, and the book is still divided into four sections to explain the coherence more clearly: understanding tourist transport: concepts and methods of analysis; the analysis, use and provision of tourist transport; managing tourist transport provision; the future. This is a deliberate attempt to provide a greater coherence to the material. Writing a text that embraces the scope, global nature and yet some of the intricacies of tourist transport is a major challenge, especially when I do not wish to simply describe transport provision, but to discuss many of the issues which affect the transport sector in relation to tourism. A new edition of the book was needed for many reasons, not least because many profound global events have occurred including the ongoing financial crisis in the US airline industry, the expansion of the climate change debate and concerns over peak oil. The collapse of a number of airlines, growing indebtedness among many other airlines and the rapid challenge posed by low-cost airlines and other innovative forms of transport provision remain ever present themes in this new edition along with new *Insights* highlighting what readers asked for – more case studies on the developing world and the challenges of accommodating future growth.

Throughout the book, data has also been updated and expanded since the first edition was published. Most of the case studies have been revised, shortened or updated as concise *Insights* where readers expressed a clear interest in their use, and in other instances new examples have been included to broaden the scope and range of material. Particular thanks go a number of colleagues at Stirling and elsewhere for their input to the book with new Insights and especially the new Chapter 9 by Susanne Becken at Lincoln University who is eminently qualified to write on the subject of climate change and future energy issues in tourist transport. Thank you Susanne for your very valuable input and for writing Chapter 9. One notable difference in this edition is the greater reference to the use of the car and the problems of managing car-based tourism and leisure traffic as more and more attention is emerging in the literature. The challenge of planning for a growing dependence upon the car and aviation is also emphasised whilst a refocusing of Chapter 2 has led to a greater initial emphasis on how to understand contemporary issues in transport and tourism through different methods and approaches researchers use in practice to understand transport and tourism. Low-cost airlines are an undeniable theme that appears at different points throughout the book, as does a greater use of commercially available transport data along with an indication of where such data can be updated electronically (i.e. the Web) and the problems in its use. Since 1998 much of the data has become publicly available on the Web, making the global nature of tourist transport much more apparent. This has also led to a much stronger focus on the e-travel revolution and the way technology has transformed the transport sector along with a greater focus on contemporary issues such as crime, safety, security and the problems of tourist travel, epitomised by the sustainability debate. This is also reflected in a completely revised future prospects chapter with a much greater emphasis on good practice examples and innovative schemes for tourist transport provision. Whilst the book has also discussed much of the new literature now appearing in the growing range of transport journals, this is increasing at an almost exponential rate such that only key studies relevant to the arguments presented are included.

The literature base in transportation has also expanded rapidly with the continuing outputs from academic journals such as *Transportation Research* (versions A, B, C, D, E and F on the psychology of transport), the *Journal of Air Transport*

Management, Transport Policy and the *Journal of Transport Geography*. In common with other areas of research, the range and nature of data sources has also expanded dramatically, often contributing to an information overload for researchers. This is made worse by the availability of material on the Web, where the quality and authenticity of the data cannot always be checked or guaranteed. In that context, books such as this offer an important synthesis for students and researchers because a wide range of sources are cited and referenced in an area dispersed across social science, management and other cognate disciplines (e.g. economics).

Existing studies aimed at National and Higher National courses in the UK and general texts published in North America contain common elements concerned with tourism and transport and many of these books deal with the topic admirably in an empirical sense. Yet the relationship between tourism and transport is rarely discussed in any degree of depth in the popular tourism textbooks. Such books do not consider what is meant by a tourist transport system and how the needs of the traveller are incorporated into management systems beyond a simplistic level. Recognised undergraduate tourism textbooks generally pay very little attention to the tourism–transport interface, reiterated in the research monograph by Lumsdon and Page (2004a). For this reason an introductory text that builds on three previous iterations may help to stimulate some thought and discussion on the role of transport in tourism and vice versa.

This book is also part of the established series – Themes in Tourism – published by Pearson Education. The main aim of the series is to introduce and systematically discuss a range of concepts and ideas related to a tourism theme that are integral to the field of tourism studies within a spatial analytical context. This is developed through the use of supporting Insights whilst the fundamental principles of tourism are emphasised throughout. The book is also designed to be a starting point for those interested in research on transport studies and tourism, because the content and bibliography may serve as an introductory review for more advanced degree-level students. Although the bibliography is by no means exhaustive, many of the most significant studies are reviewed.

Academics write books for many different reasons. In this case, the continued paucity of texts and articles which consider transport and tourism in the academic literature has meant that the existing literature remains either very rudimentary or highly specialised and technical. In some cases research on transport and tourism is no more than a few paragraphs or chapters found in many of the established tourism textbooks. This has meant that the topic has not been recognised, nor has it gained the significance it deserves. After my involvement in Air New Zealand's Consensus Forecasting Exercise in October 1996 it was evident that transport services were a powerful tool guiding the development of inbound and outbound tourism. In the case of Asia-Pacific, the growing significance of outbound markets and the need for reliable, accurate market intelligence and an understanding of the transport sector were vital. All too often, it is only when academic researchers engage in consultancy that they begin to understand the commercial realities and implications of the subject area they study. Subsequent involvement with other transport organisations and studies commissioned by tourism and non-tourism agencies confirmed this position all too often, where the transport–tourism interface is poorly understood.

This book is not intended to be a rewrite of the main themes discussed in existing textbooks. Instead it looks at what is sometimes construed as a mundane and specialist area of study dominated by a number of tourism-related publications. This book aims to prompt the reader to consider some of the relationships that exist in providing transport services and facilities for tourists. It is also an attempt to distil current thinking in the area from both academic and industry sources. This assessment of transport and tourism does not claim to present a comprehensive review of the topic. It focuses on some of the key issues that transport providers, decision makers, managers and tourists face in the use, operation and management of tourist transport. If the book raises the profile of transport issues in tourism and stimulates debate amongst its readers, reviewers and critics then it will have succeeded in establishing a consensus of opinion on tourist transport as a legitimate area of study. Published reviews of *Transport and Tourism* certainly stimulated a debate and, despite minor criticisms (inevitable with any book), its continued success at a global level reiterates that transport is important to tourism and I hope that the new edition of this text will encourage researchers to debate the issue further. Inevitably some people will question some of the ideas raised here, but this can only assist in fostering more discussion in an area frequently overlooked in the tourism literature. The comments and feedback of former reviewers of the first and second edition of *Transport and Tourism* were very helpful and have been acknowledged and addressed in this enlarged version. Thank you for your input.

Of course certain people have helped to shape the thoughts and ideas in this book. My thanks go to many people and organisations that have helped, including Dimitrious Buhalis, Michael Hall, Linda Walker and Karen Thompson. Other organisations that helped and gave time to assist with my requests include: Singapore Changi Airport; easyJet; Professor Les Lumsdon, SUSTRANS, P&O Cruises, Orient-Express, Romeo Matutina at the Airport Council International, ICAO, Leslie Vella at the Malta Tourism Authority, Queensland Rail, National Express, Mr Steven Stewart at Stagecoach, Riddell Graham at VisitScotland, Paul McCafferty at Scottish Enterprise, Paul Fidgeon at Thames Valley University, Sebastian White at JetBlue Airways, and the various libraries that provided help with material. The Thomas Cook archivist, Mr Paul Smith, and the London Transport Collection all provided illustrative material which is duly acknowledged. I am also indebted to Neil McLaren who retyped parts of the manuscript.

Since my move to Scotland in 2000 a variety of other colleagues have helped shape some of the ideas dealt with in this book. In particular, Michael Hall has been a good sounding board and source of advice as well as offering great encouragement, especially for all those very formative books. A number of other people also deserve a special mention for helping with the first, second and third editions and in no particular order of importance they are: Richard Gibb of the University of Plymouth, Rigas Doganis of Cranfield University, Roy Wood, the late Thea Sinclair of the University of Nottingham, Bruce Prideaux of the University of Queensland, Mark Orams of Aukland University of Technology, Dr Hugh Sommerville formerly at British Airways, Professor Derek Hall, the Scottish Agricultural College, Ayr, Scotland, and Jon Green at Red Funnel Ferries, Southampton. The academic libraries at the University of Sussex, Surrey University, University of Westminster, Plymouth University, Edinburgh University, Glasgow University and Strathclyde University yielded important research material cited in this text. In addition, the British Library has been a constant source of discovery and assistance in reconstructing some of the formative influences on the subject. Lastly, I would like to acknowledge the support of Andrew Taylor at Pearson Education who supported the new edition of this book in the Themes in Tourism series and turned it into reality as well as Matthew Smith who commissioned the first edition. Both were a great source of encouragement and excellent publishers to work with over the years – thanks for all your input and help. No thanks can be complete without a mention of three special people – Jo, Toby and Rosie – for hours of fun and perseverance with that odd transport enthusiast (so I am told!).

Stephen J. Page
Scottish Enterprise Forth Valley Chair in Tourism
Division of Marketing
Stirling Management School
University of Stirling
Stirling
Scotland
FK9 4LA
December 2008

Acknowledgements

We are grateful to the following for permission to reproduce copyright material:

Figures
Figures 1.1 and 1.2 adapted from *The Social and Economic Benefits of Air Transport*, Air Transport Action Group (ATAG 2008); Figure 1.6 adapted from Lamb, B. and Davidson, S. (1996), 'Tourism and transportation in Ontario, Canada', in *Practising Responsible Tourism: International Case Studies in Tourism Planning, Policy and Development*, New York: Wiley (Harrison, L. and Husbands, W., eds) pp. 261–76, copyright © 1996, this material is used by permission of John Wiley & Sons Inc.; Figures 1.7 and 4.1 from Lumsdon, L. and Page, S. J. eds (2004), *Tourism and Transport*, p. 7 and p. 32, with permission from Elsevier; Figure 2.3 'East Coast mainline route network operated by National Express', image courtesy of National Express; Figure 2.4 redrawn from Seristö, H. and Vepsäläinen, A.P.J. (1997) 'Airline cost drivers: Cost implications of fleet, routes, and personnel policies', *Journal of Air Transport Management*, 3(1), pp. 11–22, with permission from Elsevier; Figure 2.5 from Thompson, I.B. (2002) 'Air transport liberalisation and the development of third-level airports in France', *Journal of Transport Geography*, Vol. 10(3), pp. 273–85, with permission from Elsevier; Figure 2.7 from Queensland Rail; Figure 3.6 adapted from Charlton, C., Gibb, R. and Shaw, J. (1997), 'Regulation and continuing monopoly on Britain's railway industry in the UK post-privatisation', *Journal of Transport Geography*, 5(2), pp. 147–53, with permission from Elsevier; Figures 4.3a and 4.3b from *TEN-STAC European Scenario Project* (TEN-STAC 2003) maps by IWW (Institut für Wirtschaftspolitik und Wirtschaftsforschung, Karlsruhe, Germany), produced in the framework of the TEN-STAC study commissioned by the European Commission; Figure 4.5 from EuroRAP risk rate map, AA, copyright © Road Safety Foundation and © Crown Copyright, all rights reserved, licence number 399221; Figure 5.1 from 'Figure G.1: Air transport freedom rights', which first appeared in *Asia Pacific Air Transport: Challenges and Policy Reforms* (Finlay, C., Sien C.L. and Singh, K. eds 1997), p. 193, reproduced with the kind permission of the publisher, Institute of Southeast Asian Studies, Singapore, http://bookshop. iseas.edu.sg; Figure 5.5 from Véronneau, S. and Roy, J. (2008) 'Global service supply chains: An empirical study of current practices and challenges of a cruise line corporation', *Tourism Management*, 30, August, pp. 289–300, Figure 1, with permission from Elsevier; Figure 6.1 from Page, S. (2003), *Tourism Management*, pp. 118–310, with permission from Elsevier; Figure 6.5 adapted from Buhalis, D. (2003) *e-Tourism:*

Information technology for strategic tourism management, Pearson Education Ltd, Figure 1.2; Figures 6.6, 6.7 and 6.8 from Buhalis, D. (2004) 'eAirlines: strategic and tactical use of ICTs in the airline industry', *Information and Management*, 41(7), September, pp. 805–25; Figure 8.1 from Lumsdon, L.M. (2006) 'Factors affecting the design of tourism bus services', Figure 1, *Annals of Tourism Research*, 33(3), pp. 748–66, with permission from Elsevier; Figure 10.5 adapted from Seristö, H. and Vepsäläinen, A.P.J. (1997) 'Airline cost drivers: Cost implications of fleet, routes, and personnel policies', *Journal of Air Transport Management*, 3(1), pp. 11–22, with permission from Elsevier.

Tables
Table 2.4 from Page, S.J. (2003) *Tourism Management*, with permission from Elsevier; Table 3.4 from *EU Energy and Transport in Figures, Statistical Pocketbook 2007/2008* (European Commission, Directorate-General for Energy and Transport 2008), Eurostat, © European Communities, 2008; Table 3.7 from Hooper, P. (2002) 'Privatisation of airports in Asia', *Journal of Air Transport Management*, 8(5) pp. 289–300, with permission from Elsevier; Table 4.2 from 'World Traffic Statistics', Airports Council International (ACI), Geneva, Switzerland; Table 4.6 from *Asia-Pacific Air Traffic: Growth and Constraints*, Air Transport Action Group (ATAG 2001); Table 5.1 from Lee, D. (2003) Concentration and price trends in the US domestic airline industry: 1990–2000, *Journal of Air Transport Management*, 9(2), pp. 91–101, with permission from Elsevier; Table 6.2 from Buhalis, D. (2003) *e-Tourism: Information technology for strategic tourism management*, pp. 53–4, Pearson Education Ltd; Tables 6.3 and 6.4 from Buhalis, D. (2004) 'eAirlines: strategic and tactical use of ICTs in the airline industry', *Information and Management*, 41(7), September, pp. 805–25; Tables 6.5 and 6.6 from Malta Tourism Digest, http://www.mta.com.mt, copyright © of the Malta Tourism Authority and reproduced with permission; Table 7.1 adapted from *Annual Report* (BAA 2007) http://www.baa.co.uk, with permission from BAA; Table 8.1 from *Annual Environmental Report* (British Airways 1992) p. 8, British Airways; Table 8.2 from Lumsdon, L. (1996) *Cycling opportunities: Making the most of the national cycling network*, pp. 5–6, Stockport: Simon Holt Marketing Serviceson; Tables 9.1 and 9.3 adapted from Scott, D., Amelung, B., Becken, S., Ceron, J. P., Dubois, G., Goessling, S., Peeters, P. and Simpson, M. (2007), *Climate Change and Tourism: Responding to Global Challenges*, United Nations World Tourism Organisation and United Nations Environment Programme © UNWTO, 9284401709; Table 10.3 from *Cairngorms National Park Visitor Survey Final Report* (Lowland Market Research/Cairngorms National Park Authority 2004), Cairngorms National Park Authority; Table 10.4 adapted from Seristö, H. and Vepsäläinen, A.P.J. (1997) 'Airline cost drivers: cost implications of fleet, routes, and personnel policies', *Journal of Air Transport Management*, 3(1), p. 21, with permission from Elsevier.

Photographs
Plates 1(a), 1(b), 4.4 and 4.6 Thomas Cook; Plate 2.1 National Express; Plate 2.3 Stagecoach Group; Plate 2.4, 7.2, 7.6 and 7.8 JetBlue Airways; Plates 2.5, 2.6, 2.7 and 10.5 easyJet; Plates 3.2, 4.3, 8.5 and 10.6 Dr Joanne Connell; Plate 6.3 Visitmalta.com; Plates 7.3, 7.4, 7.5 and 7.7 the Civil Aviation Authority of

Singapore; Plates 8.3 and 8.4 Transport for London, London Transport Museum; Plates 9.1 and 9.2 Susanne Becken; Plate 10.4 P&O Cruises.

Text

Extract on pages 153–4 adapted from *Annual Report of ICAO Council*, 2002 and 2007, ICAO (International Civil Aviation Organization), reproduced with the permission of ICAO; Insight 4.2 adapted from Walker, L. and Page, S.J. (2005) 'The contribution of tourists and visitors to road traffic accidents: a preliminary analysis of trends and issues for Central Scotland', *Current Issues in Tourism*, 7(3), pp. 217–41; extracts on pp. 234 and 242 adapted from Centre for Regional and Tourism Research, Denmark, http://www.crt.dk/trends, Carl Marcussen; Insight 6.1 adapted from Buhalis, D. (2004) 'eAirlines: strategic and tactical use of ICTs in the airline industry', *Information and Management*, 41(7), September, pp. 805–25; extract on pp. 256–7 from House of Commons Transport Committee (2008) *Twelfth Report 3 November 2008, The Opening of Heathrow Terminal 5*, Crown Copyright material is reproduced with the permission of the Controller of HMSO and the Queen's Printer for Scotland; extract on pp. 262–3 from Tae, H., Oum, J. Y., Chunyan, Y. (2008) 'Ownership forms matter for airport efficiency: A Stochastic frontier investigation of worldwide airports', *Journal of Urban Economics*, 64(2), pp. 422–35, with permission from Elsevier; Insight 7.2 from Professor Michael Hall; Newspaper Headline on p. 333 from Hastings, M. 'Addressing binge flying is vital for the climate', *Guardian Weekly*, 11 May 2007, p. 9, copyright Guardian News & Media Ltd 2007; Insight 10.1 from Karen Thompson.

In some instances we have been unable to trace the owners of copyright material, and we would appreciate any information that would enable us to do so.

Understanding tourist transport
Concepts and methods of analysis

1

Introduction

Introduction

Transport is acknowledged as one of the most significant factors to have contributed to the international and domestic development of tourism. In Cooley's (1894) treatise on 'the theory of transportation', transport was acknowledged as one of the key features underpinning social and economic development, not only to overcome the physical constraints of distance, but also to meet human needs for movement across time and space including travel for the purpose of tourism. Even very early examples of tourism, dating to the Roman and Medieval period, required the evolution of transport, particularly its mechanisation and use of technology so that travel and tourism could occur. Without the infrastructure and the mode of transport, then, tourism could not possibly occur. Our desire to travel is underpinned by three distinct methods of human transport: self-propelled modes (e.g. walking); augmented modes (using technology or tools to amplify our bodily effort, such as skiing) and fuelled modes (especially motorised transport) (Stradling and Anable 2008). What these three modes of transport suggest are that without the infrastructure and the mode of transport, then tourism could not possibly occur. As Stradling and Anabele (2008) argue, the three notions of propulsion, combustion and consumption are what characterise modern day travel, and this can be directly related to tourism as a form of conspicuous consumption. Therefore no study of tourism can ignore the critical role which transport plays in terms of the interrelationships and interconnections that exist with tourism. It remains one of the silent elements of tourism research, not least because it is widely taken for granted and not given its rightful place in current and future evaluations of tourism growth and development. Tourism has become one of the most visible signs of human movement at a global level, benefiting from increased prosperity, a desire to travel and the benefits which new transport technology has brought to aid increased accessibility of destinations to tourists and other travellers. Without transport and its associated infrastructure, human mobility for the purpose of tourist travel would not occur, and certainly not on the massive scale which is documented in current statistics and reviews of tourism performance as shown in Insight 1.1. This provides a broad overview of how international tourism is growing and the implications for long-term prospects for tourist travel.

The global scale of travel and tourism

According to the World Travel and Tourism Council the international tourism industry employed over 231 million people indirectly and generated over 10 per cent of world GDP. In 2003 the United Nations World Tourism Organisation (UN-WTO) recorded that 694 million tourists travelled abroad (down from a peak of 703 million in 2002), which generated US$474 billion in tourist spending and a significant demand for tourist transport. By 2007, the number of international tourists had risen to 898 million, a 6 per cent growth on 2006. Such a growth in international arrivals was estimated to have generated US$ 856 billion in tourist receipts. In global terms, the expansion of international tourism continues to generate an insatiable demand for overseas travel and UN-WTO has forecast that by 2020 international tourism will have risen to 1.6 billion arrivals. Europe remains the most visited of all regions of the world, with half of all global tourist receipts and almost two-thirds of international arrivals. Even so, the fastest growing regions for tourist travel in 2007 were: the Middle East (13 per cent), Asia Pacific (10 per cent), Africa (8 per cent), the Americas (5 per cent) and Europe (4 per cent). Despite the impact of recent crises such as SARS and global terrorism, the tourism industry has a strong resilience and ability to bounce back although the current credit crunch is widely viewed as a much deeper problem for the world economy, potentially signalling the shift to a recession. The world economy up to 2007 had experienced almost 25 years of sustained growth in GDP, and GDP is widely seen as a key driver of the demand for travel, so when GDP begins to fall, it is natural to see a contraction in travel, particularly leisure travel that depends upon discretionary spending.

At a global level, much of the demand for tourism and travel between regions is dominated by urban centres, particularly world cities and what are now being termed mega-cities. For example, the United Nations has suggested that by 2020 the number of world cities with over 20 million people will have risen to 16, of which 10 will be in Asia-Pacific. This population growth combined with a growing tourism industry will see major changes in the existing patterns of global tourism and will certainly impact upon the demand for tourist travel at a global level. Existing and future patterns of tourism will therefore be shaped by the demand from people wishing to travel and this will be reflected in new demographic trends and growing affluence in expanding economies as existing patterns of tourism are reshaped.

In the case of air travel in Asia, existing patterns of travel will continue to see massive changes in the volume and scale of tourist travel, not least with respect to the investment and infrastructure needs of Asia, observed as long ago as 2003 (Page 2003), especially in China in terms of airport expansion, with forecasts of 8–10 per cent GDP growth per annum over the next 10 years. This is expected to equate to around 10–15 per cent growth in traffic per annum if forecasts are accurate. As the new middle classes in these regions begin to achieve greater mobility through improved affluence, the transport needs for tourism will see massive growth and tourism will be within reach of new groups of people. Therefore, as the expanding population and affluence in regions such as Asia begin to reach fruition, they will certainly be major consumers of domestic and international tourist transport. But the immediate prospects for travel due to the credit crunch could see some of these forecasts amended as the economic conditions may lead to a contraction of travel in the short term. For example, estimates by the International Air Transport Association suggest that in 2008, profits among global airlines may be hit by around US$2 billion, dropping to around US$ 9.6 billion for 2007/8 as people travel less frequently or not at all. However, these underlying trends in global tourism also raise issues about the underlying changes and trends which have shaped transport and travel in the early twenty-first century to which attention now turns.

What global changes are affecting travel for tourism and why does it assume a critical role in modern society?

Since the late 1990s, the world has experienced many major trends affecting both the economic and social life of many countries and probably one of the most profound is the growing importance of globalisation. Transport has been a key element in achieving the greater global interconnectedness of different areas and regions as transport connects different places and destinations: put simply, transport connects the origin and destination. But in a globalised world where space and distance no longer act as the major constraint on economic activity, in the way Cooley (1894) observed, and reiterated in many subsequent geographical analyses of transport, technology and transport have had a profound impact on making our globalised world work effectively. This is particularly the case for tourism, as broadly speaking nowhere on the globe is more than 24 hours' travel from anywhere else and technology has enabled companies and people to interact on a global scale.

But globalisation is not a new process confined to the late twentieth century. According to Friedman (2005), three eras of globalisation can be discerned:

- The first relates to when Columbus set sail in 1492 and ended in the early 1800s and is largely associated with growing exploration and discovery of other places.
- The second dates from the early 1800s and is explained by the development of a critical mass of global trade so that companies expanded into global entities, often related to the Imperial ambitions of their host country to exploit underdeveloped resources as well as new markets. In the twentieth century, the development of mass markets to consume these new products and goods combined with the emergence of modern day marketing to assist in the further development of this globalisation process when many brands were initially pioneered.
- The third dates from the late 1990s with the rise of web technologies to allow people and businesses to collaborate on a global scale.

This process of globalisation since the late 1990s has been explained by Friedman (2005) as the result of several profound changes, events, trends or innovations that changed the world. These have had a major impact on the role of transport in relation to tourism, as the following points suggest:

- The rise of the personal computer and windows software and networks (including the use of Netscape as an internet browser) has allowed the technological connectedness to occur between people and countries. For tourism, this has opened up new horizons and awareness of opportunities to search the Web to see where to travel and how to book. In the late 1990s the pace of technological innovations with the PC have also seen the tourism industry as one of the pioneering sectors to embrace the new technology. For example, the introduction of new technology has led to online booking, online check-in for air travel and changes to the way business is conducted.
- Workflow software has allowed businesses to collaborate on a global scale and has meant global supply chains have emerged creating a greater international dimension to work activity generating a greater demand for international business travel.
- Outsourcing has allowed organisations to manage business processes with technology at a distance irrespective of location. For example, this generated the

demand for call centre location in India and other low labour cost regions, to reduce business costs for many such business processes. This has also seen more business opportunities emerge in newly industrialising countries alongside the growth of a new middle class with a travel ethic and interest in outbound travel.

- The growth of China as a global economic power which has completely overtaken the tourism sector as a leading outbound market and destination, was reflected in the massive growth rates in the demand for air travel.
- The rise of 'in-forming', which is the ability of the individual to use technology via a PC to build and develop their own personal supply chain, empowering individuals through the Internet – information, knowledge and the searching/self-servicing of personal travel needs – has created a generation which is web-enabled and more aware of how to access the opportunities to travel. This makes travel a readily accessible and available commodity that is no longer just dependent upon agents and working hours of businesses to plan and book trips.
- The rise of the wireless society, where the desk of the worker now goes anywhere with them via the PC or laptop (or growing numbers of personal devices) so that workers are mobile and able to work while they travel, creating new opportunities for combining travel and work in a more flexible manner.

These trends according to Friedman (2005) contributed to the flattening of the globe, meaning that as these trends/innovations converge, there has been a revolution in the market for travel and tourism: the rise of new industrialised countries (including the rise of the post-Communist Eastern Europe as a destination and outbound market) has seen a redefinition of the economic power base on a global scale. The trends and innovations listed above coalesced to act as 'tipping points' so that a global web-enabled society has emerged with little conventional regard to geography and boundaries or language to shape the nature of economic activity. These new economic realities also shape the pattern of travel and tourism. This has meant that globalisation has made the world more open to more people to travel: no longer is it a westernised privilege. Technology has also cut through other barriers whilst the way people manage businesses and organisations has shifted management from the concept of command and control of people and resources (as discussed in Chapter 2 in its broad form) to one where effective management is also about getting people to connect and collaborate in a globalised world. Even so, one of the potential constraints that may dampen demand for transport and tourism is the rising price of oil which increases the unit costs of energy to facilitate tourist mobility.

Oil, travel and transport

Most forms of transport for tourism are dependent upon oil as the basis for energy and this has seen sharp rises and fluctuations in recent years to over US$100 a barrel. Much of the growth in in the post-war period in transport and tourism has been predicated on relatively cheap oil, since between 1947 and 2007 the median price of crude oil only exceeded US$19.04 per barrel for half of the time, typically only exceeding US$22–28 a barrel in times of war or Middle East conflict. However, in the period since 1970, prices averaged US$32 a barrel as demand increased from developing economies and due to a weak US dollar. This has also been compounded by limited spare capacity to meet short-term demand. There is also a growing concern by researchers that peak oil production at a global level has been exceeded, placing a potential premium on future supplies of oil (Becken 2007). Consequently, with transport still largely dependent upon fossil fuels for energy, there are potential concerns about the future provision of cheap transport, particularly air travel, as inflationary pressures resulting from greater concerns for climate change and green technologies alongside rising oil prices may dampen some elements of demand. So the previous growth in transport and tourism is not as readily assured as in the era of cheap travel, although the tourism sector is well known for its innovative behaviour to develop new models of production and supply that can reduce its cost base. But as energy is a dominant element for transportation, this poses many challenges (a theme to which we will return in the book). At this point, however, it is useful to briefly focus on what is meant by the term tourism sector and how transportation fits into it.

But what do we understand by the term tourism?

Even though there is an ongoing controversy over the extent to which tourism can be defined as both an industry and a service activity (see Leiper 2008 for example), it is widely recognised that tourism combines a broad range of economic activities and services designed to meet the needs of tourists. It is also evident from some of the recent studies of air transport (e.g. ATAG 2000, 2008; Graham et al. 2008) that the tourism sector is a broad, all-encompassing term which includes accommodation, catering, transport and ancillary services. Therefore using the term tourism can tend to obscure the wider significance of the transport sector in tourist travel due to the tendency to generalise its role and significance. For example, Figure 1.1 shows that if one looks at the air transport sector as a component of this wider tourism sector, it is a complex amalgam of interests comprising producers and consumers, of which the airline industry includes a wide range of stakeholders. The same can be said for other transportation sectors that are involved in transporting tourists or in the mobility of tourists. Likewise, if one then considers the interrelationship between air transport and tourism from an economic perspective (Figure 1.2), the wider significance of direct tourist spending on transport and the indirect benefits in terms of employment and other spin-offs is self-evident. All too often there is a tendency by analysts and researchers to overlook these fundamental relationships that become more obvious when an economic perspective is taken and critical relationships between consumers and producers are highlighted.

Consequently, transport provides the essential link between tourism origin and destination areas and facilitates the movement of holidaymakers, business travellers, people visiting friends and relatives and those undertaking educational and health tourism. Transport is also a key element of the 'tourist experience' (Pearce 1982; Moscardo and Pearce 2004) and some commentators (e.g. Middleton 1988; Tourism Society 1990) view it as an integral part of the tourism industry.

Transport can also form the focal point for tourist activity in the case of cruising and holidays that contain a significant component of travel (e.g. coach holidays and scenic rail journeys, see Dean 1993). Here the mode of transport forms a context and controlled environment for tourists' movement between destinations and attractions, often through the medium of a 'tour'. The integral relationship that exists

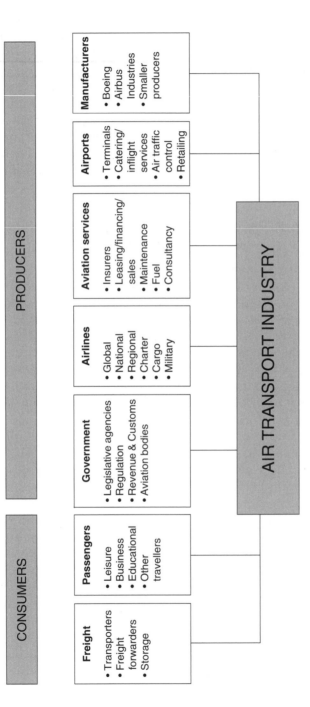

Figure 1.1 The structure of the air transport sector: its constituent parts, producers and consumers

Source: Developed from ATAG (2000).

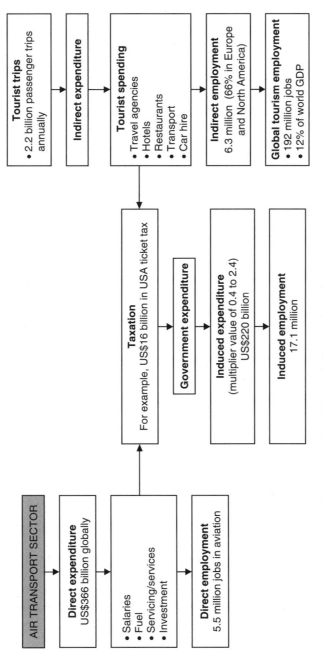

Figure 1.2 The economic impact of the global aviation and tourism sector

Source: Developed from ATAG (2008).

between transport and tourism is demonstrated by Lamb and Davidson (1996: 264), since

> transportation is one of the three fundamental components of tourism. The other two are the tourism product (or supply) and the tourism market (or demand). Without transportation, most forms of tourism could not exist. In some cases, the transportation experience is the tourism experience (e.g. cruises, scenic and heritage rail trips, and motorcoach, automobiles and bicycle tours).

Thus, the mode of transport tourists choose can often form an integral part of their journeys and experiences, a feature often neglected in the existing research on tourism. However, the interface of transport and tourism does raise the much wider conceptual problem of what is and what is not tourism transport (D.R. Hall 1997). Whilst it is readily acknowledged that there are specialised, dedicated forms of tourism transport (i.e. tourist coaches, charter flights and cruise liners), there are also other forms of transport which are used by both hosts and tourists to varying extents. For example, urban buses, metro systems and scheduled flights to tourism regions are used simultaneously by tourists and local residents and in some cases this can cause competition. Where tourist use of transport modes does occur, competition with other users has wide-ranging economic, environmental, social and political implications for destination areas. The basic difficulty is that few public sector organisations have the resources or inclination to address the issue of tourist–non-tourist use of different forms of transport: they are typically viewed as *passengers*. Therefore, even though tourist use of transport can be conceptualised at one level, making the distinction is not necessarily feasible in practice. This remains a constant problem that pervades the tourist–transport interface. However, this should not in itself preclude the academic analysis of transport and tourism. This can be done in three ways: through an overview of the development of the area of study (i.e. the transport–tourism nexus, which focuses on how the two subjects are interconnected); through an analysis of the recent scientific literature (i.e. academic journals in transport and tourism studies); and also by looking at how transport has been viewed in existing textbooks on tourism.

Tourism studies and tourist transport

The evolution of the transport–tourism research nexus

Much of the research literature and publications which are reviewed throughout this book, in common with many syntheses of new research themes, is a product of the last 30–40 years. This often marks the expansion and growing specialisation of subjects within social science and the humanities, which in turn have generated new subjects and disciplines. It is widely acknowledged that the interest in transport–tourism interconnections and synergies is largely a product of the late 1980s and 1990s. Yet there are important antecedents which have contributed to the development of this research interest, principally from two subject areas: Economics and Geography (to which we will return in Chapter 2). Although there is not space within this book to provide a detailed review of the evolution of transport studies research and the themes which are now pursued by tourism researchers, it is helpful to provide some historical context to the tradition in studying these subject areas: this is because the subject does have antecedents that do pre-date the 1980s when modern transport studies research and tourism were firmly established as academic subjects in universities. As Table 1.1 shows, one of the early studies by an economist can be dated to 1894 in a scholarly journal, although, as Kirkcaldy and Dudley Evans (1913: x) observed a specific 'transport studies' curriculum did develop, where 'The new Universities and Schools of Economics having included transport in the curriculum for their commerce degrees [in the UK], it has come to be treated as a branch of economics deserving of accurate, scientific inquiry and study'.

Similarly, the University of British Columbia, Canada has a long tradition of teaching transportation studies that can be dated to 1929 while examples of an early interest in transport studies exists in other countries across the world. The growth in textbooks in the 1920s and 1930s together with journal articles which illustrate how transport developments led to passenger growth really mark the firm development of the subject in this period. A number of post-war illustrations of studies by geographers and economists also continued this interest in 'transport studies' that saw many universities begin to establish centres of teaching and research in this area in the 1960s and 1970s. However, few tourism specialists (with a number of exceptions such as Lickorish and Burkart) pursued the tourism–transport research agenda until the 1970s.

It is widely argued that at a scientific level progress in a subject area such as tourism studies may be gauged by the higher-level research activity published in the leading peer-reviewed scientific journals, such as *Tourism Management*, the *Journal of Travel Research* and *Annals of Tourism Research*. However, transport and tourism also has a significance for the transport studies literature where a number of notable journals exist, such as the *Journal of Air Transport Management*, the *Transportation Research* series of journals (issues A to F), *Transport Policy* and a number of other cognate subject areas (e.g. the *Journal of Transport Geography* and *Transport Economics)*. As Lumsdon and Page (2004b: xiii) noted, this had not produced a large literature on the interconnections between transport and tourism studies. The number of articles published in those journals with a specific tourism focus as opposed to an indirect focus (e.g. air travel) are limited. In the period 1994–2003 only six tourism-related articles featured in the *Transportation Research* series of journals. In contrast, a recent search of the key electronic databases such as Elsevier Science's ScienceDirect.com that combines the transport and tourism journals yielded 111 hits for transport and tourism-related topics in 2005 which increased to 143 in 2008, of which a substantial proportion made only a limited reference to transport. A lesser number of hits emerged from a more wide-ranging search of the CABI Leisure, Recreation and Tourism Abstracts database (now renamed LeisureTourism) in May 2004, with around 90 items, though many were not research-based pieces in key tourism journals. In the period 2005 to 2008, a further 90 items were published but many were on emerging themes such as climate change, legal issues, health and consumer-related themes. This is interesting when looking at ScienceDirect, which lists a growth from 4731 articles (May 2004) on tourism-related topics published since 1982 to 5371 (October 2008). Even so, if one looks at the main tourism journals for the complete years 1982–2008, in *Tourism Management* some 42 papers have been published on transport and tourism but only 21 were research papers, whilst for *Annals of Tourism Research*, of the 33 references

Table 1.1 Illustrations of emerging research interest in transport and tourism to 1970

Year	Publication	Focus on transport and tourism
1894	Cooley, H. 'The theory of transportation', *Publications of the American Economic Association* 9 (3): 13–148.	A wide ranging review of human mobility and the principles of transport.
1913	Kirkcaldy, A. and Dudley Evans, A. *History and Economics of Transport*. Pitman: London.	A review of the economic history of transport with a global and national focus. A preliminary textbook for commerce students studying transport.
1920	Sykes, F. 'Imperial air routes', *The Geographical Journal* 55 (4): 241–62.	A regional description of the principal Imperial air routes to be developed in the aftermath of the First World War.
1928	Brunner, C. *The Problems of Motor Transport: An Economic Analysis*. E. Benn Limited: London.	A text outlining the transport problems posed by the expansion of car ownership and use.
1929	Fenelon, K. *Transport Coordination: a Study of Present Day Problems*. P.S. King: London.	A review of the management challenge of integrating a growing variety of transport options.
1933	Ogilvie, I. *The Tourist Movement*. Staples Press: London.	One of the first tourism texts to review the subject and its growth using statistics. Improvements in transportation are also noted.
1933	Burchall, H. 'Air services in Africa', *Journal of the Royal African Society* 32 (126): 55–73.	Documents the emergence of commercial air services in Africa, their organisation, management and Imperial air routes.
1935	O'Dell, A. 'European air services June 1934', *Geography* 20 (3): 196–200.	A review of the emerging geography of the fledgling European air route network.
1941	Currie, A. 'Economic aspects of air transport', *The Canadian Journal of Economics and Political Science* 7 (1): 13–24.	A preliminary review of the economics of air travel and its operation in Canada.
1941	Smith, S. *Air Transport in the Pacific Area*. Institute of Pacific Relations: New York.	A review of the challenge of providing air services in a large maritime environment.
1944	Van Zandt, J. *The Geography of World Air Transport*. The Brockings Institution: Washington.	A global synthesis of air route provision prior to the end of the Second World War.
1945	Eiselen, E. 'The tourist industry of a modern highway, US16 in South Dakota', *Economic Geography* 21: 221–30.	A seminal paper which highlighted the important role of the car and road development in creating linear tourism activity as well as in shaping visitor behaviour.
1946	Stuart, F. and Baird, H. *Modern Air Transport*. John Lang: London.	An overview of trunk air routes, competition and operating costs of aviation.
1949	Little, V. 'Control of international air transport', *International Organisation* 3 (1): 29–40.	A seminal paper on the importance of the 1944 Chicago Convention which helped to shape the International Air Transport Association and attempts to create multilateral agreement on the exchange of air rights.
1953	Lester, A. 'The sources and nature of statistical information in the special fields of statistics: International air transport statistics', *Journal of the Royal Statistical Society* Series A 116 (4): 409–23.	A seminal paper outlining the statistical sources available to document the 20-fold increase in air passenger kms travelled 1937–51 using ICAO statistics dating to 1932. It also documents expanding air speed records 1911–48, since the 25 mile per hour record of the Zeppelin in 1911.
1956	Ullman, E. 'The role of transportation and the basis for interaction' in W. Thomas (ed) *Man's Role in Changing the Face of the Earth*. University of Chicago Press: Chicago, 862–88.	A seminal article which indicated that 'transportation is a measure of the relations between areas and is therefore an essential part of geography', marking out the antecedents of transport geography.
1957	Wheatcroft, S. *The Economics of European Air Transport*. Harvard University Press: Cambridge, MA.	The first major review of the economics of air travel.

Table 1.1 (*Continued*)

Year	Publication	Focus on transport and tourism
1958	Kish, G. 'Soviet air transport', *Geographical Review* 48 (3): 309–20.	A detailed review of the geography of Soviet air transport based on Aeroflot's routes on a domestic and international scale.
1958	Lickorish, L. and Kershaw, A. *The Travel Trade*. Practical Press: London.	An in-depth review tourism in the UK and some overseas countries, illustrating the growth in travel since the 1930s.
1962	Burkart, A. 'Advertising and marketing in the airline industry', *Journal of Industrial Economics* 11 (1): 18–32.	A seminal publication which introduced the importance of marketing as a key element in the expanding market for air travel.
1964	Caves, R. *Air Transport and its Regulators*. Cambridge University Press: London.	An important text outlining how the international airline business operates, the role of marketing and the importance of regulation.
1966	Sealy, K. *The Geography of Air Transport*. Hutchinson: London.	This is a classic study which has stood the test of time.
1970	Williams, A. and Zelinsky, W. 'On some patterns of international tourism flows', *Economic Geography* 46 (4): 549–67.	This paper uses different geographical concepts/tools to explain the flows of international tourism.

Source: Stephen J. Page.

to transport and tourism only 10 could be classified as research articles. This illustrates the limited attention that both tourism and transport researchers devote to scientific research to advance knowledge in this area. This has added little to the conceptual development of the area of research. Even in 2008, with the expansion of research activity in tourism, substantive studies of transport and tourism are noticeably absent from the key journals, although a number of emerging themes in niche areas have attracted considerable levels of activity. So how have the tourism textbooks approached this subject, since they distil down the scientific literature to make it accessible to a wider audience?

The majority of influential tourism textbooks are a product of the 1980s and early 1990s, and although there has been a flood of more recent texts none would seem to rival the earlier texts that have been published in numerous editions or reprinted (e.g. McIntosh 1973; Burkart and Medlik 1974, 1975). The rapid expansion in the number of tourism textbooks published is one indication of the emergence of the subject as a serious area of study at vocational, degree and postgraduate level throughout the world, although cynics also point to publishers recognising this as an area worthy of commercial exploitation and still in its infancy. Hence a proliferation of tourism textbooks globally has accompanied the area of study as they are tailored to international and local audiences.

As many national governments recognise the contribution tourism can make to GDP and national economic development, the expansion of their tourism industries has led to a consideration of the immediate and long-term human resource and training requirements. New courses have developed to fill a niche in the educational marketplace and these have generated a demand for course materials to meet the international expansion of tourism education (Goodenough and Page 1993; Airey and Tribe, 2005). The range of early textbooks for tourism studies has generally been written from a North American perspective (e.g. Lundburg 1980; Mathieson and Wall 1982; Mill and Morrison 1985; Murphy 1985; Gunn 1988; McIntosh and Goeldner 1990), a European perspective (e.g. Foster 1985; Lavery 1989; Laws 1991; Ryan 1991, 2003; Witt et al. 1991) or an Australasian perspective (e.g. Pearce 1987, 1992; Collier 1989; Leiper 1990; Bull 1991; Hall 1991; Perkins and Cushman 1993), with few widely available student texts written from an Asian or less developed world perspective, although there are some notable exceptions (e.g. Hall and Page 1996, 2000).

Since the 1990s the situation has changed little, with transport usually relegated to a passive or descriptive chapter in most books even when more recent books are examined. Indeed there have been a number of more specialist texts developed from a transport studies perspective, as new editions of previous books (e.g. Hanlon 1996, 2004; Doganis 2001, 2002; Graham 2001) have a wider use in tourism studies in setting the scene for air transport. However, they do not specifically meet the detailed needs of students of tourism given their subject material and focus on economic issues almost exclusively along with policy analysis.

What an examination of the existing textbooks indicates is that travel and transport is a topic frequently cited in relation to its role as a facilitator of the expansion of tourism, as new technology (e.g. the railway and jet engine) and novel forms of marketing and product developments (e.g. package holidays) have contributed to the development of tourism as a mass consumer product. Collier (1994) provides an interesting insight into tourist transport, arguing that there are three needs to fulfil:

- transporting the tourist from the generating to the host area;
- transport between host destinations;
- transport within host destinations.

Collier (1994) also classifies tourist transport on several bases (e.g. public or private sector transport; water/land/air transport; domestic and international transport and mode of transport). This classification is expanded in Figure 1.3, which

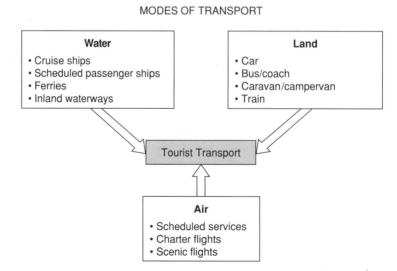

Figure 1.3 Classification of tourist transport
Source: Adapted from Collier 1994.

outlines the main modes of transport available and typifies the approach used in most tourism texts, although the issue of scenic flights is commonly omitted. Hall (1991: 22) highlights the significance of transport since 'the evolution of tourism in Australia is inseparable from the development of new forms of transport' and 'a clear relationship exists between transport development and tourism growth' (Hall 1991: 80). The development and expansion of tourist destinations are, in part, based on the need for adequate access to resort areas, their attractions and resources. Hence the relationship between transport and tourism is usually conceptualised in most tourism textbooks in terms of accessibility. Even so, in most existing tourism texts transport is at best relegated to the descriptive, to fulfil the needs of students and to act as a balance to other subjects within the tourism curriculum.

Hobson and Uysal (1992: 209), however, argue that major steps in the development of tourism have been linked with advancements in transport:

> The system . . . creates the structural linkage between origins and destinations . . . [but] the traditional focus on modes of travel often overlooks the underlying reason for the growth of transport communication; that is, the infrastructure that supports and sustains continued growth in the ability of people to travel.

Tolley and Turton (1995) point to the shrinking of distance by modern forms of international transport and four major phases can be discerned in the evolution of transport technology:

- the transition from horse and windpower;
- the introduction of the steam engine;
- the development of the combustion engine;
- the use of the jet engine.

While such innovations in technology have meant that global shrinkage has occurred (McHale 1969), with reduced journey times, cost reductions and improved capacity, Wackermann (1997: 35) asserts that the transformations which have taken place as a result of this economic opening up (and globalisation) of the recreational sector, supported by high-performance means of transport and communication, have made societies less dependent on natural resources and the limitations of distance or of time. Hobson and Uysal (1992) maintain that it is infrastructure which is crucial. They argue that supporting infrastructure has not been able to keep pace with tourism development and therefore congestion may be the biggest constraint facing planners in the new millennium.

A number of other textbooks (e.g. Holloway 1989; Mill 1992 and subsequent editions) have sought to develop this relationship one stage further, by discussing the historical development of tourist travel and accessibility, and the principles governing tourism's expansion within the context of different forms of tourist transport (e.g. air, road, rail and sea travel). Yet tourism studies does not have a monopoly on the analysis of transport for tourists. Textbooks on transport studies indirectly discuss the movement of tourists. Many of the transport studies texts from the 1970s, 1980s and 1990s are written from a disciplinary perspective such as economics (e.g. Stubbs et al. 1980; Glaister 1981; Bell et al. 1983; Banister and Button 1991; Findlay et al. 1997) whilst other texts focus on the operational, organisational and management issues associated with different forms of transport (e.g. Button 1982;

Faulks 1990; Button and Gillingwater 1991). However, the 'tourist' is rarely mentioned in these books as the term 'passenger' is usually substituted. In fact, a text on transport geography (Tolley and Turton 1995) is a case in point. The tourist receives only limited attention in Hoyle and Knowles' (1992, 1998) texts, with one chapter devoted to tourism, leisure and recreational travel (Page 1998), a feature also repeated in Knowles et al. (2008) with the chapter by D. Hall (2008). The difficulty here is that the term 'passenger' fails to distinguish between the reasons for tourist movement, implying an impersonal contractual relationship where operators move people between areas on transport systems which are only concerned with the throughput of passengers. In reality, a different situation exists, with transport operators equally concerned with many of the issues facing the tourism industry, particularly customer care and the tourist's experience whilst travelling. For many airline managers and other transport operators the burning issues of today are safety, security, competition, profitability and customer tastes. Due to the choice of transport available and the competitive environment for tourist travel in free market economies, transport operators recognise the importance of ensuring that the travel experience is both pleasurable and fulfils consumers' expectations. In state-planned economies, both the demand and supply for tourist transport is regulated by the state and a different political and ideological agenda affects the availability of tourist transport compared with free market economies.

Halsall (1992) identifies the overlap between transport, tourism and recreation, arguing that in reality it is often difficult to distinguish between tourist and non-tourist use of different forms of transport, the exceptions being dedicated forms of tourist transport such as charter flights and cruises. Former national rail operators such as British Railways (hereafter BR) did not use the term 'tourist', preferring to distinguish between 'business' and 'leisure' travellers when identifying their potential passenger market. Thus, the tourist is not explicitly recognised as such, but is regarded as a passenger. In contrast, some tourism researchers recognise the tourist trip as an important feature to examine in its own right (Pearce 1987; S.L.J. Smith 1989) (see Plates 1.1 and 1.2), although it receives only scant attention due to the simplistic notions of the tourism–transport relationship. Consequently, the relationship between tourism and transport is rarely discussed in the context of the 'tourist experience'.

Both transport and tourism studies fail to provide an explicit and holistic framework in which to assess the transportation of tourists. For this reason it is possible to build on the complementarity of these two areas of study to identify the concept of the 'tourist transport system', which highlights the integral role of transport in the 'tourist experience'. This also has the potential to accommodate different approaches to the analysis of tourist travel and transport. What is a 'tourist transport system'?

●●●● The tourist transport system: a framework for analysis

To understand the complexity and relationships that coexist between tourism and transport, one needs to build a framework which can synthesise the different factors and processes affecting the organisation, operation and management of activities associated with tourist travel. The objective of such a framework is to provide a means of understanding how tourists interact with transport, the processes and

(a)

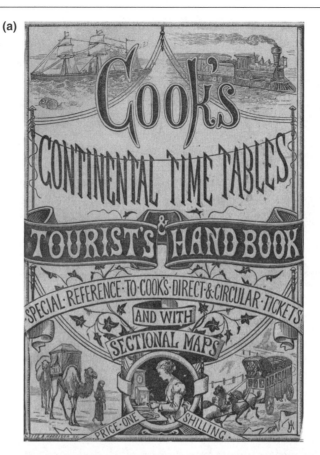

(b)

Plate 1.1 Tourist sightseeing and use of motorised transport such as the train and car have a long history as the two plates show: (a) This is the first issue of the 1873 Thomas Cook Continental Railway Timetable to aid passengers travelling to and in Europe by rail. It is still published on a monthly basis today as the European Rail Timetable © Thomas Cook; (b) A group of tourists about to commence a sightseeing tour of Berlin in 1912 ©Thomas Cook

Source: Thomas Cook

Plate 1.2 Tourists can also focus on transport as the main focus of the experience as shown with this group of visitors queuing for up to three hours for a 20 minute ride on a San Francisco cable car

Source: S.J. Page

factors involved and their effect on the travel component of the overall 'tourist experience'. Any such framework for analysing tourist transport needs to incorporate the tourist's use of transport services from the pre-travel booking stage through to the completion of the journey and to recognise the significance of the service component. It also needs to incorporate the different modes of transport used by tourists (e.g. air travel by scheduled or charter service, sea travel using ferries or cruise ships and land-based transport including the car, train, coach, motorcaravan, motorbike and bicycle).

One methodology used by researchers to understand the nature of the tourism phenomenon is a systems approach (Laws 1991). The main purpose of such an approach is to rationalise and simplify the real-world complexity of tourism into a number of constructs and components that highlight the interrelated nature of tourism. Since tourism studies is multidisciplinary (Gilbert 1990), a systems approach can accommodate a variety of different perspectives because it does not assume a predetermined view of tourism. Instead, it enables one to understand the broader issues and factors that affect tourism, together with the interrelationships between different components in the system.

According to Lumsdon and Page (2004b: 1):

the development of a theoretical framework of analysis has focused on a systems approach. The tourism system is defined by McIntosh et al. (1995: 21) as a 'set of inter-related groups co-ordinated to form a unified whole and organised to accomplish a set of goals'. Mill and Morrison (1985), in explaining the tourism system, highlight the exchange process between consumers and suppliers by way of four integrating components: the market, the travel element, the destination and the marketing mechanism. These elements are linked, in the first instance, by flows of information followed by visitors travelling between originating and receiving destinations. The processes, which enable this to happen, through, for example, travel intermediaries and transport providers facilitate the tourism experience.

This is reaffirmed in a seminal study on tourism as a system by Leiper (1990), where a system can be defined as a set of elements or parts that are connected to each other by at least one distinguishing principle. In this case, tourism is the distinguishing principle that connects the different components in the system around a common theme. Laws (1991: 7) developed this idea a stage further by providing a systems model of the tourism industry in which the key components were the inputs, outputs and external factors conditioning the system (e.g. the external business environment, consumer preferences, political factors and economic issues). As external factors are important influences upon tourism systems, the system can be termed 'open', which means that it can easily be influenced by factors aside from the main 'inputs'. The links within the system can be examined in terms of 'flows' between components and these flows may highlight the existence of certain types of relationships between different components (Figure 1.4). For example:

● What effect does an increase in the cost of travel have on the demand for travel?
● How does this have repercussions for other components in the system?
● Will it reduce the number of tourists travelling?

A systems approach has the advantage of allowing the researcher to consider the effect of such changes to the tourism system to assess the likely impact on other components.

Leiper (1990) identified the following elements of a tourism system: a tourist; a traveller-generating region; tourism destination regions; transit routes for tourists travelling between generating and destination areas; and the travel and tourism industry (e.g. accommodation, transport, the firms and organisations supplying services and products to tourists). In this analysis, transport forms an integral part of the tourism system, connecting the tourist-generating and destination regions, which is represented in terms of the volume of travel. The significance of transport in the tourism system is also apparent in the model developed by Laws (1991), where a series of smaller sub-systems were also identified (e.g. the transport system) which can be analysed as a discrete activity in its own right whilst also forming an integral part of the wider 'tourism system'. Thus, a 'tourist transport' system is a framework that embodies the entire tourist experience of travelling on a particular form of transport.

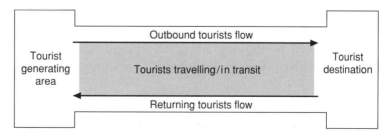

Figure 1.4 A tourism system

Source: Redrawn from Page 1994.

Despite having such a framework, Lumsdon and Page (2004b: 3) point to a number of problems that make comparisons between the way tourist and transport trips are treated by researchers. This leads to problems of coordinating data, agreeing on what is being measured and a gap between the commonly used forms of transport and tourism data at different spatial scales (see Figure 1.5). As Lumsdon and Page (2004b: 3) indicated:

the definitions, which have been almost universally applied in transport studies, are not formulated similarly in tourism. In transport, for example, a trip involves a movement of a person between two places in order for activities to be undertaken . . . In transport studies, a trip can be undertaken by using one mode of transport only or several modes. Furthermore, the trip can be divided into trip legs, each leg being a section of the overall trip made by one mode. The duration of the trip is the time between the start and finish of a journey. A tour refers to more than one trip from an originating zone to other places, but finally returning to the base destination zone. Tourism studies draw on a parallel framework but the conceptual base and definitions often differ. For example, the terms 'trip' and 'tour' are less clearly specified in tourism than in transport studies. Journey purpose is also defined differently in that transport trips can be made for work, leisure, and educational purposes whereas tourism trips include business, pleasure, visiting friends and relatives, health and religion. There are currently attempts to harmonise conceptual frameworks and data collection, mainly in relation to long distance travel, but they are still in gestation. For example, in the European Union the Methods for European Surveys of Travel Behaviour (MEST) and the DATELINE studies are seeking to co-ordinate survey design, procedures and sampling across EU member states.

For this reason the systems approach has some analytical value because it enables one to understand the overall process of tourist travel from both the supplier's and purchaser's perspectives whilst identifying the organisations that influence and regulate tourist transport, although it does not address the data limitations which exist between measuring the scale, volume and nature of tourist travel using different modes of transport. This is aptly summarised by Lamb and Davidson (1996: 264–65), who highlight the principal relationships that exist between the tourist, transport and their overall experience where

the purchaser of the tourism product *(the tourist)* must experience the trip to access the product, the quality of the transportation experience becomes an important aspect of the tourist experience and, therefore, a key criterion that enters into destination choice. Poor service, scheduling problems, and/or long delays associated with a transportation service, for example, can seriously affect a traveller's perceptions and levels of enjoyment with respect to a trip. Tourists require safe, comfortable, affordable, and efficient intermodal transportation networks that enable precious vacation periods to be enjoyed to their maximum potential.

This highlights the importance of:

- the tourist;
- the integral relationship between the transport and overall tourist experience;
- the effect of transport problems on traveller perception;
- the tourist's requirement for safe, reliable and efficient modes of transport.

SCALE OF ANALYSIS

DOMESTIC

	Local	Regional	National	International
Transport	• Local authority traffic counts • Travel behaviour studies • Transport operator on-board surveys and diary analysis • Recreational traffic counts (e.g. Loch Lomond and Trossachs National Park) • EURO-RAP road traffic accident data by organisations in each country • Consultants report s, unpublished on specific transport themes • Specialist transport providers and agencies for cycling (e.g. Sustrans), boating, coach, rail and air travel	• Scottish Executive administered traffic counts • Government transport statistics in reports such as Annual Transport Statistics and specially themed reports • Regional development agencies and regional governments	• Government White Papers (e.g. 2003 Airports Policy in the UK) • Specific operators in the airline, rail, coach/bus and sea sector, usually as in-house studies in the public/private sphere	• European Commission Eurostat publications • Privately commissioned and Omnibus Studies by consultancy companies selling the findings commercially • Industry body reports (e.g. Air Transport Action Group) • Statistical sources produced by agencies such as IATA, ICAO • Regional transport groups such as the Association of Asia Pacific Airlines and Association of European Airlines • United Nations statistical sources and reports • Specialised reports from trading blocs such as APEC, ASEAN and NAFTA
Tourism sector	• Local tourist boards • Local authority-commissioned studies and feasibility studies and regional and national government agency-commissioned studies	• Regional tourist boards	• National tourism organisations	• Tour operators in-house data, e-tourism portals and providers (e.g. Expedia, lastminute.com) • World Tourism Organization • World Travel and Tourism Council • Pacific Asia Tourism Association

Figure 1.5 Statistical sources in tourist transport studies

One recent study by Hyde and Laesser (2008) examining the concept of the vacation has highlighted the important role of transport in tourist decision-making associated with destination choice behaviour. Hyde and Laesser (2008) proposed that a vacation is a live human experience, and elements of that experience will unfold in a logical manner. They suggest that vacations have three typologies:

● Stay-put vacations, focused on one destination.
● Arranged touring vacations, typically involving touring several destinations in multiple locations.
● Freewheeling touring vacations where few stops on the itinerary have been pre-planned.

In each typology, transport will be crucial in terms of the pattern of activity which the individual/group undertakes. The typology acknowledges the wide variety of tourist travel for holidays as well as the importance of the transit trip to a destination, use of transport in the destination and importance of the supply of transport infrastructure in destination areas (e.g. mass transportation and hire cars).

These relationships are developed by Lamb and Davidson (1996), who explore a number of interfaces between transport and tourism. In their pioneering study of Ontario, Canada, they provide a range of examples that highlight the multifaceted nature of tourism, transport and the relationship with government (which is also discussed more fully in Chapter 3). As Figure 1.6 suggests, by adopting a modal approach to transport (e.g. rail, air, bus/coach and marine-based forms of transport) it is possible to demonstrate some of the functional roles transport infrastructure provides (e.g. linear corridors for tourism uses such as use of redundant rail routes). This also raises the importance of seamless travel experiences for tourists, so that different forms of transport are integrated. For example, in the case of France, the state government investment in the TGV is a clear recognition of the role of intermodal transport for tourism (i.e. how different modes of transport can work together to create a seamless journey, a feature reiterated by the OECD (1992)). Figure 1.6 is also important in emphasising how the tourism industry can harness transport linkages to develop transport-related products (e.g. scenic touring routes by car or bicycle or creation of new products). But achieving a suitable level of investment in transport infrastructure to allow tourism to thrive and develop also poses many challenges for policy-makers and planners. As Lamb and Davidson (1996: 271–2) observe, many of these challenges are timeless since they affect many destinations globally (not just in Ontario), particularly in relation to road-based tourism, including:

● *the quality of infrastructure*, since Ontario's highways are continuing to deteriorate;
● *road congestion*, especially at locations such as Lake Ontario, which may deter visitors from exploring such attractions and scenic routes;
● *signage* to encourage the spontaneous visit and to facilitate the unplanned visit.

Other initiatives related to tourist transport that Lamb and Davidson (1996) review include:

● improving intermodal connections;
● developing stronger linkages between ferry and other transport modes;
● the development of new linear land and water corridors that integrate various forms of transport to explore scenic areas.

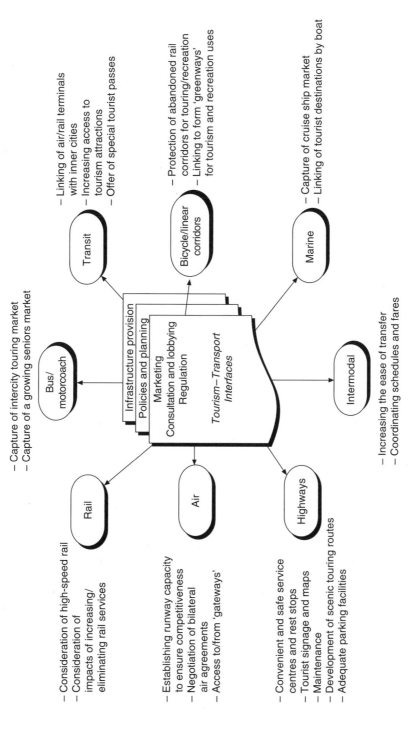

Figure 1.6 Linkages between tourism and transport

Source: Adapted from Lamb, B. and Davidson, S. 'Tourism and transportation in Ontario, Canada', in L. Harrison and W. Husbands (eds) *Practising Responsible Tourism: International Case Studies in Tourism Planning, Policy and Development*, Copyright © 1996, New York: Wiley, 261–76. This material is used by permission of John Wiley & Sons Inc.

One important tourism relationship which is worth emphasising is that coach tours encourage overnight stays and so can stimulate spending en route. Well-developed scenic touring routes therefore need to be supported by road infrastructure, accommodation and stopping points as lookouts. In Ontario, the transport ministry oversees highway support services such as signage, tourist information centres and traffic management systems. While Lamb and Davidson's (1996) invaluable study identifies the links between transport and tourism, it also highlights the need for regions or states to consider the concept of seamless transport systems for tourists. This means that the individual transport networks which exist for each mode of tourist transport need to be planned and integrated into a holistic framework. This will ensure that the tourists' experience of transport is a continuous one which is not characterised by major gaps in provision and a lack of integration between gateways and destinations (Palhares 2003). For instance, airports need to be linked to their central tourist districts so that visitors transfer from one mode of transport to another with relative ease after long flights when tiredness and disorientation can mar their experience. Recognising such linkages in terms of tourism can also yield invaluable business opportunities (e.g. the growth in airport shuttle companies) where ancillary transport operators can attract business by the provision of convenient door-to-door services for travellers.

Reconceptualising transport and tourism: a new approach?

According to Lumsdon and Page (2004b: 4) the principal issues in attempting to overcome the problems of not only measuring but conceptualising tourist trips and the transportation element can be framed in terms of the utility of tourist trips – or what makes them different from other types of trip. These, by their very nature, often involve a trip to an unfamiliar place or area and a limited amount of information may be available on the options available. Here the availability of information to the traveller combined with their accessibility is critical. This led Lumsdon and Page (2004b) to distinguish between:

- Transport *for* tourism, where it is a means to an end, being very utilitarian, and the level of satisfaction is related to cost and speed of travel, so the mode of travel has no direct intrinsic value in itself. Thus, as Prideaux (2000a) noted, travel has traditionally been viewed as a cost rather than a benefit, almost as an opportunity cost.
- Transport *as* tourism, where the transport mode is the containing context for travel such as a cruise and a basis for the tourist experience. Here the travel cost principle in transport for tourism does not apply where the transport is the main benefit, or at least many of the attributes associated with the mode of transport are beneficial.

As Figure 1.7 shows, these two interconnected approaches to transport and tourism may be expressed as a continuum, as developed by Lumsdon in its most recent form and published elsewhere (Lumsdon and Page 2004b). This is more to do with the distinction between transport *for* tourism offering low intrinsic value within the overall experience and transport *as* tourism offering a higher intrinsic value. Here the concept of speed and mobility combines with a desire for a functional

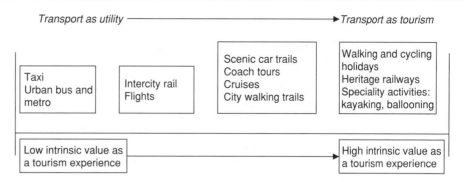

Figure 1.7 The tourist transport continuum

Source: Reprinted from *Tourism and Transport*, p 7, L. Lumsdon and S.J. Page (eds) (2004), Copyright © 2004, with permission from Elsevier.

travel experience in moving people from A to B, such as tourists travelling on a package holiday, which characterises one end of the continuum. This moves through to the other end of the scale, where cycling or cruising characterises the transport *as* tourism where the mode of transport is designed as pivotal to the tourist experience. At an operational level, this can be expressed in a more complex manner to integrate not only the tourism system approach but also the features developed in Figure 1.8 so that a more all-embracing view is possible on how transport and tourism are intrinsically linked. Figure 1.8 also highlights a series of vital interconnections involving the travel experience comprising a series of transitionary phases from initial departure from home through to arrival at a port of departure and arrival in the destination through to the return trip. At each point, the critical linkages associated with transport are highlighted that combine both the potential for multi-modal tourist travel experiences and the possible interaction between transport for tourism and transport as tourism during a holiday or tourist experience. This also highlights the continuum through from recreational travel (i.e. up to 24 hours) to the experience of travelling as a tourist, even on more extended business trips or longer exploratory trips such as backpacking for extended time periods. It also shows that recreational activities on holiday in a destination may involve the experience of transport from a purely utilitarian perspective or from a transport as tourism perspective (e.g. a whale-watching experience using a marine form of transport combined with a tourist activity). To illustrate the features of a high-quality transport as tourism service, Insight 1.2 examines the importance of luxury travel, where the transport element is a key component of that experience.

INSIGHT 1.2

Luxury train travel: the definitive tourist transport service

Luxury tourism, defined as consuming an expensive and high-quality experience was the norm among the travelling elite in the eighteenth, nineteenth and early twentieth century. It included the Grand Tour, travel on luxury cruise liners and travel on the early commercial airlines. As these products and experiences have become more widely available, tourism businesses have sought to push back the boundaries of luxury travel to cater for the ▶

increasing demand for such experiences. Among some of the novel experiences are: travel to exclusive tourist resorts, tailor-made packages including private jets with the emphasis on comfort, service, relaxation, sumptuous quality and attention to detail and exacting standards. Some analysts have argued that the consumption of luxury is about emotion, with the key factor being the experience rather than the nature of the product. In surveys of luxury, the elements of travel and tourism are often rated as amongst the highest elements of people's wish list, illustrating the significance of the concept of luxury, perception and consumption in relation to travel and tourism.

In the luxury market, a tailored experience with a high degree of customisation is about making a dream turn into reality. The 2007 CapGemini Merril Lynch wealth survey noted that there were 9.6 million people globally with assets in excess of US$1 million and this was rising, especially in newly industrialising countries.

One area which has seen significant growth in recent years has been the luxury train market, often epitomised by the Orient Express. Some of the most notable luxury train products include: the Royal Canadian Pacific, the GrandLux Express (USA), the Blue Train in South Africa, the Trans Siberian Express, the Ghan in Australia, the new Danube Express in Central Europe and the Royal Scotsman (now owned by Orient Express) in the UK. With many of these services priced at the upper end of the market, they are designed to be luxurious, comfortable, and appealing to the luxury traveller. But probably the most well known is the Orient Express.

The Orient Express began in 1883, with a service inaugurated by George Nagelmackers of Belgium on a service from Paris to Romania. This was the start of Compagnie des Wagons-Lits et des Grands Express Européens, based on the sleeping cars used in the USA. Patronage was by the rich and famous with the term the 'Train of Kings' used in the 1890s. The Simplon Tunnel constructed under the Alps and linking Switzerland and Italy opened in 1906, and saw the train extended initially to Milan and then Venice. Its heyday of use was in the 1920s and 1930s when its prestige increased as the rolling stock was upgraded. Owing to the Second World War the service was interrupted, but it was reinstated after 1945. It continued as a semi-luxurious service until 1962, when it was replaced by a standard sleeper service from Paris to Istanbul. In 1977 two sleeper carriages were acquired at auction by entrepreneur James Sherwood of SeaContainers, followed by a further 35 being acquired and restored. In 1994 Sherwood reinstated the Orient Express from Victoria Station in London, comprising 1920s and 1930s Pullman carriages for the London–Folkestone section with coach connections through the Channel Tunnel and original Wagon-Lits carriages for the continental Europe section. The trains run for the season March–November and, in 2003, carried 18,000 passengers.

Much of the appeal of these tourist services relates to heritage, the halcyon days of a bygone era, as the following extract from the Orient-Express brochure *A World of Distinction* (2004: 3) infers:

For over a century, travel upon the Orient-Express has epitomized European elegance and continental chic. Today the experience is as fresh, as magical and as effortlessly elegant as ever. Orient-Express now includes a stylish collection of international travel experiences. This brochure introduces you to train journeys and cruises that remain resoundingly true to the spirit of the original Orient-Express, and to some of the most distinctive hotels in the world, each with its own story to tell, and each offering a cultural experience without parallel. These are journeys of genuine distinction, of rare authenticity. They are triumphant proof that the golden age of travel lives on.

This Insight highlights the real premium prices that a tourist transport service with personal service can command, with attention to the finest detail, exquisite surroundings, and above all a memorable experience of distinction. Thus a re-creation of a tourist service emphasising the bygone era can yield a good return for a company with vision and the resources to make a long-term investment in the product and service.

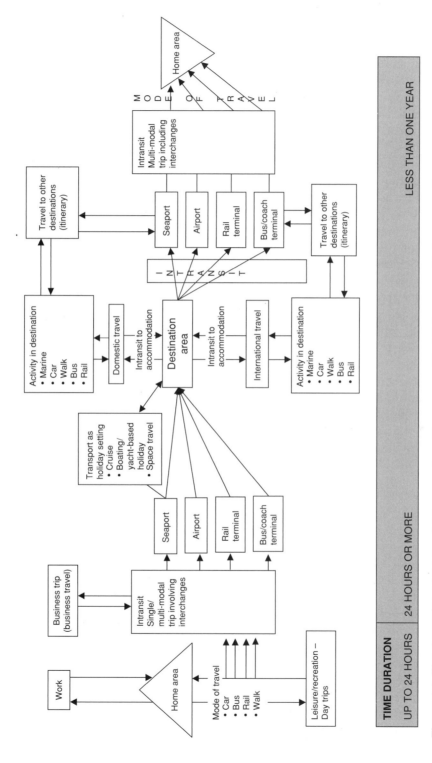

Figure 1.8 The dynamics of the tourist transport continuum – critical linkages and inter-connections

●●●● The nature and scope of tourist transport: modes of travel

Figure 1.9 shows that during any recreational or tourist trip tourists may encounter and use different forms of transport. Although this may seem self-evident, it is useful to briefly outline some of the key characteristics of tourist transport, which can be divided into a simple classification (Table 1.2). It is also evident from Table 1.2 that access to tourist transport is dependent upon the available disposable income to purchase travel options, which varies by social groups and in and between countries. Whilst walking has no direct charge for recreational purposes when staying in a destination area, access to transport to reach a destination will depend upon the distance involved, income available, ownership of transport and other factors such as willingness to travel. Cost becomes a key factor in many travel choices and Table 1.2 highlights how important the developed–less developed world differences are in tourist transport options, where income levels, affluence and patterns of consumption are markedly different. These factors affect access to transport for tourism according to cost and availability.

What is notable from the transport studies literature is that these different forms of transport may have a degree of substitutability, which means that no one mode has a monopoly on tourist travel, unless the infrastructure and availability of travel options are limited by government policy or a reluctance of the public/private sector to provide a service. Therefore, Figure 1.9 highlights a range of options available to tourists in many destinations, expanding upon the principles developed in Figure 1.8. Here transport may be a central feature of the tourists' activity patterns and focus of their leisure time, since it assists with the mobility from the accommodation to the attractions and activities. This would serve to illustrate how a high degree of substitutability may also occur in tourist transport use even in a destination, where weather conditions may impact upon the modal choice, while policy issues (i.e. a car-free destination) may condition what the visitor can access via available transport modes.

What is an overwhelming yet relatively poorly studied element is the car. This now dominates recreational and non-recreational travel in most developed countries, as later chapters will show, and offers considerable flexibility in accessing destination areas. It has the potential to cross borders and natural obstacles (e.g. seas) using other modes of tourist transport (e.g. car ferries, tunnels or bridges). We tend to overlook the fundamental importance of the car in terms of air travel and its significance in facilitative short-haul travel. Table 1.2 also shows that there is considerable scope for novel ideas and innovations in the development of tourist transport options which feature as transport for tourism. Competition between different forms of tourist transport is also important, which highlights the significance of substitutability in transport for tourism, where price, demand, supply and relative cost become critical components. In addition, modes of tourist transport are complementary and the linkages shown in Figure 1.8 need to be seamless if the experience of travelling is to be more than what Gunn (1994) described as a necessary evil of travelling, to reach a destination as transport for tourism.

In addition to these arguments, D. Hall (1999) argued that there are also more profound questions raised by the discussion of tourist transport, notably that leisure and tourism mobility raises issues of inequality and can exert substantial

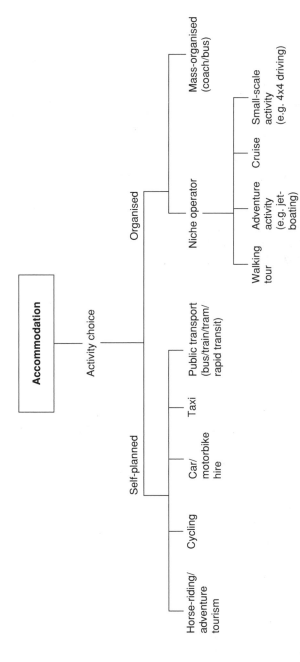

Figure 1.9 Transporting the tourist in the destination

Table 1.2 Examples of tourist transport – characteristics and classification

Location of mode	Form	Infrastructure requirements	Access to population	Cost	Transport for tourism Yes ✓ No X	Transport as tourism Yes ✓ No X
Land	Walking	● Tracks ● Paved surfaces ● Way-marked areas ● Public access	All able-bodied	None	X	✓ ● Hiking ● Strolling ● Guided walks
	Cycling	● Roads ● Tracks ● Cycle paths	All able-bodied	Bicycle purchase or hire	✓ ● Cycling holidays ● Day trips	✓ ● Cycling tours
	Car	● Vehicles ● Roads ● Bridges ● Ferries ● Tunnels ● Petrol/diesel	Licensed drivers	Cost of purchase or hire	✓ ● Travel to destination ● Travel in destination	✓ ● Touring holiday
	Coach (Express)	● Scheduled services ● Vehicle ● Terminal	All able-/non-able-bodied	Relatively low	✓ ● Travel to destination	X
	(Tour)	● Vehicle ● Terminal ● Same as car requirements	All able-/non-able-bodied	Modest	X	✓ ● Set itinerary
	Bus	● Scheduled services ● Same as car requirements	All able-bodied	Low	● ✓ ● Travel to destination ● Travel in destination	✓ ● Sight-seeing ● Open-top bus tours
	Rickshaw/ motorbike/ motorised bike	● As for car requirements plus service provision	All able-bodied	Low		
	Rail	● Scheduled services ● Rail network ● Terminal/ stations ● Inter-connections ● Locomotive/ carriages	All able-bodied	Low to medium	✓ ● Travel to destination ● Travel in destination	✓ ● Steam tours ● Vintage heritage tours
Sea	Ferry	● Port ● Docking area ● Terminal buildings ● Access by road	All	Low to medium	✓ ● Sea crossing	✓ ● Short sea cruises
Inland water-ways	Sailing boat	● Waterway ● Pier/access ● Road	All	High/hire	✓ ● Port to port	✓ ● Cruise
	Narrow boat	● As for sailing boat requirements ● Canal	All	Hire	X	✓ ● Holiday
Sea	Cruising	● Same as ferry	All	High	X	✓

Table 1.2 (*Continued*)

Location of mode	Form	Infrastructure requirements	Access to population	Cost	Transport for tourism Yes ✓ No X	Transport as tourism Yes ✓ No X
Air	Scheduled flight	• Terminal • Runway • Aircraft	All	Low to high (low cost to first class)	✓ • Business travel • Holiday travel	X
	Charter flight	• Same requirements as scheduled flights	All	Low to medium cost	✓ • Holiday trip	X
	Sightseeing flight	• Same requirements as scheduled flights	Visitors in destination mainly	High	X	✓ • Scenic areas • Glacier flights
	Helicopter flight	• Infrastructure landing area urban or rural	All	High	✓	✓
	Balloon flight	• Take-off area • Ground crew • Mobile location • Area free of hazards	Visitors or recreationalists	High	X	✓
	Space travel	• Shuttle aircraft • Space programme	Millionaires	Very high	X	✓

externality effects on host communities, as it brings large numbers of people to environments which may not necessarily be able to sustain their activities. It also raises new debates that are germane to the growing concern about the environmental effects of transport, including tourists and residents competing for road space, congestion charging and competition for public transport use. Such critical issues transcend the conceptualisation of tourism and transport due to the effects of transport and tourism on localities. Adding to the existing analysis of transport in tourism, D. Hall (1999: 181) also identified four generally accepted geographically expressed roles for tourism transport:

- in linking the source market with the host destination;
- in providing mobility and access within the destination;
- in providing mobility and access within an actual tourist attraction;
- in facilitating travel along a recreational route.

This explains some of the linkages illustrated in Figure 1.8 and some of the underlying issues which are developed through the book on impacts, inequalities and how transport when linked with tourism can act as an agent of social and economic change. In addition, one perspective which has become more prominent in recent years is the analysis of transport and tourism in developing destinations, which expands upon Hall's (1999) study. Destination development, developed in the transport-tourism literature, is worth considering at the initial stage of the book, even though it will resurface at different points later on.

Tourism and destination development: a critical role for transportation?

The issue of transport as a key element of destination development has a well-established place in tourism studies dating back to the seminal work by Gilbert (1939) on the evolution of resorts, in which transport and new technology (e.g. the railways) played a major part in expanding the accessibility of the destination (i.e. the place) to a wider population. If transport is such a critical element of the growth of destinations, it is important to understand what in fact a destination is. Tourist destinations are a mix of tourism products, experiences and other intangible items promoted to consumers. At a general level, this concept of a destination can be developed to represent geographically defined entities such as groups of countries, individual countries, regions in a country, a rural area, a resort or a wide range of experiences created by tourism marketers. Increasingly, the notion of a destination is something perceived by consumers, although most conventional definitions emphasise the geographical element of a specific place. From a tourist's perspective, a destination may usually be classified into: conventional resorts; environmental destinations; business tourism centres; places one stops at en route to another place; a short-break destination and day-trip destinations. In essence, destinations are places which tourists visit and stay at. Whatever way one approaches the concept of a destination (i.e. from an industry-supply perspective or from the consumer's viewpoint), there are six interrelated components which comprise a destination, often refereed to as an amalgam of the six *As*:

● Available Packages;
● Accessibility;
● Attractions;
● Amenities;
● Activities; and
● Ancillary Services.

In this context, transport infrastructure and accessibility are two critical elements which Ritchie and Crouch (2003) highlight as facilitating destination development. Even so, the role of transport in this facilitating role has attracted very little attention from researchers (the most notable exception being Prideaux 2000a). Prideaux (2000a) characterised the role of transport in shaping destination development around a number of key concepts already highlighted in this chapter, focusing on the notion of a destination as the framework for analysing transport and tourism:

● as a staging post for travel elsewhere;
● as a focal point for international and domestic tourism flows building on Leiper's (1990) arguments on a tourist transit route and flows;
● as a focus of perceived and actual travel time to get to a specific holiday destination;
● as a focus for transport networks which tourists use to travel within the destination and provision of interconnections to travel onwards to other destinations;
● as a focus for inbound tourism, particularly for tourist arrivals by air.

These ideas developed by Prideaux fit with the notion of transport as being one of the key levers for achieving resort and destination growth, a feature reiterated in

VisitScotland's (2007) *Tourism Prospectus* where transport is viewed as a staple underpinning to any potential growth which the tourism economy can achieve. Prideaux (2000a) pointed to the very influential study by Kaul (1985: 496) which acknowledged that

> transport plays an important role in the successful creation and development of new attractions as well as the healthy growth of existing ones. Provision of suitable transport has transformed dead centres of tourist interest into active and prosperous places attracting multitudes of people.

These ideas were developed further as a series of postulates which are simplified in Figure 1.10 to demonstrate the critical linkages between tourism and destination development as a virtuous circle. In each postulate, the relationship between transport and tourism and its critical role in a destination context is highlighted implicitly or explicitly (although they do overlook the crucial role of price as a determinant of travel demand–see Chapter 2 for further discussion) according

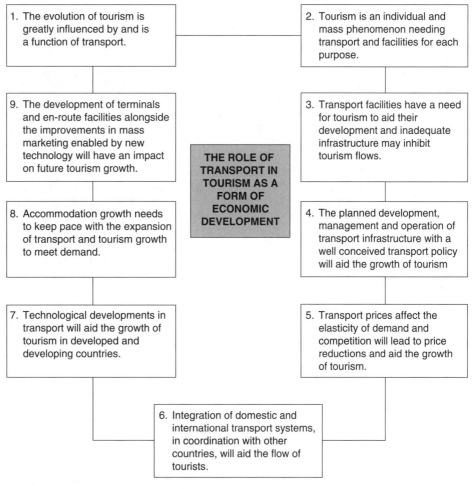

Figure 1.10 The role of transport in tourism resort development

Source: Developed and modified from Kaul (1985).

to Prideaux, given the competitive global market which exists for travel and tourism products and services. Insight 1.3 highlights the important role of transport in destination, focusing on one country with an expansionist tourism strategy and demonstrating how it views transport as one of the key levers for future growth.

INSIGHT 1.3

Developing tourist transport infrastructure to expand tourism: Turkey's tourism strategy to 2023

In 2007, the Ministry of Culture and Tourism launched the new tourism strategy for Turkey to 2023. It fits with the country's 9th Development Scheme, an economic development strategy to 2013. The strategy recognises that a focus on the development of mass tourism has led to:

● geographical concentration of tourism on the Mediterranean and Aegean Coast;
● distorted urban development patterns;
● environmental and infrastructure problems.

The new strategy seeks to address these problems by creating a Master Plan for tourism in Turkey by establishing nine tourism development areas, seven thematic tourism corridors, 10 tourism cities and five ecotourism zones by focusing investment and public sector interventions on areas of priority. This is to be supported by improving transport infrastructure by building motorways, establishing cruise ship and yacht marinas and fast links. The plan states that 'transportation is a bridge that connects tourists to tourism centres which serve as focal points of consumption' requiring better integration of transport modes, as well as linking arrivals in gateways with fast and efficient onward transport to destinations through new airport development and improved interregional railway links. Road transport is also prioritised as a key area for investment as the route network is below the EU average in both length and coverage. New tourist destinations will be created through new road development and connections to other destinations. This will involve two levels of road route development: motorways and segmental split highways (access roads). The plan seeks to increase tourism to 63 million visitors by 2023 in order to expand the tourism economy to US$86 million. The ambition is to establish Turkey as a world brand in tourism and to be in the Top 5 receiving countries for overseas visitors. This seems to be a massive expansionist programme for a destination that has already faced many problems linked to tourism.

So how does this book aim to integrate the ideas which have been raised in this first chapter in order for the notion of tourist travel to be more fully understood in the study of tourism?

The structure of the book and its approach

In view of the objectives of the *Themes in Tourism* series this book is not intended to be a comprehensive review of transport for tourism. It is designed as a framework in which the reader can gain a clearer understanding of the tourist transport system and some of the ways in which one can analyse its provision, operation and the factors influencing it. One of the inherent problems with such a book is the inevitable tension between whether it is viewed as a tourism- or transport-oriented text. It reflects the problem of achieving a balance between writing a book on a wide-ranging topic that embraces two huge subject areas – tourism and transport. It inevitably requires a compromise to be reached between what is studied and discussed and the level of detail available on specific issues.

The book is primarily written from a tourism perspective but also has a wider transport audience in mind. Even so, the book does also pose other issues such as how the relationship between tourism and transport is conceptualised and viewed by the author and readers. From one perspective, tourism can be viewed as initiating demand that requires the provision of transport, such as the widening of holiday provision in the nineteenth century and inter-war years in the UK (Page 2003, 2009). The result is that the travel component becomes either the transport for tourism or transport as tourism option or a combination of each, as discussed above. Yet another perspective also exists, namely that transport is the instrumental element in facilitating the expansion of tourism (i.e. as a facilitator). This is epitomised by the rise of the low-cost airline phenomenon in the USA heralded by Southwest Airlines and in the UK by Laker's Skytrain concept and latterly through budget airlines such as Ryanair and easyJet, and in Asia more recently through Air Asia based in Malaysia. Here the emphasis in approaching the study of the interrelationships between tourism and transport is the impact the transport mode has on tourist travel, with the tourist trip the main focus.

Throughout this book a combination of these approaches is implicitly used to illustrate some of the key relationships and interconnections and interactions between tourism and transport. But as innovations and developments in the demand and supply of tourism opportunities and changes in transport provision are continuous, apportioning the explanation of a specific relationship to either of these perspectives is not necessarily a simple process. A multitude of factors and processes are at work, making classifications and simple explanations of the transport and tourism phenomenon far from easy. In each case, the approach one adopts may in fact have underlying explanations associated with government policy, explicit or implicit, in seeking to facilitate or develop the tourism or transport sector or a combination of both.

One objective of this book is to overcome the existing perception of tourist transport as a passive element in the tourist's experience that has to be endured to reach a destination area (cruising and touring excepted). The actual process of travelling is an integral part of the tourist's experience even though it is perceived as less important than the activities and pursuits of tourists in the destination. The book offers a number of perspectives of tourist transport that the reader may find a useful starting point for further research on transport and tourism. One underlying theme emphasised throughout the book is that transport for tourism constitutes a 'service' that is increasingly judged by consumers and providers in relation to the quality, standards and level of satisfaction it engenders. For this reason, both a systems approach and an emphasis on the multidisciplinarity of tourist transport help to transcend the rather fragmented view of this aspect of tourism studies. This multidisciplinarity is critical to providing a deeper understanding of how transport and tourism need to be understood in a more holistic and integrated manner.

Furthermore, this also helps in identifying some of the contributions that different subject areas aside from tourism or transport studies can make to the analysis of transport and tourism rather than adopting a narrow analysis which simply focuses upon what a limited number of transport or tourism researchers have looked at in the past two decades.

In Chapter 2, the multidisciplinarity of tourist transport is examined, drawing upon the concepts and approaches which illustrate how they can be used to understand contemporary issues in tourist transport, with a number of applied illustrations from economics, geography, marketing and management of contemporary themes in transport and tourism. These contemporary themes are also addressed throughout the book so a greater relevance and application of concepts and principles are illustrated through short insights and examples. Each area of study highlighted in Chapter 2 provides a useful insight into the specialised nature of research on tourism and transport studies that is rarely discussed in terms of the way each complements our understanding of the tourist transport system. As Leiper and Simmons (1993) show, researchers from different disciplines consider various aspects of tourism depending on their background and focus and this inevitably means that they consider specific inputs, outputs and external factors to affect the tourist transport system. For this reason it is useful to examine some of the common approaches and concepts used by different disciplines in analysing contemporary issues in tourist transport.

Chapter 3 considers the role of transport policy and planning, its effect on operational and consumer issues and the progress towards a common transport policy in the EU. It also examines how government policy can affect the development of tourist transport systems. This is followed in Chapter 4 by an analysis of the demand aspects of tourist travel and the data sources available to tourism researchers. The chapter also reviews methods of forecasting future tourist travel. Chapter 5 looks at the supply of tourist transport, focusing on the supply chain and how companies with transport interests seek to exercise control over the distribution and quality of tourist travel services. In Chapter 6 the focus is on the management of tourism supply issues, especially the implications of new technology and e-travel. In Chapter 7 the management theme is developed a stage further with a focus on transport infrastructure – the role of the airport as a terminal facility where airlines and travellers interact as part of the tourist experience. In Chapter 8 the human and environmental impact of tourist travel and the operation of different modes of tourist transport are discussed, examining the potential for developing sustainable tourist transport. This is followed by Chapter 9 outlining one of the greatest constraints on tourist travel – climate change and global warming and the implications of changes in the availability of energy. This is a new chapter written by Susanne Becken who has worked extensively around this important theme which has major significance for the tourist as a consumer, the tourism and transport industry and governments and other public sector bodies seeking to minimise the detrimental environmental effects of leisure and non-leisure travel. Chapter 10 concludes the book, examining some of the main issues that are likely to affect tourist transport in the next decade, particularly the role of globalisation and privatisation in transport systems. Other issues such as service quality are also reviewed in tourist transport systems.

Questions

1 To what extent is tourist transport considered an area of study in transport and tourism studies?
2 What are the main linkages between transport and tourism?
3 What is the value of a systems approach to the analysis of tourist transport?
4 What are the main features of a tourism system?

Further reading

Lamb, B. and Davidson, S. (1996) 'Tourism and transportation in Ontario, Canada', in L. Harrison and W. Husbands (eds) *Practising Responsible Tourism: International Case Studies in Tourism Planning, Policy and Development*, Chichester: Wiley.

McIntosh, R.W. (1973) *Tourism Principles, Practices and Philosophies*, Columbus OH: Grid Inc. This is often attributed as the first tourism textbook to be published for a tourism studies audience.

The concept of a tourism system is dealt with in: Laws, E. (1991) *Tourism Marketing: Service Quality and Management Perspectives*, Cheltenham: Stanley Thornes.

Leiper, N. (1990) *Tourism Systems: An Interdisciplinary Perspective*, Palmerston North: Massey University.

Wheatcroft, S. (1978) 'Transport, tourism and the service industry', *Chartered Institute of Transport Journal*, 38(7): 197–206.

Websites

For tourism data see: www.world-tourism.org
For the World Travel and Tourism Council research see: www.wttc.org
For the Air Transport Action Group (ATAG) see: www.atag.org

2

Understanding contemporary issues and approaches in transport and tourism in the twenty-first century

●●●● Introduction

Tourism, like transport studies, is a multidisciplinary field of study that has borrowed and refined concepts and theories from other subjects as it establishes itself as a legitimate area of academic study. This poses a number of problems for researchers when exploring the relationship between transport and tourism in the context of tourist transport systems. For example, what approaches and methods of study should one use to analyse tourist transport systems? In most cases research is based on those social science disciplines with an interest in tourism and/or transport studies. This has an important bearing on the analysis of tourist transport systems because the types of question a researcher asks, and the focus of their work, are often determined by their disciplinary background. In other words, each subject area has its own range of concepts and way of viewing the world that builds upon the knowledge and research in that area. For this reason, this chapter commences with a broad overview of some of the key issues associated with transport and tourism in the twenty-first century to highlight what types of concepts and approaches are needed to understand them.

●●●● Contemporary issues in tourist transport in the twenty-first century

As Figure 2.1 shows, understanding the themes and issues associated with tourist transport spans many subject areas. Whilst this list of themes is by no means comprehensive, it does highlight two key points: to understand each theme requires a distinctive set of concepts and approaches, and increasingly these themes cannot artificially be divided into different subject areas because of the interconnections between them (see Preston and O'Connor 2008 for a detailed discussion of these interconnections). Nevertheless, for reasons of simplicity, Figure 2.1 identifies the broad themes which have an associated set of questions which this chapter and others will seek to address, through the contribution made by different subject areas to the analysis of tourism and transport issues. One area notably absent from the discussion is transport history, with its own journal – the *Journal of Transport History*

Area of interest	Tourism/transport industry/operations and management	Consumer/ traveller	Environment

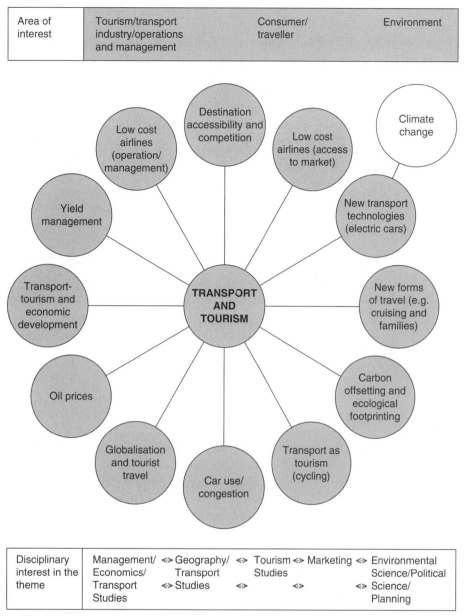

Disciplinary interest in the theme	Management/ Economics/ Transport Studies	<>	Geography/ Transport <> Studies	<>	Tourism Studies	<>	Marketing	<>	Environmental Science/Political <> Science/ Planning

<> Disciplinary connections/shared interest.

Figure 2.1 Contemporary themes in tourist transport to 2015

(e.g. see Baronowski 2007 for a discussion of the links between transport and tourism history). Whilst history does not explicitly deal with contemporary issues, some of the themes and issues discussed in this chapter have historical antecedents as illustrated in relation to car-based tourism (Prideaux and Carson 2009). What is becoming increasingly clear is that the pace and speed of change in transport and tourism is such that historical analysis may be interesting because sometimes issues come full circle, as the UK railway system shows: it was initially developed by

Plate 2.1 National Express InterCity 125 high speed train, used on long-distance routes such as Inverness to London Kings Cross, an eight-hour journey ©National Express

Source: Image courtesy of National Express

private investors and railway companies, then nationalised and then re-privatised (Plate 2.1)

Whilst many subject areas have made distinctive contributions to the study of tourism, no one discipline is all-embracing enough to understand the complexity of the tourist transport system. Social science subjects such as social psychology, sociology, and business and management studies have an interest in tourism and transport studies but there is a relative paucity of published research analysing the tourist transport system. However, for the purpose of this chapter, there are a number of subject areas identified for consideration since they have made a direct contribution to the analysis of tourist transport systems. These are:

- economics;
- geography;
- marketing;
- management.

Although other cognate areas such as logistics, planning, environmental science and behavioural sciences (e.g. psychology) do have a bearing, these are discussed throughout the book where their contribution is evident. However, the discussion in this chapter emphasises the main subject areas whose contribution is documented and concludes with a focus on management that provides a practical setting in which the contribution of each subject area is harnessed for a practical purpose – the management of tourist transport systems and different components within the system.

It must be stressed that this chapter does not attempt to provide a comprehensive review of the literature and main areas of research on transport and tourism. A wide range of books have already been published in economics (e.g. Doganis 2001, 2002), geography (Hoyle and Knowles 1998; Knowles et al. 2007) and marketing (Shaw 2003, 2007) that provide an insight into tourism and transport, although none have developed a particular focus on the transport–tourism relationship in its widest sense. The approach adopted here is to outline briefly the main principles each subject uses and to illustrate the distinctive approach it takes towards the analysis of tourist transport with appropriate applied and practical examples. Since this book can only be an introductory text, readers are directed to specialised studies for a more detailed insight into particular issues such as aviation (e.g. Graham et al. 2008).

The economist and tourist transport

The economist's approach to the analysis of tourist transport is based on two distinct areas of research: transport economics (e.g. Starkie 1976; Beesley 1989 (see Table 2.1)) and tourism economics (e.g. Bull 1991; Sinclair 1991; Sinclair and Stabler 1997), and each area of study uses similar concepts to understand how the tourist transport system functions. For this reason it is useful to consider what issues are examined by economists as a basis for a more detailed discussion of the concepts they use.

Economic issues in analysing tourist transport

According to Craven (1990: 3) 'economics is concerned with the economy or economic system . . . [and] the problem of allocating resources is a central theme of economics, because most resources are scarce'. Therefore Craven (1990: 4) argues that economics is the study of methods of allocating scarce resources and distributing the product of those resources, and the study of the consequences of these methods of allocation and distribution.

Table 2.1 Recent books on transport economics

General Texts

K. Button (ed.) (2003) *Recent Developments in Transport Economics*, Cheltenham: Edward Elgar Publishing.

T. Francis (ed) (2004) *Turning the Corner? A Reader in Contemporary Transport Policy*, Oxford: Blackwell Publishing.

R. Hall (ed) (2003) *Handbook of Transportation Science*, New York: Springer.

D. Hensher and A. Brewer (2000) *Transport: An Economics and Management Perspective*, Oxford: Oxford University Press.

S. Holloway (2008) *Straight and Level: Practical Airline Economics*, Aldershot: Ashgate.

P. Mccarthy (2001) *Transportation Economics*, Oxford: Blackwell Publishing.

H. Mohring (ed) (1994) *The Economics of Transport*, Cheltenham: Edward Elgar.

E. Quinet and R. Vickerman (2004) *Principles of Transport Economics*, Cheltenham: Edward Elgar.

K. Small and E. Verhoef (2007) *The Economics of Urban Transportation*, London: Routledge.

H. Stevens (2003) *Transport Policy in the European Union*, Basingstoke: Palgrave.

B. Vasigh, K. Fleming and T. Tacker (2008) *Introduction to Transport Economics*, Aldershot: Ashgate.

Source: Developed from Li (2008).

What is meant by scarcity and resources? The term 'scarcity' is used to illustrate the fact that most resources in society are finite and decisions have to be made on the best way to use and sustain them. Economists define resources in terms of:

- natural resources (e.g. the land);
- labour (e.g. human resources and entrepreneurship); and
- capital (e.g. synthetic aids to assist in producing goods);

and collectively these resources constitute *the factors of production* that are used to produce commodities. These commodities can be divided into:

- goods (e.g. tangible products such as an aircraft); and
- services (e.g. intangible items such as in-flight service – see Laws and Ryan 1992);

and the total output of all commodities in a country over a period of time, normally a year, is known as the *national product*. The creation of products and services is termed *production* and the use of these goods and services is called *consumption,* as discussed in Chapter 1. Since, in any society, the production of goods and services can only satisfy a small fraction of consumers' needs, choices have to be made in the allocation of resources to determine which goods and services to produce (Lipsey 1989). The way in which goods and services are divided amongst people has been examined by economists in terms of the distribution of income and the degree of equality and efficiency in their distribution. Many of these issues are dealt with under the heading of 'microeconomics', which Craven (1990: 4) succinctly defines as:

> the study of individual decisions and the interactions of these decisions . . . [including] consumers' decisions on what to buy, firms' decisions on what to produce and the interactions of these decisions, which determine whether people can buy what they would like, whether firms can sell all that they produce and the profits firms make by providing and selling.

Microeconomics is therefore concerned with certain issues, namely:

- the firm;
- the consumer;
- production and selling;
- the demand for goods;
- the supply of goods.

Economists also examine a broader range of economic issues in terms of *macroeconomics,* which is concerned with:

> the entire economy and interactions within it, including the population, income, total unemployment, the average rate of price increases (the inflation rate), the extent of companies' capacities to produce goods and the total amount of money in use in the country (Craven 1990: 5).

Therefore macroeconomics is mainly concerned with:

- how the national economy operates;
- employment and unemployment;
- inflation;
- national production and consumption;
- the money supply in a country.

Within micro- and macroeconomics both transport and tourism economists examine different aspects of the tourist transport system, which is based on the analysis of the concepts of demand and supply. However, prior to examining these concepts, it is pertinent to briefly examine the link between transport, tourism and economic development.

Transport, tourism and economic development

Irrespective of the critical role which transport plays in tourism, the economist's interest in transport is primarily focused on its role in creating economic benefits for the economy. Where transport systems operate efficiently, they can improve accessibility, create beneficial impacts and improve the mobility of people and goods. For example, Vahrenkamp (2006) examined the 1933–45 period in Germany where the concept of the Autobahn was also used as a tool to promote tourist travel. Where systems are inefficient, they may constrain economic development. This was one of the findings of the Eddington Report (HM Treasury 2006). The report examined the role of transport in sustaining the UK's productivity and competitiveness and argued that *transport and economic growth are coupled together and vital to the health of the economy: such arguments are rarely compatible with pro-sustainability.* The report highlighted the importance of large urban centres for economic activity and as a focus of transport activity, with 89 per cent of congestion delays occurring in urban areas and the need to address problems in:

● congested urban areas and their catchments;
● key inter-urban corridors;
● key international gateways;

reflecting the advice and arguments put forward by the wide range of industry bodies and transport economists/geographers during the consultation process. The report paid considerable attention to road issues, arguing that if we reduce travel time for businesses, it could generate cost savings: this pursues a simple economic argument that government subsidies for road building and road transport are good for the economy and development as this is the dominant mode of transport.

At a macroeconomic scale, some studies suggest that transport may account for around 10 per cent of a country's GDP as well as over 10 per cent of household expenditure. So it has a significant impact on national economies, enabling consumers and producers to be accessed easily, while being a key element in economic development. This is often most visible at a regional scale where transport infrastructure investment and provision may be used to pump-prime the economic development process. If tourism is brought into the equation, then the role in GDP and economic activity increases. The relationship between transport, tourism and economic development is a greatly debated area, with many transport organisations arguing that there is a broadly positive relationship between GDP and demand for transport. This is especially the case with air travel. But whilst transport may improve connectivity and accessibility for tourism, it can also have a negative effect if it makes outbound travel more attractive and inbound travel does not compensate for such effects. In other words, the UK's travel account runs in deficit because of the accessibility of outbound travel opportunities while other sectors of the economy point to the benefits offered by improved access and connectivity.

Where transport may also inhibit economic development is in situations where congestion leads to costs associated with delays, adding to higher costs of production. Nevertheless, transport is viewed as a prerequisite to achieve economic development, particularly where that development is related to tourism. Not only is this a function of infrastructure provision (e.g. roads, ports, airports and railways), but this infrastructure needs to be harnessed to provide an efficient connection between the tourist and destination if it is to gain a competitive advantage so that tourism can develop. In fact a number of early studies in tourism (e.g. Kaul 1985) recognised the link between transport, infrastructure and the economic development of tourism. More recent research by tourism economists have begun to model the importance of transport in explaining the economic development of tourism, building on Kaul's ideas, measured through the impact on tourist arrivals as reflected in Khadaroo and Seetanah's (2007) study of Mauritius. This reiterates the importance of other studies demonstrating the crucial role of transport infrastructure (e.g. Prideaux 2000a, b) in promoting destination development.

The demand for tourist transport

Within economics, the concern with the allocation of resources to satisfy individuals' desire to travel means that transport economists examine the *demand* for different modes of travel and the competition between such modes in relation to price, speed, convenience and reliability. Economists attempt to understand what affects people's travel behaviour and the choices they make in relation to transport (i.e. travel choice modelling) as something that is rarely consumed for its own sake: it is usually demanded as a means of consuming some other goods or service (i.e. commuting to work or the travel component of a holiday). Indeed, travel behaviour research combines psychological and economic research (Ortuzar et al. 1998). According to Mill (1992: 83–4), the demand for tourist transport is also characterised by:

- its almost instantaneous and unpredictable nature, which requires operators to build overcapacity in the supply to avoid dissatisfied travellers;
- the variability in demand, ranging from *derived demand* (where tourist transport is a facilitating mechanism to achieve another objective, such as business travel) to *primary demand* (which is the pursuit of travel for vacation purposes);
- non-priced items (e.g. service quality, reliability and punctuality).

Transport economists have developed mathematical models to analyse the trip-making behaviour of travellers (e.g. Ortuzar and Willumsen 1990), the factors influencing demand and why variations occur in the trip-making behaviour of consumers due to relationships between socioeconomic factors (e.g. age, income, profession and family status) and the effect of macroeconomic conditions (e.g. the state of the economy). In contrast tourism economists have examined the demand for travel and tourist products, recognising the significance of demand as a driving force in the economy. This stimulates entrepreneurial activity to produce the goods and services to satisfy the demand (Bull 1991), and a large popular literature exists on examples of entrepreneurship that have generated successful tourist transport ventures (e.g. see Calder 2002 on low-cost airline ventures, Gittel 2003 on Southwest Airlines and Peterson 2004 on Jet Blue). More specifically, tourism economists examine the *effective demand* for goods or services, which is the aggregate or overall demand over a period of time. Since income has an important effect on tourism demand, economists measure the impact using a term known as the *elasticity of demand*. As Bull (1991: 37) has shown, it is measured using a ratio calculated thus:

$$\text{Elasticity of demand} = \frac{\text{Percentage change in tourism demand}}{\text{Percentage change in disposable income}}$$

in relation to two equal time periods. The significance of this concept is that the demand for goods to fulfil basic needs (e.g. food, water and shelter) is relatively unchanging or *inelastic* whilst the demand for luxury items, such as holiday and pleasure travel, is variable or *elastic,* being subject to fluctuations in demand due to factors such as income or price. Thus, elasticity is used to express the extent to which tourists are sensitive to changes in price and service. For example, primary demand is usually more elastic than derived demand. In tourist transportation, researchers recognise the importance of price, which is acknowledged as a more complex issue than income, due to the varying impact of exchange rates, the relative prices of destinations and the high level of competition between destinations for tourists. Furthermore, the different elements that comprise the tourism product (e.g. transport, accommodation and attractions) are complementary, and it is difficult to separate out one individual item as exerting a dominant effect on price since all are interrelated in terms of what is purchased and consumed.

To assess the impact of price on the demand for tourism, economists examine the *price elasticity of demand,* where an inverse relationship exists between demand and price (Bull 1991). For example, it is generally accepted that the greater the price the less demand there will be for a tourism product due to the limited amount of the population's disposable income that is available to purchase the product. Price-elasticity is calculated thus:

$$\text{Price-elasticity} = \frac{\text{Percentage change in quantity of tourism product demanded}}{\text{Percentage change in tourism product price}}$$

However, as Wensveen (2007) argues, in terms of air transport, elasticity of demand is significantly affected by competition among airline companies, the distance over which tourists travel and the motivation to travel. For example, over short distances, tourist travel is relatively price inelastic because there is less opportunity to cut price to stimulate additional demand. In addition, leisure travel is more elastic than business travel because it is more flexible and less time sensitive.

Other contributory factors that influence the demand for tourism, particularly leisure travel (Figure 2.2) include the impact of tourist taxation, the amount of holiday entitlement available to potential tourists as well as the effects of weather, climate and cultural preferences for holidaymaking which are expressed in terms of seasonality. These factors also need to be viewed in the context of the economics of each specific mode of tourist transport (e.g. rail, coach, air and sea travel) to understand how demand is incorporated into the operator's supply of the service. In view of the variation between different modes of transport, readers should consult more detailed studies (Stubbs et al. 1980; Glaister 1981; Button 1982; Bell et al. 1983; Doganis 2002; Hibbs 2003; Holloway 2003; Wensveen 2007; Vasigh et al. 2008).

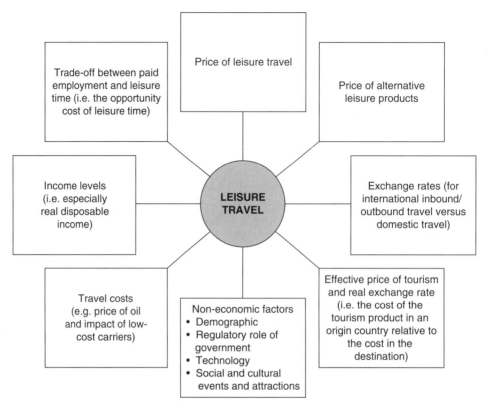

Figure 2.2 Factors affecting the demand for leisure travel

The supply of tourist transport

Economists are also interested in the *supply* of a commodity (e.g. tourist transport), which is often seen as a function of its price and the price of alternative goods. Price is often influenced by the cost of the factors of production, but in the case of tourist transport it is difficult to identify the real cost of travel. For example, state subsidies for rail travel in some European countries are used to support the supply of services in the absence of a major demand for social reasons (Whitelegg 1987). Similarly, aviation enjoys relatively favourable treatment in view of its exemption from taxation on aviation fuel in most countries. As a result of subsidies, the price charged may not always reflect the true cost, particularly where tourist transport providers use cross-subsidies in their operations. Cross-subsidisation implies that profits from more lucrative routes are used to support uneconomic and unviable services to maintain a route network (Figure 2.3), thereby increasing the choice of destinations. According to Bull (1991: 78), the supply of tourist transport can be characterised by:

- major capital requirements for passenger carriage (e.g. the cost of aircraft, passenger trains and ferries);
- government regulations and restrictions to monitor the supply, which is determined by state policy;
- competitive reaction from other businesses involved in tourist transport;
- a high level of expertise required to operate and manage tourist transport enterprises.

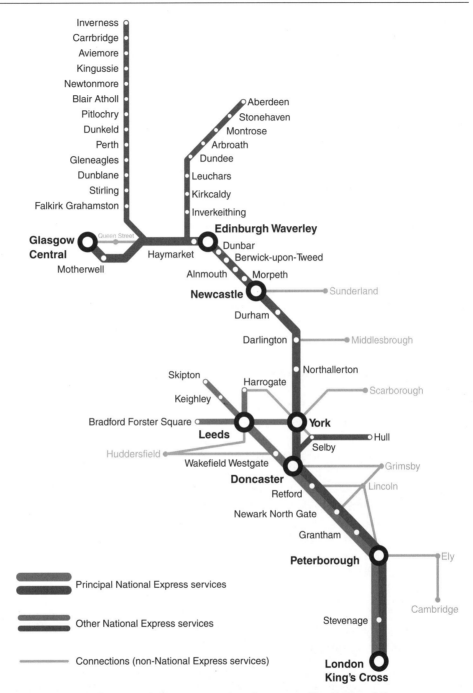

Figure 2.3 East Coast mainline route network operated by National Express

Source: Image courtesy of National Express

Bull (1991) suggests that the principal questions which economists are interested in from the supply side are:

- what to produce;
- how to produce it;
- when, where and how to produce it.

From the transport operator's perspective, the main objective in supply terms is to maximise profitability from the available capacity, which is usually expressed in terms of the *load factor*. Transport companies can maximise passenger revenue by minimising costs and pricing their product or service at a competitive rate.

According to Doganis (2002), airline costs can be divided into direct costs (e.g. flight operations, including salaries, expenses, fuel, oil, insurance and rental/lease costs, maintenance and depreciation) and indirect costs (e.g. station and ground expenses, passenger services, ticketing, sales and marketing and administration) (see Figure 2.4). In terms of the typical airline costs of operation, Doganis (2002) noted that these would comprise: aviation fuel (12–13 per cent), cabin/flight crew salaries (14 per cent), airport/en-route costs (9 per cent), aircraft ownership/lease costs (up to 13 per cent) and ticketing (16–17 per cent). Doganis also noted that a wide range of other factors affected the cost structure of airlines, including the management approach and corporate strategy as well as how airlines operated their aircraft (i.e. long-haul versus short-haul operations, and fleet type).

Certain travel markets are very price sensitive, which means that consumers may be easily persuaded to switch to another operator or mode of transport if the price rises beyond a critical level (the demand for youth travel on express coach services is a good example of a price-sensitive market). As Page (2009a) shows, the rise of low-cost coach services such as the Megabus brand in the UK and North America has created a new range of price-sensitive travellers. Despite price sensitivity, airlines and other modes of transport distinguish between scheduled routes, which operate a regular, timetabled service and charge higher fares, and charter services operated on behalf of tour operators to carry holidaymakers who have purchased a transport-only component or package holiday from the tour operator. The price differential for scheduled and charter passengers is reflected in the passenger load factor that the scheduled airline needs to reach to achieve a profit. Scheduled routes charge a higher tariff but operate on a lower load factor compared to charter flights, where a lower unit cost is charged but a higher load factor (often 90 per cent) is needed to yield a profit. Seasonality in the demand for tourist transport services may affect the load factor, and peak usage at popular times means that transport operators use premium pricing to manage the supply and maximise profit to offset losses in times of limited demand. To illustrate the importance of pricing, Insight 2.1 examines the issue in relation to air travel.

INSIGHT 2.1

The pricing of air travel

According to Hanlon (2007) the way in which airlines price their products is a complex process, with a multitude of fares available according to when one travels; whether travel is off-peak or peak; the class of travel; the length of stay at a destination and whether it includes a Saturday night in Europe. In addition, when and where the ticket is purchased influences the price, together with a host of other factors. For example, Wensveen (2007) pointed to the importance of passenger preferences, the number of passengers on a route, the financial status of the travellers, the prices charged by competitors and passenger expectations of price as determinants of airline pricing. Even though there is extensive variation in fare levels across routes, fare levels generally taper with distance so that the fare per km

is lower on a long-haul route than a short-haul route. But global anomalies exist. For example, fare levels in Europe have been higher per route km than in North America, whilst
fare levels between Europe and Asia-Pacific have been lower than between Europe and
Africa. In the USA, Milman and Pope (1997) highlight the inherent problem associated with
the demand for air travel. It is described as stochastic, meaning that the number of reservations and actual trips may vary, implying that airlines need to price their product so as to ensure that sales and seat prices maximise revenue for each departure. Because airline fares
can vary and offer so many possible fare classes for one route, it raises the issue of price
discrimination.

Hanlon (2007) examines the role of price discrimination, where the producer (the airline)
charges different prices for various units of the same commodity where there are similar
unit costs in the cost of supply. In this instance, peak and off-peak costs are not a form of
discriminatory pricing because the price differential reflects the extra costs of meeting peak
demand. Discriminatory pricing exists where prices differ more than costs, especially when
price–cost margins vary and some customers are paying a higher differential. In many
cases of price discrimination the major factor is the difference in demand elasticity. The principal explanation advanced in the economics literature is related to the inverse elasticity
rule: the firm charges more where the demand is low and less where it is high (Hanlon
2007). Firms need to be able to prevent customers who have paid low prices from reselling
to those who would be charged high prices.

A yield management system linked to the airline's computer reservation system employs
complex algorithms combined with historical booking data to forecast the scenario that enhances revenue from the seat allocation. By restricting the availability of lower-priced fares,
airlines are able to safeguard against revenue dilution in an environment where many of the
costs of airline operation are relatively fixed for each departure (see Figure 2.4). The innovative simulation model discussed by Belobaba and Wilson (1997) includes the role of passenger choice behaviour and a yield management system was employed to evaluate the

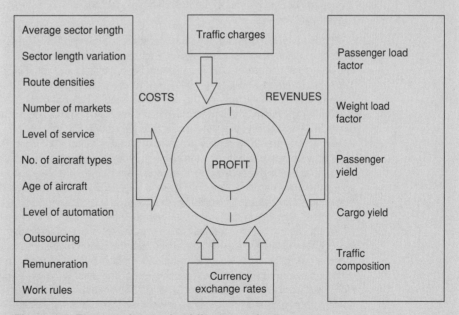

Figure 2.4 The cost factors in airline operations

Source: Redrawn from Seristö and Vepsäläinen (1997). *Journal of Air Transport Management*, 3(1), Airline
cost drivers, pp. 11–22, Copyright © 1997, with permission from Elsevier.

impact on market shares, traffic and revenues of each competing airline in a hypothetical market situation. Simulation has to be undertaken given the commercial sensitivity of airline data and competition. A model was therefore used that included four fare options for a typical US domestic airline market (full coach fare through to a 14-day advance purchase, non-refundable excursion fare priced at 40 per cent of the full fare). Historical booking data was used to forecast demand on future flights and to optimise fare class booking limits.

The simulation exercise highlighted a 'first mover' advantage, where the airline that initiates yield management (YM) gains the competitive advantage. This results in a better fare mix of traffic and, especially, protects seats for late-booking, high-fare passengers. More interesting was the finding that the airline without YM can in fact be hurt in terms of revenue by not having a YM system. The carrier with a YM system is able to dump unwanted low-fare passengers on to the flights of the carrier without YM, filling up that carrier's capacity and leaving it without adequate last-minute seat availability for the highest-fare passengers (Belobaba and Wilson 1997: 9).

Airlines are able to prevent people reselling airline tickets by making them non-transferable. Airline research shows that business travellers have relatively price-inelastic demand and are not able to book far in advance. In contrast, the price-elastic traveller can book a long time in advance and be flexible, and their concern is with the benefit of travelling at a lower price. Such price discrimination provides airlines with opportunities to segment the market with price discrimination and reason for travel as major factors in the segmentation. Indeed Belobaba and Wilson (1997: 3) confirm that:

> the practices of differential pricing and yield management, although confusing to most airline passengers, have, over the past decade, been embraced by most airlines. The incremental revenues generated by these practices contribute to the coverage of the predominantly fixed operating costs of a scheduled flight departure. By offering a range of fare options at different price levels on the same flight, airlines attempt to segment the total demand for air travel according to the different sensitivities to price and the need for travel flexibility of business and leisure travellers. To ensure that low-fare leisure passengers do not consume all of the seats on high-demand flights, airlines employ yield management (YM) systems.

These yield management systems forecast the demand for flights and calculate the number of seats that should be available for sale at each fare class to maximise flight revenues. A number of studies have estimated the benefits to individual airlines (e.g. Belobaba 1987; Weatherford and Bodily 1992), where revenue gains of 2–5 per cent occur from implementing a YM system. Yet the studies also indicated that if another competitor implemented a YM system both saw improvements in revenue, indicating the ability of carriers to catch up. This suggests that YM is not a zero-sum game and that YM may force passengers to pay fares nearer to what they are prepared to pay rather than lower fares resulting from competitive pressures between the carriers. From the consumers' perspective, discriminatory pricing that is enhanced by YM is undesirable if the price is raised for some, but desirable if the price declines. However, there is a general trend in pricing airline tickets, where those most affected by discriminatory pricing (e.g. businesss travellers) bear higher costs. In contrast, those high costs of travel help to subsidise the costs borne by discount travellers. Of course, problems occur when the market share of the more lucrative business travel fares decline for a particular airline, reducing the cross-subsidisation that the high-revenue passengers contribute to the overall profitability of its operation.

Whilst business travellers often complain of the discriminatory pricing used to justify higher standards of service, comfort and flexibility in reservations, much of the cost is often borne by businesses as an expense rather than by individual travellers. Whether such pricing enhances or hinders competition depends upon the perspective one takes. For example, discriminatory pricing can allow airlines to experiment with fare levels. Yet it can also be viewed as a tool that companies with a dominant market position can use to weaken the ▶

competition whilst increasing prices in other markets. Thus, where such competition occurs, travellers who can be flexible in terms of travel arrangements for their journey enjoy a high degree of price elasticity. As a result airlines set fares at cost plus a low profit margin for travellers with a high degree of price elasticity.

Although this is desirable for the consumer, it assumes that competitors cannot sustain business at low profit margins if their scale of operation is not able to carry such marginal pricing. In fact some notable examples, such as the Laker Sky Train that was engaged in a price war on the lucrative North Atlantic routes in the 1970s, complained of one other form of pricing – predatory pricing.

Predatory pricing occurs where a dominant business pursues a policy of eliminating, deterring or restricting competition. This usually involves selling at below cost to destroy the competition. Whilst Hanlon (1996) debates the rationality of such a policy, since the losses for the dominant business are much greater than for the competition, the dominant business will expect to recoup the losses once the competition is removed. In some cases an outright takeover or merger is more rational, but predatory pricing may ease the way to a takeover depending on the personalities in the organisations involved. In the USA, a paper by Areeda and Turner (1975) developed a surrogate measure of predatory pricing: it exists where the price is set below a business's short-run marginal cost. A marginal cost is generally seen as the 'addition to total cost resulting from the last unit of output. It refers to those elements of cost that can be avoided or escaped if the last unit is not produced' (Hanlon 1996: 172). Yet in air transport, the marginal cost may be low and seats are a perishable commodity that cannot be stored if supply is greater than demand. For airlines, the marginal cost is low for filling an unsold seat when the flight will depart even if the aircraft has seats left unsold. Even where low fares are sold to attract travellers to fill seats that would otherwise remain empty, these are still priced above the marginal cost. (See Hanlon 2007 for more discussion of how to assess predatory pricing and the mechanisms to assess marginal costs.) Non-price forms of predatory pricing can also be used by airlines seeking to stifle competition by increasing supply so that competitors find it difficult to break into a market where supply exceeds demand. Without regulation, computer reservation systems (CRSs) and frequent flyer programmes (FFPs) may also disadvantage smaller airlines unable to access CRSs and offer FFPs at the same reward rate on routes facing competition, although one option may be direct selling via the Internet (see Chapter 6 for more detail). Since FFPs have been used to target customer loyalty among high-yielding passengers (e.g. first and business class), the gains may be very high, for although they may only comprise 20 per cent of passenger volumes they may contribute 50 per cent of revenue.

Discussion of the pricing of air travel illustrates that principles of economics underpin the economic behaviour of airlines. In addition, the free market economy can result in a wide range of competitive situations. In practice, there is often regulation by national and supranational organisations responsible for air travel such as the Civil Aviation Authority in London and the European Commission in Brussels. These bodies seek to adjudicate between what is acceptable and unacceptable competition and what constitutes predatory behaviour. As Hanlon (1996: 183) rightly concludes:

> The crux of the matter is to find the dividing line between genuine revenue-enhancing yield-management techniques and practices aimed directly at undermining the economics of a competitor's operation . . . The Civil Aviation Authority approaches the problem by tracking fare developments and trends over time on a selected number of routes.

Although such monitoring can assist in the process of establishing predatory pricing, the volume of seats sold at each fare level also needs to be considered. Where predatory behaviour occurs on international routes, this falls outside the jurisdiction of national regulatory bodies and investigations can take a long time to institute. Despite the suspected existence of predatory behaviour, it is often difficult to distinguish from aggressive competitive behaviour.

Economists also have an interest in macroeconomic issues associated with the supply of tourist transport services and the structure of the market system in which companies operate. For example, economists have examined the effect of company strategy in the tourism and transport sectors in response to market competition that may affect the management, operation and provision of services to consumers. These different market conditions may range from near-perfect competition to a situation where the three following conditions may occur (see Bull 1991: 60–5 for a more detailed discussion):

- *oligopoly*, where the control of the supply of a service is by a small number of suppliers;
- *monopoly*, where exclusive control of services is by a single supplier;
- *duopoly*, where two companies control the supply of services.

For the consumer, such activities may have a significant effect on the choice, price and degree of competition that occurs. In some cases, a monopoly situation or a variant may lead to anticompetitive practices and may not necessarily be in the public's interest. As discussed earlier, transport and tourism economists have also retained an interest in the macroeconomic effects of tourist transport on national economies. Such considerations have an important bearing on public or private sector investment decisions when examining the costs and benefits of building new tourist transport infrastructure (e.g. a new airport). Issues related to the employment-generating potential of new tourist transport infrastructure and the effect on income generation for local economies feature prominently in these investment decisions (often to the detriment of socio-environmental impacts – see Chapter 8). Economists also use complex research techniques such as multiplier analysis (see Archer 1989) to evaluate the secondary or indirect economic benefits of additional tourist expenditure for local areas. There is also a growing awareness among economists of the environmental costs of tourist transport (Banister and Button 1992; Perl et al. 1997).

Geography and tourist transport

Within geography, the study of tourist transport has largely been undertaken by transport geographers (see Knowles 1993 for an excellent review of recent studies in transport geography and Knowles et al. 2008) and tourism geographers (Pearce 1990, 1995a). The main concern of geographers when considering tourist transport can be related to three key concepts that characterise the study of geography:

- *space*: *area*, usually the earth's surface;
- *location*: the position of something within space;
- *place*: an identifiable position on the earth's surface.

Geographers are therefore interested in the spatial expression of tourist transport as a vital link between tourist-generating and tourist-receiving areas. In particular, geographers are concerned with the patterns of human activity associated with tourist travel and how different processes lead to the formation of geographical patterns of tourist travel at different scales, ranging from the world to the national (e.g. country), regional (e.g. county) and local levels (e.g. an individual

Table 2.2 Recent books on transport geography

W. Black (2003) *Transportation: A Geographical Analysis*, New York: Guildford Press.

J. Bowen (2010) *The Economic Geography of Air Transportation*, London: Routledge.

G. Giuliano and S. Hanson (2004) *The Geography of Urban Transportation*, New York: Guildford Press.

P. Headicar (2009) *Transport Policy and Planning in the UK*, London: Routledge.

R. Knowles, J. Shaw and I. Docherty (eds) (2008) *Transport Geographies*, Oxford: Blackwell.

J.P. Rodrigue, C. Comtoiu and B. Slack (2009) *The Geography of Transport Systems*, 2nd edn, London: Routledge.

R. Tolley (ed) *Sustainable Transport*, London: Routledge.

P. White (2008) *Public Transport: Its Planning, Management and Operation*, London: Routledge.

place). Previous geographical research on transport has looked at its role in different regions, its impact on economic development in terms of accessibility, the effect on the environment and the role of policy-making (see Farrington 1985). In many of the popular transport geography textbooks (e.g. Hay 1973; Lowe and Moryadas 1975; Adams 1981; White and Senior 1983; Barke 1986; Hoyle and Knowles 1992, 1998; Tolley and Turton 1995) there are a number of fundamental concepts that geographers use to analyse the spatial components of transport (see Table 2.2). Geographers have typically analysed travel as a response to satisfy a human desire for movement and the spatial outcome of such journeys. They have also considered the spatial variables in the transport system (e.g. location and places) and how these affect the costs and production of other social and economic activities. For the geographer, transport facilitates the process of movement that has economic and budgetary costs, whilst behavioural factors (e.g. perception and preferences for particular forms of transport) determine the journey in terms of the available infrastructure and routes. In analysing the transport system, geographers have considered:

- the linkages and flows within a transport system;
- the location and places connected by these linkages (usually referred to as 'centres' and 'nodes');
- the system of catchments and relationships between places within the network (modified from Taafe and Gauthier 1973).

In some respects transport tends to be viewed by geographers as a passive element in a tourism context rather than as an integral part of tourism and recreational activity. But a number of geographical papers published in the *Journal of Transport Geography* (e.g. Hall 1999) raise issues related to access to tourist transport, equity, and concerns of disadvantage and social exclusion (see Hine and Mitchell 2003). In fact comparatively little progress has been made by researchers in this area of study since the influential studies undertaken in the 1960s and 1970s by geographers (e.g. Wall, 1971; Patmore, 1983). Whilst useful syntheses such as that of Halsall (1992) provide bibliographies of past studies, few of the studies reviewed by Halsall (1992) were written by geographers in the 1980s and 1990s explicitly to develop an understanding of the way in which transport facilitates and in some cases conditions the type of recreational and tourism activity that occurs. Much of the research activity by geographers in the

1990s published in the *Journal of Transport Geography* has been preoccupied with air travel (Chou 1993; Shaw 1993; Feiler and Goodovitch 1994; O'Connor 1995) and other emerging themes (e.g. Robbins and Thompson 2007; Thompson and Schofield 2007) as well as a special issue of the *Journal of Sustainable Tourism* (Volume 5(4) 2007) in which geographers contributed to a number of papers on transport, tourism and climate change. The continued neglect of transport in the analysis of tourism has also been compounded by the perception of other geographers who did not concede the importance of tourism as serious areas for research until the late 1980s and 1990s (Hall and Page 1999). Even then, it is often relegated to a minor research area despite the rapid growth in tourism and recreational courses in most countries.

Texts such as Tolley and Turton (1995) do at least highlight the need to consider tourism in the context of transport geography. Yet even these authors do not devote much space to the topic, and few other studies have sought to place transport for recreation and tourism on the research agenda beyond the notable occasional studies by the Transport Study Group of the Institute of British Geographers (Halsall 1982; Tolley and Turton 1987). Where previous studies exist (e.g. Halsall 1992) the emphasis has been on modal forms of recreational and tourist travel (e.g. land-based transport and the use of trails, water-borne transport and heritage transport for nostalgic travel – see Page 1993a, 1994a). This does not adequately develop the contribution that geographers can make to the management, planning and development of transport for recreational and tourist travel.

However, one notable contribution by geographers relates to the analysis of spatially contingent processes of change affecting global tourist transport globalisation.

●●●● Globalisation and tourist transport

According to Janelle and Beuthe (1997: 199), 'In its simplest form, globalization refers to the increasing geographical scale of economic, social and political interactions. These include . . . the expanding mobility of capital and investment transactions, and the growth of tourism, global conferences and sporting events.' One of the most notable manifestations of globalisation is the major role of multinational corporations (MNCs) and trading blocs (e.g. the EU, Association for Asia Pacific Economic Cooperation, APEC and North Atlantic Free Trade Area, NAFTA) and the role of non-governmental organisations. The increasing trend towards government restructuring of public sector activities (i.e. the privatisation of airlines and railways) has provided transport companies in the private sector with global opportunities for operating services. For example, both Schiphol Airport in Amsterdam and the British Airports Authority in the UK now manage overseas airports, as their specialist skills have led them to form private sector management companies to take advantage of these changes. These organisations now represent companies with the characteristics of MNCs, operating in borderless economies as they follow market opportunities globally and the capital, skill and resources follow the businesses they establish. Communities and nations have businesses with less of a stake in the place where they operate, as they are increasingly footloose, with many examples (e.g. Stagecoach in the UK) withdrawing from such ventures when they no longer fit with their corporate objectives. There has also been a growth in strategic alliances in the tourist transport sector (Debbage 2005; Page 2004) as airlines, in particular, seek to develop a global reach and interconnections with other carriers. The formation in the 1990s of the three large airline alliance groupings, namely:

- Oneworld (American Airlines, British Airways, Cathay Pacific, Finnair, Iberia, JAL, Lan Chile, Malēv, Qantas and Royal Jordanian);
- Sky Team (Aeroflot, Aero Mexico, Air France, Alitalia, KLM, Czech Airlines, China Southern, Continental Airlines, Delta, Korean Air and NWA); and
- Star Alliance (Air Canada, Air China, Air New Zealand, All Nippon Airways, Asiana, Austrian Airlines, bmi, LOT Polish Airlines, Lufthansa, SAS, Shanghai Airlines, Singapore Airlines, South African Airlines, Spanair, Swiss, Thai Airways, Turkish Airlines, United Airlines and US Airways),

is estimated to account for over 50 per cent of world air passenger traffic.

The spatial implications of globalisation for tourism and the transport links that result relate to improved accessibility for major global cities and competitive advantages for their tourism economies. Janelle and Beuthe (1997: 201) point to changes resulting from globalisation that include:

- longer and more customised transport links;
- greater sensitivity to the timing of connections, arrivals and departures; and
- greater reliance on communication and computer networks,

as global operators achieve economies of scope from their production. This also places a greater reliance on multi-modal transport and interconnections if one re-examines Figure 1.8 in a global context. For example, many of the airline groups also have strategic alliances with ground operators, car hire companies and other operators as they see opportunities for enhancing profits from seamless travel. Not surprisingly, globalisation as a process involves more than the simple internationalisation of a firm's production, and includes the global competition among MNCs and other tourism and transport businesses. Even within individual countries, Thompson (2002) found that despite attempts to liberalise air transport to end the monopoly position of Air France, the company took over those businesses which challenged its dominance, leading to a quasi-monopoly. MNCs are key elements in the global tourist transport industry and their control of supply may inhibit demand in more peripheral locations where the market is inadequate to justify service provision on a simple economic profit/loss basis. In the case of third-level airports in France (i.e. those providing mainly domestic flights (see Figure 2.5)) Alpine routes saw their route structure reduced to the single destination of Paris (Orly). As a result, Thompson (2002) argued that the TGV (Trans Grand Vitesse) had become the lowest cost alternative to air travel. In contrast, Romăn et al. (2007) examined competition of high-speed train with air transport on the Madrid–Barcelona route and found only 35 per cent of the market would be rail-based, pointing to the cost disadvantages of rail when the investment and infrastructure costs were included. This highlights the importance of case by case analysis of the impact of competition on traffic demand.

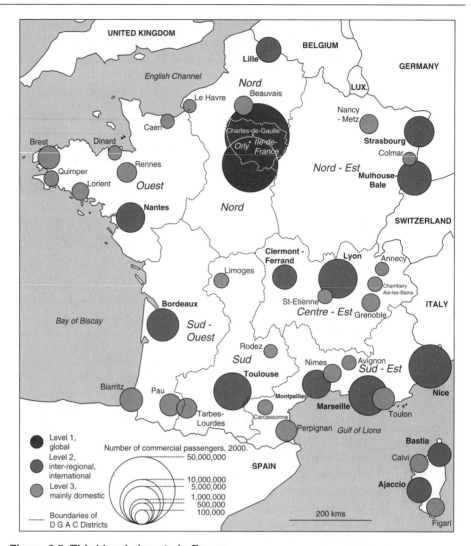

Figure 2.5 Third-level airports in France

Source: Thompson (2002). Reprinted from *Journal of Transport Geography*, 10(3), Thompson I. B., Air transport liberalisation and the development of third-level airports in France, pp. 273–85, Copyright © 2002, with permission from Elsevier.

Tourism geography and tourist transport

According to Pearce (1979), geographical research on tourism initially focused on:

● the spatial analysis of the supply and demand for tourism;
● the geography of tourist resorts;
● tourist movements and flows;
● the analysis of the impact of tourism;
● the development of models of tourist space to understand the evolution and expression of tourism in specific locations.

Since the 1970s tourism research has examined the patterns and processes associated with the development of international and domestic tourism, as discussed and debated by Hall and Page (2002, 2006). One particular skill that the geographer has contributed to the study of tourism is the ability to synthesise (i.e. sift, search and make sense of) the approaches and analyses of tourism phenomena undertaken by other disciplines. During the 1980s geographical research on tourism moved from a traditional concern with regional case studies and descriptions of tourism in particular locations to a more systematic and analytical approach (Hall and Page 1999, 2002). This is reflected in the recognition of how a spatial perspective can contribute to the analysis of tourism. How have geographers viewed tourist transport?

According to Mansfeld (1992: 58), 'the use of various modes of transport in getting to the destination has several spatial consequences' associated with the distance travelled, amount of time involved in travelling and the mode of transport used. In many cases geographers have not distinguished, or have not found it easy to distinguish, between tourist and recreational travel. Pearce (1990: 28) acknowledges that advances in transport technology have altered the patterns of tourist flows and made tourist travel more flexible and diffuse. Prior to the expansion of car ownership and mass air travel, the patterns of tourist travel were linear. It was constrained and confined to transport corridors (e.g. river-bank railway lines) or the destinations served by sea. As the following discussion shows, the car has been a major catalyst in making patterns of travel more diffuse.

The car and tourist travel

In the post-war period the growth of car ownership has not only made the impact of recreational and tourist travel more flexible, it has caused overuse at accessible sites. This ease of access, fuelled by a growth in road building and the upgrading of minor roads in many developed countries, has been a self-reinforcing process leading to overuse and a greater dominance in passive recreational activities. Probably the most influential study of car usage among recreationalists was Wall's (1972) study of Kingston-upon-Hull in 1969. Wall identified the two principal types of study used to analyse recreational activity – namely site studies (of particular facilities or areas) and national studies such as the widely cited Pilot National Recreation Survey (British Travel Association and University of Keele 1967, 1969). Wall supplemented data from the national survey with a regional sample of 500 Hull car owners in 1969. Whilst the results are now very dated, his study highlighted the importance of seasonality and timing of pleasure trips by car and the dominance of the car as a mode of transport for urban dwellers. It also highlighted the role of the journey by car as a form of recreation in itself as well as the importance of the car as more than just a means of transport. In fact the study has a degree of similarity with other studies that followed, such as Coppock and Duffield's (1975) survey of recreation and the countryside. This focused on patterns and processes of recreational activity in Scotland and mapped and described patterns of recreational travel, especially those of caravanners. At the same time, the study noted the tendency for many recreationalists not to venture far from their car at the destination, a point reiterated by Glyptis' (1981) innovative and seminal study of recreationalists, using participant observation in Hull. Wall (1971) also found that the majority of pleasure trips were day trips less than 100 km away from Hull, being spatially concentrated in a limited number of resorts along the Yorkshire coast and southerly part of the region. Other research (Wager 1967) highlighted the versatility of the car and its use to venture into the reaches of the North York Moors National Park. Other researchers' findings (e.g. Burton 1966) explained the attraction of the car to recreationalists in that it allowed them to enjoy the countryside and observe its visual characteristics rather than have physical contact with it, whilst Chubb (1989) examined the role of the car in cross-border travel in the Great Lakes region of North America, with the use of the car, recreational vehicles and the straight-line and circuit routes that existed as well as the nature of these flows (see Chubb 1989 for more detail).

Research by Eaton and Holding (1996) identified the growing scale of such visits to the countryside by recreationalists in cars. In 1991, 103 million visits were made to National Parks in the UK (Countryside Commission 1992), the most popular being the Lake District and Peak District parks. In terms of car usage, car traffic was estimated to grow by 267 per cent by the year 2025 from the levels current in 1992 (Countryside Commission 1992). In fact, the greatest impact of rising car usage has been seen in the decline in the use of public transport for recreational trips. Yet many National Parks seem unlikely to be able to cope with the levels of usage predicted for the year 2025, given their urban catchments and the relative accessibility by motorway and A-roads in the UK. Eaton and Holding (1996) review the absence of effective policies to meet the practical problems of congestion facing many sites in the countryside in Britain. Whilst schemes such as the Sherpa Bus routes in Snowdonia National Park have been introduced (Mulligan 1979) they have not been incorporated into any wider policy objectives for transport. This combines with a failure to design public transport to suit the needs and perception of users to achieve reductions and solutions to congestion in National Parks. As Regnerus et al. (2007) demonstrate, in Veluwezoom National Park in the Netherlands traffic management measures to address the negative effects of the car using 'carrot measures' (e.g. public transport and footpaths) as well as 'stick measures' (such as road charges and access charges) are used to manage the car. Thus, it is clear that the car poses a major problem, not only for urban areas and its use by commuters and recreationalists, but also in terms of the sheer growth in volume in areas not designed for large numbers of cars. This problem is especially acute when spatially concentrated at 'honeypots' (locations that attract large numbers in a confined area) within National Parks.

Planning and management issues associated with tourist car use

Within the UK, it is estimated that around 40 per cent of all mileage travelled in the car is for leisure, particularly as people travel further to engage in leisure activities (Department for Transport, Local Government and the Regions 2001). As leisure activities tend to be more dispersed in nature than commuting trips, this raises numerous issues for those sites/locations that attract car-based leisure traffic. Among the problems that occur are congestion, pollution, increased risk of accidents (Dickinson et al. 2004) and a decline in the quality of the visit experience.

Within a leisure context, Dickinson et al. (2004: 105) point to leisure travel initiatives that have been devised to address problems associated with the car:

- encouraging travel closer to home, to local as opposed to regional facilities;
- containment/restriction strategies (i.e. road closure at the Peak District National Park Goyt Valley Scheme in 1970 began with the closure of a two-mile stretch of

road on summer Sundays and Bank Holidays and provision of a Park and Ride facility);
- generation of traffic on uneconomic public transport routes;
- improving opportunities for cycling and walking, as the National Cycling Network, promoted and in part developed by Sustrans has done, as discussed in Chapter 8);
- private sector initiatives.

Among the key features in implementing these initiatives, as the UK pressure group Transport 2000 has argued, are:

- the need for promotional activities to raise awareness of alternatives;
- the need to make alternative access easier than using the car (substitutability of transport mode);
- meeting the needs of users of alternative sustainable transport modes;
- a review of car parking provision to limit spaces.

One option that Dickinson et al. (2004) point to is the development of Local Leisure Plans to identify gaps in provision so that alternative travel modes to the car can be developed (also see Chapter 8 on the link to sustainability). One other area of managing car traffic is through the use of parking policy measures (Beunen et al. 2006). Such measures may include: changing the number of available parking spaces, changes to the location of parking spaces, parking controls and the fees charged for parking. In National Parks, such measures may be combined with the use of key gateways to encourage visitors to park their vehicles and reduce vehicle flows (Beunen et al. 2007), a feature also noted by Connell and Page (2008). These demand-management measures also need to be accompanied by public acceptance of such changes alongside publicising their benefits.

Congestion

Stopher (2004) pointed to global increases in car ownership, where the example of the UK saw ownership rise from 30 per cent of households in 1960 to 70 per cent in 1995, with the fastest growth being in multiple car ownership for many households. In 2000 the USA had also exceeded one car per licensed driver in urban areas, illustrating the sheer scale of the car's prevalence in advanced industrialised societies. Whilst policy-makers seek out solutions to reduce the inevitable congestion associated with car usage, numerous options have been used, such as congestion charging that is now being used in London, and has been investigated for potential implementation in the Lake District in the UK (Eckton 2003), using a charging tollbooth cordon.

In a provocative analysis of congestion, Stopher (2004) points to congestion being less of a ubiquitous phenomenon, but one more limited to time and space. Stopher classified congestion into:

- *recurring forms,* which occur at the same place and same time every day, particularly amongst commuters or on school runs due to peaking of demand;
- *non-recurring forms,* often arising from temporary conditions such as road works or interruption to the normal transport network (e.g. a diversion), explained in terms of a bottleneck.

Stopher argues for the car to be viewed as a positive entity, in much the same way that the road user lobby groups do, but with a caveat that the car has provided unparalleled mobility and levels of economic development. He adds that the car is here to stay as a personalised form of transport. Rather than agreeing with policy shifts to encourage people to change from the car to public transport, he points to the futility of such initiatives. The alternative that is presented is for public transport to provide niche products (e.g. commuter use, tourist use and other uses). Whilst highly controversial, Stopher identified more 'sensible policy directions' for transport in the early twenty-first century that encompass the car, including arguments that consider:

- encouraging the development and use of less polluting and sustainable engines for cars;
- accepting that car congestion will never be eliminated and that, as levels rise, policy interventions should be aimed at managing this congestion;
- niche markets are best served by public transport, as widespread switching from the car will not occur without system-wide investment in public transport to improve ridership;
- road pricing may be a better option to pursue than congestion charging, with a view to supporting fuel-efficient, low-emission car use, varying the pricing of time/day/location;
- adding additional road capacity which should be carefully scrutinised given the trend towards improved mobility, use of new infrastructure but not a reduction in congestion.

Ultimately, Stopher argues that public transport does not hold the answer to congestion, since it is not a new phenomenon (though it is in relation to the car), but that policies designed to more carefully manage our use of the car would be more worthwhile than trying to resurrect public transport usage that fitted the needs of previous societies and their economies. But what does this mean for tourist travel use of the car? A study by Shailes et al. (2001) of tourists' travel behaviour in relation to congestion noted that half of the respondents they surveyed took evasive action to avoid congestion. This they did by trip timing and diversion to other routes, although interestingly those not enjoying their trip attributed it to congestion, highlighting avoidance behaviour.

Tourist use of the car for urban destinations: the impact on historic cities

Within the urban tourism literature (see Hall and Page 2002) a great deal of interest has been directed towards the understanding and analysis of tourist mobility and the pressures this poses for urban areas in terms of visitor flows and the demand for space to accommodate cars, coaches and other forms of transport. This has also produced conflicts with local residents, workers and tourists themselves, where competition develops for space to accommodate vehicles, sometimes leading to restrictive or expansive measures to try and harmonise the needs of all users. Transport within many urban destinations can also be a constraining factor, where the scale of the city, its attractions and products are not adequately interconnected by efficient transport and signposting to encourage the tourist to visit the wider city environment. This leads to what is invariably observed as tourist bunching, crowding or spatial congregation in the most accessible honeypot locations and a lack of dispersion to the wider urban environment. In other words, inadequate transportation provision may prevent cities offering their wider attributes to the visitor and, therefore, it congregates urban tourism in a limited number of districts as opposed to allowing a wider range of resources and activities from reaching their tourist potential.

The significance of transport as a mode of travel to allow visitors to access urban areas is evident in the case of London, where 73.2 per cent of the 13.5 million international visitors in 1997 arrived by air. Some 52.7 per cent arrived into London Heathrow, illustrating the significance of urban centres as gateways. A further 12.6 per cent of arrivals were into Gatwick with an additional 7.9 per cent arriving via London Stansted, London City Airport and Luton Airport.

In contrast, many *secondary* urban destinations, especially historic cities outside of gateway regions, receive many of their visitors by road. For example, Manete et al. (2000: 14) cite the following visitor arrivals by road: Rimini (80 per cent), Canterbury (56 per cent), Barcelona (46 per cent), Glasgow (41 per cent), Paris (40 per cent) and Amsterdam (35 per cent). Coach travel is important for historic cities such as Jerusalem (52 per cent), Toledo, Spain (35 per cent) and Paris (17 per cent). Orbasli and Shaw (2004) note that the arrival of visitors by motorised transport has a significant impact on the historic quarters of cities, which are not designed to accommodate vehicles. In addition, car parking has become a major problem in these cities, and whilst underground car parking may be visually less obtrusive it can conflict with archeological remains. This is problematic when 70 per cent of visitors arrive by road, as is the case in many UK historic cities (English Historic Towns Forum 1994). And many of these destinations are described by Orbasli and Shaw (2004) as victims of their own success, such as Venice (see Page and Hall 2002 for a detailed case study and resulting management measures). Not only does the traffic problem impact upon the visitor experience, but it also alienates local residents who have to live with the problem, an issue raised earlier in Chapter 1 by D. Hall (1999).

This is complicated by the third role for transport in urban tourist trips – mobility within urban areas. The London Tourist Board found that 91 per cent of international visitors used the London Underground during their visit in 1997 and 51 per cent used London's buses. In contrast, 30 per cent of international visitors used taxis to travel within the capital, 23 per cent used suburban trains, and between 11 and 15 per cent utilised the hop on–hop off sightseeing buses. Only 4 per cent of visitors used the Docklands Light Railway, while 12 per cent travelled in a friend's car at one point during their trip. This reaffirms the integral role of public transport and tourist travel. This is sometimes accompanied by congestion and overuse of the inner city by car users that conflict with pedestrian flows. One option may be to further develop tourist transport options such as hop on–hop off sightseeing buses that offer flexibility, novelty and convenience, and thus reduce car use. These problems are accentuated by the existence of seasonality in visitor arrivals and the need to manage excursion traffic such as coach-borne visitors. Congestion also generates additional pollution from vehicles. Some cities, such as Groningen in Northern

Holland, are virtually car-free, using bicycles instead, to protect the historic city and, in other contexts, the public sector has implemented a range of actions to manage traffic:

- promoting alternative travel methods such as rail;
- limiting private car use by payment parking methods;
- park and ride schemes to promote private car traffic switching to public transport at key locations outside the city centre;
- reorganisation of the road network and provision of pedestrian zones;
- the development of cycling and pedestrian tracks to reduce traffic congestion, noise and pollution and to improve the quality of the urban environment for residents and visitors alike;
- information on websites and in printed form for visitors;
- tourist coach control systems for managing organised groups;
- greater integration of local land use and transport planning;
- enhancement of local and gateway networks, with direct public transport services, including enhanced interchange facilities for people with special needs.

One interesting example of the application of urban transport measures to address tourism can be found in Manete et al. (2000), who provide case studies of Amsterdam, Barcelona, Canterbury, Glasgow, Jerusalem, Paris, Rimini, Rome, Toledo and the Alpine region – North Tyrol – Salzburg.

What emerges from the existing but limited literature on the interrelationships between transport and urban tourism is the necessity for more active management measures to address many of the issues raised above in order to balance the needs of residents, businesses, visitors and other stakeholders. A recent Archway (2008) *Good Practice Guide: Transport*, focused on access and regeneration of historic walled towns, points to many key principles for positively planning for the tourist car by prohibiting or limiting its use. This is relatively easy where a walled city has a limited number of gateways to control access to the historic centre. The principles of restraining the length of stay may include parking control measures to limit demand (i.e. CCTV, cardboard clocks and scratchcards, parking meters, pay and display meters, as well as more radical measures such as controlled entry). The UK Tourism Society's response to the Government Task Force on Tourism and the Environment (English Tourist Board/Employment Department 1991) highlighted the impact of the car in many such locations by commenting that:

> no analysis of the relationship between tourism and the environment can ignore transportation. Tourism is inconceivable without it. Throughout Europe some 40 per cent of leisure time away from home is spent travelling, and the vast majority of this is by car . . . Approaching 30 per cent of the UK's energy requirements go on transportation . . . [and] the impact of traffic congestion, noise and air pollution . . . [will] diminish the quality of the experience for visitors.

Various management solutions exist, but their adoption and implementation in many contexts pose political problems as stakeholders worry about the possible short-term impact on local businesses and the loss of visitors if the scheme developed diverts visitors to other areas/localities.

Tourism geography, transport and analytical concepts

Both air transport and car travel have provided new opportunities for more flexible patterns of travel although, as Sealy (1992) suggests, air travel and the expansion of international tourism are largely a nodal transport system dependent upon the airports (the nodes) and the flights (the flows) serving them. In the case of the Mediterranean, Pearce (1987) indicates that the expansion of charter airlines has provided a closer link between the tourism markets and potential destinations, and the increase in the geographical range of charter aircraft (i.e. increased flying time) and reduced costs of air travel have led to an expansion in the scale and distribution of tourism in the Mediterranean.

One further concept that tourism geographers have examined is the patterns of tourist transport – namely the tour. A tour is a tourist-oriented form of travel and Pearce (1987) examines the patterns and flows of tourist traffic in terms of preferred routes of travel. In the case of New Zealand, Forer and Pearce (1984) examine the tour itineraries of coach operators to provide information on the patterns of travel and circuits of coach tours. They found that on the North Island of New Zealand a series of linear tours existed between the major gateways – Auckland and Wellington – with tourists visiting popular resorts and attractions en route. On the South Island, a more complex series of looped tours existed. Many of these originated and ended at Christchurch (the second largest gateway) as tourists explored the diverse range of landscapes and scenic locations associated with National Parks such as Mount Cook, Westland and Fiordland. Pearce and Elliot (1983) developed a further statistical technique – the Trip Index – to examine the extent to which places visited by tourists were major destinations or just a stopover. The Trip Index was calculated thus:

$$\text{Trip Index} = \frac{\text{Nights spent at the destination}}{\text{Total number of nights spent on the trip}} \times 100$$

A Trip Index of 100 means that the entire trip was spent at one destination and a value of zero would mean that no overnight stay was made on the entire journey.

Other features that the tourism geographer has examined in terms of tourist transport include the use of the private car and public transport (Halsall 1992). Pearce (1990) also notes the importance of transit services from airports to city centres, as well as tourist use of transport to tour sites in major cities such as the London Underground system. In fact the Docklands Light Railway that connects Central London to London Docklands has also become a popular form of tourist transport in its own right (Page 1989b, c, 1995a).

Thus, geographers have undertaken research on tourist transport systems at different spatial scales in 'terms of mode, routes and types of operation (e.g. scheduled/non-scheduled)' (Pearce 1990: 29) and the spatial patterns, processes and networks that facilitate tourist travel, thereby making destinations more accessible. To illustrate how geographers can produce a synthesis of different disciplinary perspectives (e.g. environmental science) and the application to tourist transport, Insight 2.2 looks at recreational boating. The Insight highlights how the coexistence of recreational and tourist use of a particular form of tourist transport – boats – can generate a range of problems which require solutions that can be addressed from a management perspective (discussed later in the chapter).

INSIGHT 2.2

Tourist and recreational boating on the Norfolk Broads

The Norfolk Broads (hereafter the Broads) is the UK's largest wetland region. It is located in East Anglia and was created in the medieval period through a series of flooded peat diggings. The region comprises a wetland area focused on a number of rivers such as the Bure, the Yare and the Waveney and their tributaries in the eastern part of Norfolk and northern part of Suffolk. Although the region, with 200 km of tidal rivers and 3640 ha of water space, is not large, it is an area of natural beauty used for intensive recreational boating. It was identified as a potential candidate for National Park status but was not included under the original designations. In 1989 the area was accorded virtual National Park status when the Broads Authority was established by the 1988 Norfolk and Suffolk Broads Act. This granted the Broads Authority the same autonomy as a National Park in terms of finance, policy and administration and thus it receives a 75 per cent grant from central government (Glyptis 1991). Recreational boating dates back to the 1870s when the early wherries (local sailing vessels that carried cargo) began to carry passengers for pleasure. In the 1880s, John Loyne pioneered the hire boat industry and in 1908 the present H. Blake & Co. was established to rent purpose-built vessels to visitors who travelled to the area by rail. Thus, the use of transport for recreational day use and for much longer holiday use led to the development of a particular form of recreation and tourism that was water based and transport dependent. In 1995 boat companies owned 1481 motor cruisers and launches that were hired to approximately 200,000 visitors a year, although the number of boats hired fluctuated during the 1980s and 1990s. A number of environmental concerns have developed over the past 30 years related to their use. The total number of licensed recreational boats using the Broads now exceeds 13,000 (combining motor cruisers, yachts, launches, workboats, sailing and rowing craft). The two most serious concerns are:

1 Erosion of river banks and the destruction of the protective reed fingers, which have implications for all river-bank users and farmers.
2 Enrichment of the nutrient content of the water with nitrates and phosphates. This has contributed to the process known as eutrophication, which leads to an excessive growth of a limited number of plant species and the extinction of the diverse range of flora and fauna.

The Norfolk Broads is a recreational resource under pressure. Given the region's proximity to the urban centres in South East England, the Midlands and towns in East Anglia, access to this series of interconnected linear parks has undoubtedly contributed to these pressures. In essence, there are two competing arguments for and against the continued growth and development of recreational boating in the Broads. On the one hand, there is the physical environmental debate that emphasises the damage motor boats cause to the local ecosystem through their wash turbidity, as their propellers cause a suction effect on the river bed. This also affects reed beds and causes abrasion on the river banks as well as polluting the water through petrol and oil emissions. However, boats alone are not the main cause of environmental damage, as agricultural fertilisers and domestic sewage are also a major contributor to overenrichment and species extinction problems. Anglers may also be equally to blame for damage to river banks. Yet the problem with the hire boat industry is that it is spatially concentrated and heavy usage occurs at weekends in the northern parts of the river system (e.g. Thurne Mouth and the middle reaches of the River Bure at Horning and Wroxham/Hoveton and to a lesser degree the lower reaches of the River Ant). This places intense pressure upon attractions within that region, especially during the very short summer season. For example, a Broads Authority boat movement census in 1994 highlighted that on one peak Sunday in August there were 6296 craft movements recorded at 14 census points. In contrast, the upper reaches of many rivers are protected by their relative inaccessibility and in a few cases by low bridges.

▶

In contrast to the environmental arguments, there are powerful economic arguments for continuing to promote the development of recreational boating. The hire boat industry is estimated to contribute £25 million to the local economy and generates approximately £9000 for the economy for each boat rented (Broads Authority 1997). The Broads Authority found that a study by the East of England Tourist Board estimated that in 1998 tourism contributed £146.6 million, 82 per cent from staying visitors and 18 per cent from day visitors. This supported 3107 full-time jobs and there were over 1 million trips to the Broads by staying visitors and 1.3 million by day trippers (Broads Authority 2004). Furthermore, recreational and tourist spending indirectly contributes to 5000–5500 jobs in the hospitality sector, local tourist attractions as well as in the local marine industry. Even though boating was in recession within the area in the 1990s, boatyard diversification to develop facilities for the needs of visitors (e.g. the construction of accommodation) also posed planning problems for the Broads Authority, since such diversification changes the traditional image of the area.

Given these two competing arguments over recreational boating, it is pertinent to ask who is responsible for decision making and planning for boating in this region. Much of the decision-making is fragmented across a number of public and private sector bodies, each with particular powers, responsibilities and visions relating to boating. These include:

- National government, working through the Countryside Commission (now Natural England), has debated the issue of the most appropriate administrative structure for the region, which led to the Broads Authority being established. Yet other government departments such as the Department for Environment, Food and Rural Affairs have a very different view of the region's function from the Countryside Commission, which is not recreational or conservationist in focus.
- The Broads Authority can regulate planning proposals for new boatyards and extensions to existing ones. It can also develop new waterside facilities such as public moorings in accordance with its overall management plan (Broads Authority 1997).
- The Great Yarmouth Port and Haven Commissioners are responsible for all navigation on the Broads and rivers. They license boats and have imposed speed restrictions, enforced by river inspectors. They can also regulate river traffic charges.
- The Regional Development Agency for the area (East of England Development Agency) and East of England Tourism promote the region to visitors together with local districts. Each body has a degree of choice over the image it chooses to portray and the markets it targets, and could even advocate alternative tourist activities in the region.
- The hire boat companies and their marketing agencies have undertaken publicity campaigns to try to influence the behaviour of visitors and encourage a greater consciousness of the natural environment. Boat companies could restrict the number of vessels hired at particular places, and at certain times, if they felt it was in their long-term interests.
- A variety of other bodies have responsibilities, such as the regional water authority (Anglian Water), whilst the National Rivers Authority has powers over water quality and land drainage. There are also a large number of pressure groups that have a strong lobby function, such as the National Farmers' Union, the Nature Conservancy Council and the local Broads Society. Although no one group has direct influence over the hire boat industry, they can exert pressure on decision-makers in other bodies to influence planning outcomes.

This Insight illustrates that it is not so much the volume of boats but rather the intensity of use in time and space as well as the behaviour of users that conflicts with the natural environment. For this reason it is worthwhile focusing on the possible solutions to the recreational problems that this form of transport poses. There is no all-embracing solution that will deal with the conflicts. Coexistence with the fragile ecosystem is therefore a major challenge for recreation management. Environmental deterioration is not a problem that can be solved quickly, but the Broads Authority has a management plan for the area that is viewed as a long-term vision for the Broads (Broads Authority 2004). The 1981 Wildlife and ▶

Countryside Act has also highlighted the problem of reconciling agricultural and commercial practices with environmental conservation. Since any form of management for the Broads needs to be accompanied by objectives that inform the strategic direction, sustainability is a prime concern for the region (Broads Authority 2004). The Broads Authority has developed a number of policies to address the issue of coexistence of the recreational boating industry with the Authority's underlying objective, which is to foster sustainable management and development. Each of these policies not only requires coordination of the various agencies involved with the hire boat industry, but also an ongoing dialogue with all parties affected by the Broads management plan. By fostering an ongoing partnership between public and private sector groups, the management plan will remain a workable strategy for the future and ensure the boating industry is an integral but managed element of tourism and recreational activities available in the region. The Insight also illustrates that there is a growing concern over management of the impacts of recreational boating and that sustainable policies and practices are developed in relation to recreational and tourism transport systems.

Marketing and tourist transport

When one considers the contribution of economics and geography to the analysis of tourist transport, it is evident that a wide range of research papers and books exist. In the case of marketing, the number of studies focused on tourist transport is limited because there is a tendency for marketing to be more visible and results oriented than based on the academic analysis of good practice, although a number of seminal studies focused on air transport do exist (e.g. Shaw 2004, 2007, 2008). Promotional material and advertising campaigns constitute a major investment in time, money and creative thinking, with companies reluctant to highlight good practice that might undermine their future business potential. According to Horner and Swarbrooke (1996) the diversity of transport modes used in tourism (i.e. air, rail, water, road and off-road transport) makes it difficult to generalise about transport and marketing. This is further complicated by the private, public and voluntary sector organisations involved in transport for tourism that all have different marketing objectives. In addition, a conceptual problem exists: sometimes transport may be sold as a self-contained product, sometimes as part of a large composite product (e.g. an inclusive tour). In order to understand how marketing is integral to the analysis of tourist transport, it is therefore useful to examine the principles used in marketing and the activities undertaken by marketers.

How is marketing used in tourist transport?

According to Kotler and Armstrong (1991), marketing is a process whereby individuals and groups obtain the type of products or goods they value. These goods are created and exchanged through a social and managerial process which requires a detailed understanding of consumers and their wants and desires so that the product or service is effectively delivered to the client or purchaser. Within tourism studies, there has been a growing interest in marketing (e.g. Middleton 1988; Jefferson and Lickorish 1991; Laws 1991; Horner and Swarbrooke 1996; Seaton and Bennett 1996; Lumsdon 1997a) compared with transport studies, which has tended

Table 2.3 Marketing and distribution channels used by selected tourist transport operators in the UK

	Form of media							
						Internet		Customer loyalty scheme
Operator	Print/ magazines	Billboards	TV	Radio	Direct mail	Website	Online agency	
National Express	✓	X	✓	X	X	✓	✓Trainline.com	✓
Virgin Trains	✓	✓	X	✓	✓	✓	✓Trainline.com	✓
easyJet	✓	✓	✓	X	X	✓	X	X
P&O	✓	✓	✓	✓	✓	✓	X	X
BA	✓	✓	✓	✓	✓	✓	✓Opodo	✓

to employ marketers when required to deal with such issues, reflected in the paucity of texts on the topic. More recently, new marketing-for-tourism texts have begun to incorporate material on marketing transport services, although this usually tends to focus on airlines (Horner and Swarbrooke 1996; Seaton and Bennett 1996; for generic issues Middleton and Clarke 2001). In transport studies, marketing has assumed less importance than operational and organisational issues, but there is a growing awareness that 'transport operators are seeking to augment their basic product with add-on services that generate more income but also satisfy more of the consumers' needs' (Horner and Swarbrooke 1996: 319), and there are many mechanisms through which they seek to influence the consumer to purchase the product. For example, with low-cost airlines, large-scale billboard advertising, newspaper advertising and promotions combine with many other forms of distribution and promotion including the Internet, and a number of examples are shown in Table 2.3. Gilbert (1989) considers the growth and establishment of marketing within tourism and the critical role of a consumer orientation amongst transport providers. For example, British Airways explained its financial turnaround from a loss of £544 million in 1984 in terms of a greater marketing orientation based on recognising customer needs and attempting to satisfy them (Gilbert 1989). In this respect, marketing has a fundamental role to play in analysing tourist transport. Within marketing, three key areas exist:

- strategic planning;
- marketing research;
- the marketing mix.

Strategic planning

Within any business or company, there is a need to provide some degree of order or structure to its activities and to think ahead. This is essential if companies are to be able to respond to the competitive business environment in which they operate. For this reason a formal planning process, known as *strategic planning*, is necessary. According to Kotler and Armstrong (1991: 29), strategic planning can be defined as 'the process of developing and maintaining a strategic fit between the organisation's goals and capabilities and its changing marketing opportunities'.

Businesses need to be aware of their position in the wider business environment and how they will respond to competition and new business opportunities within an organised framework. To illustrate how strategic planning operates and its significance to tourist transport, it is useful to focus on the structured approach devised by Kotler and Armstrong (1991). The first stage is the definition of an organisation's purpose, which requires a company to consider:

- What business is it in?
- Who are its customers?
- What services do its customers require?

The stage following the setting of objectives and goals is termed the *business portfolio*. Here the company analyses its own products or services in terms of its own business expertise and how competitors' products and services may affect them. This is frequently undertaken as a SWOT analysis, which considers:

- the Strengths;
- the Weaknesses;
- the Opportunities;
- the Threats

of its products and services in the business environment.

Part of the wider strategic analysis of the business environment will also involve environmental scanning to try and understand what will be driving future change in a company's marketing activity (i.e. driver analysis). This involves a wide-ranging analysis of informal and formal sources of information to understand key uncertainties which will shape the future. Figure 2.6 is one illustration of this environmental scanning approach based on a summary of some of the principal drivers of change which will affect the marketing of air travel. Figure 2.6 illustrates that technology, the political environment (e.g. terrorism), economic, demographic and environmental factors all coalesce to generate uncertainty.

For those operators who may wish to develop a strategy that incorporates an element of organisational growth and expansion, a number of options exist. As Horner and Swarbrooke (1996: 325) show, these can be divided into:

- *Marketing consortia*, where a group of operators cooperate to create and develop a product such as the European joint railway ticket, permitting rail travel on different European railways.
- *Strategic alliances*, where different businesses agree to cooperate in various ways. This has varied by sector in the tourism industry, but may involve marketing agreements or technical cooperation. However, in the airline industry, Gallacher and Odell (1994) observed that 280 alliances existed among 136 airlines, 60 per cent of which were formed after 1992 and, as discussed earlier, the airline sector has three principal alliances: OneWorld, SkyTeam and the Star Alliance. Hanlon (1996: 201) outlined the nature of such alliances amongst airline companies, which included joint sales and marketing; joint purchasing and insurance; joint passenger and cargo flights; code sharing; block spacing; links between frequent flyer programmes; management contracts; and joint ventures in catering, ground handling and aircraft maintenance. The strategic value of such alliances is reconsidered in Chapter 6, as they can result in 'horizontal alliances . . . [involving] firms selling the same product . . . vertical alliances . . . [being] those

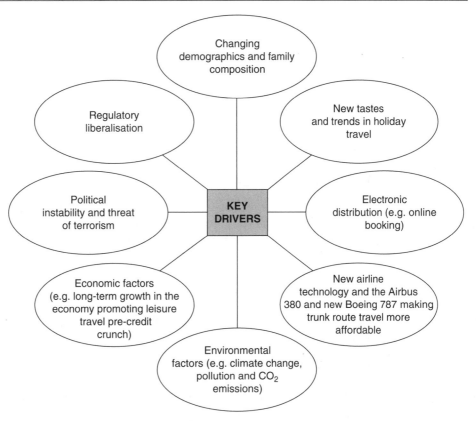

Figure 2.6 Drivers of change in the marketing of leisure air travel
Source: Developed from Shaw (2008).

with suppliers, distributors or buyers. And external alliances . . . with potential entrants or with the producers . . . in other industries' (Hanlon 1996: 204). The main concern for governments, as Chapter 3 will show, is that the transport industry may be overconcentrated in a limited number of companies or consortia that could eventually lead to market domination and higher prices. For example, Youssef and Hansen's (1994) study of the Swissair and SAS alliance indicated that on the main hub routes – Copenhagen, Stockholm and Oslo to Geneva – competition was severely reduced. Consequently, the alliance had yielded higher profits for the airlines on the hub-to-hub routes, although the subsequent demise of Swissair was a notable casualty of the global aviation crisis.

- *Acquisition*, which is the purchase of equity in other operations, such as the Scandinavian company Stena's acquisition of European ferry operations, especially in the UK (prior to its acquisition by P&O).
- *Joint ventures*, where operators seek to create new carriers.
- *Franchising*, where major operators use their market presence and brand image to extend their influence further (or to reduce costs of operation on more marginal routes) by licensing franchisees to operate routes using their corporate logo and codes.
- *Ancillary activities*, the development of which adds value to the operator or organisation's core business. For example, many European ferry operators now offer inclusive tour operations or short-break cruise options.

According to Middleton and Clarke (2001: 379) the strategic issues that arise in passenger transport for tourist operators are:

- forecasting demand;
- finding ways to reduce marketing costs;
- building corporate product and brand strengths;
- relationship marketing;
- strategic linkages and alliances,

which are issues addressed at different places in this book.

Marketing research

This process is often seen as synonymous with market research but as the following definition by Seibert (1973) implies, in reality it is a much broader concept as 'marketing research is an organised process associated with the gathering, processing, analysis, storage and dissemination of information to facilitate and improve decision-making'. It incorporates various forms of research undertaken by organisations to understand their customers, markets and business efficiency. The actual research methods used to investigate different aspects of a company's business ultimately determine the type of research undertaken. The main types of research can be summarised into the following categories:

- market analysis and forecasting, used to measure the volume, value and likely changes in markets;
- consumer research, to examine specific market segments or the ability to position oneself at a specific point in the marketplace (see Petrick 2004 for an example);
- product/price-based studies to assess the price sensitivity consumers have for specific products (see Downward and Lumsdon 2004, for example);
- distribution research, which examines distributor awareness of products;
- evaluation studies, which can include customer satisfaction studies.

Clearly marketing research allows the company to keep in touch with its customers to monitor needs and tastes that are constantly changing in time and space. Since the 1990s, the transport sector has adopted many of the market research techniques used in the commercial sector to develop a better understanding of their consumers, especially tourists, so that the services and products provided are market-led. However, the actual implementation of marketing for tourist transport ultimately depends on the 'marketing mix'.

The marketing mix

The marketing mix is 'the mixture of controllable marketing variables that the firm [or company] uses to pursue the sought level of sales in the target market' (Kotler cited in Holloway and Plant 1988: 48). This means that for a given tourist transport organisation such as an airline, there are four main marketing variables which it needs to harness to achieve the goals identified in the marketing strategy formulated through the strategic planning process. These variables are:

- *Product formulation* – the ability of a company to adapt to the needs of its customers in terms of the services it provides. These are constantly being adapted to changes in consumer markets.

- *Price* – the economic concept used to adjust the supply of a service to meet the demand, taking account of sales targets and turnover.
- *Promotion* – the manner in which a company seeks to improve customers' knowledge of the services it sells so that those people who are made aware may be turned into actual purchasers. To achieve promotional aims advertising, public relations, sales and brochure production activities are undertaken. Not surprisingly, promotion often consumes the largest proportion of marketing budgets. For transport operators, the timetable is widely used as a communication tool, whilst brochures and information leaflets are produced to publicise products. Some of the other promotional tools used to increase sales include promotional fares, frequent flyer programmes (Beaver 1996) and 'piggy-back promotions where purchasing one type of product gives consumers an opportunity to enjoy a special deal in relation to another product' (Horner and Swarbrooke 1996: 322).
- *Place* – the location at which *prospective* customers may be induced to purchase a service – the point of sale (e.g. a travel agent).

As marketing variables, production, price, promotion and place are normally called the four Ps. These are incorporated into the marketing process in relation to the known competition and the impact of market conditions. Thus, the marketing process involves the continuous evaluation of how a business operates internally and externally and can be summarised as 'the management process which identifies, anticipates and supplies customers' [see the section of this chapter on management studies] requirements efficiently and profitably' (UK Institute of Marketing, cited in Cannon 1989). To illustrate the importance of marketing, particularly promotion, Insight 2.3 about Queensland Rail in Australia emphasises how a product in decline can be revitalised and repackaged for the tourist.

INSIGHT 2.3

Marketing tourist transport: Queensland Rail

In the state of Queensland in Australia the rail services are state owned. The railway company Queensland Rail has sought to inject a new lease of life into its loss-making, long-distance passenger services by repackaging its services to meet a niche demand amongst tourists. Research by Dann (1994) explained the resurgence of interest in rail travel as a function of nostalgia amongst tourists, a feature also emphasised in the context of heritage tourism by Swarbrooke (1994). Furthermore, Prideaux (1999) cites the research by Taylor (1983) that identified the speed, comfort, amenities and sociability of train travel as appealing for tourists.

Although long-distance passenger services commenced in 1885 in Queensland, with luxury services being added in the 1930s (e.g. the *Sunshine Express),* followed by air-conditioned carriages in the 1950s (e.g. the *Sunlander* operating between Brisbane and Cairns in 1953), the post-war period saw a decline in rail travel. Road transport, notably the rise of the private car, and the expansion of air travel led to a decline in services. The extensive network of passenger services contracted as routes were reduced, lines closed and services cancelled. Although rail sought to introduce innovations to stem the flow of traffic (e.g. car-carrying wagons), its decline mirrored the future of rail in many other countries up to the ▶

1980s (Kosters 1992). This led to a downward spiral of declining passenger numbers and declining services. In addition, Prideaux (1999) pointed to:

- The slow nature of train travel (e.g. in 1997 travel by air between Brisbane and Cairns took *2.5* hours compared to 32 hours on the *Sunlander).*
- Infrequent services, with the *Sunlander* operating six times a week in 1961 and three times a week in 1997.
- Passenger carriages were designed for longevity and recent fashions and tastes are not reflected in 1950s rolling stock.
- The train is inflexible compared to the car, with its convenience and wide availability.
- Concessionary fares for pensioners have not yielded a great deal of revenue and gener-ated intense competition in the peak season, also affecting the image of the railway.
- Lack of investment in new rolling stock and new technology, until the introduction of the *Spirit of Capricorn* in 1989 and upgraded track in the 1990s. The introduction of a tilt-technology on the *Spirit of Capricorn* in 1997 (similar to the ill-fated British Rail Advanced Passenger Train in the 1970s and 1980s) reduced the journey time for Brisbane to Rockhampton from 9 hours 25 minutes to 7 hours at a total cost of AU$139 million. There are now two tilt train services from Brisbane to Rockhampton/Bundaberg and Cairns.
- An absence of promotion due to public sector principles that did not emphasise commer-cial practices until the late 1990s.
- A perceived lack of reliability in keeping to the published schedules.
- Rail travel was expensive and not price competitive with air travel.
- Competition from long-distance coaches, following the deregulation of the sector in 1985. Price and departure flexibility among coach operators combined with mass media advertising and their attractive multi-sector price structures for tourist travel, severely dented rail's market share.

While Queensland Rail sought to address some of these issues in the 1990s, the loss of traditional clientele meant the search for new markets after the state government's corpo-ratisation of Queensland Rail in 1995. This followed the reorganisation of long-distance rail services in the late 1980s into a new group – Traveltrain. Tourism was seen as an area for expansion, with two services – Sunshine Rail Experience and Kuranda Scenic Railway, which departs from Cairns and traverses scenic gorges and travels through virgin rainforest and the jungle village of Kuranda. By 1994, 500,000 passengers a year were travelling on the Kuranda Scenic Railway, making it Australia's sixteenth-largest tourist attraction that same year, exceeding visits to the Great Barrier Reef.

Following the success of the *Queenslander* tourist train in 1986, the *Spirit of the Outback* and the *Spirit of the Tropics* were introduced in 1993 to help offset losses on other long-distance services. In 1995 the *Savannahlander* was brought in and subsequently won tourism awards. But how has Queensland Rail been able to turn an ailing railway company into a successful tourist venture?

One of the tools used by Queensland Rail (http://www.traveltrain.co.au) was the develop-ment of promotional themes to sell individual services via its tourism arm – Australian Adventures, where a number of market segments were carefully nurtured, and these have received high customer satisfaction scores, with 8.8 out of 10 for the Kuranda Scenic Railway (Queensland Rail 2003, http://www.qr.com.au). According to Prideaux (1999), these included:

- *Long-distance rail services* (e.g. the *Sunlander)* using traditional routes developed in the nineteenth century from Brisbane to Rockampton to Townsville and Cairns. In 1995 the *Sunlander* underwent a AU$2.8 million refit with themed carriages and public entertain-ment areas. This was accompanied by a reimaging of these services to convey a restful travel experience full of discovery and attractions.
- *Nostalgia,* where the former *Midlander* service from Rockhampton to Winton was re-launched as the *Spirit of the Outback* in 1993. An elimination of pensioner concessions

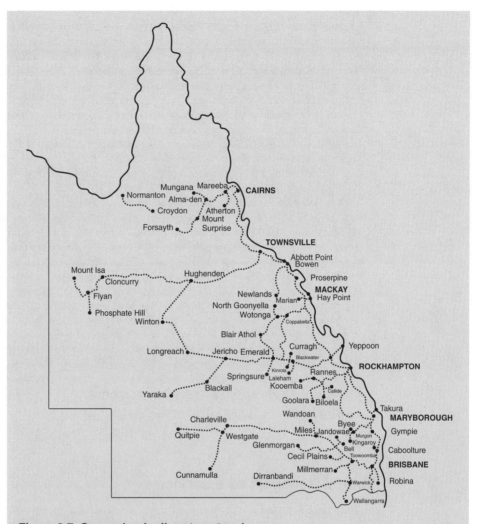

Figure 2.7 Queensland rail route network

Source: Queensland Rail

on this service combined with a strong appeal to nostalgia characterised the marketing of this service.

- *Trains as* tourist *attractions*, as epitomised by the Kuranda Scenic Railway, with the *Gulflander* and *Savannahlander* also marketed in the same way. These utilise a range of heritage themes (e.g. mineral mining) and a strong emphasis on nostalgia.
- *Rail-touring,* using daytime travel along the Queensland coast between Brisbane and Cairns and overnight stays in motels along the lines of the 1962 Sunshine Rail Experience.

The routes for these are shown in Figure 2.7.

Following corporatisation, Queensland Rail only received state subsidies to operate services the state deemed were important from a public welfare perspective (see Chapter 3 on government policy). The move towards profitability was underwritten by a 10-year AU$4 billion capital works programme to assist with the corporatisation (O'Rourke 1996). Long-distance passenger services remain unviable, with a large network and high costs of operation. The *Sunlander* contributes 34 per cent of Traveltrain's gross revenue, ▶

followed by the Kuranda Scenic Rail service with 19 per cent. However, tourism ventures have not noticeably reduced operational losses on long-distance rail services due to what Prideaux (1999) considers to be Queensland Rail's inability to market its services. Until recently travel sales could only be made through railway offices and not through travel agents. However, alliances with tour wholesalers proved to be a major step forward.

Prideaux (1999) also points to the desire of Queensland Rail to reposition itself in the tourism sector, and in 2008 the company was offering the following services and ticket sales through its Australian Adventures division on Australian-wide services: Queenslander Class on the Sunlander; the Tilt Train; the Spirit of the Outback; the Westlander; The Gulflander; the Kurander scenic; the Savannahland; the Inlander; the Ghan; the Indian Pacific; the Overlander; and the XPT high-speed intercity train (Sydney–Melbourne–Brisbane) based on the highly successful British-built Intercity 125 train.

Clearly Queensland Rail is still developing the marketing of its services, with opportunities to expand this role through packaged rail tours, the sale of a rail experience, moving Queensland Rail from a promotional to a more sales-oriented role, and using new marketing strategies to enhance the marketing effect. Continued service improvements on board trains combined with a higher degree of cost recovery need to be a financial target for Queensland Rail. This can be achieved by increasing the profitability of its existing and forecast markets (e.g. tourists) and by developing a more sophisticated marketing philosophy, perhaps with a stronger emphasis on service quality. In 2008, QR won the prestigious recognition for the *Sunlander* service of being one of the world's Top 25 rail journeys.

As the Insight shows, marketing has a certain degree of synergy with economics, as an understanding of economic concepts and the way in which the marketplace works is fundamental to marketing. But the application of marketing principles to the tourist transport system requires a recognition that one is dealing with a service and the tourist experience which is embodied in the concept of the service encounter.

Further reading: Queensland Rail (2003) *http://www.qr.com.au*

Tourist transport as a service

Gilbert (1989) noted the growing importance of service quality and consumer satisfaction in tourism in the late 1980s. In the context of tourist transport, what is meant by a service? Defining the term 'service' is difficult due to the intangibility, perishability and inseparability of services. Kotler and Armstrong (1991: 620) define these three terms as follows:

- *Service intangibility* – a service is something that cannot be seen, tasted, felt, heard or smelt before it is purchased.
- *Service perishability* – a service cannot be stored for sale or use at a later date.
- *Service inseparability* – a service is usually produced and consumed at the same time and cannot be separated from providers.

Van Dierdonck (1992) argues that the intangible nature of a service is determined by the fact that, unlike manufactured goods, a service is provided and consumed at the same time and same place, making it difficult to define and communicate its form to customers. Even so, it is possible to identify six core elements in a service if it is defined as a product, where each element affects customer perception of the service:

- the image of the service;
- the image of personnel with whom customers interact;

● image differences within the same sector as the service *provider* (e.g. how a service compares with those offered by its competitors);
● the customer group targeted;
● the influence of the physical environment in which the *service* is delivered (e.g. the building);
● the working atmosphere in which the service is formulated, designed and delivered (modified from Flipo 1988, cited in Van Dierdonck 1992).

In one of the few studies of the marketing of transport in a tourism context, Middleton and Clarke (2001) point to the specific services offered to tourists as transport combining:

● service availability;
● cost in comparison to competitors on the same route;
● comfort and speed;
● ambience;
● convenience and ticketing arrangements;
● contact with staff;
● image and positioning of each operator.

An alternative view of a service is that it constitutes a process rather than an end product, which actually disappears once it has been made. In this respect, a service can be conceptualised as a process that responds to the diverse needs of consumers. Since consumers are not homogeneous it is difficult to standardise a product to meet every need. The process of providing a service tailored to meet precise and varied needs is integral to the concept of responsive service provision.

Researchers such as Poon (1989) have argued that the challenge for tourism-related enterprises, such as transport providers, is to respond to the growing sophistication of tourists so that the entire tourism experience meets the expectations of the consumer. In this context, three key issues that emerge are service quality, customer care and the service encounter (Gilbert 1989). From the consumer's perspective, critical incidents (Bitner et al. 1990) in the service process (e.g. where the service delivery breaks down) have been used to analyse the consumer's service encounter and how they view it under adverse conditions. If we accept there is a consensus amongst marketing researchers that service provision needs to be seen as an ongoing process, how does this process operate? Cowell (1986) examined this process as a four-stage system (see Figure 2.8) with the provider trying to offer a service in response to actual or perceived customer demand. The process is based on the following concepts: consumer benefit, the service concept, the service offer and the service delivery system.

The consumer benefit

At the outset, the supplier of a service tries to understand what the consumer wants and how they may benefit from the service. At this stage a detailed understanding of consumer behaviour is required that recognises the relative importance of the factors influencing the purchase decision (Qaiters and Bergiel 1989). These include social, economic, cultural, business and family influences and how they condition and affect the attitudes, motives, needs and perceptions of consumers. In the case of tourist transport services, a significant amount of research on the social psychology of

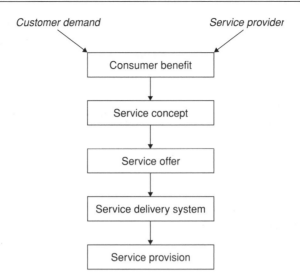

Figure 2.8 The service process
Source: Based on Cowell 1986.

tourists has examined what holidays tourists choose, the mode of transport selected and the factors affecting their decision-making as consumers (Javalgi et al. 1992; Mansfeld 1992). Following the consumer benefit stage, the service provider translates the assessment of consumer demands into a service concept.

The service concept

At this point the supplier examines the means of producing a service and how it will be distributed to consumers. Marketing research at both the consumer benefit and service concept stage is essential to assist in identifying the specific market segment to target and the nature of the consumer/producer relationship (e.g. is the service to be sold direct to the public or via a different distribution channel such as a travel agent?). Lastly, the producer identifies and develops the image that is to be associated with the service. Having established what the service will comprise in concept form, it is developed further into the service offer.

The service offer

At this point the service concept is given more shape and developed within precise terms set by managerial decisions, which specify:

- *the elements* – the ingredients;
- *the form* – how it will be offered to consumers;
- *the levels of service* – what the consumer will expect to receive in terms of the quality and quantity of the service.

The composition of the service elements is discussed in detail by Gronroos (1980). The form of the service concept also needs to be considered in terms of how the corporate image will be communicated to the public. Furthermore, the service levels, the technical aspects of service quality and how it is rendered also need to be assessed as part of the service offer. Despite the significance of the service offer, there is little evidence to suggest that consumers judge service quality in a definitive way. For example, Lovelock (1992a, b) acknowledges that services such as tourist transport, which have a high degree of customer contact, need to be recognised when entering the last stage – service delivery.

The service delivery system

This is the system that is developed to deliver the service to the customer and will comprise both the people responsible for different aspects of the service experience and the physical evidence such as the transport and environment in which it is delivered (Bitner 1992). The tourist's experience of these components is embodied in the *service encounter* (Laws 1991). It is in the service delivery system that barriers may occur in the provision of a satisfactory encounter (see Thornberry and Hennessey 1992) and a great deal of marketing research has been directed to identifying deficiencies, critical incidents and ways of overcoming dissatisfaction in this area (Bitner et al. 1990). The pursuit of excellence in service delivery (Peters and Waterman 1982; Berry and Parasuraman 1991) has meant companies monitoring what the consumer wants and then providing it. In this context marketing assumes a critical role in terms of both research and communication with customers. Quality of service provision may help to develop customer loyalty in the patronage of tourist transport. As the competitive market for tourist transport intensifies, the demand for service delivery systems that are customer centred is likely to be an important factor in affecting tourist use of transport services. For example, a number of transatlantic all-business-class airline services have been developed to try and build a high-quality, loyal customer base with a good value product compared to its competitors. The consumer is a key player in the service process, being an active participant and important judge of quality (Zeithmal and Berry 1985). It is therefore essential to consider how transport providers can integrate many of the perspectives discussed in the chapter so far to meet customers' needs and to run a tourist transport business successfully. Attention now turns to the contribution that management can make.

●●●● Management studies and tourist transport

Having examined the role of other disciplines and their contribution to the analysis of transport, it is useful to consider one area that draws the others together and harnesses their skills. That area is management. Here it is pertinent to examine what management is, its rationale, the principles that guide managers and the factors which can impact upon the need to manage. This is followed by a case study of airline management and the significance of many of the perspectives developed already (marketing, economics and geography) in the success of low-cost airlines, Insight 2.4, which provides an integrating role for this chapter as in reality all of these perspectives coexist and are interrelated.

In a purely abstract academic context, management is concerned with the ability of individuals to conduct, control, take charge of or manipulate the world to achieve a desired outcome. In a practical business setting, management occurs in the context of a formal environment – the organisation (Handy 1989). Within organisations (small businesses through to multinational enterprises) people are among the elements that are managed. As a result, Inkson and Kolb (1995: 6) define management as 'getting things done in organisations through other people'. In a business context, organisations exist as a complex interaction of people, goals and money to create and distribute the goods and services that people and other businesses consume or require.

Organisations are characterised by their ability to work towards a set of common objectives (e.g. the sale of holidays to tourists for a profit). To achieve their objectives, organisations are often ordered into specialised groupings to achieve particular functions (e.g. sales, human resources management, accounts and finance) as departments. In addition, a hierarchy usually exists where the organisation is horizontally divided into different levels of authority and status, and a manager often occupies a position in a particular department or division at a specific point in the hierarchy. Within organisations, managers are grouped by level in the organisation:

- *Chief Executive Officer* (CEO) or *General Manager* at the top who exercises responsibility over the entire organisation and is accountable to a Board of Directors or other representatives for the ultimate performance of the organisation.
- *Top managers* are one level *down* from the CEO and their role is usually confined to a specific function, such as marketing or sales. They may act as part of an executive team that works with other top managers and the CEO to provide advice on the relationship between different parts of the organisation and contribute to corporate goals.
- *Middle managers* fill a niche in the *middle* of the hierarchy with a more specialised role than the top managers. Typically they may head sections or divisions and be responsible for performance in their area. In recent years corporate restructuring has removed a large number of middle managers to cut costs and placed more responsibility on top managers or the level below – first-line managers.
- *First-line managers* are the *lowest* level of manager in an organisation, but arguably perform one of the most critical roles – the supervision of other staff who have non-managerial roles and who affect the day-to-day running of the organisation.

Managers can also be classified according to the function they perform (i.e. the activity for which they are responsible). As a result, three types can be discerned:

- *Functional managers* manage specialised functions such as accounting, research, sales and personnel. These functions may be split even further where the organisation is large and there is scope for more specialisation.
- *Business unit, divisional, or area managers* exercise management responsibilities at a general level lower down in an organisation. Their responsibilities may cover a group of products or diverse geographical areas and combine a range of management tasks, requiring the coordination of various functions.
- *Project managers* manage specific projects that are typically short-term undertakings, and may require a team of staff to complete them. This requires the coordination of a range of different functions within a set time frame.

The goals of managers within organisations are usually seen as profit driven but, as the following list suggests, they are more diverse:

- Profitability, which can be achieved through higher output, better service, attracting new customers and by cost minimisation.

● In the public sector, other goals (e.g. coordination, liaison, raising public aware-ness and undertaking activities for the wider public good) dominate the agenda in organisations. Yet in many government departments in developed countries pri-vate sector, profit-driven motives and greater accountability for the spending of public funds now feature high on the agenda.
● Efficiency, to reduce expenditure and inputs to a minimum to achieve more cost-effective outputs.
● Effectiveness, achieving the desired outcome; this is not necessarily a profit-driven motive.

In practical terms, however, the main tasks of managers are based on the manage-ment process, which aims to achieve these goals. Whilst management theorists differ in the emphasis they place on various aspects of the management process, there are four commonly agreed sets of tasks. McLennan et al. (1987) describe these as:

1 *Planning*, so that goals are set out and the means of achieving the goals are recognised.
2 *Organising*, whereby the work functions are broken down into a series of tasks and linked to some form of structure. These tasks then have to be assigned to individuals.
3 *Leading*, which is the method of motivating and influencing staff so that they per-form their tasks effectively. This is essential if organisational goals are to be achieved. Leadership is a critical role in the success of any enterprise, but has been attributed to the success of key low-cost airlines such as Southwest Airlines (Gittel 2003) and Ryanair (Evans et al. 2003).
4 *Controlling*, which is the method by which information is gathered about what has to be done.

Managing requires a comparison of the information gathered with the organisa-tional goals and, if necessary, taking action to correct any deviations from the over-all goals.

Fundamental to the management process is the need for managers to make deci-sions. This is an ongoing process. In terms of the levels of management, CEOs make major decisions that can affect everyone in the organisation, whereas junior managers often have to make many routine and mundane decisions on a daily basis. Yet in each case decisions made have consequences for the organisation. To make decisions managers often have to balance the ability to use technical skills within their own particular area with the need to relate to people and to use 'human skills' to interact and manage people within the organisation, and clients, suppliers and other people external to the organisation. Managers need these skills to communicate effectively to motivate and lead others. They also need cognitive and conceptual skills. Cognitive skills are those that enable managers to formulate solutions to problems. In contrast, conceptual skills are those that allow them to take a broader view, often characterised as 'being able to see the wood for the trees', whereby the manager can understand the organisation's activities, the inter-relationships and goals and can develop an appropriate strategic response (Inkson and Kolb 1995).

In recent years there has been a growing recognition that to perform a manage-rial task successfully a range of competencies are needed. A competency, according to Inkson and Kolb (1995: 32) is 'an underlying trait of an individual – for example a motive pattern, a skill, a characteristic behaviour, a value, or a set of knowledge – which enables that person to perform successfully in his or her job'. The main motivation for organisational interest in competency is the desire to improve management through education and training. Competencies can be divided into three groups:

- understanding what needs to be done;
- getting the job done;
- taking people with you.

Whilst the concern with competencies questions the traditional planning, organising, leading and control model as a description of the management process, an overriding emphasis on the skills managers need to perform tasks also has inherent problems. Research has shown that the view that such skills are generic and can be generalised to all situations is incorrect. In fact, human skills are very much related to personality and individual style and conceptual skills are based on the natural abilities of individuals. However, a certain degree of training and development as well as everyday learning may assist managers to improve their effectiveness. What is critical is the manager's ability to be adaptable and flexible to change, particularly in fast-moving areas such as tourism.

Change is a feature of modern-day management and any manager needs to be aware of, and able to respond to, changes in the organisational environment. For example, general changes in society, such as the decision of a new ruling political party to deregulate the economy, have a bearing on the operation of organisations. More specific factors can also influence the organisational environment:

- *Socio-cultural factors*, which include the behaviour, beliefs and norms of the population in a specific area.
- *Demographic factors*, which are related to the changing composition of the population (e.g. birth rates, mortality rates and the growing burden of dependency where the increasing numbers of ageing population will have to be supported by a declining number of economically active people in the workforce).
- *Economic factors*, which include the type of capitalism at work in a given country and the degree of state control of business. The economic system is also important since it may have a bearing on the level of prosperity and factors that influence the system's ability to produce, distribute and consume wealth.
- *Political and legal factors* that are the framework in which organisations must work (e.g. laws and practices).
- *Technological factors*, where advances in technology can be used to create products more efficiently. The use of information technology and its application to business practices is a case in point.
- *Competitive factors*, which illustrate that businesses operate in markets and other producers may seek to offer superior services or products at a lower price. Businesses also compete for finance, sources of labour and other resources.
- *International factors*, where businesses operate in a global environment and factors that obtain in other countries may affect the local business environment.

- *Change and uncertainty* are unpredictable in free market economies, and managers have to ensure that organisations can adapt to ensure continued survival and prosperity. Change continually challenges all organisations and change in any one factor within an organisation can affect how it functions. Various techniques can be used to help to overcome internal resistance to change within organisations. As Kotter and Schlesinger (1979) observe, these include:

  - education and communication;
  - participation and involvement;
  - facilitation and support;
  - negotiation and agreement;
  - manipulation and co-optation;
  - explicit and implicit coercion.

Change may be vital for organisations to adapt and grow in new environments and the introduction of information technology is one example where initial resistance within businesses had to be overcome, with remarkable success where the technology is harnessed as the example of Megabus and internet bookings show. Initially the company expanded in the UK (Plate 2.2) and then rolled out an expansion of the idea to major cities in the eastern seaboard of the USA (Plate 2.3). Increasingly, managers are not only having to undertake the role of managing, but also the dynamic role of 'change agent' especially as the low-cost revolution moves from air travel to other sectors of the tourism production system and transport sector.

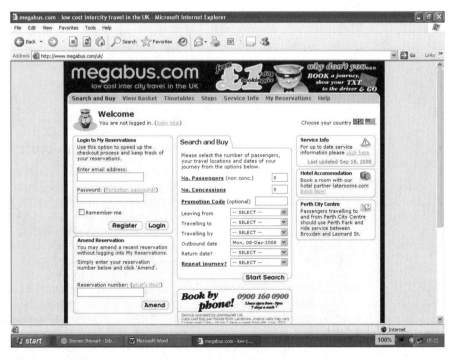

Plate 2.2 Megabus website and the low cost revolution in coach travel ©Stagecoach
Source: Stagecoach Group

Plate 2.3 A megabus double decker on the new low-cost Chicago–New York service ©Stagecoach
Source: Stagecoach Group

Managers have to understand how systems and organisations work and function to create desirable outcomes. It is the ability to learn to manage in new situations where there are no guidelines or models to follow that Handy (1989) views as the way people develop, especially in a managerial role.

INSIGHT 2.4

Airline management and the low-cost revolution in air travel

The airline industry developed as a commercial enterprise during the 1930s as technological advances in aviation enabled companies to develop regular passenger services, cross-subsidised by the provision of air freight and postal services. In the post-war period, modern-day air transport emerged as an international business, providing services and products for a diverse group of users including scheduled and non-scheduled (charter) transport for air travellers and cargo transport for businesses. The airline industry is a truly global business and in 2002 commercial world passenger air transport generated 3.2 billion revenue passenger kilometres (RPKs) (Boeing Commercial Airline Group 2003). The growth in global passenger travel by air has risen consistently, with the exception of 9/11 and SARS, with Airbus and Boeing anticipating average annual rates of growth in air travel of 5 per cent through to the year 2022, led by growth in the Asia-Pacific region. This will see a reversal after three years of negative growth in 2001–4 as RPKs recover and by 2022 the number of RPKs is expected to double to 8.4 billion and the number of aircraft in service will also double. Such a rate of growth is not new for the airline industry, since it has a history of dramatic change over a short period of time dating back to the introduction of commercial aviation services in the 1920s and 1930s.

▶

Airline management as a concept

Airline management is a concept that all commercial airline companies have taken seriously due to the rate and pace of change in the competitive global business environment in which they operate. It is also a volatile business, where unpredictable external factors (for example the Gulf War, 9/11, SARS and terrorism) can dramatically affect companies' ability to attract customers and may threaten their profitability – 'the bottom line'. Consequently, airline management may loosely be defined as the process whereby individual (and groups of) airlines seek to organise, direct and harness their resources, personnel and business activities to meet the needs of their organisation and customers in an effective and efficient manner. In the case of the airline industry, the ability to respond to change and to adapt is a key challenge for management. Profitability of the airline is the principal objective of privately owned airlines. Yet many airlines began life as state-owned enterprises, due to the capital-intensive nature of this business activity, which requires a steady and predictable long-term stream of revenue to absorb the high capital and operating costs. The airlines of many smaller countries are still subsidised and maintained for political reasons. For example, state ownership of airlines persists in order to ensure the prestige of the national carrier in international relations, to maintain a degree of control over tourist arrivals, and to provide competition with other carriers to prevent a monopoly or duopoly situation from arising (Doganis 2001). Therefore airline management may, in some cases, be motivated by political factors that outweigh the forces of the free market system and normal competition.

To understand the scope and process of airline management (see the excellent books by Doganis (2001, 2002), who was CEO of a European airline, for more detail), a focus upon the issues that all airlines have to deal with on a day-to-day basis (operational issues) and on a longer-term basis (strategic issues), together with the marketing of airlines, illustrates the wide range of issues and problems which require management to ensure the airline is functioning in an efficient and effective manner. In reality, the management process for airline companies is a continuous activity that requires a predetermined structure to ensure that all the business activities are adequately integrated to meet the needs of internal customers and external business needs (i.e. those of the customer or purchaser of services and products).

Airline managers not only have to oversee, coordinate and direct the activities of airline operations (domestic and international airline business), they also have to manage diverse activities that affect the organisation's main business (for example ground handling, planning, human resource management and reservations). For the organisation to operate in an effective manner, airlines typically allow different elements to operate as separate business units, with a general manager reporting to a management board. This helps to achieve a degree of integration within the organisation whilst delegating responsibility for specialised functions to individual business units. However, before considering the management issues typically affecting international and domestic airlines, it is important to realise that 'airline managers are not free agents. Their actions are circumscribed by a host of national and international regulations. These are both economic and non-economic in character and may well place severe limitations on airlines' freedom of action' (Doganis 1991: 24). As a result, regulation is a major factor affecting the business environment.

According to Gittell (2003) it is apparent that a new mode of airline organisation and production created a new business model in the low-cost airline sector. This model is far more complex than the simple low-cost approach that will be examined later in this Insight: it is a philosophy and approach, in much the same way that Total Quality Management dominated airline philosophy and service in the 1990s, driven by a very influential CEO. The Southwest model has been emulated by the new start-ups in the low-cost sector in Asia following some of these principles. Amongst the key points that highlight success in the aviation sector are:

● *Leadership* by visionary and new management practices emulating from the CEO creating an organisational culture where staff work effectively as teams, and teamwork across traditional work boundaries characterised the success of the airline.

▶

- *Strategic* vision and focus, with a core focus on point-to-point traffic and route development rather than seeking to develop head-on competition on trunk routes and at hubs.
- *Coordination* of airline activities, with an emphasis on high performance relationships within and outside the organisation. Southwest has developed a range of practices to allow coordination. Traditionally the airline sector is broken down into 12 functions (pilots, flight attendants, gate staff, ticketing, operational staff, ramp staff, baggage handling, cargo, mechanics, refuelling, cleaning and catering). At Southwest there are 10 organisational practices to coordinate all these diverse staff and tasks, so teamwork and a focus on making things work distinguishes the airline from its competitors. Its key principles are: to have shared goals, shared knowledge and mutual respect, achieved through relational coordination, with frequent communication, timely communication and problem-solving communication.

Management of the organisation is therefore seen as being vital to the airline's success in an increasingly competitive environment.

The global airline business

The recent experiences of the international airline industry would indicate that whilst collectively it lost US$2.7 billion in 1990, due in part to the Gulf War and the recession, the mid-1990s saw these fortunes change for many of the top airline companies and then dip again in the new millennium. Indeed many US airlines have faced difficult trading conditions since 2001, some operating in Chapter 3 bankruptcy protection. For example, United Airlines, the world's second largest airline, reported net losses of US$2.73bn in the second quarter of 2008, compounded by oil costs. Although the Asia-Pacific region continues to offer the greatest growth prospects for airline operators (see Page 2004 for a detailed analysis), the international aviation marketplace is heterogeneous in nature. For example, the airline industry in Canada, Australia and New Zealand can be considered similar in that each has few dominant airlines, few high-volume routes, and relatively large, but thinly populated geographic expanses to serve (Go 1993: 180) although this situation has changed with the introduction of low-cost operators. In contrast, Europe used to comprise three major carrier segments (scheduled, regional and charter carriers) but now has a fourth – low-cost carriers – whilst the international trend is towards a few large transnational airlines dominating and controlling the business as global operators. British Airways' goal in the 1990s was to become a global carrier and it has entered into strategic alliances to overcome competition by cooperating with other partners, but its fortunes altered dramatically on its short-haul and domestic routes with the onset of low-cost operators, and a failed attempt to counter declining market shares with its own low-cost airline – Go – has seen it lose some of its previous dominance due to financial problems and its sale to its competitor – easyJet. Within Europe strategic alliances have resulted from the establishment of a single continental aviation market. Other airlines have pursued a strategy of vertical and horizontal integration (see Chapter 6 for more detail) to diversify their business interests in aviation so that they now operate subsidiary companies offering airport catering, passenger services, tour wholesaling, aviation maintenance facilities, pilot training, computer reservation systems, taxi services, property development and quality service training in addition to the core function of running an international airline. In this context, many airlines have adapted different management responses to the changing global environment for the airline industry as discussed earlier, which can be critical to survival. Indeed, the 2008 credit crunch in the US airline industry saw over 26,000 job cuts to reduce costs, whilst cutting seat capacity and charging fees for ancillary services (e.g. additional baggage).

Airline marketing and management

One of the principal concerns of airline managers is the matching of the supply of services with the actual and forecast demand. Such a concern underpins all aspects of airline management and planning because without a fundamental understanding of marketing and planning it is not possible to address issues such as aircraft selection, route planning, scheduling, product planning and pricing, advertising and long-term strategy, since each area requires an analysis of demand. The demand for airline services is also directly related to supply, since qualitative factors such as the quality of airline service (on the ground and in-flight) affect its supply features. Airline planning is therefore part of the management process, with supply adjusted to meet demand. The more competitive and unregulated the market, the greater the degree of planning and adjustment needed to match supply and demand. This is normally undertaken under the auspices of the marketing process. Such issues pose an even greater challenge for airline managers since the growing global competition for air travel has meant the new millenium is proving to be the decade of the air traveller as a consumer: not only have airlines been forced to reduce operating costs to compete for business, but they have been required to focus on the needs of their customers. If managers ignore the needs of their customers their companies are unlikely to remain key players in the global airline business.

A common misconception in airline management during the 1970s was that marketing is simply about selling the final product. Airline marketing is now more complex than was recognised in the 1970s, since it is vital to the management process of deciding what to produce and how it should be sold. Thus

> the role of airline marketing is to bring together the supply of air services, which each airline can largely control, with the demand, which it can influence but not control, and to do this in a way which is both profitable and meets the airline's corporate objectives (Doganis 1991: 202)

If the essence of airline marketing is to satisfy customer needs, the airline needs to be market oriented, as opposed to being dominated by an operational bias. For example, British Airways explained its financial turnaround from a loss of £544 million in 1981/82 to a profit of £272 million in 1983/84 in terms of its greater marketing orientation, based on recognising customers' needs and setting about satisfying them although, in its current restructuring exercises, market positioning also has a role to differentiate it from the competitor. Other airlines, such as Scandinavian Air Services (SAS), have used marketing and a focus on service quality to retain a competitive edge.

The role of marketing in the management of airline services can be summarised as a four-stage process:

1 Identify markets and market segments using research methods and existing data sources and traffic forecasts.
2 Use the market analysis to assess which products to offer. This is known as product planning. At this stage, price becomes a critical factor. Therefore product planning is related to:
   (a) market needs identified from market research;
   (b) the current and future product features of competing airlines and the cost of different product features;
   (c) assessing what price the customers can be expected to pay for the product.
3 Develop a marketing plan to plan and organise the selling of the products. Sales and distribution outlets need to be considered, together with a detailed programme of advertising and promotion.
4 Monitor and review the airline's ability to meet service standards, assessed through sales figures, customer surveys, analysis of complaints and long-term planning to develop new service and product features.

Many of these issues are exemplified in the success of the low-cost airline operations that now compete aggressively with both scheduled and charter services.

The low-cost phenomenon equals innovative use of economics, marketing, geography and management. ▶

Table 2.4 Key characteristics of low-cost carriers that make them more competitive than other carriers

- Some carriers have introduced single/one-way fares not requiring stopovers or Saturday night stays to get advanced purchase (APEX) prices
- No complimentary in-flight service (no frills), which often reduce operating costs by 6–7 per cent
- One-class cabins (in most cases)
- No pre-assigned seating (in most cases)
- Ticketless travel
- High-frequency routes to compete with other airlines on popular destinations and up to three flights a day on low-density routes
- Short turnarounds, often less than half an hour, with higher aircraft rotations (i.e. the level of utilisation is higher than other airlines) and less time charged on the airport apron and runway
- The use of secondary airports where feasible (including the provision of public transport where none exists)
- Point-to-point flights
- Lower staffing costs, with fewer cabin crew as there is no complimentary in-flight service, which also reduces turnaround times due to the lack of cleaning caused by food service
- Flexibility in staff rostering, a lack of overnight stays for staff at non-base locations and streamlined operations (e.g. on some airlines toilets on domestic flights are only emptied at cabin crew requests rather than at each turnaround to reduce costs)
- Many of the aircraft are leased, reducing the level of depreciation and standardising costs
- Many airline functions are outsourced, such as ground staff and check-in, minimising overheads and reducing overhead costs by 11–15 per cent
- Standardised aircraft types (i.e. Boeing 737s) to reduce maintenance costs and the range of spare parts that need to be held for repairs
- Limited office space at the airports
- Heavy emphasis on advertising, especially billboards, to offset the declining use of travel agents as the main source of bookings
- Heavy dependence upon the Internet and telephone for bookings
- Small administrative staff, with many sales-related staff on commission to improve performance (as well as pilots in some cases)

Source: Page (2003a). Copyright © 2003, with permission from Elsevier.

There is a growing academic literature now emerging on the low-cost revolution in air travel (e.g. see Childs 2000) as many smaller secondary airports compete to attract low-cost operators (see Francis et al. 2003; Gillen and Lall 2004; Francis et al. 2004) that have remodelled many of the airport–airline relationships. The competition afforded by low-cost operators (Franke 2004) in contrast to the larger network carriers such as British Airways has led to a redefinition of many of the principles of airline management. Some of the characteristics of low-cost airline operation can be seen in Table 2.4, which illustrates:

- In economic terms, how to run the operation much more cheaply and efficiently, passing on the saving to customers.
- In geographical terms, using lesser-known, smaller airports (secondary airports) to reduce landing costs, opening up new tourism markets to short breaks and a new geography of leisure travel have evolved as low-cost airlines expand their networks, services and the type of destinations served (Plate 2.4). The competition with charter and scheduled carriers is self-evident, as well as the new locations it has developed (see Williams 2001 and 2008 for a debate on whether low-cost carriers will replace charter carriers).
- In terms of marketing, innovative low-cost airlines lead in fares, internet selling, billboard and newspaper advertising, combined with high-profile public relations activity by the CEOs of the airlines and a management style to make the organisation work in a rapidly expanding business environment (see Plates 2.5, 2.6 and 2.7)

Plate 2.4 Terminal areas such as Terminal 5 at New Yorks JFK airport has many of the hallmarks of quality design and thought for the tourist experience in a spacious and airey building ©JetBlue Airways

Source: JetBlue Airways

Plate 2.5 The low-cost airlines have used highly visible colour schemes and branding to differentiate their service, as shown here in the easyJet and GO fleet just after the easyJet–Go merger ©easyJet

Source: easyJet

Plate 2.6 The easyJet brand has used a distinctive colour scheme and utilises all opportunities to reinforce the brand, with logo use on aircraft engines and all other visible areas of the fuselage ©easyJet

Source: easyJet

The success of airlines such as Ryanair, Southwest and, in Asia, Air Asia (with the lowest operating costs in the airline industry) has created a model that many other airline managers now scrutinise to see how it can be developed/adapted for their own organisations. The sheer scale of the success of one company – easyJet – really highlights the importance of this new business model.

As Page (2004) observed from easyJet data, the airline has followed the Southwest model of operation after commencing flights in 1995 from Luton Airport, a secondary UK airport. Data from the company website (http://www.easyjet.co.uk) indicates that in 2007 it carried 37 million passengers, almost double the volume of 2003. This astonishing growth from 30,000 passengers in its first year of operation (Table 2.5) makes it one of the larger low-cost carriers, further consolidated in 2002 when it purchased British Airway's low-cost carrier – Go – in August 2002. It attributes much of its success not only to streamlined business operations but in making substantial savings through e-distribution, making it one of the largest tourism e-tailers in Europe as over 90 per cent of its business is booked online. This streamlined business model has been examined by Barrett (2008) who examined the cost advantages low-cost carriers have over full-service carriers on short-haul routes. They typically enjoy a 49 per cent cost saving per seat due to higher seat density on-board, lower station costs (i.e. terminal costs) and outsourcing of their handling tasks.

Some of the principal differences in low-cost airlines are attracting a growing interest from academics and some of the studies provide useful further reading (e.g. Lawton 1999; Sull 1999; Mason 2000, 2001; Reynolds-Feighan 2001; Gillen and Morrison 2003; Barrett 2004).

Clearly marketing is a key component of airline business strategies in the 1990s and a number of airlines have decided to withdraw from non-core activities, such as the hotel business, baggage handling, ground-support activities and catering. This has sometimes been

Plate 2.7 The development of low-cost airlines has often been a result of the entrepreneurial talents of individuals, as in the case of easyJet and its founder Stelios Haji-Ioannou ©easyJet

Source: easyJet

Table 2.5 easyJet passenger numbers, 1995–2007

Year	000s of passengers
1995	30
1996	420
1997	1,140
1998	1,180
1999	3,670
2000	5,996
2001	7,664
2002	11,400
2003	20,300
2004	24,300
2005	29,558
2006	32,953
2007	37,200

Source: easyJet, www.easyjet.com.

▶

a response to spiralling costs, which may be controlled through the use of contracted-in services. Airline management has attracted very little attention from management researchers with a number of notable exceptions (e.g. Oum and Yu 2000; Janic 2007; Wensveen 2007; Lumpé and Kearney 2008), probably because it remains a complex industry to understand fully unless one has worked closely with an airline organisation. Such organisations are wary of outsiders due to the highly competitive nature of their business and the prospect of 'insider knowledge' being used to the advantage of other airlines. A great deal of the available research data on airlines and their management remains confidential to the individual organisations and their employees, and only commissioned management consultants are usually privileged to consult it.

Despite these constraints, the airline industry is in a constant state of flux, adapting to changing trends. Even low-cost carriers have different management and business models for their operations. For example, Barrett (2008) points to the cost savings Ryanair has in comparison with easyJet. It has lower staff costs due to higher staff productivity (i.e. a lower number of staff per aircraft and no overnight stays for cabin crew). Computer reservation systems, controlled by the global airlines (for example AA) now offer these organisations unparalleled control over passengers' choice of services, allowing them to become brokers of other travel services. This is transforming the airline business by offering a profitable business activity that may outstrip the actual profitability of individual airline operations. This has meant that airline managers need to be versatile, adaptable and more willing to view their business activities as part of a global travel and tourism industry. As customers' expectations increase, technological advances in aircraft design (for example the Boeing 777 and other medium-sized aircraft) may see the cost of air travel stabilise, if the cost of aviation fuel remains fairly constant.

The future shape of the global aviation industry is likely to contain a limited number of global mega-carriers, with smaller airlines integrated into their operations by strategic alliances and other devices (for example part ownership by the larger carriers). A more hierarchical system of route provision is also likely to evolve and airlines will be forced to deal with greater volumes of passengers using a 'hub and spoke' system of provision to achieve efficient operations (see Chapter 6 for more detail), with passenger volume tied to aircraft type. The major constraint on this rapidly evolving business activity for airline managers will be the availability of uncongested airspace and airports with sufficient capacity. This is already affecting air travel in Europe and the USA, whilst the environmental lobby regularly opposes airport expansion near major urban centres. Airline managers will need to be increasingly focused on ensuring that their operational requirements can be fulfilled and their environmental impacts monitored and minimised to reduce local opposition to air transport. For example, many airports have introduced bans on aircraft that do not meet noise emission levels. These managerial issues have to be addressed and accommodated within the day-to-day operation and longer-term planning by airline managers so that passengers are not adversely affected by delays, congestion and inadequate planning.

●●●● Summary

This chapter has shown that different disciplines have developed a range of concepts and distinctive approaches to the analysis of different aspects of the tourist transport system. The Insights have highlighted how these concepts can help us to understand different features of the tourist travel experience and the interaction of the consumer and producer in tourist transport systems. The economists' analysis of tourist transport systems is based on the demand and supply issues associated with the use and provision of different modes of transport and the implications for the future (i.e. forecasting, which is dealt with in Chapter 4). In contrast, the geographer has largely focused on the spatial analysis, organisation and distribution of tourist patterns of travel, whilst the transport geographer has considered the policy, management and planning issues associated with the provision of transport, sometimes in combination with economists (see the contributions in Banister and Button 1992). In marketing, the interest in tourist transport is developing within the existing literature, although the contribution should not be understated because marketers have identified the importance of a more consumer-oriented focus for tourist transport provision. The concern for service quality that has emerged in the marketing literature has started to permeate tourist transport provision, particularly in the airline sector (see Laws 1991 for a fuller discussion). In the case of management, tourist transport is often viewed as a practical and process-oriented activity that is fundamental to the organisation, with control, leading and planning functions necessary to ensure a vibrant, profitable and functional business organisation.

It is clear from the discussion of the contributions made by economists, geographers, marketers and management studies to the analysis of tourist transport systems that these contributions need to be integrated into a more coherent framework, which is possible if a systems approach is adopted. In reality, the decision-making functions undertaken by transport operators and public sector organisations associated with tourism and transport invariably use a variety of economic, geographical, marketing and management principles in their everyday work to plan and develop tourist transport services. The concern with enhancing the tourists' travel experience, so that it meets with the preconceived notion of service quality and provision, has become a concern not only for operators but also for government policy-making. It is the issue of government policy-making and its effect on tourist transport systems that is the focus of the next chapter.

Questions

1 What concepts characterise the way economists, geographers, marketers and management researchers approach tourist transport?

2 Prepare a SWOT analysis for a tourist transport service with which you are familiar.

3 How is the use of yield management assisting tourist transport operators to maximise their revenue?

4 What are the main qualities needed to manage a tourist transport business?

Further reading

The following titles are a good starting point from which to examine the contribution each discipline makes to the analysis of tourist transport.

The economist

Dwyer, L. and Forsyth, P. (eds) (2006) *International Handbook on the Economics of Tourism*, Edward Elgar: Cheltenham.

Gray, H. (1982) 'The contribution of economics to tourism', *Annals of Tourism Research*, 9: 105–25.

The geographer

On the role of the geographer, see:

Hall, C.M. and Page, S.J. (2006) *Geography of Tourism and Recreation: Environment Place and Space*, 3rd edn, London: Routledge.
Mansfeld, Y. (1990) 'Spatial patterns of international tourist flows: towards a theoretical approach', *Progress in Human Geography*, 14(3): 372–90. This provides an interesting approach to the analysis of tourism flows.

Marketing

Gilbert, D. (1989) 'Tourism marketing: its emergence and establishment', in C.P. Cooper (ed.) *Progress in Tourism, Recreation and Hospitality Management*, Vol. 1, London: Belhaven, 77–90. This provides a good insight into the development of tourism marketing.

Management

On the problem of managing transport and tourism in the countryside, especially the car, see:

The Countryside Agency (2003) *Transport in Tomorrow's Countryside*, Cheltenham: The Countryside Agency.

On the evolution of modern aviation see:

Rhoades, D. (2003) *Evolution of International Aviation*, Aldershot: Ashgate.

and on the factors which affect the success and failure of new entrant airlines see:

Gudmuudsson, S. (1999) *Flying Too Close to the Sun*, Aldershot: Ashgate.

and for a recent analysis of airline alliances see:

Kleymann, B, and Seristö, B. (2004) *Managing Strategic Alliances*, Aldershot: Ashgate.

The role of government policy and tourist transport: regulation versus privatisation

Introduction: governments, transport and tourism

The development of tourism in specific countries is a function of the individual governments' predisposition towards this type of economic activity. In the case of outbound tourism, governments may curb the desire for mobility and travel by limiting the opportunities for travel through currency restrictions (such as in the case of South Korea in the 1980s) whilst still encouraging inbound travel. Similarly, in the former USSR under communist rule, the opportunities for domestic tourism were controlled by limiting the supply of holiday infrastructure. However, such examples are not the norm because most governments seek to maximise the domestic population's opportunities for mobility and travel by the provision of various modes of transport to facilitate the efficient movement of goods and people at a national level. In fact, the development of transport to facilitate inbound tourism is often motivated by governments' desire to increase earnings from tourist receipts, especially in less developed countries seeking to modernise their post-colonial economies (see Scheyvens 2002).

This chapter examines the role of government policy in relation to tourist transport provision and how it can affect various modes of transport. The concept of transport policy is introduced and its meaning discussed in relation to political variants of transport policy in free market economies. Emphasis is placed upon different political ideologies and how these have affected transport policies for tourism with the rising tide of privatisation in many societies. The significance of transnational organisations such as the EU and progress towards transport policies in aviation and rail travel are discussed alongside other measures to liberalise global transport and tourism services.

To achieve a government's objectives for transport to facilitate tourist travel, policies are formulated to guide the organisation, management and development of tourist and non-tourist transport (Starkie 1976; Knowles 1989; Enoch 2003). This is normally followed by specific planning measures that seek to implement the policies (Banister 1994). As Lay (2005: 161) shows, transport planning passes through four key stages:

- the political stage, which considers broad social and economic goals, planning at a conceptual and policy level;
- the development stage, which considers such factors as land use and transport levels of service, planning at a strategic and systems level;

- the transport stage, which considers transport demand management and infrastructure provision options, such as planning at a corridor level;
- the facility stage, which considers planning at an implementation stage.

These stages of planning will often require national governments to invest in – or encourage private sector organisations to invest in – new infrastructure that may be dedicated to tourist travel (and cargo), such as airports. At the point of investment decision-making, Mackie and Nellthorp (2003) point to the role of transport appraisal, which helps to determine if a specific project goes ahead. They identify three influences on this appraisal process, including what the public thinks, the findings of an economic appraisal and the political context which illustrates a key point that decision-making is not always rational. Politics have a key role to play in project appraisal, making policy and project assessment a complex process.

Conversely, and more typically, governments may need to develop policies and planning measures that expand and develop national, regional and local infrastructure to accommodate tourist and recreational travel alongside commuting and non-tourist travel (Jeffries 2001). D. Hall (1997) rightly highlights the conceptual problem of distinguishing between what is tourist transport and what is not. Government policies often highlight this problem since whilst specialised, dedicated forms of tourist transport exist (e.g. tourist coaches, package flights and cruise liners), there are other forms of transport shared by hosts and tourists to varying extents. For example, urban buses and metro systems may be used by tourists, but their *raison d'être* is primarily for local transport, and this is reflected in generalised transport policies that often do not accommodate use by tourists. In Singapore the state-subsidised mass rapid transport system is integrated with local bus services to provide the population with an efficient public transport system, and in London the underground metro system is used by 3 million people a day, a proportion of whom will be tourists. As Orbasli and Shaw (2004) point out, the £3.5 billion Jubilee Line Extension (JLE) to Stratford in East London was also recognised for its potential to link the tourist districts in West London with the growth of East London as a tourist destination and its potential to assist in urban regeneration (Evans and Shaw 2001), although, as Page and Hall (2002) argued, East London had not benefited substantially from the growth in tourism due to poor transport and strategic planning decisions. Again, the area's potential to harness long-term and sustainable tourism benefits from the 2012 Olympics hinges upon investment in transport links to harness the regenerative benefits that such an event might bring to the area (despite the economic costs for London ratepayers and UK taxpayers – see Page 2009 for a more detailed discussion). Yet like many other metro systems it offers incentives for tourist use through the provision of 'tourist explorer tickets'. Indeed there are few forms of transport that tourists are unlikely to use but the separation of tourist and non-tourist use is not usually an issue for policy-makers. In a theoretical and more abstract context, research by sociologists interested in tourism, such as Urry (1990) and his work on the *tourist gaze*, invokes notions of post-tourism, where all transport is potentially for and of tourism as the tourist gaze is supported by tourist travel (D. Hall 1997).

The transport policies developed by national governments are influenced by their changing attitudes, outlook and political ideology. This often manifests itself in terms

Table 3.1 The scope and extent of the Scottish Executive's involvement in national transport planning and management in Scotland

- Aviation is a reserved issue for the UK government (though rail links serving airports are in the Scottish Executive's remit)
- ScotRail rail franchise, costing £250 million a year
- Network Rail in Scotland, £300 million a year
- Direct funding to vital air services (Barra, Campbeltown and Tiree to Glasgow) and operation of 10 airports in the Highlands and Islands
- Ferry subsidies to the Northern Isles, Clyde and Hebrides services
- Provision of the Bus Operator Grant
- Encouraging 'Smarter Choices in Travel'
- International connectivity by air and the Air Route Development Fund, administered by Scottish Enterprise
- International connectivity by sea is a matter for the private sector
- Cross-border connectivity
    - advice to UK government on rail franchises
    - 148 short-haul flights per week day Scotland to London, of which 98 are London–Edinburgh/ Glasgow
    - promotion of rail as a more sustainable option and use of Air Route Development Fund to reduce reliance upon London-based connecting flights

Source: Adapted from Scottish Executive (2006a).

of the level of expenditure on capital investment, infrastructure provision and policies to *facilitate* (Department of Employment/English Tourist Board 1991) or *constrain* tourist travel. Griffith (1989) discusses the effect of international airways sanctions as an example of government policies formulated to achieve a political goal against South Africa. As Table 3.1 shows, in Scotland many aspects of transport policy have been passed to a devolved government. What Table 3.1 shows is the scope and extent of state involvement in national transport policy and planning along with its significance for tourism. Table 3.2 shows that many of the key issues affecting national transport planning in Scotland also have major implications for tourism.

Likewise, when governments fail to acknowledge that policies and action are required to facilitate the development of tourist transport systems, capacity problems and bottlenecks may develop where tourism is imposed on inadequate national infrastructure. Gormsen (1995: 82) documented the situation in China in the mid-1990s where

> serious capacity problems can be observed, not only for the airline companies, but also for railways, road traffic and river navigation, despite the fact that since the establishment of the PRC [People's Republic of China] all of these systems have been improved to a large extent.

As Table 3.3 shows, whilst the railway network, asphalt roads and air capacity expanded under government direction in 1949–87 (see Hayashi et al. 1998 for a review), the growth in patronage has outstripped supply as 'undercapacity at all levels of the transportation system remains a problem. Foreign tourists who must pay higher prices than citizens of China . . . receive preferential travel on the public transportation lines' (Gormsen 1995: 84). In an attempt to improve the efficiency of domestic air travel the state airline, Air China, was divided into seven regional airlines after 1985 and by the late 1990s over 30 domestic carriers were operating,

Table 3.2 Scottish Executive (2006b) Scotland's national transport strategy

The strategic outcomes to achieve the vision identified as making a fundamental difference in delivering a world class transport system are:

- Improved journey times and connections
- Reduced emissions
- Improved quality, accessibility and affordability across public transport.

In terms of tourism, the document makes the following observations:

- The vast majority of visitors to Scotland travel by car
- We are travelling more by plane
- Air travel is predicted to rise 150% 2004–30 (UK 2003 White Paper on Air Travel and the 2006 Progress report)
- Road traffic is forecast to increase 12% 2005–10 in Scotland and 22% 2005–15
- Tourism is one driver of the demand associated with increases in real incomes, economic growth and rising personal travel
- The number of international destinations reached from Scotland 1999–2005 rose from 32 to 71 and international ferry links carried 10 million passengers a year
- The Rosyth–Zeebrugge ferry crossing has carried 700,000 passengers since its inception in 2002
- A major challenge is to ensure cross-border and international connections for visitors, particularly with the demand for road travel
- The visitor experience of public transport provision remains an area for future action by the Transport Directorate
- Improvements in the transport sector are seen as critical for tourism to improve international arrivals, including the pump-priming subsidy for new air routes via the Air Route Development Fund to reduce connections via London (although this is being replaced by a new scheme after 2007 which will only apply to the EU)
- It agrees that simply adding more airport capacity is not sustainable but strategic investment and improvements at key gateways is supported
- In the sea sector, the cruise liner, leisure craft and ferry sector all contribute to tourism and it will continue to support ferry routes to Northern Ireland, Ireland and mainland Europe and beyond
- Cross-border road links are seen as vital for domestic tourism with a £3 billion capital investment programme in trunk road and rail networks
- It should maintain an active interest in high-speed services to London (but it is a reserved issue for Westminster)
- Improving journey times is seen as assisting in reducing perceived peripherality of remote communities for tourists and residents
- It is committed to the use of road pricing
- It is supporting the UK government Emission Trading Scheme for road and aviation transport
- There is recognition of the benefit of an improved journey experience for tourism in getting to and travelling around Scotland.

Source: Based on the Scottish Executive (2006b).

many at a loss or in need of major capital investment. However, in 2001 these policies were revised following a series of crashes, so the deregulated structure was consolidated into three groups (see Zhang and Round 2008):

1 *Air China Group* had 118 aircraft, 329 routes (of which 286 were domestic), comprising Air China, China Southwest, China National Aviation Corporation, Zhejiang and Dragonair, and an asset value of US$6.94 billion and 20,235 staff.

2 *China Eastern Group* had 118 aircraft and 437 routes (of which 383 were domestic), comprising China Eastern Airlines, Yunan Airlines, China Northwest and Great Wall Airlines, and a capital value of RMB473 billion and 25,109 staff.

3 *China Southern Group* had 180 aircraft and 606 routes (of which 512 were domestic), comprising China Southern Airlines, China Northern Airlines and Xinjiang Airlines, and a capital value of RMB500 billion and 34,089 staff. This company has most of the domestic connections in China.

Table 3.3 The development of China's transport system, 1949–87

Year	Number of public vehicles			Rail (1000 km)	Road (1000 km)	Number of passengers (millions)				
	Trains (1000)	Buses (1000)	Aircraft			Rail	Road	Water	Air	Total
1949	3	17	–	30	32	103	18	15	0.27	137
1952	5	19	45	35	55	163	45	36	0.02	245
1957	8	34	105	43	121	312	237	87	0.07	638
1962	10	47	245	55	263	741	307	163	0.17	1221
1965	10	60	287	58	304	412	436	113	0.27	963
1970	11	75	293	70	411	524	618	157	0.22	1300
1975	14	173	357	77	511	704	1013	210	1.39	1929
1978	15	257	382	85	647	815	1492	230	2.31	2539
1980	16	351	393	86	662	921	2227	264	3.43	3417
1985	21	795	390	95	750	1121	4764	308	7.47	6200
1987	23	1115	402	99	982	1124	5936	389	13.10	7464

Source: Adapted from Gormsen (1995) based on the National Statistics Bureau, China's Statistics Publishing House, 1989 and Historical Statistics by Provinces, China 1949–90, National Statistics Bureau, China's Statistics Publishing House, 1990.

Around 81 per cent of China's aviation market is now catered for by these groups' policy decision to deregulate domestic travel in the 1980s by allowing airlines to start up in order to stimulate competition. Despite overcapacity, unnecessary competition and price wars, 25 regional airlines are not directly under the Civil Aviation Administration of China (CAAC). In the case of China it is evident that, even when policies are put in place to expand infrastructure, demand can often outstrip supply. In the case of air travel, continuous growth in demand since consolidating the company structure is apparent from the following summary for 2006:

- China has 1279 air routes, 1000 of which are domestic.
- China contains 133 airports, serving 132 domestic cities and 75 overseas.
- In 2006, 186 million domestic passengers travelled on China's airlines, 66 per cent of which were on domestic routes.
- In 2005–06, the Chinese aviation market grew by almost 16 per cent.
- The composition of the Chinese aviation market in 2006 was: 49 per cent business travel; 40 per cent for tourism; and 10.5 per cent to visit family, highlighting its crucial role for both business travel and tourism.

The CAAC has frozen any new applications for additional airlines until 2010 due to congestion at Beijing Capital Airport. In 2008, 24 airlines were licensed to operate in China and the CAAC sees an optimum number as ranging between 20 and 30. The continuous growth in demand, as an expanding global economic power, is reflected in the investment in infrastructure to support air travel. In 2007, there were 140 airports and a capital investment programme to 2020 of US$18.5 billion will see 40 new airports come on stream. This reflects the forecasts within the airline industry that predict that the intra-Asia airline market will represent one-third of all air travel by 2020. This is one explanation why China's airlines have been able to join the international airline alliances, as discussed in Chapter 2.

As Banister (1994) observes, forecasting the demand for transport planning is an Achilles' heel that has not improved even with growing technical sophistication in the methods used. Whitelegg (1993: 160) may have highlighted one of the problems that needs to be recognised in a European context: 'leisure, recreation and tourism trips are major growth areas in travel behaviour'. Page (1998) also argues that from a spatial perspective tourist and recreational travel cannot easily be modelled and explained using conventional models and principles in transport geography. This is because it does not conform to principles of distance optimisation and least-distance patterns of travel. Therefore, government policy cannot necessarily assume that tourists will seek to use infrastructure developed for national economic goals. As Chapter 2 noted, the car may be the principal agent driving tourist and recreational trips, but this will rarely feature in cost–benefit assessments. This is because the seasonality of use makes such assessments less attractive, despite the pressures which such use pose to the infrastructure in peak seasons, as noted by Connell (2004) using traffic count data. In their analysis of VFR (visiting friends and relatives) journeys, Cohen and Harris (1998) found that the car was more cost competitive when a group of people travel together (despite group discounts on long-distance rail trips), even though the potential exists to transfer weekend trips, as Duffell and Harman (1992) also observed. As the distances people travel by car increases, there are obvious environmental consequences. Thus, the UK's Department of Transport (1987: 1) observed:

> tourism and leisure depend heavily on travel and transport. In Britain, travelling by road represents the dominant mode for visitors to get to and from their final destinations or to see places of interest . . . [and] the tourism industry, in common with many other industries, also depends heavily on roads for the transport of the goods and services people need

In the UK roads are assuming an even greater role in the patterns of tourist activity, despite problems associated with congestion in urban areas, and in France it is the most popular mode of travel for domestic tourism (Trew and Cockerell 2004). This is particularly evident when the traditional holiday season commences, as in the first week of August in France and the first week of July in the Netherlands. For example, in the first weekend of the school holidays in the Netherlands, around an additional 750,000 vehicles will use the roads for holiday purposes. These problems also affect rural areas, as is the case in National Parks.

Managing the car: Yosemite National Park

One recent example of the attempt to manage the impact of car recreational traffic on the natural environment can be seen in Yosemite National Park, California. An early example of a National Park, it has seen progressive growth in vehicle traffic since 1917. The experiences of another US National Park – Yellowstone, highlight a similar pattern of growth. In 1922, Yellowstone received 98,000 visitors, of whom 50 per cent stayed overnight, 1500 of them in hotels. A further 50,000 stayed overnight camping next to their cars, which is termed auto-camping and expanded rapidly after the First World War in the USA. This illustrates the type of recreational and tourist use which emerged in many US National Parks as the car made them more accessible. By the 1980s the General Management Plan for Yosemite (see *www.nps.gov*) sought to develop measures to manage the effects of such growth, subsequently revisited in the 2000 Final Yosemite Valley Plan, given the impact of human activity on the Yosemite Valley where 1000 buildings now exist and 30 miles of road have generated over 1 million vehicle movements a year. As with all forms of tourism and recreation management, the US National Park Service seeks to balance the objectives of enhancing the visitor experience with protecting the environment as well as improving visitor understanding of the environment. This is in juxtaposition with the stated objectives of reducing traffic congestion and crowding in the area (Yolonda et al. 2008). The 1980 Plan pointed to the debate on whether parking should be expanded or limited, and highlighted successful cases of US National Park Service projects in reducing access by vehicle at Devil's Postpile National Monument, California, and Zion National Park, Utah, where early morning and late evening access by car was permissible but at other times public transport options were implemented. The Yosemite Plan in 2000 developed an additional 550-space car park out of Yosemite Valley for busy periods and a shuttle bus to take able-bodied visitors into the park to reduce car congestion, with the provision of additional pedestrian and cycle trails. Similar problems also exist in many British National Parks, such as the North Yorkshire Moors, which had 2.8 million private vehicle day visits per year, a further 1.9 million car-based holiday visits taken outside the Park, and 2.5 million taken inside the Park, with only 450,000 visiting by public transport.

On a European scale, the growth in car ownership 1970–2006 (Table 3.4) per 1000 inhabitants exhibits a clear upward trend (apart from Bulgaria), as does the growth in the motorway network compared to rail, illustrating the nature of the challenge for policy-makers, as discussed in Chapter 2. Policy formulation in relation to tourism may very well have to examine radical measures including road pricing (Steiner and Bristow 2000) and de-marketing the car (Wright and Egan 2000), which in turn requires a more in-depth analysis of tourists' car use (Taplin and McGinley 2000) to feed into evidence-based policy-making. One option may be the promotion of sustainable alternatives in destination areas (Holding 2001; Tolley 2003) in an attempt to address the dependence upon the car in city environments (Murray and Graham 1997; Newman and Kenworthy 1999; Lumsdon and Tolley 2004), although in rural areas this may be more problematic with scenic areas (Lew 1991).

In the Republic of Ireland, the former Department of Transport and Tourism (now split into different Ministerial portfolios) recognised that:

> the development of an enhanced internal transport network fully integrated with appropriate access infrastructure and services is a fundamental requirement for the future development of the tourism industry. This requires the provision of good quality access transport services and facilities together with a satisfactory internal transport infrastructure and services (Government of Ireland 1990: 24)

Although the quotation from the Government of Ireland highlights the interrelated nature of transport and tourism, in practice the responsibility for transport and tourism is often fragmented. It is frequently dispersed across different government departments, and where little interdepartmental liaison occurs there is poor coordination of policies affecting tourist transport (see Banister and Hall 1981 for a public policy perspective), if it exists at all.

Table 3.4 Motorisation rate of passenger cars in Europe, 1970–2006

Number of passenger cars per thousand inhabitants %

	1970	1980	1990	1995	2000	2005	2006	Change 05/06
EU-27			345	381	427	459	466	1.5
EU-15	183	293	405	435	478	503	508	1.1
EU-12			140	191	243	296	307	3.6
Belgium	213	320	387	421	456	468	470	0.5
Bulgaria	19	92	152	196	245	329	230	−30.0
Czech Republic	70	173	234	295	335	386	399	3.4
Denmark	218	271	309	320	347	362	371	2.4
Germany	194	330	461	495	532	559	566	1.2
Estonia	22	86	154	269	339	367	413	12.4
Ireland	132	215	228	276	348	400	418	4.4
Greece	26	86	170	207	292	387	407	5.1
Spain	70	201	309	360	431	463	464	0.3
France	233	354	476	481	503	499	504	1.0
Italy	189	313	483	533	572	590	597	1.2
Cyprus	97	175	304	335	384	463	479	3.4
Latvia	17	66	106	134	236	324	360	11.4
Lithuania	14	72	133	199	336	428	470	10.0
Luxembourg	212	352	477	556	622	655	661	0.9
Hungary	23	94	187	218	232	287	293	2.4
Malta				487	483	525	535	1.9
Netherlands	195	320	367	364	409	434	442	1.8
Austria	160	297	388	452	511	503	507	0.8
Poland	15	67	138	195	261	323	352	8.6
Portugal	49	129	171	255	336	397	405	1.9
Romania	2	11	56	99	127	156	167	7.3
Slovenia	87	218	294	357	435	479	488	1.7
Slovakia	36	110	166	189	237	242	247	2.2
Finland	155	256	388	371	415	462	475	2.7
Sweden	283	347	419	411	450	459	461	0.4
United Kingdom	231	277	361	378	425	469	471	0.4
Croatia				158	253	312	323	3.7
Former Yugoslav Republic of Macedonia				145	148	124	127	2.5
Turkey				49	65	80	84	5.1
Iceland	199	375	468	445	561	625	641	2.6
Norway	177	301	380	386	411	437	445	1.8
Switzerland	223	355	442	457	492	518	519	0.3

Notes: Passenger car stock at end of year *t* has been divided by population on 1 January of year *t* + 1.

Source: © European Commission, Directorate-General for Energy and Transport (2008), *EU Energy and Transport in Figures, Statistical Pocketbook 2007/2008*

Public sector involvement in the tourist transport system at national government level is designed to facilitate, control and in some cases regulate or deregulate the activities of private sector transport operators with a view to 'looking after the public's interests and providing goods whose costs cannot readily be attributed to groups or individuals' (Pearce 1990: 32). (Also see Chapter 5 on airline deregulation.) Economists explain such interventions as a need to rectify market failure, where transport markets do not operate in a fair manner and work against the consumer's interest due, for example, to a dominant position in the market. This was the reason why the UK government's Competition Commission investigated the UK's largest airport operator – British Airports Authority (BAA) in 2007. In 2008, the Commission required BAA to sell a number of its airports following its report (Competition Commission 2008). This is because BAA handled 60 per cent of all UK air passenger traffic but controlled 90 per cent of the capacity in South East England and 84 per cent in Scotland. A lack of competition was deemed to be not in the public interest and the company will reveal its final range of airports it will offer for sale in 2009, which are likely to include: London Gatwick, London Stansted and either Edinburgh or Glasgow in Scotland.

Since the private sector's primary role is revenue generation and profit maximisation from the tourist transport system, the government's role is to promote and protect the interests of the consumer against unfair business practices, and to ensure that safety standards are maintained to protect the interests of employees in large- and small-scale transport operations. Oum (1997: 3) argues that in the case of Asian airlines:

> government policy makers and bureaucrats regulating the airline industry would agree that their long-run objectives are essentially two-fold: to attend to the needs of consumers (the travelling public and air cargo shippers) and to ensure a strong and viable airline industry within the country.

The role of government policy and tourist transport

The term 'policy' is frequently used to denote the direction and objectives an organisation wishes to pursue over a set period of time. According to Turner (1997), the policy process is a function of three interrelated issues:

- the intentions of political and other key actors;
- the way in which decisions and non-decisions are made;
- the implications of these decisions.

Policy-making is a continuous process and Figure 3.1 outlines a simplified model of the process that is applicable to the way tourism transport issues are considered by government bodies. Hall and Jenkins (1995) examine the issue of policy-making in a tourism context. The journal *Transport Policy* offers many relevant articles on this issue with regard to different aspects of transport. National policy is normally formulated by government organisations with economic and social factors in mind, without an explicit concern for tourism, even though transport networks are used for tourist and non-tourist travel. The development and shape of transport policy is partly affected by the existing infrastructure, which has resulted from major public and private sector investment to achieve general and specific transport objectives. It may also be the case that other government policies (e.g. defence) affect transport. For example, many innovations in civil aviation have been developed as a spin-off from defence policy, particularly military research and development or the availability of surplus aircraft for charter work that spurred the package holiday business into action in the 1960s. In addition, defence infrastructure is sometimes used for civilian purposes, as in the case of the former Eastern Europe (D. Hall 1993a). Changes to the underlying infrastructure cannot be executed quickly because of the

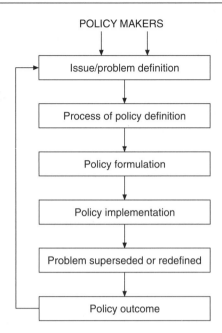

Figure 3.1 The policy-making process

major capital costs, planning procedures and the time delay in responding to the demand for such changes. For example, the expansion of an airport to accommodate a forecast growth in tourist arrivals may take between five and 10 years from its inception to the completion stage. Such developments also have to be set against the increased environmental impact (e.g. noise, pollution, waste and greater numbers of tourists – see Chapter 8) resulting from additional flights (see Somerville 1992). Transport policy is a reactive element of government activity as changes in society and the demand for tourist and non-tourist travel require a certain degree of continuity and change in policy to meet historical patterns of demand and new trends. What political and ideological principles affect transport policy?

National transport policies have been characterised by a range of approaches that span a spectrum from a free market orientation to those based on planned resource allocation (Farrington 1985). The market-oriented view has been pursued on the premise that centralised state control of transport produces an unwieldy and often unresponsive service requiring unnecessarily high subsidies from state taxation. By introducing a greater degree of private sector involvement and competition it is argued that improved services should result and the need for public subsidies should diminish. In contrast, supporters of the regulated planned response towards state involvement in transport have pointed to classical economic theory which recognises that, in a free market economy, supply imperfections result. State intervention in the market economy is justified to rectify supply imperfections on social efficiency and environmental grounds to avoid inequalities in accessibility. For example, lobby groups like the Transport and Tourism Forum in Australia (*www.ttf.org*) provide a coherent argument for such interventions to assist transport and tourism businesses such as additional investment in transport infrastructure to develop access to the Sydney Olympic Games, support following the collapse of Ansett Australia and to offset the effects of SARS. The organisation's principal argument is that: *tourism has a symbiotic relationship with transport and infrastructure.* In situations where inadequate levels of demand exist to support a viable service, state subsidies may be required to provide access for communities on social grounds (Whitelegg 1987). Thus, government intervention in transport activities, either directly or through other agencies to coordinate different parts of the transport system, is essential to bring order to the different components of the system so that they operate in harmony as illustrated in Insight 3.1 which examines transport and tourism in Mongolia.

INSIGHT 3.1

Transport and tourism policy issues in Mongolia

Mongolia is a land-locked country which is located between China and Russia, in Central Asia. Tourism is a key development objective in Mongolia, that saw expansion of visitor numbers from the 1990s in niche areas such as adventure tourism and ecotourism (Yu and Goulden 2006). Prior to 1990 all travel was strictly controlled under communist rule, with most visitors from other communist bloc countries. In 1989, 236,000 visitors, largely from the Eastern European countries, visited Mongolia and between 1990 and 1997 visitor numbers fell sharply with the decline of the communist system. From 1998 onwards, visitor numbers recovered but did not reach pre-1989 levels until 2003. A National Tourism Board was established in 1995 and in 1999 a Tourism Master Plan was developed followed by a Strategic Tourism Development Plan to cover the years 2000–05. In addition, 2003 was 'Visit Mongolia Year' although SARS adversely affected attempts to increase arrivals.

One of the principal obstacles to expanding tourism in Mongolia is transport, particularly access and domestic travel. This is because Mongolia has only 11,200km of road, of which only 1500km are paved (i.e. sealed/tarmac). Almost 7000km are earth tracks, and many of the bridges crossing rivers are of wooden construction. Most roads connect the capital – Ulaanbaatar with other centres. Since communism, much of the former state-owned transport infrastructure and operators have been privatised or operate in competition with state-owned enterprises. There is a limited rail network, with links to Russia and China used for much of the country's trade and freight.

Given the vast distances involved in tourist travel in Mongolia, adverse weather conditions and poor roads most domestic and tourist travel is by air. Almost 98 per cent of traffic is routed via Ulaanbaatar's Genghis Khan International Airport and 17 regional airports also exist, serve by small aircraft. Only four airports have paved runways, with gravel runways in other locations unsuitable for pressurised jet aircraft. The main airline services are provided by the state-owned Mongolian Airline, MIAT, which dates to 1956 using Russian-made aircraft. Only five aircraft service the country's airline needs, which reached a crisis point in 2005 when its domestic fleet (Antonov An 24s) were grounded after they had to be retired from service. This left the company with no domestic aircraft (although it did continue to operate international services with an A310 and 737–800). Whilst a private airline, Aero Mongolia, filled some loss of capacity with three F50 turboprops and an F100 jet, it severely affected domestic tourist travel. This also occurred alongside potential plans to privatise MIAT and to consider ceasing domestic loss-making flights.

This poses many challenges for the Ministry of Road, Transport and Tourism and the range of infrastructure problems as well as access issues if it wishes to increase international and domestic tourism. It also indicates how volatile transport issues are in relation to tourism development, where adverse weather can curtail flights and travel arrangements.

As Insight 3.1 indicates, the level of intervention needed to achieve this coordinating function depends on the political views of the government and its policy objectives, which are subject to changing attitudes and external influences upon policy formulation, such as shift towards greater levels of privatisation. So how have these principles been applied to transport policy in the past and what effect have they had on the tourist transport system?

●●●● Interpreting transport policy: implications for tourist travel

According to Button and Gillingwater (1983), in Europe and North America transport policy has affected the tourist transport system in a number of ways, although it is based on two underlying economic principles:

- allocative efficiency (the use of resources and the price mechanism to achieve efficient access to transport and travel);
- political obligations (the need for the state to protect the public interest in transport provision).

These principles have had an important effect on the provision of transport for tourist travel in terms of the development, expansion and regulation of different modes of transport to facilitate access to tourism resources. Modes of transport that enable mass travel developed at different times in Europe and North America but the effects were similar in terms of making tourist travel more available. Technological innovations and their commercial exploitation (e.g. the motor car), and their diffusion to different social groups during the late nineteenth and twentieth centuries, have been shaped by transport policy to achieve the twin goals of allocative efficiency and political obligations.

In historical terms, the principles of allocative efficiency and political obligations have been interpreted in different ways by governments, and Button and Gillingwater (1983) identify four distinct phases in transport policy:

- *The Railway Age*, which, in the UK, led to heavy investment in the provision of infrastructure that made seaside resorts accessible to the working classes after the 1870s. Government promotion of railways in the private sector dominated the period, except during wartime (1914–18) when state control emerged to coordinate and manage the railways in the 'national interest' of efficiency.
- *The Age of Protection*, which characterised the 1920s and 1930s, saw the emergence of road transport, particularly the rise of the private car and coach travel in an unplanned manner. For example, Davidson and Sweetman (2003) point to major changes in consumer use of transport in early twentieth century USA. Between 1916 and 1930, ridership of streetcars (trams) dropped in many cities as car use expanded. In Washington, around one-third of the 600,000 population owned cars by 1924, making around 103,000 trips into the central business district. By 1932, there were 24 million car owners in the USA and car competed with public transport and provided new opportunities for recreation and leisure use. This led governments to intervene in the marketplace to avoid massive cost cutting amongst private operators as competition intensified due to the growing number of small transport operators. Such intervention was justified on the basis that the effects of major competition might have led to a reduction in the number of operators, following a price war to secure passengers and market share. It was expected that this would be followed by a much reduced route network and

poorer levels of service. In the USA, this was characterised by the 1935 Motor Carriage Act, which protected the Greyhound Bus operations, providing one major operator with a virtual monopoly on inter-urban bus travel. Greyhound operations emerged from the Maserba Transportation Company in the 1920s and were a notable survivor in the 1920s as over 1000 operators collapsed due to competition as well as the depression.

- *The Age of Administrative Planning*, which emerged in the post-war period (i.e. after 1945) and superseded the Age of Protection, saw the private car emerge as a potent force for tourist and recreational travel. One consequence was the growing financial weakness of railways, although urban growth continued to dictate the need for large, efficient urban passenger transport systems. The nationalisation of railway networks and other forms of public transport epitomises this era in transport policy. The 1960s saw a growing burden of state subsidies to support public transport and some attempts to radically restructure the transport network (e.g. the Beeching Report in the UK and subsequent rationalisation of the rail network). In the UK, the 1968 Transport Act sought to reorganise public transport and one consequence for tourist travel was the establishment of the National Bus Company, with the responsibility for express coach travel. In the USA, the 1962 Urban Mass Transportation Act provided federal grants for two-thirds of public transport projects. Efficiency in provision was interpreted by government policy in terms of integration and coordination of transport planning, which reduced wasteful competition (Button and Gillingwater 1983).

- *The Age of Contestability* has characterised the period since the early 1970s in the USA (and the 1980s in the UK), based on the pursuit of the principle of deregulation to achieve 'allocative efficiency in transport policy' (Farrington 1985). By creating efficient transport operations and reducing public subsidies (see Plate 3.1) the private sector is seen as the main panacea for efficient transport operations (Knowles and Hall 1992). In the UK the sale of the state-owned airline, British Airways, and its emergence as a profitable private sector company is cited by supporters of this political philosophy as one of the main successes of privatisation and deregulation. It is interesting to note that the UK/North American experience in transport policy in the 1970s and 1980s has not been adopted and endorsed in many other European countries, where the state remains committed to investment in tourist transport systems.

More recent developments in transport policy in the late 1990s have contributed to a *new era*, the public–private partnership (PPP) approach, characterised in the UK by PPP such as the London Underground, in an attempt to draw more investment into aged infrastructure. In Australia, the Tourism and Transport Forum lobbied government to gain acceptance of this model of infrastructure funding for transport and tourism projects. Whilst privatisation remains a real issue, a measure of government involvement in large public transport systems has characterised much of the debate on tourist transport. In the UK context, Banister (1994: 68) identified the essential need to recognise that 'society is now in transition from one based on work and industry to one in which leisure pursuits dominate – the post-industrial society'. The implication is that policy making needs to recognise the significance of meeting the transport needs of this society (Glaister et al. 2006; Stevens 2004).

As Banister (1994: 69) explains, 'many of the policies have been justified on . . . criteria, such as ideology (for example deregulation), democracy (for example widening

Plate 3.1 Public Service Obligation operated railways such as the Inverness route through the Cairngorms National Park can use tourist traffic in the summer to help offset public subsidies, whilst still serving local needs as shown at Blair Atholl Station, Perthshire

Source: S.J. Page

share ownership), efficiency (for example private enterprises are more efficient than public ones), and accountability'. The Treasury was the prime mover in these new policy directions, constraining expenditure on investment and renewal of transport infrastructure by the state: this is a theme we will return to later in the chapter in relation to the ideological mantra associated with rail privatisation in the UK, given the scale of state subsidies needed to maintain franchises post-privatisation. The emphasis in policy was a shift from state investment in public transport to investment in roads to meet a demand for car use. Whilst the government increasingly turned to the private sector for capital and investment in the 1990s, it merely provided expenditure that was required in the 1980s to keep up with demand. Banister (1994: 70) acknowledges that

> In the early 1980s there was a concern over the increasing levels of public support for bus and rail services with subsidy levels for each amounting to about £1,000 million. The market philosophy is to ensure that all services are provided at a level

and a price which is determined competitively. Intervention should only take place when the market is seen to fail, for example, for social need, but even then the intervention should be specific and that there should be no cross subsidisation between services.

The policy changes since the 1980s are characterised by:

● transferring transport from the public sector to the private sector through privatisation or denationalisation;
● the introduction of competition into public transport services and greater regulatory reform;
● the pursuit of greater levels of private capital in the large transport infrastructure projects such as the Channel Tunnel and Skye Road Bridge in Scotland and the Queen Elizabeth Bridge on London's M25 orbital motorway.

In fact privatisation is not a process in government policy-making that is confined to the UK and USA: it has been adopted in many countries, but as the example of UK airport policy shows (Insight 3.2), it is largely a private sector activity with the state setting out the strategic framework for growth and management given the expansion in the 1990s of the low-cost airline model (see Groß and Schröder 2007).

INSIGHT 3.2

UK airports policy

In 2004 the UK Department for Transport (*www.dft.gov.uk*) issued its White Paper outlining the strategic direction for airport development to 2033, after a lengthy consultation process, where 500,000 responses were received from stakeholders. The resulting policy acknowledged the key challenge – to balance the impacts of airports with the benefits expansion would bring, which was a matter for planning bodies. The arguments put forward for an expansion were:

● UK air travel increased five-fold in 1970–2002, from 32 million to 189 million passengers.
● By 2020, growth will be to 350–460 million passengers.
● Half the population now flies once a year, 70 per cent of whom are headed overseas (though this finding is debatable, since it depends upon how one calculates participation rates).
● The economy increasingly depends upon air travel (for exports, tourism and inward investment), which supports 200,000 direct jobs and 600,000 jobs indirectly, and contributes £13 billion to UK GDP.
● Aviation links peripheral communities (supported by Public Service Obligation Services as discussed by Williams and Pagliari 2004).
● It facilitates international tourism.
● The evidence suggests that the demand for air travel will continue to grow to 2033 (though this is dependent upon appropriate infrastructure to accommodate demand).

The counterbalancing argument (which seems much weaker in the weight given to its significance) was that:

● Airport capacity cannot be added to regardless of environmental cost, so that a balanced approach is needed to address environmental issues that include:
  – noise (though it was argued that the new generation of aircraft are 75 per cent quieter than 1960s jet aircraft);
  – limiting the area affected by noise pollution;

▶

- promoting research into low-noise aircraft (though the UK's main role here is through its engine manufacturer – Rolls-Royce);
- using noise-related landing charges;
- insulating affected properties from noise whilst also reducing the effect of blight on properties.

The government's policy position towards specific airport projects outlined in its consultation phase in 2002 were announced in the 2003 White Paper, which is summarised in Table 3.5. The table represents the most significant airport development programme in the UK since the military expansion of 1939–45 (and some expansion plans are based on former military facilities). What is highly debatable in this policy is the implicit acceptance of the powerful arguments by the UK industry stakeholders such as the airlines, tourism industry and other lobby groups (also see the discussion in Chapter 8 by the House of Commons Select Committee on sustainability and airport policy). However, since much of the regional growth in air travel in the UK has been promoted by low-cost airlines for point-to-point travel, competing with rail and coach, one has to consider why environmental impacts will be incurred when an expansion of land-based travel (i.e. high-speed rail) may fulfil much of the expected demand. There is a simple and effective political-policy response. The aviation sector is largely a private sector activity in the UK that creates employment, whilst taxes on air travel generate tax revenue. Furthermore, the airline sector in the UK enjoys lower fuel duty rates than other modes of transport, and so does not necessarily pay the real environmental and economic costs of operation. Similar arguments have also been lobbied in the case of road transport, where road-building costs have historically been subsidised in the UK by taxpayer revenue at the expense of public transport.

The Department for Transport (2006a) *The Future of Air Transport: Progress Report* launched in December 2006 as a follow-up to the 2003 White Paper on Airport Policy examined the factors affecting demand that are focused on:

- Trade and freight transport demand.
- International competitiveness.
- Aviation's direct contribution to economic development.
- People's aspirations to travel (which are based on the Department for Transport (2006b) *Attitudes of, and Experiences Towards Air Travel* study which underlined the strong aspirations of the UK population flying in the future given that 15 per cent had flown at least three times in the previous year. Affordability and rising incomes were seen as key drivers of these aspirations although 70 per cent recognised the impact of such activity on the environment.

On the basis of these factors which were seen as shaping demand, revised projected demand forecasts were produced for air travel to 2030 under two assumptions:

1 Unconstrained demand, where demand would rise from 228 million passengers per annum (MPPA) in 2005 to 490 million in 2030.
2 Constrained demand, where there is an assumption that by 2010 passengers will be paying for the effects of climate change, providing forecasts of traffic increasing from 228 MPPA in 2005 to 465 million MPPA in 2030.

The implications of these demand forecasts for one part of the UK – Scotland – are that traffic may grow to:

- 20.2 MPPA at Glasgow and 26 MPPA at Edinburgh in 2030;
- 6 MPPA at Prestwick in 2030;
- 5.3 MPPA at Aberdeen in 2030;
- 1 MPPA at Inverness by 2010,

which will have implications for infrastructure provision if these volumes of traffic are to be accommodated.

Table 3.5 Government airport policy in the UK in 2003

Option for development/expansion	Support	Not supported	Comments: key Infrastructure Development
SCOTLAND			
New central airport		✓	
Edinburgh Airport	✓		• New runway • Safeguard land • Terminal/stand capacity
Glasgow International Airport	✓		• Runway expansion • Land safeguarding
Glasgow Prestwick	✓		• Runway/terminal expansion
Dundee Airport	✓		• Expand terminal
Inverness Airport/Highland Airports	✓		• Terminal expansion/ capacity growth
WALES			
Cardiff International Airport	✓	✓	• Expand – determine locally
New airport in/around Severn Estuary			
NORTHERN IRELAND			
Belfast International Airport	✓		• Development in existing boundaries to meet demand
Belfast City Airport			• Northern Ireland authorities to review cap
City of Derry Airport			• Review future with Northern Ireland/Eire authorities
ENGLAND			
Manchester Airport	✓		• Develop terminal capacity
Liverpool John Lennon Airport	✓		• Improve surface access • Expand as planned • Runway lengthened
Blackpool Airport			• Decide locally
Carlisle Airport	✓		• Encourage development
Newcastle Airport	✓		• Support 360m runway expansion
Teesside International Airport	✓		• Terminal facilities and runway length
Leeds Bradford International Airport	✓		• Additional terminal capacity • 300m runway extension • Minimise noise impacts
Humberside International Airport	✓		• Attract new traffic but will be in competition with new airport at Doncaster Finningley
New Midlands' airport near Coventry/Rugby		✓	
Birmingham International Airport	✓		• Expand as opposed to new Midlands Airport • New 2000m runway • Stringent limits on noise
East Midlands Airport	✓		• Expansion of passenger/ freight traffic • Strict noise controls

(Continued) ▶

Table 3.5 Government airport policy in the UK in 2003 *(Continued)*

Option for development/expansion	Support	Not supported	Comments: key Infrastructure Development
			• No support for second runway/land for runway but will review • For local use
Coventry Airport/ Wolverhampton Business Airport/civil use of RAF Cosford			
Bristol International Airport	✓		• Runway extension and new terminal
New airport north of Bristol		✓	
Bournemouth International Airport	✓		• Add capacity to terminal
Exeter International Airport	✓		• Decide locally and constraints to expansion
Plymouth			• No consultation undertaken – decide locally/regional
Newquay Airport	✓		
Gloucester/Filton Airports	✓		
London Stansted	✓		• By 2011/12 a second runway at Stansted • Strict noise controls • Minimise impact on heritage and countryside • No support for second and third runways
London Heathrow	✓		• Development supported subject to strict environmental limits and a new runway during 2015–20 with land safeguarded for runway • Air quality issues to be addressed
London Gatwick Airport	✓		• Safeguard land for a wider runway in case conditions for the Heathrow runway cannot be met • Will not act to overturn the planning agreement preventing the second runway before 2019 • Do not support the option for two new runways
Luton Airport	✓		• Support up to one runway but not two
Second hub in South East		✓	
New airport at Cliffe, Kent		✓	• Due to the ecological impact, safety risk and viability
Alconbury		✓	

Other airports with scope for expansion to meet demands: London City, Norwich, Southampton, Southend, Manston and potential at Lydd, Shoreham and Biggin Hill

Source: Compiled from text in the government White Paper, *The Future of Air Transport 2003*, HMSO 2003.

Whilst some expansion of airport capacity is inevitable, perhaps more radical policy measures might have looked at promoting modal switching from short-haul air to rail given the success of similar schemes in France with the TGV (Page 2002a, 2003), although politically this is less acceptable given the inherent investment needs of the rail sector. Nevertheless the government's Ten Year Plan 2000 for the period 2000–10 outlined some plans for investment in public transport (including private sector elements), with road investment of £20.8 billion 2001/2–2010/11, rail with £64.1 billion and £26.9 billion in London. These plans are likely to see some potential enhancement as the country enters recession in 2008, as infrastructure projects are earmarked for state investment as a means of reflating the domestic economy based on the principles articulated by Maynard Keynes in the 1920s, to generate state-led employment opportunities. Thus, even where policy seeks a private sector role, such as with airports, the wider public sector role still requires substantial investment in supporting infrastructure such as roads and rail. The competing and increasing investment needs of the transport sector are one reason why many governments have sought to reduce a state role in areas such as aviation that require massive investment. For this reason, it is interesting to focus on Asia-Pacific aviation, which had not seen a major role of private investment until the 1980s and 1990s.

Privatisation in Asia-Pacific aviation

The Asia-Pacific region is one of the fastest-growing regions of the world for scheduled air travel. In the period 1980–90 commercial air traffic expanded by 7.95 per cent per annum compared to 5.8 per cent growth per annum in North America, and these trends would have continued had it not been for a number of global crises in air travel such as 9/11, SARS and terrorism. Despite such crises, the region is becoming the world's most important airline market, a feature evident from the forecasts by Airbus and Boeing. Oum (1997: 1), however, argued that 'even though the major airlines of Asia belong to the world's fastest growing airline market, they have remained relatively small in terms of network size, traffic volume and operating revenue, compared with major carriers in the United States and Europe'. Part of this is related to the restrictive bilateral agreements that also protect the home market, with only limited privatisation prior to the 1980s and a number of key developments post-1988. There has been considerable research in the aviation sector that compares the productivity of airlines under government control with their subsequent performance as privately owned enterprises and similar arguments have been applied to airport policy (Hooper 2002). Most of the studies indicate superior performance under conditions of privatisation (Findlay and Forsyth 1984; Oum 1995) although not in every case (Oum and Yu 1995).

Table 3.6 indicates that prior to 1985 there were isolated cases of privatisation but much of the privatisation occurred post-1985. For example, whilst the case of Singapore Airlines indicates that the government remains the majority shareholder, it is largely a private airline. In Oceania, the majority of airlines are privately owned, though many of the smaller airlines of the Pacific Island states remain state owned to retain a degree of control over tourist arrivals (Forsyth and King 1996)

Table 3.6 Airline privatisation in the Asia-Pacific region, 1985–95

Airline	Country	1985 ownership		1995 ownership	
		Private	Public	Private	Public (%)
American Airlines	USA	X		X	
Aeromexico	Mexico		X	X	
Aero Peru	Peru		X		20
Air Canada	Canada		X	X	
Air China	China		X		100
Air Lanka	Sri Lanka		X		100
Air New Zealand	New Zealand		X	X	
Air Nugini	Papua New Guinea		X		100
Air Pacific	Fiji		X		79.6
Air India	India		X		100
All Nippon Airways	Japan	X		X	
Ansett Australia	Australia	X		X	
Avianca	Colombia	X		X	
Biman Bangladesh	Bangladesh		X		100
Canadian Air International	Canada	X		X	
Cathay Pacific Airways	Hong Kong	X		X	
China Airways	Taiwan	X		X	
Continental Airways	USA	X		X	
Delta Airlines	USA	X		X	
Garuda	Indonesia		X		100
HAL (Hawaiian)	USA	X		X	
Indian Airlines	India		X		100
Japan Air Systems	Japan	X		X	
Japan Airlines	Japan		X	X	
Korean Air	South Korea	X		X	
Ladeco	Chile	X		X	
Lan Chile	Chile			X	
Malaysia Airlines	Malaysia		X		30
Merpati	Indonesia		X		30
Mexicana	Mexico		X		35
Northwest Airlines	USA	X		X	
Pakistan International	Pakistan		X		57.4
Philippine Airlines	Philippine		X		33
Qantas	Australia		X		75
Royal Brunei	Brunei		X		100
Saeta Air Ecuador	Ecuador	X		X	
Singapore Airlines	Singapore		X		54
Thai International	Thailand		X		93.7
United Airlines	USA	X		X	
Vietnam Airlines	Vietnam		X		100

Source: Based on Forsyth (1997a).

and for strategic reasons related to accessibility and the independence of major carriers. In Pacific South American states, airlines have been privatised as well as those in North America, Canada and Mexico. In Asia, the situation is mixed. Whilst some states have privatised their airlines and others intend to do so, a considerable number remain state owned. Most of the privatised companies are the large successful airlines. As Forsyth (1997a: 53) observes:

> there is a strong correlation between per capita income levels and private ownership. In the richer countries in the region, such as Japan, Korea, Singapore,

Taiwan, Malaysia, along with the colony of Hong Kong, all the airlines are privately owned. By contrast, there are few examples of private ownership of airlines in the poorer countries,

whilst a number of governments have allowed the introduction of private airlines (e.g. Asiana in Korea, Sempati in Indonesia and Dragonair in Hong Kong) to compete on international routes as well as low-cost airlines such as Air Asia.

Where privatisation has occurred, it can take a number of forms:

● listing on the stock market (JAL and Singapore Airlines);
● sale of the airline to other companies in the same country;
● sale of the airline to strategic shareholders.

Privatisation also allows overseas investment in airlines through direct investment by shareholders and equity holdings through strategic alliances. In contrast, there has been less interest in the privatisation of airports in Asia, with only Australia taking Britain's lead in privatising all of its airports. The argument advanced to justify privatisation of airlines is the efficiency gains that will result. In the case of airports, it is widely recognised that the greatest proportion of costs are capital as opposed to operating costs. Therefore the potential for efficiency gains is limited (a more detailed discussion can be found in Chapter 7). However, some of the aspects of airport operation that private firms may perform efficiently include:

● terminal operation;
● retail outlet operation;
● building and operating runways;
● contracted-out services.

As Hooper (2002) shows, a number of models of privatisation have also been used in the airport sector in Asia (Table 3.7). Whilst the data in this table may now seem dated, what is important is the diversification of privatisation models used to fund individual projects. However, Forsyth (1997a: 62) maintains that 'investment policy, and ownership of the main facilities may best be left to the public sector' although this has certainly not been heeded by policy-makers. In an Asia-Pacific context, privatisation has certainly opened up the opportunities for the region's airlines to become part of a global aviation industry through foreign investment, alliances and cooperation motivated by commercial motives in the absence of state policies to protect state airlines. As Wheatcroft (1994: 24) argues, 'in the long term, the privatisation of airlines seems certain to contribute to a reduction in protectionism in international aviation policies'.

Since changes in transport policy within individual countries have repercussions both on tourism and on other countries, attention now turns to the role of policy formulation and development amongst transnational organisations such as the European Union and ASEAN. The single European Act has sought to introduce greater competition and a reduction in state subsidies to achieve greater efficiency in transport provision (see the special issue of the *Journal of Air Transport Management* 3(4) 1997 on this theme). Even this is not without problems, as the example of the Common Transport Policy indicates.

Table 3.7 Airport privatisation schemes in Asia – a snapshot in 2001

Model	Cases	Comments
Service concessions Contracting-out	Seoul's Inchon International Airport	Marketing function outsourced during construction phase
Management contracts	Seoul's Inchon International Airport Jakarta's Soekarno-Hatta International Airport	Majority owned by government 30-year concession awarded to Amsterdam Schiphol Government's stated objectives were to improve efficiency
Multiple concessions	BAA's six airports in China	Established as a joint venture majority owned by the government of China
BOT scheme (BOOT, BOT, etc.)	Macau International Airport	Majority owned by the regional government
	Seoul's Inchon International Airport	Commercial developments associated with the airport (e.g. hotels)
	Terminal 3 at Manila's Ninoy Aquino International Airport	25-year concession to build terminal. Piatco joint venture company includes Frankfurt airport operator Flughafen Frankfurt
	Cambodia-Pochentong Airport, Phnom Penh	Upgrading works under a 20-year concession for works costing $250 million
	Bangalore International Airport, India	Development officially started in January 2001
Long-term leases (LDO, etc.)	India's four main airports	Government to decide on successful tender
BOO	Cochin International Airport	Majority owned by government of Kerala
Capital markets	China-Xiamen, Hongqiao Beijing Capital, Guangzhou Baiyun International, Huangtian International Airports	The companies are usually majority owned by the regional government, but it is notable that airlines also own significant stakes of their hubs
	Malaysia Airports Sdn. Bhd.	Majority owned by national government with 30–50 year concession agreement subject to discretionary regulation
Joint venture	Kansai International Airport	Majority owned by government

Note: BOOT = Build own operate and transfer back to state
    BOT = Build operate and transfer back
    BOO = Build own operate lease
    LDO = Long-term leases

Source: Reprinted from *Journal of Air Transport Management*, 8, P. Hooper, 'Privatisation of airports in Asia', pp. 289–300, Copyright © 2002, with permission from Elsevier.

●●●● Towards a common transport policy for the European Union: the case of rail travel

In the case of aviation, the EU policy

has changed dramatically over the last decade after a move from aviation markets being a series of heavily regulated, discrete bilateral cartels, dominated by nationally owned flag carriers, to a structure which promises by the end of the century to have become a liberalised multinational civil aviation market (Button 1997: 170).

Accordingly, Button (1996) views this as evolving into an institutional structure similar to that which developed in the USA (see Chapter 5). Aviation was initially excluded from the EU's Common Transport Policy in 1957, with individual countries regulating their own domestic aviation markets. In the international arena, bilateral service agreements were used to regulate air travel. Policies existed that regulated scheduled fares, market entry and service provision. Changes have occurred in the EU aviation market:

● Individual countries (e.g. the UK) did not free the market entirely; instead the procedure for allocating licences was more liberal. Other countries such as France, Italy and Germany have been more reluctant to institute domestic liberalisation.
● Since the mid-1980s bilateral agreements have been liberalised between member states (e.g. the UK–Netherlands agreement in 1984), which relaxed market entry restrictions. Changes on the UK–Ireland routes indicate that lower fares resulted.
● External changes, such as the USA's 'open skies' policy, have assisted EU member states in developing more liberal bilateral agreements.
● In the late 1980s the EU began to develop a common policy following court rulings that led European politicians to consider liberalisation measures (Stasinopoulos 1992, 1993) and the introduction of the Third Package measures (see Papatheodorou 2002).

Since 1998 competition rules have been applied to aviation. The EU's three air transport liberalisation packages aimed at removing restrictions on access, price and capacity. The First Package in January 1988 was modest and agreed to a move towards a single market. The Second Package in June 1990 removed 'government to government capacity-sharing arrangements, introduced in stages the notion of double disapproval of fares and prevented governments discriminating against airlines, provided that they conformed with technical and safety standards' (Button 1997: 172). The final element, the Third Package, launched in January 1993, led to a regulatory framework which emerged in 1997 that is similar to the US domestic market. In other words, since 1997, full cabotage has been permitted and fares are no longer regulated. Foreign ownership amongst EU carriers can occur although the EU has reserved the right to intervene in the market under certain circumstances: to freeze the market if it becomes unbalanced and to prevent downward spirals on air fares (see Button 1997 for more detail). Aviation, however, is not the only area for action by the EU, as rail travel is now considered.

Rail transport and rail networks are state owned in all member states of the EU (despite changes in the UK), and they receive subsidies to assist with the operation of uneconomic services. Yet there are certain governments (e.g. the UK and Sweden) that have sought to introduce greater competition, aspects of privatisation and a more explicit market orientation for rail passenger transport after many years of state control. In many countries, state ownership of rail transport has meant that national railway networks have a dependence upon public sector subsidies due to the enormous infrastructure and investment needs of the sector, which has traditionally been associated with a close relationship with national governments.

The close relationship between the management of railways and the interests of national governments has meant that policy-making has been largely inward looking and focused on national rather than EU-wide concerns. Gibb and Charlton (1992) have confirmed this view in their analysis of the EU's role as an organisation intended to foster cooperation in transport policy between its member states. They found that in the case of rail travel, the wider considerations of the EU have been undermined by the vested interests of national governments in their own rail networks. As a result, the EU has made little progress towards developing a common rail policy due to two principal objectives of EU transport policy that consistently cause conflict:

- the desire to liberalise rail transport to achieve free trade policies in the move towards the Single European Market;[1]
- the need to harmonise the conditions of competition in rail services in pursuit of social intervention policies.

The EU 'Proposal for a Council Directive on the Development of Community Railways' (COM (89) 564 final), which was finalised in July 1991, embodied these principles. It proposed that railway operations and infrastructure should be the responsibility of two separate organisations, so that railway companies can make commercial decisions about long-distance passenger services. This is designed to facilitate an expansion in international rail passenger services where the user entering a national network pays a user fee, thereby reducing the possibility of cross-subsidisation of railway networks by national governments. Whilst the EU aimed to introduce freedom of access to national railway networks across its member states, the changes required by national governments to achieve these objectives imply an end to the highly regulated environment in which state-managed railway enterprises operate. The prospects for providing access to national railway networks and the introduction of competitive operations are remote, due to the challenge to existing national markets and services.

The EU and rail travel

In the EU, rail travel has experienced a relative loss of market share to road since the 1970s. With the decline in infrastructure for rail operations and to seek to reverse the declining fortunes of rail, the EU Common Transport Policy set out a number of goals that subsequent directives needed to meet:

- to open up EU markets for rail;
- to develop interoperability of high-speed and conventional rail systems;
- to set out the conditions within which state aid could be provided.

Since only 5 per cent of EU rail revenue was derived from international, cross-border services (€13 billion), much of the attention focused on improving the

---

[1]In the Single European Act passed in June 1987 railway transport was not included.

competitiveness and financial management of member state operations to reduce debts and to help separate operations from government control to make financial matters more transparent. For example, Directives in 1995 (Directive 95/18/EC and 95/19/EC) addressed some of these concerns as well as outlining public service obligation (PSO) conditions where subsidies could be provided which were €35 billion at a time of contraction in the EU rail network.

Interestingly, the 1996 White Paper, *A Strategy for Revitalising the Community Railways,* identified the need for states to separate infrastructure and operations and was the foundation of further Directives in 1998, adopted in 2001 – the Rail Infrastructure Package – also allowing new operators to work EU networks. Directive 2001/14/EU also clarified the manner of charging for the use of infrastructure for operators and in September 2001 the White Paper, *European Transport Policy for 2010,* outlined a further 60 measures to make transport policy more user oriented to increase rail usage by 40 per cent in 1998–2010. The 2001 White Paper also planned more consumer rights regulations to make rail more user driven. However, the main focus of EU investment and policy has been on developing a pan-European high-speed rail network.

The EU high-speed rail network

Much of the EU's concern has been focused on the creation of a Trans-European Network System (TENS) to establish a high-speed transport road and rail network. After 1994 nine rail projects were developed for completion by 2005 to increase rail modal switching from car and air to rail so that rail could achieve a market share of 23.5 per cent by 2010 on trunk routes (compared to 60.2 per cent by car and 16.5 per cent by air). In 2001 the EU outlined its priorities for TENS rail projects to foster trans-European cooperation in passenger services to attempt to repeat the THALYS success. However, critics point to the shortcomings of the TENS approach (Van Excel et al. 2002), which are still evaluated in national terms to achieve some of the wider TENS objectives of:

- maximising transport efficiency;
- improving transport safety;
- environmental improvement;
- strategic mobility and environmental, economic improvement;
- implementation of the Single Market;
- contribution to external dimensions, such as network development, integration and cooperation (*Source*: European Commission 1998, *www.europa.int*),

and research has evaluated the level at which such infrastructure projects should be measured (Vickerman 1995), with a tension between straight economic appraisal and more strategic impacts at an EU level as well as non-economic objectives (Van Excel et al. 2002). The TEN-T project is to be reviewed in 2010 in relation to its original objectives, while new plans for 2020 will also be developed (Van Reeven 2005).

But much of the EU transport policy work, particularly in the area of rail, makes implicit assumptions about the benefits and impact upon tourism as well as the role for the nation state in formulating an effective policy for tourist transport.

●●●● Formulating state-level tourist transport policy

The Organisation for Economic Cooperation and Development (OECD) Tourism Committee, formed in 1948, pursued tourism as a vehicle for economic cooperation and development during the post-war reconstruction of Europe. One of its principal objectives is to provide advice and information to member countries on the issues commonly faced by government tourism administrations. Its reports and activities are particularly influential in shaping and influencing government policies on tourism, particularly the issue of globalisation and obstacles to improving member state's tourism competitiveness. Many OECD countries possess relatively mature tourism destinations and so improving their global competitiveness involves policy developments such as the greater linking of different cross-cutting policies across government to improve tourism performance. One such area is transport and tourism, particularly the improvement of infrastructure (OECD 2008a: 15).

The OECD has argued that effective state policies for tourist transport should be integrated so that tourism and transport concerns work in harmony rather than in isolation. These policy issues are predominantly concerned with issues of competition, accessibility and destination development. Transport policy needs to consider tourism as a related activity that is directly influenced by the objectives pursued in national, regional and local transport policy. In fact Sinclair and Page (1993) examined the role of policy formulation in a transfrontier region (the Euroregion – in North East France and South East England) in relation to transport, tourism and regional development. This is an interesting example where cross-border cooperation and planning for transport assisted in coordinating the variety of bodies involved in implementing tourism and transport planning in two different countries. It also illustrates how a wider policy-making framework can assist in the recognition of the vital link between transport planning and tourism to promote economic development in local areas.

Yet translating policy objectives into a planning framework may pose particular problems for tourist transport systems, since the political philosophy of national governments can lead to different approaches to funding and development of transport infrastructure projects. For example, the case of airport development highlights the inherent tensions and a trend towards airports being operated as commercial enterprises. This means that infrastructure provision now based in the private sector, with the UK government's market-led philosophy also applying to complementary infrastructure provision through PPPs. This was demonstrated by the public/private sector partnership between the former British Rail and the BAA's £300 million Heathrow Express rail-link project to connect Heathrow and Paddington in London (see Chapter 7). According to May et al. (2005: 238) integration in transport can be achieved by:

- integrating the policy instruments used across different modes of transport;
- integrating policy instruments associated with the provision of infrastructure, management, pricing and information provision;
- integrating land use planning with different transport schemes and measures;
- linking policies not currently aligned with transport such as health, education and other areas (e.g. tourism);
- integrating the activities of different public bodies and authorities in large urban areas.

As May et al. (2005) argue, policy instruments to achieve integration can involve a wide range of options that can be grouped under six headings: infrastructure provision; management and regulation; attitude change; pricing; land use; and information provision. From a policy perspective, their effectiveness will depend upon their ability to influence or alter a number of underlying factors (e.g. the number of journeys undertaken, length of journey, mode of transport used, timing and routing). In most studies of transport integration, May et al. (2005) point to two underlying principles: the pursuit of synergy (i.e. how policy instruments interact to give a positive outcome) and the removal of barriers (i.e. those factors which may be obstacles to effective implementation such as institutional, financial, political and practical barriers). For example, in the example of the London Congestion Charge influencing road user behaviour, a number of complementary strategies as alternatives to road use had to be developed (e.g. prioritising bus use of roads, improving the frequency of rail schedules, expanding rail infrastructure).

Where countries do formulate a tourist transport policy, the following issues should be taken into account in its implementation through planning measures:

- *The management of tourist traffic* in large urban areas (see the London Tourist Board 1987: 61–3, on managing transport used by visitors, particularly the problems of coach parking, which is also discussed by the Bus and Coach Council 1991) and small historic cities (see Page 1992a for a case study of Canterbury). In 1997 the English Historic Towns Forum (1997) established a Code of Practice for coach tourism to address the issue amongst its members in line with growing concerns about managing tourists and non-tourists and traffic in town centres (Page and Hardyman 1996).

- *The management of tourist and recreational traffic in rural areas* (see Sharpley 1993; also see the Department for Rural Affairs in the UK 2004 Rural White Paper Review, *Transport, www.defra.gov.uk/rural* for a discussion of the issues, along with its 2002 *Review of English National Park Authorities* on the same website and its arguments for a greater examination of local transport plans to assist with transport planning in these sensitive environments and the need to work with transport operators and visitors to reduce car-based visits to extend choice and reduce environmental pollution).

- *The promotion of off-peak travel by tourists* to spread the seasonal and geographical distribution of tourist travel and the resulting economic, social, cultural and economic impacts of tourism. For example, in late 2006, a collaborative venture between tourism partners in Budapest entitled Budapest's Winter Invasion sought to address seasonality by providing incentives for visiting (e.g. three nights for the price of two) with a free pass to visit the city's museums and unlimited travel by public transport.

- *Maximising the use of existing transport infrastructure* and the use of more novel forms of tourist transport together with the provision of new infrastructure on the basis of long-term traffic forecasts.

- *Integration of transport modes* (see Stubbs and Jegede 1998) as evident from the UK's Department for Transport move towards an integrated transport strategy and illustrated by Insight 3.3 in relation to tourism and transport in Hong Kong.

- *More integration between the public and private sector* rather than the fragmentation that has arisen from privatisation in the UK rail network.

INSIGHT 3.3

Integrated transport provision for tourism – Hong Kong

According to the Hong Kong Planning Department, transport is a key prerequisite for achieving the strategic development aims of the Special Administrative Regional (SAR) government to support tourism, as one of the four cornerstones of its economy. The Planning Department identified the importance of understanding visitor characteristics, mode of transport chosen and how they used transport to travel in Hong Kong. This was seen as critical to future transport planning exercises given the crucial role of tourism to the economy. For example, visitor arrivals have grown from almost 10 million in 1995 to 16 million in 2002 and 25 million in 2006. With a high annual growth rate in visitor arrivals, mainly by air and with increasing numbers from mainland China, understanding transport needs was important to plan future transport services and capacity. With most visitors staying around three days, we need to understand the tourism requirements in terms of use of private transport, organised tours, taxis and other forms of public transport.

Given Hong Kong's expansion as a global financial and business centre, located on a land area of $1104km^2$ with a population of 6.9 million in 2004, developing forms of mass transit to transport residents and tourists efficiently and safely was a high priority.

Government policies have prioritised mass carriers whilst controlling private cars (Tang and Lo 2008). Since the 1970s, Hong Kong has had a mass tourist railway and an electrified overground railway and a key pillar of Hong Kong's transport policy is an integrated public transport system. Basic principles behind the state management of transport services include inter-modal coordination, particularly between bus and rail that underpin the transport network.

The Planning Department Study (2003) noted that most visitors use the mass tourist railway and taxi to explore Hong Kong followed by coach transfers, public buses, airport express links and the harbour ferries. This will inevitably have changed since the opening of Hong Kong's newest mega-attraction – Hong Kong Disneyland, with its own dedicated rail service. To accommodate future growth in tourism until around 2030 Hong Kong opened its new airport in February 2007 and the former Kai Tak site is currently being developed into a new cruise terminal. This reflects an expanding market sector for the tourism sector, with its own transport and infrastructure needs.

The Planning Department (2003) study rightly acknowledged that tourist trip patterns are very different to domestic work and school trips that may be able to avoid peak period usage. The Department expected the current transport network to be able to cope with tourism demand although potential arrivals by road in the future may cause major impacts. Among the improvements recommended to enhance the visitor's experience of travelling in Hong Kong were: improved seating around popular tourist attractions and transport nodes; improvements to the pedestrian environment; better signposting; and increased integration of public transport at major tourist attraction. In addition, better information was seen as vital to encourage visitors to tour around the SAR to create a more 'tourism-friendly transport environment'. What this Insight demonstrates is that Hong Kong not only recognises the symbiotic relationship between transport and tourism, but sees an important value-adding process which can enhance the visitor travel experience and satisfaction levels by attention to detail and investing in measures to promote easy access and travel. This is particularly significant when the SAR land use planning model has helped to cluster tourism activities for large visitor volumes at 'tourism nodes'.

●●●● Privatisation and the UK rail system: lessons for governments

Tourist and recreational use of rail services remains a poorly understood area of tourism research, with the exception of examples of transport for tourism such as the Orient Express or sightseeing excursions as discussed in Chapters 1 and 2. According to Halsall (1982) and Page (2003b) tourism and leisure rail travel generate a number of journey types typically including more than one category:

- The use of dedicated rail corridors that connect major gateways (airports and ports) of a country to the final destination, or as a mode of transit to the tourist accommodation in the nearby city.
- The use of rapid transit systems and metros to travel within urban areas.
- The use of high-speed and non-high-speed intercity rail corridors to facilitate movement as part of an itinerary or city-to-city journey, typically for business and leisure travel. These journeys may cross country borders in the EU and form part of a pan-European network.
- The use of local rail services outside of urban areas, often used in peak hours by commuters to journey to/from mainline/intercity rail terminals en route to other destinations.
- The use of peripheral rail services that serve remote communities in the tourist season for scenic sightseeing and special interest travel.

A study by OGM (2002) for the EU on *The Development of International Rail Passenger Markets and Policy* expanded the scope of the market for such services,

Plate 3.2 Car parking pressures in rural areas such as National Parks remain a major challenge for transport planners as shown in Widecombe car park, Devon. Do you accommodate the volume or try to de-market the area by non-provision of parking areas?

Source: Dr Joanne Connell

identifying five detailed segments at an international level that were also relevant to domestic trips:

- *regional cross-border services* for commuting or tourist trips, typically 80–90 km in duration. These services are used by EU citizens living in border areas of one member state but who work in another;
- *long-distance intercity services* for leisure and business travellers;
- *high-speed services* for leisure and business travellers where a dedicated link has been provided (e.g. the Brussels–Paris link) and that has seen a major modal shift from car and air to high-speed rail travel with the THALYS service capturing 53 per cent of the traffic between Brussels and Paris;
- *regular niches* such as night trains and car-sleeper services, with a notable growth in the German market of 10 per cent per annum since the restructuring of services;
- *occasional services* such as winter sport destinations or coastal resorts.

But how has privatisation affected this market for tourist travel in the UK?

The pre-privatisation era and tourist and leisure use of rail

Turton (1992a) provided a broad overview of the various factors that affected the organisation and management of pre-privatisation passenger services (Figure 3.2), the impact of government policy and the relative importance of rail versus other modes of transport. Potter (1987) argues that the main determinants of the demand for rail travel are:

- speed;
- cost;
- comfort;
- convenience;
- access to stations;
- the image of the service.

These affect the perceived quality of the service and are often judged in relation to competing modes of transport.

In terms of tourist demand, Turton (1991) reports that the Long Distance Travel Survey (1979–80) found that rail had a 20 per cent share of all long-distance trips (those over 40 km). According to Jefferson and Lickorish (1991), the number of domestic tourists using rail to reach their holiday destination in Great Britain dropped from 13 per cent in 1971 to 10 per cent in 1985 and 8 per cent in 1989. For journeys to the European mainland that included a sea crossing, 8 per cent of British tourists travelled by BR in 1986. In 1991/2, the business traveller using InterCity (long-distance, high-speed rail services) comprised:

- 23 per cent of InterCity passenger volumes;
- 35 per cent of receipts; and
- approximately 8 per cent of the UK long-distance travel market.

According to Green (1994) InterCity accounted for 8 per cent of all long distance trips in the UK and 52 per cent of these trips were classified as 'leisure travel' (which includes tourist travel). A further 27 per cent of travellers were undertaking business trips that could also have an element of tourism since some of these trips would involve an overnight stay away from the traveller's normal place of residence.

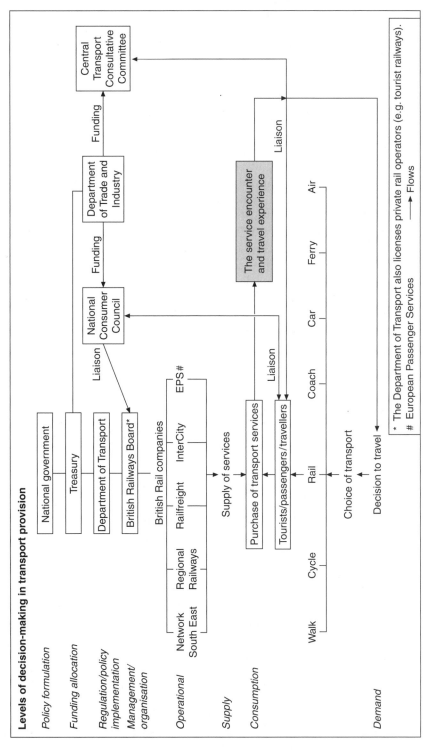

Figure 3.2 The tourist rail system pre-privatisation

Source: Adapted from Page 1994.

Rail travel in the UK, as with the rest of the EU, had seen a significant drop in public support and patronage since the 1970s as competition with other modes of transport (e.g. air, car and coach travel) eroded rail's market share. How far is this a result of government policy as opposed to changing attitudes and preferences amongst travellers, and the extent to which it is due to the decline in the use of rail for tourist trips, is debatable, since this appears to be a unique feature of the UK. However, wider investment policy in rail also had a role to play, as analysts now acknowledge. For example, in the 1970s and early 1980s BR penetrated the domestic long-distance holiday market, selling over 170,000 'Golden Rail Holidays' per annum by the late 1980s (Lavery 1989), but its share of the long-distance travel market continued to decline, despite attempts to diversify its product base. A significant proportion of tourists in the UK use trunk rail routes (Figure 3.3) and inter-urban travel dominates the traffic flows (Turton 1992b) since much of the demand emanates from the main towns and cities, which also contain many of the UK's main tourist gateways. Those rail routes that experienced the greatest volume of traffic were the electrified east and west coast main lines, linking London and Scotland with many of the UK's major towns and cities. Feeder services from rural areas to the main trunk routes and cross-country express services during periods of peak demand (e.g. summer services from inland towns and cities to coastal resorts) provide additional services connecting most destinations to the rail network. Within the overall demand, different segments are discernible (e.g. youth travel, business travellers, the elderly and disabled people), each of which generates its own patterns of demand. The provision of such rail services is subject to the prevailing policy objectives of the national government.

Government regulation of rail services in the UK prior to 1994: the Department of Transport

The Department of Transport was the government department responsible for regulating rail travel and it licensed a number of tourist railways until privatisation measures in 1994. It also licensed railways operated on a seasonal basis to meet the demand for scenic and nostalgic journeys (Halsall 1992). Since 1981 government policy in the UK has rolled back the role of the state in the regulation of public transport through selective measures of privatisation as discussed earlier (e.g. the 1985 Transport Act – Knowles 1985, 1989) in an attempt to develop a greater degree of commercialism in service provision. For example, BR's government subsidy was cut by 60 per cent in the period 1983–89. For BR, this meant that it had to adopt a greater degree of market-led planning towards rail services.

Rail privatisation in the UK

According to Gibb et al. (1996: 35), 'the process leading to the privatisation of British Rail (BR) actually started in the early 1980s and has been a more protracted process than most political commentators credit' and 'BR has been better prepared than most industries for privatisation as a result of a restructuring process that began well before the strategy and timetable for privatisation became clear'.

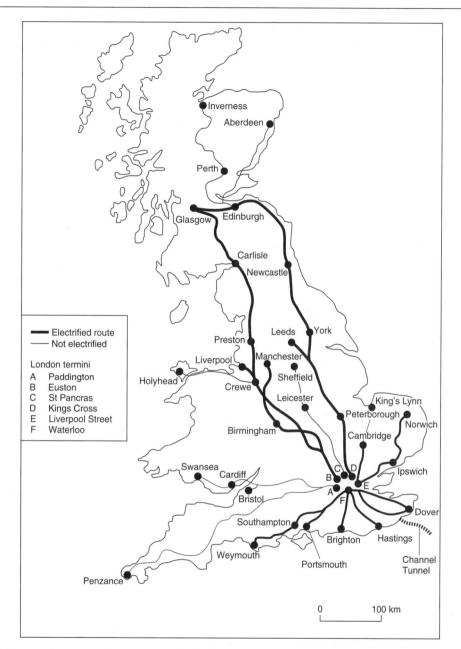

Figure 3.3 Trunk railway routes in the UK

Source: Adapted from Page 1994.

Although privatisation dates to the post-1992 period when there was an 'underlying neoliberal philosophy – seeking to reduce government involvement and to encourage a free market driven by competition' (Gibb et al. 1996: 37). A number of commentators examine privatisation in detail (i.e. Gibb et al. 1996, 1998; Wolmar 1996; Charlton et al. 1997) and readers are directed to their lucid analyses (as well as the excellent papers by Shaw 2000; Murray 2001; Wolmar 2001 and Casson 2004). But it is also pertinent to outline some of the principal changes that have occurred and the implications for tourist rail travel.

In 1992 the Department of Transport announced its plans to implement government policy objectives by introducing further measures to privatise the railway system (Department of Transport 1992a, 1992b, 1993). Whilst seeking to reduce government subsidies for rail travel, a hybrid solution was sought to introduce private sector investment and involvement. Gibb et al. (1996: 38) show that 'up to 1982 the railways had been run as five geographical units. This was replaced with five business sectors – InterCity, Network South East, Regional Railways, Parcels and Freight'. Yet privatisation plans paradoxically were not necessary on financial grounds by the early 1990s, since InterCity and Freight were operating without subsidy and the Department of Transport's (1992a) *New Opportunities for the Railways* acknowledged that BR was the most efficient of any European railway. At the time of privatisation, the existing business units were not selected as the best option for sale. Instead the Department of Transport's (1992a) proposal intended to sell both Freight and Parcels to the private sector, the breaking up of passenger services into franchises to be operated by the private sector, the provision of rights of access to the rail network for private operators of Freight and passenger services (overseen by a Regulator), the separation of track and train services with one part of BR becoming a track authority (Railtrack) with responsibility for running the track and infrastructure, and opportunities for the private sector to purchase or lease stations (Gibb et al. 1996: 43).

The Department of Transport's (1994) *Britain's Railways: A New Era* outlined the final structure of the privatised railway industry, where BR was compartmentalised into independent businesses, each cooperating on a commercial and contractual basis. As Charlton et al. (1997) argue, the government's desire to break BR's monopoly was enacted using the concept of a *common carrier*, which avoided the provision of new infrastructure. By separating ownership of infrastructure from service provision, the common carrier could provide customers with access to its resources – the companies that compete to offer rail services to the public. In this case Railtrack was the common carrier but after it got into financial trouble its successor (Network Rail) is less profit driven. The rail industry now comprises a series of companies that operate rail services or support services. Not only is this a complex operational structure (Charlton et al. 1997), as a result of privatisation 92 businesses emerged and 67 were offered for outright sale. The train-operating companies (TOCs) were offered as regionally based franchises through a tendering process. Railtrack was also responsible for central timetabling, train planning, signalling and the structural condition of the 2500 stations leased to TOCs. Charlton et al. (1997) argue that government intervention and regulatory action have effectively prevented competition. Most TOCs are still supported by government subsidies to procure rolling stock and access to track with some exceptions such as the former GNER East Coast franchise (now operated by National Express).

In a competitive context, Charlton et al. (1997: 152) observe that BR's monopoly has been replaced by an oligopoly due to horizontal and vertical integration (see Chapters 5 and 6 of this book on supply issues) where corporate interests have acquired TOCs, franchises and rail businesses as the recent range of franchises (see the Office of the Rail Regulator, *www.rail-reg.gov.uk*) show, with a post-privatisation industry structure emerging initially as shown in Table 3.8. Studies have examined the

Table 3.8 Company groups within the rail industry according to their function

Function	Description
Central	Consultancies, research and telecommunications services
TOC	Train-operating companies running passenger services
BRIS	British Rail Infrastructure Services (e.g. track renewal and maintenance)
BRML	British Rail Maintenance Limited (e.g. rolling stock maintenance and construction)
ROSCO	Rolling stock leasing companies
GoCo	Railtrack, Union Railways and European Passenger Services (EPS) The ownership of these businesses was transferred to central government prior to privatisation. Union Railways was charged with planning the high-speed rail link from London to the Channel Tunnel. Union Railways and EPS were combined as part of the deal with LCR in 1996 to develop the high-speed rail link.

Source: Adapted from Charlton et al. (1997).

utility of such an approach (e.g. Adamson et al. 1991) and critics of privatisation have argued that lack of government investment is responsible for the poor performance of the nationalised railway company. Yet within the European railway industry, it is widely acknowledged that BR operated one of the most efficient railway networks in Europe, in view of the level of staffing and government subsidy provided per passenger kilometre travelled, highlighting the effect of politics and policy.

The tourist rail experience post-privatisation

One of the leading innovators under nationalisation was InterCity and the CEO, Chris Green (see Vincent and Green 1994), helped to turn the operation into a customer-focused enterprise based on three key principles which recognised a hierarchy of needs that can be developed a stage further under privatisation. Under privatisation, competing rail franchises on long-haul routes (e.g. the East Coast franchise and Virgin Trains West Coast mainline franchise) took on these principles, to ensure that all customers, rather than only premium customers (e.g. business travellers) enjoyed a high-quality experience. InterCity had refined a trail-to-train model (Figure 3.4) using market research and a consumer focus. Competition has seen the introduction of value adding and more attention to detail, with a wide range of leisure travel.

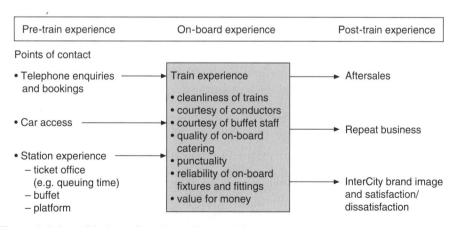

Figure 3.4 InterCity's 'trail to the train' model
Source: Based on Vincent and Green 1994.

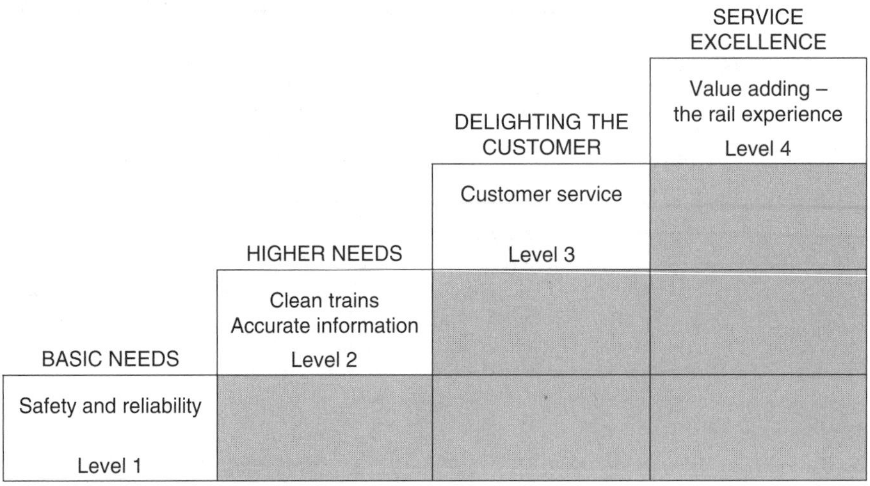

		DELIGHTING THE CUSTOMER	SERVICE EXCELLENCE
			Value adding – the rail experience Level 4
	HIGHER NEEDS	Customer service Level 3	
BASIC NEEDS	Clean trains Accurate information Level 2		
Safety and reliability Level 1			

Figure 3.5 Model for customer service

Source: Developed and expanded from Vincent and Green (1994); author; GNER in-house rail brochures.

Prior to privatisation, InterCity had been able to reach Levels 1–3 in terms of service delivery (Figure 3.5), but post-privatisation it is apparent that innovations in service delivery assisted with reaching Level 4 in models of rail service delivery with improvement on the principles in Levels 1–3. Under privatisation, developments at each stage of that model occurred, including the pre-train experience:

● e-travel options (i.e. booking via the Internet or via Trainline.com);
● National Rail Inquiry call centre;
● more approachable staff to help at stations for long-distance services;
● clearer branding of the rail product offered by each franchise.

The on-board rail experience offered:

● a redesigned team approach on long-distance services to remove hierarchical management and demarcation of duties;
● greater information during service interruptions to keep passengers informed and to maintain satisfaction levels;
● the introduction of packages to offer more on-board value in restaurant and buffet cars;
● investment in new and refurbished trains;
● more interaction with passengers to generate repeat business.

The post-train experience included:

● increased attention to customer ratings, with a quarterly National Rail Survey;
● monitoring of customer services;
● expansion of services to meet service demands.

The impact of privatisation and some of these changes (Figure 3.6) coincided in the UK with what some commentators such as Shaw et al. (2003) called a renaissance in rail travel, as the economy revived up until late 2007. For example, by 2008 there were around 3 million journeys a day on the UK rail network, resulting

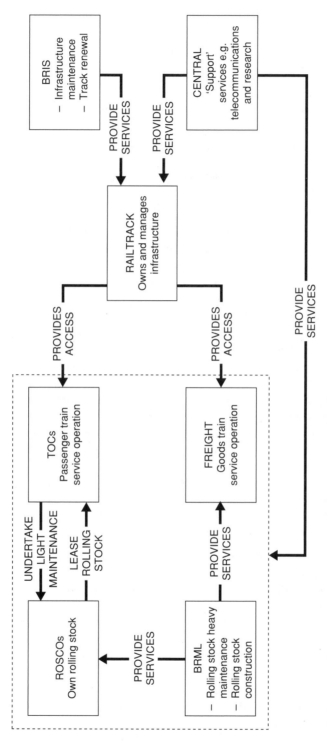

Figure 3.6 Interactions in the newly privatised railway industry in the UK post-privatisation

Source: Adapted from Charlton et al. 1997.

Table 3.9 Passenger journeys on selected long-distance UK rail operators with a recreational and tourist market, 1996/7–2006/7

Franchise	1996/7	1997/8	1998/9	1999/2000	2000/1	2001/2	2002/3	2006/7
				(Million passenger journeys)				
Virgin Cross Country	12.0	12.5	13.8	14.5	13.7	14.9	17.8	23.4
First Great Western	15.0	16.4	16.9	18.0	18.6	19.2	20.2	76.3*
Gatwick Express	3.7	3.7	4.5	4.4	4.7	4.3	4.2	5.1
GNER	11.9	13.7	13.9	15.9	13.6	14.5	14.6	17.6
Virgin West Coast Trains	13.2	14.9	15.9	16.6	15.3	16.4	15.2	19.8

*The massive increase in the First Great Western ridership figures are due to the company acquiring several other franchises

Source: Developed from the Strategic Rail Authority; Office of the Rail Regulator

in over 49 billion passenger kms travelled a year, a 43 per cent growth 1998–2008. As Table 3.9 shows, on the more defined tourist and leisure long-distance services, demand has risen sharply in many cases, despite some fluctuations. Increased competitive pricing using APEX tickets, internet booking and phone sales have also helped to nurture leisure markets, especially the golden market (over 60-year-olds) with Leisure First Class tickets and discount cards. The use of customer charters has also provided a clearer link between customer expectations and performance, refining the concept introduced by British Rail in 1992 (see Page 1994a, 1999 for more detail). In fact JetBlue (*www.jetblue.com*) has launched a Bill of Rights for customers setting out how they will treat customers when things go wrong and what type of compensation they offer. Whilst this is now standardised in the EU, there remains a grey area with airlines citing operational difficulties or other potential problems where they do not have to provide statutory compensation under Article 17 of Regulation [EC]261/2004 establishing common rules on compensation and assistance to passengers in the event of denied boarding and of cancellation or long delay of flights (see EU.com for more detail).

What the experience of privatisation shows is that many of the business principles that characterised the InterCity culture by 1994 in UK rail travel have been implemented and expanded upon post-privatisation, including the following points which hold true a decade after the demise of InterCity:

● High-speed passenger rail businesses must be market led and customer driven.
● Operations and production are clearly vital to the efficient and safe running of a railway, but they must be subordinate to the customer and the market if they are to survive.
● Customers' needs have to be thoroughly understood and acted upon by all staff.
● Good customer service is a key concern for all those who work for InterCity (and post-privatisation with the new TOCs – see Table 3.10 for a list of TOCs).
● Consistent standards of customer service are essential to a national brand under pressure from competition.
● Giving customers added value is paramount for repeat business (Vincent and Green 1994: 117).

The service encounter begins at the point when the ticket is purchased and includes the time spent waiting at the station through to the completion of the journey. The experience on board the train is also deemed to be one of the most memorable

Table 3.10 Train operating companies in the UK

Arriva
C2C
Chiltern Railways
Cross Country
East Midland Trains
First Great Western
Gatwick Express
Heathrow Express
Hull Trains
Island Line
London Midland
Merseyrail
National Express
Northern Rail
One
Stansted Express
ScotRail
Southeastern
SouthWest Trains
Southern
First Capital Connect
Transpennine Express
Virgin Trains

NB. This will inevitably change as franchises are changed – an updated list of franchises and TOCs can be found on the website of the Office of the Rail Regulator (*www.rail-reg.gov.uk*) together with operational data for each company.

aspects of the journey and an integral part of the service encounter (Prideaux 1990). Shilton (1982) suggests that while it is difficult to quantify the quality aspects of travel, additional advertising accounted for half of the increased patronage of the long-distance travel market in the early 1980s, and this has been repeated under privatisation with the use of e-products.

The following points summarise the key findings of the discussion of rail privatisation in relation to tourist transport:

● Marketing research has become an important part of the strategic planning process for a tourist transport service, particularly when attempting to assess what tourist and non-tourist travellers require from a rail journey. This has a critical role in establishing a benchmark for service quality to ensure minimum standards of provision are met with value adding now a key feature of competition with other TOCs and low-cost airlines.

● Government has adopted a long-term policy favouring privatisation under the guise of improving consumer choice and service quality, citing the transformation in former state-owned enterprises that have been privatised and are more customer led. Yet as Charlton et al. (1997) indicate, turning policy into reality has been problematic due to internal contradictions associated with the logic of inducing effective competition in rail travel. It has also led to most franchises remaining unprofitable, a current concern in government, as failure is rewarded with more subsidies.

● In the 1970s and 1980s tourist use of railways in the UK declined but there is potential for increasing the number of journeys involving air and rail for distances of 500–1000 km with the Channel Tunnel, although low-cost airlines have filled some of this niche.

- The introduction of the passenger charter is a direct consequence of government policy towards public service provision and has led to a greater emphasis on service quality in the tourist transport system. However, most refunds are only rail vouchers for more rail travel – not cash rebates.
- For international tourists visiting the UK the changes since privatisation are complex, confusing and not visitor friendly; many cannot take advantage of APEX tickets (nor can premium-priced travellers), and they may view rail as expensive.
- The long-term implications for rail service provision outside of the main conurbations are less clear. The integrity of the existing network is in question as many of the TOCs operate under a subsidised regime and a series of privately owned monopolies have replaced BR's monopoly. However, it is worth considering Whitelegg's (1998: 21) comment on the London Underground, which received no government subsidy operating grant and is now the subject of a PPP. It is an indication of what can happen if a private sector ideology dominates public transport as 'two and a half million journeys are made . . . every day [now 3 million] . . . Travelling on it is also a very unpleasant experience . . . A poor-quality public transport system sends out strong signals to those seeking work, tourists and inward investors. They are less likely to choose London as a destination if their experience of moving around is one of delay, overcrowding, inconvenience and misery.'
- Government policy can radically affect the way in which transport services are delivered to tourists and non-tourists, as well as ensuring that a simplistic or complex operational structure exists.
- The degree of privatisation and the model chosen in transport policy determine the style of competition and likely benefits that will result for consumers. Yet with many franchises protected from competition and receiving subsidies it is far from competitive on the local services and away from lucrative long-distance trunk routes.
- Speakman (1996: 47) argues that 'the process of rail privatisation is . . . a serious threat to UK tourism. The recent controversy about the proposed withdrawal of the West Highland Sleeper Service focuses on the degree to which rail travel is still . . . a vital part of the region's tourism product'. The privatisation process may also mean a loss of discounted travel and accommodation arrangements for tour operators. This is serious for rail companies since Speakman (1996) estimated that 40 per cent of rail travel is leisure based, which is probably still the case nearly a decade later. In Scotland since 2004 the Plus Bus Initiative (bus–train ticket) has assisted in greater rail–bus integration but its marketing and promotion has been low-key.

Policy measures to improve the trade in tourism and transport: GATS

One of the principal problems which continue to affect the development of a global transport and tourism sector is the existence of obstacles to free trade. Trade liberalisation has been identified as one policy direction which exists to enable destinations and destinations to engage more fully in the global tourism economy. Trade liberalisation in tourism services has become part of the multilateral trade agenda as part of the General Agreement on Trade in Services (GATS) where tourism and travel-related services (hotels and restaurants; travel agencies and tour operator services; tour guide services and other services) represents the first multilateral agreement to have an impact upon the sector.

The issue of GATS is complex but its ultimate purpose is to liberalise trade in services by the elimination of trade barriers, enhancing trade between countries, especially developing countries. It sets out to liberalise services by a three-tiered approach to liberalisation: through general provisions relating to all members; setting rules for specific industry sectors such as tourism and through national schedules of commitments on market access. In tourism, the market access focus is particularly important because it focuses on the global nature of tourism as a form of trade, covering four dimensions of tourism supply: cross-border trade; consumption abroad; commercial presence (which covers all forms of foreign direct investment); natural persons (people travelling internationally to provide services). GATS seeks to address policy constraints on tourism in many countries including foreign ownership limits, airline access rights and those associated with anticompetitive behaviour (Lee et al. 2002). Suitable policy mechanisms in many developed countries include legislation and bodies which routinely review some of these issues including the impact of major acquisitions and mergers on industry sectors such as tourism to avoid anticompetitive behaviour (e.g. the US antitrust legislation and the EU Competition Commission and similar institutions in many member countries). Running alongside the GATS negotiations in tourism, members of ASEAN (the Asian Economic Cooperation Organisation) pursued a phased introduction of liberalisation measures in 2008 for a single aviation market (initially in air freight) and a phased implementation to all passenger services by 2015 similar to the experiences of the EU discussed earlier in the chapter.

Summary

It is evident from the analysis of government policy towards tourist transport that it is often subsumed under the wider remit of national transport policy-making, rather than being seen within an integrated planning context where the relationship between transport and tourism is recognised, a feature which the OECD has highlighted for greater government action. Different political ideologies affect the continuity in investment decisions for transport planning and development, and this often leaves future governments with a legacy in view of the timescale involved in major tourist transport infrastructure projects coming to fruition. This is certainly the case with rail travel following privatisation and the election of a Labour government with a greater concern for public transport to supplant the insatiable appetite for car use in the UK, but despite an impressive growth in tourist and leisure use the car remains dominant. The influence that governments exercise on tourist transport systems to regulate the efficient movement of people cannot be viewed in a vacuum: it is not isolated from the operation, management, provision and consumption of tourist transport services. Some governments have concerns over striking a balance between healthy competition and actions described as predatory pricing (Morrison 2004). The example of the tourist rail travel system in the UK has used controlled competition (Shaw and Williams 2004), which has not led to most franchises operating profitably as some policy analysts suggest. This objective was naïve to say the least, as Page (2003) shows that most EU countries have a substantial rail industry, though EU policy has made these subsidies more transparent. In the UK state re-intervention with the creation of Network Rail to improve infrastructure highlighted the fallacy of private sector solutions where state neglect created an impossible backlog of maintenance and repair work.

Clearly, the situation in any tourist transport system is both dynamic and in a constant state of flux as government policy, the business environment and the requirements of the consumer are forever changing, as the post-privatisation situation in the UK shows. For the innovative transport provider, staying abreast of these developments is a major challenge, although day-to-day operational and management issues assume great importance in an economic activity where the logistics of moving large numbers of people from origin to destination areas for business and pleasure require much skill and organisation. Not surprisingly, the formulation and implementation of government transport policy is often viewed as a long-term issue for any tourist transport operator as their concern for the efficient management and operation of profitable services consumes the time of their operations staff. It is the corporate strategists and planners who have a long-term view of their future position in the marketplace and the means of achieving strategic planning objectives. Even so, where governments pursue private sector solutions based on tendering and short-term franchises, long-term planning and policy issues are replaced by an overriding concern for the bottom line – profitability and retaining the contract – though in the UK extra subsidies have partly addressed this issue. This runs contrary to wider strategic goals such as those espoused by the Wales Tourist Board (1992) which argues that:

> the provision of the basic tourism infrastructure upon which the industry depends . . . covers [the] fields of roads, public transport, information provision and visitor facilities. Accessibility from the principal visitor markets is crucial in determining the number of visitors . . . The quality of . . . facilities [and infrastructure] will undoubtedly influence the visitor's perception of Wales.

Such issues are of less concern for a fragmented and diverse transport sector that often fails to recognise the vital contribution tourism and recreational traffic makes to its business. Even so, an understanding of consumer demand for tourist travel services is a fundamental requirement for tourist transport operators wishing to plan their supply of services in the short to medium term. For this reason, the next chapter examines the demand for tourist transport services and some of the data sources available to assess this issue.

Questions

1 How do governments ensure that transport policies are formulated to accommodate the tourist and leisure traveller?

2 Is the privatisation process now affecting many components of tourist transport services at a global scale?

3 How will the rail privatisation process affect the travel experience for tourists and leisure travellers?

4 Why do governments of less developed countries still retain state ownership of tourist transport services?

Further reading

Competition Commission (2008) *BAA Airport Markets Investigation*, London: Competition Commission. (*www.competition-commission.org.uk*).

Department of Transport (1994) *Britain's Railways: A New Era*, London: Department of Transport.

Enoch, M. (2003) 'Transport Practice and Policy in Mauritius', *Journal of Transport Geography*, 11(4): 291–306.

Findlay, C., Sieh, L. and Singh, K. (eds) (1997) *Asia Pacific Air Transport*, Singapore: Institute of South East Asian Studies (http://www.Iseas.edu.sg/pub.html).

Gibb, R., Lowndes, T. and Charlton, C. (1996) 'The privatisation of British Rail', *Applied Geography* 16(1): 35–51.

Gibb, R., Shaw, J. and Charlton, C. (1998) 'Competition, regulation and the privatisation of British Rail', *Environment and Planning C: Government and Policy*, 16(6): 757–68. This contains a wealth of detail on each aspect of the newly privatised railway system. It also sets out the TOCs' plans for each franchise it operates.

Hall, C.M. and Jenkins, J. (1995) *Tourism and Public Policy*, London: Routledge.

Knight, S. and Johnston, H. (1998) *The Comprehensive Guide to Britain's Railways*, Peterborough: EMAP.

Lee, M., Fayed, M. and Fletcher, J. (2002) 'GATS and tourism', *Tourism Analysis*, 7(2): 125–37.

Morrison, W. (2004) 'Dimensions of predatory pricing in air travel markets', *Journal of Air Transport Management*, 10: 87–95.

Good overviews of privatisation also exist in:

Murray, A. (2001) *Off the Rails: Britain's Great Railway Crisis: Cause, Consequences and Cure*, London: Verso.

Shaw, J. (2000) *Competition, Regulation and the Privatisation of British Rail*, Aldershot: Ashgate

Vincent, M. and Green, C. (eds) (1994) *The InterCity Story*, Somerset: Oxford Publishing Company.

Wheatcroft, S. (1994) *Aviation and Tourism Policies*, London: Routledge/World Tourism Organization.

Wolmar, C. (2001) *Broken Rails: How Privatisation Wrecked Britain's Railways*, London: Aurum Press.

See also the special issue of the *Journal of Air Transport Management*, 3(4) (1997) on aviation deregulation in Europe.

On the geographical effects of deregulation, see:

Burghouwt, G. and Hakfoort, J. (2002) 'The geography of deregulation in the European aviation market', *Tijdschrift voor Economische en Sociale Geografie*, 93(1): 100–106.

On the economics of rail pricing for access to infrastructure, see:

Nash, C., Coulthard, S. and Matthews, B. (2004). 'Rail track charges in Great Britain: The issue of charging for capacity', *Transport Policy*, 11(4): 315–27.

The analysis, use and provision of tourist transport

4

Analysing the demand for tourist travel

Introduction

Leisure travel has become a key feature of the leisure society that now characterises many developed countries and is also beginning to affect developing countries as their middle classes develop the travel bug. In a more theoretical context, Urry (2001) described the mobility issues that underpin tourism, and what he called 'transports of delight', as an element of leisure-related travel. One corollary of this is that tourist travel has become a global activity and it is assuming a much greater role in the leisure habits of developed societies now that holidays and overseas travel have become much more accessible to all sections of the population. Conversely, large sections of society in developing countries do not have such access, since their daily lives revolve around meeting their everyday needs such as food, shelter, health, water and employment. Even though this situation is changing for some segments of the population in newly industrialising nations, it is not the norm. Yet in many western nations, tourist travel has been accompanied by the time–space compression discussed in Chapter 1, where perceived access to places on a global scale now seems much easier.

This growth in travel also poses many challenges for the transport industry since understanding the demand for tourist transport is a critical part of the strategic planning process for transport operators and organisations associated with the management and marketing of transport services for tourists. At government level, accurate information on the use of tourist transport infrastructure is critical when formulating transport policies and particularly in assessing the future demand by mode(s) of transport. At the level of individual transport operators, it is necessary to have a clear understanding of the existing and likely patterns of demand for tourist transport, to ensure that they are able to meet the requirements of tourists, particularly the peak demand. This means that for transport providers high-quality market intelligence and statistical information are vital in the strategic planning process and day-to-day management of transport, so that the services offered are responsive and carefully targeted at demand, cost effective and efficient. Ultimately, most transport companies seek to operate services on a commercial basis so that supply matches demand as closely as possible, but there are also situations in which such services are subsidised to meet social objectives not related to tourism. In such situations, tourism is really an added bonus for subsidised services such as rail, bus or air services to more remote and peripheral regions with a highly seasonal tourism industry. For example, in El Salvador, public transport costs are set at around US$0.25 to give wide access to transport and tourist use is clearly not an intended use, being primarily designed for the domestic population.

The types of information required by decision-makers associated with tourist transport provision are usually gathered through the marketing research process (see Chapter 2) and are likely to include the following:

- the demographic and socioeconomic characteristics of tourist travel demand (e.g. age, sex, family status, social class, income and expenditure);
- the geographical origin and spatial distribution of demand in the generating region;
- the geographical preferences, consumer behaviour and images of tourists for holiday destinations and tourist travel habits, including the duration of visit;
- when it is likely to occur (e.g. temporal and seasonal distributions of use);
- who is likely to organise the holiday (e.g. independently or as part of a package);
- the choice of transport likely to be used in the tourist transport system;
- future patterns of demand (e.g. short- and long-term forecasts of tourist travel);
- government policy towards tourist transport operations;
- the implications of tourist travel demand for infrastructure provision and investment in tourist modes of transport (e.g. aircraft, airports, passenger liners, ferries and ports).

The purpose of this chapter is to examine a range of the main types of data sources available to assess the demand for tourist transport at different spatial scales, from the world scale down to individual countries. International and domestic sources of data are introduced for transport and tourism, with the emphasis on the relative merits and weaknesses of each source. As most tourism textbooks tend to focus on definitions of tourism, tourists and ways of measuring tourism *per se*, rather than on the implications of tourism statistics for assessing the demand for tourist transport, the discussion here is more focused on transporting the tourist. Building on the issues surrounding data sources, Insight 4.1 examines low-cost airlines. Another Insight examines how to integrate different data sources in relation to research on one specific problem in tourist transport – road safety and road traffic accidents (RTAs) to show how data sources need to be linked together to analyse an issue. The implications for managing the demand for international and tourist transport systems are also emphasised. Lastly, the role of forecasting the demand for tourist transport is discussed in relation to the assessment of future growth scenarios for tourist travel. This is important because it enables travel organisations (e.g. tour operators) and transport providers to plan ahead to remain competitive and anticipate tourist travel requirements.

The international demand for tourist travel: understanding why people travel

Ryan (1991) discusses the economic determinants of tourism demand that are associated with the purchase of an intangible service, usually a holiday or transport service, which comprises an experience for the tourist (see Chapter 2). The consumption of tourist transport services as part of a package holiday, or as a separate service to meet a specific need (e.g. a business trip or a visit to see friends and relatives), has manifested itself on a global scale in terms of the worldwide growth in international tourist travel. Amongst the economic determinants of the growth in international tourism are rising disposable incomes and increased holiday entitlement in developed countries. Transport operators have stimulated demand by more competitive pricing of air travel and other forms of travel for international tourists. This has been accompanied by the 'internationalisation' and 'globalisation' of tourism as a business activity (see Witt et al. 1991; Meethan 2004), as global tourism operators emerge through mergers, takeovers, strategic alliances (e.g. airlines cooperating and code sharing on routes), investment in overseas destinations and diversification into other tourism services. One consequence is that tourist transport operators view the determinants of tourist travel as crucial to their short- and long-term plans for service provision. Whilst internationalisation was primarily about international links and operations, globalisation is a more embracing notion, which involves a different form of organisation and cuts across conventional concepts like the nation-state. Globalisation has had a profound effect on transport and tourism because it has aided the interconnectivity of places physically and remotely using new information communication technologies.

Aside from the economic determinants of the demand for travel, Ryan (1991) emphasises the significance of psychological determinants of demand in explaining some of the reasons why tourists travel. Although there is no theory of tourist travel, a range of tourist motivators exists (Pearce 1992; Ross 1994). Ryan's (1991: 25–9) analysis of tourist travel motivators (excluding business travel) identifies reasons commonly cited to explain why people travel to tourist destinations for holidays. These include:

- a desire to escape from a mundane environment;
- the pursuit of relaxation and recuperation functions;
- an opportunity for play;
- the strengthening of family bonds;
- prestige, since different destinations can enable one to gain social enhancement amongst peers;
- social interaction;
- educational opportunities;
- wish fulfilment;
- shopping.

Although it is possible to identify a range of motivators, it is also possible to classify tourists according to the type of holiday they are seeking and the travel experience they desire. For example, Cohen (1972) distinguished between four types of tourist travellers:

- *the organised mass tourist* on a package holiday; they are highly organised and their contact with the host community in a destination is minimal;
- *the individual mass tourist*, who uses similar facilities to the organised mass tourist but also desires to visit other sights not covered on organised tours in the destination;
- *the explorers*, who arrange their travel independently and who wish to experience the social and cultural lifestyle of the destination;
- *the drifter*, who does not seek any contact with other tourists or their accommodation, seeking to live with the host community (see Smith 1992).

Clearly such a classification is fraught with problems, since it does not take into account the increasing diversity of holidays undertaken and inconsistencies in tourist behaviour (Pearce 1982). Other researchers suggest that one way of overcoming this difficulty is to consider the different destinations tourists choose to visit, and then establish a sliding scale similar to Cohen's (1972) typology, but which does not have such an absolute classification. P. Pearce (1992) produces a convincing argument that highlights the importance of considering the tourist's destination choice. By establishing a blueprint for tourist motivation, Pearce (1992: 113) argues that:

> Tourism demand should not be equated with tourism motivation. Tourism demand is the outcome of tourists' motivation as well as marketing, destination features and contingency factors such as money, health and time relating to the travellers' choice behaviour . . . Tourism demand can be expressed as the sum of realistic behavioural intentions to visit a specific location . . . [which is] reduced to existing travel statistics and forecasts of future traveller numbers. Tourist motivation is then a part rather than the equivalent of tourism demand.

In other words, transport providers need to recognise the traveller's choice, behaviour and travel intentions at destinations to understand fully the wider transport requirements beyond simple aggregate patterns of travel statistics.

●●●● Motivation, tourist transport research and psychological issues

Motivation has been described as one of the principal explanations of why people travel and, in its purest sense, motivation is the driving force behind human actions. According to Prentice (2005: 262) 'motivation is about the causes of personal action in tourism and other activities'. It is therefore the starting point for studying tourist behaviour and beyond that for understanding systems of tourism including the use of transport modes and their meaning (Moscardo and Pearce 2004: 29), although such approaches to transport research diverge from the existing and large literature on travel behaviour that is predominantly based on economic appraisals of travel. Consequently, according to Moscardo and Pearce (2004: 30) the literature on tourist transport is significantly different from the prevailing economic analysis of behaviour since:

- it focuses on the traveller and different markets to examine the different travel choices made in relation to leisure and tourism;
- it considers traveller choices and mode of travel, which may be multi-modal during any tourist trip and have a great deal less predictability than commuter travel behaviour in time, space and modal use;
- the literature is very dispersed and lacks any real clear conceptual framework, or theoretical framework, as discussed in Chapters 1 and 2.

Moscardo and Pearce (2004) identify the relevant literature on this area of motivation and the psychology of mode of tourist travel in relation to a number of areas of research including visitor satisfaction (Noe 1999) and benchmarking of service provision (Kandampully et al. 2001), along with more qualitative approaches to route mapping by visitors (Oliver 2001). In addition, trip planning, route choice and the activities of specific market segments such as the senior market (Black and Rutledge 1995; Black and Clark 1998) have attracted, attention. The social psychology of travel is clearly a complex area, as Van Middlekoop et al.'s (2003) analysis of tourist choice of travel mode amongst Dutch travellers suggests: life-cycle factors and use of the car for domestic trips is important but number of children and use of accommodation affect modal choice. An interesting study by Wansink and Ittersum (2004), which examined the stopping decisions of travellers, highlighted the importance of tourist behaviour based on need recognition and desire to consume a service en route and the information search travellers go through in selecting stopping points during land-based travel that inevitably involves an evaluation and choice function. This provides a clear justification for the research by Moscardo and Pearce (2004), which identified the significance of life-cycle factors and the need for psychographic studies to understand the motives behind travel as well as their behaviour during the travel process, which really underpins modal choice and travel behaviour research.

Figure 4.1 is a very helpful framework which examines the tourist–transport interface from a motivation perspective that reinforces many of the arguments

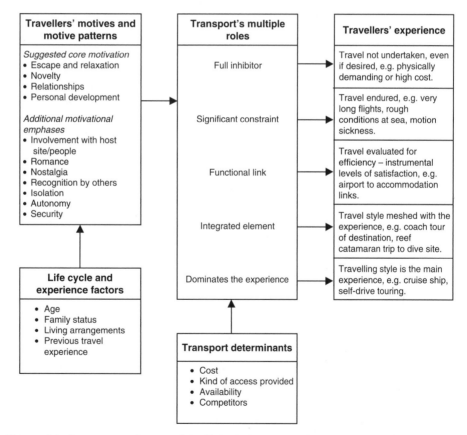

Figure 4.1 A conceptual map of the links between motivation, life cycle, transport roles and the travellers experience

Source: Reprinted from *Tourism and Transport*, p. 32, L. Lumsdon and S.J. Page (eds) (2004), Copyright © 2004, with permission from Elsevier.

presented in Chapter 1 – that a continuum exists ranging from no travel in some cases to transport and tourism through transport for tourism. The figure emphasises the significance of life-cycle factors and group motivation into core and additional emphases, developing a classification of the multiple roles of transport, where different experiences result. These are a complex series of interactions where the style of travel is shaped by numerous motivational factors, and even with a mode of travel such as car-based transport Figure 4.1 illustrates that different factors motivate the self-drive market versus the non-self-drive market amongst car-borne travellers in Northern Queensland.

The implication of such research on motivation and demand is that governments and transport operators need to recognise what economic, social and psychological factors are stimulating tourist travel. All too often the social and psychological perspectives have been overlooked in economic analyses of travel. But as Prentice (2005: 276) argues, 'No single paradigm or model is likely to explain all tourism behaviour. No single typology is likely to have more than specific relevance'. This may help in establishing the different types of travellers and their preferences for various destinations and specific activity patterns on holiday. Tour operators selling holidays need to recognise the complexity of tourist motivation to travel and airlines need to understand the precise effect on the availability of aircraft. In particular, they must be able to rotate and interchange different aircraft in a fleet to meet daily and seasonal travel requirements through complex logistical exercises. For airports, the expected number of passengers, use of airspace and runways need to be planned in advance (see Chapter 7) and they need to take account of where there is going to be a long-term growth in demand. As Prentice (2005: 268) suggests, 'tourism is in fact both multi-motivational and made up of multiple groups of tourists, many of whom are experienced as tourists and versatile in their use of tourism'. This also means that infrastructures such as airports have to consider future investment and development plans. More specifically, transport operators will need to understand the range of motives and expectations of certain types of traveller since the level of service they provide will need to match the market and the requirements of travellers. Operators need to understand not only the dimensions of demand, but the market segments and the behaviour and expectations of consumers that they will need to accommodate in providing a high-quality tourist experience (see Plate 4.1).

Throughout much of the chapter the emphasis is on establishing patterns of tourism demand. In addition we need to remember that 'A conceptual rethink is also required if tourism is no longer an exceptional part of people's lives' (Prentice 2004: 268) as the boundaries between work, leisure and tourism are blurring in many western societies. Leisure, like tourism, has its own transport requirements, some of which overlap with tourism and we should not forget the significance of domestic tourism, which Pearce (1995a) argues is 10 times greater than international tourism in numerical terms. However, all too often data sources on domestic tourism are poorly documented and irregular in terms of survey timing. Therefore, prior to discussing international tourism, one example of domestic tourism in China is used to illustrate the type of patterns of tourist activity that developed in spite of a limited transport system.

Plate 4.1 A former London Transport routemaster (now operated by FirstBus) at Trafalgar Square, London. Tourists make extensive use of the 1960s buses as they are icons of the London tourist transport product, but they are being phased out by Transport for London

Source: S.J. Page

● ● ● ● Domestic tourism patterns in China: development amid infrastructure constraints

There is a growing research literature on tourism in China (e.g. Lew and Yu 1995; C.M. Hall 1997; Ryan and Huimin 2009) and a wide range of articles have been published in academic journals, particularly those with an Asia-Pacific focus (e.g. *Asia-Pacific Journal of Tourism Research*), and increasingly in mainstream tourism journals. Much of the interest in China has been focused on its post-1979 opening up to international tourism and the effect on the demand and supply for tourism infrastructure (e.g. transport). As reviews of tourism research in China show (e.g. C.M. Hall 1997; Hall and Page 2000; Ryan and Huimin 2009), much of the effort has been expended on the urban and coastal areas, where rapid tourism development has occurred, and on the implications for the management of ancient heritage sites. Only recently has a new genre of studies emerged that begins to deal with more diverse aspects of tourism such as rural tourism (e.g. Getz and Page 1997) and domestic tourism (Zhang 1997) as well as the infrastructure requirements to support such growth. With a land area of 9326 km^2, connecting the settlements and regions has placed major demands on infrastructure investment. In 1989–2001, the state spent US$761 billion on infrastructure projects (including transport-related schemes) and in 2006–10 alone, US$200 billion was so spent on railway investment to expand the network to 70,000 kms (including a rail route into Tibet, see Su and Wall, 2009) as well as US$30 billion on the flagship Beijing to Shanghai high-speed rail link. In 2006–10, there are also plans to expand countryside roads by 300,000 km, which illustrates the sheer scale of development being undertaken.

In terms of the growth of domestic tourism in China and the history of travel, reviews (Sofield and Li 1997) highlight the significance of ideological traits in shaping tourism in post-revolutionary China. China is without doubt the largest domestic tourism market numerically. Prior to the 1970s the large proportion of domestic travel was business oriented, VFR or health related (i.e. to visit a spa). Zhang (1997: 565) highlights the problem of documenting the volume, patterns and activities of domestic tourism prior to 1970 since 'there are no statistics on tourism during this period'. Low living standards and shortages of accommodation and transport acted as constraints to domestic travel. Economic reform in China stimulated the growth of inbound tourism to help raise much-needed foreign revenue and yet, as Zhang (1997: 566) argues:

> not much attention was given to the development of domestic tourism [for the Chinese]. The improvement of facilities and supplies appropriate for domestic tourists was ignored. As the lack of adequate passenger transportation was the 'bottleneck' in the development of the national economy, demands were far from satisfied, consequently curbing the growth of domestic tourism.

One of the principal drivers of domestic tourism demand in China in the late 1980s was rising living standards, which saw the national average per capita income rise by 3.44 times that of 1979 to RMB1189 (RMB = renminbi yuan). However, in the coastal areas and large cities, rates of income were higher (e.g. Shanghai RMB4501; Beijing RMB3035). By 2007, this had increased to RMB10,493 for urban dwellers and RMB3255 for rural dwellers illustrating the massive growth in income. In fact among the top 10 per cent of income earners, there were average per capita earnings of RMB97,000 which is 55 times that of the lowest paid, illustrating the rise of the nouveaux riche in China. Airbus (2007) couched this in terms of the rise in Asia of first-generation fliers who will spend their disposable income on travel. Using statistics from China's National Tourism Administration, Zhang (1997) documents the post-1985 growth in arrivals and receipts from domestic tourism. As Figure 4.2 shows, the 1990s experienced a significant growth in arrivals that was

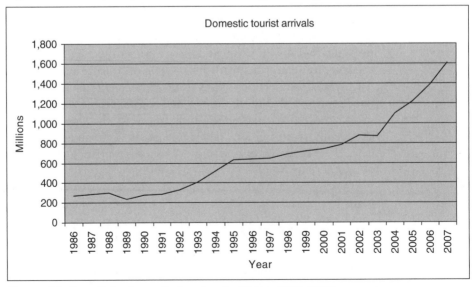

Figure 4.2 Growth in domestic tourism in China, 1986–2007

Source: Data from China National Tourism Administration.

repeated into the new millennium, with a drop in 2003 due to SARS and then a sharp rise thereafter.

Zhang (1997) explains this growth in terms of both the spillover effects of developing international tourism and expanding the opportunities for growth. In addition, the private sector began to recognise the market opportunities for domestic tourism as government policies progressively moved to the simultaneous promotion of international and domestic tourism. This was also facilitated by economic growth that enabled greater investment in domestic tourism infrastructure. The development of a socialist market economy system after 1992 has generated economic growth of 9 per cent in China's GNP (Gross National Product) per annum which has only slipped just below this rate due to a global slowdown (compared to 3–4 per cent for the world economy in 2008). Patterns of consumption by China's population have risen in parallel with this and domestic tourism has been a major beneficiary. For example, between 1990 and 1995 domestic arrivals grew by 17.62 per cent whilst average receipts increased by nearly 52 per cent. Domestic tourism arrivals reached 640 million in 1996, an increase of 2.286 times the arrivals in 1990. Between 1996 and 2007, the average domestic tourism expenditure rose from US$37.5 per capita to US$70.64 in 2007, which is indicative of this massive expansion in consumer spending on tourism services. As shown in Chapter 1, a buoyant economy has continued to fuel a growth in demand for domestic travel.

To explain such a growth in domestic travel, one needs to examine a greater co-ordinated level of development amongst the constituent parts of the tourism industry (especially in transport). For example, by 1995 China had 1.39 million km of road and in 2004 this had grown to 1.6 million km of road, largely concentrated in urban areas. This has been accompanied by a growth in car ownership. Other major infrastructure projects such as the Beijing–Jiujiang–Jiulong and Nanning–Kumming railway projects plus other infrastructure projects such as the Beijing–Shijiazhuang and Shanghai–Hangzhou expressway projects have assisted in intercity tourist travel. The following comparisons illustrate the effect of changes in demand for expanding infrastructure provision:

- In 1990, there were 437 civil aviation routes, 385 of which were domestic; in 2006 there were 1336 routes, of which 1068 were domestic.
- In 1990, China had 94 airports; by 2006 there were 142 airports.
- In 1990, China had 503 civilian aircraft; in 2006 it had 1614 civilian aircraft.

Greater mobility resulting from the growth in other forms of urban transport has favoured domestic travel. Yet as Hilling (1996: 225) explains:

> the relatively flat terrain of a number of the larger cities (Beijing, Shanghai, Tianjin) undoubtedly favours cycling, as does the serious inadequacy of public transport in the face of rapidly rising demand and urban roads which cannot easily accommodate larger vehicles – in Beijing an estimated 12 per cent of the urban road network cannot take buses.

This is supported by Zhang (1997: 568), who argues that 'the transportation capacity is still not satisfactory, and the basic infrastructure needs further improvement'. Against these constraints, one also has to recognise that in the early 1990s the Chinese government began to introduce a national holiday system allowing employees 7–15 days' annual leave based on length of service. This combined with the gradual introduction of a five-day week to generate opportunities for long-distance domestic travel. However, in 2002, a quarter of all domestic travel occurred in the Golden Week holidays in February, May and October (King 2004) which has stimulated mass travel. This holiday is designed to encourage domestic tourism and the impact on domestic tourism (Figure 4.2) is evident as the volume of travel has grown 250 per cent between 1996 and 2008 and the style of travel has evolved from mass packaged travel to now include self-drive travel as car ownership has increased from 14.3 million private cars in 1996 to 182 million in 2006, mainly concentrated in the growing urban areas. This meant that many destinations had to introduce temporary parking areas to cater for the vast increase in demand. In 2008, the top destinations during Golden Week were Beijing and Hong Kong. In Golden Week, about 6 million domestic tourists visited Beijing, boosted by visits to see the Olympic venues, with one venue recording 500,000 visits in one day. In terms of domestic air travel, Golden Week saw domestic airlines carry 4.3 million passengers, a growth of almost 15 per cent on 2007. These volumes of demand are also apparent in other holiday periods, such as the 25-day Spring Festival in March 2007 when 100 million people travelled to venues by train. In terms of tourist travel in China, transport remains the dominant element of expenditure in growing consumer income in the main cities. If one also adds the use of transport at destinations for sightseeing, then transport accounts for a significant element of tourism expenditure. The 1990s can therefore be characterised as the decade in which domestic travel for pleasure began to develop, and recent experiences of Golden Week would infer that it continued after 2000. As Zhang (1997) explains, travel is associated with the acquisition of new knowledge and understanding in Chinese society, but he adds that most Chinese people are not affluent enough to travel extensively, a feature reiterated by several analysts examining China's economy and its ability to stimulate international travel (since GDP, Gross Domestic Product, is much lower per capita than the US$5000 disposable income deemed to be critical to stimulate outbound travel). However, the volume of travel has doubled from 16.6 million in 2002 to 40.9 million in 2007, though it is still a fraction of domestic travel and analysts expect outbound travel will continue to grow at over 20 per cent per annum as China is expected to be one of the top outbound markets by 2020.

This is confirmed in forecasts by the Boeing Commercial Airline Group (2003) and Airbus (2003, 2007) which show that these growth trends are not likely to abate until 2026. As Airbus (2003) indicated, China's domestic aviation market is expected to achieve average annual growth rates of 8.5 per cent to 2022, which will require huge increases in infrastructure and aircraft. Such growth rates highlight the importance of demand management (Taplin 1993) to accommodate the volumes involved. China's airport authorities continue to seek overseas capital to assist in the investment programme. The situation described by Ballantyne (1996: 20) still holds true for domestic air travel since 'China's airlines have become vibrant and yet the size of tourism demand in China is of a scale many people find hard to recognise and comprehend'. However, one further consideration in relation to transport and domestic tourism is the pressure posed by international tourism on the same resources. For example, China increased its importance as a destination, becoming the world's fourth most popular and fastest growing destination in 2007. China was also ranked fifth in terms of receipts, achieving 4.3 per cent of world tourism receipts. In addition, China remains the powerhouse of economic growth in Asia, having recorded an average of 9 per cent growth in GDP over the past 25 years, which affects travel, albeit domestic travel.

This raises a further debate: whether tourism demand can be stimulated by infrastructure development in developing countries, given the rising demand from an expanding economy. Hilling (1996) outlines two schools of thought which are pertinent here.

●●●● Infrastructure development in developing countries: experiences from Asia-Pacific

First, the supply-led school of thought has traditionally viewed demand as following the provision of infrastructure (White and Senior 1983). A more recent explanation and now widely used model in transport provision is that it should be a response to demand. Hilling (1996) explains that in supply-led models, development would occur where a latent demand existed. In the demand-led model now coming increasingly into vogue due to the enormous cost of transport infrastructure investment, such as in China, tourism use of infrastructure is seen as a new market to support the demand for infrastructure investment. But it is not the case that infrastructure is being provided in advance of demand. In China, a demand-led model probably characterises the situation affecting the domestic tourism market, with economic cost–benefit criteria assuming a higher priority in infrastructure development decisions, given the scarcity of resources to meet all transport needs. Other experiences from across the Asia-Pacific region also highlight the range of challenges which many countries face.

According to Chin (2005), the focus on China and India as two of the powerhouses of GDP growth in the ASEAN region obscures a wide range of experiences among the countries. There are three types of country according to Chin (2005): low income economies, middle income economies and high income economies, each of which have very different routes and experiences of transport and infrastructure development. Among the low income countries, such as Cambodia and Myanmar, dilapidated road networks and the provision has been supply-led with a limited element of privatisation. In the case of Indonesia, major growth in car ownership has also posed demand-management problems and radical solutions such as state-subsidised busway investment have been used to keep the urban areas moving. Similar issues of congestion affect the Philippines, particularly Manila where tourist use of the jeepney model of private sector transport provision is well known. Vietnam, in contrast, has around half of its roads in poor condition even though road is the main method of transport in an economy experiencing above average GDP growth and a rapidly expanding tourism economy (Page 2009). In medium-income economies such as Malaysia, the state has employed a more systematic approach to transport for tourism development, building projects into its National Development Plans with a very well developed urban public transport system to support the rapid increase in urbanisation. For example, the country has one of Asia's best expressway networks of roads and an airport policy based on hub and spoke operations (see Chapter 5 for more detail) anticipating demand with its major investment in Kuala Lumpur International Airport to create an Asian hub. In high income countries such as Singapore, the state has needed to adopt a major infrastructure investment programme to retain its economic advantages so that tourism growth can be accommodated through airport capacity and an integrated transport network to move high volumes of travellers.

For the remainder of this chapter the emphasis is on the dimensions of international tourism demand, due to its global significance. A focus on international tourism will illustrate the interrelationship between government policy and tourism demand as well as the implications for developing transport systems that both domestic and international travellers can use. However, the 'analysis [of international tourism] is complicated by the paucity of appropriate data' (Pearce 1987: 35). So, what sources of data are available to assess the demand and use of different modes of tourist transport?

Data sources on international tourist travel

The analysis of tourism, tourists and their propensity to travel and previous travel patterns is 'a complex process . . . involving not only the visitor and his movements but also the destination and host community' (Latham 1989: 55). Tourist transport providers will often have statistical information relating to their own organisation's services and tourist use. But how can a new entrant into the tourist transport business examine the feasibility of providing a transport service? What statistical information on tourist transport is available? How is it gathered? And who publishes it?

On a global scale, Hilling (1996: 1) acknowledges that:

> there are vast differences in the availability of transport, indeed there is a stark contrast between a relatively immobile Third World and the highly mobile advanced economies . . . much of the infrastructure is poorly maintained and in disrepair and is inadequate for present needs without the complication of growth of demand in the future.

The global discrepancies that exist in transport provision obviously have a major impact on the tourism-generating potential and patterns of demand which result. One of the best sources to document such trends is the *United Nations Statistical Yearbook*, which records much of the growth in car ownership worldwide. At a regional level, the United Nations Economic and Social Committee for Asia produced the *Statistical Abstract of Transport in Asia* (United Nations 2003), which documents trends in Asian transport 1990–2000 and the *Statistical Yearbook of Asia and the Pacific* (United Nations 2007) for all forms of transport with some domestic and international tourism statistics also recorded. An abstract of air transport and tourism data for selected Asian countries is shown in Table 4.1, which highlights many of the data problems of gaps in information and the problems of linking transport and tourism data together, although it does help to demonstrate underlying patterns of growth where data exists.

What does emerge from an examination of international data sources on transport is that the developed regions of North America, Europe and Oceania comprise 26 per cent of the earth's land area, have around 15 per cent of the population and contain 60 per cent of the world's commercial vehicles. Africa is notable for its underprovision and Japan is responsible for 64 and 67 per cent respectively of Asia's commercial and passenger vehicles. Whilst newly industrialised countries (NICs) such as Thailand, South Korea and Brazil have experienced increased mobility, the gap between developing and developed countries is certainly great and reflected in terms of patterns of international tourism demand, with India needing around US$320 billion of additional infrastructure investment by 2012 to maintain current

Table 4.1 Trends in air transport and tourism for major Asian countries, 1990–2004/5

Country	Civil aviation passengers (000s)	Domestic air (million pax km)	Total pax by air (million pax km)	International tourist arrivals (000s)	International tourist departures (000s)
Brunei					
1990	307	–	487	377	–
1995	916	–	2,403	498	–
1996	857	–	2,712	–	–
1997	1,088	–	2,906	–	–
1998	877	–	2,972	–	–
1999	808	–	2,563	–	–
2000	864	–	3,001	984	–
2002	–	–	3,715	–	–
2004	–	–	–	–	–
China					
1990	16,596	17,879	23,048	10,484	–
1995	47,565	50,304	64,204	20,034	4,520
1996	51,770	54,477	70,605	22,765	5,061
1997	52,277	57,183	72,964	23,770	5,324
1998	53,481	58,642	75,823	25,073	8,426
1999	55,853	60,698	85,730	27,047	9,232
2000	61,892	–	97,054	31,229	10,473
2002	–	–	126,870	–	–
2004	–	–	178,230	46,809 (2005)	–
India					
1990	10,862	7,767	16,722	1,707	2,281
1995	14,261	9,964	21,880	2,124	3,056
1996	13,395	10,119	22,317	2,288	3,464
1997	16,526	11,920	24,620	2,374	3,726
1998	16,547	11,775	24,722	2,359	3,811
1999	16,005	11,115	24,215	2,482	–
2000	17,339	–	26,212	2,649	–
2002	–	–	28,667	–	–
2004	–	–	40,302	3,915 (2005)	–
Indonesia					
1990	9,223	6,104	14,581	2,178	688
1995	15,977	9,343	24,754	4,324	1,782
1996	17,139	10,152	25,081	5,014	2,076
1997	12,937	8,048	23,718	5,185	–
1998	9,603	6,205	15,974	4,606	–
1999	8,047	5,215	14,544	4,728	–
2000	9,485	–	16,764	5,064	–
2002	–	–	18,419	5,002 (2005)	–
2004	–	–	–	–	–
Japan					
1990	76,224	48,010	100,501	3,236	10,997
1995	91,797	59,824	129,981	3,345	15,298
1996	95,914	62,763	141,812	3,837	16,695
1997	94,998	66,950	151,048	4,218	16,803
1998	101,701	68,794	154,402	4,106	15,806
1999	105,960	71,334	162,798	4,438	16,358
2000	108,413	–	176,628	4,757	–
2002	–	–	168,739	–	–
2004	–	–	164,976	6,728 (2005)	–

(Continued)

Table 4.1 Trends in air transport and tourism for major Asian countries, 1990–2004/5 *(Continued)*

Country	Civil aviation passengers (000s)	Domestic air (million pax km)	Total pax by air (million pax km)	International tourist arrivals (000s)	International tourist departures (000s)
South Korea					
1990	223	81	40,416	2,959	–
1995	254	94	69,019	3,753	–
1996	254	94	78,178	–	–
1997	280	94	83,427	–	–
1998	64	–	62,613	–	–
1999	59	–	72,439	–	–
2000	86	–	83,955	–	–
2002	–	–	92,175	5,322	–
2004	–	–	96,583	6,022 (2005)	–
Malaysia					
1990	10,242	2,513	11,862	7,446	14,920
1995	15,418	3,624	23,431	7,469	20,642
1996	15,118	4,485	26,862	7,138	23,333
1997	15,592	4,694	28,698	6,211	26,165
1998	13,654	3,979	29,372	5,551	25,631
1999	14,985	4,455	33,708	7,931	26,067
2000	16,561	–	35,658	10,222	–
2002	–	–	36,923	–	–
2004	–	–	–	16,431 (2005)	–
The Philippines					
1990	5,639	1,862	10,390	1,025	1,137
1995	7,180	2,397	14,374	1,760	1,615
1996	7,263	2,284	15,132	2,049	2,121
1997	7,475	2,426	16,392	2,223	1,930
1998	3,944	1,585	7,503	2,149	1,817
1999	5,004	1,888	10,292	2,171	1,755
2000	5,444	–	13,063	1,992	–
2002	–	–	14,216	–	–
2004	–	–	–	2,623 (2005)	–
Thailand					
1990	8,201	1,804	19,757	5,299	883
1995	12,771	2,966	27,053	6,952	1,802
1996	14,078	3,303	29,801	7,244	1,845
1997	14,236	3,194	30,827	7,294	1,660
1998	15,015	3,291	34,340	7,843	1,412
1999	15,951	3,288	38,345	8,651	1,686
2000	17,392	–	42,236	9,509	1,909
2002	–	–	48,337	–	–
2004	–	–	–	–	–
Vietnam					
1990	89	72	–	250	–
1995	2,290	1,118	4,094	1,351	–
1996	2,108	1,070	3,948	1,607	–
1997	2,527	1,273	3,922	1,716	–
1998	2,373	1,273	3,867	1,520	–
1999	2,600	1,308	4,042	1,782	–
2000	2,881	–	4,383	2,140	–

(Continued)

Table 4.1 *(Continued)*

Country	Civil aviation passengers (000s)	Domestic air (million pax km)	Total pax by air (million pax km)	International tourist arrivals (000s)	International tourist departures (000s)
2002	–	–	7,101	–	–
2004	–	–	9,367	–	–
Hong Kong					
1990	–	–	–	6,581	2,043
1995	–	–	–	10,200	3,023
1996	–	–	–	12,974	3,445
1997	5,957	0	20,283	11,273	3,758
1998	12,203	0	42,964	10,160	4,197
1999	12,593	0	43,907	11,328	4,175
2000	14,393	–	50,248	13,059	–
2002	–	–	53,148	–	–
2004	–	–	–	–	–
Singapore					
1990	7,046	0	31,600	4,842	1,237
1995	10,779	0	48,400	6,422	2,867
1996	11,841	0	53,647	6,608	3,305
1997	12,981	0	55,459	6,531	3,671
1998	13,316	0	58,174	5,631	3,745
1999	15,283	0	65,471	6,258	3,971
2000	16,704	0	71,786	6,977	–
2002	–	–	75,620	–	–
2004	–	–	–	7,080 (2005)	–

Source: Developed and adapted from United Nations (2003, 2007).

levels of growth in economic activity, including tourism given the obstacles to growth identified in Chapter 3 by OECD (2008).

Aviation statistics

One immediate problem that confronts the researcher interested in tourist transport is the absence of international statistics which monitor every mode of tourist travel on an up-to-date basis. For example, organisations such as the International Civil Aviation Organization and International Air Transport Association (*www.iata.org*) publish annual statistics on international air travel for their members' airline operations. In the case of ICAO, its 2007 Annual Report summarises the state of airline operations for the 190 contracting states, which are:

● In 2007, the world's airlines carried 2,260 million passengers, a rise of 5.5 per cent on 2006, which equates to a 6 per cent rise in international air traffic and a 4 per cent rise in domestic traffic.
● The traffic was distributed between North American airlines (33 per cent), Asia-Pacific airlines (29 per cent), European airlines (27 per cent), Latin American, Caribbean and Middle Eastern airlines with 4 per cent each, and African airlines with 2 per cent of the traffic.
● The trend in passenger loadings had grown from 65 per cent in 1993 to 71 per cent in 2002 with a drop in 2001 to 69 per cent largely due to the after-effects of 9/11 rising to 76 per cent in 2006 and 77 per cent in 2007.

- In 2007, 41 per cent of scheduled traffic volumes (including freight and mail) were dominated by airlines based in the USA (31 per cent), Germany (5 per cent), the UK (5 per cent) and Japan (6 per cent) with large domestic markets.
- For international scheduled traffic, the market was dominated by American airlines (17 per cent), Germany and the UK (7 per cent each) and Japan (6 per cent).

(*Source*: ICAO (2002, 2007) *Annual Report of ICAO Council*, reprinted with permission.)

The issue of airline profitability has become a massive one for many airlines, especially in the USA, as discussed in Chapter 2. This is because since 9/11 the global airline industry reported losses for each year up to the end of 2006. In contrast, 2007 was a year of returning to profitability for the global airline sector, with net profits of US$3.8 billion, almost two-thirds generated in Europe and a third in Asia-Pacific, with the USA still reporting losses of around US$600 million. This reflects the fact that many airlines have had significant problems post-9/11 due to their cost structures and manner of operation (Doganis 2001, 2002). For this reason, it is interesting to examine which airlines are the most profitable.

The most successful airlines in 2003 (i.e. those in net profit) were those with a diversified portfolio of passenger and freight business (e.g. Lufthansa, Singapore Airlines and Cathay Pacific), with some freight-only operators (e.g. Federal Express) although what is notable is the dominance of Asian operators in the Top 25 despite the impact of SARS. This reflects their overall productivity and lower cost basis, as Oum and Yu's (1998) study of airline competitiveness in 1993–8 found – Asian carriers, notably Singapore Airlines (but excluding Japan Airlines, JAL and All Nippon Airways) had lower unit costs than major US carriers. Many of these differences were attributed to lower input costs, giving Asian carriers (excluding the Japanese carriers) a significant cost advantage, although exchange rate fluctuations can lower competitiveness if a home currency appreciates for an international carrier and may lower its cost competitiveness. A comparison with 2003 shows that in 2007 the situation had changed little in terms of the ranking of profitable airlines; what had changed was the level of profitability, which had increased significantly for the top airlines. For example, the top two airlines reporting profits in 2007 were Lufthansa with over $2.4 billion and Air France with US$2 billion followed by Singapore Airlines with US$1.4 billion, British Airways with US$1.3 billion and Emirates with US$1.2 billion. Interestingly, Ryanair slipped down the rankings between 2003 and 2007 from sixth to eleventh place, but is still a major player as the company benefited from its business model of low-cost operation, while in 2007 easyJet was ranked twenty-first.

In terms of the scale of passenger activity at the world's major airports, data for the top 10 airports in 2003 based on data from Airport Council International (*www.aci.org*) highlights the dominance of US airports and a number of European hubs (Table 4.2) but in contrast to 2004, Beijing now enters as a major airport in ninth place. The data is unable to identify tourist and leisure trips, being a broad measure of terminal passengers and international travel, and for this reason it is an amalgamation of passenger traffic including people boarding/disembarking and in transit at specific airports. Such data is dependent upon the willingness of airports to report statistical information on passenger flows and therefore it is only indicative of the scale of travel at an aggregate level. Not surprisingly, the data in Table 4.2 confirms Hillings' (1996) identification of

Table 4.2 Passenger traffic at the world's top 10 airports for 2007[1]

Airport	Passenger traffic
Atlanta, USA	89 million
Chicago, USA	76 million
London Heathrow, UK	68 million
Tokyo, Japan	67 million
Los Angeles, USA	62 million
Dallas/Fort Worth, USA	60 million
Paris, France	60 million
Frankfurt, Germany	54 million
Madrid, Spain	52 million

[1]Total passengers enplaned and deplaned, passengers in transit counted once.

Source: Copyright © Airports Council International (ACI), Geneva, Switzerland, reproduced with permission.

a world transport gap, although in the case of China this is now being closed up along with the massive growth in India.

In contrast, aviation statistics collected by national aviation organisations such as the UK's Civil Aviation Authority UK Airports outline the origin and destination of all terminal passengers. This data relates to air transport movements at UK airports and is based on the operators' requirement to report each service they operate, passengers uplifted and discharged. Only data on direct flights is recorded. This is only an indication of the relative importance of passenger flows between the UK and other countries. As in Table 4.2, it is not possible to distinguish between arrivals and departures or the regional breakdown of flights. However, Western European travel flows dominate UK travel patterns, which comprised nearly two-thirds of the total passenger movements to and from the UK. This is followed by the USA and a range of other destinations throughout the rest of the world. To illustrate what these statistics mean at the level of one country and the importance of aviation statistics in trying to understand tourism and leisure demand, Insight 4.1 examines the demand for low-cost air travel in the UK. This develops and expands upon the Insight in Chapter 2 on low-cost airline management, focusing on demand issues.

INSIGHT 4.1

The growth of the demand for low-cost airlines in the UK

There has been a sustained debate among industry analysts, the media and academic researchers on the rise of low-cost airlines (LCAs) in the UK and Europe. Airbus (2007) documented the scale of such airline development where 13 airlines controlled 25 per cent of the market in the USA in 2007, while in Europe 44 airlines controlled 30 per cent of the market, 10 controlled 20 per cent of the market in Latin America and 43 in Asia controlled only 12 per cent of the market. In other words, there was considerable scope for further development of this market in emerging countries, but especially in Latin America and Asia. Much of the debate has surrounded their impact on tourist travel behaviour, destination development and competitive behaviour within the aviation sector. For example, Bel (2009) points to the impact of Ryanair on Girona-Costa Brava airport in Spain which saw passenger traffic grow from 500,000 in 2002 to nearly 5 million in 2007, a 770 per cent increase. Ryanair accounted for almost 88 per cent of the airport's passenger traffic, reflecting its corporate strategy of focusing on secondary airports which their business model for flight operation is ▶

based upon. This Insight reviews the evidence of a report in the UK by the Civil Aviation Authority (CAA) in November 2006, *No Frills Carriers: Revolution or Evolution*? This succinctly summarises some of the main issues associated with the growth of LCAs, which the CAA entitle 'No Frills' due to the low-cost model that has also been employed more widely in the airline sector. The CAA report is useful in debunking many of the myths associated with LCAs.

Much of the impetus to develop low-cost models of airline operation are attributed to Southwest Airlines in the USA and their growth as a leading US domestic carrier as discussed in Chapter 2. The use of point-to-point routes with no interlining associated infrastructure to transfer passengers across a network combined with a standardised fleet, lower costs of production and higher staff productivity, use of regional airports, and a simplified fare structure helped create one of the US's most innovative airlines. The use of yield management systems to maximise review and profitability, load factors and the business mix combined with direct sales by phone and the Internet generated a wide range of new travel as well as encouraging passengers to switch from full-service carriers on domestic routes.

Regulation in the European Union up until 1986 (when the UK–Ireland routes were deregulated to allow more competition) limited the potential for LCAs to begin operation. It was not until 1992 that the European Union introduced the 'Third Package' or airline deregulation which facilitated carriers from any member state to fly any route throughout the EU, as discussed in Chapters 2 and 3. This removed frequency restrictions on routes and obstacles to where airlines could operate as well as liberalising fares. Whilst Ryanair began operation in 1986 on UK–Ireland routes, much of the expansion in the UK and EU market for LCAs occurred after 1992, largely in line with how the expansion occurred in the USA following airline regulation, replicating the low-cost model of operation developed by Southwest Airlines.

The significance of the LCA in the UK–EU market is reflected in the following CAA statistics:

- In 1996, no frills airlines comprised 3.1 million passengers on UK–EU traffic whilst full-service carriers composed 42.2 million and the charter market 23.8 million.
- In 2005, no frills airlines comprised 51.5 million passengers on the UK–EU market, followed by full-service carriers with 47.2 million and the charter airlines with 25 million passengers.
- In 1996, no frills airlines carried 1.2 million domestic passengers in the UK domestic market whilst full-service carriers had 30.9 million (charter airlines share was negligible).
- In 2005, no frills airlines carried 26 million domestic passengers in the UK, with full-service carriers at 26.1 million passengers.
- For 2005, no frills airlines carried 77.5 million passengers from UK airports, capturing 42 per cent of the UK–EU traffic and 49 per cent of the domestic market.

In 2005, CAA figures show that despite a wide range of LCAs operating in the UK, Ryanair and easyJet dominated the market. Whilst Ryanair and easyJet dominate the UK–EU market, their position in the UK domestic market has slipped by 25 per cent in 2000–5. In the international UK–EU market, the competition is larger (i.e. spread amongst more LCAs). What is also notable in the CAA (2006) report is the questioning of the contention, often associated with media reports, that the LCAs had significantly increased the growth rate of passenger traffic.

The CAA modelled passenger traffic data for UK airports in 1950–2005 (including long-haul traffic) and identified the following trends from annual growth rates and the use of a 10-year moving average trend.

- The first period, 1950–74, was characterised by very high average annual growth rates of around 14 per cent per annum, with a 7 per cent contraction in 1973 due to the first oil price shock.
- Growth continued in 1975, albeit at a slower average rate of 5.8 per cent per annum in 1975–2005, which was relatively stable through time despite a number of fluctuations. ▶

The CAA data shows that there was *no* acceleration in traffic growth after the mid-1990s, although external factors (e.g. 9/11, SARS) may mask such growth. To overcome this, CAA looked at the UK–EU and UK domestic market in detail.

- In the UK–EU and UK domestic aviation market, CAA data shows that, at the most, no frills airline activity may have accelerated growth by 0.7 per cent a year, assuming a start point of 1996, and if 1998 is taken as the start point, there is no marked impact on growth due to no-frills airlines. This is in spite of strong GDP growth and a more favourable macroeconomic environment compared to the 1975–96 period.

So what does this mean for the LCA market and tourism?
CAA and other data suggest that LCAs base their development upon:

- Traffic generation or traffic stimulation, inducing people to travel who may otherwise have gone by other modes.
- Traffic substitution or traffic abstraction, where people switch airlines thus affecting air-line market shares. A notable example in the UK was the rebranding of British European to FlyBe, from a full-service to no-frills model.
- Studies have indicated that 30 per cent of LCA passengers may be diverted from exist-ing airlines and 70 per cent are stimulated (DETR 2000). Likewise an ELFAA (2002) study broadly concurred with this finding, suggesting these carriers gained 60 per cent of their business through traffic generation and 40 per cent from traffic substitution.

Consequently, LCAs have grown at the expense of full-service and charter airlines which in the UK domestic market contracted by 4.8 per cent per annum during 2000–5 whilst LCAs grew by 35 per cent per annum. In the UK–EU market, drivers of change have been over-seas holiday homes purchased (rented by UK residents), changing patterns of leisure travel and preferences for destinations. The charter airline market was the greatest loser in this sector. Therefore, despite these examples of how LCAs have affected routes in different ways, much of the perceived success of the LCA sector has not been as a result of a mas-sive acceleration of traffic growth year on year. A large proportion of the growth has been by traffic generation and traffic switching (e.g. the rise of business travellers using LCAs as more flexible travel arrangements are permitted), since CAA data shows that around 20 per cent of the market for LCAs is now amongst business travellers. In essence LCAs have ex-panded at the expense of full-service and charter airlines but even this has not led to aggre-gate traffic growth in excess of 7.2 per cent during 1993–2000. The high growth rate of LCAs in 2000–05, of 32.5 per cent in traffic per annum, should not be used as a surrogate for overall traffic growth which is buoyant but not at the rates achieved in 1950–75. One use-ful conclusion from the CAA study is that an analysis of the 15 densest European charter routes in 2000–05, shows LCAs taking up to 50 per cent of the market from charter airlines on routes such as Malaga, Alicante and Faro.

It is apparent from the CAA data that EU countries with the largest LCA presence are ex-periencing the fastest rates of traffic growth. Whilst a range of factors may explain this trend, such as market maturity, GDP growth, VFR links and the novelty value of new destinations, the wide range of new destinations poses many competitive pressures for the UK's domes-tic tourism industry.

Source: Developed from CAA (2006).

A study by Peeters et al. (2006) has extended our understanding of the demand for tourist travel in Europe as part of a project funded by the EU. It modelled data for 29 states in Europe to provide forecasts of traffic growth to 2020. Figure 4.3a provides an illustration of the scale of international tourist air travel within Europe in 2000. Among all the modes of land-based travel, air exhibits the greatest poten-tial to grow from the pattern in 2000, which is dominated by UK and German

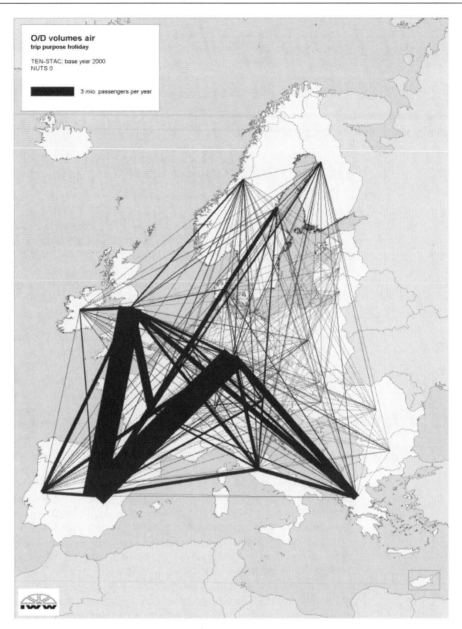

Figure 4.3a International tourism origin-destination transport volumes (number of trips) for the trip purpose holiday for air in 2000

Source: IWW (TEN-STAC 2003) in Peeters *et al.* 2006

holiday travel to Spain. When this pattern is extrapolated and forecast to 2020 (Figure 4.3b) the growth in demand for holiday trips by air is expected to grow from 875 million tourism journeys in 2000 to 1371 million by 2020, a growth rate of 2.3 per cent per annum. These expected patterns of growth also raised serious concerns in the Peeters et al. (2006) study which examined the environmental effects of such growth, with air accounting for a significant proportion of greenhouse gas emissions compared to rail, coach and ferry travel. Figure 4.3b also indicates that

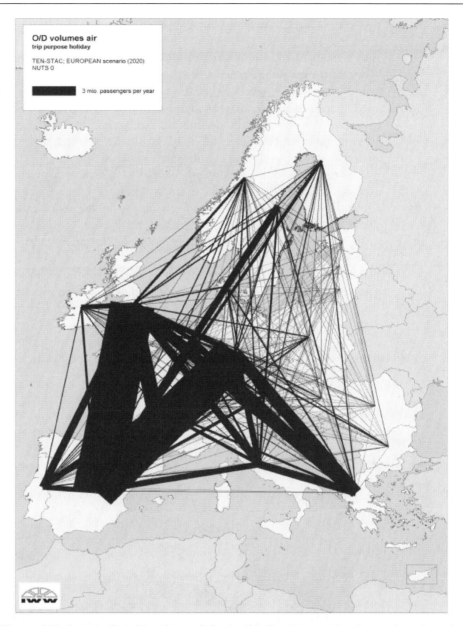

Figure 4.3b International tourism origin-destination transport volumes (number of trips) for the trip purpose holiday for air in 2020

Source: IWW (TEN-STAC 2003) in Peeters *et al.* 2006

air will continue to intensify its volume of tourist travel within the EU, raising issues over the eco-efficiency of air versus other modes of transport, given the dominance of tourist-related air travel in terms of the external cost in terms of climate change.

Bus and coach travel statistics

In contrast to air transport, road-based bus and coach travel is sparsely documented with the exception of the UN *Statistics Yearbook*, which provides a generic overview. Coach travel usually refers to inter-urban, rural or urban-based trips. To complicate matters, the analysis of statistics for tourist or leisure use of these services amalgamates bus and coach, which is very unhelpful given that a number of distinct forms of bus/coach service exist for tourists including their use of domestic and international scheduled coach services, coaches for group travel and different companies who use coaches and buses for sightseeing in destinations. In recent years, innovations in the destination sightseeing services have seen all-day excursions operating on a hop on/hop off basis as well as the development of dedicated airport shuttle services and tailor-made services.

At the EU level, the *Energy and Transport in Figures* (*www.europa.eu*) documents trends since 1970 and other useful studies are *Jane's Urban Transport Systems Handbook* (*www.janes.co.uk*) along with many of the periodicals published on the bus and coach industry that provide market intelligence. On a global scale, however, the most useful is the data generated by the Union Internationale des Transport Publics (*www.uitp.com*) and the data from individual operators (where it exists). The scale of this industry in the EU is often underestimated, some of which is supported by tourism, since the bus and coach sector employs around 10 million people; although with a few notable exceptions (e.g. Downward and Lumsdon 1999) it remains a poorly understood sector by researchers. According to the North West Regional Development Agency (NWRDA) study in 2008 on Coach Tourism in England's North West, the coach market was predominantly based upon 60–70 year old travellers who:

● took 2 million trips a year to the region;
● spent £120 million a year as a result of coach tourism in the region;
● accounted for around 1:20 of all domestic staying trips in NW England;
● visited two dominant locations: Blackpool (50 per cent) and the Lake District (30 per cent).

Plate 4.2 Lomond Shores, Loch Lomond which is a gateway to the Loch Lomond and Trossachs National Park and a key stopping point for coach tourists
Source: S.J. Page

The market has seen increased pressure from low-cost airlines although the luxury end of the market still has considerable potential for growth along with special interest tours (e.g. seeing behind the film set of a popular drama series). Combined with forecasts of an ageing population, the NWRDA report suggests this may be an opportunity for the coach market along with the increasing investment in higher specification vehicles.

Rail travel statistics

Rail travel is comparatively well documented with a number of annual surveys (e.g. Jane's World Railways, United Nation's reports) and data from the UIC (*www.UIC. asso.fr*), which is the worldwide railway association. Other studies such as the OECD's (2002) *Trends in the Transport Sector 1970–2000* and OECD (2005) *OECD in Figures 2005 – Transport* provide useful time series data, as do the EU's *Energy and Transport in Figures*.

Cruising and ferry transport statistics

The *United Nations Statistics Yearbook* is a good starting point for maritime transport, but there are clear differences between what is a tourism-only activity (e.g. cruising) and the use of ferries to cross natural barriers (e.g. seas and lakes) for tourism and non-tourism purposes. Most governments provide statistical data on ferry crossings that are compiled from government and private-sector owned ports and services. For example, in Scotland's Highlands and Islands many of the services are supported by PSOs although they have a high level of tourist usage in the summer season. Indeed, as Connell (2005) has shown in the case of Tobermorey on the Isle of Mull, the demand induced by film-related tourism from a programme such as *Balamory* (*www.bbc.co.uk/cbeebies/balamory/*) can mean that normal provision is unable to meet demand in peak seasons when additional tourist pressures are added to normal timetabled services (Plate 4.3).

As Table 4.3 shows, the main ferry routes within Scotland's Highlands and Islands serve a very dispersed series of islands and this is a feature mirrored across the world where island tourism depends upon such linkages, given the limitations on air services where demand or supply of services is limited by infrastructure. Recent traffic patterns on these routes suggest continued growth, with Caledonian McBrayne services carrying 5.3 million passengers a year including 1.1 million cars while the Scotland–Northern Ireland international ferry route carries around 2 million passengers a year, with demand highly seasonal and reflected in enhanced summer sailings and limited winter services. To meet new EU guidelines on the provision of PSO grants for such routes, the Scottish Executive identified the need for a public tender process that could be operated by:

- tendering the entire network;
- tendering specific routes or a group of routes.

whilst the final form of service delivery may include a vessel-owning company (with vessels leased to operators at full cost), a vessel owned or leased that is not dissimilar to the model presented in Chapter 3 on the rail industry ROSCOs (rolling

Plate 4.3 The ferry services to the Islands of Scotland have a limited capacity in summer that cannot easily be adjusted to accommodate a surge in demand, as was experienced in 2003 and 2004 with the *Balamory* television programme

Source: Dr Joanne Connell

Table 4.3 Principal ferry services to Scotland's Highlands and Islands, 2002

- Services to Orkney and Shetland from Aberdeen and Scrabster (currently provided by P&O but transferring to NorthLink) including Aberdeen–Lerwick (Shetland), Aberdeen–Stromness (Orkney) and Scrabster–Stromness
- Shetland inter-island ferry services including Lerwick–Bressay, Mainland–Yell, Yell–Unst, Yell/Belmont–Fetlar, Mainland–Whalsay, Mainland–Out Skerry, South Mainland–Fair Isle, West Mainland–Foula and West Mainland–Papa Stour
- Orkney Island services from the mainland to Eday, Stronsay, Sanday, Flotta, Hoy, Graemsay, North Ronaldsay, Papa Westray, Westray, Rosay, Egilsay, Wyre and Shapinsay
- Services from Shetland to the Faroe Isles and Bergen in Norway
- The services in the Firth of Clyde (currently operated by Caledonian MacBrayne), including Wemyss Bay–Rothesay, Colintraive (Cowal)–Rhubodach (Bute), Largs–Cumbrae, Gourock–Dunoon, Gourock–Kilgreggan–Helensburgh and Protavadie (Cowal)–Tarbert (Kintyre)
- Western Ferries' service between Gourock and Dunoon
- The services to Islay, Colonsay & Gigha (currently operated by Caledonian MacBrayne), including Kennacraig (Kintyre)–Port Ellen and Port Askaig (Islay), Tayinloan (Kintyre)–Gigha and Oban–Kennacraig–Colonsay
- The services to Mull and the Inner Hebrides (currently operated by Caledonian MacBrayne) including Oban–Craignure (Mull), Lochaline–Fishnish (Mull), Tobermory (Mull)–Kilchoan (Ardnamuchan), Oban–Coll–Tiree, Fionnphort (Mull)–Iona and Oban–Lismore
- Argyll and Bute Council ferry services (Appin–Lismore and Islay–Jura)
- The services to Skye, Raasay and the Small Isles (currently operated by Caledonian MacBrayne) including Mallaig–Armadale (Skye), Sconser (Skye)–Raasay and Mallaig–Eigg–Muck–Rum–Canna
- The services to the Outer Hebrides (currently operated by Caledonian MacBrayne) including Oban/Mallaig–Castlebay (Barra)/Lochboisdale (South Uist), Uig (Skye)–Lochmaddy (North Uist), Otternish (North Uist)–Leverburgh (Harris), Uig–Tarbert (Harris) and Ullapool–Stornoway
- Highland Council's Corran ferry and its (directly provided) Camusnagaul–Fort William service, Mallaig–Inverie (provided under contract to Highland Council), Cromarty–Nigg (supported by Highland Council and others) and Glenelg–Kylerhea (a commercial and seasonal service across the narrows)

Source: Scottish Executive (2002: 31–2).

stock companies). A recent inquiry into ferry services in Scotland in 2008 by the Scottish Government's Transport, Infrastructure and Climate Change Committee received evidence that observed its critical role in the visitor experience and as a means of accessing island tourism destinations confirming Rigas' (2009: NP) comments that 'tourism is very often the major financial activity of island economies . . . transport services play a critical role, as they not only offer the means to reach the destination, but also become part of the touristic experience. The EU, having recognised this fact, aims to support the socio-economic cohesion of these regions, through a number of policies, such as public service obligations (PSO)'. Rigas' (2009) study of Greece points to the 90 seaports and 24 airports serving the region of the Aegean, with seven companies providing ferry connections between Athens and the Aegean Islands. Sea captures around two-thirds of the traffic compared to air with one-third of the market.

Here transport policy set at a pan-European level has a definite effect on how tourist services are delivered on the ground and yet few analysts make the crossover here between transport delivery and the direct effect on tourism (although, from public consultation on such issues, it is clear that residents on these islands affected by such changes are very concerned about the impact on access and their tourism industries as these services are a lifeline).

In contrast to the ferry sector, data is more problematic for the cruising sector (Plate 4.4) as the excellent reports by Peisley (2006) demonstrate. These should be a vital starting point for any researcher interested in global or regional issues in cruising (Gibson 2006). Peisley points to the data sources available from the large cruising companies such as the Carnival Corporation, Royal Caribbean and Star Cruises Group, although most data comes from individual ports. In the USA, the Cruise Lines International Association (CLIA) (*www.cruising.org*) noted in 2003 that its members saw 9.52 million cruise passengers travel, up from 8.6 million in 2002. By 2005, Peisley (2006) observed that these figures had risen to 14.5 million, illustrating the continued growth of around 8 to 10 per cent per annum. In the USA, the cruise business was worth around US$30 billion and C$1.8 billion in Canada. A CLIA press release pointing to research it commissioned from TNS Plog Research (*www.cruising.org/CruiseNews/News*) provided a profile of likely cruise ship passengers in the USA, who were aged 35–54, with 76 per cent married and 44 per cent college graduates; families are also a key segment in this market (with 18 per cent bringing children). Many of the cruising population are frequent travellers, undertaking around 3–4 trips a year, and they spent twice as much as the average US traveller, around US$5135; they spend between 16 and 20 nights away on cruises. Some 89 per cent still book via travel agents. In the UK, VisitBritain's Foresight publications (*www.visitbritain.co./research*), *The Cruiseline Boom* (May 2006) highlighted the increase in the number of UK ports handling cruise ships for inbound tourism. 'Port of call' passengers (where a cruise ship arrives and departs and where shore excursions take place) have a strong presence in Scotland. In 2006, VisitBritain reported that Invergordon was ranked third in the UK with over 40,000 port of call passengers, after Guernsey and Dover, with Lerwick ranked fifth (25,000 passengers), the Clyde placed sixth (with just under 25,000 passengers), Kirkwall ranked seventh (23,000 passengers), and Leith, Edinburgh was ranked ninth with just under 20,000 passengers a year.

Plate 4.4 Advertising for cruises comprise a key element of the tourist experience as this poster advertisement for Cunard White Line tickets from 1937 suggests in terms of the imagery used ©Thomas Cook

Source: Thomas Cook

These statistics underpin what Peisley (2006) identified, that the USA dominates global patterns of cruising with relatively smaller volumes in the UK, although he points to the problems of obtaining realistic estimates of global cruising. Recent trends (see Chin 2008, for example) also illustrate the growth in river cruising (Plate 4.5) such as along the River Nile as former products and experiences are rediscovered by a new generation of travellers, the Victorians having developed such tastes from the innovative packages and tours of Thomas Cook. A number of academic studies highlight these historical patterns in the Pacific (e.g. Douglas and Douglas 1996) and South East Asia (Douglas and Douglas 2000), whilst more recent analyses have examined a wide range of themes from economic impacts through to the behaviour of cruise ship tourists

Plate 4.5 The potential of linear corridors such as rivers for tourism and leisure are well known, as is the case with pleasure traffic on the River Thames in London
Source: S.J. Page

(Bull 1996; Dwyer and Forsyth 1996; Morrison et al. 1996; Moscardo et al. 1996; Dickinson and Vladmir 1997; Burt 1998; Wood 2000, 2004; Chase and McKee 2003). Therefore, a blend of these academic studies that contain original primary research and those studies which are a commentary of the existing data sources assists in understanding the nature of cruising as a tourism phenomenon which has emerged as a key segment of the transport as tourism market. Yet to fully understand the nature of tourist travel, these studies have to be examined in tandem with the prevailing tourism statistics.

Tourism statistics

Within an international context, tourism statistics provide an invaluable insight into:

- tourist arrivals in different regions of the world and for specific countries;
- the volume of tourist trips;
- types of tourism (e.g. holidaymaking, visiting friends and relatives and business travel);
- the number of nights spent in different countries by tourists;
- tourist expenditure on transport-related services.

Such information may indicate the order of magnitude of tourist use of transport systems and their significance in different locations (Plate 4.6). In this context, Latham and Edward's (2003) seminal study on tourism statistics is essential reading, since it provides a useful insight into the complex process of assessing the demand for international tourist transport. Studies by Latham and Edwards (1989, 2003), Jefferson and Lickorish (1991), Veal (1992) and Lennon (2002) document

Plate 4.6 One of the major challenges of gathering accurate tourism statistics is to understand that tourist itineraries and places they visit may be varied, which was compounded by the rise of the car as a means of travel as illustrated by this early example of a personalised tour available by chauffer-driven car by Thomas Cook ©Thomas Cook

Source: Thomas Cook

the procedures associated with the generation of tourism statistics, which often use social survey techniques such as questionnaire-based interviews with tourists at departure and arrival points.

Unlike respondents in other forms of social survey work, tourists are a transient and mobile population. This raises problems related to which social survey method and sampling technique one should use to generate reliable and accurate statistical information that is representative of the real world. Due to the cost involved in undertaking social surveys, it is impossible and impractical to interview all tourists travelling on a specific mode of transport. A sampling framework is normally used to select a range of respondents who are representative of the population being examined. Whilst there are a number of good sources which deal with this technical issue (see S.L.J. Smith 1989 and Veal 1992), it is clear that no one survey technique and sampling framework is going to provide all the information necessary to enable decision-makers to reach strategic planning decisions. It is possible to discern three common types of tourism survey:

- pre-travel studies of tourists' intended travel habits and likely use of tourist transport;
- studies of tourists in transit or at their destination, to provide information on their actual behaviour and plans for the remainder of their holiday or journey;
- post-travel studies of tourists once they have returned to their place of residence.

Clearly there are advantages and disadvantages with each approach. For example, pre-travel studies may indicate the potential destinations that tourists would like to visit on their next holiday, but it is difficult to assess the extent to which holiday intentions are converted to actual travel. In contrast, surveys of tourists in transit or at a destination can only provide a snapshot of their experiences to date rather than a broader evaluation of their holiday experience (Plate 4.7). One interesting survey instrument that, in part, addresses the potential weaknesses associated with surveys of holiday experience would seek to assess the tourists' previous travel behaviour and their changing travel behaviour through time. Where retrospective

Plate 4.7 Transport can be used to stimulate event tourism, as in the case of the Thomas the Tank engine roving event that tours the UK steam railways

Source: S.J. Page

post-travel studies are used, they often incur the problem of actually locating and eliciting responses from tourists that accurately record a previous event or experience. Each approach has a valuable role and generally individual transport operators and tourism organisations use the approach appropriate to their information needs.

The most comprehensive and widely used sources of tourism statistics that directly and indirectly examine international tourist travel are produced by the UN–World Tourism Organization (WTO) and OECD (Pearce 1987, 1995a). National governments also compile statistics on international tourism for their own country (inbound travel) and the destinations chosen by outbound travellers. These are normally commissioned by national tourism organisations as a specialist research function, though it depends upon each country and how the management of public sector tourism is organised. WTO publishes a number of annual publications, including the *Yearbook of Tourism Statistics* (published since 1947 as *International Travel Statistics*, then as *World Travel Statistics*, and now as *World Travel and Tourism Statistics*). This has a summary of tourism statistics for almost 150 countries and areas, with key data on tourist transport, and includes statistical information in the following order:

- world summary of international tourism statistics;
- tourist arrivals;
- accommodation capacity by regions;
- trends in world international tourism arrivals, receipts and exports;
- arrivals of cruise passengers;
- domestic tourism;
- tourism payments (including international tourism receipts by countries calculated in US$ millions, excluding international fare receipts);
- tourism motivations (arrivals from abroad and purpose of visit);
- tourism accommodation;
- country studies that examine the detailed breakdown of tourism statistics collected for each area, including tourism seasonality.

In addition to WTO, OECD produces *Tourism Policy and International Tourism in OECD Member Countries*. Although the data collected is restricted to OECD countries (BaRon 1997), it deals with other issues such as government policy and barriers to international tourism.

International tourist travel: trends and patterns

Both WTO and OECD statistics are compiled by each agency from returns and data that national governments supply according to the criteria laid down by each organisation. International tourist arrivals have risen from 25 million in 1950 to 593 million in 1996 and 694 million in 2003, 903 million in 2007 and 924 million in 2008 (see Figure 4.4). Between 1990 and 2000 world arrivals grew 42 per cent, which is a good rate of growth given the prevailing global economic conditions that had a bearing on different tourism regions as annual growth rates compound to give this pattern of sustained growth. For example, in 2006–07, arrivals grew by 6.6 per cent, while tourist receipts grew by 5.6 per cent to US$85 billion.

A key feature of Figure 4.4 is the continued dominance of Europe, although the relative position of Europe in world arrivals has declined in successive years as the

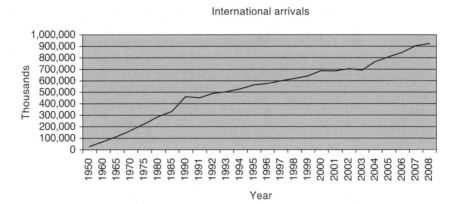

Figure 4.4 International tourist arrivals 1950–2008

importance of Asia-Pacific increases. However, continued dominance as an origin and destination area for tourism is due to the fact that its population contains segments with a high disposable income and a highly developed tourism infrastructure.

The East Asian Pacific (EAP) region continued to experience a rapid growth in arrivals between 1986 and 1996, with 87 million arrivals, which reached 131 million in 2002 and dropped to 119 million in 2003 due to the effect of SARS: this recovered and rose to 184 million in 2007, comprising 20 per cent of all arrivals. Africa received 20.6 million arrivals in 1996 and 30 million in 2003 rising to 44 million in 2007, accounting for 5 per cent of all arrivals. The Middle East received 15.3 million arrivals in 1996 and 30 million in 2003 and 48 million in 2007. Tourist arrivals are not distributed evenly in each region, with some countries and their destinations performing better than others. Hoivik and Heiberg (1980) argue that up to four-fifths of all international flows were between Europe, North America and Japan, and one-twentieth between other countries in the world. Pearce (1995a) has examined these flows in more detail and Rowe (1994) listed the country-to-country flows in order of magnitude, although these are now very dated given the expansion of China and India as two examples. In 2007, Europe still dominated the overall market share with 52 per cent of arrivals but East Asia Pacific supplanted the Americas into third place, with 20 per cent of all arrivals compared to the Americas with 16 per cent.

Whilst such patterns are well established in international tourist travel, the growing significance of EAP and outbound/intraregional travel needs to be recognised. Although the existing Europe–Americas dominance of flow remains marked, the growth of arrivals in other regions is a noticeable feature, particularly outside of Europe and the Americas. Although WTO (1992) did provide a summary of tourist transport, it stopped publishing tourist transport statistics in its summary and a full compendium of tourism statistics in 1996, so it is unfortunately no longer possible to investigate the role of transport and arrivals. This exemplifies the problem facing tourism researchers in developed countries and, particularly, in developing countries (Weaver and Elliot 1996; O'Hare and Barrett 1997; Scheyvens 2002), where inadequate data exists beyond general aggregate statistics that do not investigate the tourism–transport interface.

Problems in using transport and tourism statistics

Researchers encounter numerous problems in using transport and tourism statistics, some of which were introduced in Chapter 1. The principal problem relates to the purpose for which the statistics are collected, which in most cases are for government recording purposes or for industry groups. Not surprisingly, these are rarely suitable for researchers who seek to answer specific research questions that are more specific than the generic nature of many statistics. In addition, the statistics rarely link transport and tourism together, which is one reason why many academic researchers use their own survey instruments to collect statistics to examine research issues. Yet here the sample sizes are often small and selective in geographical coverage, offering little more than an insight into a region, market segment or mode of transport. Non-governmental organisations (NGOs) such as the WTO and UN do attempt to provide universal coverage but these statistics are not only dated in many cases, but can rarely offer insights at the local level. Researchers need to be aware of the limitations of the statistical sources they use and acknowledge who the statistics are collected for, the methodologies used and the inherent weaknesses. Developing a better understanding of the tourism–transport–leisure interface requires that statistics are collected with a clear purpose in mind and the end user needs to be clearly identified. Many national and regional tourism surveys, which often have a question on mode of travel/transport used, are inevitably sample surveys and they need to be treated with caution, since they are frequently aggregated to provide national estimates. Ultimately, researchers need to use as many different data sources as they can access, triangulating them to try and corroborate their findings and to establish some measure of the volume, patterns and activities of visitors using different forms of transport during their tourism activities. To illustrate how this can be undertaken with reference to a specific research problem – tourist road safety and traffic accidents – a recent study of Scotland is examined in Insight 4.2.

INSIGHT 4.2

Developing the tourist–transport interface: using complementary statistical sources to understand tourist road safety and accidents in Scotland

Linda Walker and Stephen J. Page,[1] University of Stirling

A substantial literature on road traffic issues now exists in the wider transportation and safety science literature, and tourism researchers have only belatedly begun to recognise both the importance and contribution that visitors make to road-related injuries. Much of the literature has been from a broad range of disciplines spanning tourism, transport and safety science as discussed in detail in Walker and Page (2005). Many of the studies are characterised by a case study or at best a single country-based approach, but data remains one of the most problematic areas in terms of its availability, reliability and comparability. In this Insight, collaborative research with the Central Scotland Police Force to examine the dimensions, scale and nature of tourist-related road traffic accidents (RTAs) has assisted in

[1]This Insight is derived from a more substantive research paper by L. Walker and S. J. Page (2005) 'The contribution of tourists and visitors to road traffic accidents: a preliminary analysis of trends and issues for Central Scotland', *Current Issues in Tourism*, 7(3): 217–41.

▶

using official statistics that need to be supplemented through primary data gathered by key agencies (such as the police) to augment and supplement existing analyses of RTAs whilst relating the findings to available tourism data. Whilst inconsistencies inevitably arise through incomplete data, problems of data linkage and geographical coverage of data, it is evident that such research advances our understanding through a multidisciplinary approach to a multifaceted problem – namely why and how tourists have RTAs in one part of the UK – Central Scotland.

Road traffic accidents and tourists

According to Paixao et al. (1991), those dying through trauma are more likely to be younger (32 per cent in the 20–29 group and 80 per cent were under 50) and male, with road traffic accidents accounting for a large number of these deaths. Hargarten et al. (1991) attributed 26.8 per cent of injury deaths to motor vehicle accidents. The 'everyday' nature of road traffic accidents combined with our reliance on, and relationship with, road transport, particularly cars, tends to encourage us to trivialise the associated risks (Mitchell 1997), despite road traffic accidents being a major cause of death and injury for tourists and non-tourists alike.

Road traffic accidents in the UK

Britain has a good record of road safety, with death rates from road traffic accidents amongst the lowest in Europe (EuroRAP 2002). Indeed, in Scotland, mortality rates from car accidents more than halved from 1980 to 2002, both in actual numbers and in standard-ised rates; emergency admittance rates to hospitals as a result of RTAs demonstrate a sim-ilar pattern (ISD Scotland 2003). Despite these decreases, road traffic accidents are still the main cause of accidental deaths in the under-45s in Scotland (ISD Scotland 2003).

EuroRAP and road safety

According to Lynam et al. (2003), EuroRAP established a pilot programme in 2001 to exam-ine three themes at a European level:

- a comparison of death rates on road networks in different European countries;
- mapping and analysis of fatal and serious injury accident rates in Great Britain, the Netherlands, Sweden and Catalonia;
- inspection of the safety quality of the road networks and extent to which the infrastruc-ture protects road users from death and serious injury when accidents occur.

(The technical report that outlines these approaches can be accessed at *www.eurorap.org*.) One of the outcomes of the detailed analysis are risk rate maps as shown in Figure 4.5, illustrating the statistical risk of death and serious injury occurring on Britain's motorways and major roads. What the research by EuroRAP suggests is that:

9% of deaths outside built-up areas are on motorways, 19% on dual carriageways, 38% on single carriageways of national or regional importance and 34% on other single car-riageways. The fatal and serious accident rate of the A-road network is about four times that of the national motorway network (Lynam et al. 2003: 170).

Figure 4.5, derived from the most recent EuroRAP research, illustrates that Scotland has a much less dense road network at the motorway and A-road (trunk road) level than England and Wales. This is partly a function of population density, the rural nature of the environment outside of Central Scotland and the geographically dispersed nature of settle-ment in the Highlands and Islands of Scotland and the Borders area (south of Glasgow and Edinburgh). In terms of the risk rating of the roads by EuroRAP, it takes a stretch of road and calculates the incidence of fatal and serious injury accidents according to previous recorded incidents. Although Figure 4.5 indicates that the Central Scotland area has only two routeways with medium risk (i.e. the M9, A9(M) and A9, A811 and A84), these are major transit routes through the region to the Highlands of Scotland. Within Figure 4.5 accident ▶

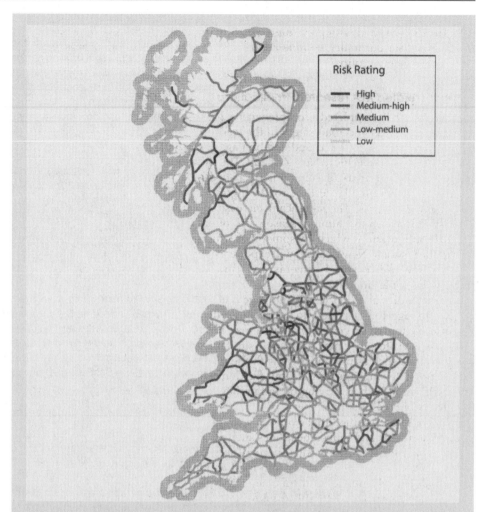

Figure 4.5 EuroRAP risk rate map of roads in Great Britain, 1999–2001

Source: Copyright © Road Safety Foundation and © Crown Copyright. All Rights Reserved.
Licence number 399221.

blackspots are not identified, although these are more localised in terms of their accident rating, such as the Dunblane roundabout at the end of the M9 that has amongst the most accidents for a roundabout in Central Scotland. EuroRAP data is useful in the identification of stretches of road with poor safety performance that leads to high levels of death and serious injury, which complements much of the work of local authorities and road safety groups (see Broughton and Walker (2009) on motorcycle riders).

Tourist-related RTA research

Wilks (1999) completed a comprehensive literature review dealing with international tourists and road safety in the lead-up to the 2000 Sydney Olympics. This was later revised and updated by Page et al. (2001) prior to presenting an analysis of data specific to New Zealand. The New Zealand study is of particular interest due to areas of commonality between Scotland and New Zealand: left-hand drive, similar terrain and roads, highly variable weather conditions and climatic variations. The significant increase in caravan/campervan traffic on dual carriageway roads in the summer season also offers many similarities, as does the road configurations that are sometimes winding, with a significant camber, so that the visitor to New Zealand will experience similar hazards to those of visitors to Scotland. The use of speed cameras and rural accident blackspot notices also provide similarities.

The studies by Wilks (1999) and Page et al. (2001) deal specifically with overseas/ foreign tourists; they do not consider the domestic tourist. Although the domestic tourist or visitor to an area may not have the same challenges as an overseas visitor, they may have some similar issues. Overseas visitors may face difficulties such as unfamiliarity with the road regulations of the host country and possible language barriers, but the domestic and overseas visitor will both face hazards such as driving on unfamiliar roads and distractions such as the novelty of breathtaking scenery.

It could be assumed that overseas visitors are more likely to be involved in road accidents, and indeed headlines such as 'Tourist road hazard' (*Scotsman* 2001) or 'Tourist caused crash' (*Evening Times* 2001) would tend to reinforce this view. However, a recent study of road accidents involving tourists in rural Scotland would not support this view; Sharples and Fletcher (2001) analysed postcode data from 'STATS19' forms for 1999 and 2000 in rural areas of Scotland. The STATS19 forms are completed by police in the event of any road traffic accident resulting in injury. Prior to 1999 it would not have been possible to differentiate non-UK residents from UK residents with unknown postcodes due to lack of coding. Using post-1999 data, they found that accidents increased in times of higher visitor numbers but that the accident rate per vehicle mile was similar and that 'There is no evidence that the foreign and UK visitor drivers are markedly more likely than local drivers to be involved in an accident' (Sharples and Fletcher 2001: i). Yet the cause of accidents was found to vary between the UK drivers and foreign drivers, as may be expected:

> For the average driver who was at fault, loss of control, negotiating a bend, or going too fast for the conditions of the road were the main causes. However, for foreign drivers who were at fault, the most frequent causes were driving on the wrong side of the road, turning, and crossing the centre line (Sharples and Fletcher 2001: ii).

Although caution must be taken in utilising this data, as its collection is very much dependent on the accurate completion of forms in what may be difficult or traumatic situations, it does allow an insight into differences in the nature and type of accidents involving various groups. Until recently it was likely that most overseas tourists driving in Scotland would have had a great deal of driving practice before reaching the Central Scotland Police Force area due to the main ports of arrival being outside the area. But the opening of ferry crossings at Newcastle and, more recently, at Rosyth in Central Scotland, has meant that more overseas visitors can bring their car over straight on to Scottish roads.

Tourists and visitors are likely to be more at risk from road accidents not purely due to unfamiliarity or their own behaviour, but the very fact that people tend to drive longer distances on holidays and day trips (DLTR 2001). This will increase their exposure to accidents. However, overall risk will be determined for an individual traveller by the number of accidents per unit of traffic (EuroRAP 2002). Using this measure, serious and fatal accident rates are four times higher on A-roads than on motorways in Britain (EuroRAP 2002) and, as Scotland has fewer motorways but a higher proportion of road per capita (DfT 2003), the risk for locals and visitors alike should, theoretically, be heightened. To date there has not been sufficient research to appreciate the reason why Scottish A-roads appear to have lower fatal and serious accident rates than the national A-roads. This however should be seen in the context that the majority of road deaths occur outside built-up areas on single carriageway roads (EuroRAP 2002).

Data sources

The data used has been taken from STATS 19 data supplied by the Central Scotland Road Accident Investigation Unit (CSRAIU); in the four-year period 1999–2002 there were 2841 road traffic accidents in the Central Scotland Police Force Area involving 4842 vehicles and 7384 casualties. The data does not allow tourists to be specifically identified; however, one ▶

of the fields captured in the data is postcode information. This information can then be used to distinguish 'locals' (i.e. those living within the Central Scotland Police Force area) and 'visitors' (i.e. those living outside of the Central Scotland Police Force area). Of the records, 21 per cent had to be dismissed from the analysis due to being identified as containing incomplete information, leaving records for 3831 drivers/vehicles and 5826 casualties identifiable as 'visitor' or 'local'.

This data will not show the entire extent of road incidents in the area as they may not be recorded for various reasons, such as the minor nature of the incident or due to those involved not wishing to notify the authorities. The data set also suffers from incomplete records on postcode fields. Unfortunately, this may result in a disproportionate number of 'visitor' records being excluded as it is likely that local postcodes will, at least in part, be known by the police whereas non-local areas, including overseas ones, will be unknown and, therefore, less likely to be recorded. There was concern expressed in the Sharples and Fletcher (2001) report that, although there had been some evident improvement, the STATS 19 forms, on which their report and this Insight are based, are not completed accurately much of the time. In a fifth of the records used here the postcode fields were entered as 'unknown' or left blank and, although there is no way of knowing for certain what their contents should have contained, it is likely that a large number of these will be from outside the local area.

Estimates of tourists and day visitors for the region – Central Scotland – are taken from Scottish Tourism Economic Activity Model (STEAM) figures, a supply-based assessment of visitor numbers to the area, commissioned by the former Area Tourist Board and public sector to measure visitor activity. The data is consistent with the police district in the main since the one Area Tourist Board region has several sub-regional STEAM reports that provide estimates of tourism activity at a local level. However STEAM figures do not include people travelling through the area and commuters; but those identified as 'visitors' for the purpose of this study will include these groups.

The Central Scotland region

The Central Scotland Police Force area is based in east-central Scotland in the area known as the Forth Valley, covering the three local council areas of Stirlingshire (including almost half of the Loch Lomond and Trossachs National Park), Clackmannanshire and Falkirk District (with a few marginal boundary differences). The population base in this area is approximately 279,480 consisting of:

Clackmannanshire	48,077
Stirlingshire	86,212
Falkirk District	145,191
Total	279,480

In terms of tourism, there is a large variance between the three areas, with Stirlingshire having the most recognisable 'tourism brand' (Page and Hall 2002) and the other districts having weakly developed tourism industries (Table 4.4). As the majority of usable data in the study pertained to UK residents, background data from the DTLR (2001) helps to develop a

Table 4.4 Tourism in the Central Scotland Police Force area

Local authority area	Overnight visitors	Day visitors	Total visitors	Average per day
Clackmannanshire	347,560	35,060	382,620	1,048
Stirlingshire	2,652,890	2,985,540	5,638,430	15,448
Falkirk District	1,095,510	253,990	1,349,500	3,697
Total	4,095,960	3,274,590	7,370,550	20,193

Sources: STEAM; Walker and Page (2005); Scottish Enterprise Forth Valley.

▶

clearer understanding of possible differences in behaviour between visitors and locals. There are several fundamental differences between general 'everyday' travel patterns and holiday/day trip patterns. Holiday trips tend to be longer than average trips; 44.2 miles against an average for all purposes of *6.6* miles. Unsurprisingly, as distance increased so did the likelihood that a trip was for holiday purposes, with visiting friends being the most likely reason for trips over 50 miles. Car journeys for holiday or day trip purposes have the highest level of occupancy compared to other purposes with an average of 2.3 passengers; compared, for example, with commuting trips with an average of 1.2 or shopping trip average of 1.6 (DTLR 2001). This is likely to have implications for casualty numbers in the event of an accident, theoretically at least there is likely to be a higher number of casualties per accident for visitor-driven cars due to these higher car occupancy levels. UK data suggests that men are more likely to travel longer distances by car (DTLR 2001) and are more likely to hold a driving licence, particularly in the older age groups (DfT 2003). This will make their exposure rates to accidents higher than those of women. Although there is no clear evidence to suggest that men drive more on holiday than women, as tourists visiting Scotland tend to be in the older age groups (VisitScotland, 2002) there is likely to be a correspondingly high proportion of male drivers.

Findings of the research

Using the driver postcode and the accident grid reference, 'accident to home' distance can be calculated. This would indicate that the mean average distance from home is 21.75 km but the modal distance for accidents was 2 km from home, meaning that the majority of drivers were very local to the accident area. Although this study is centred on the Central Scotland Police Force area, the calculations for 40 km away from home were made to allow comparison to the 'definition' of a local in the Sharples and Fletcher (2001) report; the argument put forward for this distance was based on the National Travel Survey data (see Sharples and Fletcher 2001: 25). This allowed a triangulation 'check' on the data. Some 89 per cent of accidents occurred within a 40 km distance from home; this was comparable to the Sharples and Fletcher report, which had 87 per cent 'local only' drivers and 8 per cent 'mixed local and non-local' (2001: 29).

Visitor drivers are involved in 28 per cent of accidents occurring in the Central Scotland Police Force area; however, they are proportionately more likely to be involved in serious or fatal accidents (see Figure 4.6).

Although over the course of the year, visitor drivers, are involved in 28 per cent of all accidents, they show a slight rise in April then a larger rise in June, peaking in July before descending again in August. This mainly coincides with Easter and Summer holiday periods, although visitor accidents as a percentage of total accidents in August only make up 28 per cent of the total, the average as shown in Figure 4.7.

Road types also showed significant differences between local and visitor driver accidents, with visitors more likely to be involved in an accident on A-, A(M)- or M-classified

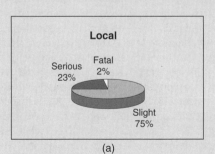
(a)

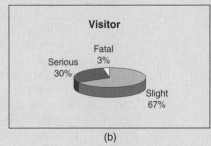
(b)

Figure 4.6 Level of severity of accident for (a) local and (b) visitor drivers

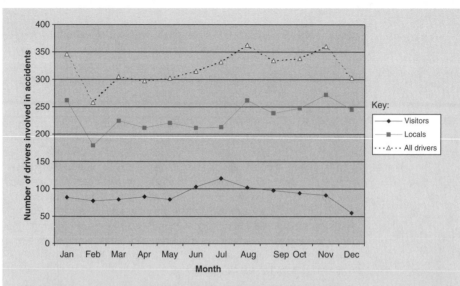

Figure 4.7 Seasonal distribution of road traffic accidents

Table 4.5 Road type where accident occurred for local and visitor drivers

Road type	Local (no.)	Visitor (no.)	Local (%)	Visitor (%)
Motorway	123	126	4.4	11.8
A(M)-road of motorway standard	24	10	0.9	0.9
A-road	1294	677	46.5	63.3
B-road	498	119	17.9	11.1
C-road	59	7	2.1	0.7
Unclassified road	788	131	28.3	12.2
Total	2786	1070	100.0	100.0

roads (see Table 4.5). This again is likely to be due to exposure rates with visitor drivers more likely to stick to main routes due to unfamiliarity with local roads.

As 66 per cent of tourists to Scotland (VisitScotland 2003) are aged over 35, a higher average age for accidents may be expected. For non-UK drivers there was insufficient data, but of the 40 identified as non-UK drivers, the mean was 40 years and the modal age was 38 years.

Although the cause of accident must be treated with caution due to the very subjective nature of completion of reports in difficult situations, it does give some indication of the differences between local and visitor drivers, with local conditions being more significant for visitor drivers. However, perhaps more important is the type of accident impact experienced. This insight shows that the EuroRAP research is a useful start in identifying the likely risks for all drivers, but this then needs to be related to the risks that tourists face as drivers and how a blend of tourism, transport and other data is required to investigate a transport and tourism problem. The data can also be used to look at future resourcing issues for planners, local government and central government with reference to investment programmes to improve tourist and non-tourist road safety. However, to anticipate likely cost–benefit savings from additional investment to make safety improvements, it is often necessary to use such data to forecast likely growth in tourist traffic. For this reason, attention now turns to the issue of forecasting.

●●●● # Forecasting the demand for tourist transport

According to Jefferson and Lickorish (1991: 101), forecasting the demand for tourist transport is essential for commercial operators, 'whether in the public or private sector . . . [as they] will seek to maximise revenue and profits in moving towards maximum efficiency in [their] use of resources'. Archer (1987: 77) argues that:

> no manager can avoid the need for some form of forecasting: a manager must plan for the future in order to minimise the risk of failure or, more optimistically, to maximise the possibilities of success. In order to plan, he must use forecasts. Forecasts will always be made, whether by guesswork, teamwork or the use of complex models, and the accuracy of the forecasts will affect the quality of the management decision.

Reliable forecasts are essential for managers and decision-makers involved in service provision within the tourist transport system to try and ensure adequate supply is available to meet demand, whilst avoiding oversupply, since this can erode the profitability of their operation. In essence, 'forecasts of tourism demand are essential for efficient planning by airlines, shipping companies, railways, coach operators, hoteliers, tour operators . . .' (Witt et al. 1991: 52).

Forecasting is the process associated with an assessment of future changes in the demand for tourist transport. It must be stressed that 'forecasting is not an exact science' (Jefferson and Lickorish 1991: 102), as it attempts to make estimations of future traffic potential and a range of possible scenarios, which provide an indication of the likely scale of change in demand. Consequently, forecasting is a technique used to suggest the future pattern of demand and associated marketing activity is required to exploit the market for tourist transport services.

According to Jefferson and Lickorish (1991: 102) the principal methods of forecasting are:

- 'the projection by extrapolation, of historic trends' (i.e. how the previous performance of demand may shape future patterns);
- 'extrapolation, subject to the application of . . . [statistical analysis using] weights or variables';
- and structured group discussions amongst a panel of tourism transport experts may be used to assess factors determining future traffic forecasts (known as the Delphi method).

Bull (1991) recognises that the range of tourism forecasting techniques is determined by the methods of analysis they employ. There are two basic types of forecasting method: those based on qualitative techniques, such as the Delphi method, which Archer (1987) argues are considerably less rigorous than quantitative forecasting methods, using techniques developed from statistics and economic theory.

Bull (1991: 127–8) classifies the quantitative techniques forecasters use in terms of the degree of statistical and mathematical complexity based on:

- time-series analysis of trends (e.g. seasonality in travel), which involve simple statistical calculations to consider how past trends may be replicated in the future;
- economic theory models, used in econometrics (see Witt and Martin 1992).

Clearly, in an introductory book such as this there is insufficient space to consider the detailed technical aspects of forecasting that are reviewed in a number of other good sources (e.g. Archer 1987; Witt and Martin 1992; Witt and Witt 1995; Frechtling 1996; Sinclair and Stabler 1997; Song and Witt 2000). The important issue to recognise here is that in forecasting, a number of variables are examined which relate to factors directly and indirectly influencing tourist travel. These variables are considered according to their statistical relationship with each other. Bull (1991: 127) notes that the most common variables used are:

- number of tourist trips;
- total tourist expenditure and expenditure per capita;
- market shares of tourism;
- the tourism sector's share of gross domestic product.

Depending on the complexity of the methodology employed, the forecasting model may examine one dependent variable (e.g. tourist trips) and how other independent variables (e.g. the state of the national and international economy, leisure time, levels of disposable income, inflation and foreign exchange rates) affect the demand for tourist trips.

Approaches to forecasting can also be classified according to what they are attempting to do. For example, time-series models of tourism, using statistical techniques such as moving averages (see Witt and Martin 1989: 6), may be easy and relatively inexpensive to undertake, but they are 'non-causal'. This means that they do not explain what specific factors are shaping the trends: they only indicate what is happening in terms of observed trends. In fact, there is also evidence that non-causal techniques have been more accurate than more complex econometric models (Witt et al. 1991). Econometric models are termed 'causal' since they are searching for statistical relationships to suggest what is causing tourist trips to take a certain form, thereby producing particular trends. Thus, the level of complexity involved in causal modelling is considerably greater.

Usyal and Crompton (1985: 14) provide a good overview of different methods used to forecast tourism demand, concluding that:

Qualitative approaches when combined with quantitative approaches enable forecasts to be amended to incorporate relevant consumer demand data. When used alone quantitative models have conceptual limitations. Typically they are philosophically blind . . . Lack of appropriate data means that they are unable to incorporate an understanding of consumer motivations and behaviour which explain tourism demand and may cause it to shift unpredictably in the future.

Ultimately, forecasting attempts to establish how consumer demand for tourist transport has shaped previous trends and how these may change in the future, often over a 5- to 10-year period. On a world scale, the detailed study by Edwards and Graham (2000) *Long Term Tourism Forecasts to the Year 2005*, and subsequent updates, remains an invaluable and widely cited source that examines the future demand for tourism. This can be used to assess how the demand for tourist transport will change on a global basis and within different countries over the next decade. However, industry organisations such as the Air Transport Action Group commission specialist agencies to produce forecasts whilst the major airline manufacturers also produce forecasts (Airbus 2003; Boeing Commercial Airline Group 2003). For this reason, some of the key findings from ATAG's forecasts for Asia-Pacific air travel (ATAG 2001) are examined, given its significant growth potential in world aviation to 2012 and beyond.

Air transport traffic forecasts in Asia-Pacific to the year 2014

ATAG was established in 1990 as an industry coalition aimed at developing 'economically beneficial aviation capacity improvements in an environmentally responsible manner'. It is concerned to lobby bodies to ensure that the future growth in air travel can be accommodated through appropriate investment in airports and air traffic management. The organisation recognises that its impact has been greatest in Europe, North America and Asia through a range of its publications; most of its reports are also available on the Internet (*www/atag.org/atag/Index.htm*). Given ATAG's values and objectives, the report it commissioned from IATA (International Air Transport Association) in 2001 provides a detailed analysis of Asia-Pacific traffic forecasts to 2014 (*www.atag.org*) as shown in Table 4.6.

According to ATAG (2001), there will be limited growth in the world market for air travel as many markets have matured, but Asian international traffic will rise from 32.5 per cent of global traffic in 1999 to 36.1 per cent by 2014. Much of this growth will be dominated by the development of the Chinese aviation market, as its share of domestic and international traffic increased from 9.9 per cent in 1985 to 16.1 per cent in 1999 and is forecast to grow to 24.6 per cent by 2014, as shown in Table 4.6. Thus, China will be a key driver of Asian aviation demand to 2014. ATAG (2001) outlined the key drivers of air travel to 2014 as:

- short-haul high-density routes such as those in growth triangles, for example Singapore–Kuala Lumpur and Bangkok;
- medium-haul routes, especially city pairs within Asia and those in north Asia;
- long-haul routes between Europe, the USA and the Pacific region as well as within the region from South East Asia.

Table 4.6 Domestic and international traffic in Asia, 1985–2014

	Annual passengers in millions			Average annual rates of growth	
	1985	*1999*	*2014*	*1985–99*	*1999–2014*
China	15.4	69.6	214.7	11.4	7.8
Japan	60.1	139.5	195.8	6.2	2.3
Taiwan	10.7	52.4	101.1	12.1	4.5
South Korea	7.5	38.4	83.0	12.3	5.3
Hong Kong SAR	9.3	29.1	71.4	8.5	6.2
Thailand	6.8	25.7	59.3	10.0	5.7
India	13.4	24.4	57.5	4.3	5.9
Singapore	8.6	21.7	51.4	6.8	5.9
Malaysia	6.7	18.4	39.3	7.5	5.2
Indonesia	5.0	1.2	27.2	50.9	6.1
The Philippines	6.4	9.0	20.9	37.9	5.8
Vietnam	0.1	4.3	19.2	29.5	10.5

Source: ATAG (2001).

ATAG points to trunk routes in each of the three categories above, but what will dominate intra-regional travel in the region are the trunk routes between:

- Japan and South Korea;
- Japan and Hong Kong;
- Hong Kong and Taiwan.

The result would be that Japan is displaced as the main driver of Asian aviation demand by 2014 if these forecasts are achieved, which in terms of scale means that there would be a tenfold increase in passenger volume 1985–2014. For example, China could achieve a 208 per cent increase from 69.6 million passengers in 1999 to 214.7 million in 2014. Thus, in 2014, ATAG (2001) argues that 88 per cent of international scheduled Asian traffic will be intra-Asian (233 million passengers) whilst the main intercontinental routes will be Asia–Europe and Asia–North America. To accommodate this growth, ATAG indicated that airlines in Asia will have to accommodate growth by increasing load factors, better seat densities, increasing the number of non-stop flights as opposed to stopping services and having larger aircraft – all of which may help increase occupied seats per departure.

This research has also been expanded upon more recently by Airbus (2007) *Global Market Forecast 2007–2026*, pointing to the compound growth in global air travel of 4.9 per cent per annum and the demand for 24,000 new aircraft by 2026, 31 per cent of which will be from Asia. Much of the Airbus analysis is predicated upon the growing urbanisation of Asia and rise of the megacities (i.e. by 2015 there will be 30 cities with over 10 million population worldwide). By 2026, in terms of RPKs (route passenger kilometres), Asia will be the leading region for air traffic, to over 3500 billion RPKs followed by just over 2500 billion RPKs.

This is a useful starting point to consider the relationship between demand, supply and the role of forecasting. Such research also highlights the significance of using various data sources and techniques to assess future demand. As Witt and Witt (1995) conclude in their seminal review of tourism forecasting methods, future developments in forecasting need to make improvements in model building and to use a range of methods to produce forecasts.

Alternative approaches to understanding future demand for tourism and transport services: scenario planning Stephen J. Page and Ian Yeoman

One criticism of tourism demand forecasting as an approach is that it is not sophisticated enough to accommodate the impact of tourist behaviour change and the impact of events as Song and Li (2008: 217) acknowledge:

> Considering the enormous consequences of various crises and disasters, events' impact evaluation has attracted much interest in tourism demand forecasting research. It is crucial for researchers to develop some forecasting methods that can accommodate unexpected events in predicting the potential impacts of these one-off events through scenario analysis.

This points to the importance of scenario analysis as a valid technique to further enrich our understanding of transport and tourism futures. Other studies such as Prideaux et al. (2003) reaffirmed the necessity of considering scenario analysis given the problems of forecasting in foretelling the impact of events and the significance of developing the domain often identified as tourism futures research. In short, scenario planning is the process of predicting multiple, plausible and uncertain futures (Heijden et al. 2002), and so is well suited to address some of the potential shortcomings of futures research which is almost entirely based upon forecasting in Tourism Studies. Forecasting pre-supposes a degree of certainty in futures research whereas scenario planning seeks to incorporate the principle that nothing is certain in the future and is well suited to strategic planning (Bunn 1993).

A scenario planning approach to the future argues that nothing in the future is certain or predictable with regard to transport and tourism, given the current concerns and uncertainty over global issues such as climate change (Gössling 2003) and the future of oil as a fuel as Chapter 9 will show. A wide range of 'futures' research methods help us to consider how possible policy shifts may be needed to facilitate the ongoing development of a nation's tourism sector. These global issues will have a national and local impact upon transport and its ability to facilitate tourism growth in the future. In other words, the current thinking which dominates our ability to understand how tourism and transport interact and facilitate tourism growth will inevitably change in the next 15 to 20 years. Therefore, tourism will be affected by a range of new challenges and different potential scenarios such as the future role of transport and CO_2 emissions by 2030 in the UK (Hickman and Bannister 2007) and the role of policy measures in this debate which will directly affect different modes of tourist transport and propensity to travel.

There are critics of the need for scenario analysis and the need to apply it to understand future tourism growth because conventional thinking by many politicians is that the problems of future mobility and global warming will be addressed by technology, a largely optimistic anthropocentric interpretation. This philosophical position argues that there is no need to plan for major changes in the future of travel and tourism resulting from potential constraints. This thinking is shaped by the pursuit of competition and growth in tourism where virtually every country in the world is now a beneficiary of tourism growth and development, and so the view that tourism may be different in form, shape and volume in the future (i.e. smaller in scale and volume) is not necessarily a stance adopted by political decision-makers, given the short-term political time horizons in which they think.

Scenario planning as a method of analysis

Scenario planning is increasingly being used by organisations to consider the uncertain elements in the business environment to try and improve our foresight, to challenge our existing assumptions about how the world works (Schnaars 1987). The UK Cabinet Office Performance and Innovation Unit (2001) sets out a range of general principles which underpin futures work which is more than simply forecasting or predicting the future. It embraces a wide variety of techniques to help create choices based on looking at alternative possibilities framed around three key questions: what may happen (possible futures), what is the most likely to happen (probable futures) and what would we prefer to happen (preferable futures). In their review of different definitions of scenario planning, Duinker and Greig (2007: 209) concluded that the commonality was the 'idea that scenario-building does not focus on making predictions or forecasts, but rather on describing images of the future that challenge current assumptions and broaden perspectives'.

A substantial literature emanating from management science and the development of scenario planning in the 1960s and 1970s from the work of the Rand Corporation and Stanford Research Institute (e.g. Chermack et al. 2001) exists epitomised by studies such as Heijden (2005) and other studies such as Lindgren and Bandhold (2003) where the emphasis is upon using scenario analysis to effect change in corporate strategy. More all-embracing overviews such as Wilson and Ralston (2006) and Ringland (2006) seek to emphasise how learning about the future and uncertainty can use a variety of tools, which are discussed below in more detail. Ringland (2006) provides a detailed background to the development of scenario planning as a subject, including the work of large organisations such as Shell and the way in which scenario planning can be developed to craft a number of diverging stories about the future using uncertain events and driving forces to better understand the future within organisations. Duinker and Greig (2007: 210) argue that scenario planning performs two important functions: 'risk management, where scenarios enable strategies and decisions to be tested against possible futures, while the other is creativity and sparking new ideas' which is reviewed in detail by Lang (1998). One notable example which Ringland (2006) illustrates, is how one transport organisation – British Airways – has used this process in its futures research. More specialist overviews by Ringland (2002) focus on the public sector whilst other authors have embraced the term scenario learning (Fahey and Randall 1997) as a conceptual approach in scenario analysis.

The journals *Futures* and *Long Range Planning* also carry a range of academic and practitioner articles on this highly applied and problem-solving area of management research while there have been wider applications across the natural sciences (e.g. Duinker and Greig 2007 and its role in improving environmental impact analysis) and other areas of social science and each application is characterised by different conceptual approaches to developing scenarios. Cornish (2004) provides an overview of the wide range of futures techniques which can be harnessed which include: environmental scanning, trend analysis, trend monitoring, trend projection, scenarios, polling, brainstorming, modelling, gaming, historical analysis and visioning (i.e. looking more than 10 years ahead) and this aspect of scenario planning according to Schoemaker (1995) is a highly disciplined method for imaging possible futures and asking questions such as 'what if'. This broad range of techniques illustrates how scenario planning fits into the wide continuum of futures research methodologies. Calantone et al. (1987) distinguished between four forms of forecasting and the merits of each approach, including: exploratory forecasting based on extrapolating past trends using regression and similar techniques; normative, integrative and speculative forecasting (each of which are reviewed in detail by Song and Li 2008). What Prideaux et al. (2003) emphasise is that forecasting has a limited role to play beyond the short-term horizon of around 5–10 years. This is due to the implicit use of equilibrium and stability in such models as opposed to more uncertainty and complexity. It reflects the need to acknowledge the certainty of uncertainty given the maxim of history that change rather than equilibrium dominates human society, where events and the unexpected cause change. This perspective of the longer term horizon means that risks to tourism growth are more certain than continued growth based on past experiences, particularly given the significance of global warming.

Within scenario planning a range of scientific standpoints exist (see Bradfield et al. 2005 for more detail) along with a range of practices, each with their own tools and techniques. There are also a variety of hard to soft techniques, each having objectives ranging from intuitive and learning outcomes for the organisation through to more analytical methods that offer more certainty than ambiguity. The challenge is in harnessing the most appropriate tool for the task in hand and in integrating a range of tools to understand different dimensions of the research problem being investigated.

A study by Lyons et al. (2002) provides one example of how to examine the future of transport in the twenty-first century – through their Transport Visions Project (*www.trg.soton.ac.uk/research/TVNetwork*) – which sought to understand the diversity of factors that will shape transport demand in the new millennium. Much of the initial research has considered how changing values in society and different lifestyles may shape future demand and how policy makers may have to respond. What is recognised is that a culture of travel and migration will continue to prevail as mobility remains a central tenet of developed economies (and developing economies). This will require more collective forms of transport (i.e. public transport) to be expanded on major urban corridors whilst the diversity of individual demand that is car based will continue (as discussed in Chapter 3). The car, with its ability to offer flexibility and to accommodate trips with variable time and space impacts, will continue and therefore policy, more precise measures of demand and statistical sources will be critical in a growing climate of evidence-based policy decision-making (i.e. evidence to support decisions as opposed to simple political expediency and philosophy that characterised the short-term policy objectives which dominated transport policy in the nineteenth and twentieth centuries). Lyons et al.'s (2002) paper is interesting because it shows how the diversity of approaches to understanding future demand and how policy needs to be shaped to affect supply is critical for tourism and leisure provision, not least because the future shape of society will affect how society exercises its right to mobility and travel (also see Chatterjee and Gordon 2006; Page et al. 2010).

Summary

This chapter has shown that the demand for tourist transport can be examined from a range of accessible data sources published by NGOs such as the WTO and OECD, which may be complemented by more detailed studies by individual researchers, consultancies and transport operators interested in understanding the needs of their customers. As previously emphasised, the demand for tourist transport can be directly influenced by government policy to expand both incoming tourism and outbound tourism, although this has important consequences for infrastructure provision and the supply issues in tourist transport, which are dealt with in subsequent chapters. In the case of China, the demand for domestic travel is of a scale that many planners, operators and researchers would find difficult to visualise and conceptualise. This is also the case if one looks at air travel forecasts for Asia-Pacific over the next decade or beyond. Growth in demand has major implications for infrastructure and the use of transport modes. Even a minor growth in demand in China has major consequences for tourist travel, given the large base population and distances involved in domestic trips. Whilst data on domestic tourism in China is notoriously difficult to access outside of China, existing studies do point to the significance of diverse data sources in reconstructing patterns of demand and expected future growth. In this respect, WTO data can only be a rudimentary starting point for any analysis of demand. As the Insight on road safety and traffic accidents illustrated, a variety of other data sources (which do not always correspond with each other) are vital in understanding the human dimension of tourism demand.

Many airline companies have set their sights on penetrating emerging markets such as Asia-Pacific at a time of relative stagnation in other mature travel markets, as illustrated by both tourism and traffic data. Such strategies are based on forecasts of the likely growth in the Japanese outbound market, since companies need to establish how future investment programmes in new routes and infrastructure can be justified. Yet as Burns (1996) argues, statistical growth in tourism is not necessarily an indication of widespread cultural and cognitive changes towards holiday and overseas travel.

It is not surprising that large tourist transport operators employ forecasting experts in-house and use a variety of transport analysts to ensure that they receive the best sources of market intelligence to understand how tourism markets are performing and changing to remain competitive. Such information inevitably remains confidential, even though forecasting is not an exact science that is able to offer definitive answers on how particular tourist markets will perform over a 5- to 10-year time span. Yet the demand for tourist transport should not be viewed in isolation from supply issues. The tourist transport system operates through the interplay of government policy, consumer demand and the supply of transport services. For this reason, the next two chapters consider the supply of tourist transport services from two perspectives: how to understand supply issues and how they are subsequently managed.

Questions

1 What are the main published sources of data available to researchers to assess the demand for domestic and international travel?

2 Why do private and public sector tourist transport providers commission research on the demand for their services?

3 Why do tourist transport organisations undertake forecasting?

4 What are the main types of forecasting technique which researchers use when assessing the future market potential for tourist transport services?

Further reading

Some of the following studies are now quite dated but remain amongst the most accessible and helpful in introducing themes and issues.

In terms of international tourism statistics, the most accessible synthesis of trends is:

BaRon, R. (1997) 'Global tourism trends to 1996', *Tourism Economics*, 3(3): 289–300.

On forecasting and tourism data consult:

Archer, B.H. (1987) 'Demand forecasting and estimation', in J.R.B. Ritchie and C.R. Goeldner (eds) *Travel, Tourism and Hospitality Research*, New York: Wiley, 77–85.

Song, H, Witt, S. and Li, G. (2009) *Advanced Econometrics of Tourism Demand*, Routledge: London.

On the problems posed by the car in relation to National Parks see: Transport for Leisure and Smith, A. (2001) *Experience and Best Practice in the Planning and Managing of Transport within National Parks and Areas of Outstanding Natural Beauty in England and Wales*, Scottish Natural Heritage Commissioned Report FOONC10, SNH, Edinburgh.

and National Parks in England and Wales Transport Policy Statement on the issues and problems (*www.nationalparks.gov.uk/enpaa/whatsnew/transportpolicystatement.htm*).

Websites

There follows a useful range of websites that have transport and tourism statistics.

United Nations: www.un.org

European Union: www.europa.eu

World Tourism Organization: www.world-tourism.org

Cruise Lines International Association: www.cruising.org

Department for Transport, UK: www.dft.gov.uk

Air Transport Action Group (ATAG): www.atag.org

International Civil Aviation Association (ICAO): www.icao.org

Airport statistics can be found at Airport Council International: www.aic.org

5

Analysing supply issues in tourist transport

Introduction

In Chapter 4 the demand for tourist transport was discussed in terms of the commercial opportunities it affords operators that are able to understand and harness it. To meet the demand for tourist transport, businesses and operators can employ a range of concepts to analyse what they need to do to match supply to demand. For this reason, the next two chapters examine supply issues in two discrete and yet interrelated ways. First, this chapter considers some of the broader issues affecting the supply of tourist transport, particularly a conceptual framework in which both the traveller's and the transport provider's perspectives are considered to try and maximise the commercial and non-commercial opportunities within the tourism industry. Second, Chapter 6 discusses how operators and the transport sector employ particular management tools (e.g. logistics and information technology applications) and business strategies to provide the tourist as a user and consumer of the transport system with a range of opportunities to enhance their overall tourist experience. Whilst the two chapters examine supply issues in different ways – looking at the complexity of analytical and operational issues separated into discrete sections – in reality one needs to view these two elements in a holistic manner as they are intertwined in the real world.

It is also important to emphasise the broader tourism context in which tourist transport exists. The study by Harris and Masberg (1997) that examined vintage tram operations in 26 North American cities indicates how the supply of a mode of transport can be harnessed for tourism and yet is not able to generate tourism without appropriate infrastructure to support it. Harris and Masberg (1997) argue that whilst trams may constitute a cultural icon influencing tourists to visit a destination, a pool of attractions is needed to get visitors to use trams to tour within the destination. In other words, the supply of transport itself is not sufficient to stimulate tourism development but can be a catalyst if it is integrated as part of a wider strategy to develop attractions, accommodation and an urban tourism experience (Page 1995b). This example serves to illustrate the significance of developing various approaches and concepts that promote a broader understanding of transport supply issues. A similar argument can also be developed for transport modes, such as car hire, that support tourist activities (see Loverseed 1996), although in a number of cases where transport is the tourist experience (e.g. cruising and vintage railways), supply issues may assume an even greater significance as the entire experience is

Plate 5.1 Coach parking in small historic cities, such as Canterbury, needs to be located so as not to conflict with local residents' use of the city, which led to the conversion of a Council site to a coach park and new tourist route into the city away from the congested areas around the Cathedral Precincts
Source: S.J. Page

directly dependent upon the service the operator provides (Plate 5.1). Sakai (2006: 266) highlights a key role in the analysis of supply issues – namely the provision of tourism infrastructure, such as roads, bridges, ports and airports as:

> The provision of tourism infrastructure is of particular importance to the long-term environment of tourism growth. Expanded facilities are needed to accommodate anticipated growth and to maintain a relatively uninterrupted service level (Sakai 2006: 266).

In fact Sakai (2006) pointed to industry estimates that between 2004 and 2014 capital investment in infrastructure (some of which will be tourism-specific) may reach US$1402 billion. So the key message is that ongoing investment in transport and infrastructure is needed to ensure the continued efficiency and competitiveness of tourism destinations.

There is a relative paucity of research on supply issues in tourism and transport studies (Eadington and Redman 1991). Witt et al. (1991: 155–6) consider that:

> [the] subset of transport studies that directly relates to tourism is relatively neglected . . . [and] it is a major task of research to bring together the work done in transport studies with that more specialised work on tourism . . . [as] many of the relevant studies are privately commissioned and often not widely disseminated.

The absence of any synthesis of supply-related research which integrates tourism and transport into a more cohesive framework led Sinclair (1991: 6) to argue that the 'literature on transportation and its implications for domestic and international tourism merits separate analysis'. The efficient management and operation of transport systems for tourists require that demand issues are analysed in relation to supply since the two issues coexist and they determine the future pattern of use and activities within the tourist transport system.

The supply of tourist transport has been dealt with in various popular tourism textbooks (e.g. Holloway 1989; Lavery 1989), which consider the characteristics, principles and organisation associated with each mode of tourist transport. In a book such as this, it is inappropriate to reiterate the empirical discussion of different modes of transport in these publications since it would inevitably result in a descriptive listing that is documented elsewhere (Collier 1994).

The chapter commences with a discussion of theory related to supply issues; this is followed by a framework that develops the context in which both the traveller's and the transport provider's perspectives are considered in relation to an underlying concern for service quality. The concept of transaction analysis is introduced as a method of understanding the central role of transport in the supply of tourist travel. Transaction analysis assists in assessing the transport supplier's involvement in the distribution chain and the ways in which they may influence and control the chain and service quality in the supply of transport services. To illustrate the extent of one transport operator's involvement in the distribution chain, an Insight based on Singapore Airlines is examined (Insight 5.1).

● ● ● ● Theoretical perspectives on tourism and transport supply issues

Despite the rapid growth in research studies in tourism in the 1980s and 1990s, those publications that make a contribution to the advancement of knowledge and our understanding of the subject are still comparatively few. This is certainly the case in relation to supply issues, and one explanation may be related to the fact that:

> Tourism supply is a complex phenomenon because of both the nature of the product and the process of delivery. Principally, it cannot be stored, cannot be examined prior to purchase, it is necessary to travel to consume it, heavy reliance is placed on both natural and human-made resources and a number of components are required, which may be separately or jointly purchased and which are consumed in sequence. It is a composite product involving transport, accommodation, catering, natural resources, entertainment, and other facilities and services, such as shops and banks, travel agents and tour operators (Sinclair and Stabler 1997: 58).

Thus, many businesses supply components that are combined to form the tourism product, and because they operate in different markets it makes it difficult to analyse supply issues. In fact, it proves even more complex when seeking to separate out one element of the tourism product (i.e. transport) to identify the range of supply issues affecting an individual element.

Probably the most influential and pertinent publication to date that assists in addressing supply issues in a theoretical framework is a synthesis of *The Economics of Tourism* (Sinclair and Stabler 1997). Sinclair and Stabler infer that one can explain how firms operate under different conditions and therefore it may be possible to identify factors which affect supply issues in relation to tourism in general, and transport in particular. For example, Hofer et al. (2009) examine the impact of financial distress (e.g. Chapter 11 protection from bankruptcy in the USA) on airline pricing strategies: some airlines reduced prices during periods of distress while others did not, reflecting the complexity of pricing and the response of competitors. In markets with a large number of competitors, some airlines became more risk-assertive in the way they priced products and in general terms; the relationship between firms facing financial distress and air fares was a negative one. Whilst it is not possible to present a detailed analysis here, the main principles outlined by Sinclair and Stabler (1997) are discussed as they focus on four market situations:

- perfect competition;
- contestable markets;
- monopoly;
- oligopoly.

In this discussion, attention is directed to the transport sector.

Perfect competition

In economic models of conditions of perfect competition, a number of assumptions exist:

- There are a substantial number of consumers and firms, implying that neither can affect the price of an undifferentiated product.
- There is free entry to and exit from the market, assuming that there are no barriers.

Sinclair and Stabler (1997) explain how a perfect market operates and how prices are derived, with the tendency towards a break-even price in a situation where consumers derive a benefit. However, in the real world, many economists believe that markets are not perfectly competitive.

Contestable markets

In this situation, there are 'insignificant entry and exit costs, so that there are negligible entry and exit barriers. Sunk costs which a firm incurs in order to produce and which would not be recoupable if the firm left the industry, are not significant' (Sinclair and Stabler 1997: 61). Owing to technology, information and supply conditions are available to all producers and, whilst producers cannot change prices instantaneously, consumers can react immediately. The key principle here is that new and established firms are able to challenge rival businesses through pricing strategies. Firms in contestable markets are seen to operate in a similar way to those in perfect markets, since they charge similar prices for a product; existing operators cannot charge more than average cost because more competitors would enter the market. Owing to low sunk costs and low entry/exit barriers, rivals establish to compete. As Debbage and Alkaabi (2008: 149) argue, it was the theory of the contestable market which provided the intellectual justification of airline deregulation in the USA.

Monopoly

This is probably best described as the opposite of perfect competition, where a major business or firm is able to exercise a high level of control over the price of the product and level of output. The implications are that firms operating in a monopolistic market charge prices above the average cost of production to generate high profit levels, so consumers pay a price higher than that which would exist in a competitive market. In many countries, domestic air and rail networks operate under monopoly conditions even though it can be against the interests of consumers.

In some cases a monopoly condition may be more beneficial than competition, as in the case of deregulation in the transport industry. In such situations an influx of new entrants following deregulation may lead to smaller firms being taken over by larger businesses (see the next section on airline deregulation in the USA). An interesting study by Pitfield (2007) of airline alliances and their immunity from US antitrust legislation found that such alliances led to a decline in competition, contrary to popular belief. Indeed, Open Skies Agreements were heralded as providing more open access for competition. In October 2008 at its Agenda for Freedom Summit the IATA called for many of the current bilateral agreements between countries to be scrapped in favour of greater deregulation of markets to give greater market access via improved Freedom of the Skies (see Chapter 6 for more detail).

Sinclair and Stabler (1997) examine scenarios where monopoly conditions may be beneficial to the wider public good in tourist transport operations. Where governments have privatised state transport interests, one outcome has been a greater degree of concentration of operations amongst a small number of operators. However, where monopoly situations exist, regulation by the state is normally imposed to prevent higher prices and supernormal profits. Interestingly, Fageda and Fernández-Villadangos (2009) indicate the point where monopoly switches to competition on airline routes, which bears a relationship to the volume of traffic and demand for services.

Oligopoly

An oligopoly exists where a limited number of producers dominate the transport sector. Williams (1995: 163) highlights the situation in relation to tourism and transport since 'tourism has a highly dualistic industrial structure which is polarised between large numbers of small firms (typically in retailing, accommodation services) and a small number of large companies (for example, in air transport)'.

In an oligopoly, each firm controls its price and output levels and there are entry and exit barriers. An oligopoly market situation is characterised by supply conditions dependent in part upon the output and pricing decisions of competitors. In an ideal world, oligopolies prefer prices to be set at levels where the profits are maximised for all producers in that industry sector. If the firms colluded to set prices, it could lead to a monopoly and higher profits for producers if they restricted the supply. Sinclair and Stabler (1997) point to the impact of inter-airline pricing and route-sharing agreements to achieve joint profits in an oligopolistic situation. In an oligopolistic market, producers can alter output and prices whilst taking account of their competitors' likely reactions.

In their overview of the air travel market, Sinclair and Stabler (1997: 81) argue that:

> Although a domestic monopoly or oligopoly structure has been common, with a single state-supported airline or a small number of competing airlines, deregulation has made some markets competitive in the short run. In the international market some routes are competitive, being served by many carriers. Most of the others are served by at least two carriers, indicating an oligopolist market, although a few routes are served by a single carrier which may be tempted to exercise monopoly powers.

In terms of the remaining transport sectors, Sinclair and Stabler (1997: 81) conclude that:

> The structures of the bus, coach and rail sectors are similar to that of air travel in that they too experience the problems of high capital costs, fixed capacity, peaked demand, the need for feeder routes to sustain profitable ones. Some state support and regulation characterise these modes.

It is apparent that where a large number of small firms operate in the transport sector a competitive market exists. In contrast, where a limited number of firms operate, akin to an oligopoly or, at the extreme, a monopoly, different conditions affect the supply of transport services for tourists. What emerges from the excellent analysis of supply conditions in tourism is that various criteria influence the competitive conditions which exist in different markets, and factors such as the degree of market concentration or price leadership affect the extent and nature of interfirm competition. For example, French (1996b) examines the advent of 'no frills' airlines in Europe and the effect on the market. The European Low Fares Airline Association (ELFAA) (2002) report summarised the benefits of low-cost airlines for the consumer following the liberalisation of airline markets in Europe (discussed in Chapter 2) in terms of:

- increased choice for consumers;
- lower fares, especially on trunk routes;
- removal of restrictive pricing practices, with one-way fare pricing;
- greater accessibility of travellers with the use of secondary airports;
- greater benefits for regional development through secondary airport development and destination development associated with such growth (e.g. the growth of new destinations such as Charleroi in France, Gdansk in Poland and Knock in Ireland) and a greater tax take from tourism in these new destinations from airline and tourism;
- a spreading of the weekly and annual patterns of demand and seasonality through midweek cheap travel options with low-cost airline air fares.

In a similar vein, the Channel Tunnel is a new market entrant and has had an impact on the cross-Channel ferry market. Here the competition led to a reduction in yields with a competitive price war. The result has been a greater degree of concentration in the ferry market with the merger of P&O and Stena Line. Similar arguments have also been seen in the deregulated bus and coach market in the UK and across Europe with the concentration of the industry into a small number of large operators (e.g. Firstbus, Arriva and Stagecoach). In fact, the UK coach market has been subject to even greater concentration with the National Express network effectively controlling the majority of long-distance coach routes in England and Wales. In Brazil, however, after a period of economic liberalisation, the aviation market was re-regulated in 2003 due to the problems of over-competition (similar to the problems which faced the US airline sector – see more discussion later in this chapter) (Bettini and Oliverira 2008). This was an interesting development for Latin America, since Brazilian airlines control about 35 per cent of the air traffic in the region. Thus, in any analysis of transport supply issues, a range of criteria needs to be investigated in different market conditions. These are based on Sinclair and Stabler (1997: 83):

- the number and size of firms;
- the extent of market concentration;
- entry and exit barriers;
- economies/diseconomies of scale and economics of scope;
- costs of capital, fixed capital and costs of operation;
- price discrimination and product differentiation;
- pricing policies (e.g. price leadership, price wars and market-share strategies).

The final two points are examined in more detail in Chapter 6 since they are concerned with the strategies businesses pursue in competitive markets. In the case of the first five points, which pertain to market structures, Sinclair and Stabler identify a range of data sources available to researchers. Yet competition as a concept has been developed a stage further with key studies such as Porter (1990) using the notion of competitive advantage, based on the strategies which businesses and nations pursue. In the context of tourism and transport, such work has helped to shape further studies that have identified how competitiveness has been shaped by the types of supply-led investment and actions which governments take in terms of policy decisions to facilitate transport-led tourism growth (Chapter 3).

Competitiveness, transport and tourism: key relationships

The link between transport and the competitiveness of nations was developed in Porter's (1990) influential study which highlighted how places were able to compete with each other, and transport was a key element of the access to markets and attractiveness of places. Subsequent research developed such interests in a destination context through benchmarking (which is the comparison of how one compares to competitors) of performance in tourism and how far transport helps to explain the existing level of performance. This is an explicit concern with the supply of transport infrastructure and a recent evolution of research in this area is the Travel and Tourism Competitiveness Monitor developed by the World Economic Forum (WEF) in Switzerland (WEF 2008). This is a comparative study based on a combination of 58 variables derived from a Global Executive Opinion Survey of one or two respondents per country plus hard data for 28 of the variables employed. The data is aggregated to produce 14 pillars with three sub-indexes with assistance from WTTC (World Travel and Tourism Council), UN-WTO and IATA for relevant tourism/aviation data. For example, three of the pillars relate specifically to transport (i.e. air transport infrastructure, ground transport infrastructure and tourism infrastructure). The approach follows the WEF established methodologies used to assess competitiveness to understand why some countries become prosperous and others lag behind.

The Travel and Tourism Competitiveness Report in 2008 constructs a Travel and Tourism Competitiveness Index (TTCI) for 130 countries where tourism and destinations are ranked and evaluated in terms of their competitiveness. The use of destination competitive measures and indices is part of a wider shift towards performance measurement. The results for 2008, like 2007, ranked Switzerland on a range of indices in a country where its massive investment in public transport is seen as key attribute of developing a prosperous tourism sector. What is also interesting is how these types of competitiveness study are used by different destinations and policy-makers to try to address perceived weaknesses in their investment in transport and tourism infrastructure. What this shows is how a report which seeks to benchmark destination performance can be used to highlight areas for further development in terms of transport and accessibility. Even so, wider policy debates raised in previous chapters on issues such as privatisation and state deregulation of the transport sector can have a major impact on the supply of tourism services, as the following case of airline deregulation in the USA will show.

●●●● The state and the supply of tourist transport: airline deregulation in the USA

Air travel provides an interesting example of how government policy (see Chapter 3) has led to different effects upon the supply of transport services for tourists. Sealy (1992) identifies two approaches:

1 a regulated transport system where a country exercises sovereignty over its airspace;
2 a liberalised and unregulated system characterised by an open-skies policy,

which is somewhat problematic for a global industry that still has many protectionist and regulated environments in some instances.

In Chapter 3, it was clear that various historical and political factors may explain the aviation policy in a given country. The regulations governing airline operations by international bodies such as ICAO and IATA (see Holloway 1989; Mill 1992) and bilateral agreements were influential in shaping air travel in a regulated environment until the late 1970s (see Figure 5.1). In addition to IATA (the United Nations body that facilitates the international regulation of air travel), national governments play an active role in regulating air travel (see Graham 1995).

The experience of domestic airline deregulation in the USA in 1978 led to a complete re-evaluation of the supply of air travel in terms of its organisation, operation and regulation by the state (see Milman and Pope 1997 for an up-to-date analysis of the US airline industry). Deregulation in North America was also a test bed for aviation strategies subsequently developed in Australia and those planned for the EU (Debbage 2005). The case of the US domestic airline market is also interesting because 'it is more highly developed and more extensively used in the United States than in any other part of the world' (Graham 1992: 188). For example, in 2002 air

1st Freedom: Right of transit without landing.

2nd Freedom: Right of technical stop (e.g. refuelling).

3rd Freedom: Right to set down traffic from home state.
4th Freedom: Right to pick up traffic bound for home state.

5th Freedom: Right to pick up and put down traffic between two foreign states
as an extension of routes to/from home state.

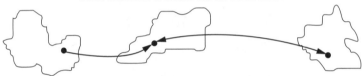

6th Freedom: Unofficial right to pick up and put down traffic between foreign states
via home state (by combining 3rd and 4th Freedom rights).

7th Freedom: Right to pick up and put down traffic between two foreign states.

Figure 5.1 Freedoms of the air

Source: Redrawn from 'Figure G.1: Air transport freedom rights', which first appeared in *Asia Pacific Air Transport: Challenges and Policy Reforms*, edited by Christopher Findlay, Chia Lin Sieh and Karmjit Singh (1997), p. 193. Reproduced with the kind permission of the publisher, Institute of Southeast Asian Studies, Singapore, http://bookshop.iseas.edu.sg.

travel in the US exceeded 644 million RPKs (route passenger kms). According to Button and Gillingwater (1991), the implications for the supply of tourist transport can be examined in relation to:

● the corporate response of airline companies to the new competitive environment for air travel;
● the effect on the functioning of the transport system;

- the effect on consumers, service provision and service quality;
- the impact upon complementary infrastructure (e.g. airports).

To understand the impact of deregulation of the domestic market for air travel in the USA, it is pertinent to examine the regulatory framework prior to and following deregulation as a context in which to consider the changes in the supply of air services.

Airline regulation in the United States

In the USA, the evolution of the US airline industry has been discussed in detail by Ben-Yosef (2005) and airline regulation can be dated to the passage of the 1938 Civil Aeronautics Act and the subsequent formation of the Civil Aeronautics Board (CAB) in 1946 that licensed routes and airline operations, regulated the pricing of fares and monitored safety issues. Federal regulation of civil aviation was firmly established within a government department. It also limited the number of domestic carriers until the 1970s to avoid excessive competition. Despite such measures, the post-war boom in domestic and international air travel in the USA was facilitated by a buoyant economy, innovation in aircraft design, reduced travel costs and stable fares maintained by the CAB. In addition, the CAB provided subsidies for local service carriers so that small communities could be connected to the emerging inter-urban trunk network of air routes, to achieve social equity in access to air travel. This also facilitated the development of major airlines as the CAB guaranteed loans for carriers that invested in new aircraft to serve such routes. To reduce subsidy payments, carriers were gradually awarded more lucrative longer-haul routes with a view to carriers cross-subsidising the shorter feeder routes from small communities to connect with trunk routes. These developments occurred against the background of pressure from the airline industry to increase fares in the 1970s, which appeared to place the consumer at a disadvantage. In 1975, the CAB began to relax some of its restrictions on the operation and pricing of charter aircraft to compete with scheduled flights, permitted discounted fares and licensed new transatlantic carriers prepared to offer low fares. This provided the background for the 1978 Airline Deregulation Act, which established greater flexibility in route licensing and abolished the CAB in 1984. As Goetz and Sutton (1997: 239) argue, 'the Act stripped the CAB of its authority to control entry and exits, fares, subsidies and mergers'. As a result, some of the CAB functions were transferred to the Department of Transportation, including responsibility for:

- the negotiation of international air transport rights and licensing of US carriers to serve the airline market;
- the monitoring of international fares;
- the maintenance of air services to small communities;
- consumer affairs and complaints;
- airline mergers.

In contrast, the Federal Aviation Administration powers included:

- the promotion of air safety and use of navigable air space;
- regulations on the competence of pilots and airworthiness of aircraft;
- the operation of air traffic control (ATC) systems.

From these regulatory responsibilities it is evident that the structure of the US airline business comprises:

- airlines;
- airports and ATC providers;
- aircraft manufacturers (e.g. Boeing and its acquisition of McDonnell Douglas);
- consumers;
- third parties, such as government agencies (e.g. FAA and Department of Transportation).

As Debbage (2004) observed, much of the theoretical justification for airline deregulation in the USA originated from the contestable markets arguments (Bailey and Baumol 1984) and this affected the airline industry by creating a competitive environment. For example, Shaw (1982: 74) identifies the following structure for airline companies:

- the majors (also called the 'legacy' airlines to distinguish them from the new generation of low-cost airlines and new entrants to the market);
- the nationals – based on a regional network;
- new entrants;
- small regional and commuter airlines that provide the short-haul link-ups with the majors to feed into the networks of their partner airlines.

The effects of deregulation on the supply of tourist transport services

Within the literature on the supply of tourist transport, one area that has been well researched is airline deregulation (Goetz and Sutton 1997; Button et al. 1998; Debbage 2005). This has focused on the controversy over the effects of such measures on the commercial environment for airline operations, but there is not space within this chapter to review the specialised range of papers generated by researchers on this topic. One approach is to consider a limited number of issues that are constantly referred to by researchers. According to the US Department of Transportation, following deregulation the number of carriers serving the USA increased from 36 in 1978 to 72 in 1980 and 86 in 1985, dropping to 60 by 1990 (including air cargo carriers). However, a range of factors such as financial insolvency, mergers and acquisitions reduced the number of operators to 10 carriers of regional or national scale by 1988. This was followed by a period of consolidation, and by 1991 the situation had worsened, with both PanAm and Eastern Airlines having faced bankruptcy: the existing carriers had either prospered or lost market share to competitors. By 2002 there were 14 major airlines, 28 national carriers and around 32 regional carriers although entry to/exit from the market will always leave these statistics subject to variation, with 74 carriers operating (FAA 2003) which had risen to around 90 in 2007.

Thus, a 62 per cent increase in the number of domestic travellers carried on US airlines during 1978–90 was followed by a greater degree of concentration and integration in the airline business. The number of enplanements (i.e. the number of people boarding an aircraft) rose from 526 million in 1995 to 769 million in 2007, two-thirds of which were enplaned at large hubs. Milman and Pope (1997: 4) argue that in the late 1990s:

> the US airline operates in an oligopolistic market structure . . . [and] in recent years, access for airlines new to the industry has become more difficult due to the limited availability of terminal space and gates, a lack of departure and landing slots at major airports, and price competition from the dominant carriers.

Goetz and Sutton (1997: 239) examine the effects of concentration in the airline industry post-deregulation in detail, noting that 200 carriers were absorbed or went bankrupt in 1983–88, with the nine largest airlines (American, United, Delta, Northwest, Continental, USAir, TWA, PanAm and Eastern) responsible for 92 per cent of domestic revenue passenger miles. By 1995, 'the industry has been transformed from a regulated oligopoly of ten trunk carriers controlling 87 per cent of the market [in 1978] to an unregulated oligopoly of eight major carriers controlling 93 per cent in 1995' (Goetz and Sutton 1997: 239). This is an interesting situation given the rationale for deregulation: that it would lead to a situation of perfect competition with no major economies of scale or barriers to entry. However, a major challenge to these oligopolistic behaviours was the rise of low-cost carriers which took over 30 per cent of the domestic market by 2007, up from only 7 per cent in 1990. Such new forms of competition were focused on the major urban trunk routes which challenged the situation in the mid 1990s. Between 2000 and 2005, legacy network carriers reduced their share of the US domestic airline market from 62 per cent to 48 per cent. Graham and Goetz (2008) point to the impact on the airline network, with restructuring. For example, American Airlines acquired TWA in 2001 and US Airways merged with American in 2005. In November 2008, Delta and Northwestern Airlines merged, with a global network serving 375 cities in 66 countries and 75,000 employees. This makes the airline the largest globally, with a presence in every US hub. The integration of the two companies is expected to take up to two years to complete.

Goetz and Sutton's (1997) excellent synthesis of deregulation observes that whilst average air fares (in constant dollars) have declined since 1978, discount pricing and fare wars have also reduced fares, a feature reiterated by Lee (2003). The result is that higher fares have been levelled for short-notice business travel; but under conditions of severe discounting, some fares have dropped below cost levels. However, airlines servicing more peripheral routes where one airline dominates have set fares 18–27 per cent higher, on average, than on trunk routes. Even so, recent US data would indicate that US airlines face a double-edged sword: since 2000, costs have risen for many carriers, but yields have dropped whilst load factors (i.e. the occupancy rate of seats on each departure) have risen to almost 80 per cent. Largely as a result of discount fares, domestic passenger volumes have increased dramatically under deregulation as shown earlier. In the period 1978–93, an 87 per cent growth occurred, with passengers increasing from 256 million to 478 million. Flight departures in the same period also grew from 5 million to 7.2 million. But between 1990 and 1993 airlines in the USA made record losses of US$13 billion – the largest losses ever in history (Goetz and Sutton 1997), which have continued in recent years. For example, in 2002 the FAA (2003) reported that the US majors made a US$9.9 billion loss compared to US$5.3 billion in 2001, whilst the nationals made a loss of US$161 million in 2002 and the larger/medium regional carriers had losses of US$34 million. In contrast, the regional and commuter lines made a US$159 million profit. In 2008, IATA has predicted almost US$6 billion losses in the US airline industry. Since 2002, almost half of all US domestic capacity has been restructured or the carriers have been operating under Chapter 11 protection. Graham and Goetz (2008) show that the legacy carriers responded to the challenge posed by the low-cost airline phenomenon and their rising market share by:

- reducing labour costs;
- merging (as in the case of the Delta and Northwestern merger in November 2008 which was estimated to generate an additional US$2 billion in revenue and cost savings);
- reducing fares and cabin service;
- introducing e-booking;
- introducing their own low-cost carriers or what have been termed 'carriers within carriers' with lower costs than their parent carriers (Graham and Vowles 2006) such as United's Express brand. Morrell (2005) examined the activities of different parent companies (and their spin-off-with the launch date) which included: Delta (Delta Express which commenced operation in 1996 and ceased in 2003 and its replacement was Song, launched in 2003); United (Ted, 2004); Continental (CALite, 1993 which closed in 1995); United (Shuttle which commenced operation in 1994 and ceased in 2002); US Airways (Metrojet, launched in 1998 and ceased operation in 2002). As Morrell (2005) found, those legacy carriers which operated low-cost carrier offshoots, made little progress in closing the cost/productivity gap with low-cost carriers such as Southwest. Many of the offshoots were to target low-cost competition but rarely were profitable.

What has deregulation meant for the structure and provision of services through American airline networks?

The spatial effects of deregulation

From the transport geographer's perspective, a distinctive spatial structure in air travel has emerged in the USA (see Chou 1993; Shaw 1993), whereby the major US airlines have developed a hub-and-spoke structure as spatial and commercial strategies for organising airlines' operations in a deregulated environment. This contrasts with the CAB regulation era where inter-urban routes were often 805 km or more in length and little attention was given to integrating the route networks amongst operators. However, in a deregulated environment where cost reductions are a central element of the commercial strategy, least-cost solutions and network maximisation are a priority to achieve efficient operations. Airline services need to be responsive to demand and there has been a greater emphasis on airlines connecting all the nodes in their network. In this context, a hub-and-spoke system of provision may enable airlines to serve a large number of people over a wide area, the hub acting as a switching point for passengers travelling on feeder routes along the spokes that cannot support a trunk route.

Figure 5.2 illustrates the volume of traffic through major airports in 2006 and shows the dominance of the key hubs, particularly Atlanta, Chicago, Dallas-Fort

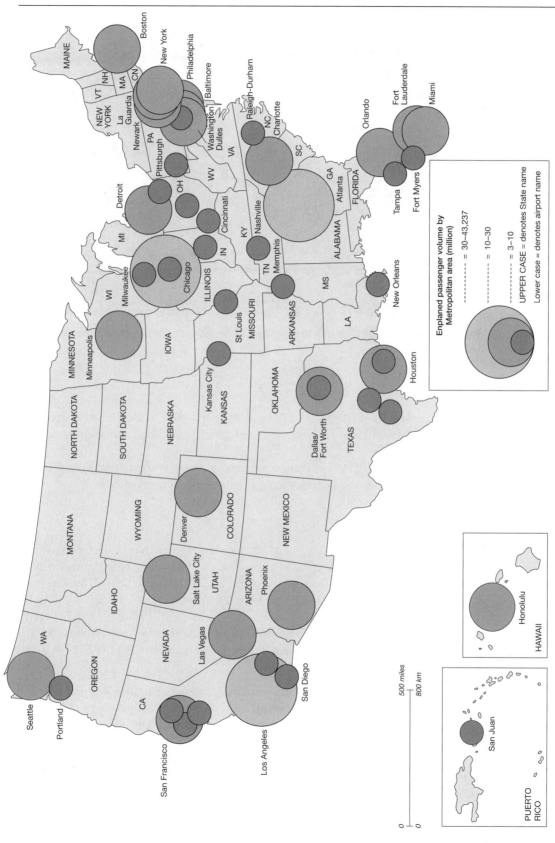

Figure 5.2 Enplaned passenger volume by US metropolitan areas in 2006

Source: Data from FAA 2007.

Plate 5.2 Large terminal areas are needed to service aircraft at core hubs such as Los Angeles

Source: S. J. Page

Worth, Los Angeles (Plate 5.2), Las Vegas, Phoenix, New York, Houston, Newark, Detroit, Minneapolis and Denver, with in excess of 15 million enplaned passengers a year.

Goetz and Sutton (1997) explain the spatial patterns of deregulation in terms of core–periphery concepts. They distinguish between two types of hub:

- domestic hubs;
- international gateways.

They also expand upon Shaw's (1993) analysis identifying the international gateways (Plate 5.3) as funnels for international services and connections to domestic destinations but they do not function as domestic hubs. The gateways are mainly located in coastal cities whilst the domestic hubs are the focal point for the domestic system, and Dresner and Windle (1995) raise a range of issues related to such developments. In terms of the geographic concentration in the airline industry that occurred post-regulation, Goetz and Sutton (1997: 244) argue that:

> Between 1978 and 1993, every domestic hub core except Cleveland experienced an increase in single carrier concentration. In 12 of the 22 hub cores as of 1993, one carrier accounted for more than 60 per cent of their traffic, and 9 hubs reported more than 70 per cent concentration. These high levels of concentration at hub cores reflect the increases in both hub and spoke operations and industrial consolidation. Once entry and exit regulations were removed and carriers adopted hub-based networks, carriers concentrated traffic, personnel, and infrastructure at key points in their systems. The development of 'fortress hubs' – cities

Plate 5.3 Under deregulation, hubs such as Los Angeles have assumed an even greater role both as international gateways to the USA and as hub cores for hub-and-spoke operations

Source: S. J. Page

where no other carriers were able to establish beachheads of operation – emerged as a key strategy for major airlines facing competitive threats from new entrants into the industry.

Interestingly, Lee's (2003) analysis of deregulation post-1978 noted that this spatial pattern of aviation meant that more passengers had to change planes via hubs (i.e. 80 per cent had direct flights in 1978 but this dropped to 64 per cent in 2000). At the same time, recent developments in the expansion of low-cost airlines have provided new airline strategies that challenge the hub-and-spoke principle (Figure 5.3). The point-to-point services of the low-cost airlines such as Southwest Airlines have proved significant, now ranked fifth in market share of US air traffic in 2001 with 15.7 per cent of the market. What Table 5.1 shows is that whilst mergers and acquisitions continued apace during the 1990s and into the new millennium, there had not been a noticeable concentration of carriers with a monopoly control, with a few exceptions (Lee 2003). As discussed earlier, one of factors these has been the impact of low-cost airlines such as Southwest.

Following deregulation, there has been considerable debate amongst researchers over the effect on consumers (tourists and non-tourists). For example, Kihl (1988) argues that deregulation led to a decline in service quality as smaller communities not directly connected to trunk routes faced fare increases and less frequent services. Goetz and Sutton (1997) observe that 'smaller turboprop carriers' have replaced jet services and service quality has declined. It is clear that airline mergers may have led to a decline in the number of carriers serving some communities, but Jemiolo and Oster (1981) maintained that any changes in service provision to less-accessible

I: Trunk route services – no connecting services

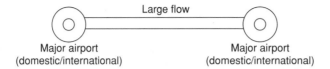

II: Trunk route with hub-and-spoke operation using alliances

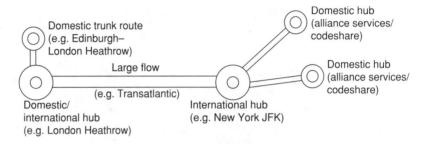

III: Trunk route service with integrated hub-and-spoke operation

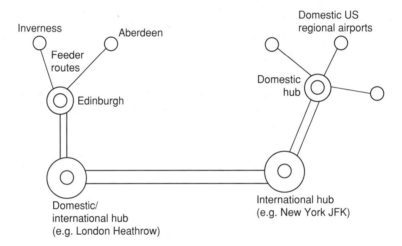

IV: Point-to-point international services, no onward connections

Figure 5.3 Schematic diagram of airline strategies in route planning and provision

V: Low-cost domestic routing – point-to-point, secondary airports

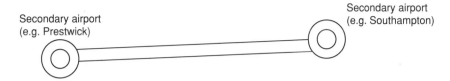

VI: Low-cost international routing – point-to-point, hub to secondary airport

VII: Low-cost international routing – point-to-point, secondary to secondary airport

VIII: Conventional mega carrier – international network, multiple destinations with alliance/codeshare/own services

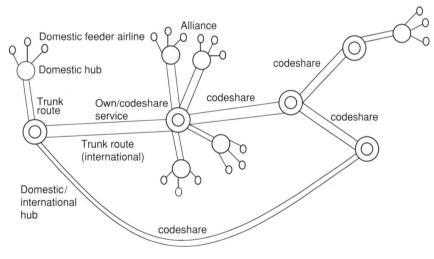

Figure 5.3 *(Continued)*
Source: Page 1994a, 1999.

Table 5.1 Number of top 1000 airport-pair routes served by carrier

	1990	1991	1992	1993	1994	1995	1996	1997	1998	1999	2000
Large network carriers											
American	667	662	686	612	616	517	516	502	511	531	551
Continental	455	535	540	508	536	444	444	443	437	426	423
Delta	624	651	663	633	669	662	696	668	671	696	679
Northwest	412	451	43	396	423	429	412	426	438	439	430
TWA[a]	303	342	369	350	371	351	322	333	335	331	372
United	515	547	537	452	500	492	514	484	507	542	591
US Airways	520	508	471	458	473	409	407	416	397	412	452
Low fare, niche and other carriers											
Southwest	140	158	178	186	263	268	328	328	324	359	377
America West	179	220	226	212	218	229	253	236	244	253	269
AirTran[b]					4	16	19	16	93	95	107
ATA	3	4	7	18	30	36	30	37	56	65	86
Frontier					3	19	25	37	45	53	80
Midway[c]	169	92			8	38	29	39	43	51	65
Alaska	48	41	39	50	44	45	47	44	41	45	42
Vanguard					2	12	25	17	17	22	30
Sun Country[c]										24	29
Spirit			2	6	9	9	4	6	12	21	26
Midwest Express	16	15	12	14	21	20	23	21	23	25	24
National										12	23
JetBlue											13
Carriers acquired during 1900s											
Morris Air				37	17						
ValuJet[b]				8	50	110	35	55			
Reno Air			14	33	36	36	54	68	43		
Carriers declaring bankruptcy during 1990s											
Eastern	329										
Carnival			3	8	11	17	14	18	15		
Braniff	5	6	12	45	65						
Kiwi			4	9	14	12	3	16	9		
Western Pacific						20	37	49			

Notes: Includes carriers with at least 1 per cent of total route passengers and carriers serving 15 or more of the top 1000 routes during at least one year in the sample period. Data from the fourth quarter of each year.

[a] Acquired by American in 2001.

[b] Operations combined in 1997.

[c] Declared bankruptcy in 2001.

Sources: DOT DB1A Database, 1990–2000.
Reprinted from *Journal of Air Transport Management*, 9(2), D. Lee, 'Concentration and price trends in the US domestic airline industry: 1990–2000', pp. 91–101, Copyright © 2003, with permission from Elsevier.

communities were a result of recession and greater fuel costs rather than deregulation. Yet Goetz and Sutton (1997: 252) argue that 'small communities overall have experienced frequent interruptions in service and many have been dropped from the air network altogether', a feature emphasised by Kihl (1988). Of 514 non-hub communities with an air service in 1978, 167 had lost their service by 1995, with only 26 communities gaining a new service. The Airline Deregulation Act 1978 did include provisions for Essential Air Service subsidies so that small communities were still served.

Debate has also centred on the effect of deregulation on passenger safety (Moses and Savage 1990). Golich (1988) asserts that the development of hubbing operations led to a decline in safety as more services and take-offs/landings were concentrated into specific areas, increasing the potential for accidents. However, the US civil aviation statistics for the period 1975–90 show that the number of fatalities actually dropped from 663 to 424, whilst the rate per million aircraft miles flown has remained constant at 0.001 for scheduled services (see Abeyratne 1998; Braithwaite et al. 1998 for the situation elsewhere) and these figures have changed little up to 2008 (see *www.ntsb.gov/aviation*).

Following deregulation and the growth in new entrants to the domestic airline market, consumer complaints increased to a peak of 40,985 in 1987 but dropped to 6106 for 1991 and 4629 in 1995 (US Bureau of the Census 1996) and in the period to 1997 they rose again to just over 6000 per annum. Yet by 2003 they stabilised at 5980 although they were substantially lower than the 9466 in 2002 according to US Department of Transportation statistics. The most commonly reported sources of dissatisfaction in 2008 were:

- flight problems, such as cancellations and delays;
- baggage problems;
- reservations, ticketing and boarding;
- problems associated with refunds;
- customer service issues such as unhelpful employees, inadequate meals and poor cabin service;
- incorrect or incomplete information about fares;
- disability issues;
- overselling;
- frequent flyer problems;
- discrimination;
- advertising;
- animals (US Department of Transportation 2008).

Airlines have exercised greater control over their workforces since deregulation, in pursuit of continued increases in productivity and greater economies of scale (Humphries 1992), despite the success of the model of low-cost production used by Southwest as the notable success story of deregulation (Gittell 2003).

The changes brought about by deregulation have also had a pronounced effect on the US airport system as the demand for air travel has continued to grow despite constraints on the supply of airport capacity (Sealy 1992). Deregulation and the development of trunk routes and hubs have intensified congestion at major US airports, a feature confirmed with the ACI data on the world's largest airports and also in this chapter with the data in Figure 5.2.

What the case of airline deregulation in the USA shows is that the supply environment can be dramatically affected by the change in policy and a new competitive environment results when airlines adopt new strategies to airline provision as outlined in Figure 5.3. Therefore, in summary, Table 5.2 provides an overview of some key debates surrounding deregulation in the US airline industry, that celebrated 30 years of operation under this policy environment in 2008 attracting a great deal of public interest given the ongoing financial problems facing many domestic carriers. In fact the US Government Accountability Office looked at whether re-regulation of the

Table 5.2 Summary of the advantages and disadvantages of deregulation of the US domestic airline market

Advantages

- Price drop in cost of air travel (1950–78, prices fell by 2.8 per cent; 1978–93, prices dropped by 1.7 per cent)
- Growth in passenger traffic from 275 million passenger enplanements in 1978 to 769 million in 2007
- Increased frequency on flights on trunk routes, as low-cost airlines introduce point to point routes to improve accessibility and challenge oligopolistic behaviour of legacy carriers
- Greater competition

Disadvantages

- Rise in consumer concerns over service standards, delayed flights, mishandled baggage, involuntary 'bumping' of passengers off overbooked flights
- Concerns over the safety of an ageing fleet which led to several airlines grounding aircraft in March 2008 to complete safety checks to comply with Federal Aviation Administration guidelines
- Lack of a recognition of the business impact of the airline industry as having special characteristics that do not fit well with deregulation: excessive price competition on some routes has made operations too unprofitable even to recover the costs of operation
- The failure of US airlines to reinvest in new fleets for domestic operation due to profitability and affecting their efficiency in terms of fuel consumption and emissions
- Declining profitability and declining yields amidst greater volumes of travellers
- Major casualties across the sector with 165 airlines collapsing/merging or operating in Chapter 11 bankruptcy protection 1978–2008
- Concerns about the effect on seasonal tourism markets that are not on major trunk routes (e.g. ATA Airlines and Aloha Airlines in Hawaii (the latter ceased operation after 60 years) collapsed in 2008 leaving only Hawaiian Airlines and a number of other carriers as the main operators, reducing competition as more airlines face bankruptcy due to unviable business models due to excessive price competition

Source: Various.

domestic market might be appropriate in 2005, but concluded it was not necessary, given the successes of this model in some other markets such as the US–Caribbean leisure market (Warnock-Smith and Morrell 2008). Having outlined some of the principal theoretical considerations affecting the supply of transport for tourism and how they have been applied in one market, attention now turns to a conceptual framework – the supply chain. This enables one to recognise the theoretical issues and to appreciate how the criteria associated with competitive markets may affect the organisation and delivery of supply by individual transport operators such as airlines.

The supply chain in tourist transport services

Prior to the innovative synthesis by Sinclair and Stabler (1997), there was an absence of detailed research on the supply of tourism and transport services. This has acted as a major constraint on the development of literature in this area, and with the exception of research by transport economists, economists' interest in supply issues has been limited, if not peripheral to the main studies in the area (Sinclair and Stabler 1997). The situation has been compounded by the image of supply research in tourism and transport studies, which is sometimes perceived as descriptive, lacking intellectual rigour and sophisticated methods of study, since 'generally there is little research on the tourism [and transport] industry and its operation which is analytical in emphasis' (Sinclair and Stabler 1991: 2). This is perpetuated by the treatment of supply issues in many general tourism texts that broadly discuss 'passenger transportation', since there are methodological problems in differentiating between the supply and use of transport services by the local population for travel to work, leisure and recreational travel purposes and more specific tourist use. In fact, Sinclair and Stabler (1997: 70) argue that 'categories [such] as transport are very broad and benefit from disaggregation into sub-markets with different structures and modes of operation'. Thus, it is not surprising to find that research has focused on established areas of tourism and transport supply, notably:

- descriptions of the industry and its operation, management and marketing
- the spatial development and interactions that characterise the industry at different geographical scales (Sinclair and Stabler 1991: 2).

Studies of transport systems within tourism research have been characterised by a preoccupation with how their operations are organised to provide a service to travellers and how the international nature of transport facilitates tourism activities and development. This approach to research on tourist transport systems is rooted in economics, as emphasised in Chapter 2, based on the concept of the 'firm', developed by Coase (1937) and discussed further by Buckley and Casson (1987).

In the context of tourism and transport supply, Buckley (1987) notes that the analysis of a firm or company is characterised by certain relationships within the organisation and with its purchasers or consumers. The external process of selling a product or service involves a transaction between two parties following an agreement to purchase, often though not exclusively using a monetary transaction. Commercial transactions are based on agreed conditions and enforced within a framework of contractual obligations between the parties. Therefore transaction chains develop to link the tourist with the suppliers of services in tourism and the 'tourism product or service' is defined as the sum of these transactions (Witt et al. 1991: 81). Such research highlights the significance of the 'chain of distribution' for transport and tourism services, which is the method of distribution of the service from production through to its eventual consumption by tourists. A more general discussion of the distribution chain in tourism can be found in Holloway (1995).

Transaction analysis

Buckley (1987) describes some typical transaction chains for tourism that identify the integral role of transport services in linking origin and destination areas as shown in Chapter 1 with Figure 1.8. The nature of the specific supply chain depends upon a wide range of factors that are internal and external to individual firms in the transport sector. For example, what is the primary force driving the supply system? Is it driven by pull factors, where a tourist destination may market a region and supply transport services on a state-owned airline to stimulate demand for tourism? Or is it driven by push factors, where the tourist generates the demand, and the transport and accommodation sectors respond to this as a commercial opportunity? The overall business environment, government predisposition to tourism and planning constraints may have a moderating influence on the supply system. In addition, transaction analysis illustrates the significance of 'agents' in the system, corporate policy in transport provision and contractual arrangements in the supply chain.

Much of the existing knowledge available on these issues has been generated through interviews with managers in each sector of the transport industry about their commercial practices (e.g. contracting arrangements, profit margins and global strategies). It is rare to find researchers being given access to commercial information on supply (and demand) issues, due to the confidential and sensitive nature of the data, and the perceived threat it might pose to a company's competitive advantage if rival operators obtained such information. In some cases this amounts to paranoia among companies, as media coverage of the British Airways and Virgin Atlantic libel case in 1992–93 highlighted. The result is that the relationship between transport supply and tourist use remains poorly understood, with commercial research primarily concerned with the effect of pricing transport services, the behaviour of consumers (see Gilbert 1990) and the outcome in terms of use and profitability for producers. It is within this context that Buckley's (1987) research proves useful in understanding the nature of relationships which may exist in the supply chain.

From Buckley's four chains (Figure 5.4), it is evident that a variety of distribution systems exist for the sale and consumption of transport services by tourists (Barnes 1989). One of the critical issues in the distribution system for the seller is access to superior information on available services, so that these can be sold to the consumer. There are various studies documenting tourism and transport retailing (e.g. Holloway and Robinson 1995), where the agent or broker is normally paid a commission on their sales. The travel agent comprises a convenient one-stop location for tourists to buy tourism services as an inclusive package, which includes transport and accommodation, usually marketed through the medium of a brochure. The packaging of these products or services (much of the literature interchanges these terms) by wholesalers (e.g. tour operators) reduces the transaction costs to the tourist of purchasing each element independently (Laws 1995). Thus, a travel agent normally receives around 10 per cent commission on the sale of a holiday marketed by a tour operator, but the overall cost to the consumer is markedly lower than arranging the same components independently. However, in the case of air tickets, commissions to agents are declining as airlines seek to reduce this expense in competitive market conditions. The tour operator is able to reduce the number of transactions involved by packaging a holiday, thereby making economies in the supply through wholesale purchasing and by entering into long-term contracts with the suppliers of accommodation and transport services. Not only does this have benefits for the price charged to the purchaser, but it has more beneficial effects for the supplier as a number of intermediaries or brokers in the chain are eliminated by large tour operators and airlines that control a significant part of the distribution system. This was the

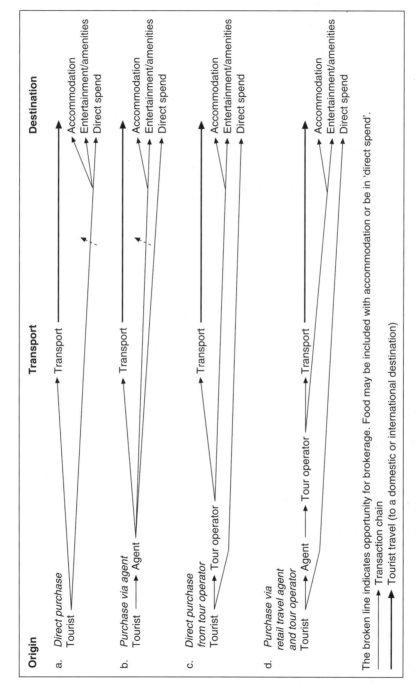

Figure 5.4 Four types of tourism transaction chain
Source: Adapted from Page 1994, 1999 and based on Witt et al. 1991.

focus of innovative research by Bote Gomez and Sinclair (1991), who discuss the nature of corporations controlling the transaction chain to:

● maximise profit by eliminating costs;
● reduce the price to the consumer to boost market share;
● increase their level of concentration in the tourism industry.

Company strategies often pursue horizontal and vertical integration in the tourism and transport sectors, not only to control the production process of tourism services but also to improve efficiency through economies of scale and long-term profitability. Although there are various economic theories to explain integration (see the excellent review by Bote Gomez and Sinclair 1991), the two terms – vertical and horizontal integration – have received little detailed analysis (Sinclair 1991).

Integration in the tourism sector: implications for the supply of tourist transport

According to Bote Gomez and Sinclair (1991):

● Integration is based on the concept of common ownership, which may involve the coordination or control of the production process or may have no direct effect on it.
● Horizontal integration occurs where two enterprises with the same output combine to increase the companies' control over output. It can occur through mergers, acquisitions, collaboration, franchising agreements and more complex contractual arrangements, and may induce concentration in the same business.
● Vertical integration occurs when an enterprise with different interests and involvement in the supply chain acquires or merges with companies contributing inputs to its activities, or where output purchasers provide a ready market for the service. This has the advantage of decreasing economic uncertainty in the supply system and the avoidance of problems related to contract breaking.

The significance of integration in the tourism industry and the implications for tourist transport has been well documented by Sinclair (1991). It is evident that:

> the transport function is an important point in the exchange of rights in the tourism transaction chain. If this function is subcontracted to an independent operator this delicate and central function can go out of control; hence the close integration of transport with other facilities in the integrated multinational company to ensure a degree of control in the distribution system in the supply of transport services to tourists (Witt et al. 1991: 83).

Buckley (1987) notes that integration in tourist transport operations, especially vertical ownership, may help to reduce costs where higher load factors can be guaranteed for associated companies. Transaction analysis highlights not only the driving force in the supply system but also raises questions that researchers may wish to address in relation to specific companies and their role in tourist transport.

Transaction analysis also provides an opportunity to consider the changing patterns and processes shaping the tourist transport system and the growing internationalisation of the supply chain. One of the growing issues in the globalisation of tourism supply is a reflection of the development of mass leisure tourism markets, which have been subject to the process of internationalisation. Williams (1995: 163) argues that the 'internationalisation of tourism activity and investment has to be seen in the more general and increasingly rapid process of globalisation of international investment'. As a result, transnational business interests have developed in the tourism industry. Williams (1995: 164) suggests that 'firms' competitive strategies are based on seeking cost leadership, product differentiation, and focusing on market niches; under certain circumstances these may dictate the internationalisation of tourist activity and investment'. Such research is underpinned by the earlier findings of Dunning (1977) that transnational development in sectors of the tourism industry such as transport is due to firms entering international markets for offensive and defensive reasons when using recognised brand names. They aim to establish location-specific advantages and to reduce risk by using the existing business advantages of an established company.

More recent research by Meethan (2004) has indicated that the natural development of the transaction research is the development of production and consumption chains of services, where bundles of services and commodities are purchased and consumed across time and space. This highlights the globalised nature of tourism activity, of which transport is a key component, and provides many of the inter-sector linkages helping to make tourism a globalised activity when the activities of transnational companies are considered. One of the enabling factors that help companies to achieve these linkages is information technology (discussed in more detail in Chapter 6). Company behaviour is critical here as the pursuit of global business strategies and ambitions helps to explain why companies seek alliances and cooperative approaches to develop a global reach. The transport sector is key here as both an element of an integrated portfolio of business interests and an enabling factor in seeking to develop market shares of tourists, using various business tools such as hubs and spokes in air travel or visible methods of branding (Shaw and Williams 2004).

●●●● New research agendas in tourism supply research: tourism supply chain management

A more recent study by Tapper et al. (2004: 1) described the concept of tourism supply chains, moving the research agenda along in transport and tourism research as

> all the goods and services that go into the delivery of tourism products to consumers. It includes all suppliers of goods and services whether or not they are directly contracted by tour operators or by their agents . . . or suppliers (including accommodation providers: Tourism supply chains involve many components – not just accommodation, transport and excursions, but also bars and restaurants, handicrafts, food production, waste disposal, and the infrastructure that supports tourism in destinations.

Many of these supply chains are managed by business-to-business relationships, using what is known as supply chain management to improve the performance and output in the chain. There is also some overlap here with other research on tourism distribution channels, but TSCM (tourism supply chain management) is more specific to the management of tourism supply since it focuses on a series of approaches to help manage the supply chain to meet tourist needs, particularly the end product as well challenges such as seasonality. Above all better coordination of the supply chains assists in improving relationships in the system as well as overall profitability and competitiveness. In the large tour operator sector, oligopolistic business relationships mean that SCM can be used to assist in profitability, quality assurance and improvement of market share. This raises the issue of travel chains.

A study by Schiefelbusch et al. (2007) examined the notion of the tourist chain of services as part of SCM, identifying ways in which the use of the car as a mode of travel for leisure can be substituted by other forms of transport during trips. Whilst the underlying objective in this study was the enhancement of sustainability objectives in tourism, it did highlight how the transport element in the supply chain needed to be used as a basis for planning transport trips to reduce impacts. A further study by Véronneau and Roy (2009) shifted the focus in SCM to the macro scale from individual travel, to look at global service supply chains in cruising. The study highlighted the importance of a well coordinated supply chain to ensure cruise ships are efficiently supplied throughout their journey. Above all SCM research focuses on meeting the customers' needs. In the cruise ship sector, vessels with over 4000 passengers and almost 1500 crew require supply chains able to service their supplies needs, carefully aligned to set itineraries and onboard tactical planning to ensure day-to-day operations run smoothly, as Figure 5.5 shows. What is interesting from Véronneau and Roy's (2009) study is the global nature of the sourcing of supplies and the economies of scale achieved through such practices. They define the supply chain management of a cruise ship as 'the timely coordination of supply in anticipation of demand in support of support to service delivery excellence' (Véronneau and Roy 2009: 128). These supply chains tend to be more reactive in their planning and management because of the time-compressed manner to which cruise ship schedules operate using very complex supply chains, where replenishment is a critical element to ensure the on-board experience, given the dependence upon food and beverages as a key element of the visitor experience (Teye and Leclerc 1998).

Introducing a corporate quality control system may help to minimise customer dissatisfaction, particularly if the organisation employs and trains staff to deal with the service encounter as an ongoing process, rather than viewing the services as a series of discrete elements over which they have only limited control. Yet even in a corporate quality control system, employees have to recognise the limit of their responsibilities and be able to refer customers to the relevant personnel empowered to deal with an interruption in the service requested.

Where the tour operator and purchaser of the transport service are unable to directly control the inputs and outputs throughout the system, one option may be to develop a contractually administered quality control system. Here all parties involved in the supply chain may make a contractual commitment to supply services to a certain standard to avoid weak links in the system (e.g. poor quality food and service on board an aircraft) that can affect the tourist's impression of the entire service. All parties involved need to agree on a particular quality principle (e.g. the British Standard 5750 for service systems that some transport operators, such as P&O Stena, already employ) to implement throughout the supply chain, using performance indicators to ensure that the necessary standards are being reached. One way of examining the supply chain in the case of tourist transport operators that are public

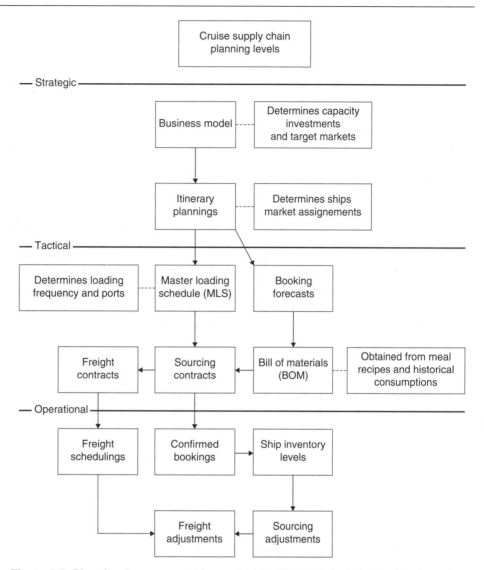

Figure 5.5 Planning for consumable products with dependent demand on board a cruise ship

Source: Reprinted from *Tourism Management*, 30, S. Véronneau and J. Roy, 'Global service supply chains: An empirical study of current practices and challenges of a cruise line corporation, pp. 289–300. Copyright © 2009, with permission from Elsevier.

companies is to examine their annual report. For this reason it is pertinent to consider the role of such data sources, their purpose, and how they may be used.

Analysing annual reports: company accounts

An annual report is used by companies to provide a review of the year's activities and it contains company accounts that are prepared within accounting guidelines in force in the country where the head office is based. For example, in the case of SIA (Singapore International Airlines), the accounts must be deposited in Singapore.

Bird and Rutherford (1989) argue that company accounts contain messages that use specialist jargon to deal with a complex situation. Once the specialist jargon is decoded by the reader, company accounts provide an insight into the financial performance of businesses. There are two key elements within company accounts:

- a balance sheet;
- a profit and loss account.

Within the balance sheet, items of value (assets) are listed and any claims against them are set out. A claim is a liability, such as an unpaid bill. Assets are divided into fixed assets, which are those acquired for use within the business, and current assets, comprising cash and other items that are to be converted into cash. Liabilities within the accounts are also divided into current liabilities, where settlement will be made within one year, and long-term liabilities to be settled after one year. It should be recognised that a balance sheet only provides a snapshot of an organisation's activities at one point in time. Analysts therefore tend to consider company accounts over a three- to five-year period to give a more realistic assessment of an organisation's business performance.

There is a great deal of debate amongst accountants over the reliability of such documents, due to the degree of creative accounting that characterises them. In other words, critics argue that company accounts only record what a company wants to state publicly about its activities. In fact, one can argue that the flexibility and vagueness of accounting rules in relation to the preparation of company accounts and financial results means that they are no longer an absolute measure of success. Manipulation of the profit and loss account and the balance sheet to report flattering results that meet corporate investors' and stock markets' expectations have contributed to the pressure for creative accounting. Notwithstanding these limitations associated with company accounts within published annual reports, they provide an important public relations function for companies and offer an insight into the organisation, operation and scale of a company's activities and their involvement in supply chains.

INSIGHT 5.1

Singapore Airlines and the supply of tourist transport services

An interesting way to identify the extent to which integration exists within the tourist transport system is to consider one company and its activities. The case of Singapore Airlines (SIA) provides a useful example since it is based within one of the fastest-growing tourism markets. As a tourist transport operator, SIA has been widely regarded as Singapore's premier enterprise, formed in 1947, developing as the national flag carrier in 1972 and privatised after 1985. Its performance has been consistently profitable (Bowen 1997) and its close relationship with the government has meant it has developed a synergy with the Singapore Tourism Promotion Board to assist with the development of inbound tourism.

Sikorski (1990) provides a detailed analysis of how SIA was developed and financed as well as its route to privatisation. This Insight focuses on SIA's annual report to illustrate the scope and involvement of one company in the supply chain for transport and tourism services. The company comprises a complex range of aviation businesses, including SIA Cargo (the third largest cargo carrier in the world), Singapore Airport Terminal Services and SIA Engineering. The Singapore government still holds a controlling share of 57 per cent of the airline through Temasek Holdings. The airline has a fleet of around 98 aircraft and a route

▶

network that serves 65 cities and they employ over 14,000 staff: their reputation for having one of the newest aircraft fleets is reflected in the average aircraft age of around 6.5 years.

The SIA annual report

The SIA annual report for 2006/07 (*www.singaporeair.com*) comprises 178 pages. As a source of information on tourist transport, it contains a significant amount of public relations material which complements the statistical information on the airline. As an accessible data source for researchers, it is a baseline of information from which further research can be undertaken. The initial statistical highlights within the report provide an executive summary of the company accounts, but it is the discussion of the SIA group activities that is the most informative in terms of airline operations and integration within their business activities.

The general operational review discusses the company's performance as SIA's group activities saw its operating profit rise 61.6 per cent in 2007/08 to S$5,972.5 million. The profit before tax increased 11.5 per cent in 2007/08 to S$2,547.2 million. Passenger traffic increased by 4.2 per cent from 18,346,000 in 2006/07 to 19,120,000 in 2007/08 and the overall load factor increased to 80.3 per cent. At the same time, yields increased 11 per cent per passenger km.

In terms of the financial aspects of the company's performance, the following are included, which are standard aspects for most companies:

Financial review

Auditors' report

● Profit and loss accounts
● Balance sheets
● Cash flow statements
● Notes to the accounts
● Half-yearly reports of the group
● Ten-year statistical record of the company
● Information on shareholdings
● Share prices and turnover

Source: Adapted from SIA (*www.singaporeair.com*).

Product and service development

SIA's reputation as a global leader in the airline industry for product and service development saw the introduction in 2003 of non-stop direct flights with the new Airbus A345 it has named the Leadership: this was followed in 2008 by the introduction of the A380, new large long-haul aircraft, as Singapore Airlines was the first airline to put the aircraft into regular service. This is part of the company's ongoing policy of leadership in the global airline industry, which led to its introducing the new Krisworld in-flight entertainment system. This trend-setting innovation is an individual entertainment system with 22 video channels at the seat of every passenger. Whilst other airlines have attempted to introduce such technology, it has been characterised by in-flight service breakdowns. Krisworld is a state-of-the-art technology that has proved popular with passengers, allowing customer choice in relieving the tedium of long-haul air travel. Many other airlines subsequently followed SIA's lead. Yet there is also a debate on the extent to which such investment strategies will continue to be the lead for the airline sector as, on medium-haul routes, low-cost options are competing with established airlines. Whilst SIA continues to receive accolades for innovation in airline travel, its policy of continuous improvement to services and product development (including regular customer satisfaction surveys) indicates the competitiveness of international travel, particularly in the business and first-class sectors, making it a market leader though, as with all airlines, the economy sector is constantly evolving. This may be why the airline has taken a lead in establishing a low-cost airline – Tiger Airways – to compete with the newly established Valuair in Singapore.

▶

Integration in SIA group activities

The global scale and distribution of airline services has now become increasingly depend-ent upon computer reservation systems (CRSs) for marketing (see Chapter 6). These sys-tems have been developed by airlines and account for the majority of airline bookings in North America and Europe. SIA has participated in this recent expansion in CRS technol-ogy (Archdale 1991) and internet booking to extend its products to retail travel agents and customers.

The subsidiary and associated companies of the SIA group highlight the involvement in the tourist transport system, particularly:

- tour wholesaling (package holidays) – Tradewinds;
- air transport (SilkAir, Tiger Airways and a 49 per cent stake in Virgin Atlantic Ltd and a 25 per cent stake in the Great Wall Airline Company);
- airport services (catering, airport ownership, security services) – SATS as well as hold-ings in 21 companies across Asia;
- duty-free sales (including a 76 per cent stake in Singapore Airport Duty Free);
- hotel ownership (e.g. a 20 per cent stake in Ritz-Carlton, Singapore);
- airport bus services;
- aircraft leasing;
- CRS (Abacus Travel Systems);
- airline software development;
- aircraft engineering and maintenance;
- hotel and property ownership (SIA Properties);
- quality service training;
- Singapore Flying College;
- cargo.

The activities of SIA's subsidiary companies are reported separately in the annual re-port, although the majority of the document focuses on SIA. SIA also produces an individual breakdown of the profitability of its three principal activities:

- airline operations;
- airport terminal services;
- engineering services.

It is evident that company annual reports can be a useful data source from which to ex-amine not only integration in the tourist transport system but also the performance of indi-vidual companies. Annual reports are an accessible data source that can be obtained direct from public companies' head offices. Although the amount of detailed information contained within annual reports may be somewhat daunting and complex, analysis of such sources will yield important insights into the commercial, operational and supply aspects of different tourist transport operators.

Yet even though annual reports for individual companies are of interest, there are growing numbers of industry associations that provide data on the transport and tourism sector combining data from their members to illustrate trends across the sector concerned. These provide equally valuable data on the supply issues and, in some cases, can assist in identifying regional and global issues as well as performance and relationships across the sector. However, how does the supply of tourist transport provision fit with the activities and needs of tourists as consumers and tourism businesses as well as the role of the state as a provider of infrastructure?

Linking together tourism, transport and policy issues

Having outlined a range of issues associated with the supply of transport and infrastructure to support tourism growth and development, it is useful at this juncture to try and explain how these issues fit together, particularly in view of the state's role in managing and influencing supply through policy measures. As Chapter 3 discussed, state intervention in transport infrastructure may have many motives, including social equity and economic development motives such as growing tourism. As the example of airline deregulation in the USA suggests, this has occurred alongside the increased personal mobility and concerns over consumers' interests being safeguarded. The new focus in many governments in the period since the 1980s has been on redefining the role of the state in the supply of transport infrastructure and services. Deregulation has not meant withdrawal of the state, just a new way of approaching supply. As Shaw et al. (2008) argue, this is part of the hollowing out (i.e. privatisation/deregulation) and filling-in role of the state (i.e. setting out new functions to replace old ones) such as a former command and control style of public transport provision. For example, the UK bus industry has seen a market-oriented approach using privatisation and contractual agreements to manage the supply. This is a development of the transaction analysis approaches, with a more focused role on individual aspects of supply. Equally, the state also has to think more clearly about how it engages with measures of demand management to control issues of unregulated access and the growth of a crisis in mobility (i.e. congestion on roads and in air space). Shaw et al. (2008) have described this as a re-engagement of regulation in some areas where demand management measures are needed (such as the London congestion charge on car use in the central area of the city). More theoretical interpretations of these changes have been described by Giddens (2000) as the third way, a mix of political philosophies from capitalism and socialism to reach compromise to achieve solutions, especially competition as a basis for achieving economic progress as well as seeking to gain the centre ground from a political and managerial perspective. The blend of neoliberal and welfarist theories means that market principles are applied to transport supply increasingly in many countries. This has led in some cases to greater state regulation (as opposed to less) to achieve specific economic, social and environmental goals. From a tourist transport perspective, this means that provision cannot simply be characterised as a state-deregulated approach or state-regulated approach as opposing views: policy and provision becomes a more complex political process which the tourism industry has to be cognisant of in its own business strategies and activities.

Summary

The analysis of tourist transport issues has attracted comparatively little research in contrast to the analysis of demand issues. The rise of transaction analysis is a useful way to view the supply chain in tourist transport systems and the contractual relationships that exist between consumers and suppliers. However, more recent theoretical syntheses of tourism supply issues by economists (Sinclair and

Stabler 1997) highlight the importance of understanding the competitive conditions and markets in which tourist transport businesses operate. It is this more theoretically derived analysis that begins to advance the supply side beyond simple descriptive studies. The discussion highlights the dominant influence of the tour operator sector in the supply of package holidays and the purchase of transport services on behalf of customers at discounted prices. The ability of tour wholesalers to negotiate discounts with transport operators reflects the capital-intensive nature of the tourist transport business and the need to achieve high load factors to improve profitability. This reflects the indivisible nature of transport operations discussed in Chapter 2, where airline companies cannot operate half an aircraft if it is only 50 per cent full. The fixed costs of transport operations (e.g. repayments on loans to purchase capital equipment) mean that the incremental costs of selling existing capacity on a transport service are low once it has reached its break-even point. This is one explanation of the reduced price of airline tickets and stand-by fares as it is more efficient to sell a reduced-priced ticket if the carrier has capacity than to underutilise the capacity. The contractual relationships associated with the supply of tourist transport are often negotiated up to six months in advance and a great deal of market planning goes into the provision of a service.

The provision of services that meet certain quality standards is one of the reasons why labour costs are so high in the supply of tourist transport services. It is a labour-intensive activity that requires staff contact with travellers to ensure their needs are met at each stage of travel. Employees cannot easily be substituted where a service is dependent on face-to-face contact with customers. Employee training and corporate human resource management policies are assuming an important role in ensuring that the supply of tourist transport services is based on a sound understanding of service quality, maximising customer satisfaction and developing programmes with incentives to foster customer loyalty. Analysis of company reports provides a useful source to assess both the role of the transport operator's involvement in the supply chain and their development of more sophisticated ways of serving the customer's needs.

The example of SIA highlights how important these issues are for a market leader in the tourist transport business. The degree of vertical and horizontal integration within a company such as SIA highlights the significance of annual company reports. SIA has certainly ensured that its involvement in the supply chain enables it to develop more sophisticated ways to meet the needs of its customers.

Questions

1 How does the concept of a supply chain affect the analysis of the tourist's 'travel experience'?

2 Can the market for tourist transport ever operate in conditions of perfect competition?

3 What is the value of using company annual reports to understand the operational and organisational structure of tourist transport providers?

4 How can the case study approach be used for an analysis of tourist transport providers?

Further reading

Doganis, R. (2001) *The Airline Business in the 21st Century*, London: Routledge.

Giddens, A. (2000) *The Third Way and its Critics*, London: Polity Press.

Ioannides, D. and Debbage, K. (eds) (1998) *The Economic Geography of the Tourist Industry: A Supply Side Analysis*, London: Routledge.

Sinclair, M.T. and Stabler, M. (1997) *The Economics of Tourism*, London: Routledge. Although this is a difficult text for the uninitiated economist, it is well worth reading for detail on supply issues.

Witt, S., Brooke, M. and Buckley, P. (1991) *The Management of International Tourism*, London: Routledge. This is a good general introduction on supply issues.

Websites

A good source on the prevailing conditions in financial reporting, especially the preparation of annual reports in the UK, can be found on the website of the Chartered Institute of Management Accounting (CIMA): www.cima.org.uk

The Singapore Airlines website can be found at: www.singaporeair.com

Managing tourist transport provision

6

Managing supply issues in tourist transport

Introduction

The provision of tourist transport services by public and private sector organisations is a complex process, requiring a wide range of human resource skills and managerial abilities and a sound grasp of the transport business and how it operates. In recent years, meeting the needs of consumers (travellers) has also assumed a higher priority in the supply of services. In Chapter 5, the conceptualisation and analysis of tourist transport supply issues highlighted the significance of understanding the broader strategic and contextual issues that affect the way different forms of transport supply perform in the marketplace. In this chapter, the emphasis is on a number of issues highlighted by the Singapore Airlines Insight in Chapter 5 (Insight 5.1), namely how successful transport providers can produce, manage and operate efficient supply systems to meet tourist needs. In particular, the chapter focuses on the mechanisms and tools used by operators to manage supply issues, together with the role of the public sector. This provides a comparison of the different objectives pursued by private sector operators, such as airlines, railway companies and cruise lines. Private sector operators are motivated by the financial performance of the business, to ensure that an efficient operation delivers products to its customers. In contrast, the public sector agencies directly and indirectly associated with the provision of tourist transport services are often not motivated by profit as discussed at the end of Chapter 5. Such organisations frequently have a more strategic view and are concerned with planning, coordination and liaison functions to ensure tourist transport provision meets public policy objectives at various spatial scales. The chapter commences with a review of strategy used by transport operators such as airlines to improve supply issues and competitiveness – particularly alliances and the role of cooperative industry groups such as the Association of Asia Pacific Airlines (AAPA) representing the leading airlines in Asia. The discussion then turns to one of the most important tools used by transport providers in the late 1990s and new millennium – information technology (IT) and the rise of e-travel – using a detailed Insight of the airline sector (Insight 6.1). The supply of transport services in destination areas is then reviewed.

● ● ● ● Business strategies and the transport sector

According to Evans et al. (2003: 9) strategy is one of the most important factors determining the success or failure of tourism businesses. They point to the use of the term strategy by Mintzberg, who identified that it may constitute: a plan; a ploy; a pattern of behaviour; a position in relation to someone else; or a perspective. This involves a range of strategic elements including identifying long-term objectives as identified in Chapter 2 in relation to marketing. In particular, it requires different courses of action – strategic alternatives to be recognised and planned for at different levels within organisations from the strategic level of the CEO or board through to the tactical level of middle managers or at the operational level of customer delivery. This very hierarchical approach does not, however, account for the success of strategic approaches by airlines such as Southwest where empowering staff to work as teams and to work towards set corporate objectives around the company vision of the CEO has questioned many of the established approaches to managing organisations.

Shaw and Williams (2004) point to the strategic reactions of tourism companies to competition in the marketplace that has differing implications for the transport sector. Inter-modal competition is a key element of transport (except in cases of monopoly provision or one mode of transport such as a ferry to cross between two islands with no air access). Shaw and Williams (2004) show that where contestable markets exist, such as in the airline sector in the USA, different strategies may result. Evans et al. (2003) point to the influential work of Porter in setting out the strategic reactions in maintaining a competitive advantage that could involve differentiation (i.e. making your product look different and more attractive to the competitor) or one of cost leadership, or the use of either approach to set out a narrow focus on the market such as one segment. Shaw and Williams (2004) indicate that the most common response to competition is either cost competition (i.e. reducing the price) or through product innovation which may combine cost savings with technology. These strategies are often combined in the most successful companies by innovation to maintain a competitive edge. As Page (2003) indicated, innovation implies change of some sort and can be divided into a number of areas: diffusion of new ideas, products or processes; adoption by individual organisations; and levels of innovativeness. Much of the existing research on innovation emerged after Schumpeter's study (1952), which identified five principal routes to innovation as shown in Figure 6.1. This is important when seeking a leadership role as exemplified in Chapter 5 in the case of Singapore Airlines and may involve significant investment costs. Similar cases exist in the rail sector, with the introduction of new trains by Virgin Trains in the UK in 2002–03, with the electric Pendolino tilting train introduced for future high-speed operations and new cross-country diesel Voyager trains led the market. This inevitably involves a balance in strategy between risk and uncertainty and success. For example, process innovation is apparent in the use of internet sales for low-cost airlines to reduce production costs, whilst product innovations such as the non-stop A345 Leadership and A380 by Singapore Airlines, combined with branding to differentiate the product offering, provide a competitive advantage. Innovation has to be a continuous process as competitors are constantly seeking new products or niches, and only through process or product innovation can this edge be maintained. One other way in which companies in the transport and tourism sector have sought to maintain this edge is through forming strategic alliances to cooperate rather than compete.

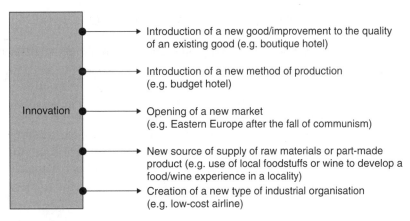

Introduction of a new good/improvement to the quality of an existing good (e.g. boutique hotel)

Introduction of a new method of production (e.g. budget hotel)

Opening of a new market (e.g. Eastern Europe after the fall of communism)

New source of supply of raw materials or part-made product (e.g. use of local foodstuffs or wine to develop a food/wine experience in a locality)

Creation of a new type of industrial organisation (e.g. low-cost airline)

Figure 6.1 Types of innovation in tourism

Source: Page 2003a, based on the ideas of Schumpeter 1952, Copyright © 2003, with permission from Elsevier.

Strategic alliances and cooperation

There is a well-developed literature in both tourism and management that examines the way in which companies have overcome the problems of fragmentation of the tourism product to cooperate and form alliances and collaborative arrangements to progress business objectives within the private sector and between the public and private sector. At a destination level, such partnerships seek to improve the competitive position of the destination, and transport may be a critical part of that process of development. In the tour operator/transport sector this may be a partnership to deliver the product. Despite problems of defining exactly what forms cooperation may take in every case, there is a recognition that one of the most commonly used forms is the alliance (Bennett 1997; French 1997b), which is examined below in relation to airlines.

Evans (2001) provides one of the most useful studies in this area, identifying strategic alliances particularly amongst airlines (e.g. Oum and Park 1997; Iatrou and Oretti 2007; Pitfield 2007; Tieran et al. 2008) that highlight a range of motives, objectives and different outcomes. Evans (2001) summarised the process of collaborative strategy formulation into internal drivers (i.e. risk sharing, economies of scope and scale, accessing assets such as limited slots at airports and shaping the competition) along with external drivers (i.e. the changes induced by information technology and turbulent economic climates, rapid product and market changes as well as global competition). Despite the success of some alliances and collaborations, they can be very unstable and subject to churn (i.e. partners enter and leave as business needs and objectives change). This highlights what Evans et al. (2003) point to as strategic fit, the need for partnerships to be workable as well as being able to offer compatability, commitment and a sense of partnership.

Airline alliances

There is a very clear link between the use of IT in tourist transport sectors and the development and expansion of airline alliances, which were briefly discussed in Chapter 2. French (1997b: 99) argues that much of the growth of alliances was only made possible with the growth of technology. Bennett (1997) views such developments in the context of a growing globalisation of the tourist transport business, indicating that 60 per cent of alliances were formed between 1992 and 1996. But this phenomenon within the aviation industry is not as new as Bennett (1997) implies, since French (1997b) traces the development back to the 1970s. However, it is the speed of this development that is critical to the aviation industry worldwide and which has implications for tourist supply issues, particularly the formation of airline alliances in the 1990s as shown in Chapter 2. French (1997b) points to the principal data source for analysing airline alliances and their current status – the survey published each year in the June issue of *Airline Business*. It is therefore an important reference source to trace the evolution, changing status and dynamics of alliances (*www.airlinebusiness.com*).

Bennett (1997: 214) distinguishes between two types of alliance:

- *Tactical partnerships*, comprising a loose form of collaboration designed to derive marketing benefits, characterised by code sharing and exemplified by the hub-and-spoke system of air travel in the US domestic airline market. This is reflected in the smaller feeder and regional airlines being aligned with key hub-based carriers.
- *Strategic partnerships*, where an investment or pooling of resources by partners aims to achieve a range of common objectives focused on the partners' strategic ambitions. Bennett (1997: 214–15) describes strategic alliances as incorporating 'shared airport facilities (check-in lounges), improved connections (synchronised schedules), reciprocity on frequent flyer programmes, freight co-ordination and marketing agreements (code-sharing and block selling)'.

Bennett (1997) outlines the principal motivations that may explain why airlines enter into strategic alliances, and reiterates many of the points developed by Evans (2001):

- to achieve economies of scale and learning, principally to improve profitability and perhaps also to benefit from economies of scope (Hanlon 2003);
- to gain access to the benefits of the other airline's assets;
- to reduce risk by sharing it;
- to help share the market, which may help reduce incapacity in mature markets and could reduce competition;
- speed in reaching the market given the structural changes occurring in the airline industry (e.g. deregulation and privatisation – see Chapter 3).

According to Morley (2006) airlines enter into such alliances for the following reasons:

- to get economic benefits such as productivity gains;
- to gain competitive advantages from improved customer service;
- cost reductions from sharing lounge facilities, terminal facilities and block space sales on aircraft from partners and code sharing and pooling;
- joint purchasing allows additional cost savings;
- economies of scale and scope in marketing activities;
- more connected route network for passengers and greater choice of destinations;
- expanding market access for individual airlines and growth where restrictions to access may apply (also see Hannegan and Mulvey 1995; Alamdari and Morrell 1997a).

In terms of the direct impact on tourism, Morley (2006) points to a potential 2.5 per cent increase in visitor arrivals to Australia as a result of alliances operating among airlines serving Australia. For full service airlines, strategic alliances are now a vital business model and part of how the airline industry operates and manages its competitive activities. Bennett (1997: 222) reiterates concerns that 'less competition equates with less choice, while improved economic circumstances for airlines are tantamount to higher prices'. Inevitably alliances are part of the trend towards a number of mega-carriers dominating the airline industry as part of the globalisation process in tourism. Yet as Hsu and Shih (2008) show, alliance membership and activity has improved network connectivity for passengers, improving accessibility from high to medium traffic airports through to low traffic airports: whilst such travel may involve more transfers overall, they argue that it involves less travel time for the passenger. In the case of one of the larger alliances, the Star Alliance, Holtbrügge et al. (2006) argue that such alliances help partner airlines to compete more succesfully. The Star Alliance (a non-equity alliance) formed in 1997, has integrated functions to assist member airlines with procurement, marketing and other activities, but the human resource functions of member airlines still have very divergent approaches (also see Wang and Horsburgh 2007 for more details on the three main alliances: OneWorld, Star Alliance and SkyTeam). A key feature which has assisted the growth of alliances is technology.

In crisis management terms, the example of SARS and the experience of one airline – SIA – illustrates many of the features of a strategic response to a crisis (Ritchie 2004) and how technology has helped airlines to communicate better with their customers. The company evaluated the strategic alternatives, selecting a number of strategies (cost reduction measures and capacity reduction), whilst maintaining good communication with travellers and deploying resources (e.g. health kits) to allay fears, along with collaboration with stakeholders (e.g. airport authorities and health agencies) and the media, and the resumption of normal service after the SARS epidemic. One of the central tenets of its communication strategy was the use of technology, namely the company website, and this is a fitting introduction to the next section – information technology – since as Knowles et al. (2001) rightly noted: 'technology will shape the future of marketing programmes, product design and corporate strategies' in the tourism sector, which has had a major impact on the transport sector.

●●●● Information technology and supply issues in tourist transport: a role for logistics and IT?

It is widely acknowledged that society has entered the 'information age' and that this has had implications for transport provision (Hepworth and Ducatel 1992). One of the immediate impacts for tourist transport providers is that up-to-date information flows are now vital when a supply chain exists, and the transport provider is just one component of the overall tourist product. As Christopher (1994: 12) observes, the customer service explosion means there is a need for 'consistent provision of time and place utility. In other words, products do not have value until they are in the hands of the customer at the time and place required'.

Christopher (1994) argues that logistics of service delivery are of paramount importance and enable organisations to add value and deliver a consistent product. Logistics is a vital concept to recognise, particularly when IT is also introduced, since IT and logistics enable transport providers to achieve their objectives in a competitive environment. According to Quayle (1993: 9):

> Logistics is the process which seeks to provide for the management and coordination of all activities within the supply chain from sourcing and acquisition, through production where appropriate, and through distribution channels to the customer.

Logistics provides a competitive advantage by offering a strategic view of operational issues and an understanding of the links in the supply system. It also assists in the coordination of the service delivery function, and transport in its own right is a vital element of logistics in moving the customer nearer to the product in a tourism context. Logistics is documented in detail by Quayle (1993) and Christopher (1994) and performs a vital role in providing the link between the marketplace and operating activity of the business. Figure 6.2 outlines the business functions which fall within the remit of logistics. What emerges from Figure 6.3 is that information flows are a critical component in logistics and the management of supply issues in transport.

Within the literature on IT in tourism, the seminal study by Sheldon (1997) is fast becoming the key reference source, replacing the earlier work by Poon (1993). The tourist industry generates large volumes of information that needs to be processed

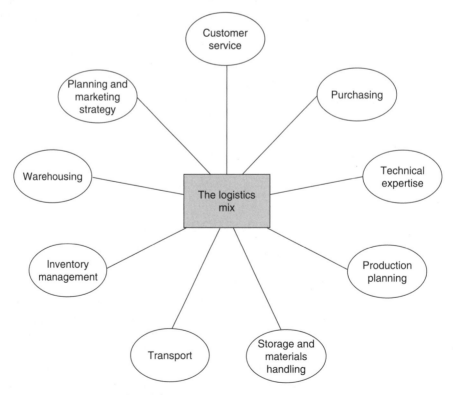

Figure 6.2 The scope of logistics

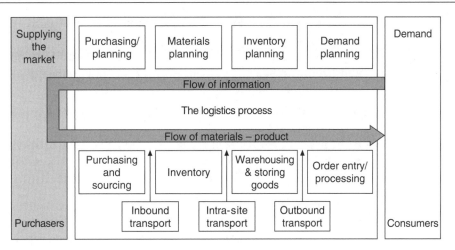

Figure 6.3 The logistics process

and used within a logistics context. For example, Sheldon (1997) notes that each airline booking generates 25 transactions that need processing. In Sheldon's (1997) model of tourism information flows, there are three main agents involved: travellers, suppliers and travel intermediaries. For the purpose of the discussion here, it is the supplier's use of IT to handle, utilise and manage these information flows that is of interest. From a transport supplier's perspective, information is essential to allow the organisation to function and for different departments to make decisions about corporate objectives, their consumers and competitors. It can also be harnessed in the marketing function (see Chapter 2). Sheldon (1997) cites the example of the airline industry, which makes extensive use of IT in a wide range of contexts, including:

- global distribution systems (GDSs) (see WTO 1994);
- frequent flyer databases;
- yield management programmes (see Chapter 2);
- distribution and marketing of their products;
- the design, operation and maintenance of aircraft and luggage handling;
- check-in systems at airports.

Although other transport sectors involved in tourism also make use of IT (including train operators, car rental agencies and coach and cruise ship operators), it is probably most highly developed in the airline sector, due to large investment in capital and the highly competitive nature of the business. In that sense, IT is seen as integral to gaining a competitive edge and, in the case of SIA, in maintaining continuous product innovations. For example, on its Megatop-747s, all passengers have access to an in-flight telephone to make credit card calls from air to ground.

Sheldon (1997) traces the development of IT in the airline industry, where it is primarily seen as a means of improving the efficiency of operations and of management functions. The airline sector first developed computer technology in the form of computer reservation systems in the 1950s. It is impossible in a book such as this to trace the rapid development of IT in the airline industry and all the other transport sectors, although it is pertinent to outline the current state of the art in IT and its organisation.

Following the rapid growth in CRSs (Knowles and Garland 1994) in the 1970s and 1980s (Archdale 1991), Sheldon (1997) outlines the typical configuration of an airline CRS. It comprises:

- a central site housing the computer systems driving the CRS (often up to 10 mainframe systems);
- the network hardware at the central site and computer staff to maintain it;
- a series of front-end communication processors to process information and online storage devices at the central site.

This is complemented by satellite communications to remote communication concentrators (RCCs) in key cities that relay data from the earth station. This is then relayed to reservation terminals and airports, providing rapid communications.

One of the major changes in the late 1980s and 1990s has been the move from CRSs, which contained only airline information for the proprietary airline, to systems containing data for multiple airlines. Sheldon (1997) traces the development of CRSs into what have now been called global distribution systems (World Tourism Organization 1994), such as the Asian GDS, Abacus. Table 6.1 outlines the principal developments contributing to the development of GDSs.

GDSs are CRSs that are affiliated with airlines. There has been a great deal of debate over the impact of airline affiliation on the competitiveness of air travel in North America. Sheldon (1997) argues that, following legislation, rules now exist to ensure all airlines are represented on GDS screens. According to Sheldon (1997: 25), the significance of major GDSs in 1996 was as follows:

- Sabre   US$1500–2000 million
- Apollo   US$1100+million
- Abacus   US$650 million
- Amadeus   US$600 million
- System One   US$500 million
- Worldspan   US$500 million
- Galileo   US$400 million.

Table 6.1 The development of GDSs

1976	Three North American airlines began to offer their systems – Apollo (United Airlines), Sabre (American Airlines) and PARS (TransWorld Airlines) – as well as offering US travel agents terminals to access their systems
1981	Eastern Airlines established System One Direct Access (SODA)
1982	Delta Airlines launched its DATAS II
1987	In Europe, Galileo and Amadeus were formed and offered to travel agents. In Asia, Abacus was formed and also offered to travel agents
1988	Japan Airlines formed Axess
1990	System One was purchased by a non-airline company – EDS. The merger of PARS and DATAS II resulted in the formation of Worldspan. In Japan, All Nippon Airways and Abacus formed Infini
1993	Galileo and Apollo were merged to establish Galileo International
1995	System One merged with Amadeus

Source: Based on Sheldon (1997: 24).

Although a CRS will show only one airline's schedules, a GDS has the advantage of showing data on multiple carriers, including:

- flight schedules and availability;
- passenger information;
- fare quotes and rules for travel;
- ticketing.

Since the advent of GDSs airlines have also established 'a presence on the Internet and [are] using that as an important distribution channel especially to consumers' (Sheldon 1997: 27). By accepting payment by credit card, airlines have harnessed a developing technology to complement GDSs and traditional distribution channels.

Sheldon (1997) also discusses other airline IT applications, which include:

- baggage and cargo handling systems;
- cabin automation (e.g. entertainment systems, visual route systems on in-flight screens using geographical positioning system equipment);
- safety systems;
- decision support systems;
- flight scheduling and planning;
- crew scheduling and management;
- gate management and control.

Sheldon (1997) also examines the developments in IT that have been introduced into land transport operations to help the logistics of fleet management in relation to car rental and other innovations which improve the tourists' travel experience. However, the most dramatic revolution induced by the IT revolution is e-travel.

E-travel and the transport and tourism sector

E-tourism has been defined by Buhalis (2003: xxiv) as 'the digitisation of all the processes and value chains in tourism, travel and hospitality . . . industries that enable organisations to maximise their efficiency and effectiveness'. Here technology has enabled consumers and businesses to use information communication technologies (ICTs) to communicate and interact as shown in Figure 6.4. Figure 6.4 also shows that the e-tourism revolution has spread across all sectors of the tourism industry, but it has had a pronounced impact on sectors such as transport and travel agents given the distribution channels they now access to reach the customer direct. One of the clear indications of this development is in the use of online buying from websites to access a wide range of suppliers. As Buhalis (2003) has shown, ICTs have led to developments in customer relationship management (CRM) through the information virtual organisations hold on consumers, but also in continually interacting with customers. What ICTs have also done is to revolutionise the experience through CRM by not only increasing selling opportunities by gaining customer attention, but also through building familiarity with an organisation, brand awareness and product information relevant to the customer's needs.

As Buhalis and Licata (2002) show, changes from the GDS era induced by e-commerce and the Internet have led to a new generation of e-mediaries as single suppliers (i.e. BritishAirways.com) and multi-supplier sites and online agencies (i.e. expedia.com). The online agencies have certainly developed a diverse range of products for e-travel consumers, with transport a core component. One consequence

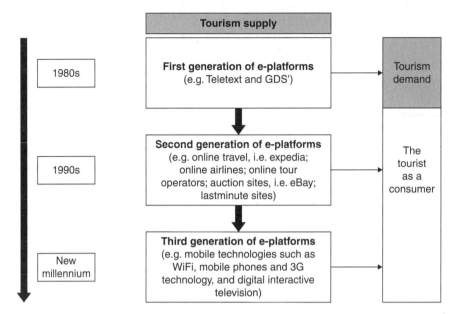

Figure 6.4 Evolution of three generations of e-tourism

of the growth in online booking via the different options available is that British Airways decided to close two call centres in February 2004 due to online booking on ba.com for short-haul traffic, of which 46 per cent is now booked on that website. ICTs also help businesses to compete globally for business as opposed to the more geographically defined markets in the 1970s and early 1980s.

Much of this development has occurred through the convergence of technology, as Buhalis (2003) has shown (see Figure 6.5), as tourism and transport operations harness this new technology to achieve a competitive advantage. As Table 6.2 shows, many of the competitive issues raised earlier in this chapter can also be addressed by ICTs, since they allow a more timely strategic reaction to the complex

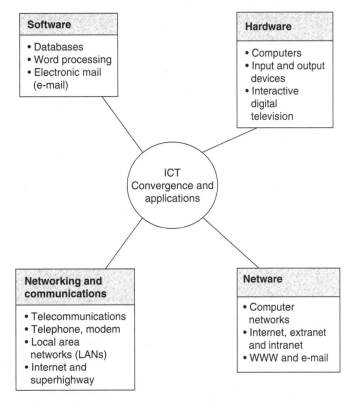

Figure 6.5 ICTs in tourism: the components and convergence

Source: Developed and modified from Buhalis 2003.

Table 6.2 Using ICTs to develop competitive advantage

Strategies	
Cost leadership	Use ICTs to reduce the cost of customers or suppliers Reduce cost of business processes Increase cost efficiency Ensure competitive pricing Decrease supply costs and ease supply Maximise resources utilisation especially for fixed costs
Product differentiation	Use ICTs to develop unique products and add value Differentiate products/services of a company Reduce differentiation advantage of competitors Use information as a product itself
Focus	ICT-enhanced segmentation and targeting Develop relationship marketing Aim to develop mini-market segments Enhance the ability to create niche markets
Time	Provide timely solutions to consumer and trade problems Maximise interaction and reduce response times Enable just-in-time initiatives, reducing stock and distribution costs

(Continued)

Table 6.2 Using ICTs to develop competitive advantage *(Continued)*

Strategies	
Speedy reaction	Proaction and reaction are important Business at the speed of thought
Marketing research	Use ICTs to interact with consumers Continuous marketing research Scenario building and testing
External environment	Interact with external environment and appreciate influence Set indicators and sensors React first
Innovate	Identify and develop new niche markets and products Create new products and add value to existing products Re-engineer business processes Use ICTs for communicating with consumers and partners
Promote growth	Geographical expansion Operational expansion to gain from economies of scale Develop networks and partnerships to gain economies of scope Promote horizontal, vertical and diagonal integration
Alliances	Develop virtual organisations and concentrate on core business Integrate value chain Develop flexible network of partners based on ICTs
Outsourcing	Outsource non-core business to partners
Efficiency	Redesign processes to maximise output with minimum resources Reduce time required for development and delivery of product
Quality	Standardisation and quality-control systems Offer before, during, after service
ICT platform	Integrate all internal and external processes Develop info-structure and info-space
Loyalty	Provide incentives to create loyalty Add value through personalised interactions with consumers Develop relationship and 1-2-1 marketing
Fight competition	Use ICTs to avoid substitution and barriers to entry Establish entry barriers Effect switching costs and mechanisms Build closer relationships with suppliers and customers Limit access to distribution channels

Source: Based on O'Brien (1996); Robson (1997); Peppard (1993) in Buhalis (2003: 53–4).

and increasingly volatile trading environment that characterises global tourism. To reiterate the points made above, ICTs allow continuous innovation through more careful targeting of niche products using technology and a growing complexity and scale of operations, as virtual collaboration and partnerships are now more commonplace through vertical and horizontal integration. The application of ICTs in the transport sector is illustrated in Insight 6.1.

So what is the future of e-travel?

An annually updated study on e-travel in Europe by Carl Marcussen can be found at *www.crt.dk/trends*, which is helpful in trying to understand the nature of and

INSIGHT 6.1

The use of ICTs by airlines

Dimitrious Buhalis, University of Bournemouth[1]

ICTs contribute towards efficiency, productivity and competitiveness improvements of both inter-organisational and intra-organisational systems. There is evidence, however, that well-managed ICTs can generate tremendous value for organisations (Chalk et al. 1987). Clear strategic goals and commitment are prerequisites for the development of an appropriate e-commerce strategy and the development of websites and other technological solutions. This Insight primarily concentrates on scheduled and no-frills airlines, as charter airlines use different distribution mechanisms to display their availability and prices. However, the distinction between these types of airlines is increasingly becoming unclear, as each type of carrier is trying to enter another's market. However, low-cost airlines as new entrants have been much more technologically innovative, and these innovations are identified in the analysis.

Many low-cost carriers rely exclusively on ICTs for displaying their availability and for communicating and transacting with their clientele and a number of these providers of ICT services are shown in Table 6.3. ICTs are equally important in operations management and contribute to the optimisation of procedures and processes (Gudmuudson and Rhoades 2001; Goh and Uncles 2003) as well as for softer service elements such as in-flight entertainment and customerservice. Indeed, airlines see the Internet as a major opportunity to tackle distribution costs and to re-engineer the structure of the industry.

As shown in other parts of the book, low-cost airlines emerged in both Europe and the US, seeking lower input costs using simple distribution strategies for communicating with their clientele. Internet early adopters, including both well-established and newly founded airlines, identified a clear opportunity. easyJet and Ryanair (see Creaton 2005), for example, derived the vast majority of their bookings through the Internet by 2002 and passed on their cost savings to consumers. No-frills airlines, empowered by the Internet and other

Table 6.3 Airline ICT providers

GDSs and IT providers	
Sabre	*www.sabre.com*
Worldspan	*www.worldspan.com*
Amadeus	*www.amadeus.com*
Galileo	*www.galileo.com*
Airline systems	
IBM	*www.ibm.com/solutions/travel/*
Lufthansa	*www.lsyna.com/*
LIDO	*www.lido.net/*
Open Skies Navitaire	*www.navitaire.com/index.htm*
SITA	*www.sita.net/*
NCR/Teradata	*www.teradata.com/solutions/travelindustry.asp*
ORACLE	*www.oracle.com/industries/traveltransportation/*
International Air Transportation Association (IATA)	*www.iata.org/*
Inflight Catering Association	*www.ifcanet.com*
Airport Technology	*www.airport-technology.com/*

[1]This Insight is a shortened and updated version of the author's paper 'eAirlines: Strategic and tactical use of ICTs in the airline industry', *Information and Management*, 41(7), September 2004, 805–25, which is recommended reading.

ICT tools, made the industry re-engineer itself as it introduced a number of ICT-enabled innovations, including:

- electronic/paperless tickets;
- transparent and clear pricing led by proactive and reactive yield management;
- single fare tickets with no restrictions on staying or Saturday night rules;
- commission capping and publication of net fares;
- financial incentives for self-booking online;
- auctions and online promotions;
- powerful customer relationship management systems;
- online and context-relevant advertising.

The strategic and tactical role of ICTs for airlines

From a strategic point of view, airlines use technology to develop and manage their business model as well as to monitor the external environment and competition, undertake revenue analysis, forecasting, maintain historical data, predict demand, and design desirable products. ICTs are critical for monitoring and forecasting the performance of strategic business units and for deciding which markets airlines should penetrate and how. Routes and crew planning, frequency of service, choice of aircraft and developing relationships with strategic partners are key functions supported by ICTs. Similarly, strategic pricing and yield management are also supported by running complex algorithms to establish best performance and profitability levels.

ICTs also allow airlines to reduce their dependence on intermediaries and that has direct strategic implications for their partners and strategic alliances. Branding and communication of principles are also critical for airlines at the strategic level. Managing communications with all stakeholders, including investors, press, employees and customers, is of paramount importance. ICT-enabled communications assist airlines to interact with all their stakeholders and to update them with regard to their initiatives and developments. Many carriers used their websites as main information points following the 11 September 2001 attacks, as well as for other disturbances in their services emerging from their external environment, such as SARS as discussed above.

ICTs are critical for the operational management of airlines, as illustrated in Figure 6.6. There are several requirements including check-in, allocation of seats, generating a number of reports and orders, such as flight paths, weather forecasts, load and balance calculations, manifests for airport immigration and security authorities, in-flight catering orders and crew rotas. ICTs also assist a number of functions including inventory and reservations management as well as ticketing. Airlines have bases and distributors around the world and need efficient coordination and communication with stations, branches, distributors, and customers globally. Interaction with distributors, travel agencies and other distributors can determine levels of sales whilst efficient invoicing and revenue collection is critical for both cash flow and profitability. Finally, airlines have been investing in customer relationship management programmes in order to improve their direct communication and to manage their loyalty clubs. Increasingly, e-ticketing instigates paperless transactions, whilst offering significant savings (Shon et al. 2003). Tactical pricing, yield management and special offers and promotions are all facilitated by constantly assessing traffic and by taking both proactive and reactive measures to adjust demand and supply. ICTs also facilitate e-procurement and management of suppliers and partners on a regular basis. Most airlines use standardised software to undertake those functions and to generate the reports.

Airlines had to invest significantly in their ICT systems in the late 1990s in order to develop interfaces with consumers and the travel trade and on an ongoing basis. The level of investment in ICTs illustrates their critical role. ICTs have emerged from a pure infrastructure department to a critical enabler of the entire range of airline business processes. ICTs

Generic airline management	Strategic airline functions
• Strategic and operational management • Finance and accounting • Employee productivity and crew management (rota and training) • Relationships with partners and alliance integration • Business management and reporting • Safety and security procedures	• Strategic business unit management • Routes planning and market assessment • Monitoring of competitors • Strategic pricing and yield management • Branding and communication of principles • Distribution strategy • Partnerships and alliances • Capacity and aircraft decisions
Interface with consumers, partners, agencies, other distributors and ticketing	**Tactical planning and running the business**
• Inventory management and distribution of tickets • Customer profiling, customer service and communication with consumers • Management of inventory and bookings through GDSs and the Internet • Customer relationship management • Managing loyalty clubs • Reservations management, ticketing and electronic ticketing • Operational management • Tactical pricing and yield management • Promotions, special offers and targeted campaigns • eProcurement and management of suppliers and partners • Communications and transactions with stations, branches, distributors and customers globally • Invoicing and revenue collection • Co-ordinating with partners and alliance members	• Reservations and revenue support • Check-in procedures and seat allocation • Gate management and reporting to authorities • Management of in-flight catering • Airport passenger handling • Cargo management • Baggage handling and monitoring • Pricing, ticketing, revenue and yield management • Networking and schedule development • Scheduling, operational management and control • Crew management and control • Maintenance management and control • Procurement of materials and equipment • Co-ordination of stations and hubs • Weather, fuel and rota reports and manifests • Critical incident management and corrective mechanisms

Figure 6.6 eAirlines ICT-empowered functions

Source: Buhalis 2004.

effectively determine the competitiveness of airlines, as they are embedded in every single element of the airline value chain, as illustrated in Figure 6.7.

Horizontal collaboration with other airlines

The vast majority of airline investment is concentrated on distribution, as it is becoming one of the most important elements of airline marketing strategy and competitiveness. Distribution strategies determine all other elements of the marketing mix. Air fares are modified by commission costs and reservation fees. The product itself is determined, since CRSs facilitate the development of hub-and-spoke systems as well as code-share agreements. Promotion is also influenced, as online and offline promotional campaigns primarily aim to increase traffic to airline websites.

ICTs will not only formulate all elements of the marketing mix of airlines in the future, but will also determine their strategic directions, partnerships and ownership. The global alliances, such as the 'Star Alliance', are only possible because of the coordination that can be achieved through harmonised ICT systems or through effective interfaces. In ▶

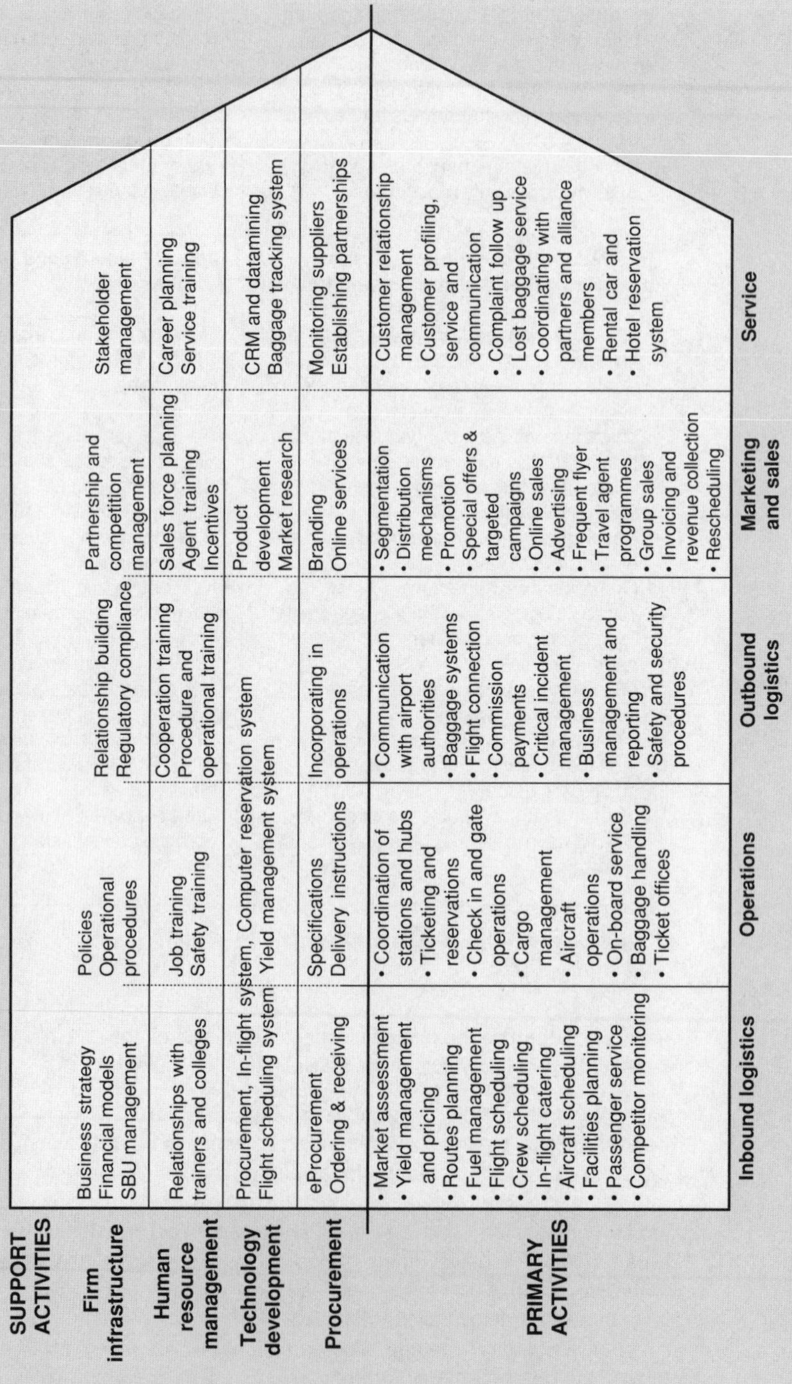

SUPPORT ACTIVITIES	Inbound logistics	Operations	Outbound logistics	Marketing and sales	Service
Firm infrastructure	Business strategy, Financial models, SBU management	Policies, Operational procedures	Relationship building, Regulatory compliance	Partnership and competition management	Stakeholder management
Human resource management	Relationships with trainers and colleges	Job training, Safety training	Cooperation training, Procedure and operational training	Sales force planning, Agent training, Incentives	Career planning, Service training
Technology development	Procurement, In-flight system, Computer reservation system, Flight scheduling system, Yield management system		Product development, Market research	Product development, Market research	CRM and datamining, Baggage tracking system
Procurement	eProcurement, Ordering & receiving	Specifications, Delivery instructions	Incorporating in operations	Branding, Online services	Monitoring suppliers, Establishing partnerships

PRIMARY ACTIVITIES	Inbound logistics	Operations	Outbound logistics	Marketing and sales	Service
	• Market assessment • Yield management and pricing • Routes planning • Fuel management • Flight scheduling • Crew scheduling • In-flight catering • Aircraft scheduling • Facilities planning • Passenger service • Competitor monitoring	• Coordination of stations and hubs • Ticketing and reservations • Check in and gate operations • Cargo management • Aircraft operations • On-board service • Baggage handling • Ticket offices	• Communication with airport authorities • Baggage systems • Flight connection • Commission payments • Critical incident management • Business management and reporting • Safety and security procedures	• Segmentation • Distribution mechanisms • Promotion • Special offers & targeted campaigns • Online sales • Advertising • Frequent flyer programmes • Travel agent programmes • Group sales • Invoicing and revenue collection • Rescheduling	• Customer relationship management • Customer profiling, service and communication • Complaint follow up • Lost baggage service • Coordinating with partners and alliance members • Rental car and • Hotel reservation system

Figure 6.7 ICT-enabled airline industry value chain

Source: Buhalis 2004.

effect consumers receive a seamless service, collect frequent-flyer miles and enjoy privileges from different carriers in all continents simply because ICTs provide the 'infostructure' for close collaboration. Hence ICTs are also instrumental for the globalisation of the airline industry.

Connecting with consumers and all stakeholders through the Internet

The proliferation of the World Wide Web in the mid-1990s changed the airline business dramatically and enabled new business models to emerge. By 1998, most airlines already hosted websites to inform consumers and to support itinerary building, fare construction and reservations. They enhanced their interactivity with consumers and built relationship-marketing strategies as well as frequent-flyer systems. Websites also assisted airlines to launch another communication and purchasing channel in order to reduce the power and costs of conventional intermediaries such as travel agencies and GDSs.

Air transportation accounts for approximately 65 per cent of all travel e-commerce. It is estimated that internet bookings contribute about 5 per cent of the total airline sales globally. However there are great variations between regions and carriers. The figures quoted for American carriers are significantly greater, as a result of a greater penetration of the Internet. In the USA 11 per cent of the airlines' seats are booked online on carriers' websites. No-frills carriers in the USA are clear front-runners, with 41 per cent of their seats booked online.

No-frills airlines are using their websites to attract and communicate directly with consumers. There are a number of reasons for this, as demonstrated in Table 6.4, which

Table 6.4 Reasons for no-frills airlines' success in internet bookings

Simpler product	• Often A–B–A itineraries and tickets • One class of service • Each segment priced individually • No catering on board • No pre-allocation of seats
Simple distribution channel	• Single distribution channel through own call centres and Internet • Financial incentives to book online and disincentives for phone bookings • Net rates across all channels • No commitment to existing distribution channel members • Partnership with popular offline media, such as newspapers
Advanced CRM and aggressive direct marketing	• Email- and SMS-driven customer relationship management (including the use of engagement with social networking sites) • Aggressive banner advertising policies • Context-based advertising • Data and e-mail acquisition through online and offline campaigns
Aggressive pricing and yield management	• Individual priced seats • Minimal fare restrictions • Proactive and reactive pricing • Provocative pricing, starting from offering free flights
Advanced information technologies	• No legacy systems • No commitment to global distribution systems • Paperless office and efficient procedures • Interconnectivity with technologically advanced partners
Dynamic packaging and value added services	• Proactive approach in selling complementary services, such as hotels and car rentals through white labelling • Additional value-added services such as destination guides

builds upon Insight 2.4 on airline management. At the end of 2002 a number of innovative scheduled carriers achieved more than 30 per cent of their bookings on their websites and aimed to achieve 50–70 per cent by 2005 – primarily achieved by offering their best fares only on their websites. For example, British Airways' Internet site currently achieves over 1.5 million visits per month, whilst the average growth of online bookings has been 11 per cent per month. BA aims to achieve 80 per cent of customer trip transactions as well as 100 per cent of executive club transactions on its internet site now.

Several structural changes in the industry have emerged as a result of the ability of airlines to communicate directly with consumers. The most useful feature is the ability to promote distressed capacity at discounted rates at the last minute. Following the events of 11 September 2001 and the consequent global unrest, most airlines were able to promote heavily discounted fares via electronic mail and auctions. As a result, they managed to sell a significant proportion of their perishable seats, contributing directly to the bottom line. Industry experts explained that this should be regarded as direct profit, as airlines would otherwise have lost this revenue.

The ability to disintermediate travel agencies has also enabled airlines to cut down commission rates. Airlines initially in the USA, and increasingly globally, reduced their commission rates (from 10–12 per cent to 7–0 per cent), whilst they also introduced 'commission capping' (e.g. $50 per ticket). Major airlines quote savings of several million dollars. In addition, electronic ticketing and ticketless travel have gradually reduced distribution, fulfilment and labour costs whilst increasing efficiency. Continental Airlines is often quoted as an example of an airline that decreased its cost by $20 million simply by reducing commissions to travel agencies and introducing electronic ticketing.

ICT-empowered strategic alliances

Interviewees suggested that ICTs and the Internet have gradually enabled new types of strategic alliances and have forced airlines to collaborate and compete *(coopete)* simultaneously. Alliances support the integration of their frequent-flyer programmes and benefits. They also provide access to business lounges and allow endorsement waivers to enable passengers to switch between airlines. Alliances support code sharing, optimisation of capacity and yield, as well as a certain level of collaboration. Cooperation is also extended to sharing systems and ICT expertise. Almost half of the airlines within alliances are already sharing systems with their partners and another 20 per cent plan to do so to help offer customers seamless services. Outsourcing has increased across all airlines and 85 per cent of carriers have already outsourced all or part of their ICT functions. Airlines need to develop stronger alliances and meaningful networks of wealth creation if they are to survive global competition in the future. Business strategies and alliances management will therefore need to refocus and include ICT solutions as part of their core competency, their collaboration infostructure, and brand drivers. Only then will alliances be able to maximise their contribution and their impact in the marketplace. Business interconnectivity requires technical interoperability and airlines need to agree on technological standards and common approaches.

ICT and the airline of the future

Airlines are one of the most interdependent organisations in the travel industry. Therefore they need to use technology strategically to integrate their operations and control and coordinate all their business and management functions. Figure 6.8 demonstrates that networked airlines of the future will take advantage of the Internet as well as intranets and extranets to communicate with all their stakeholders, to improve their internal efficiency and effectiveness and interact with all their stakeholders productively. Implementing enterprise resource planning can help airlines integrate all facets of their business and maximise their performance. Developing successful extranets will also allow airlines to develop effective collaboration channels with all their partners.

Managing the entire supply chain electronically can allow all partners to benefit by reducing costs, increasing transaction accuracy and optimising efficiency. There is evidence that

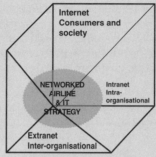

CONNECTING WITH ALL STAKEHOLDERS THROUGH THE INTERNET

Consumers
- Information, itineraries, reservations
- Special offers, auctions
- Frequent-flyer clubs and redemptions
- Personal preferences
- Check-in facilities
- Operational updates
- Baggage systems and WorldTracer

Stakeholders
- Shareholders
- Environmental groups
- Journalists and newsletters
- Place spotters and aviation enthusiasts
- Value added

INTERCONNECTING PARTNER SYSTEMS AND EXTRANETS

eProcurement: transactions and information flows with suppliers
- Extranets
- Reports for Air Traffic Control, Customs and airport authorities
- Reports for suppliers
- eProcurement tools and software
- Marketplace
- Baggage systems and WorldTracer

Distribution, marketing and sales support with partners
- Computer reservation systems
- Global distribution systems
- Dedicated travel trade portals & systems
- General sales agencies systems & extranets

Horizontal collaboration with other airlines
- Extranets between alliance members

INTERNAL AIRLINE SYSTEMS

Sales and marketing support
- Computer reservation systems
- Global distribution systems
- Reservations and revenue management
- Decision support systems

Operational systems
- Flight schedule management systems
- Operations control
- Flight watch
- Station control systems
- Baggage handling and monitoring systems

Resource management systems
- Maintenance control
- Crew management systems

Internet Consumers and society

NETWORKED AIRLINE & IT STRATEGY

Intranet Intra-organisational

Extranet Inter-organisational

Figure 6.8 The networked airline of the future

Source: Buhalis 2004.

e-procurement is developing rapidly and it seems that other extranet applications will be emerging soon to facilitate communications and interaction with customs, immigration, airport, air traffic control and civil aviation authorities. Technologies can improve the entire customer travelling experience. Frequent travellers demand speedier check-in processes and a higher degree of flexibility and control over their own travel arrangements. e-ticketing and paperless communications are expected to improve customer service by reducing the level of bureaucracy, by increasing flexibility, and by speeding up all processes. Self-service kiosk applications will increasingly support travellers make travel reservations, check in, receive boarding passes, select seats, check frequent-flier miles, request upgrades, purchase a ticket, print e-ticket receipts, or check bags – all without waiting in line for an agent. ICTs will therefore be used dynamically before, during and after the travel experience to serve passengers and to reinforce the airline brand. Sigala (2008) discusses the most key operational benefits of self-service check-in, including:

- cost savings (including less staff needed and collection of customer data electronically);
- improved customer service (reducing the need for queuing, greater flexibility of where and how to check in, reduction in crowding);
- revenue opportunities to sell and promote complementary tourism products.

The ability of travellers to connect from virtually anywhere with their wireless devices and adapt their itinerary is expected to be one of the most widely used services. Wireless solutions will empower airlines to communicate with their passengers virtually anywhere, anytime. Wireless and mobile devices, such as mobile phones, personal digital assistant (PDAs) and laptops, are already used for searching and booking flights, altering flight arrangements, retrieving updated arrival and departure information, checking in and selecting seats. The Star Alliance allows members to download timetables and booking agents to their PDAs.

Implications

ICTs play a critical role in the strategic and operational management of airlines. They not only contribute to the formulation of all elements of the marketing mix, but they will also determine the strategic directions, partnerships and ownership of airlines. It can therefore be predicted that technology will facilitate and support the successful airlines of the future. As ICTs are instrumental in rearranging airline alliances and concentration, it is also likely that technology may provide a major motivation for mergers and collaboration. ICTs are already instrumental for the globalisation and concentration of the airline industry. Further integration and consolidation seems inevitable. ICTs will enable airlines to establish global networks, to serve their customers better and to communicate with their partners more efficiently on a global basis. They will need to provide the 'info-structure' for closer collaboration with all stakeholders available. Hence, the networked airline of the future will take advantage of the Internet, intranets and extranets to strengthen its position, reinforce its brand and contribute to its profitability.

Questions

1 How has the airline industry changed its use of ICTs since the 1990s?
2 What are the main features which give low-cost airlines a competitive edge?
3 What will the distribution system of the airline of the future look like?

market for e-travel. According to Carl Marcussen (2008), the demand for e-travel in Europe is continuing to grow at a dramatic rate. It was worth €13.9 billion in 2003, rising to €24.7 billion in 2006 and could exceed €26 billion in 2008, equivalent to 6.5 per cent of the European travel market. The main category of travel purchases in 2007 was air travel (56 per cent), followed by hotels (17 per cent), and package tours (14.5 per cent). Marcussen found that in 2007 the shares of the online travel market were: the UK 30 per cent; Germany 19 per cent; France 14 per cent. Direct sellers accounted for some 65 per cent of online sales in 2007 and intermediaries some 35 per cent. Yet once the tourist reaches a destination, their travel experience is also important, aside from how they have purchased their holiday or trip, and for this reason attention now turns to the destination and tourist transport provision as discussed in Chapter 1 and 8.

The supply of tourist transport in destination areas

The supply of tourist transport services in the destination is one area neglected in Buckley's (1987) transaction analysis. Two studies that do deal with this issue are Teye's (1992) study of Bermuda and Heraty's (1989) examination of the supply-related problems that characterise less developed countries (LDCs). Two notable studies in this area were by Prideaux (2000a, b), which identified the transport–destination development linkages as developed in Chapter 1. In these studies it was noted that accessibility was critical to destination development as a range of transport and infrastructure is progressively developed so that different forms of tourism development can occur, from local or day-tripper markets initially through to regional, national and international markets. Surprisingly, few studies have made the critical links that Prideaux noted, that the rate of destination growth was dependent upon investment in infrastructure and transport services if new markets are to be accessible to destination areas. A more recent study by Prideaux (2004) observed that the development of Cairns as an international tourist destination was contingent upon the opening of its international airport, so that the perception of peripherality within an Australian context was reduced once an international airport was expanded as opposed to a more local facility. What Prideaux (2004: 90) rightly argued was that:

> Although often overlooked, it is apparent that the transport system can exert a major influence over the shape and direction that tourist development takes in a destination. As the distance between destinations and origins increases, the significance of transport, including both its cost and availability, becomes increasingly important . . . Transport's role is therefore one that lies in the background, noticed only when it is inadequate to the task or falls short of the expectations of the traveller.

Visitors expect good destination-specific transport systems and they form an important part of the tourist's overall experience of travel. Heraty (1989), in the context of the LDCs, remains one of the few studies in terms of how the supply of tourist transport needs to meet both the expectations and requirements of visitors if the service encounter in the destination is to reach minimum standards. Leinbach (1995) reiterates the poor state of research on transport and less developed countries, whilst a more recent study by Wade et al. (2001) on Tanzania does highlight the constraints imposed on tourism development through poor infrastructure, most notably roads, and Turton and Mutambirwa (1996) and Turton (2004) have reviewed the situation in relation to air travel in Zimbabwe.

Although some of the problems Heraty (1989) examined are unique to LDCs, the general issues raised also have implications for developed countries. The issues that highlight tourists' expectations in the developed world and the maintenance of service quality include:

- *Airport transfers.* Tourists arriving in a destination after a tiring flight require convenient and comfortable transfer vehicles. The tendency to use a limited number of transfer vehicles to shuttle a large number of different tour groups to a dispersed range of hotels often adds to the inconvenience associated with long-haul travel in LDCs. The trend towards the use of baggage trucks to transport tourists' baggage to hotels due to the lack of space on old vehicles is disconcerting for tourists and can cause delays due to misdelivery.
- *Sightseeing tours.* For LDCs receiving high-spending tourists, one lucrative tourist transport service that offers potentially high profits to private operators is sightseeing tours (see Plate 6.1). Visitors from developed countries expect coaches with air-conditioning and a public address system, vehicles that are safe and give good all-round visibility. In many cases the capital cost of such vehicles is prohibitively high for private operators in LDCs, who are forced to import them. Yet where they are available they significantly enhance the tourists' experience. Well-trained tour guides, able to provide commentaries and answer questions in a variety of languages, are also an important asset. Guides who are able to convey the local culture, history, customs and lifestyle to visitors will be able to contribute to the tourists' pleasant memories of their holiday. Adequate stopping places at cafes, restaurants or clearings with toilets and refreshment facilities also have a part to play.

Independent travel by tourists in destination areas

The more adventurous tourist often wishes to travel on local public transport systems and adequate information needs to be made available (e.g. timetables). The

Plate 6.1 In Central London, sightseeing buses compete with public service vehicles in conveying visitors on both the road and in terms of passengers
Source: S.J. Page

use of hire cars is also a major tourist service in LDCs, and they need to be supplied according to a code of good practice. Heraty (1989: 289) suggests that good practice should include:

● high-quality vehicle standards, insurance and contract conditions;
● provision of tourist-oriented maps and leaflets;
● signposting of routes to tourist attractions and sights;
● training for the police in dealing with tourist drivers;
● action to address road-based and car-related crime affecting tourist hire cars;
● safety standards for mopeds where governments permit tourists to hire such transport;
● incentives to encourage short-stay visitors (e.g. cruise ship passengers) to venture away from the port to visit other locations;
● licensing and regulation of taxi companies and drivers to prevent tourists being exploited.

From the transport policy-makers' perspective, Heraty (1989: 290) notes that a range of problems needs to be addressed at government level to facilitate tourist travel in destination areas, including:

● Import duties may need to be relaxed to facilitate the acquisition of new vehicles and to make them more affordable and able to absorb 'standing costs' (when the vehicle is off the road) as tourist use declines outside of the peak season.
● Roads and tourist transport infrastructure need to be maintained to reduce wear and tear on vehicles.
● Skilled mechanics and vehicle drivers need to be trained to ensure an adequate supply of labour to meet demands.
● Traffic congestion related to peak seasonal demand by tourists needs to be managed.

● Sufficient transport operators need to be licensed to prevent limited competition and cartel-type operations resulting under prohibitively expensive situations.

A review by Grant et al. (1997) also outlines the transport policies and strategies that local authorities need to develop in order to facilitate a more efficient supply of tourist transport services. They highlight the practical and organisational issues involved in the development of specific forms of tourist transport and in meeting the needs of users (e.g. car based, coach borne, pedestrians, people travelling on public transport) and the needs of sightseers and the importance of integration (May and Roberts 1995). Many of these issues are also apparent in the case of small islands.

Tourist transport and small islands: the case of Malta

A large literature now exists on tourism and small islands (e.g. Lockhart et al. 1993; Hall and Page 1996) and most of the studies highlight the management issues associated with tourism, notably the limited land area, resource base and dependence upon imports, leakage out of the economy, MNC control of the tour operator and accommodation sector in some instances, human resource management issues associated with training, education and indigenous skills. Yet what is not reviewed in any detail is the link between tourism, visitor use of island-based transport and the issues associated with sustainability (see Chapter 8 for a more detailed discussion of this issue). In simple terms, the limited land area of small islands combined with the influx of visitors poses many logistical issues of moving large volumes of visitors around a relatively constrained infrastructure. What is of interest in the case of Malta, an island in the southern Mediterranean, is the high usage of public transport by visitors and the ongoing monitoring of usage and trends by the national tourism organisation, the Malta Tourism Authority (MTA), which has a very detailed research base on tourism (see *www.tourism.org.mt*). At the same time, the island has been suffering from the pressures of rising car ownership (Attard 2005; Attard and Hall 2003) which rose 116 per cent in 1985 to 2000. Despite this and a relative drop in domestic patronage of the radial pattern of bus routes, radiating from the capital, Valletta, the bus network is a popular means of tourist travel.

In terms of the island's development as a tourist destination, previous studies have traced its evolution, development and expansion in the 1960s and 1970s (Lockhart and Ashton 1987). Visitor numbers have grown from 12,500 arrivals in the 1950s when the island was a military base for the UK, to 186,000 after independence in the 1960s to 728,000 in the 1970s. A noticeable change in the period since the 1980s is the diversification of its source market, which was predominantly UK visitors (76 per cent) to the position in 1993 when 49 per cent of visitors were from the UK, with other European markets (Germany, France, The Netherlands) diversifying the visitor mix. Overall, Malta's visitor market comprises around 1 per cent of Mediterranean tourist arrivals, which generates 24 per cent of the island's GNP, 22 per cent of government income, and over 41,000 jobs. In 1998, the island's tourism economy generated £M109 million (€271 million) based on 194 accommodation establishments with 40,000 bedspaces. The recent pattern of visitor arrivals is shown in Table 6.5, which highlights the dependence

Table 6.5 Tourist arrivals/departures by air and by sea, 1995–2007

Year	1995	1996	1997	1998	1999	2000	2001	2002	2003	2004	2005	2006	2007
AUSTRIA	20,095	15,909	17,913	23,741	29,027	28,119	27,670	24,448	28,416	24,030	26,393	23,540	20,384
BELGIUM	22,008	21,879	25,567	25,146	28,349	26,713	23,695	24,018	23,724	31,434	28,730	29,077	26,456
DENMARK	17,500	16,702	15,769	14,553	17,276	17,086	18,194	17,427	17,747	20,039	22,665	23,947	27,986
FRANCE	72,876	64,453	62,457	72,512	73,264	75,809	82,669	80,101	76,384	87,129	82,607	73,400	75,149
GERMANY	187,761	184,110	193,020	203,199	212,430	204,749	160,262	142,106	125,811	135,138	138,217	125,810	130,049
ITALY	97,384	89,439	90,190	90,558	92,726	92,522	93,564	100,875	94,175	102,169	92,406	112,548	113,651
IRELAND*	—	—	—	—	—	—	—	—	—	—	17,247	15,378	28,130
LIBYA	37,186	50,950	39,289	37,509	44,968	43,268	31,017	22,783	20,218	12,831	10,662	9,198	9,259
NETHERLANDS	45,526	48,928	52,238	56,534	65,345	64,168	50,756	44,395	40,810	38,446	37,102	37,833	34,783
NORWAY	6,942	6,745	6,478	6,711	10,024	9,136	10,777	9,786	11,825	16,351	15,515	15,167	15,313
FINLAND	5,552	7,082	5,672	4,583	4,242	5,802	5,939	4,306	5,147	6,759	8,261	10,575	12,438
RUSSIA	10,593	13,596	21,339	23,717	16,223	18,780	22,054	22,919	21,096	19,697	16,647	21,770	22,909
SWEDEN	8,537	9,891	11,329	14,150	19,065	20,051	17,424	11,738	12,017	25,705	26,112	23,964	31,545
SWITZERLAND	18,502	19,900	17,924	24,776	23,448	21,982	24,365	20,375	22,110	22,846	20,274	21,403	22,023
UK	461,159	398,899	436,899	448,763	422,368	428,780	451,530	444,335	459,565	452,880	482,615	431,339	482,404
USA	10,945	11,969	14,924	17,641	18,558	19,269	19,986	20,080	20,657	18,720	18,136	16,970	20,423
OTHERS	93,405	93,336	100,153	118,147	136,917	139,478	140,243	144,122	146,899	141,854	152,529	158,267	170,608
TOTAL	1,115,971	1,053,788	1,111,161	1,182,240	1,214,230	1,215,712	1,180,145	1,133,814	1,126,601	1,156,028	1,170,610	1,124,233	1,243,510

*Prior to 2004: tourist arrival data.
2004 onwards: tourist depature data.
Source: Malta Tourism Digest, http://www.mta.com.mt, copyright © of the Malta Tourism Authority and reproduced with permission.

upon the UK market, with almost 500,000 arrivals a year followed by smaller numbers from other European countries alongside a growing cruise ship arrival market. The peak tourist season for arrivals is April–August, when around 43 per cent of arrivals occur, although markets such as the UK also have an all-year presence. In the case of the dominant market, the UK, some 10.7 per cent of its expenditure is on public transport, which may seem small, but travel costs on the island by bus are low.

To illustrate the issues of sustainability and transport, the island's population created a density of 1200 people km^2 and tourism adds an additional 100 people km^2. The current transport supply on the island, as discussed earlier, highlights the dominance of the private car, but also illustrates the number of hire cars, coaches/minibuses contracted by tour operators to shuffle visitors from the airport to their hotels (and for guided tours) along with the large number of public service buses. The island's bus fleet is a tourist transport mode for two reasons. First, the island has a simple hub-and-spoke network, with all buses operated to/from the hub in the capital city – Valletta (Plate 6.2). Second, the ageing fleet of vintage buses (Plate 6.3) offers a visitor attraction in its own right, providing easy access to most tourist accommodation and offering a convenient way to tour the island's tourist sites and sights. There are over 500 buses serving 91 routes from Valletta and in 2007 around 5 per cent of UK tourist expenditure was on public transport. For example, Table 6.6 illustrates the ongoing monitoring by the MTA of tourist use of transport on the island, from road usage, usage of public transport, car hire, use of taxis, in 2007.

Plate 6.2 Valletta bus station in Malta acts as a hub for the island's well-developed bus route network, where every service is routed in and out of the hub and serves the routes as spokes in much the same way that airline services operate. Tourists and residents use these services on a regular basis

Source: S.J. Page

Plate 6.3 A Maltese bus illustrating the historic attraction for visitors of these meticulously restored vintage vehicles that operate across the island and are well utilised by tourists ©Malta Tourism Authority

Source: Visitmalta.com

Table 6.6 UK visitor use and rating of transport and infrastructure in Malta, 2007 (%)

	Very good	Good	Not so good	Poor	Very poor	Usage level
Physical aspect						
Car hire	25.1	44.8	19.1	6.8	4.1	25.0
Taxi	30.9	44.2	17.9	4.7	2.3	36.3
Public transport	39.1	40.4	14.7	4.3	1.5	76.9
Service aspect						
Car hire	30.4	43.4	18.4	4.8	3.0	22.9
Taxi service	35.1	44.1	14.7	3.6	2.5	32.2
Public transport	37.8	43.9	13.7	2.7	1.9	67.4

Source: Malta Tourism Digest, http://www.mta.com.mt, copyright © of the Malta Tourism Authority and reproduced with permission.

Public transport scores very well and illustrates that, on average, over 70 per cent of UK visitors use public transport at least once during their stay and rate it highly. The significance of a well-developed and easy-to-use public transport system on a small island highlights how a large visitor market can be accommodated in a sustainable manner in relation to its transport needs and usage. A simple system, where all buses go to/from a hub, makes usage simple and effective. It is certainly a model that other islands could use, and it reduces some of the pressure which visitors may place, through car hire usage, on an island that is facing a high car ownership level, congestion in some of the main towns and problems of car parking at peak times. These issues are common to all small islands, and the Maltese example illustrates how an integrated strategy for transport on a small island with a high dependence upon tourism needs to examine all the options available to reduce tourist car use and to make more sustainable use of existing infrastructure.

● ● ● ● Summary

This chapter has examined some of the principal issues facing transport providers in the new millennium in managing the supply of services and associated operational issues. In particular, it has emphasised how various transport providers, such as airlines, have used the two major tools, ICTs and logistics, to improve the flow of information to assist in the management and delivery of services to customers. The growing importance of ICTs is demonstrated by the competition between international airlines (Oum and Yu 1998) and the greater use of IT to gain competitive advantage. This also applies to the role of infrastructure providers discussed in the next chapter, in optimising the use of the facilities (see Haghani and Chen 1998) to gain cost savings and optimal use of major sunk costs in infrastructure.

The other tools now being harnessed in terms of strategic management by transport providers such as airlines are the growing use of alliances and strategic partnerships. This is a function of enhanced competition in the marketplace (Charlton and Gibb 1998), a feature discussed in considerable detail in the context of air transport in the EU (Graham 1998) and Australia (Hooper 1998), rail travel in the UK (Knowles 1998), coach travel in the UK (White and Farrington 1998) and the US railway industry (Jahanshahi 1998). Competition is a theme running throughout this book and is not simply confined to any one chapter. In fact competition is now assuming a greater importance as many governments seek to deregulate former state-planned transport systems (e.g. Cline et al. 1998), placing a greater emphasis on individual transport businesses to meet the needs of tourists in a competitive environment where all the tools available are needed to operate in a cost-efficient and safe manner (Braithwaite et al. 1998).

Despite the emphasis on aviation, due to its dominant effect on the tourist sector, the example of land-based supplies issues on small islands and in the less developed world is frequently overlooked as peripheral to the main concern of transport planners and researchers. Yet, as this chapter has shown, the tourist experience does not stop when the tourist disembarks from an aircraft and leaves an airport terminal. Thus, as Chapters 5 and 6 show, the integration and linkages between air transport and land transport need to be viewed as part of the seamless travel experience, particularly in cases where package holidays are produced and sold by organisations with a horizontally integrated tourism and transport operation (e.g. Thomson Holidays, as discussed in Chapter 5). In fact there is growing evidence from research that the issue of safety is also assuming a growing importance for the transport sector in individual countries. Recent research on the wider issue of tourist safety (Abeyratne 1998) and accidents and injuries on transport as a form of recreational activity (e.g. jetboating and white water rafting) also needs to be set in the wider context of tourists' experience (Page 1997). As a result, this chapter does illustrate that the supply issues facing the transport operator cover a diverse range of fields, from business operations, including IT and logistics, through to safety and management of the services provided to ensure the company operates in a profitable and sustainable manner.

Yet as the discussion by Heraty (1989) suggests, the supply of tourist transport services in destination areas needs to be carefully targeted at the market both to ensure customer satisfaction and to maximise revenue generation for private sector transport operators. As the study by Heraty (1989) indicated, and more recently that by Prideaux (2004), where there is a significant demand for a destination, government action may need to be taken to develop the infrastructure if tourist development is to be promoted. Understanding the expectations and motives of visitors confirms the importance of setting the demand and supply for tourist transport services in a systematic framework where the wider issues and interrelationships can be understood. In this context, the next chapter considers the specific implications of supply and demand for infrastructure development.

Questions

1 What is the role of logistics in transport service provision?

2 How do transport companies utilise ICT in the sales of transport?

3 How have the World Wide Web and online sales affected the transport sector?

4 What problems do tourist transport operators face in less developed countries?

Further reading

Abeyratne, R. (1998) 'The regulatory management in air transport', *Journal of Air Transport Management*, 4(1): 25–37.

Braithwaite, G., Caves, R. and Faulkner, J. (1998) 'Australian aviation safety: observations from the lucky country', *Journal of Air Transport Management*, 4(1): 55–62.

Buhalis, D. (2003) *e-Tourism*. Harlow: Prentice Hall.

Goetz, A. and Sutton, C. (1997) 'The geography of deregulation in the US airline industry', *Annals of the Association of American Geographers*, 87(2): 238–63.

Hilling, D. (1996) *Transport and Developing Countries*, London: Routledge.

On strategic issues see:

Evans, N., Campbell, D. and Stonehouse, G. (2003) *Strategic Management for Travel and Tourism*, Oxford: Butterworth-Heinemann.

On the growing Asian air transport market see:

Page, S.J. (2004a) 'Air travel in Asia', *Travel and Tourism Analyst*, 3: 1–56.

Many interesting books on small islands now exist but a number of key studies are:

Attard, M. (2005) 'Land transport policy in a small island state: The case of Malta', *Transport Policy*, 12(1).

Ioannides, D., Apostolopoulos, Y. and Sonmez, S. (eds) (2001) *Mediterranean Islands and Sustainable Tourism Development: Practices, Management and Policies*, London: Continuum.

Wilkinson, R. (1987) 'Tourism in small island nations: a fragile dependence', *Leisure Studies*, 6: 127–44.

7

Managing tourist transport infrastructure: the role of the airport

Introduction

The development of tourism requires a transport infrastructure to facilitate the free movement of tourist traffic, and much of the research in this context has focused on modal forms of travel (e.g. rail travel, air travel and car-based trips). One of the fundamental links that has been overlooked in the tourist transport system is the way in which demand and supply are brought together and managed, and the infrastructure used to ensure the system functions efficiently. In both the transport and tourism literature, terminal facilities, which provide the context in which the tourist embarks on the mode of transport (to ensure the interaction of supply and demand takes place smoothly), have been largely overlooked. It is also widely recognised from a psychological perspective that the 'holiday experience' begins when the tourist arrives at a terminal, ready to embark on a journey (Plate 7.1). In fact some commentators even suggest that the experience effectively begins when the traveller leaves their home environment.

This chapter examines the challenge of managing the interaction of supply and demand for tourist travel with reference to one type of terminal facility – the airport. The chapter commences with a discussion of the management challenge posed by terminal facilities, emphasising the organisations involved in the management process. This is followed by a discussion of the locational and planning issues associated with airport development, particularly access to markets. Future development plans for world regions experiencing a rapid growth in tourist travel are then discussed, as arrivals are likely to outstrip existing airport capacity. Airports are probably the most complex environments and systems in which this interaction occurs and yet they often remain poorly understood in a tourism context, even though the links between 'tourism and aviation are becoming more explicitly recognised, and these links are having a role in government's aviation policy formation'. Even so, as Forsyth (2008: 82) also suggests, 'while the links between aviation and tourism are obvious, they have not been given much attention' and this is particularly the case in relation to airports. As Ashford et al. (1991: 1) argue, 'the airport forms an essential part of the air transport system, because it is the physical site at which a modal transfer of transport is made from the air modes to land modes', and one of the most interesting and useful studies is by Graham (2001, 2003, 2009). As Graham (2003: 1) suggested:

> Airports are an essential part of the air transport system. They provide all the infrastructure needed to enable passengers and freight to transfer from surface to

Plate 7.1 Purpose-built terminals, such as Liverpool Street in London, require spacious concourses and well-lit and signposted information such as departure boards, given that tourist and leisure traffic connects to the boat trains to Harwich in Essex for the Hook of Holland sailing to The Netherlands
Source: S.J. Page

air modes of transport and to allow airlines to take off and land. The basic airport infrastructure consists of runways, taxiways, apron space, gates, passenger and freight terminals and ground transport interchanges

and have a wide range of commercial facilities within them, along with external facilities that are highly profitable, such as car parks. As Brihla (2008: 168) argues:

The airport's key function is the provision of infrastructure needed to allow airlines to safely take off and land and to facilitate passenger and freight transfer from surface to air mode. In order to fulfil their role, airports bring together a wide range of aeronautical and non-aeronautical facilities and services including air traffic control, security, fire and rescue, handling and a diversity of commercial facilities ranging from shops and restaurants to hotels, conference services and business parks. In addition to this central role within the air transport sector, airports hold a strategic importance to the regions they serve due to their interaction with the overall transport system (such as rail and road networks) and the substantial employment opportunities and economic development which they encourage.

The scope of the airport's activities and significance from a tourist and tourism industry perspective relates, according to Graham (2003), to the different type of customers that the airport services, which include:

● *passengers*: scheduled, charter, business, leisure and transfer passengers;
● *the tourism industry and other sectors*: airlines, tour operators, freight forwarders ad general aviation services;

- *other stakeholders and interested parties*: tenants and concessionaires, visitors, employees, local residents and businesses each of which have their own needs and characteristics requiring specific services and relationships to be built and maintained with the airport as an organisation

and from a tourism demand perspective, Brilha (2008: 168) suggests that

> Basic passenger segmentation considers two main travel purposes, namely business and leisure . . . Business passengers were generally thought to be more time conscious, more demanding on facilities and services and more in need of flexible travel arrangements. They would travel for shorter periods and be less sensitive to price fluctuations. On the other hand, the common perception of the leisure passenger was someone who was travelling for longer periods of time, usually in a group of family with children, being very price sensitive but being less demanding for services . . . However, air transport industry and tourist profiles have greatly evolved, reflecting increased disposable income, added experience from travel frequency, vast information and social and cultural changes in society

which is reflected in the impact of low-cost carriers which have induced new forms of demand as passengers can now travel more often for the same disposable income. As will be discussed later, this has also changed the way some airports view tourism, since the attraction of low-cost carriers to relatively undeveloped and small, regional locations can have a major impact on destination development as discussed in Chapter 5.

But why focus on air travel rather than other types of terminal? Graham (2009) identifies three reasons why an analysis of airports is important, namely their commercialisation, privatisation and globalisation. What literature does exist is airport specific and ports, bus/coach terminals and railway terminals have not attracted much attention, with a notable exception being Bertolini and Spit (1998). However, in Chapter 3 the importance of the terminal environment for InterCity rail travel was discussed, albeit briefly, in relation to service quality and the travel experience. In terms of scale, ATAG (1993) provided a convincing argument for a focus on air travel: in 1993 the volume of air travel worldwide was equivalent to one-fifth of the world's population travelling once a year, which has increased in developed countries as the contentious arguments have previously suggested – up to 50 per cent of the UK population flew once a year (see ATAG's website *www.atag.org* and the World Tourism Council website *www.wttc.org* for an up-to-date assessment). Therefore, whilst some of the principles and issues discussed in this chapter relate solely to air travel, some of the broader issues (i.e. developing a customer-focused approach) have a wide application to the management of the tourist–transport interface that occurs in transport terminal facilities (see Graham 2001 for a more detailed discussion).

The management challenge of tourist transport terminals: airports

To the uninitiated, occasional traveller, terminal facilities can be a bewildering, seemingly chaotic and unnerving experience (a theme explored in more detail in Chapter 8). The semblance of chaos is conveyed by Barlay (1995: 48):

> The airport cavalcade can baffle or startle the inexperienced passenger. Laden with suitcases and packages, calm and rational people grow uptight, defensive

Plate 7.2 Check-in desks at JFK Terminal 5 for JetBlue Airways ©JetBlue Airways
Source: JetBlue Airways

with aggression, fail to allow themselves time to familiarise themselves with the layout or study the free guides to terminals.

The entire psychology of travel and the change in the behaviour of the traveller in airports (e.g. tunnel vision or airport syndrome) embraces a whole series of emotions amongst the diversity of passengers: 'joy, grief, anxiety, expectations, aggravation, yearning and fulfilment'. From a tourists' perspective, numerous factors affect their experience, according to Barlay (1995: 49), and where award-winning airports exist (e.g. Changi Airport, Singapore) they are a major draw-card for airlines and passengers since the following factors are important to travellers:

● speed of check-in (see Plate 7.2);
● efficiency of passport control, customs clearance and security screening (Plate 7.3);
● luggage retrieval;
● availability of shops, duty-free goods and associated services (Plates 7.4 and 7.5);
● a spacious and relaxed environment in which to wait prior to boarding the air-craft, highlighting the importance of service provision at airline terminals (Correia et al. 2008). Some of these passenger concerns also relate to supply-side issues surrounding the efficiency of airport operations (see Tovar et al. 2009), particularly ground handling services (Schmidberger et al. 2009).

In 2008, a survey by travelsupermarket.com which examined travellers' airport experiences, blamed heightened level of stress upon: flight delays and cancella-tions, lengthy queues and strict security measures, a feature examined by Nie et al. (2009). The issue of congestion at airports has certainly assumed a greater

Plate 7.3 Security screening of passengers at Changi Airport, Singapore

Source: Civil Aviation Authority of Singapore

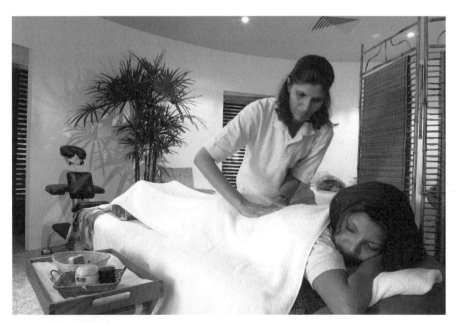

Plate 7.4 One of the innovations for long-haul travellers at Changi Airport, Singapore is the introduction of a massage service

Source: Civil Aviation Authority of Singapore

Plate 7.5 Provision of business services via a specialist centre for business travellers whilst they are intransit can help maximise a traveller's productivity and offer convenience

Source: Civil Aviation Authority of Singapore

role in policy-related debates on air travel, as observed by Winston and de Rus (2008), given the growing concerns about the performance of aviation infrastructure with the major growth of airport hubs and the relationship with national ambitions for becoming major international tourist destinations (Lohmann et al. 2009; Vesepermann et al. 2008).

From the airport's perspective, operational issues dominate its everyday working, most notably evident in 2008 with the opening of London Heathrow's Terminal 5 at a cost of £4.3 billion – described as a 'national embarrassment' by the House of Commons Transport Committee (2008: 3)

BAA opened Heathrow's fifth terminal for business on 27 March, after six years of construction at a cost of £4.3bn, on time and within budget. Passengers had been promised a 'calmer, smoother, simpler airport experience'. Multiple problems, however, meant that on the first day of operation alone, 36,584 passengers were frustrated by the 'Heathrow hassle' that Terminal 5 (T5) had been designed to eliminate. What should have been an occasion of national pride was in fact an occasion of national embarrassment. Problems were experienced with the baggage system, car parking, security searches and aspects of the building itself. When the baggage system failed, luggage piled up to such an extent that it was transported by road to be sorted off-site. According to British Airways, 23,205 bags required manual sorting before being returned to their owners. We found that most of these problems were caused by one of two main factors: insufficient communication between owner and operator, and poor staff training and system testing. Over the course of our inquiry, we were pleased to find that steps were being taken at all levels to address the problems at the source of T5's problems.

As this example shows, the management challenge is to recognise the tourists' needs and to minimise likely problems whilst ensuring the terminal operates as a smooth series of complex systems. This has even led to the development of an industry-practitioner journal – the *Journal of Airport Management*, launched in 2007 to disseminate best practice and to understand the growing complexity of airport management as a subject since, as the report noted, the experiences of Terminal 5 were not unique. Similar problems were found by the House of Commons Transport Committee (2008: 5) to have occurred at 'Denver Airport in particular (1995) experienced serious problems with its baggage handling system. Kuala Lumpar's airport (1997) and Hong Kong International (1998) also experienced problems, notably with lack of staff familiarity'.

Doganis (1992: 7) defines airports as complex industrial organisations that

act as a forum in which disparate elements and activities are brought together to facilitate, for both passengers and freight, the interchange between air and surface transport.

In some countries, for a range of historical, legal and other reasons, the scope of airport activities can vary from the highly complex and all-embracing to the very limited. In physical terms, Doganis (1992: 7) defines an airport as:

Essentially one or more runways for aircraft together with associated buildings or terminals where passengers are processed; the majority of airport authorities own and operate their runways, terminals and associated facilities, such as taxiways or aprons.

Doganis goes on to distinguish between the three principal activities of airports:

● essential operational services and facilities;
● traffic-handling services;
● commercial activities

although 'at most, if not all, airports, the major consideration must be passenger flows' (Ashford et al. 1991: 27), and this in itself requires management measures to ensure smooth operation (e.g. pricing and flow management – see Matthews 1995). This comprises a broad range of activities within any airport environment, whether in an international gateway airport, a regional or local airport:

● ground handling (Soames 1997; Caves 1994) (see Plate 7.6);
● baggage handling (de Neufville 1994);
● passenger terminal operations;
● airport security;
● cargo operations (see Plate 7.7);
● airport technical services;
● air traffic control (where applicable – see Majumdar 1994, 1995);
● aircraft scheduling (take-off/landing slot allocation);
● airport and aircraft emergency services;
● airport access

Plate 7.6 Gate Gourmet servicing and provisioning a flight prior to departure ©JetBlue Airways

Source: JetBlue Airways

that are described in detail by Ashford et al. (1991) and subsequent editions in what remain the principal study on airport operations. Figure 7.1 highlights some of the relationships which need to be managed in the airport system so that the airport–airline–traveller interactions occur in a professional and smooth manner. Figures 7.2 and 7.3 also illustrate the spatial interactions in the airport system, indicating how the airport enables an aircraft to take off/land and to unload and load passengers. As part of these functions, it enables travellers to change their mode of transport and be processed efficiently (e.g. ticketing and documentation).

Each of these functions impinges upon the management of the tourists' experience of the terminal facilities. Airport growth on a global scale has been discussed in previous chapters and readers should consult appropriate websites that can give an up-to-date assessment of the passengers handled at airports (e.g. see *www.ACI.aero*) given that there are over 1000 airports worldwide. Of the top 25 in terms of passenger volume, the majority are located in the USA followed by Europe and Asia-Pacific. Of the top 30 airports, the majority are located in the USA, confirming a pattern similar to that observed by Sealy (1992). This is again followed by Europe and Asia-Pacific.

Globally, the management of airports is affected by government policy (see Hanks 2006) that, in part, determines the pattern of ownership. As Oum et al. (2005: 109) argue:

Historically, airports were owned and operated by governments. Since the mid-1980s, however, significant changes have occurred in the way airports are owned, managed, and operated. With the exception of the US, corporatization,

Plate 7.7 Apron at Changi Airport, Singapore with cargo loading/unloading, since freight is the other very lucrative aspect of airport revenue that counterbalances an overdependence upon passenger revenue

Source: Civil Aviation Authority of Singapore

commercialization and privatization of airports have become the worldwide trend. The motives for ownership and institutional restructuring via commercialization and privatization are diverse, but normally include easier access to private sector financing and investment, and improved operational efficiency. The commercialization and privatization have taken different formats/models in different countries.

As Doganis (1992) observes, there are four main types of ownership:

● *State ownership with direct government control*, characterised by a single government department (i.e. a Civil Aviation Department) that operates the country's

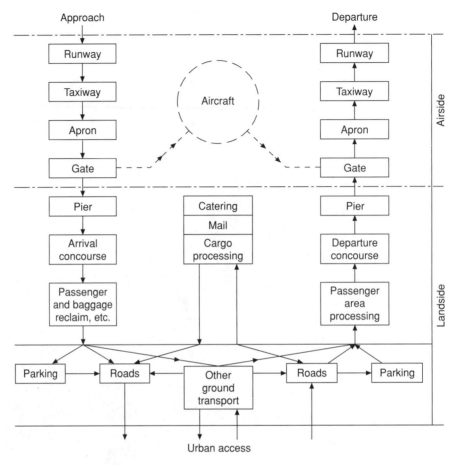

Figure 7.1 An airport system

Source: Based on Ashford et al. 1991.

airports. The alternative to a centralised government pattern of control and management is localised ownership such as municipal ownership.

- *Public ownership through an airport authority*, usually as a limited liability or private company. For example, the British Airports Authority (BAA) was one of the early examples of a national airport authority. Aer Rianta in the Republic of Ireland is another such example. There are also cases of regional airport authorities in the USA.

- *Mixed public and private ownership* is an organisational model adopted at larger Italian airports, where a company manages the airport, with public and private shareholders.

- *Private ownership* was a model of limited appeal prior to the wave of privatisation in the 1980s. One of the early examples in the UK was London City Airport in London's Docklands, opened in 1987 (Page 1987, 1989b, 1991; Page and Fidgeon 1989). However, Doganis (1992) points out that the major impetus to private ownership was the privatisation of BAA in 1987.

According to Oum et al. (2008), countries considering privatisation should transfer majority ownership shares to the private sector and mixed ownership of airports

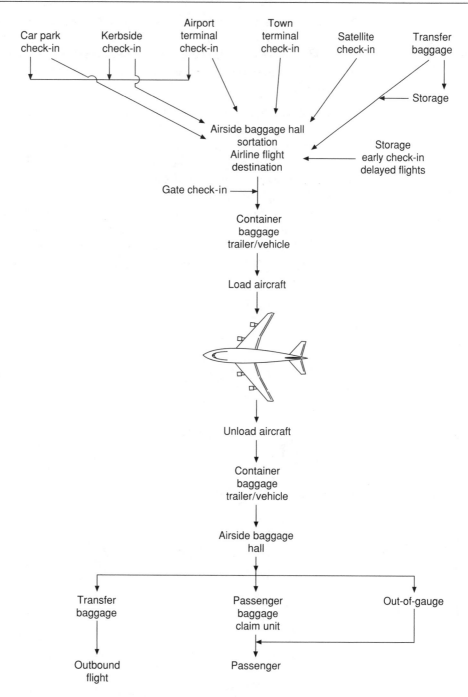

Figure 7.2 Luggage loading and unloading in the airport system

Source: Based on Ashford and Moore 1992

with a government majority ownership should be avoided in terms of improving airport efficiency. Furthermore, in cities with multiple airports, privatising one or more would improve the overall efficiency of the airport sector. Oum et al. (2008: 423) provide an excellent overview of the state of airport ownership and progress towards privatisation as:

All major Australian airports have been privatized . . . In Asia, Mumbai and New Delhi airports in India have been privatized, whereas minority stakes of Beijing Capital International Airport, Shanghai Pudong Airport [and] Malaysia Airports Holdings Bhd . . . have been sold to private investors. Tokyo's Narita International Airport was corporatized in 2003 and is expected to be privatized in the near future. Many airports in other Asian countries, South Africa, Argentina, and Mexico have also been and/or are in the process of being privatized partially or wholly. In contrast to this worldwide trend of privatization, however, the United States and Canada have not embraced the privatization policy. In Canada, the federal government has retained ownership of its major national airports, but

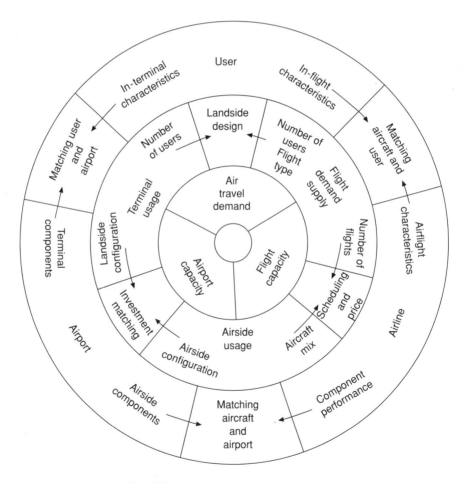

Figure 7.3 Airport relationships

Source: Based on Ashford *et al.* 1991

commercialized these airports by transferring their management and operation to 'not-for-profit' locally-based airport authorities under long term lease contracts. In the United States, airports have remained mostly municipal or regional government-owned and operated. However, the government ownership and management of the US airports are considered to be rather different from those of other countries in that there is substantial private sector involvement in management decisions concerning key airport activities and capital investment decisions . . . Although not strictly following the worldwide privatization trend, many airports in the United States have in recent years begun to be organized as quasi-privatized airport authorities. These airport authorities are similar in nature to that of Canadian airport authorities, insofar as they are not-for-profit/non-shareholder entities that re-invest retained earnings into future airport development programs and are by-and-large financially self-sustaining.

Yet such policy variations do not exist in a vacuum. As Forsyth (2003) indicated in the case of Australia, sudden policy changes in relation to crises can occur. In Australia, a policy of price caps on major privatised airports to limit aeronautical charges were temporarily removed in 2001–02 after the crisis in the aviation industry with the collapse of Ansett Australia, Qantas' dominance of the domestic market, the entry of Virgin Blue and the later impact of 9/11, which added impetus to this need for change. In mid-2002 the government announced that smaller airports were also to be deregulated and price regulation was to be replaced by price monitoring (but price capping could be reintroduced if airport behaviour on charging was not satisfactory).

In generic terms, Doganis (1992) argues that a prime function of airport management is to determine the objective of any economic and management strategy for an airport by addressing four questions:

- Should airports be run as commercially oriented profitable concerns?
- How should one improve airport economic efficiency?
- Should profits from larger airports be used to cross-subsidise loss-making smaller airports?
- Should airports be privatised?

These four questions essentially raise the issue of what form of airport ownership a government deems important and the prime objectives that will affect the economic strategy each airport pursues. This in turn will require very different management strategies. For example, airlines and bodies such as IATA still claim that airports are public utilities when arguing against increased airport charges.

It is useful to examine a number of specific issues associated with airport management that will then be exemplified by a case study of BAA. As Doganis (1992: 45) rightly argues, 'matching the provision of airport capacity with the demand while achieving and maintaining airport profitability and an adequate level of customer satisfaction is a difficult task'. One of the principal problems facing any airport manager is that of planning. The time lag between the decision to build and the opening of a new airport terminal is five to ten years, as the case of Heathrow airport's Terminal 5 illustrates. The planning inquiry cost £80 million, 700 people gave evidence and it took 100,000 transcripts of evidence, lasted for 524 days and took eight years from its initial application to approval. This was one of the last delays for the UK government for major infrastructure projects, which has led it to introduce a new Planning Bill for large infrastructure projects being subjected to the powers of a Infrastructure Planning Commission to speed up decision-making; this has been criticised for overriding the democratic process and serving the needs of industry and the wider economy without adequate measures to safeguard the needs of the community and environment.

In addition, planners also need to ensure forecasts of future growth are within realistic bounds so that terminal facilities can accommodate demand for at least another decade. However, for any airport development, probably the most fundamental issues to understand are:

- costs;
- the economic features of airports;
- sources of revenue;
- methods of charging and pricing airport aeronautical services (see Forsyth 1997b; Reynolds-Feighan and Feighan 1997);
- the type of commercial strategy to adopt (see Freathy 2004);
- potential sources of commercial revenue (see Zhang and Zhang 1997; Tovar and Martín-Cejas, 2009);
- the most appropriate management structure for an airport as a commercial/non-commercial organisation;
- financial performance indicators (see Gillen and Waters 1997; Hooper and Hensher 1997; Graham 2001) and the recent development of benchmarking (Francis et al. 2002; Sarkis and Talluri 2004) (based on Doganis 1992; Ashford and Moore 1992; author).

Costs and economic characteristics of airports

Research undertaken in the 1980s and reported by Doganis (1992) identified the following costs of airports based on an analysis of European airports, which remains the most widely cited study within the academic literature, and found that:

- *Staffing* accounts for 42 per cent of costs; it is normally the major operational cost for most airports. However, the impact of increased security costs for BAA in 2006 meant that its security staff increased 70 per cent as 2200 additional officers were recruited.
- *Capital* charges comprise 22 per cent of costs; they include interest payments on commercial loans and the cost of depreciation of capital assets.
- *Other operational items* (e.g. electricity, water and supplies) comprise 11 per cent of costs.
- *Maintenance* accounted for 9 per cent of costs whilst *administration* resulted in 4 per cent of costs.

These costs are listed in Table 7.1 for the British Airports Authority for 2006–07, which was purchased by the Spanish group Ferrovial in June 2006. In 2006/7, BAA's income from its operations was £489 million which rose to £656 million in 2007 and it employed over 10,000 staff, almost 2000 of whom were in the World

Table 7.1 Operating costs for BAA in 2006–07

	2007 (£ million)	2006 (£ million)	% change 2006–07
Staff costs: wages and salaries	595	544	9.3
Other staff costs	209	235	−11.1
Retail costs	41	40	0.7
Depreciation	326	299	9.1
Maintenance	184	153	19.7
Rent, rates and utilities	1125	117	7.7
Capitalised costs	(94)	(75)	(25)
Total	1500	1424	5.3

Source: Adapted from BAA (2007) Annual Report, *www.baa.co.uk*.

Duty Free chain. The data in Table 7.1 shows that the company's flagship airports in London (Heathrow, Gatwick and Stansted) account for over two-thirds of revenue generated by the BAA Group. Almost 50 per cent of its revenue comes from airlines, with retail the next most important source of revenue. However, BAA made a strategic decision to focus on core activities and to sell its World Duty Free business to help repay its debt from financing the purchase of BAA. This sale was completed in May 2008 and the company received over £500 million for the business. This is in spite of the retailing sector's massive growth and given that as a company, BAA receives more income from retail activities than its airline charges category, with almost 20 per cent from its World Duty Free business established in 1997. These stores cover an area of 15,000 m^2 and sell 14,000 products. BAA's World Duty Free business was based on two elements: its core product range of duty-free products and a more impulse-driven tax-free range of merchandise. Overall, retail and airport revenue comprise over 80 per cent of the group's income. This is notable as Graham (2001) observed that 51 per cent of European airports derived their income from aeronautical sources, which was around 50 per cent in London but much higher in the regional airports. This may well be a function of the London market's social mix of passengers and nature of the traffic mix, with less emphasis on the price-sensitive travellers whose numbers have grown in the regional airports.

Doganis (1992) also draws attention to the differences between US and European airports; airport costs are reduced by airline rental or lease agreements on terminal facilities in the USA. Likewise, many US airports are not directly involved in baggage handling, which is left to airlines. But financing costs for US airports tend to be a major element of expenditure, often 44 per cent of total costs if depreciation is included, although staff costs tend to remain at approximately 22 per cent. Even so, the scale of airport operations are evident from the example of Heathrow Airport which is served by 80 airlines, employs 72,000 staff directly and supports over 100,000 associated jobs indirectly.

Two of the principal economic characteristics of airports are that:

● Economies of scale exist as the volume of traffic increases, though congestion can lead to increases in unit costs.
● Development programmes for airports increase unit costs, particularly when new terminals are opened and are operating below their design capacity.

Airport revenue

According to Ashford and Moore (1992), airport revenue can be divided into two categories:

1 *operating revenues*, which are generated by directly running and operating the airport (e.g. the terminal area, leased areas and grounds);
2 *non-operating revenues*, which include income from activities not associated with the airport core business,

whilst Doganis (1992) divides it into aeronautic or traffic revenues and non-aeronautical or commercial revenues.

In terms of *aeronautical revenues,* a range of possible revenue sources exist (though not all airports necessarily collect or use the revenue in a set way):

● landing fees;
● airport air traffic control charges;
● aircraft parking;
● passenger charges;
● freight charges;
● apron services and aircraft handling (where the airport provides such services) such as air bridges used to connect aircraft and passengers at the departure gate (Plate 7.8).

In terms of *non-aeronautical revenue*, Doganis (1992) outlines the following sources:

● rents or lease income from airport tenants;
● recharges to tenants for utilities and services provided;
● concession income (e.g. from duty-free and tax-free shops);
● direct sales in shops operated by the airport authority;
● revenue from car parking where it is airport operated;
● miscellaneous items;
● non-airport-related income (e.g. through land development or hotel development).

Within a European context, Doganis (1992) noted that aeronautical revenue accounted for 56 per cent of revenue and non-aeronautical revenue for 44 per cent of income. In the USA the situation was slightly different, with airports generating more revenue from commercial sources (e.g. concessions 33 per cent; rents 23 per cent; car parking 4 per cent; other non-aeronautical sources 17 per cent; and aeronautical fees 23 per cent). CIPFA (1996) provides a range of detailed data for all UK airports.

Pricing aeronautical services

According to Doganis (1992), aeronautical fees (i.e. those costs commercial aircraft have to pay to land at an airport) will continue to remain a crucial element of airport finances since they can be adjusted to offset revenue losses. The impact of such fees on airlines varies from nearly 20 per cent of airline operating costs to less than 2 per cent. This directly affects the price the consumer pays for their ticket. Landing fees continue to be a key source of revenue (Ashford and Moore 1992). Doganis

Plate 7.8 Air bridges are used to connect the passenger to the aircraft for a smooth transition but the cost of use has meant many low-cost airlines board passengers via aircraft steps to save costs and improve the efficiency of boarding ©JetBlue Airways
Source: JetBlue Airways

(1992), Ashford and Moore (1992) and Basso and Zhang (2008) identify a range of approaches to charging fees, including:

- a fixed rate per tonne multiplied by a unit charge;
- a rate per tonne with weight-break points, with fees increasing in steps;
- single fixed charges irrespective of size of aircraft, which are used to fund the following types of services:
  - air traffic control facilities;
  - landing facilities such as the runway and taxiways;
  - parking of the aircraft on a stand or apron for a specified time, after which a separate fee is levied;
  - use of aircraft gates, airbridges and terminal facilities (though increasingly airports are levying departure taxes to pay for the use of such facilities by travellers);
  - take-off facilities.

The CIPFA (1996) compared the landing charges for an international inbound flight using a Boeing 737-400 at various UK airports in 1994/5. A comparison of Cardiff and Gatwick indicates that the combined cost of the landing fee and passenger facility charge levied to land at Cardiff at 9.30 am in June was £1814.35. This equates to a revenue per passenger of £12.10. The same flight would cost £2589 to land at Gatwick at the same time, with a revenue per passenger of £17.26. Such variations are marked within the airport system in the UK. However, as Doganis (1992) notes, each airport has in place its own levels of rebates/surcharges for flights and airlines, so these may not in fact be the true costs once such factors are taken into account. In Europe, additional surcharges apply for the use of aircraft that do not meet noise requirements (see Chapter 8 and Insight 8.1 on British Airways and research by Perl et al. (1997) on pricing such impacts). Doganis (1992: 69–111) outlines many of the issues associated with pricing airport charges and this should be read in conjunction with Toms (1994) and the study by Forsyth (2003).

Commercial strategies for airports

With the move towards privatisation in the UK and other countries, airport managers have had to adopt more commercially driven business principles when looking at the best strategy to adopt in managing airport infrastructures and services. Carter (1996), for example, points to the growing trend towards airport privatisation so airports can seek private sector finance to invest in the development strategy needed to compete in the new millennium. In fact Carter (1996) describes the move from a simple public utility view of airports towards a management-led approach that is more commercially driven. This reflects the three main economic benefits of a management-led approach:

- improvements to overall operating efficiencies;
- introduction of new management styles and marketing skills (which are discussed in more detail later in the chapter);
- an ability to make better long-term investment decisions and to access a wide range of investment sources to develop the airport's potential.

As Skapinker (1996: I) argues, 'most of the world's airports have barely begun to exploit their full commercial potential'. Even so, the proportion of world airports which are privatised is still low, at less than 10 per cent. In many cases, seeking to generate additional revenue from non-aeronautical sources is far more attractive to many airport managers than resorting to increases in landing fees.

Doganis (1992: 112–13) argues that, in establishing a commercial strategy for future development:

> Airport owners and operators have to make a choice between two alternative strategies. They can follow the *traditional airport model* . . . where airports see their primary task as being to meet the basic and essential needs of passengers, airlines, freight forwarders and other direct airport customers or users. The alternative strategic option is that of the *commercial airport model.*

In the commercial model, revenue maximisation from a wide range of customers offers the airport manager greater flexibility in the finance available to invest in a demand-led approach to airport development. In many ways the traditional model epitomises the government-managed approach, characterised by Athens airport in the late 1980s (Doganis 1992: 113). In contrast, Frankfurt airport exemplifies the commercial model, which requires airport managers to recognise a number of discrete markets amongst airport users:

- passengers (departing, arriving and those transferring between flights);
- the airlines, which are major consumers of space for storage, maintenance, staff and catering;
- airport employees;
- airline crews;
- meeters and greeters;
- visitors to airports;
- local residents;
- the local business community (based on Doganis 1992: 115).

As a result of recognising the business opportunities afforded by these groups, there is potential to derive income from activities and services that these users require.

According to Freathy (2004) airports in Europe have had to deal with a range of issues that required a strategic response, including:

- declining aeronautical revenues (i.e. Heathrow and Gatwick increased charges by less than the rate of inflation in recent years as government policy was seeking to increase inbound tourism);
- a decline in state control and a corresponding rise in privatisation;
- abolition of the duty-free market for intra-regional EU travel;
- changing patterns of consumer behaviour, exemplified by the rise of low-cost airlines as a source of cheap travel;
- the World Health Authority proposal to ban the sale of tobacco at airports as a duty-free product, which would affect what Freathy (2004) identified as a market worth US$2.19 billion;
- the rise of the terrorist threat on a global scale.

Freathy (2004) also acknowledged that airport managers had adopted different strategies to address the challenge that these issues posed to their business, including:

- steps to preserve their customer base by absorbing some additional costs from duty-free changes;
- greater segmentation of the customer base;
- cooperative agreements between airlines and airports and between retailers and airports;
- greater diversification of the airport product base, including the export of intellectual capital and expertise such as BAA's management of duty- and tax-free shopping at Pittsburgh airport up until 2017;
- increased market concentration in airport retailing.

Income can be derived from rents from service providers and concessionaires that offer services on the airport premises as well as from involvement in those activities identified above (e.g. retailing, car parking and aircraft-related services). Developing the most appropriate organisational structure to manage the airport also needs to take into account the relationship with government bodies (i.e. should a commercial approach be developed?):

> the pressures for change, not least of which are those that relate to the personalities and abilities of individuals with directional responsibilities within the organisation . . . [and whether] the airport authority assumes . . . a brokering function with minimal operational involvement in many on-airport activities (the US model) to direct operational involvement in many of the airports' functions (the European model) (Ashford et al. 1991: 13).

For example, if a commercial model is pursued, it will require an organisational structure that is responsive to change. Ashford et al. (1991) review the various management structures adopted by airports. Doganis (1992) and Ashford and Moore (1992) point to the preoccupation of airport managers with operational issues prior to the onset of the commercial model. As a result, airport management was traditionally organised into functional areas (e.g. security, finance, administration, human resource management, engineering and so forth). Each area was headed by a specialist manager reporting to the airport manager. The problem with such a structure was that commercial activities did not assume a clear focus, with different aspects of business dispersed across each of the airport's functional areas. The result was that no one assumed responsibility for pursuing a commercial strategy. Yet this situation has changed dramatically in recent years as the improvements in airport management have been accompanied by the rise of airport marketing.

Airport marketing

According to Graham (2003: 178),

> Airport marketing as a concept at most airports did not really exist until the 1980s. Prior to this, the role of the airport as a public service meant that very often airport management would merely respond to requests for new slots . . . the airports considered it was solely the role of the airline to identify opportunities for new or expanded services . . . Airport promotion tended to be very basic, typically consisting of the production of a timetable and publicity leaflets and a reactive approach to the media.

However, the 1990s stimulated the process of airport marketing due to a number of key developments associated with the rise of a more commercial focus in airport management that follows wider trends in business, where marketing is a core activity of any organisation that seeks to communicate with its customers effectively. Key changes which occurred in the 1990s that promoted the development of airport marketing (also see Jarach 2005) were:

● The growing deregulation of air transport, especially airports and the need to compete with other airports for business.
● The demands of the low-cost airlines for a new approach to airline management and marketing (as discussed in the next section below), requiring different marketing techniques to attract their business.

- Market expansion in air travel and a growing sophistication among travellers and a shift from a supply-led market which was capacity-led to one where the customer was able to exercise more choice about what they wanted and where they wanted to travel from.
- Greater moves towards privatisation and commercialisation of airports as businesses which inevitably requires the harnessing of commercial tools such as marketing (alongside management) to grow the business to meet new customer segments (e.g. low-cost travellers) and a recognition that airport travellers as well as other stakeholders – i.e. the airline business (e.g. airlines, tour operators and other bodies), passengers and associated groups (e.g. tenants, concessionaires, employees and residents) – outlined earlier in this chapter, were in fact customers.
- A recognition that the demand for airport services was increasingly being analysed using marketing concepts such as products (e.g. leisure and business travellers) or market segments, each of which had specific requirements from airports. For example, passengers will be greatly affected by accessibility, choice of flights, ease of use, cost of parking and airlines using the airport. In contrast, Graham (2003: 184) argues that airlines will be affected in the choice of airports they serve by the market demand for the service (i.e. catchment), availability of slots for take-off/landing, the competition, fees and other costs of using the airport, transfer connections available as well as other considerations such as environmental restrictions.

What these influences suggest is that the airport was increasingly being looked at in terms of being a product. As Kotler et al. (2005) explain, the product can be split into a number of components as shown in Figure 7.4. Figure 7.4 shows that the core product is service benefit which consumers or other stakeholders are seeking from the product; the actual product is the element which actually provides the benefit whereas the augmented product is the way in which additional value or services can be built around the core and actual product to attract specific markets and audiences. It is at the augmented level, according to Graham (2003), where much of the competition between airports occurs. Yet as Graham (2003) also shows, the notion of airports as products is complicated by the composite nature of the product, with airports really comprising large commercial centres. For example, the tourist may see the airport and airline product as one element, which leads Graham to distinguish

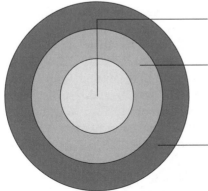

CORE AIRPORT PRODUCT, which is the consumer benefit sought from the product

ACTUAL AIRPORT PRODUCT, which is the element of the product that delivers the benefit such as the product feature, brand and quality

AUGMENTED AIRPORT PRODUCT, which is the element of the product that will distinguish one airport from another through key features such as marketing incentives to low-cost airlines to be based there and for the passenger, the range of quality of shops

Figure 7.4 The airport as a product

between 'raw' and 'refined' features: the raw are the physical and more tangible elements such as the runway and terminal buildings and intangible elements such as staff and customers. The refined elements are the intangible and tangible elements combined with the different services provided inside the airport and by the airline.

One of the most noticeable developments in marketing for many airports has been the use of market research techniques to understand the nature and characteristics of the markets which the airport serves as well as the customer's satisfaction with services. This has also been combined with a greater use of branding (see Halpern and Niskala 2008) to attract carriers in more peripheral regions in Northern Europe. Branding has been used as way to provide a greater level of distinctiveness to what is an intangible product to many consumers, but which seeks to achieve three key outcomes:

● recognition
● preference
● loyalty.

Yet one key development that has tested existing models of airport management and required greater use of marketing tools, particularly at developing secondary airports, is the rise of low-cost airlines.

A new relationship in airport management: the impact of low-cost airlines

As the earlier chapters in this book have shown, one of the most far-reaching changes affecting the supply of tourist transport provision, particularly in terms of contestable markets, is the low-cost airline. This has not only provided competition for other airlines but has added increased competition for other modes of travel and has affected how some airports deal with these carriers. Francis et al. (2004) point to the effect of low-cost airlines in Europe that are expected to increase their market share of short-haul traffic from its current 6 per cent to 25–33 per cent by 2010. The implications for airport management go far beyond the capacity requirements of a new breed of providers. The low-cost airline management strategies are very different in the way they approach cost. This has challenged the conventional approach by which airports and airlines negotiate contracts on access rights and charges. As many of these airlines have focused on secondary airports due to the point-to-point services they offer, they have often targeted airports with fewer than 1 million passengers, many of which airports are still state owned and not highly profitable. Francis et al. (2004) point to the examples of where the low-cost revolution has led to massive increases in passenger use, such as the entry of Ryanair at Charleroi, easyJet at Luton and Bmibaby at East Midlands airport. In some cases subsidies have been offered at the initial entry of the airline to attract them. For example, Ryanair agreed to operate from Charleroi airport in 2001 with six routes and a base there and it led to a growth in the airport's traffic from 200,000 passengers in 2000 to 773,000 in 2001 and 2.2 million in 2006. However, as Echevarne (2008) shows, this led to an investigation by the European Commission in relation to the preferential treatment the airline received on passenger handling and landing charges (i.e. 50 per cent of the standard rate). The investigation found that the European Commission deemed some aspects of the state aid from the airport compatible with EU Transport Policy to develop secondary airports and to make better use of under-utilised infrastructure. In addition, the incentives paid to assist with the start-up costs were allowable. However, the reduced airport charges and handling fees were not permissible on all but one route. This use of state aid led the European Commission to require Ryanair to pay back the aid to the Walloon government. This led to an appeal by Ryanair and an agreement in 2008 regarding the payments. What this example shows is that the regulatory environment is problematic and whilst it has been debated whether such subsidies are anti-competitive and discriminatory, that has not stopped the continued growth of the low-cost model. But the low-cost airlines have very different requirements due to their focus on cost reduction. For example, airports have had to provide apron and gate space and parking stands near to the departure due to tight turnaround times. In some cases, airports have invested in low-cost terminals, such as JetBlue's new terminal at JFK Airport, New York at a cost of US$875 million. This has a capacity of 20 million passengers a year with 26 gates and the ability to handle 250 flights a day. In France, Marseille Provence airport has also invested in a low-cost terminal at a cost of €16.4 million in 2006, with a capacity of 3.7 million passengers a year, by converting a former cargo terminal. The fit-out for the terminal is low-cost and basic to reflect the demand for low-cost services. As Echevarne (2008) argues, low-cost travel has also had a knock-on effect for airport management, where such passengers require a greater range of car parking provision and good public transport access. Furthermore, low-cost airlines require fewer check-ins, simple luggage handling, and no airbridges as they prefer to use the front and back doors of their aircraft to unload passengers quickly to reduce cost. In addition, the use of self-powered manoeuvring at airports is preferred to being pushed away by airport vehicles at additional cost.

The implication for airports is that they have not always been able to charge the rates they would like to attract this business. Indeed, some low-cost carriers have viewed the spare capacity at these airports as opportunities to drive costs below airport marginal costs. These airports have had to reconsider their commercial strategies, balancing additional non-airline revenue against the losses on aeronautical charges and in some cases offering subsidies. In Scotland, the Scottish Executive (now the Scottish government) also provided a £6 million fund to attract low-cost airlines to increase inbound travel to offset such costs, although this can also increase outbound travel, thereby being a zero-sum game for a country's tourism industry. Such strategies that have sought to expand smaller regional airports based on low-cost operators have, as Francis et al. (2004) show, been highly volatile in Europe where 30 low-cost services have been withdrawn since 1998. For the airports, this may also pose an equity issue for existing full-service carriers that seek to gain parity with new start-up airlines or, in some cases, withdraw completely.

One notable area of development in the low-cost market is the issue of airport retailing which can be viewed in marketing terms as a retail offer (Figure 7.5). According to Skapinker (1998a: VI), 'an airport is, in many respects, the ideal environment for retailers. The potential customers are affluent, or reasonably so, and are often on the lookout for presents for family or friends. Above all they

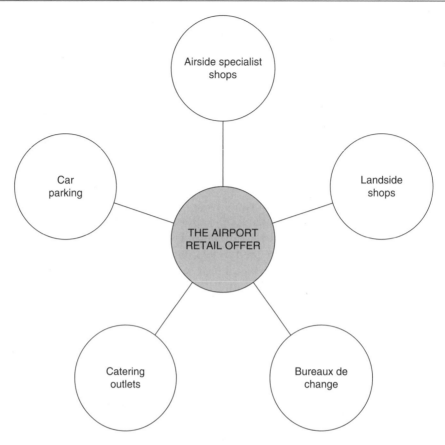

Figure 7.5 The airport retail offer

are trapped'. However, one of the criticisms which Skapinker (1998a: VI) reports is that:

> some airline executives are unhappy about the way shops are taking over large areas of airport terminals . . . [which] means there is less space for airline facilities, such as check-in desks . . . passengers become absorbed in their shopping, do not hear departure announcements, and arrive late at gates, delaying flights.

As Geuens et al. (2004) noted, airport shoppers are not a homogeneous group, but have four discernible motivations for shopping in airports:

● functional motivations, based on price, convenience and quality shopping;
● social motivations, including interaction with others sometimes to offset insecurities;
● experiential motivations based on the convivial environment and atmosphere created for the shopper;
● travel-related motivations; including being out of one's normal place of residence, present- and souvenir-purchasing behaviour and a desire to spend the last amount of foreign currency

although Geuens et al. (2004) noted that three types of airport shopper could be discerned: mood-related shoppers, the apathetic and indifferent shopper, and the shopping lover. Echevarne (2008) points to research which suggests that initial concerns by airport managers that the rise of low-cost travellers would lead to diminished retail spend have not eventuated. The behaviour of such travellers is not dissimilar to the full-cost traveller, since extended check-in times and dwell time in terminals has seen retailing revenue hold up. Globally such retail revenues are estimated to be worth US$25–30 billion and the areas for future growth are China and India. Echevarne (2008: 190) summarised the impact of low-cost carriers (LCCs) on airports, where specific benefits have occurred:

> Commercial activities that have particularly benefited from LCCs are, for example, food and beverage services (bars and restaurants) and car-rental services. Since most LCCs charge for food and beverages served on-board, many passengers tend to eat at the airport or even purchase food and beverage to consume during the flight. This, combined with the fact that passengers are being asked to arrive early at the airport in order to have enough time to complete the increasingly lengthy security measures, has resulted in a significant increase in the average revenue per passenger on these concessions. However, this tendency has also spread to larger airports too, as a result of the increasing numbers of legacy carriers charging for in-flight catering. Consequently, airports have focused on the development of food courts. For example, Marrakech, a popular LCC destination in Morocco, developed a food court following the theme of the rich and varied local gastronomy for which this tourist region is known. Car-rental concessions have also benefited from LCC passengers. This is a direct result of the trend towards independent travel, which sees passengers booking their flights, ground transportation and accommodation themselves using the Internet.

However, for many larger airports, their concern is also for the way their competitors perform, which has led to the development of numerous measures of performance.

Airport performance: the use of benchmarking

The development of commercial opportunities, most notably retailing and concessions, has been a major result of the more commercially driven model of development. Hsu and Chao (2004) evaluated the relationship between space allocation in airport terminal buildings involving commercial and public space, and IATA monitors the provision for public service areas such as check-in, queuing, circulation space, baggage claim and other public areas, given the desire of many airports to maximise the amount of commercial space available in terminals.

Yet how can an airport evaluate the success of its management and business strategy? Ashford and Moore (1992) cite the earlier work of Doganis and Graham (1987) *Airport Management: The Role of Performance Indicators*, which evaluated the performance of 24 leading European airports based in 11 countries. They examined five key areas in airport management:

- costs;
- revenue;
- labour productivity;
- capital productivity;
- financial profitability.

The basic principle is to assess whether the resources being used at a given airport are effective, efficiently employed and able to achieve the desired outcome. For example, a study in 2007 for the Tourism and Transport Forum (TTF) entitled *Assessing the Impact of Airport Privatisation* examined the effects of privatisation and the impact on productivity and performance. It found that labour force productivity improved post-privatisation, while operating costs dropped by 7 per cent and employee costs dropped 15 per cent. It also observed that

> Improved returns from aeronautical and non-aeronautical assets through competition and . . . [the] . . introduction of private sector business development and management techniques in the area of in-terminal commercial activities (such as in airport retail, branding, marketing, etc) as well as overall commercial management (TTF 2007: 16)

had occurred which contributed to improved financial performance. Privatisation had also led to major increases in forecast investment levels in Australia's airports (see Insight 7.1). This report highlights the shift during privatisation, towards a greater demand from airport managers to understand their competitors and how they are performing which has seen the development of research on benchmarking (see Doganis 1992: 159–87 for more detail on operationalising performance indicators and Graham 2009 on airport benchmarking).

Benchmarking

Benchmarking has become a fashionable term in both transportation and tourism research in recent years (Kozak 2004; Lennon et al. 2006), with much of the work undertaken for commercial organisations. Benchmarking is described as a performance improvement technique concerned with understanding how other similar ventures are performing and it has sometimes focused on the concept of 'best practice' to look outside of an organisation to see what others do better and to find ways of incorporating that into one's own operation (Francis et al. 2002). Whilst a substantial literature exists in management and transportation (e.g. see a review in Oum et al. 2003 on this subject), it has been used in a somewhat specific way in the airport sector by commercial organisations and academics to measure and compare airport performance. Much of the early work in this area (see Graham 2009 for a detailed discussion) has focused on the concept of work load unit (WLU), which has equated to each passenger or 100 kg of freight processed at an airport. Other bodies such as governments and international aviation agencies have also developed measures of performance, such as the Airport Council International's annual economics survey and IATA's Airport Monitor. This has built on the early work of Doganis and others as it becomes a more mainstream activity to measure how different airports

INSIGHT 7.1

Airport privatisation: international experiences – UK, Mexico and China

Many examples of airport privatisation point to the initial development of this model of management in the UK and for this reason it serves as useful starting point to understand the nature of airport privatisation and how it has been adopted in other countries. In 1985 the British government produced its White Paper *Airports Policy* (HMSO 1985), which Doganis (1992: 27) interpreted as stating that:

(a) airports should operate as commercial undertakings;
(b) airports' policy should be directed towards encouraging enterprise and efficiency in the operation of major airports by providing for the introduction of private capital.

The ensuing 1986 Airports Act then turned BAA into a limited company, BAA Plc, which was floated on the Stock Exchange in 1987. This was then organised into a single company operating seven airports: London Heathrow, London Gatwick, London Stansted, Southampton, Glasgow, Edinburgh and Aberdeen. The 1986 Act also led to the UK's largest regional airports (with a turnover exceeding £1 million) becoming public limited companies and being detached from their former local authority owners. In New Zealand, the three largest airports were also privatised in 1988 as individual corporations (see Doganis 1992: 28–33 for an analysis of the costs, benefits and issues of airport privatisation), whilst in South Africa a semi-privatised model has been pursued (Prins and Lombard 1995). Yet it is the BAA model that remains widely cited for its commercial success since the 1980s and its ongoing financial success which is a model that many other airport organisations seek to emulate. The organisational abilities of BAA have seen it develop its range of non-operational activities, including:

● airport management;
● retail management;
● property management;
● project management.

In the field of non-aeronautical services, it is BAA's retail activities that have attracted a great deal of interest from analysts although these have now been disposed of. However, other countries have followed this route to airport management as the examples of Mexico and China will briefly show.

Mexico began a process of deregulation of its state-owned transport sector in the late 1980s with the privatisation of two carriers – Aeromexico in 1988 and Mexicana in 1989. In the late 1990s the process of privatisation was started with the airport sector. Initially 58 federal airports were regrouped into five sub-groups and four groups were open to private competition. The airports with the highest volume of passenger and freight business were privatised. The state still has a controlling stake in the privatised airport groups. Even though traffic volumes fell in 2001–06, the revenue from the privatised airports grew and state stakes in the airport groups were subsequently auctioned on the stock markets (Galeana, 2009). However, as Galeana (2009) argues, these increases in revenue may have arisen from higher airport charges as opposed to efficiency gains.

In the case of China, Yang et al. (2008) examined the spectacular growth in airport infrastructure with 147 airports operating by 2005. Airport reforms can be dated to 1988, when three distinct stages occurred: 1988–94, a reform of airport management allowing private investment after 1994; second, 1995–2001, the emergence of joint equity and local reforms to move towards a more market-oriented focus; post-2002, a greater liberalisation of the airport industry permitting foreign capital and private capital to speed up the pace of airport development. This also led to greater freedom of the pricing of aeronautical and non-aeronautical ▶

revenue within defined state pricing guidelines. China now has an ownership structure that comprises state ownership, central government owned–controlled mixed ownership, local government owned and local government owned–mixed ownership. Overall, Yang et al. (2008) point to greater levels of competition forcing the airports to operate more along market lines but the state remains a key player controlling the sector. This has transformed many airports from loss-making ventures to more customer-orientated ventures, expanding their non-aeronautical revenue base with strong growth.

perform, especially with privatisation and shareholder interests. Having examined the scope and issues confronting airport management, attention now turns to international experiences of airport privatisation.

Airport planning and development

According to O'Connor (1995: 269), 'airports are among the most important elements of modern cities . . . in many places, the traffic at the airport reflects the vitality of the tourist industry. For these reasons, airports are critical to the vitality of metropolitan areas', a feature observed in the seminal study by Hoare (1974) of London Heathrow as a growth pole. The significance of airport planning and development has been a feature often overlooked in many analyses of tourist transport. However, a number of UK (e.g. Sealy 1976) and North American texts have examined the theme of airport development indirectly (e.g. Taneja 1988; Wells 1989) and in a more focused manner (e.g. Horonjeft and McKelvey 1983; Smith et al. 1984; Ashford et al. 1991; Ashford and Moore 1992), although probably the most up-to-date and accessible source is French (1997a). O'Connor (1996) outlines the importance of locational factors in the development of airports in Asia-Pacific, notably:

- physical and technical considerations (i.e. appropriate sites);
- economic forces, where air traffic now is a vital element in the national economy of most countries;
- the role of government in forward planning (e.g. Changi Airport in Singapore developed two parallel runways and has well-organised ground services and facilities to ensure the smooth passage of travellers, backed by high levels of investment).

In physical terms, locational factors are important (e.g. the availability of a large expanse of flat land, access to urban centres that are the source of travellers and an environment able to accommodate the noise and physical pollution from airport operations – see Upham et al. 2004). Airport developers increasingly have to seek new sites away from major population centres (see Caves and Gosling 1999 on strategic airport planning for a good overview of this area). Speak (1997) examines the example of Kai Tak, Hong Kong, which handled 21,370,000 passenger movements and 150,118 aircraft movements in 1995. The development and planning of the new Chek Lap Kok site was originally advocated in 1989, 25 km west of Hong Kong's central business district (CBD) (Figure 7.6). In 1996 an airport development authority was established to develop the project, and the airport opened in 1998.

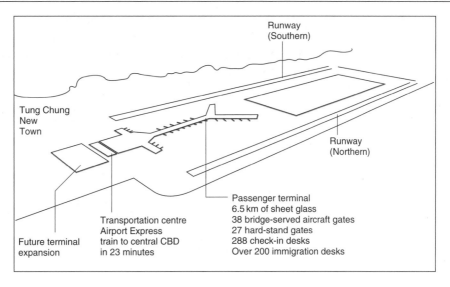

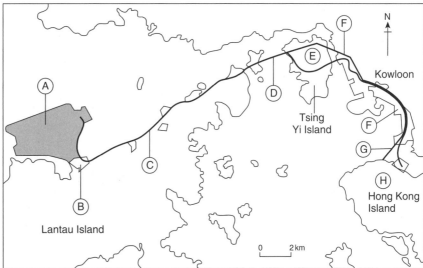

(A) Chek Lap Kok Airport
1,248 ha site built on a
man-made platform from
bedrock of 2 islands and
938 ha of land reclaimed
from the sea; cost $12.1 bn

(B) Tung Chung New Town;
cost $1.38 bn

(C) North Lantau Expressway; cost $307 m

(D) Tsing Ma Bridge; cost $1.77 bn

(E) Tsing Yi Island; cost $5.6 bn

(F) Airport Railway; cost $8 bn

(G) Western Harbour Crossing Tunnel;
cost $1.9 bn

(H) Hong Kong Island land reclamation:
cost $8.07 bn

Airport Cost: $40 bn

Figure 7.6 Chek Lap Kok airport

Source: Adapted from Hong Kong Airport Authority data.

The physical development of the 1248 ha site involved flattening a small island and land reclamation. The airport is capable of accommodating 35 million passenger movements a year using the first runway; and it could expand to a capacity of 87 million once the second runway is completed. The need for access to Hong Kong's CBD required two bridges and a dedicated airport railway to be built (Figure 7.6) and has necessitated 10 associated infrastructure projects as shown in the figure. Policy is also critical in this context, as Martin and Roman (2003) observed in their discussion of potential changes to the regulated aviation market in South America and implications for airport hub development and the wider strategic issues examined in Japan by Feldhoff (2003). At a regional level, there is scope for some military airfields to be converted to commercial use as Cidell (2003) examined, although these are often lacking strategic transport links that are critical and require substantial investment (Phang 2003).

ATAG (1993) also acknowledged the importance of surface transport access to airports (*www.atag.org/AH/Index.htm*). Amongst the principal concerns of ATAG (1993) were:

● the needs and expectations of airport users that staff should be courteous and the prices charged should be compatible with the service provided;
● the provision of user-friendly airport terminal facilities;
● provision of facilities that allow those with special needs or a disability to travel (see Chapter 8 for more detail);
● encouraging passengers to use public transport to travel to the airport to reduce environmental impacts as BAA does for passengers and staff via its airport transport strategy (see *www.baa.co.uk*). In November 2008, British Airports Authority (BAA) announced that it would contribute £230 million towards the cost of the £16 billion Crossrail project to link Heathrow Airport with the east of London and the business centre at Canary Wharf in London Docklands without requiring rail passengers to make multiple transfers between east and west London by overground and tube train. This reflects the need to ensure the smooth integration of land transportation links with the airport;
● the development of interchange facilities that do not penalise public transport users financially or make access difficult through poorly designed interchanges;
● a well-planned network of roads and dedicated airport access routes;
● adequate parking spaces that are well signposted to distinguish between short- and long-stay traffic;
● the development of rail–air services from major urban centres (e.g. London's rail–air services to Heathrow, Gatwick and Stansted and Schiphol's dedicated train service).

Whilst not all of these access issues are important for every airport, it is evident that improving access from urban centres consumes a significant element of capital budgets. For example, in 1997 Auckland International Airport in New Zealand was reported as requiring NZ$1 billion in capital expenditure over the next 15–20 years, a large proportion of which will be devoted to access issues and terminal design.

It is the process of physical planning of airports to which attention now turns. Through a focus on Denver International Airport (see Dempsey et al. 1997) it is possible to understand the procedures and processes followed to build an airport.

Denver international airport

According to Goetz and Szyliowicz (1997), Denver International Airport (DIA) opened five years late in 1995, mainly due to problems with its automated baggage system (de Neufville 1994). The cost overrun rose from US$1.7 billion to over US$5 billion, and though the airport was forecast to handle 56 million passengers by 1995, only 30 million used it in that year. It also received noise complaints from residents, despite seeking to minimise noise impacts. DIA is therefore an interesting example of how short-term problems in the planning process can emerge even where there is a systematic approach to development. In the USA, the Federal Aviation Administration (FAA) has published guidelines on the approach towards airport development. Rycroft and Szyliowicz (1980) examine the limitations of the FAA approach where access to all forms of data is not possible, and argue that it overlooks the role of power and political variables. It also assumes that planning occurs in a rational manner, whereas there is all too often a lack of agreement on the principal goals of large projects such as these. Furthermore, this approach also assumes that it is possible to derive accurate forecast demand estimates (see Chapter 4). In the wider literature on transport planning such problems remain intractable as traffic forecasts are notorious for their inaccuracy and inability to accommodate human travel behaviours (see Hensher et al. 1996). To overcome some of these problems, Maldonado (1990) and de Neufville (1991) have developed a strategic planning approach that recognises issues such as uncertainty and flexibility in future planning requirements.

The initial decision to expand airport capacity in Denver can be dated to 1974, when the political consensus was to expand the existing Stapleton International Airport. By the time deregulation occurred in the 1980s expansion was not considered feasible, given the FAA's and Denver's consultants' forecasts for future traffic growth. Forecasts suggested that the existing traffic of 25 million passengers in 1983 would grow to 56 million by 1995. Runway capacity at Stapleton had already caused a bottleneck in the national air transport system during adverse weather conditions due to runway design. Goetz and Szyliowicz (1997) provide an interesting commentary on the politics of the decision to select a site for DIA. They also examine how the airline users exacted major concessions from the developer – the city of Denver. The most serious concession was exacted by United Airlines, which sought and gained an automated baggage system to service its concourse. This concession also contributed to major delays in the airport becoming operational. Delays to the airport's opening due to technological problems associated with the baggage system added to cost overruns. The airport traffic forecasts also assumed that Denver would emerge as a major hub. But in March 1994 Continental Airlines abandoned its hubbing operation at Denver, leaving United as the main hubbing operator, whilst the FAA assumed that American Airlines might consider establishing a hub operation by 1995 (see Bania et al. 1998 on hubbing operations). The DIA project was downsized by reducing the number of runways from six to five and gates from 120 to 88 – this was made possible by the modular design of the airport.

The airport also aimed to reduce noise impacts, being located 24 miles from Denver's CBD. But according to Goetz and Szyliowicz (1997: 272–3):

In all of 1994, Stapleton received 431 noise complaints, but in the first twelve months since DIA opened the city received over 57,000 complaints. Much of this can be attributed to previously non-impacted populations now receiving some amount of aircraft noise. But it remained unclear whether these complaints indicate that the original noise contours developed in the Environmental Impact Statement are still accurate.

(The complex issues associated with environmental assessment techniques and noise pollution are discussed in more detail in Chapter 8.)

Goetz and Szyliowicz (1997) view the DIA example as highlighting the airlines' role as something that could not have been foreseen in the rational comprehensive planning model advocated by the FAA. The goals of each airline were not in sympathy with those of the city of Denver and the FAA, and the political system affected both the decision-making and implementation phases of planning. As Szyliowicz and Goetz (1995) argued, a range of actors with different strategies, agendas and purposes ensured that no one unitary actor drove the project forward. As a result, political and cognitive factors were powerful in shaping the airport development process. The ability to accommodate future risk and uncertainty also assumes a much greater role given the 'critical nature of aviation forecasts for airport planning and design and of demand forecasts' (Goetz and Szyliowicz 1997: 274). This means that the planning process needs to be able to accommodate likely errors in forecasts. Goetz and Szyliowicz (1997) also point to the need for decision-makers and planners to adapt to new business situations with flexibility rather than remaining locked into a project that may not be suitable on completion. Vested interests, political careers and an unwillingness to admit that earlier decisions may have been made on inaccurate information still affect mega-projects such as airports. A similar problem can be seen in the Civil Aviation Authority (CAA's) Swanwick air traffic system developed for the UK. This was a mega-IT project that has so far revealed 15,000 errors in the computer software which cost over £623 million and was over budget and several years late. It was envisaged that it would replace the ageing West Drayton air traffic control centre, although some critics believed it might have been abandoned if it could not be made operational (see CAA 1997 for detail on air traffic control and Swanwick). Both DIA and the Swanwick example highlight overoptimistic expectations that technology which is not tried and tested can be put into practice immediately. What emerges is a need for flexibility and constant monitoring once the decision has been taken to implement a project and a willingness to halt the project if technical problems cannot be solved. However, there are also a number of other current issues affecting global airports, notably security.

The threat of global terrorism and security issues for airports

Since the 9/11 terrorist attacks and subsequent global terrorism events (as well as health issues such as SARS), tourist security issues have become the number one concern for travellers, a feature that Gilbert and Wong (2003) found in respondents pre-9/11. Much of the pressure to reassure passengers has fallen upon airlines and airports. The airport has a significant responsibility due to its sifting and search functions to ensure passengers do not carry prohibited material or anything that could be used as a weapon on board aircraft. One noticeable feature is the tightening of security at many airports, as airports undertake public relations activities via websites to reassure passengers. In Europe, restrictions imposed on the transportation of liquids has affected duty-free sales at many UK airports due to uncertainty over the rules on liquids and travel. For example, the USA's US Transportation Security Administration illustrates the scale of the problem that now faces the travelling public with reference to terrorist threats. But in reality the risk of a terrorist attack in an airport or on board an aircraft is very small. Nevertheless the new era of airport security has been heralded with biometric measures using eyeball and fingerprint recognition tools being introduced to detect undesirable travellers (i.e. terrorists) in some countries (see the journal *Biometric Technology Today* for an up-to-date assessment of measures being implemented in different airports). Amongst the measures introduced is improved baggage scanning and perimeter security at some airports, but the impact on the travelling public has been an increase in delays and queuing at screening points.

Amongst the least known and understood issues, but one that is nevertheless important for airports as gateways, is the biosecurity risks posed by tourist travel. This is discussed in Insight 7.2 on biosecurity.

INSIGHT 7.2

Tourism and biosecurity: the challenge for airports and air travel

Professor Michael Hall, University of Canterbury

The world is increasingly mobile. Improvements in transport and communications technology, population growth, deregulation and internationalisation of the world economic system, and moves towards 'free trade' have all encouraged greater mobility of goods, services, ideas, businesses and people. Tourism is an important part of the growth in population mobility. However, increased movements of people across political and physical borders may have a number of unintended and unwanted consequences. One of the most significant of these is the extent to which travellers and the transport systems they use may act as vectors for diseases or pests, which in themselves may host or transport diseases (e.g. Russell 1987; Carlton and Geller 1993; Berkelman et al. 1994; Bernard and Scott 1995; Wilson 1995; Fidler 1996; Ginzburg 1996; Borgdorff and Motarjemi 1997; Kaferstein et al. 1997; Legors and Danis 1998; Cookson et al. 2001; Seys and Bender 2001) (Table 7.2).

In order to combat the introduction of pests and diseases many countries and regions have introduced biosecurity strategies. Biosecurity refers to the protection of a country, region or location's economic, environmental and/or human health from harmful organisms. 'Biosecurity involves preventing the introduction of harmful new organisms, and eradicating or controlling those unwanted organisms that are already present' (Biosecurity Strategy Development Team 2001a: sec.1.3). Although tourism is a major focal point for biosecurity measures there is little discussion of the significance of biosecurity measures in the tourism studies literature. Indeed, the industry itself may be unaware of the role that it plays in biosecurity management. For example, of the 122 submissions received on the *Issues Paper: Developing a Biosecurity Strategy for New Zealand* (Biosecurity Strategy Development Team 2001b) only one came from the tourism industry (Biosecurity Strategy Development Team 2002: 4).

▶

Table 7.2 What is carried by humans when they travel

- Pathogens in or on body or clothes
- Microbiologic fauna and flora on body or clothes
- Vectors on body or clothes
- Immunologic sequelae of past infections
- Vulnerability to infections
- Genetic makeup
- Cultural preferences, customs, behavioural patterns, technology
- Luggage and whatever it contains, including food, soil, fauna, flora and organic material

Source: After Wilson (1995); Hall (2004).

Biosecurity measures occur at a number of different scales, all the way from the international level, such as agreements on the movement of agricultural produce through border controls, to biosecurity practices at individual locations, such as farms. Biosecurity strategies can also be categorised in terms of their utility at the pre-border, border and post-border stages (Biosecurity Strategy Development Team 2001a, 2001b; Green 2001) (Table 7.3).

Tourism is clearly a major area of biosecurity risk and is a focal point of border control activities, many of which occur at airports as gateways, particularly in agriculturally based economies and regions. In Australia the Australian National Audit Office (ANAO) (2001: 16) estimates indicated that almost 90 per cent of seizable material arriving by mail, and more than half arriving carried by international airline passengers, entered Australia undetected.

In Australia, there has been a marked increase in the number of interceptions of pests and diseases at the border, from around 3500 interceptions in 1994 to over 10,000 in 1999 (ANAO 2001). This may be due in part to increased trade and tourism traffic, but is also a likely result of improved biosecurity strategies, particularly as with respect to surveillance the more you look the more you find. Prohibited items, that is those considered as having 'a high risk of carrying pests or diseases and which are seized, treated or re-exported', intercepted at Australian airports increased from 1000 per month in 1998 to 4000 per month in 2000, reflecting the impact of quarantine reform initiatives (ANAO 2001: 25). Just as significant is the estimated leakage rate which measures the percentage of all items that have crossed the border but which still contain or possess seizable material. According to ANAO the leakage rates for airline passengers arriving in Australia have been relatively stable since 1998, at between 3 and 4 per cent. In comparison in 2000 the estimated leakage rate for international mail was 1.2 per cent (ANAO 2001). Using these figures the ANAO in its audit of quarantine effectiveness in Australia estimates that 'in excess of half of the seizable material (or 300,000 items per year) carried by international air passengers breaches the quarantine barrier' (2001: 27).

From a tourism perspective biosecurity strategies occur at different stages of the trip cycle: decision-making and anticipation, travel to a tourism destination or attraction, the on-site experience, return travel, and recollection of the experience. Each of these five stages will have different psychological characteristics, with implications for how tourism organisations and businesses establish a relationship with the customer or, in the case of biosecurity, how biosecurity and quarantine organisations establish a relationship with the traveller and assist them in undertaking good biosecurity practice.

Central to appropriate biosecurity practice by travellers is an improved understanding of biosecurity and quarantine. Improving awareness of biosecurity may lead to a decrease in the number of prohibited items that cross a border. In Australia the ANAO (2001: 24) noted that 'Awareness of quarantine amongst Australians intending to travel, or who have travelled recently, has improved markedly' since implementation of a national campaign by the Department of Agriculture, Fisheries and Forestry to improve public understanding of, and

▶

Table 7.3 Pre-border, border and post-border biosecurity strategies

Pre-border

- Identifying threats to ecosystems
- Profiling and modelling the characteristics of damaging or potentially damaging organisms and vectors
- Identifying controls (in the country of origin) for selected organisms that pose a threat to destinations
- Analysing and predicting risk pathways for unwanted organisms
- Identifying and collating databases and expertise on unwanted organisms
- Developing systems for rapid access to appropriate data
- Developing import standards and compliance validation methodologies
- Auditing exporting countries' compliance with destination biosecurity standards
- Identifying and locating biosecurity-related risks to animal, plant and human health
- Analysis of public attitudes and perceptions of biosecurity risks and barriers to biosecurity responses in visitor-generating areas
- Development of educational programmes in exporting regions so as to reduce likelihood of introduction of unwanted organisms in imported goods
- Development of educational programmes for tourists in both generating and destination regions so as to reduce likelihood of introduction of unwanted organisms

Border

- Developing improved systems, including clearance systems and sampling methodologies, and technologies for intercepting unwanted organisms according to import standards
- Developing border containment and eradication methodologies according to import standards
- Developing profiles of non-compliance behaviour to biosecurity requirements

Post-border (includes pest management)

- Developing rapid identification techniques for unwanted organisms
- Designing and developing methodologies for undertaking delimiting surveys for new incursions
- Developing rapid response options for potential incursions of unwanted organisms
- Analysis of public attitudes and perceptions of biosecurity risks and barriers to biosecurity responses in destination areas
- Developing long-term containment, control and eradication strategies

General

- Analysis of economic and political models for the management of biosecurity threats
- Development of rapid-access information systems, collections and environmental databases on unwanted organisms
- Improve export opportunities for 'clean' products
- Development of industry and public biosecurity education programmes

Source: After Hall (2004).

commitment to, quarantine. New Zealand has also recognised the importance of the development of a communications and education programme 'to emphasise the value of biosecurity and the role travellers can play in preserving New Zealand's unique flora and fauna' (Biosecurity Strategy Development Team 2002: 11). Such measures apply not only to the international visitor but also to New Zealanders travelling abroad as 'incoming New Zealanders are responsible for 40% of border infringements by passengers' (Biosecurity Strategy Development Team, 2002: 11). As the *Issues Paper* written as part of the development of a biosecurity strategy for New Zealand noted:

> Because the actions of travellers and importers are key to successful biosecurity management, education and awareness programmes may have significant potential to

provide low cost gains in biosecurity protection. Education is possibly the major risk management tool available for biosecurity. If the level of risk consistently presented at the border is lowered, facilitation could be improved and compliance costs and general inconvenience reduced Programmes should encourage the general public to take personal accountability for protecting New Zealand's biosecurity. Attitude change may be the best way to reduce long-term risks in the face of increased trade and travel . . . Biosecurity agencies should work co-operatively with industries to develop messages and tools specific to the range of target audiences. The tourism industry is well placed to help to improve visitor awareness of the importance of biosecurity to New Zealand, and biosecurity messages could be integrated with tourism promotion campaigns (Biosecurity Strategy Development Team, 2001b: 24–5).

In Western Australia it is estimated that phylloxera could cost affected growers AU$20,000/ha in the first five years in lost production and replanting costs (Agriculture Western Australia 2000a). For many grape diseases, including phylloxera, humans are a significant vector (Pearson and Goheen 1998). One aspect of biosecurity is the use of customs and passenger declarations as a means of not only gathering customs duty and traveller information and educating travellers about biosecurity but also alerting customs officials to potential biosecurity risks. In addition to containing questions regarding the bringing of plant material, fruit or foodstuffs into the country, of potential interest to the grape growers are questions as to whether passengers have travelled to other rural areas or locations where they might have encountered grape diseases or pests. For example, the Australian incoming passenger card (Commonwealth of Australia 1999) asks visitors 'Have you visited a farm outside Australia in the past 30 days?' (It should be noted that it also asks 'Are you bringing into Australia . . . Soil, or articles with soil attached, i.e. sporting equipment, shoes, etc?') The United States customs declaration asks if the traveller or a member of the family has 'been on a farm or a ranch outside the US' (Department of the Treasury, not dated). In New Zealand incoming passengers are told that 'you must declare' if 'in the past 30 days' a visitor had been 'to a farm, abattoir or meat packing house' as well as having been 'in a forest or hiking, camping, hunting in rural areas or parkland' (New Zealand Customs Service 2001).

This Insight shows that biosecurity issues are an almost unseen element of the potential range of issues which airports and their customs staff have to deal with. This has become even more significant with the rise of concern about bioterrorism. Although biosecurity issues discussed here are significant for agriculturally based economies, they are also significant elsewhere, as the case of SARS has shown in this book, some of these issues will be returned to in the next chapter on the human and environmental consequences of travel.

●●●● Summary

There is no doubt that 'airports are complex businesses with functions that extend substantially beyond the airfield or traffic side of operations' (Ashford et al. 1991: 11). Airports provide the vital infrastructure that links:

- the airline;
- the traveller;
- air and surface transport

and they are complex systems which require clear management guidelines and structures to ensure they operate efficiently.

Since the late 1980s and 1990s the process of privatisation has swept across many of the world's airport organisations, as the public sector is unable to provide access to large sources of capital to invest in upgrading schemes. The full or partial privatisation of airport companies has also changed the airport as a travel terminal. Under privatisation, a greater focus on non-traffic revenue sources and a broad revenue strategy have transformed the airport from a waiting area and functional environment. The transformation, which has been inspired by business principles to generate revenue from retailing, has resulted in the airport mall becoming a cultural icon. The airport is often viewed as a post-modernist expression of the conspicuous consumption now pervading many developed societies, epitomised by leisure travel. In this new environment, where marketers have seized the initiative to develop products and services for a wide range of target groups (including the traveller) the airport is now firmly part of the broad travel experience. Many privatised airports have a clear marketing focus on customer needs in a market characterised by high-volume business and a captive clientele. The consumer's interests are also represented by the UK Consumers' Association publication, *Holiday Which*. Its winter 1998 survey, *Which Airport*, undertook a qualitative review of UK airports and compared value for money, access, areas in need of improvement (e.g. catering) and the best departure lounges, as well as the range of shops available. Such surveys illustrate how important the airport is now becoming in the wider travel experience.

The example of BAA also illustrated the diverse range of activities associated with airport management, the sheer scale and volume of operations, and the fact that there is now a customer-driven focus to improve the traveller's experience. Even so, large organisations such as airports cannot necessarily respond to issues as quickly as the customer would like. For example, on a flight from Scotland to London in March 1998, the author experienced an incident that highlights this issue: the ground staff held the departure up to allow an inebriated passenger on board, who was served additional alcohol during the flight and who then created difficulties during and after the flight. At the destination, ground crew were faced with this situation and it took an inordinately long time for the airport security staff to be called. Whilst this reveals total ineptitude by the airline staff for allowing a passenger on board who was unfit for travel, it also illustrates the unexpected events with which airport staff have to deal and the time delay in putting the appropriate system and action in place (see Chapter 10). It was also the airport staff who had to deal with the outcome of the airline staff's inexperience and lack of understanding of the situation. Thus, airport management embraces a wide range of operational and human interactions that affect the way travellers perceive the airport environment. Since 9/11 this situation has radically changed concerns for safety and security.

In terms of development strategies for airport growth, the example of DIA illustrates the complex interaction of factors that can affect the final outcome. Airport development involves extremely large funding, increasingly from the private sector, to meet the complex needs of airlines and travellers as well as the airport operator. To describe such entities as mega-projects is a good description, given their scale and vastness. Managing such entities once they are fully operational and meeting a broad range of customers' needs in the fast-changing world of domestic and international travel is a key challenge.

Questions

1 Why are transport terminal facilities an integral part of the tourist travel experience?

2 What are the primary functions of an airport?

3 How has the introduction of airport privatisation affected the management and operation of airports globally?

4 Is the airport of the future likely to look considerably different in terms of design, internal organisation, layout and function?

Further reading

The literature of airports and tourism is growing and the best starting point is Graham, A. (2009) *The Management of Airports*, Butterworth Heinemann: Oxford; and the *Journal of Air Transport Management*, which is an important source of research articles on the activities associated with airports.

On airport development see:

Kazda, A. and Caves, R. (2000) *Airport Design and Operation*, Oxford: Pergamon.

And for a more strategic perspective see:

Caves, R. and Gosling, G. (1999) *Strategic Airport Planning*, Oxford: Pergamon.
Forsyth, P., Gillen, D., Knorr, M., Niemaier, M. and Starkie, D. (eds) (2004) *The Economic Regulation of Airports*, Aldershot: Ashgate.

On airport marketing see:

Jarach, D. (2005) *Airport Marketing*, Basingstoke: Ashgate Publishing Limited.

Websites

On safety and security issues at airports see the following:
www.dhs.gov, the US Department of Homeland Security
www.airsafe.com, Air safety information
www.jar.janes.com, Janes Airport Review
www.dot.gov, the US Department of Transportation
www.hse.gov.uk, the UK Health and Safety Executive

8

The human and environmental impact of tourist transport: towards sustainable tourist travel?

Introduction

The international expansion of tourism and the development of transport systems to meet this demand have had a range of direct and indirect social, cultural, economic and physical impacts on both host populations affected by the operation of tourist transport, and destination areas. In the 1970s and 1980s this led to a growing concern about the impact of tourist travel on the environment, but little attention has been given to the experiences for tourists whilst in transit. As Potter and Bailey (2008: 29) argue:

> Transport, whether by road, rail, sea, inland waterway, air. bicycle, or on foot, offers many economic and social benefits but also has a wide range or direct and indirect environmental impacts. Large amounts of finite resources in the form of fuels and materials are needed to construct vehicles and transport infrastructure. Transport activities account for over 30 per cent of all energy use by final consumers and are widely predicted to be the largest contributor to the growth of carbon dioxide emissions in the twenty first century.

This chapter examines the effect and impact of tourist transport from two perspectives: the effect of travelling on the tourist's experience and the impact of transport systems on the environment. It should be read in conjunction with Chapter 9 which focuses on the issues of climate change and future energy for the transport and tourism sector. In Chapters 1 and 2 the concept of the service encounter was discussed (by using Bitner et al. 1990), recognising that dissatisfaction with tourism services is associated with three types of incident: employee failure to respond adequately to customer needs; unprompted and unsolicited employee actions; and service delivery failure (Ryan 1991: 42–3). The first part of this chapter focuses on service delivery failure, particularly how travel delays and service interruptions may contribute to the stress of tourist travel (i.e. the human effect), and some of the measures taken by transport operators to address such problems. This is followed by a discussion of environmental issues from the transport provider's perspective, including the role of environmental auditing and assessment to address the long-term implications of new tourist transport projects for the environment. The chapter concludes by considering the extent to which sustainable tourist travel and individual projects (Harris et al. 2002) may assist in identifying ways of reducing transport's impact on the environment. A landmark study in this area is Banister (1998).

● ● ● ● The human consequences of modern tourist travel

Previous chapters have shown that the tourist travel experience is a complex phenomenon. Social psychologists (Pearce 1982, 2005) and marketers are continually trying to understand the relationship between consumer behaviour (Qaiters and Bergiel 1989; Schiffman and Kanuk 1991) and tourist travel (Goodall 1991; Swarbrooke and Horner 2007), tourists' degree of satisfaction with travel services and their propensity to revisit destinations in the future. One area that has lacked serious academic research is the tourists' feelings and the trauma sometimes associated with international travel; a more detailed discussion of tourist health can be found in Clift and Page (1996), Page (2002b) and Wilks and Page (2003). In terms of foreign travel, stress is a feature often overlooked since tour operators and travel agents frequently extol the virtues of taking a holiday to fulfil a deep psychological need (see Chapter 4). Ryan (1991) notes that tourist travel experiences offer many potential avenues of research.

The stress associated with international and, to a lesser degree, domestic travel is the result of various psychological factors that are compounded by the effect of congestion on transport systems (see Barlay 1995 for a range of interesting insights into the delights of air travel). McIntosh (1990a) argues that the stress of travel could be attributed to:

- preflight anxieties;
- airside problems;
- transmeridian disturbance;
- fears and phobias;
- psychological concerns,

while in-flight health problems can also be added to the stress involved in modern-day long-haul travel (Harding 1994).

Preflight anxieties emerge when tourists commence their journey by travelling to the place of departure, often to meet schedules imposed by airlines. McIntosh (1990a: 118) suggests that the marketing of travel insurance to cover eventualities such as missed departures can also heighten the inexperienced traveller's sense of anxiety. Once at the departure point, the preflight check-in and the complex array of security checks associated with luggage can subject the traveller to a significant amount of stress in an unfamiliar environment. In addition to this is 'the apprehension . . . initially generated by preflight security . . . searches . . . [which are] a reminder of the risk of hijack and in-flight explosion' (McIntosh 1990a: 118). This has been exacerbated in many airports worldwide with increased security precautions due to global terrorism, accentuating the delays and queuing associated with the security process.

Overcrowding in terminal buildings associated with the throughput of passengers at peak times can overwhelm and disorient travellers, whereas seasoned travellers (e.g. business travellers) often have access to executive lounges and a more relaxed and welcoming environment free from some of these stressors. In fact airline business lounges are an excellent example of one such marketing tool to help relieve preflight stress.

Airside problems, including the design and layout of holding areas for passengers travelling economy class, may contribute to an impersonal and dehumanising process prior to departure, which is exacerbated by an absence of information about the nature and duration of delays. As Ryan (1991: 43) argues, 'passengers delayed in air terminals might be observed as passing through a process of arousal to anxiety, to worry, to apathy, as they become initially frustrated by delays [and] eventually reach apathy because of an inability to control events'. Even so Graham (2009) points to the diversity of traveller types and their different needs in airport settings.

Transmeridian disturbance associated with time zone changes during long-haul travel is a major problem for some travellers (Petrie and Dawson 1994; Auger and Morgenthaler 2009). The condition is often associated with a lack of sleep on long-haul flights and a sleep–wake cycle that can cause exhaustion, commonly referred to as 'jet lag' (Coste and Lagarde 2009). Travel agents may need to be sensitive in their advice to some clients as to the effect of transmeridian disturbance on those suffering from depression. Taking a long-haul holiday to forget their problems may heighten their sense of depression on east–west travel across the world's main time zones. One solution that Barlay (1995) identifies is the use of mild sleeping pills or use of melatonin. Melatonin is a 'naturally occurring neuro-hormone secreted by the pineal gland, a small pea-like organ at the back of the brain. Its rate of secretion is increased by darkness, causing the individual to feel sleepy' (Barlay 1995: 166). However, there is a medical debate on the possible side-effects of such a drug (Brown et al. 2009).

Fears and phobias associated with flying (see Abeyratne 2008) and the likelihood of political insurrections, how hospitable the host population will be and potential language difficulties in the destination region all contribute to the traveller's apprehension in transit. This stress can be alleviated by in-flight entertainment and public relations campaigns by national tourism organisations to reduce travellers' fears. The threat of terrorism or hijack is also an underlying worry for some travellers. Travellers' anxiety appears to follow a cyclical pattern, being heightened after an incident and then subsiding in response to the ensuing public relations exercises by airlines to reassure passengers of the increased security measures that are in place. Yet in extreme cases terrorism may pose a major threat to travel, which has characterised the period since 9/11.

Psychological concerns, such as loneliness and a sense of isolation, can also contribute to the traveller's feelings of anonymity during their journey, particularly if travelling alone (McIntosh 1995). The experience is often heightened on a busy jumbo jet carrying approximately 450 passengers, where an individual feels a sense of anonymity and of being confined in a strange environment 10,000 m up in the sky. Some airlines now offer Fear of Flying courses to help worried passengers overcome their fears and phobias, acting as an important tool for the worst affected travellers. Safety issues also induce a sense of unease amongst travellers following an incident such as an air crash. Although air crashes are rare occurrences (Steward 1986) in terms of the volume of passengers carried and the number of take-offs and landings undertaken, they do assume a prominent role in the psychology of tourist travel. Abeyratne (2008: 47) observed that '40 per cent of the 2.1 billion persons carried in 2006 [by air] had some fear of flying', with around 10 to 20 per cent who may experience medium discomfort and 5 to 10 per cent who may have severe symptoms. Some of the fears of flying were related to: fear of heights, being in enclosed spaces, crowding on-board, the quality of recirculated air on board aircraft, concerns over noises on board the aircraft during the flight, turbulence and a general lack of control (Abeyratne 2008).

According to Barlay (1995: 7) 'the worst pterophobia sufferers confess their debilitating fear' but as many as 80 per cent of regular fliers have apprehension when boarding an aircraft. Although few people experience outright panic, mild pterophobia can affect many passengers. On a boat, travellers reason that they could potentially swim to safety in the event of an accident. In a car or train, they feel a greater degree of control. However, travellers can choose which airline they fly with, based on their safety record, which may help overcome some of the worst effects of pterophobia. Whilst claustrophobia in the aircraft cabin may also exacerbate the anxiety passengers feel, airlines such as Singapore Airlines have recognised that gadgets such as Krisworld and high-quality catering (Frapin-Beange et al. 1994) can assist in passing the time and breaking the monotony on long-haul flights. At the destination, tourists may need reassurance when using local transport systems, where operators give the impression of being blasé or unconcerned about safety issues and passenger welfare.

In-flight health-related problems may also affect passengers on long-haul flights where immobility, reduced air pressure in the flight cabin and dehydration may occur due to the recirculation of dry air within the aircraft, and as Page (2002b) has shown, there is growing concern amongst scientists and governments over the quality of cabin air. Barlay (1995) shows that most airlines use a mix of recycled and fresh air, leading to a build-up of CO_2 that can exacerbate jet lag, nausea and the onset of migraine. Amongst the most controversial and high-profile issues that has attracted public attention is the incidence of deep vein thrombosis (DVT) associated with long-haul flights and passenger immobility combined with risk factors that make certain groups prone to this problem. It has also raised a highly critical debate over seat pitch on aircraft, as summarised by Donne (2002) in a very useful overview of the DVT issue.

Barlay (1995: 164–8) also lists a number of measures for passengers to consider to ensure a comfortable flight:

- *air pressure* – mild flu can cause extreme pressure in the ears that may be relieved by pinching the nose and swallowing, sucking a sweet or, in extreme situations, some airlines carry a decongestant which may be inhaled;
- *shoes* – comfortable footwear and regular exercise on the aircraft are essential to help prevent swollen ankles and, for those at risk of DVT, flying socks are also available from many chemists;
- *clothing* – layers of loose, roomy clothing are ideal for flying, and can be adjusted depending on the changing cabin temperatures;
- *skin dehydration* – frequent application of moisturising creams is highly recommended;
- *liquids and alcohol* – dehydration is a major problem on long-haul flights, as eyes can become dry and sore. Consumption of alcohol exacerbates dehydration, compounded by high-altitude flights. Mixing drinks (tea, coffee, non-carbonated water and fruit juice) are recommended by the British Airline Pilots Association to keep the body topped up with fluids (see Leggat and Nowak 1997 for more detail);
- *food* – eating with moderation, especially in business class and first class, is strongly recommended to avoid indigestion and the feeling of being bloated;

- *exercise* – gentle body movements can assist in avoiding the effects of tiredness and aching limbs on long-haul flights, as can walking up and down the aisles.

There is a range of other more persistent physical problems that affect the tourist's experience in transit, most notably *motion sickness.*

McIntosh (1990b: 80) provides a useful overview of motion sickness as a 'debilitating but relatively short-lived illness which indiscriminately affects air, land and sea travellers'. Yardley (1992) examines the literature associated with the concept of motion sickness, casting doubt over previous explanations of its causes and the tourist's susceptibility, and a study by Sherman (2002) updates the literature in this field, with some suggestions on preventive strategies. It is clear from the existing literature on travellers' health that this affliction is not fully understood (Oosterveld 1995). According to the US Center for Disease Control (CDC) in Atlanta (*www. cdc.gov*) it can affect up to 58 per cent of children and 100 per cent of travellers on boats in very rough conditions. But it confirms that research shows that individual susceptibility is poorly understood. What is known is that the situation occurs through sensations of head position and movement where angular acceleration or vertical acceleration in the ears sends sensory information to the body via the central nervous system. Some researchers believe it is associated with the way in which different modes of transport stimulate an alteration in the perceived stability of the travel environment (i.e. motion changes such as swaying from side to side or violent changes in altitude due to turbulence in air travel) and this affects one's sensory system. This tends to overstimulate the sensory perceptors. It may affect the traveller's perception of the environment and causes various symptoms such as drowsiness, vomiting, increased pulse rate, yawning, cold sweats, nausea and impaired digestion. Although some drug therapy may attempt to block the effects of motion sickness, no comprehensive cure exists and McIntosh (1990b: 82–3) reviews measures to assist the traveller in overcoming sea, car and air sickness. However, Barlay (1995) argues that motion sickness is now a rare event in modern passenger transport, though Barlay has obviously not experienced some of the challenging weather conditions in which airlines fly.

Yet airlines are not the only captive environments in which travel health issues arise on-board transport. According to Chimonas et al. (2008) gastrointestinal (GI) diseases such as the norovirus can have a major impact on a confined setting such as a cruise ship, reflected in the CDC's Vessel Sanitation Programme which seeks to prevent, detect and respond to GI outbreaks. According to Neri et al. (2008), norovirus episodes actually declined on-board cruise ships from 29.2 per 100,000 in 1990 to 16.3 per 100,000 in 2000 but then rose to 25.6 per 100,000 in 2005. This has caused concerns amongst health professionals and cruise ship operators with 'regimes on-board cruise ships . . . directed towards prevention, surveillance and response' (Gibson 2006: 14) given the contagious nature of the norovirus.

The experience of travel stressors and health-related problems may be severe amongst certain groups such as the elderly. McIntosh (1989) reviews the range of problems that the elderly may experience on tourist transport systems, such as immobility and confusion when a number of time zones are crossed during a journey. In view of the increasingly aged nature of tourism markets in developed countries (see Viant 1993; Smith and Jenner 1997), the welfare of elderly travellers and their service experience in transit is assuming a greater significance (McIntosh 1998) amongst the more innovative transport carriers, with specialist tour operators (e.g. Elderhost in the USA and Saga in the UK) ensuring these needs are met through transport provision. As growing numbers of senior travellers experience excellent health, it is evident that this niche market will present many opportunities for the tourist transport system (Viant 1993).

There is a growing concern for disabled travellers in the transport literature (Oxley and Richards 1995). A study by Abeyratne (1995) considers a range of international and national regulatory measures for the carriage of elderly and disabled persons by air and recent EU legislation on the disabled (see Shaw and Coles 2004 for a review of this area in tourism) has placed many obligations on businesses to make their premises and products more accessible. For example, Access Tourism (*www.access-tourism.co.uk*) points out that there are 9.7 million disabled people in the UK and improving access to businesses is a key requirement under disability legislation so they are not excluded from travelling by inadequate access to sites, facilities and infrastructure/transport. This is reiterated in the work of Tourism for All (*www.tourismforall.org*) which has a useful range of best practice case studies. Abeyratne (1995) examines the scope of the issues for airlines and airports in terms of:

- contacts with airline reservation and ticket sales agents who can advise travellers;
- specific fares, charges and related travel conditions, since some airlines require some elderly and disabled passengers to be escorted;
- accessibility of aircraft, via wheelchair or airbridges for incapacitated travellers;
- movement, facilities and services on board aircraft to ensure that the passengers' carriage can be undertaken in a way that provides a safe and comfortable environment.

In the context of the USA, Abeyratne (1995) produced a set of detailed guidelines to facilitate further the 'passage of elderly and disabled persons'. These guidelines highlight a range of policy issues for airports and airlines and the practical measures needed to facilitate the further growth in travel by disabled and elderly tourists.

With these guidelines in mind, it is pertinent to consider the measures transport operators can take to reduce the stressful experience associated with different aspects of tourist travel:

- Provision of special assistance at airports for senior travellers and disabled tourists, to reduce the stress for group organisers taking large parties of tourists abroad and the provision of a more customer-focused approach amongst UK rail companies to help such travellers.
- Development of 'fear of travelling' programmes for different modes of transport, especially air travel (see Barlay 1995 for a humorous review).
- Planners and designers can improve the structure and appearance of terminal buildings so that they are built with the customer in mind, reducing the stress of being in an unfamiliar environment. The award-winning design of the Stansted airport terminal building (London) is one example of how to incorporate these principles into new terminal buildings such as the T5 at Heathrow. Provision of accurate and up-to-date information when travel delays occur.
- Airline staff should inform travellers prior to take-off about the aircraft sounds they will hear (e.g. as wheels are retracted and the change in engine sound at the cruising altitude) to allay any fears.

- Provision of accurate in-flight advice for travellers, such as KLM Royal Dutch Airlines' *Comfort in Flight* brochure (see Leggat 1997 for more detail on the 15 airlines surveyed).
- Replacement of 'anxiety-provoking intensive security screening' (McIntosh 1990a: 120) with low-profile security checks at ports of departure to reduce the potential for passenger stress.
- In extreme cases, general practitioners may prescribe mild medication (e.g. Diazepam) to relax the traveller in flight, but this is often a last resort.

The Tourism for All website (*www.tourismforall.org.uk*) points to a useful study by Darcy (2007) which examined useful ways of improving practices for airlines so that disabled travellers were not caused to have heightened levels of anxiety, a feeling of helplessness and humiliation, which builds on Abeyratne's (1995) useful study. The US Americans with Disabilities Act follows measures in other countries to ensure disabled travellers are not excluded. One particular challenge here is what Gutierrez et al. (2005) describe as making online reservations available to disabled travellers, as there are around 50 million disabled people in the USA which represents a huge niche market if businesses are able to target their needs and meet them.

To date, research on tourists' experience of travel has focused on travellers' health, health precautions prior to departure and problems encountered at the destination (see the *Journal of Travel Medicine*). This discussion, however, has shown that throughout the transport system greater attention needs to be paid to the tourist's experience in transit, due to the range of problems that travel may engender. As Gunn (1988: 163) suggests:

> tourists seek several personal travel factors and will opt for the best combination . . . [of] comfort (freedom from fatigue, discomfort, poor reliability), convenience (absence of delays, cumbersome systems, roundabout routines), safety (freedom from risk, either from the equipment or other people), dependability (reliable schedules and conditions of travel), price (reasonable, competitive) and speed.

Thus, tourist 'transportation is more than movement – it is an experience' (Gunn 1988: 167). The operator needs to recognise this so that the total travel experience is as free from inconvenience and stress as possible. Tourist transport not only has an impact on the traveller, but also affects the environment. For this reason, the second part of the chapter considers some of the issues associated with the environmental effects of tourist transport.

● ● ● ● The environmental impact of tourist transport

During the 1980s there was increasing concern with environmental issues and the impact of different forms of economic development, particularly tourism and, therefore, concern about the transportation element as a contributor to pollution and more recently its link to climate change and global warming. This international growth in *environmentalism* has meant that there is a greater emphasis on the protection, conservation and management of the environment as a natural and finite resource. Within the tourism and transport business, this concern has emerged in the form of the concept of *sustainable* tourism, which highlights the vulnerability of the environment to human impacts from tourism and the need to consider its long-term maintenance (see Hall and Lew 1998; Page and Connell 2008). Much of the work on sustainability can be dated to the influential 1987 World Commission on Environment and Development (WCED) report *Our Common Future* (WCED 1987), which asserts that 'we have not inherited the earth from our parents but borrowed it from our children'. In other words, sustainable development is based on the principle of 'meeting the needs of the present without compromising the ability of future generations to meet their own needs' (WCED 1987).

In 1992, the World Earth Summit held in Rio de Janeiro highlighted many of these global environmental problems and the issues of global warming and climate change. One of the outcomes, as is discussed later in this chapter, was the Agenda 21 work. In 1997, the Kyoto Protocol was signed by over 100 countries pledging to cut greenhouse gases such as CO_2 that contribute to global warming. Interestingly, the USA and Australia did not ratify the Treaty, as their consumption of fossil fuels that give off emissions (and thereby aid economic growth) may have been compromised (see the Friends of the Earth review of this issue at *www.foe.co.uk*) and they were concerned that some emissions had risen since 1997 amongst countries which signed the Treaty. What has become more definite in the evidence available is the link between the contribution of aviation to global warming and the depletion of the ozone layer and addition of greenhouse gases (see the Aviation and Environment Forum for a critical debate, *www.aef.co.uk*).

A Rio plus 10 summit held in Johannesburg revisited many of the issues raised in 1992, but it is notable from a tourism and transport perspective since many briefing reports were produced on progress by different forms of transport in moving towards sustainable objectives and future objectives were outlined (see the United Nations, *www.un.org* and the World Travel and Tourism Council, *www.wttc.org*). However, it would seem that many sectors of the transport and tourism industry are of the view that the future move towards sustainability will be solved by new technology which will make travel greener and less polluting. These assessments show a somewhat intransigent position by many in the transport sector and government bodies that do not want to compromise economic growth through measures which may raise the cost of transportation. A review of the criticisms posed by the House of Commons Select Committee (House of Commons 2004) is pertinent.

The House of Commons (2004) was highly critical of the Department for Transport (DfT) in its consideration of the environmental impacts and issues associated with the Airports Policy Review discussed in Chapter 3. The committee criticisms were very significant, particularly in relation to the 'predict and provide' attitude of the DfT, which was wholly uncritical and unquestioning of the scale of the environmental impacts that the airport expansion would create. The report was extremely focused in pointing out the fundamental flaw in the government approach: it had agreed to encourage more sustainable consumption at the Johannesburg Summit but at the same time did not explain how it should (or if it should) seek to discourage air travel. The uncritical acceptance of the future demand and supply needs was a flawed and antiquated approach to transport planning, made worse by the government disputing the Select Committee's forecast of carbon emissions to 2050 that would comprise 65 per cent of domestic emissions if current aviation policies continued. This House of Commons report is essential reading for anyone who needs to understand how a number of different government departments have conflicting objectives and take different stances on sustainability, reinforcing many of the arguments presented in Chapters 1 and 3 on the lack of integration of transport policy with other relevant areas, let alone tourism and the environment.

This requires some understanding of the natural environment's ability to sustain certain types of economic activity such as transport and tourism. However, research on transport and tourism has often been considered in isolation, as the following discussion will show, although the use of research techniques such as environmental auditing and environmental assessment may help to bridge this gap and to recognise the specific impacts of tourist transport systems.

● ● ● ● Transport and the environment

Tourist transport is one component of a much wider concern for more sustainable forms of development as problems relating to the impact of transport on the environment are symptomatic of the need for more environmentally sensitive forms of development (Banister and Button 1992; Root 2003). Within the context of transport planning, there has also been a greater understanding of the complex and sometimes detrimental impact of certain forms of transport on the environment (Carpenter 1994 offers a detailed insight in relation to railways), although there is almost an acceptance of the inevitability of such impacts. The rich background environmental research on the impact of different modes of transport (TEST 1991) has focused on the implications for transport and policy-making (Department of the Environment 1991; HMSO 1997b; Docherty and Shaw 2003; Hensher and Button 2003) in relation to controversial new tourist and non-tourist infrastructure projects such as airports, new rail links, roads, bridges and major hotel complexes. This interest in the impact of infrastructure projects has led to measures for environmental mitigation. The emphasis on the environment has also led to detailed research on specific components of environmental problems induced by transport such as:

● health and safety;
● air pollution;
● noise pollution;
● ecological impacts;
● the environmental effects of different modes of transport.

An interesting study by Davenport and Davenport (2006) examined many of these issues in relation to coastal tourism destinations in terms of trends in tourist transport which have affected the natural environment of these sensitive localities through impacts resulting from:

● The increasing motorisation of tourist travel, using individualised and road-based transport in the twentieth century that led to the provision of roads and the destruction of coastal habitats to facilitate car-based and coach-based tourism. This has also required major land take in terms of car parking provision (Plate 8.1).
● Continued urbanisation of coastal areas and expansion on a ribbon pattern along the sea front contributed to by resort development, in-migration and other processes such as caravan park development.

Plate 8.1 Car parking at coastal sites can involve a major landtake to accommodate rising demand for access by car which is far from sustainable
Source: S.J. Page

- An exponential growth in the use of coastal waters for tourism experiences (see Jennings 2007), including provision of built infrastructure such as marinas, breakwaters and associated facilities.
- The growth of cruise ship tourism (as noted in Chapter 4) and the effect on destinations and the natural environment, with increasing ship size requiring increased dredging of channels to accommodate them.
- The expansion of personal leisure transport such as swimming and particularly motorised marina transport with increases in speeds of use, with yachts, motorboats and other forms of transport.

As Davenport and Davenport (2006: 290) aptly conclude: 'much of the damage already done to coastal waters is irreversible', illustrating the fragility of these environments to tourist transport. One consequence of such environmentally focused research is that policy-makers have concentrated on the direct costs and problems associated with the development of new transport infrastructure, which is now subject to more rigorous environmental safeguards to minimise the detrimental impacts. This concern for the environmental dimension has also been mirrored in tourism research.

Tourism and the environment

As discussed in Chapter 2, the increasing sophistication amongst tourists has been reflected in the development of a 'new tourism' (Poon 1989), accompanied by a greater emphasis on the consumer requirements of tourists in terms of their search for more authentic holiday experiences and individualised tourism services. One consequence of this 'new tourism' phenomenon is a greater concern for the natural and built environment in which tourism activities are undertaken and their impact in different localities. This greater awareness of environmental issues related to tourism (Gössling 2002; Holden 2007) is reflected in the rapid expansion and diversity of research on 'sustainable tourism' (Smith and Eadington 1992; Weaver 2006), which emphasises the need for a more holistic assessment of how tourist-related activities (e.g. tourist transport) affect the environment.

Recent reviews of research on the environmental dimension in tourism have identified the scope and nature of this growing body of knowledge as well as the existing weaknesses in the structure and form of such studies (Pearce 1985; Page and Dowling 2002). The recognition of the symbiotic relationship between conservation and tourism (Romeril 1985) has led to the need for a greater integration of interdisciplinary and multidisciplinary approaches to research on tourism and the environment in order to achieve sustainable tourism development, of which transport is an integral component. Central to sustainable tourism development is the need to overcome tourism's tendency on occasions to destroy the very resources on which it depends. This is the focus of the seminal study – *Tourism and the Environment* (Department of Employment/English Tourist Board 1991) – aimed at encouraging the UK tourism industry to recognise that the environment is its lifeblood and that it needs to consider the long-term consequences of tourism activity and development. Although Romeril (1989) argues that appropriate strategies and methodologies are required to understand the complex interrelationships between tourism and the environment, no universal environmental methodology appears to have been adopted by researchers in their assessment of tourism and the role of transport in affecting the environment.

It is evident from the discussion so far that tourism and tourist transport systems are consumers of the environment (Goodall 1992) since the provision of tourist infrastructure has a direct impact on the environment, particularly in destination areas. Selman (1992) and Newson (1992) discuss the concept of environmental auditing as one way of examining the extent to which tourist transport systems and their activities are environmentally acceptable. Does tourist transport cause unnecessary pollution? Can measures be taken to mitigate and reduce the harmful effects on the environment without compromising the commercial objectives of the tourist transport operator? According to Goodall (1992: 62) one needs to distinguish between the existing and the future impacts of tourist transport. Two types of research methodology can be used here:

- environmental auditing of existing transport systems and their performance and effect on the natural and built environment;
- environmental assessment to consider the impact of proposed developments in the tourist transport system,

whilst recent progress towards developing and showcasing best practice approaches, benchmarking performance and environmental management have added a range of tools that assist in the implementation of environmental measures at a company or sectoral level.

Each methodology has been developed as a multidisciplinary technique requiring an input from disciplines such as economics, atmospheric science, environmental science, geography, management studies and planning. Within these techniques, a systems approach is often used as a method of examining how different tourist transport inputs affect the environment, and how to mitigate the effects of outputs that contribute to environmental degradation (Wathern 1990).

Environmental auditing and tourist transport

Within tourism and transport literature the notable studies published on environmental auditing are Goodall (1992), Sommerville (1992) and Goodall and Stabler (1997). They are still a key starting point, and illustrate how this research technique is used as a response to the growing interest in sustainable development (Banister and Button 1992). Environmental auditing is a voluntary exercise that tourist transport operators and tour operators, which contract transport services for clients, may undertake to assess how their activities affect the environment and how they can reduce this impact by making modifications to existing business practices. Newson (1992: 100) notes that 'the term auditing, borrowed from finance, implies a thoroughness and openness which is essential in a meaningful desire to reform commercial practices' but few environmental audits have been publicised. Some examples from the field of consumer products (e.g. The Body Shop and Procter & Gamble in the UK) have followed the lead of North America in terms of consumer demand for more 'green products' (Selman 1992). Critics argue that such companies have harnessed new-found environmental awareness to gain competitive advantage and increase market share by offering environmentally friendly services and products as part of the move towards total quality management within their organisation.

Research by Forsyth (1997) raises a wider debate on tourism and environmental regulation, since auditing is a voluntary process. Forsyth surveyed 69 UK-based companies involved in tourism (e.g. tour operators, travel agents, hotels, passenger carriers, tourism associations, national tourist offices and consultancies advising companies sending tourists overseas). Forsyth argues that self-regulation is viewed as preferable in the tourism–environment debate because environmentally responsible practices can be harnessed to increase competitive advantage. Forsyth's survey was sponsored by the World Wide Fund for Nature (UK) and Tourism Concern and prior to any interviews, respondents were sent a copy of *Beyond the Green Horizon: A Discussion Paper on Principles for Sustainable Tourism*. Forsyth's (1997) results identify four main types of practice:

- cost-cutting measures (e.g. paper recycling);
- adding value to the product (e.g. information on destinations as sympathy booklets);
- long-term investment (e.g. staff training);
- legislation (e.g. tourist taxes – see Abeyratne 1993 for a fuller discussion of air transport taxes).

Businesses, however, saw themselves as powerless to effect change, given the threat of competitors who did not adopt similar measures. The main obstacles businesses perceived to developing practices compatible with sustainable tourism principles were:

- it is the responsibility of government to initiate sustainable tourism;
- it may leave businesses at a disadvantage if competitors do not embrace similar practices;

- operators are powerless to produce change;
- a potential lack of interest among customers in sustainable tourism.

The potential for businesses was in 'labelling green or sustainable tourism as quality tourism, and by acknowledging that populist market demand may lead to stereotypical approaches to minorities or ecotourism not helpful to equitable development' (Forsyth 1997: 270) and this has remained a major growth sector, as noted in Harris et al. (2002).

For those businesses which view environmental self-regulation as offering benefits to their image and product, there is evidence that if committed transport operators undertake an environmental audit it may prompt other companies to follow suit, thereby improving the awareness of environmental issues within their sector of the tourism business. The establishment of the British Standards Institution's (BSI) Environmental Management System, mirroring the BS 5750 quality system for service providers is evidence of the significance of environmental auditing as a potent force that has encouraged companies to establish a benchmark of acceptable standards of environmental management in commercial activities. Tourist transport systems are no exception to this environmental awareness and it is likely to increase given the prominence of the sustainability debate. For example, P&O European Ferries undertook a comprehensive environmental review in the 1990s and implemented environmental policies to reduce the company's impact on the atmosphere, marine environment and on shore.

Goodall (1992) identifies the role of Environmental Auditing in corporate policy-making amongst tourism enterprises (e.g. transport providers), which includes:

- *a consideration stage*, where the legislation and scope of environmental issues are considered;
- *a formulation stage*, where an environmental policy is developed;
- *an implementation stage*, where both existing and proposed activities can be considered;
- *a decision stage*, where transport operations are either modified or left unchanged in pursuit of a corporate environmental policy.

More specifically, Goodall (1992: 64) recognises that policy statements and action to minimise environmental impacts need to consider:

- the extent to which transport operations and associated activities comply with environmental legislation through company regulations;
- ways of reducing negative environmental impacts such as polluting emissions and use of energy-efficient modes of transport and equipment based on state-of-the-art technology;
- the development of environmentally friendly products;
- how to encourage a greater understanding of environmental issues amongst staff, customers and people affected by tourist transport.

Translating these principles into commercial practice is a complex process even though organisations such as the World Travel and Tourism Council (see the award scheme on *www.wttc.org*) recommend that such audits should be undertaken annually to foster more responsible forms of development (Goodall 1992). The nature and scope of environmental auditing in the tourist transport system may be determined by the objectives, commitment of senior management, and the size of their organisation to resource such an exercise. More specifically, Goodall (1992) identified a number of types of audit including tourism and transport auditing as an *activity*. Other types of audit may include *site-specific* audits for a business such as the energy efficiency of a terminal building. Audits may also be undertaken as a form of *compliance* of a company's activities with environmental legislation or how well its suppliers or *associates* meet company standards of environmental performance. Audits of specific issues, such as recycling or waste management, may be undertaken as the study by Li et al. (2003) illustrates with reference to in-flight activities. Audits of a company's *products* may also occur as a more wide-ranging *corporate* audit to assess operations across the business and in different localities to ensure consistency in environmental performance and in working towards corporate goals. One tourist transport operator that has developed a corporate audit is British Airways (see Insight 8.1) which set the pace for change and has been developed by many other airlines subsequently.

INSIGHT 8.1

British Airways and environmental management

Consumer interest in environmental issues in the late 1980s prompted tourist transport operators in the UK (e.g. P&O European Ferries and British Airways) to undertake environmental audits to provide a public image of 'environmentally conscious' companies. Purchasers of tourist transport services (e.g. tour operators such as Thomson Holidays) also undertook environmental audits to respond to this trend as previously mentioned with reference to Forsyth (1997). This Insight focuses on the extent of environmental management by one of the world's largest tourist transport operators – British Airways. The significance of British Airways (hereafter BA) as a tourist transport company has been documented elsewhere (see Laws 1991) and need not be reiterated here. BA's role in the world airline industry is reflected in its £8.37 billion turnover in 1996/7, which dropped to £7.6 billion in 2002/03 and £7.5 billion in 2003/04 but reached £8.7 billion in 2007/08. Air travel is a useful example to focus on as airline operation has a variety of impacts on the environment. These can be dealt with under the following headings.

Noise
Early tourist travel on turbo-prop and jet-propelled aircraft generated a significant noise impact during take-off, in flight and on landing (see Farrington 1995 for a discussion of the technical issues). Modern aircraft technology has reduced the level of noise in response to international conventions and legal requirements at specific airports that aim to reduce noise impacts for local communities. The sheer volume of air travel creates a persistent problem for those affected by airlines' flight paths. As Sommerville (1992) notes, since the 1970s the number of people affected by noise nuisance at Heathrow within a 35 Noise Index Number contour has dropped by almost 75 per cent, but this was accompanied by a dramatic increase in the volume of air travel. Increasingly airports are monitoring individual aircraft (e.g. their noise footprint) to ensure they meet noise regulations (see M. Smith 1989 for further information). The phasing out of older aircraft is one way of reducing the noise impact in line with recent guidelines issued by countries abiding by ICAO recommendations. From April 1995, aircraft over 25 years old were being replaced in countries observing ICAO guidelines, whilst additional regulations applied in European airspace.

As BA (2004) shows, it has made considerable progress towards noise reduction targets, with a 5.8 per cent reduction in 2002–03 (which rises to 8 per cent if Concorde is excluded) ▶

Table 8.1 Airline emissions[1]

Emission	Environmental effects	Approximate emissions (millions of tonnes)	
		Commercial aviation	Worldwide (fossil fuels)
Oxides of nitrogen	Acid rain. Ozone formation at cruise altitudes and smog and ozone at low levels	1.6	69[2]
Hydrocarbons	Ozone and smog formation at low levels	0.4	57[2]
Carbon monoxide	Toxic	0.9	193[2]
Carbon dioxide	Stable – contributes to greenhouse effect by absorption and reflection of infrared radiation	500–600	20,000[2]
Sulphur dioxide	Acid rain	1.1	10[2]
Water vapour	Greenhouse effect by absorption and reflection of infrared radiation	200–300	7,900[3]
Smoke	Nuisance – effects depend on composition	Negligible	N/A

[1]Other emissions, mainly from paints and cleaning solvents, are associated with aircraft maintenance and also from ground transport supporting the airline's operation.
[2]OECD Secretariat estimates (for 1980), from OECD Environmental Data 1989.
[3]Derived from BP Statistical Review of Energy 1991.
Aviation figures from AEA estimates apart from NO_x (Egli, *Chimia* 44, 369–371, 1990).

Source: British Airways (1992: 8). Reproduced courtesy of British Airways. For a more up-to-date assessment of the situation, readers may also like to consult the 1999 Intergovernmental Panel on Climate Change (IPCC) report, entitled *Aviation and the Global Atmosphere, www.ipcc.ch*.

and 78 per cent of its fleet already meets the new Chapter 4 noise standards (see BA Environmental Report for more detail), up from 60 per cent in 1998/9. The global distribution of noise pollution by BA aircraft at airports it uses is shown in Table 8.1, which illustrates the pattern of operations, dominated by its London bases. To further help reduce noise pollution on arrival at airports, the airline has a Code of Practice – the Continuous Descent Approach (CDA) – which seeks to reduce noise and improve fuel efficiency when it is safe to use this approach. In 2007/8, BA met its CDA guidelines for 95 per cent of daytime and 94 per cent of night time flights at Heathrow, an improvement on the 84 per cent and 88 per cent figures respectively for 2006/7.

Emissions, fuel efficiency and energy

The growing concern over global warming and 'greenhouse gases' (e.g. CFCs, CO_2, NO_x and methane) (see Chapter 9 for more detail) has meant that atmospheric pollution from aircraft has come under increasing scrutiny. BA (1992) identified the range of emissions from aviation. At a global level, BA (1997) estimated that civil aviation accounts for 400–500 million tonnes of carbon dioxide from 20,000 million tonnes of fossil fuels. This recognises that almost 50 per cent of global warming may be a consequence of man's activities, with civil aviation's contribution accounting for 3 per cent of the total effect of global warming.

BA (2003) indicated that NO_x emissions remain the main airport-related pollution issue for airlines and the combined effect of CO_2, NO_x, particles and water vapour combine to produce *radiative forcing,* that is a process resulting from airline pollution to contribute towards global warming. BA indicates that global aviation contributes about 3.5 per cent to this process, a ▶

feature also discussed in the House of Commons (2004) report as aviation is estimated to add £1.4 billion of external economic costs on the environment from pollution.

BA (2003) also indicated that in relation to CO_2 emissions, its volume of pollution fell to 15,149,000 tonnes, a 11.6 per cent drop over the period 2000/1 through to 2002/3, partly due to fleet characteristics (more energy-efficient aircraft) and improved fuel efficiency overall, which was a 25 per cent improvement on 1990 despite a slight drop in the downward trend in 2002/3. By 2007/08 this had dropped to 1,107 metric tonnes of NO_x at 1,000 feet.

Wastewater, energy and materials

In 1990, BA's expenditure on waste disposal was £1.5 million and it has pursued a corporate 'reduce, reuse and recycle' philosophy since then. Recycling of aircraft materials (e.g. waste oil, tyres, batteries and metals) has been in place since the 1950s and aluminium and paper recycling occurs, whilst water and effluent management schemes have been reviewed to ensure the quality of waste management is improved. Complex energy efficiency monitoring is also undertaken to identify energy savings. BA's use of CFCs and chlorocarbon (CC) in its engineering operations for cleaning purposes has been reviewed and alternatives are being sought, with aerosol use replaced wherever possible by trigger sprays. Deicing fluid used in BA's airport operations is biodegradable and there is evidence of a decline in its use between 1989 and 1997 (except in 1995/6). In 2003, BA announced it was reviewing waste management practices across the entire organisation, since it was a corporate priority for 2003–07, and in 2002/3 it saw a 4 per cent drop in water consumption and 61 per cent decline in fuel spills. In terms of its overall waste management processes, the airline reported that 68 per cent of its activities were associated with landfill operations, 26 per cent with treated liquid waste, 2 per cent on incineration and 4 per cent on recycling at Gatwick and Heathrow airports. In its 2004 Report (BA 2004) it outlined its objective 'to reduce waste and effluent, manage waste and effluent streams responsibly and be efficient in our use of resources', setting targets for 2004–06 'for reducing waste' per passenger, increasing recycling and recovery and limiting our reliance on landfill as a method of disposing of waste' (BA 2004: 12). In 2003/04 key initiatives undertaken by the airline in pursuit of this objective included: a waste training seminar, reviewing its packaging compliance obligations in relation to the Producer Responsibility Obligations Waste Regulations (Packaging) 1997, reviewing water discharge consents, pursuing recycling initiatives and its waste contracts prior to launching its Corporate Waste Strategy in 2004. By 2007/8, BA had increased its percentage of recycling at Heathrow and Gatwick to 30 per cent, aiming for a 50 per cent target by 2010. It also aimed to reduce the landfill waste it generates to zero by 2010, as part of a steady drop in the waste it landfills.

So how can one evaluate BA's performance in the environmental management of tourist transport? One initial issue to consider is BA's integrated approach to environmental management, so that the company complies with all existing environmental regulations. It also highlights the corporate ethos – to ensure 'all staff are responsible for safeguarding, as far as they are able, both their working environment and the greater environment surrounding our operations' (BA 1997: 51). In evaluating the scope of BA's environmental measures, it is evident that the organisation is establishing a benchmark by 'taking the lead [but] it is up to other sectors of the industry to extend the initiative' (Somerville 1992: 173). In many respects BA has led the way in this area within the airline industry and many other large global carriers have come to emphasise many of these features in their annual reports. Environmental researchers have also developed a greater interest in the future impact of tourist transport systems in terms of the requirement for additional infrastructure and its impact on the environment, which is now considered in relation to environmental assessment.

Further reading: *www.ba.com*

●●●● ## Environmental assessment and tourist transport

An understanding of the past and present effect of tourist transport systems on the environment is critical to the long-term management of environmental resources (e.g. see Han and Hayashi 2008 for a discussion of the expected environmental impacts of increasing levels of car ownership in China to 2020), but there is also a need to consider the likely effect of future transport development projects. It is within this context that the significance of research methodologies such as environmental assessment (EA) can be examined to show how future tourist transport infrastructure projects may be evaluated. Within the existing literature on the environmental impact of tourism and transport (see Farrington and Ord 1998), a number of research methodologies exist, which are documented by Williams (1987) in terms of their analytical function and the techniques they employ.

There are three levels at which EA of tourism and transport projects can be undertaken: 'identification', 'prediction' and 'evaluation'. Williams (1987) summarises five main methodologies used to assess the impact of tourism on the environment, in which transport is a significant component. These range from 'ad hoc' teams of specialists describing impacts within their professional field of study, through the 'map overlay approach' frequently employed in land use planning, to 'check-lists' of different impacts associated with physical development related to tourism, 'networks' to assess the secondary and tertiary effects associated with action relating to tourism projects and lastly, more sophisticated matrices of impacts within the confines of EA (see Wathern 1990 for a more detailed discussion). Although EA was not specifically designed with tourist transport projects in mind, it is a useful methodological tool to examine the direct and indirect effects of a project on the existing and future tourism environment within an integrated research framework. (See Department of the Environment 1989 for a guide to the scope and complex range of issues which EA in the UK must address as a legal requirement.)

A recent study by Perl et al. (1997) moves the EA research frontier forward in the methodology they devised for pricing aircraft emissions at Lyon-Satolas airport. Without reiterating the technical aspects of the study, Perl et al. (1997) highlight the three principal environmental impacts associated with airport operation: air, noise and water pollution. As Perl et al. (1997: 89) rightly argue:

> One important variation concerns the degree to which these impacts mobilise public participation in, or demands for influence over, airport planning and development . . . an impact like aircraft noise, which is spatially concentrated in certain areas, has motivated much greater public protest than the air or water pollution impacts from airports, which diffuse more broadly and mix with pollutants from other sources.

By linking EA techniques with economic cost evaluations (e.g. van Wee et al. 2003), Perl et al. (1997) estimated the cost of air pollution for 1987, 1990, 1994 and 2015. The methodology involved pricing the pollution cost from the landing–take-off cycle, which includes taxiing, idling, queuing, take-off and climbout. For 1994, Perl et al. (1997) estimated the cost of air pollution at US$3.6–6.6 million. This was projected to rise to US$9.5–17.4 million in 2015 (assuming that aircraft engineering technology did not improve). Such research can be extended to other airports and can certainly assist in scenario planning for possible environmental costs of pollution. It certainly has the potential to make EA a more systematic rather than descriptive method in dealing with tourist transport impacts. Since the initial development of EA, Strategic Environmental Assessment (SEA) has been developed (in Europe since 2001 with the EU Directive 2001/42/EC) which seeks to understand the cumulative effects of environmental impacts that can be compared within an individual EA report. In the UK this has been integrated into the notion of Sustainability Appraisal (SA) which focuses on wider notions of sustainable development (Potter and Bailey 2008).

Towards sustainable tourist transport systems

As mentioned earlier, 'sustainability' was a new-found term within tourism and transport literature in the 1990s: for services to be attractive to consumers they must now be 'sustainable' or 'green', though much of the rhetoric associated with sustainability has not led to radical changes in the operation and management of tourist transport systems – merely some readjustment to accommodate green issues in most cases. This is particularly the case where definite financial benefits can accrue to the company such as the large European tourism company TUI and its sustainable supply chain management system which has led to a focus on forward and backward linkages to implement measures for sustainable product design, sustainable procurement, sustainable production and sustainable delivery throughout the entire supply chain (Sigala 2008). As transport is fundamental to tourist travel, some researchers argue that it is not possible to make tourism sustainable without a fundamental revision of the concept of tourism, holidaymaking and the role of travel in modern society (see Krippendorf 1987 for an excellent review of this issue) which is in complete juxtaposition to the role of commercial interests that have adapted to the need for sustainable business practices. In fact, as Chapter 9 will show, concerns over the future of oil (Roberts 2005) may force a long-term re-evaluation of tourist transport policy and its supply, since the world depends upon oil for 40 per cent of its energy needs and 90 per cent of all transport energy. This does mean that we also need to re-evaluate the future of pleasure travel, because without such measures designed to introduce sustainability into the tourist transport environment debate, we are unlikely to address the root cause of the problem: the demand for tourism. However, since this is unlikely to be influenced in the short term, the immediate issue is to address the environmental impact of existing tourist travel.

The motivation to achieve sustainable tourist travel has resulted from the actions of pressure groups (e.g. Greenpeace, Friends of the Earth and Transport 2000 in the UK), and their views have permeated national governments as such groups have harnessed grassroots pressure from consumers to develop a greener economy and improve the quality of the environment. But it is at government level that commitment needs to be made to formulate, implement and resource policies to facilitate sustainable transport options (House of Commons 2004). Little attention is given to the issue of tourist transport systems as it is often subsumed in the general theme of transport, which has a bias towards domestic concerns and the effect on economic development. Chapter 9 reviews some of the more innovative and forward-looking schemes. What this shows is that central and local government has to take a leadership role to champion such issues and to put policies and plans in place to make the changes happen. The UK Tourism Society's response to the initial findings of the Government Task Force (the final report is Department of Employment/English Tourist Board 1991) suggests that:

> no analysis of the relationship between tourism and the environment can ignore transportation. Tourism is inconceivable without it. Throughout Europe some 40 per cent of leisure time away from home is spent travelling, and the vast majority of this is by car . . . Approaching 30 per cent of the UK's energy requirements go on transportation . . . [and] the impact of traffic congestion, noise and air pollution . . . [will] diminish the quality of the experience for visitors (Tourism Society 1990).

How can the sustainability concept be incorporated into the tourist transport system? According to Barbier (1988: 19, cited in Newson 1992), sustainability needs to be viewed as a process in terms of how different systems interact as:

> the wider objective of sustainable economic development is to find the optimal level of interaction among three systems – the biological and resource system, the economic system and the social system, through a dynamic and adaptive process of trade offs.

This means that economic activity, such as tourism, must try to achieve a balance with the natural environment so that the environment can support the activity without generating unacceptable impacts which affect the future resource base. To achieve this objective, the concept of sustainability needs to be built into the operation of tourist transport systems, and the following action is needed in terms of policy-making and management:

- policy formulation;
- policy implementation;
- facilitating good practice in tourist transport;
- the evaluation of sustainable transport practices.

A systems approach is useful in this context as it helps one to understand how the decision-making process associated with the regulation, organisation and management of tourist transport systems affects different elements within the system. This is exactly how the House of Commons (2006) inquiry into the London Olympics approached the issue in its report *Going for Gold: Transport for London's 2012 Olympic Games*. The importance of the tourist transport system led to the argument that

> The influence of the transport infrastructure on the millions of visitors expected will be profound. Visitor experiences on our roads, railways and the London Underground during the Games will have the potential to make or mar their visit, and their opinion of the capital (House of Commons 2006: 6).

This report really gets to the essential policy problem of how you transport millions of Olympic spectators and participants in a sustainable manner for a major event whilst ensuring the City can continue to function. One key is the provision of new infrastructure and the report noted the £692 million to be spent on transport infrastructure to prepare for the Games and the £150 million allocated for operating the transport services during the Games. However, the report also noted that to move an estimated 10 million spectators was a challenge after the UK Association of Train Operating Companies prompted a debate on the ability of the high speed javelin shuttle from London Kings Cross to Stratford to handle 25,000 passengers an hour when it stated that its capacity was probably nearer to 12–14,000, raising issues of flow management. The report also observed that London's traffic volumes would need to drop by 15 per cent on the designated Olympic Route Network if congestion was not to be a major problem. As the report concluded: 'Travelling into London must become a pleasant experience if the Olympics are to succeed', highlighting the importance of sustainability principles of managing large volumes of visitors, meeting their needs during a major event and ensuring the public transport system can cope with the additional demands without adversely affecting the visitor experience.

In terms of the sustainability concept, actions in one part of the system (e.g. policy formulation) will have repercussions for other parts of the system.

Policy formulation for sustainable tourist transport

Banister and Button (1992: 2) recognise that the 'whole question of sustainable development . . . is – and is likely to remain – a central concern of policy-makers and transport is but one element of this'. The rapid growth in long-distance passenger transport and its dominance by aviation on the international scale, together with the rapid expansion in car ownership within countries poses many problems for policy-makers attempting to pursue sustainable transport options as discussed in Chapters 2 and 3. Moreover, the underlying demand for travel seems set to continue to expand, as forecasts in Chapter 1 indicated for tourist growth and development. The social and psychological demand for travel and holidays remains a potent force in developed countries. One result of the sustainability debate for policy-makers is that the environmental impact of transport is not just a local issue: it is also a global problem, as the case study of BA indicated. This is confirmed by Banister and Button (1992: 5), who argue that 'transport is an important contributor [to the sustainable development debate] at three levels (local, transboundary and global)'. Policy formulation therefore needs to be undertaken in a context where national governments develop transport policies and coordinate their responses at a transnational and global level through agencies such as the United Nations.

However, political commitment to formulating sustainable transport policies at national level may not be compatible with other political priorities. For example, many governments have facilitated the development of tourist transport infrastructure to foster regional tourism development (e.g. Ireland – see Page 1993b) and to encourage outbound travel (e.g. Japan). In fact Wahab and Pigram (1997: 285) argue that 'a growing trend in policy making in many countries is to leave tourism to private enterprise, and current economic conventional thinking supports the role of market mechanisms'. Sustainable transport policies may require a re-evaluation of these national transport policy objectives in relation to tourism, transport and the cost to the environment. In the context of the UK (see Banister 1992 for a discussion of national transport policies in the UK), D. Hall (1993) argues that sustainable transport is neglected in policy-making since the government's White Paper *This Common Inheritance* (Department of the Environment 1991) and accompanying policies have paid little attention to transport and the environment, whilst other subsequent reports such as the Royal Commission on Environmental Pollution have been influential in providing hard evidence of the need for changes but to date only lip service has been paid to such studies. The basic premise, as discussed earlier, is that governments do not wish to see sustainability compromising the economic activities and growth of the country given the global competition for investment and development. The provocative title of Docherty and Shaw's (2008) review, *Traffic Jam: Ten Years of Sustainable Transport in the UK*, epitomises many of the concerns over the ability of one government to make a number of modest successes in the field but also a number of significant failures in government policy. This is a major concern because, as the World Travel and Tourism Council et al. (1997: 63) argue, 'Transport is the lifeblood of the travel and tourism industry and failure to take action and improve performance in this area could result in harsh penalties for travel and tourism companies and increased costs for travellers.' To avoid such penalties, the report advocates that companies should:

● use well-maintained and modern transport technology, which may reduce emissions especially in the airline sector but also in other land- and sea-based transport sectors;
● assist less developed countries to acquire technology and skills to reduce environmental emissions from tourist transport;
● develop and manage car-share, cycle or walk-to-work schemes for employees and provide incentives for successful implementation;
● provide information for tourists to encourage the use of public transport, cycle ways and footpaths;
● work with government to implement measures to reduce congestion in air transport and in urban tourism environments;
● work with governments to achieve a greater integration in planning transport modes that not only reduce reliance on the private car, but also reduce energy consumption in linking tourists to onward destinations;
● use demand management tools to assist in reducing the need for polluting modes of transport in preference for more environmentally friendly modes of transport (modified and developed from World Travel and Tourism Council 1997: 63–4).

Whilst such suggestions are helpful, in the self-regulation era companies need to be given incentives as such measures require more commitment than conducting an environmental audit. It may be that individual countries need to formulate an environmentally based tourist transport strategy with which companies can comply. In fact, D. Hall (1993) suggests that a general environmental transport strategy needs to be formulated for the UK that is in contrast to the work of the commission for integrated transport. Although tourist transport is subsumed within the wider category of transport systems, Hall does suggest that coordinated action is needed in relation to:

● regulatory mechanisms (e.g. by setting a ceiling for emissions);
● financial mechanisms (e.g. incentives to favour energy-efficient modes of travel);
● the introduction of technological advances in transport to encourage the use of more fuel-efficient engines;
● the development of an integrated and coordinated planning response to transport where land use and transport planning should minimise the distance to travel for economic and leisure activities (e.g. work and shopping).

How does this affect international tourist travel? It would appear that the likely outcome of D. Hall's (1993) strategy would be the promotion of environmentally friendly modes of travel for tourists. Yet the real issue of existing tourists' travel habits is absent from the policy objectives as it is often perceived as an international problem rather than one nation's sole responsibility.

Implementation of sustainable tourist transport policies

A range of government transport policy responses to sustainability issues is discussed in Banister and Button (1992), and one recurrent theme is the need to adopt economic policies to price transport activities so that they reflect the environmental cost (e.g. Carlsson 2002). There is growing evidence that countries are now looking at controversial measures such as road pricing, which has been developed in Singapore. One approach widely used in developed countries is the differential pricing of petrol through the level of taxation it attracts, to reduce the use of leaded petrol and to increase the consumption of unleaded petrol. In this respect, concerted international government action is needed to reduce levels of pollution from transport, with certain countries taking a lead whilst others are forced to follow suit through international pressure. Yet as Button and Rothengatter (1992) acknowledge, the global nature of transport's impact on the environment is likely to intensify, as Chapter 9 will show. The implementation of sustainable transport policies needs to be accompanied by changes in the lifestyles of tourists so that they recognise the environmental degradation which their process of travel induces (see Dickinson and Robbins 2008).

Good practice in sustainable tourist transport

The real debate over achieving sustainable tourist transport options is usually focused on the outcome: can such options really be put into practice or do they remain a stated policy objective of environmental planning that is little more than a paper exercise? In other words, how do you go about changing traveller's behaviour? There are various examples of good practice cited in the tourism literature where transport is a core component of tourism planning, so that conservation and interpretation of the environment raises tourists' awareness of natural habitats and the need for a delicate balance to be achieved between tourist use and preservation. The Tarka Project in Devon is one well-established example where a tourism strategy has achieved these objectives (see Department of Employment/English Tourist Board 1991 and Charlton 1998 for more details). However, the reliance on public and private sector transport operators to implement sustainable tourism is questioned by Wood and House (1991, 1992). Although Wood and House (1991) acknowledge that transport operators need to pursue good environmental practices, they also advocate that the onus should be placed on the tourist. Their central argument is that tourists should 'environmentally audit themselves' before and during their holiday and this principle could also be applied to aspects of business travel, although critics have pointed to the idealistic nature of such an approach. However, the environmental audit is based on a number of simple questions:

● Why go on holiday? – consider your motivations and whether you really need to travel.
● Choose the right type of holiday to meet your needs.
● Consider travelling out of season to less well-known destinations.

- Choose the right travel method and tour operator after asking what the company is doing to minimise environmental impacts.
- Consider the form of transport you will use to get to the point of departure.
- Does the tour operator contract transport companies with new energy-efficient vehicles and aircraft or are they old, noisy and less efficient?
- Is public transport, cycling (Scottish Tourist Board 1991) or walking a feasible option when you are at the destination as opposed to hiring a car?

Wood and House's (1992) *The Good Tourist in France* illustrates how tourists can make their trip sensitive to the environment, especially in their use of transport. Wood and House (1992) provide information on 'how to get there' but more importantly they undertake detailed research on each region of France so that tourist travel in the destination area can be based on sustainable options (i.e. forms of transport that do not have major environmental impacts). They outline details of operators and locations where you can hire or purchase travel services based on:

- rail travel;
- bus/coach travel;
- car travel;
- boating;
- cycling;
- walking;
- riding,

as well as contact addresses of local groups that encourage and support sustainable development. But it still comes back to finding ways of changing individual's behaviour to promote sustainable travel for leisure and tourism. This is a point reiterated by Gronau and Kagermeier (2007), who focus on the importance of individual attitudes to stimulate sustainable travel behaviour and a modal shift away from car use which depends upon:

- the quality of the alternative transport offer (especially convenience and ease of access);
- the importance of targeted marketing of individuals and groups for suppliers and service providers to communicate with their audience (a feature also highlighted by Enoch and Potter 2003);
- the attractiveness of motorised options for travel, such as the car.

These points are developed a stage further by Guiver et al. (2006) in examining government policies in the UK towards encouraging a modal shift in leisure and tourist travel from the car. As Chapter 2 pointed out, in the UK around 31 per cent of trips made by car are for leisure purposes, and the trips are longer than other utility trips (e.g. commuting). Guiver et al. (2006) review the progress which employers have made in implementing travel plans to persuade employees to switch to non-car transport and the efficacy of such tools for the tourism sector, particularly visitor attractions in destinations. According to Transport 2000, some examples of best practice exist in tourism, with the Eden Project in Cornwall, UK (Plate 8.2) implementing a travel plan to help switch trips to public transport, with its integrated shuttle service to connect the attraction with other forms of travel such as train. In fact Guiver et al.'s (2007) review of the Hadrian's Wall visitor attraction in

Plate 8.2 A sustainable visitor attraction – the Eden Project, Cornwall: it has been viewed as a sustainable project in relation to its commitment to green transport solutions

Source: S.J. Page

Northern England, found that leisure travel is characterised by high levels of discretionary behaviour (i.e. flexibility around where and when to travel in contrast to utility trips like commuting). Adding to this was the fact that visitors from outside the locality will be unfamiliar with the destination and its transport infrastructure, making switching to public transport more problematic. Leisure and tourist travel also has more intrinsic value and so the trip may also be less utility focused and can be an attraction in its own right (Robbins 2008). This is pertinent in the case of the iconic London Routemaster bus, some of which were converted in the 1970s into open-top sightseeing vehicles, as illustrated in the promotional campaign by London Transport in 1979 (Plate 8.3). This highlights the importance of sustainable destination-oriented transport services as well as the significance of marketing these options, demonstrated by the innovative poster campaign by London Transport to launch the new Piccadilly Line extension to Heathrow Airport in the 1970s – fly the Tube (Plate 8.4).

Sustainable tourist-oriented transport services in destinations

According to Lumsdon (2006), destinations have been particularly concerned to seek to reduce car use for travel to and travel within destinations, especially National Parks due to their sensitive resource base (Cullinane 1997; Cullinane and Cullinane 1999; Page and Connell 2008). As Lumsdon (2006: 749) argues, this has focused on stabilising car use where possible and encouraging bus, rail, cycling and walking as alternative transport strategies. To do this, in the case of bus services, has required the redesign of services, particularly focused on enhancing the tourist experience so that intrinsic elements of fun and sightseeing are incorporated (Downward et al. 2006). Lumsdon's (2006: 760) study pointed to the 'substantial mismatch between the needs of the utilitarian and leisure user. Thus, the common practice of designing networks primarily for utility purposes and then marketing them to the tourist is not likely to be attractive unless adapted to their needs'. This

Plate 8.3 London Transport advertisement for sightseeing tours ©London Transport Museum

Source: Transport for London, London Transport Museum

Plate 8.4 London Transport advertisement for the new Heathrow Airport extension in the 1970s – Fly the Tube ©London Transport Museum

Source: Transport for London, London Transport Museum

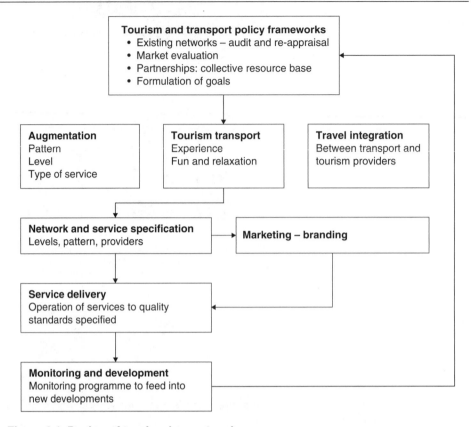

Figure 8.1 Design of tourism bus networks

Source: Reprinted from *Annals of Tourism Research,* 33, L. Lumsdon, 'Factors affecting the design of tourism bus services', p. 764, Copyright © 2006, with permission from Elsevier.

led Lumsdon (2006) to propose the model in Figure 8.1 for the development of bus networks for tourists in National Parks but it has wider relevance to tourist transport because:

● A market evaluation of demand is needed alongside a review of services (existing and potential) which might try and link into known tourist itineraries (see Page and Connell 2008 for more detail on this and Chapter 2). This also needs to be accompanied by building relationships with businesses along the routes and in destinations so as to get buy-in for the route and to help promote them as sustainable travel options.

● The services to be provided need to be tailored to tourist needs, following the notion of an augmented product as explained in Chapter 7 in relation to an airport product, so as to add value to the tourist experience and make it an attractive proposition. In some National Parks this has been accompanied by priority treatment or incentives for the visitor at the destination. However, this requires a major change in transport planning so that tourism is seen as a central feature of the planning process rather than a bolt-on to existing community-based transport planning, where routes need to be actively marketed to visitors.

● Part of the marketing process will require a form of branding to give the service a distinctive appeal to all stakeholders and to make it a essential experience for visitors.

- In transport planning terms, the service needs a definite set of standards of provision and regular monitoring alongside reviews of the service and its ability to deliver the objectives of sustainable tourist transport.

As Lumsdon's (2006) model shows, tourist travel cannot be treated in the same way as other daily utility trips.

Research on fragile tourism environments such as the Arctic has advocated the need for visitor codes of practice (Mason 1994) and Page (2003) questioned the efficacy of banning tourists from some sensitive environments to obviate the environmental impacts from the mode of transport used to travel there. Marsh and Staple (1995) reinforce such arguments in relation to using codes of practice as a voluntary measure. They argue that cruise ship passengers to such environments need to be educated about the impacts they can cause. This also extends to operators, as highlighted in 2007 by the sinking of *The Explorer* cruise ship in Antarctica. But this does not remove the very substantial environmental impacts of tourist travel to these environments and highlights the ethical dilemma in balancing business interests (i.e. profit) against environmental resources, and in most cases the tourism industry and its operators would appear to win the argument, especially when they utilise the services of academics to produce arguments and credibility for their business case. Nevertheless, tourism nearer to home also has an important but often overlooked role in sustainable transport and tourism policy debates.

According to M. Page (2006: 582)

Walking and cycling have often been seen as the 'Cinderellas' of transport policy, their needs often addressed only after the 'main' modes of private and public motorized transport have been considered . . . In the UK, which has more walking and cycling than the USA, but less than much of Europe, walking accounts for 25 per cent all journeys and 80 per cent of journeys under 1.5 km, with an average of 263 trips made per person per year predominantly on foot. Despite significant falls in usage over recent decades, more trips are made each year using cycle as the main mode (an average of 16 per person) than by surface rail (13) in the UK: However, the average distance traveled per person per year on foot has declined by 20 per cent over the last decade, and the distance cycled by 6 per cent.

Probably the most sustainable form of non-motorised transport that tourists can engage in is walking and cycling. Walking is a human necessity for the able-bodied to achieve mobility, to engage in work, social activities and non-work functions. Although the industrial and post-industrial period has seen a move towards more mechanised forms of transport such as the car, giving people a greater spatial reach and flexibility in travel patterns, walking remains a key activity in everyday life and as a tourism and leisure activity (Tolley 2003). Cycling is comparatively neglected in the tourism literature, being discussed in generic transport studies research and in leisure contexts. M. Page (2006) argues that there are a range of reasons why walking and cycling should be given a greater focus in transport planning and policy which are germane to tourism:

- Walking and cycling are energy efficient means of mobility, not reliant upon fossil fuels and not contributing to congestion.
- Walking and cycling are more sustainable travel options, contributing much less damage to the environment than motorised forms of travel, with only a limited

use of non-renewable resources and are socially equitable modes of transport because they are more widely available to many sections of the population than motorised forms.

● These modes of transport are less dangerous, with fewer accidents and injuries per distance travelled and are healthy forms of transport, since they involve physical activity and a reduction in the risk of cardiovascular disease and other diseases.

One of the underlying problems in policy terms which M. Page (2006) has identified is the reluctance of many governments to prioritise these two activities if it causes conflict with car users. Even so, significant progress has been made in the area of tourism and leisure, and Insight 8.2 focuses on cycling as a sustainable means of tourist transport with a relatively low impact on the environment.

INSIGHT 8.2

Cycling as an environmentally friendly form of tourist transport

According to Lumsdon (1996a), the market for recreational and tourist cycling can range from day trips to part-time casual usage through to long-distance touring holidays. The most likely is the occasional casual usage by tourists visiting a destination who may hire a cycle for a day (see Page 1998 for a discussion of such usage on the Norfolk Broads in the UK) or the more determined tourist who undertakes long-distance cycling holidays. Lumsdon (1996b: 5) defines cycle tourism as cycling which is 'part of or the primary activity of, a holiday trip . . . it falls within a categorisation of activity holidays'. Beyond the seminal study that incorporates cycling (Tolley 1990), there are a growing number of studies on cycle tourism (Beioley 1995; Ritchie 1997; Sustrans 1997; Schieven 1998), as the reviews by Lumsdon (2000) and Lumsdon et al. (2004) show. In a review of leisure cycling, Lumsdon (1997b) observes that the Department of Transport (1996) statistics suggest that up to 40 per cent of cycle journeys are for leisure purposes and, if other personal trips are included, up to half of all trips are for leisure. Yet as Lumsdon (2000) shows, the prevailing literature on cycle transport pays little attention to the leisure dimension (in which tourist use is subsumed). Even the UK's *National Cycling Strategy* (Department of Transport 1996) highlights the significance for non-leisure use, though, as Lumsdon (1997b: 115) shows, leisure is discussed:

> Leisure cycling has great potential for growth, it can be a stimulus to tourism, and it is a high-quality way to enjoy the countryside and a good way to introduce people to cycling for their everyday transport needs. To encourage leisure cycling there need to be small scale improvements, especially near where people live, followed by better signposting, marketing and information. Flagship leisure routes, using quiet roads or disused railway paths, can increase the profile and boost leisure cycling in town and countryside
> (Department of Transport 1996: 13 cited in Lumsdon 1997b: 115).

But who are the typical cycle tourists and what motivates them to use this form of transport? The Scottish Tourist Board's (1991) innovative study *Tourism Potential of Cycling and Cycle Routes in Scotland* indicated that cycling had grown in popularity as a recreational activity in the 1970s and 1980s, with the membership of the Cyclists' Touring Club growing each decade, as new infrastructure was provided. The Australian Cycling Resource Centre (*www.cyclingresourcecentre.org.au*), an initiative of the Australian National Cycling Strategy 2005–10 observed that cycle tourism was a niche market which involved cycling holidays, holidays where cycling was an activity undertaken, cycling day visits, cycling events

▶

(involving participation and spectators). The Countryside Commission's (1995) *The Market for Recreational Cycling in the Countryside* identified some of the main motivations for cycling, including:

● keeping fit;
● fun;
● fresh air;
● access to the countryside.

Lumsdon (1996b) simplifies the market segments involved in cycle tourism to include:

● *Holiday cyclists*, comprising couples, families or friends who seek a holiday where they can enjoy opportunities to cycle but not necessarily every day. They seek traffic-free routes and are free independent travellers not seeking a package holiday. Whilst they are likely to take their own bikes on holiday, a proportion will hire bikes and are likely to cycle 15–25 miles each day, a feature examined in New Zealand by Ritchie (1997).
● *Short-break cyclists*, who seek to escape and select packages that will provide local knowledge (with or without cycle hire) and comfortable accommodation. They are likely to travel in groups and will cycle 15–25 miles a day.
● *Day excursionists* are casual cyclists who undertake leisurely circular rides of 10–15 miles and are not prepared to travel long distances to visit attractions or facilities. They prefer quiet country lanes that are signposted. They tend to comprise 25–30 per cent of the market for cycling and are increasingly using their own bikes rather than hiring them and were dominant in the North Sea cycle route (Lumsdon et al. 2004).

However, Lumsdon (1996b) also provides a more detailed analysis of the market for cycling (Table 8.2). Lumsdon (1997b) cites the continued rise of adult cycle sales in Europe as evidence for the growth of interest in cycling for recreational purposes. Lumsdon (1997b) indicates that in Austria, Denmark, Germany, The Netherlands and Switzerland, tourism and recreational networks are now developing that also enhance the image of cycling. Similarly, Israel announced in 2005 a NIS20 million investment in cycle paths and trails to help promote tourism as well as healthy lifestyles. The Scottish Tourist Board (1991) outlines some of the constraints on and needs of cycling tourists in Scotland (Table 8.3). Table 8.3 highlights a range of needs and constraints, but probably the most important issue is that of appropriate infrastructure and opportunities for cycle tourism (Plate 8.5), an issue reviewed in New Zealand by Ritchie (1997). Although the Royal Commission on Environmental Pollution (HMSO 1994) identified the impact of other forms of tourist transport on the environment and the role of cycling as a mode of personal transport, it was recognised that it has limited environmental impact.

The UK's national cycle network
The Royal Commission on Environmental Pollution (HMSO 1994) recommended that cycle trips should be quadrupled to 10 per cent of all journeys in the UK by 2005. Wardman et al. (1997) review some of the measures needed to achieve the target of 10 per cent by 2005, using behavioural model-based research. This research has important implications for infrastructure provision. One of the important findings of the Royal Commission (HMSO 1994) was that local authorities in the UK should have a central role in meeting the 2005 targets and in infrastructure provision. In a planning context, this was to be achieved through the existing planning mechanism – the local authority's annual Transport Policies and Programme (TPP) submissions. Whilst the purpose of this was to improve the level of cycle use, it has implications for tourism, which can utilise any infrastructure put in place for residents and leisure users in local areas. It may also assist in reducing fatalities amongst cyclists (McClintock and Cleary 1996). A number of UK local authorities have appointed cycling officers, who have developed strategy documents for local use, but one of the principal catalysts for facilitating the development of a national cycle network in the UK is Sustrans.

▶

Table 8.2 Segmentation of the cycle market

Type	Profile/Nature	Use of infra-structure	Trend	Spend in local economy	Potential for growth
Day excursion					
1 Half-day and day Casual, home-based tourer	Occasional rider from home base. Singles and couples, age 24–45. Also families. Increasingly using cars to transport bikes. Cycling approx. 10–20 miles. Socio-economic spread	Using back lanes or recognised cycle trails	Sustained increase	Estimated little expenditure	High
2 Half-day and day Casual mountain biker	Occasional rider from home base. Age 24–45. Higher proportion of males and fewer families. Cycling approx. 10–20 miles. Increasingly using cars to transport bikes. Socioeconomic spread	Seeking off-road routes of easy to moderate terrain. Potential to saturate popular routes in National Parks, etc.	Estimated little expenditure	Sustained increase	Moderate/ High
3 Half-day and day Cycle hire	Infrequent rider – more likely not to have bicycle or use when on holiday. Wider age profile of 18–55. Families strong market. Cycling 10–20 miles. Socioeconomic spread	Seeking publicised off-road and quiet country routes or historic town trails, (such as Oxford, York)	Strong up-ward trend in late 1980s. Static at present with growth of cycling ownership	Spend in local facilities more	Low in most localities, high in key tourist zones, high potential in historic towns if traffic calming introduced
Holiday market					
4 'Do-it-yourself' cycle tourer	Organises day rides or cycling tours from an independent base. Keener cyclists, young people, hostellers increasingly using car to transport bikes. More likely to be professional/managerial. Use of guidebooks	Mainly country lanes	Slow growth	Higher spend in local facilities than day market	Moderate

Table 8.2 *(Continued)*

Type	Profile/Nature	Use of infra-structure	Trend	Spend in local economy	Potential for growth
5 'Do-it-yourself' mountain biker	As in (4) but seeking more strenuous routes. Fewer families and slightly younger age profile. Use of leaflets and guidebooks. More likely to be professional and managerial	Heavier impact on off-road routes in sensitive areas	Moderate and sustained growth	Not quite so high as tourers given nature of activity means less time at attractions, tea rooms, etc.	Moderate/High
6 Organised independent self-guided, cycling holidays/tourers, mountain bikes	Participants book an organised holiday (routes, accommodation, etc.) but travel as couple or group of friends. They are more likely to be professional and managerial	Companies offer towns, country lanes or mountain bike options. Impact minimal at present	Moderate growth	High spend in local economy	Moderate
7 Organised group cycling	As above, but participants make up a group for a guided tour	As above	Static	High spend in local economy	Low
8 Group holidays	As above, but booking made for group as part of multi-activity or cycling holiday. Incorporates day hire of cycle fleets by school and youth clubs	Usually minimal as leaders choose specific routes, e.g. through YHA	Static	High spend in local economy	
9 Club riders	Keen riders; knowledgeable, self-arranged, long-distance day rides and holidays	Mainly touring, minimal impact	Static	High spend on holidays	Low
10 Sports competitors	Mainstream cycling as a sporting activity	Heavy impact, e.g. Kellogg's Tour of Britain, Milk Race. Static	Limited potential for spend by spectators, media, back-up teams	Spectator sport	
11 Events riders	Cycling for charity mainly	As above	Increasing	Greater potential for spend	Moderate

Note: Estimates in the table are based on evaluation of cycle hire holiday company brochures, qualitative comment by companies.

Source: Copyright © L. Lumsdon (1996: 6–7), reproduced with permission.

Table 8.3 Characteristics and needs of different types of recreational and tourism cycling

Category of cycling activity	Characteristics of users	Main constraints	Main needs	Growth potential
Day touring	Home (or holiday-based) excursions for whole or part of day. Trips of 20 miles upwards. Mainly experienced users	Few constraints although safety reaching minor road network may be a problem. Design of roads a problem in some areas. Rail travel can be restricted	Safe town/country links, alternatives to busy main trunk roads. Improved access to rail network. Off-road cycleways	Medium/ High
Cycle hire	Casual cycling usually holiday-based for whole or part of day. Experienced and inexperienced cyclists	Lack of cycle hire centres in some areas. Problems of catering for diverse cycle types and sizes. Only a short season	Off-road cycles routes in popular areas. Improved publicity and marketing. Need for information on where to cycle	High
Cycle touring	Extended day touring requiring overnight accommodation. Mainly experienced cyclists with good knowledge	Difficulties of transporting cycles by rail. Need for alternative routes in town centres/ on trunk roads. Accommodation sometimes a problem and conflict with cars in the summer. Cycle repair shops infrequent	Good rural road network Varied accommodation from campsites to hostels. Some off-road routes. Improved tourist information	Medium/ High
Organised cycle touring	Extended day touring requiring overnight accommodation. Less experienced cyclists and overseas visitors	Difficulties of transporting cycles by rail	Need for back-up services. Quiet rural road network	High
Mountain bikes	Major growth; car-based and hire-based activity	Availability of off-highway facilities. Cost of bikes and hire. Lack of certainty about where cyclists can and cannot cycle. Conflict with other users	Extensive network of off-road routes, e.g. forestry tracks. Improved information on rights of access. Signed trails. Cycle hire	High

Source: Scottish Tourist Board (1991: 5)

Plate 8.5 The reuse and conversion of redundant railway lines like the scenic Killin-Strathyre route which is part of Route 7 on the NCN, provides a new resource for tourist and leisure cycling, in a linear resource separated from car traffic

Source: Dr Joanne Connell

Sustrans

Sustrans is a national sustainable transport and construction company operating as a charity, founded in 1977 'which designs and builds routes for people' (Lumsdon 1996b: 10). One of its early aims was to develop a 2000-mile national cycle network to link all the main urban centres in the UK, using a combination of traffic-calmed roads, cycle paths and disused railway lines and river/canal paths. This aim was realised in 1996 by a grant of £42.5 million from the Millennium Commission to create a 6500-mile route on the basis of Sustrans' original vision, which would become the UK's National Cycle Network (NCN). Initial estimates seem to indicate that the network has the potential to generate 100 million trips per annum, 45 million of which will be cycle based, of which 40 per cent will be leisure based (18–20 million journeys a year). Sustrans (1995) argued that the network has the potential to generate £150 million in tourist receipts annually and to create 3700 jobs. This has to be viewed within the context of cycle tourism, since Beioley (1995) estimated that it generates £535 million a year from leisure day trips, domestic holidays and overseas trips which is now estimated to be over £635 million a year.

In 2002 Sustrans (*www.sustrans.org.uk*) observed that by later that year 7000 miles of NCN would be open, with a target of 10,000 miles to be open by 2005. By June 2000, 4000 miles were open, by 2005 it had risen to 9000 miles and by 2007 this had reached 12,000 miles (of which 30 per cent was traffic free), which is a major achievement in sustainable transport terms. It outlined the objectives of the NCN, which were to:

1 be a catalyst for change in transport culture;
2 encourage a growth in cycling and walking for all types of trip;
3 Provide a high-quality cycle route in every town (Sustrans 2002).

▶

Sustrans (2002) also outlined the recent growth patterns in NCN usage and a number of monitoring studies are available on its website, which illustrate the modal shift it is inducing in recreational travel, with around 97 million trips made on the NCN in 2002 by cyclists and pedestrians: by 2006 this had risen to 338 million journeys. Sustrans (2002) also reviews the similarities and differences in the way it collates and measures usage versus the National Travel Survey.

The C2C (coast to coast) route illustrates the generative effect that new cycle routes can have on tourism. It is a 170-mile coast-to-coast route in Northern England (Lumsdon et al. 2004) that Sustrans (1995) estimates attracted 15,000 mainly cycle tourists in an economically marginal area (West Cumbria and the North Pennines) and contributed around £1.1 million a year to the local economy. Sustrans (1995) also has a pan-European perspective on cycle tourism, with its European Cycle Route Network. Some of the principal routes are:

- the 5000 km Atlantis route (Isle of Skye in Scotland to Cadiz in Spain);
- the 470 km Noordzee route (Den Helder in The Netherlands to Boulogne-sur-Mer in France).

Some commentators might view Sustrans' (1996) work as making a valid contribution to local Agenda 21 initiatives, with its close working relationship with UK local authorities. It is also argued that since almost 75 per cent of leisure trips on the National Cycle Network are expected to be new or switched from other modes of transport (Sustrans 1995), it can make an important contribution to sustainable tourism and community-based strategies for environmental management. In fact, the launch of the Kingfisher Trail in Northern Ireland in 1998, as part of the National Cycle Network, is evidence of how the network can also contribute to rural tourism initiatives. The Kingfisher Trail evolved from a desire to harness the popularity of the Shannon–Erne Waterway, using a network of quiet country roads. As a result the trail is marketed as an activity-based rural tourism corridor with cycling as the vital transport link. It is similar in many ways to the widely cited Tarka Trail in Devon (Charlton 1998), which is a 180-mile walking route with a 30-mile cycling route incorporated within it. According to Puncher and Buchler (2006) in North America, Canadians' participation in cycling is three times that of Americans due to various factors such as a safer cycling environment, higher costs of car ownership, better training programmes and a much more highly developed cycle infrastructure. Therefore, in the case of cycling tourism, cultural attitudes towards this form of tourist use are also important in shaping levels of participation. Therefore, how sustainable is cycle tourism?

According to Lumsdon (1996b: 10–12), there are three ways in which the National Cycle Network may contribute to sustainable tourism:

- By encouraging tourists to switch from cars to cycles at their destination, although it needs a cycle-friendly culture to implement such changes in tourist attitudes. Lumsdon (1996b) argues that this could reduce recreational car journeys at the destination by 20–30 per cent.
- By reducing car-based day excursions, particularly at honeypot attractions or sites near to resorts and urban areas. Lumsdon (1996b) views the National Cycle Network as offering tourists 'escape routes', as evidence from the UK's Forest of Dean and Wye Valley implies (Lumsdon and Speakman 1995).
- A growth in cycle-based holidays in both the short break and longer duration category by UK residents and overseas visitors.

Lumsdon (1996b) also provides a detailed study of:

- the market for cycling opportunities;
- the supply of cycling opportunities,

which is an excellent analysis of the marketing issues that need to be addressed to assist in promoting cycle tourism. However, Lumsdon (1997b: 126) views the development of a cycle ▶

culture as vital to encourage the growth of recreational and tourist cycling. Cycle tourism is able to make a valid contribution to sustainable tourism development, encouraging less environmentally damaging forms of activity to be developed. Cycle tourism is certainly beginning to assume a much higher profile in the UK but not necessarily in other countries as a matter of course. As Woodstock et al. (2007: 1085) observe:

> Cycling in many large African cities has collapsed. In Nairobi, the share of trips by bike fell from 20 per cent in the 1970s to 0.5 per cent in 2004. In many East Asian cities, although under threat, cycling retains a high modal share and the opportunity exists for this to be retained and expanded.

Woodstock et al. (2007) point to the negative associations which governments in developing countries have with cycling as a symbol of underdevelopment which raises many policy issues if this is to be promoted as a sustainable alternative for tourist and leisure use. So cycle tourism may be enjoying a growth in many developed countries as an 'active form of transport' which is non-polluting and able to complement walking as a means of sustainable transport. But how can one evaluate the extent to which sustainable tourism and tourist travel are realistic propositions in the new millennium?

The evaluation of sustainable principles for tourist transport

During the 1980s the concept of mass tourism came under greater scrutiny as a range of influential books questioned whether the economic benefits of tourism were adequately compensating for the increasing environmental impact (Krippendorf 1987). As Wahab and Pigram (1997: 287) argue:

> mass tourism, with the detriments it may inflict on the environment, has been severely criticised as a major environmental predator. It is therefore necessary that tourism adopts a different perspective that should be compatible, for all practical purposes, with the environment and the community in which it is active.

This close scrutiny of mass tourism was followed by the development of 'sustainable', 'responsible', 'green' or 'soft' tourism, growth management and a growing recognition that tourism cannot easily be managed where the carrying capacity (see Pigram 1992 for a discussion of this term) of the environment is greatly exceeded. Page (2003) has gone a stage further, arguing that tourism has an almost fatal impact on the environment if it is not managed, given its ability to take over and destroy localities. Transport is pivotal to this, since access and infrastructure provision are essential to the development of tourism in any locality as Prideaux (2000b) noted in relation to destination development needs. Marketing strategies with 'sustainable' in their title have emerged as a response to the industry interest in the environment (Middleton and Hawkins 1998), but all too often they have failed to grasp the carrying capacity and absolute numbers of tourists that different locations can support. Consequently, tourist transport has contributed to growing pressure on tourism environments by the provision of services to locations that have outgrown their carrying capacity. Therefore it is not surprising to find criticisms of the sustainable tourism movement, which has been manipulated by certain commercial interests as a new trend they can use to sell tourism and transport services to the more discerning and environmentally aware tourists. Yet as Wahab and Pigram (1997: 289) argue,

> Tourism sustainability is a byproduct of a multitude of factors that contribute to the successful present integration and future continuity of tourism at the macro

and micro level in the destination. As all socioeconomic, cultural, political and environmental factors are subject to change in time and space, sustainability is therefore a relative term and not an absolute fact.

Despite sustainability being a relative term, there is growing evidence that tour operators and tourist transport providers have seen the positive benefits of appearing to offer sustainable products, as discussed by Harris et al. (2002).

Wheeler (1992a) argues that it is difficult to visualise sustainable tourism as a realistic solution as the world is now experiencing 'megamass tourism', which is viewed as the next stage on from mass tourism. Although sustainable tourism (Wheeler 1992b) is emphasising small-scale individual tourist activities at specific locations and the substitution of the term 'traveller' for 'tourist', a rather elitist movement has developed, supported by a small number of more 'progressive tourists'. Herein lies a major contradiction in the sustainable debate: the insatiable demand for tourist travel is incompatible with the rather up-market, small-scale and expensive form of tourism that only a limited number of tourists are likely to be able to afford. As a concept, sustainability is still developing and is unlikely to lead to major changes in the tourist transport system, being more appropriate as a marketing tool for 'new tourism' (Poon 1989). In all probability, sustainable tourist travel cannot be achieved until the concept has been researched further and the fundamental problem of megamass tourism is addressed. What many studies fail to appreciate is that even when transport infrastructure exists to promote sustainable tourism, enticing tourists to use it needs to recognise the diverse range of groupings within the tourist population (Plate 8.6). For example, Dallen (2007) illustrated this

Plate 8.6 Competition on short sea crossings over the English Channel led to the introduction of hovercraft in the 1970s. The time savings achieved by this form of technology have been superseded by those offered by the Channel Tunnel. The hovercraft have been replaced by catamarans (see http://www.hoverspeed.co.uk)

Source: S.J. Page

with a study of the St Ives Bay line in Cornwall which identified a range of user groups (i.e. the regular road users, public transport reliants and train enjoyers) as well as an equally diverse group of non-users (i.e. anti-rail riders and content car drivers).

Although the design of resort areas and human-made tourist attractions able to meet the demands of mega-mass tourism may be able to deal with a high through-put of tourists in a restricted geographical area (e.g. Disneyland) there will be a growing demand for tourist transport to reach these artificial and synthetic tourism environments. This may have the temporary effect of reducing pressure on other more fragile tourism environments whilst the needs of tourists are met by these staged tourist attractions. But the real prospect of environmental damage will emerge if mass tourism trends are based on the search for a more authentic experience (MacCannel 1976). The fundamental problem of environmental impacts is likely to remain and future technological advances may offer a lifeline for the environment if staged tourism can be developed further for the mass tourist, using new ideas such as 'virtual reality' to meet the tourists' need for entertainment, excitement and pleasure.

As tourist transport operations are usually characterised by private sector ventures, voluntary agreements have typically been the basis for environmental management policies. Government organisations can assist in this process by ensuring that legislation is in place to encourage a reduction in environmental pollution from transport. Government commitment to sustainable transport policies in developed countries seems to have foundered as the decision to deregulate transport is unlikely to see such options implemented, given the reliance on profitability in tourist transport provision rather than environmental issues. Pigram (1992) argues that, in the process of policy formulation and implementation of sustainable tourism options, it is important to recognise the role of major decision-makers such as transport operators in influencing the long-term success of such schemes. Even so, Wahab and Pigram (1997: 289) identify a very worrying trend that may militate against developing sustainable tourist transport systems because:

> a growing trend in policy making in many countries is to leave tourism to private enterprise, and current economic conventional thinking supports the role of market mechanisms, the pendulum shows signs of change in theory and in application . . . countries such as Canada and the United States have reduced or abolished the role of the public sector in national tourism administration in favour of private enterprise. State tourism bodies remain as promotion agencies at the macro level.

In other words, those public sector bodies able to understand and make the links between transport, tourism and sustainability at a policy-making level are no longer able to fulfil that role. This is certainly the case in New Zealand in relation to sustainable tourism (Page and Thorn 1997, 2002) where the local authorities are charged with dealing with the implications of tourism development.

Ultimately, the tourists' desire for international and domestic travel may need to be the focus of long-term educational strategies to identify some of the problems travel, tourism and transport pose for the environment. Codes of practice may assist in that respect in all but the most sensitive environments, such as Antarctica where tourism should be prohibited, though this has ethical and human rights implications given the anthropocentric paradigm that dominates philosophical stances on tourism development (see Page and Dowling 2002 for more detail). It would seem that the economists with their cost–benefit analysis (CBA) of environmental resources miss a fundamental point here: charging for environmental damage is of little use if the resource is irreparably damaged. Whatever price you place on a resource, it cannot be recreated from its natural state and so once it is lost it has gone, as have many species of wildlife. This is the problem with using abstract tools such as CBA to address real-world situations where premises on resource use make the assumption that this generation may be prepared to trade a loss of resource at a price, but that does not really accommodate more ecocentric views where sustainability assumes you are in stewardship of the resources for future generations rather than an anthropocentric view that considers resources are ripe for use and can be degraded for human use.

One radical long-term solution may be to increase the cost of travel through a tourist carbon tax (see Tol 2007 for a discussion of the potential impact of such a tax on tourist destinations and the geography of tourist travel) and introduce government regulations to restrict the demand in order to reduce the impact on the environment. Yet there are many political and ethical objections to such an approach, since it is reminiscent of the situation in some Eastern bloc countries before the collapse of communist rule, and it would be tantamount to an infringement of individual freedom in democratic societies. Increasing the cost and restricting the opportunity to travel has other social implications because it may run contrary to the objectives of social tourism, which aims to make travel and holidays accessible to all social groups. A partnership approach between responsible transport and tour operators and governments committed to making tourists more aware of their own actions may be one way forward as case studies of good practice reported in the literature show. Instead of tourist travel being regulated, tourists should be encouraged to exercise greater restraint in their demand for travel, though it is evident that there is no short-term solution to preventing the environmental impact of tourist transport systems.

● ● ● ● Summary

The human effects and environmental consequences of tourist transport have led to a greater awareness of how tourist transport systems interact with the human and physical environment. The concept of 'sustainable tourism has burdened itself with incompatible conflicting objectives – small scale sensitivity and limited numbers to be achieved in tandem with economic viability and significant income and employment impacts' (Wheeler 1991: 95). In other words, sustainable tourism's implicit assumption that smaller-scale tourist activities will result from such developments could pose threats to the economic threshold at which tourist travel services are provided. If sustainable tourism were viewed as the only legitimate form of tourism it would have unrealistic social impacts by limiting travel to a privileged minority. This

> appeases the guilt of the thinking tourist while simultaneously providing the holiday experience they or we want. The industry is happy because the more discerning (and expensive) range of market can be catered for by legitimately opening up new areas to tourism (Wheeler 1991: 96).

This highlights the rather superficial nature of the sustainability concept (Wheeler 1994), which does not really offer any long-term solutions to the tourist and the transport provider because it fails to address the global impact of tourism, which is too large a problem for governments and transport operators to address in isolation. Even if tourist transport providers and tour operators withdrew from carrying tourists to sensitive environments, the competitive nature of tourist transport provision in market economies would mean that another rival operator, with less interest in environmental issues, might enter the market. Environmental auditing and environmental impact assessment are moving the transport business towards considering the consequences of transporting tourists to different environments (see Martin-Cejas and Sánchez 2009), but the reliance on private sector cooperation in minimising their impact may only result in action:

> where the benefits [of environmental auditing] are largely enjoyed by third parties or the general public . . . [but] if consumers' current search for quality embraces an increasing environmental awareness, the tourism industry would face demand-led pressure to adopt environmental auditing more widely (Goodall 1992: 73).

Even so, the growing interest in alternative modes of transport, such as cycling, and government commitment to funding infrastructure such as the National Cycle Network, are encouraging signs for more sustainable forms of tourism transport. Hull (2007) points to a growing shift towards a new realism in transport policy away from the predict and provide approach that typified the UK for road travel, to one where sustainable mobility is a more visible stance. But the reality of developing mass sustainable transit systems for tourist and non-tourist use still remain a way off in the UK, as Hull (2007) acknowledges. Nykist and Whitmarsh (2008) argue that what is needed is a radical systemic innovation to achieve a transition to a sustainable mobility system. But as Doll and Wietschel (2008: 4069) argue, 'transport systems perform vital societal functions, but in their present state cannot be "sustainable". Particular concerns in this respect include climate change, local air emissions, noise congestion and accidents'. The next chapter now turns to the pivotal issues facing the future development and operation of tourist transport – climate change and the long-term reliance on oil as a form of energy for transport systems. These issues may well force a more rapid change, as a major culture shift is needed in tourists' and transport providers' attitudes, so that more environmentally sensitive and sustainable tourist activities are promoted.

Questions

1 How would you classify the environmental impacts of tourist transport?

2 What is sustainability? How has it been used by tourist transport operators to market their services?

3 Is cycling the only sustainable form of tourist transport with a minimal impact on the environment?

4 What is an environmental audit? How can it help a tourist transport operator to assess impacts on the environment?

Further reading

The literature on sustainability and tourism has expanded rapidly since the 1990s. An interesting array of articles can be found in:

Page, S. J. and Connell, J. (eds) (2008) *Sustainable Tourism*, Routledge: London.

For a focus on transport, see:

Docherty, I. and Shaw, J. (2003) *A New Deal for Transport? The UK's Struggle with the Sustainable Transport Agenda*, Oxford: Blackwell, which is a good overview of the situation in the UK into the new millennium when read in conjunction with:.
Root, A. (ed.) (2003) *Delivering Sustainable Transport*, Oxford: Pergamon.

In terms of constraints on development, the case of Cuba with its interesting political history offers many lessons for other countries seeking to develop a sustainable transport system:

Enoch, M., Warren, J., Valdes Ríos, H. and Henríquez Menoyo (2004) 'The effect of economic restrictions on transport policies in Cuba', *Transport Policy*, 11(1): 67–76.

A good review of the use of environmental reports in the transport sector can be found in the following article, which argues that for a full understanding of omissions generated by transport integrated supply chain backcasting is needed to understand the impact of carbon dioxide:

Roth, A. and Kaberger, T. (2002) 'Making transport systems sustainable', *Journal of Cleaner Production*, 10(4): 361–71.
See Docherty, I., Shaw, J. and Gather, M. (2004) 'State intervention in contemporary transport', *Journal of Transport Geography*, 12(4): 257–64 for a good discussion of why the state needs to intervene in transport provision especially in relation to environmental reasons.
One interesting article on whether rail as a green travel option is enjoying a renaissance can be found in Shaw, J., Walton, W and Farrington, J. (2003) 'Assessing the potential for a "railway renaissance" in Great Britain', *Geoforum*, 34(2): 141–56.

Also see the text of the Kyoto Protocol on the United Nations Framework Convention on Climate Change (UNFCC) *http://www.unfcc.int*. A good overview of the wide-ranging environmental impacts of aviation can be found in:

Janic, M. (1999) 'Aviation and externalities: The accomplishments and problems', *Transportation Research D*, 4(3): 159–80.

Websites

The range of sites with material of interest is expanding rapidly, but the following offer a range of commercial, charitable and critical perspectives on sustainability and the role of transport.
On the development of sustainable transport and cycling see: www.sustrans.org.uk.
A critical analysis of tourism can be found at the site developed by Tourism Concern, a charity set up to promote awareness of the impact of tourism on people and their environments: www.gn.apc.org/tourismconcern
The role of lobby groups such as Transport 2000 (www.transport2000.org.uk), the Aviation Environment Federation, (www.aef.org.uk), and other groups are a useful critical perspective on policy and environmental impacts of tourism and transport.

9

Global challenges for tourism and transport: how will climate change and energy affect the future of tourist travel?

Susanne Becken, Lincoln University, New Zealand

Introduction

In the previous chapter, the impacts and consequences of transport and tourism were analysed, focusing on the environmental dimension. What should be clear from Chapter 8 is that much of the rhetoric and debate on tourist transport since the 1970s has been around the use of tools and techniques which appear to ameliorate or modify the impact of transport on the environment, such as environmental assessment and environmental auditing. However, by the 1990s it was becoming apparent from scientific studies of the impact of transport, and in particular aviation, on the environment that carbon dioxide emissions (CO_2) were having a major global environmental impact through global warming. It became clear that the case for simply making minor modifications to the way transport affects the environment was no longer acceptable. Furthermore, debates within tourism research on the long-term sustainability of continued growth in tourism globally highlighted additional pressure for governments and international organisations to re-look at the future growth agendas for transport and tourism.

This chapter builds upon the issues identified in Chapter 8, highlighting the need for a more strategic view of the future challenges which will shape tourist travel, and thereby the demand and supply of tourist transport. Key challenges identified are climate change and the future availability of oil as a key energy source for most forms of tourist transport. These two issues pose a profound challenge for future tourist travel – will it be dominated by continued growth and development based on previous experience or will we see a greater degree of constraint? This key proposition is examined in this chapter and a key feature underpinning any analysis of the future of tourist travel is an understanding of tourism growth and the demands it poses for economies.

Global tourism: challenges and imbalances

As discussed in Chapters 1 and 4, tourism has grown substantially in the past few decades. There are now almost 10 billion arrivals worldwide according to UN-WTO statistics (Scott et al. 2007). About half of these arrivals are from same-day visitors (4 billion domestic and 1 billion international) and the other half is from overnight

Table 9.1 Tourist volumes worldwide broken down by domestic and international tourism and by same-day and overnight visitors

Arrivals (billions)	Total	Domestic	International
Same-day	5.0	4.0	1.0
Over land/water	5.0	4.0	0.99
By air	0.05	0.04	0.01
Overnight	4.9	4.0	0.8
Over land/water	3.93	3.52	0.41
By air	0.82	0.48	0.34

Source: Modified from Scott et al. 2008. © UNWTO, 9284401709

arrivals (tourists) (4 billion domestic and 800 million international) (Table 9.1). Almost all same-day trips and about 82 per cent of overnight trips are by land transport, mostly by car. The largest proportion of air travel is amongst international overnight tourists (41 per cent).

As a result of strong historic growth, an increasing number of destinations have become increasingly dependent on tourism. So far, these have 'benefited particularly from a prolonged period of global and national economic growth, falling real transport prices and the rise of new tourism markets' (OECD 2008: 5). This has combined with the underlying concern of the OECD about globalisation and how these destinations will compete. Most tourism forecasts still assume further growth, and tourist destinations plan and invest accordingly (e.g. UNWTO 2001; Boeing 2005; New Zealand Ministry of Tourism 2008). Investments include major infrastructure projects that extend current transportation systems and networks as discussed in Chapter 7. Airport extensions around the world (e.g. a fifth terminal at London Heathrow and terminal extensions in New York (JFK), London Stansted, Birmingham, Dubai, Perth, and Auckland, as well as new runways planned in Atlanta, Frankfurt and Brisbane) are examples of major capital investment in the tourism transport system to expand tourism. At the same time, tourism is facing an increasing number of challenges, such as 'imbalances in the international economy, highly volatile energy prices, the threat of climate change, and environmental concerns' (OECD 2008: 5). Two of the key challenges, namely man-made climate change and the availability of (affordable) liquid fuels, are closely linked to the transport sector, and therefore to tourist travel. One of the most prominent issues affecting tourist transport is global climate change.

●●●● Global climate change

Climate change and transport

The Intergovernmental Panel on Climate Change (IPCC) defines climate change as

> Change in the state of the climate than can be identified (e.g. using statistical tests) by changes in the mean and/or the variability of its properties, and that persists for an extended period, typically decades or longer. Climate change may be due to natural internal processes or external forcings, or to persistent anthropogenic changes in the composition of the atmosphere or in land use.

This means that man (i.e. anthropogenic influences) can substantially alter the current climate by changing the atmosphere. This man-made 'change' was confirmed in the Fourth Assessment Report of the IPCC (2007), which reported that anthropogenic greenhouse gas (GHG) emissions have increased by 70 per cent between 1970 and 2004. Carbon dioxide (CO_2) is the most important GHG, making up 77 per cent of all anthropogenic GHG emissions in 2004. The concentrations of CO_2 have risen by 100 parts per million (ppm) since pre-industrial times, reaching 379 ppm in 2005. When all other GHGs (e.g. methane and nitrous oxide) are considered, the concentration of CO_2-equivalents has reached 455 ppm (IPCC 2007: 27).

Transport is a key driver of global energy demand and CO_2 emissions (about one-quarter) (OECD 2001), and it is forecast that transport-related carbon dioxide emissions will increase by up to 80 per cent by 2030 compared with 2002 (IPCC 2007). Clearly, to mitigate the impacts humans have on the global climate, measures will have to be implemented in the transport sector to reduce such growth in emissions and reverse current trends. Reducing emissions from transport, however, has proven to be extremely challenging. One reason for this is that mobility and car ownership are commonly associated with substantial psychological and social benefits (Moriarty and Honnery 2008). Due to the importance of personal mobility in modern society, most mitigation measures are focused on new technologies or traffic management rather than the reduction of demand (Table 9.2). A number of studies have shown, however, that technological changes alone will be insufficient to reduce emissions to required levels, and more fundamental transformations are required for transport to make a real contribution to global climate change mitigation (Kwon 2005; Bristow et al. 2008; Moriarty and Honnery in press).

Aviation emissions are even more difficult to address than those related to land transport, because there is no practical alternative to fully replace fossil fuel in the near future. Moreover, aircraft are operated for at least 30 years and the sector has been growing so fast that any efficiency gains were more than compensated by increased volumes. Potential for improving efficiency lies in aircraft design and engine technology (ATAG 2005; Peeters et al. 2006), air traffic management (Penner et al. 1999), optimising cruise altitude and speed (Williams et al. 2003; DeRudder et al. 2005) and the use of biofuels (Wardle 2003; Marsh 2008). For example, in February 2008 Virgin Atlantic and GE Aviation's trial of a biofuel blend of babassu (from the seeds of the babassu palm) and coconut oil led to a flight within Europe, illustrating the prospects of alternative fuel sources for aviation.

Table 9.2 Key mitigation technologies and practices for the transport sector (non-technological measures such as lifestyle changes are not included)

Mitigation technologies/practices currently available	Mitigation technologies/practices available by 2030
More fuel efficient vehicles, hybrid vehicles, cleaner diesel vehicles, biofuels, modal shifts from road transport to rail and public transport systems, non-motorised transport (cycling, walking), land use and transport planning.	Second generation biofuels, higher efficiency aircraft, advanced electric and hybrid vehicles with more powerful and reliable batteries.

Source: IPCC 2007: 10

Table 9.3 Overview of tourism transport worldwide

	Total-	Same-day (domestic and international)	Overnight: domestic	Overnight: international
Passenger-km (billion)	9,147	1,237	4,832	3,077
Average return distance (km)	938	247	1,208	4,102
Total CO_2 (Mt)	982	133	479	371
CO_2 per trip (kg)	101	27	120	494

Source: Modified from Scott et al. 2008. © UNWTO, 9284401709

Transport is an integral component of tourism and vice versa (Gössling et al. 2005). A study of European tourist transport (Peeters et al. 2004) showed that transport emissions for domestic and international tourism amounted to 250 Mt CO_2 in 2002 (relating to the then EU25 plus Norway and Switzerland). This amount is equivalent to 9 per cent of all CO_2 emissions in Europe in the same year. The same study forecast growth of 122 per cent between 2000 and 2020, with an increase in CO_2 emissions of 85 per cent. One way of trying to understand the impact of the transport and tourism sector's impact on emissions is by examining their carbon footprint (CF). The CF is a measure of a business or sector's contribution to global warming in terms of GHG emitted, either directly or indirectly. The CF of tourism has recently been assessed for New Zealand (Becken 2008) and Australia (Forsyth et al. 2008), highlighting similarly significant contributions by tourist transport in terms of CO_2 emissions.

A recent study commissioned by the UN-WTO shows that CO_2 emissions from global tourism transport are in the order of 981 Mt CO_2 (Scott et al. 2008). More than half (52 per cent) of these are estimated to be caused by air travel, while 43 per cent of emissions are from cars, and 5 per cent from other transport modes (i.e. coach, rail and water borne). Of the 981 Mt CO_2, 44 per cent are from international tourism transport, with the remainder being related to domestic travel (Table 9.3). The same study estimated tourism's overall contribution to global CO_2 emissions to be in the order of 1302 Mt CO_2 or 5 per cent of global emissions. Transport therefore constitutes 75 per cent of tourism's emissions, highlighting its central role in any measures to reduce emissions in tourism.

Implications for tourist transport?

The issue of climate change will affect tourism transport in three ways. First, tourists who become increasingly aware of the climate effects of their travel may choose to alter their holiday behaviour, for example by visiting different destinations, changing transport modes or travelling less often (but potentially staying longer). Second, climate change policies will increase the cost of tourist transport and as a result the relative attractiveness of certain transport modes and tourist destinations might change. Tourist volumes overall might reduce as well. Finally, wider socioeconomic changes are likely to affect travel behaviour, in relation to both business and holiday travel. Some of these changes are not well understood, but it seems very plausible that tourism as a social phenomenon will not escape wider changes imposed by climate change. These three impacts will now be discussed in more detail.

Changing perceptions of travel

With an increasing acceptance of climate change as a major problem and with more information on how tourism contributes to climate change, tourism has been challenged to improve its environmental performance. Media attention has increased tourists' awareness of climate change, in particular in relation to air travel (Addley 2006). An article in *The Guardian Weekly*, for example, discussed the increasing 'hypermobility' associated with cheap flights in Europe under the heading 'Addressing binge flying is vital for the climate' (Hastings 2007). Hypermobility in a tourism context can be defined as mobility that is frequent and often long distance, is a result of the growing network of airports, perceived cheap fares, better education, higher income, and more leisure time, including opportunities to leave work for longer periods (Becken and Hay 2007). The availability of cheap flights has certainly increased hypermobility amongst a growing part of society.

The 2007 Lonely Planet Annual Travellers Pulse Survey (24,500 participants) (Lonely Planet 2007) indicated that the majority of travellers are worried about carbon emissions from flying. Only 7 per cent of respondents said that they did not think aircraft carbon emissions were a concern. Recent market research in Australia and New Zealand also indicated that tourists are concerned about the environment and the impacts of their travel (Instinct and Reason 2008; Tourism New Zealand 2008).

Related to an increased environmental awareness is the willingness to pay for more environmentally friendly products and carbon compensation (or 'offsetting') schemes. Carbon compensation means that the amount of GHG produced by a tourist is reduced elsewhere, where mitigation is cheaper than reducing emissions at the activity in question. As a result, compensating schemes are set up to achieve an optimal relationship between climate protection and costs. In a recent study of Canadian travellers, 7 out of 10 reported that they would pay $10 or more for every $1000 spent on airfares. While some airlines record very limited uptake of their offsetting schemes (in the order of 1 per cent), Jetstar Australia reports an uptake by 12 per cent of its passengers (Travelmole.com, 2008). One reason for this might be the convenient online booking procedure for both flights and carbon credits.

Notwithstanding tourists' awareness and willingness to contribute financially, it remains questionable to what extent tourists really engage in pro-environmental behaviour (either in the form of offsetting or changing travel practices). A recent DEFRA study (2007) on British citizens' responses to sustainable tourism and leisure found that tourists did not consider the environment when making travel-related decisions. They also felt that environmental initiatives should not limit their ability to engage in holidaymaking. Similar responses were found amongst tourists in New Zealand (Becken 2007), although tourists also indicated that at some point changes to travel will be necessary to combat climate change.

This is very indicative of what Instinct and Reason (2008) observed, namely that the present risk of tourists changing their travel behaviour is comparatively low, but a significant number of tourists are 'sitting on the fence' and could very soon change their opinion and discontinue long-distance travel. This would severely affect a wide range of tourist destinations, amongst others island destinations and those in the Southern Hemisphere. If and when a 'tipping point' is reached will depend on a number of factors, amongst others the speed and success of international negotiations (e.g. the annual United Nations Framework Convention on Climate Change summits, such as the one in Bali in 2007) and the discourse of mainstream media.

Travel costs

Global efforts to curb CO_2 emissions will affect tourism in a number of ways. The main policy instruments for climate change mitigation include (after IPCC 2007):

- regulations and standards (e.g. vehicle emission standards)
- taxes and charges (e.g. Air Passenger Duty in the UK and carbon taxes in various European countries);
- tradable permits (as in the European Emissions Trading Scheme);
- voluntary agreements and schemes (e.g. the Tour Operators Initiative, environmental certification);
- subsidies and incentives (e.g. energy efficiency grants or adjustment of existing subsidies such as in the airline industry);
- information and education (e.g. undertaken by the UN-WTO for its member states).

All of the above policy responses have relevance for tourism, but the economic instruments are likely to have the largest impact, as they will affect the affordability of tourist transport. They will also affect the transport systems: low-fare carriers, for instance, are likely to belong to the 'losers' of climate change measures, as their business model is largely built on high-volume, low-yield travellers and very large growth rates as discussed in more detail in Chapter 2. In other words, economic measures will make the low-cost options less desirable.

The international aviation sector is of particular interest to mitigation schemes due to its large contribution to global GHG emissions (about 3 per cent in 1992; Penner et al. 1999). Several economic instruments to achieve reductions in emissions have been discussed (e.g. German Advisory Council on Global Change 2002). A charge on tickets is a straightforward option to internalise the climate-change costs of aviation. Overall, however, demand is likely to continue to grow and a ticket charge would not provide an incentive for airlines to reduce their emissions. In contrast, emission charges would be targeted at the source of impact and theoretically it is possible to charge according to the climate effect of a particular flight. Practically, the airline industry perceives that it is challenging to estimate the emissions for each flight, especially in relation to non-CO_2 emissions.

Currently, Australia and New Zealand are working on including aviation in their Emissions Trading Schemes, following the European Union's lead in 2008 with its planned introduction by 2011. There are several practical issues that remain to be solved, for example deriving a fair way for allocating emission certificates to existing airlines and procedures for allocation to new entrants (Wit et al. 2005). Depending on the specific mechanisms, it seems likely that inclusion of aviation in emissions trading would allow the sector continued growth, with GHG savings made elsewhere. In the case of the UK, the currently unaccounted emissions from international air travel would make up 22 per cent, 39 per cent or 67 per cent of the national CO_2 budget in 2050 (depending on different growth rates of air travel at 3 per cent, 4 per cent or 5 per cent), when added to national GHG accounts (Lee et al. 2005). This poses issues of fairness between aviation and other economic sectors.

The costs of buying carbon credits are likely to be passed on fully or to some degree to passengers. Higher airfares will lead to reduced demand and both airlines and tourist destinations have to prepare for decreases in tourist arrivals. As Njegovan (2006) illustrated ticket prices are not necessarily the main or only driver for air travel, but that strong cross-elasticities exist with domestic leisure prices and destination cost levels. For example, if prices at the destination increase substantially, demand for this particular destination is likely to reduce. Similarly, if prices in tourists' home country are high, travellers are less likely to go on holiday (Jensen 1998). These findings imply that the effectiveness of carbon charges for air travel need to be assessed in a wider context of price indices and also exchange rates.

The implications of higher travel costs are discussed in more detail in the sections on tourism and global oil prices below.

Wider socioeconomic changes

Tourism depends on economic prosperity and sociopolitical stability, and the UN-WTO recognises that socioeconomic changes due to climate change are likely to have substantial impacts on how people travel (Scott et al. 2008). Following the Stern Review (2006), in the long term the negative impact of climate change on global economic growth will reduce the discretionary income available to consumers, and tourism is likely to face some challenges for future growth or even maintaining existing levels of activity. Tourists are also averse to political instability and social unrest and the forecast climate change-related problems in hotspots, such as Sub-Saharan Africa, Southern Africa, Caribbean, Southeast Asia, and Bangladesh–India–Pakistan, are likely to negatively affect tourism demand. It is also conceivable that climate change will affect the way people organise their lives, ways they do business, priorities they set and the importance and style of holidays to be taken. At present, there is limited understanding of how climate change impacts will interact with, or influence some of these longer term social and market trends. Demographic changes, increasing travel safety and health concerns, increased environmental and cultural awareness, advances in information and transportation technology, and shifts toward shorter and more frequent holidays are likely to play some role (Scott et al. 2008). Set against these wider socioeconomic factors are concerns about the future availability of oil as an energy source for tourist transport as initially raised in Chapter 1, and which is now discussed in more detail here.

Availability of oil

As Chapter 1 discussed, cheap oil has been a major driver of the growth of international tourism in the twentieth century but there are now concerns that the era of cheap oil has ended. This entire issue of oil availability has been substantially neglected in tourism research until comparatively recently (Farrell and Brandt 2006; Becken 2008b) despite its critical role in facilitating tourism growth. What these studies indicate is that the tourism sector needs to begin to understand the implications of the end of cheap oil and the energy options available in the medium to long term.

The end of 'cheap oil'

Oil and gas make up 35 per cent and 21 per cent of worldwide energy use, respectively; with coal adding another 25 per cent (IEA 2006). Hence, oil is the most important energy source in many economies and it is essential for transportation, with about 95 per cent of vehicles powered by petroleum fuels (IPCC 2007). The current rate of global oil consumption is 86.1 million barrels per day (in 2007) and this is forecast to increase to 116 million barrels per day in 2030 (IEA 2008).

The question of how much oil there is on Earth has been analysed widely. Estimates vary depending on the assumptions made, but generally the so-called 'ultimate reserves' are believed to range between a total of 2000 to 3000 billion barrels (e.g. Duncan and Youngquist 1999; Hirsch 2005). Even more important are attempts to estimate how much oil there is left. Optimistic sources estimate this to be in the order of 1255 billion barrels, but there are good arguments why the remaining reserves could be as low as 854 billion barrels (Bentley 2002; Greene et al. 2006; Energy Watch Group 2007). The difference between those figures has been referred to as 'paper barrels'. These are thought to be artificially created on paper either by oil companies or oil-exporting countries for political reasons, such as increasing bargaining power within OPEC or improving shareholder values (Bell et al. 2008).

In its 'Outlook for oil and jet fuel prices', IATA (2008a) stated that there is no need to be concerned about 'peak oil', as 'known reserves would last a further 44 years at current rates of consumption with no further discoveries'. It is correct to assume that given a constant consumption of about 86 million barrels per day and an assumed ultimate reserve of 1255 billion barrels, production would theoretically last 40 years. If the reserve is assumed to be more around the 800 billion barrel mark, this would reduce to 27 years. In both scenarios, it is unrealistic to assume that demand will stay constant, as any increase in demand will reduce the remaining time of oil availability substantially. Furthermore, it is also technically impossible to maintain constant production rates until the last drop of oil has been exploited. A more realistic picture is that demand will increase faster than supply, and at some point (the peak of production) supply will decrease at an unknown rate, thereby increasing the gap between demand and supply even further. This point of 'peaking' will only be known with hindsight. However, already, in 2007 the global demand for oil was larger than production in the same year (86.1 mb/d compared with 85.6 mb/d production; IEA 2008), indicating that the peak may have been reached or even passed. It appears that the above statement by IATA (2008a) confirms the imminence of peak oil and the likelihood of drastically increasing prices and eventually shortages of oil.

The sharpness of a decline in global production after peak oil depends on many factors. One important aspect is the rate of discovery of new fields. Skrebowski (cited in Wilkinson 2007) gives the following summary of global resources: of 18 super giant fields (largely in the Middle East), 12 are in decline, 5 have some potential for growth and 1 is undeveloped. The largest 120 fields worldwide provide 50 per cent of production, and 70 per cent of production comes from fields that are more than 30 years old. Recent discoveries have been small and infrequent. The average size of newly discovered fields is only 10 billion barrels, well short of annual oil consumption and down from an average field size of new discoveries of 527 million barrels in the period 1960–70 (Energy Watch Group 2007). As Hirsch (2005) commented, we are consuming oil that was discovered decades ago.

With more and more pressure on existing oil reserves, interest in 'unconventional' oil resources has increased. As opposed to 'conventional oil' which is easily accessible with present technologies and economic parameters, the viability of unconventional oil exploration relies on technological advances and higher oil prices. The most promising new resources are oil sands (mainly in Canada), extra heavy oil (Venezuela) and oil shales (USA) (Greene et al. 2006). Other options for mitigating the risk of oil depletion are coal liquefaction (already undertaken on a large scale in South Africa) and gas-to-liquids processes (Hirsch 2005). The extraction from non-conventional resources is extremely energy intensive and results in large amounts of greenhouse gas emissions. As Farrell and Brandt (2006: 4) point out, 'the oil transition is shifting from high quality resources to lower quality resources that have increased risks of environmental damage'. The same authors argued (2006) that policies are required to balance tradeoffs between environmental disruption in return for increased economic and energy security. It is unclear at present to what extent unconventional sources will be able to meet the increasing demand for oil, and what investments and technologies will be required. What is clear is that oil prices will directly affect transport and tourism, as was apparent in mid-2008 with the massive fluctuations in price that substantially affected the input price to transportation and tourism prices.

Oil prices and tourist transport

The increasing oil prices affect tourism substantially (Plates 9.1 and 9.2), in particular the airline industry. The costs of aviation fuel have increased by 30 per cent between 2007 and 2008, and they now constitute 34 per cent on average of operating costs (IATA 2008b). In 2003, when crude oil prices were US$29, fuel made up 14 per cent of operational costs. Steve Lott from the International Air Transport Association describes the recent developments as the 'perfect storm':

> The economic slowdown in the US, the oil price and the weakness of the dollar are all conspiring to hit the aviation market. Americans are going to be thinking hard about whether they can afford to travel (Jagger 2008).

Over the last few years, airlines have been forced to pass on some of the costs to their customers, largely in the form of 'fuel surcharges'. The increase in airfares combined with higher costs of products in general has led to a reduction in demand for travel. Global air passenger travel slowed substantially in 2008, with low growth rates of 1.9 per cent in July and 1.3 per cent in August for international travellers. Load factors have also dropped from 81 per cent to 79 per cent – an indication of overcapacity and reduced demand (IATA 2008c). Even Asia Pacific carriers reported less demand than predicted, following a trend already observed during high oil prices in 2006, when Chinese airlines recorded a loss of US$320 million despite increasing capacities (Worldwatch Institute 2008). The airline industry is now expecting a net loss of US$5.2 billion for the year 2008 (IATA 2008c).

The drop in demand for air travel can largely be attributed to leisure travellers, who are more price sensitive than business travellers (Brons et al. 2002). Yeoman et al. (2007) expect that low-cost carriers will suffer most under high oil price scenarios. Moreover, price elasticities were generally found to be higher for short-distance travel compared with long-distance travel, possibly because the choices and possibilities for substitution are greater for short-haul travel (Gillen et al. 2004).

Plate 9.1 The heavy reliance upon the car for domestic tourism in many countries means dependence upon petrol is a key element for tourist mobility with predictions for peak oil

Source: ©Susanne Becken

Plate 9.2 Adventure activities for small groups such as heliskiing have a significant environmental impact in terms of their carbon footprint

Source: ©Susanne Becken

Higher oil prices also affect road transport, although car travel is generally considered to be inelastic. In a meta-analysis of price elasticities related to automobile travel, Graham and Glaister (2002) found that short-run elasticities are typically around -0.3 and long run elasticities are about -0.6 to -0.8. This means that adjustments are more evident in the long run (typically over one year). This is due to the fact that travellers are less likely to change their behaviour immediately (i.e. decrease demand), but will react more sensitively in the long run when they have had time to adjust to the new prices and are able to make alternative arrangements (Brons et al. 2002). This distinction is relevant when analysing transport behaviour by domestic tourists compared with that of international tourists (e.g. rental cars). International tourists are more likely to show short-term, inelastic behaviour in response to transport costs at their destination, as found for rental car tourists in Mallorca (Palmer-Tours 2007).

Tourists' responses to higher oil prices not only affect the transport sectors, but also destinations that depend on tourists getting there, be it by air or by land transport. The German Chambers of Industry and Commerce (DIHK) found that in the 2008 summer season some German hotels and restaurants were at risk of going out of business due to reduced domestic demand and people's reluctance to spend money on holidays in difficult times (Hansen 2008). Similarly, a study undertaken in the United States found that increased fuel costs lead to a drop in demand for hotel rooms (with an elasticity of -1.74), especially in suburban locations and hotels close to main roads (Canina et al. 2003). A scenario planning exercise by Yeoman et al. (2007) in Scotland established that 'energy inflation' may result in severe reductions in tourist arrivals in Scotland with consequences on expenditure, economic value added and employment from tourism.

New forms of tourism

From the above discussion, it is clear that both climate change and peak oil will affect how people travel, where they go, what they do and how much they will be able to spend at the destination. While the detail of such developments is not fully understood, it seems wise to consider management measures that reduce the risk of increased dependency, mis-investment, and structural lock-in into systems that may not be supported in the future. Clearly, tourism transport that relies less on fossil fuel is more likely to survive changes caused by climate change mitigation policies or increasing oil prices. Global oil prices might be the more imminent challenge that needs to be addressed to avoid large-scale interruption and decline of societies and economies (Hirsch 2005). Johnson and Cottingham (2008: 10) summarise this threat as follows:

> The impact of Peak Oil will be felt particularly strongly by industries that are dependent on abundant cheap energy. These include transport sectors such as aviation, industrialised food systems, air conditioning and refrigeration, and commodities such as plastics and pesticides. The declining availability of oil and gas means that unless a systemic transition to a post-carbon society is initiated and planned for now, it is likely to happen without our choosing – and with catastrophic impacts on the global economy, poverty levels and human development.

This implies that there are major implications for the design, development and management of future tourist transportation systems, to which attention now turns.

Transportation systems

To date, measures for reducing transport's fossil fuel dependency have largely been focused on developing new technologies (e.g. plug-in hybrid cars) and fuel sources. There are numerous examples from the tourism sector that illustrate the use of electric cars, ethanol-run buses and other alternatives such as tourist boats running on coconut oil. Many developed countries have targets in place for the production and sales of biofuels, recently amended by conditions that the biofuel is of a sustainable nature (e.g. does not compete with food production). Also, a number of airlines in partnership with aircraft manufacturers are testing the use of biofuels in the aviation industry (Marsh 2008). However, it has also been demonstrated that the role of biofuels will always be insignificant compared with the amount of liquid oil that is required to meet the demand for transportation. Patzek (2007) argued that it is absolutely impossible to replace fossil fuels with biofuels due to the low conversion rate of solar energy into usable energy by plants and the lack of space and limited resources on earth.

New systems that ensure ongoing provision of tourist transport are therefore unlikely to build on air and car travel as we know it, but will increasingly rely on electrified rail networks augmented by electric cars and buses for local travel. Already, trains offer a viable alternative to air transport on short routes, as for example demonstrated by the Eurostar which operates through the Channel Tunnel, connecting the UK with mainland Europe. More than 70 per cent of trips between London and Paris are now undertaken by train, and about 64 per cent of trips between London and Brussels (Johnson and Cottingham 2008). Given that the majority of tourist trips are domestic or intra-regional, there is substantial potential to substitute air with rail travel. The increased demand for electricity could be satisfied by expanding the use of photovoltaic technology (i.e. generating electricity based on solar radiation); an efficient energy technology when measures as output per square metre of land (Patzek 2007).

Rail networks can also be complemented by small electric cars and cycling or walking infrastructure to improve connectivity with the origin and destination of tourist trips. There are numerous examples in the tourism literature of successful cycle tourism projects. For example, Lumsdon (2000) discusses the United Kingdom National Cycle Network, which offers connected cycling routes on traffic-free trails, traffic-calm roads, and minor roads. Expanding cycle networks requires substantial investment by the public sector and its partners such as Sustrans (see Chapter 8); however, compared with roading projects, the establishment of cycling routes appears to be a very cost-efficient alternative (Becken and Hay 2007).

Clearly, a change in transport systems towards rail, electric vehicles and non-motorised forms of mobility represents a substantial shift in holiday mobility. Distances travelled by tourists would be shorter and the speed of travel would be slower. A trip to a faraway destination will become the exception rather than the rule. Travelling will also require more organisation and less flexibility. This may not resonate well with current tourists' expectations (Böhler et al. 2006). Conventional forms of travel will still be available but at a high cost. As a result these will not be affordable for everyone and not at the frequency we experience today. However, if changes in transport systems are made, in time people will be able to adjust and still be in a position to experience holidays. The dire consequences of failing to urgently reduce oil demand are outlined in the so-called Hirsch report, 'Peaking of world oil production: impacts, mitigation and risk management', Hirsch et al. (2005) note that if mitigation were to be too little, too late, then world supply/demand balance will be achieved through massive demand destruction (shortages), which would translate to significant economic hardship.

Tourism destination management

Following the change in affordability and availability of transport systems, as well as increasing environmental awareness by tourists, destinations might find themselves attracting fewer and different kinds of tourists: at the very least they will have to deal with change and greater uncertainty in their markets and appeal. To some extent this can already be observed in some long-distance destinations, for example New Zealand, where arrivals from the United Kingdom have dropped markedly and (reduced) tourism growth is only maintained due to increased arrivals from the close-by Australian market (New Zealand Ministry of Tourism 2008).

Rather than reacting to these trends, tourist destinations can proactively identify markets that are less prone to climate change and oil prices (Becken 2008). Naturally, these markets will be either intra-regional or domestic in nature and less likely long-haul international markets. For international tourism, it might be beneficial to develop lucrative niche markets with a competitive advantage. There might also be new forms of tourism, such as 'slow travel' (e.g. *www.slowplanet.com/travel*). It will become increasingly important to understand the interplay between recreation and tourism. For example, if fewer tourists leave a country (due to higher airfares) there might not only be an increased potential for domestic tourism but also for recreation. This will provide business opportunities but also require new management tools to accommodate an increase in domestic tourism in many countries.

At present, most tourist destinations seem to build on ongoing growth in international tourist arrivals, and if this does not materialise the preferred response is to increase marketing budgets. Very few destinations develop strategies to stabilise arrivals and extract more yield from arriving tourists (Becken and Simmons 2008). As noted by Johnson and Cottingham (2008), countries – especially in the developing world – should focus on formulating policies that prevent leakage and keep more tourism revenues rather than simply promoting growth. This will require a shift in how destinations think about tourism and it will also require courage by governments to implement policies that are not based on the growth paradigm. This is unlikely to happen in the near future, as governments already find it hard to 'come to grips with the complexity of advancing the objective of car traffic reduction combined with continued tourism growth' (Robbins and Dickinson 2007: 119). This will become even more challenging when not only transport growth is at risk but tourism growth in itself.

● ● ● ● Conclusion

With about 10 billion trips in total worldwide, tourism's magnitude is significant as both an economic activity but also as a consumer of tourist transport. Tourism implies mobility and the current tourism transport systems rely heavily on petroleum fuel. This makes tourism vulnerable in two ways: first as a result of its contribution to global climate change and second as a key consumer of increasingly scarce oil resources. Both challenges are likely to impose future costs on tourism transport, and coupled with an increasing environmental awareness of tourists, the viability of tourism in its current form is at risk. This chapter has demonstrated that present tourism is not particularly future-proof in the face of climate change and peak oil, and destinations run the risk of major reductions in tourism which, if not planned for, will have severe socioeconomic consequences. It is time for tourism to undertake a proactive risk assessment and investment in new transport systems that rely less on fossil fuels (see Van Mierlo et al. 2006).

In parallel, destinations are advised to gain some understanding of low-risk markets and new travel philosophies that might withstand severe changes to the affordability and availability of traditional transport systems and ways of travelling. This is reminiscent of the fundamental philosophical shift which Krippendorf (1987) called for (so that domestic tourism replaced the demand for international tourism), but has not been embraced to date by most countries and their policy-makers. Before climate change concerns among the research community, Krippendorf argued that international tourism growth was not sustainable at an international scale in relation to the increasing environmental damage it caused.

New policies and management practices should also concentrate on extracting more yield from tourism, while coping with potentially reduced tourist volumes, often articulated in terms of adding value to the visitor experience. These issues also raise many more fundamental concerns for the travel and tourism sector, not least of which is how they can plan for a future tourism sector without oil and one that has to cope with the unprecedented problem of climate change. For this reason, the last chapter of the book will focus on how the transport and tourism sector can begin to deal with a future based on uncertainty.

Questions

1 Is climate change likely to lead to changes in the way tourism operates? If so, outline ways it will change.

2 What is peak oil and how will it affect the future development of tourism and transport?

3 How will the issues of alternative fuel sources affect the way tourists travel in the future?

4 Is the debate on sustainability and transport an impossible dilemma to resolve for an economic activity dependent upon large amounts of energy?

Further reading

Becken, S. (2007). Tourists' Perception of International Air Travel's Impact on the Global Climate and Potential Climate Change Policies. *Journal of Sustainable Tourism*, 15(4), 351–368.

Becken, S. (2008). Indicators for managing tourism in the face of peak oil. *Tourism Management* 29(5), 695–705.

Becken, S. & Hay, J. (2007). *Tourism and Climate Change – Risks and Opportunities*. Cleveland: Channel View Publications.

The future

10

Prospects and challenges for tourist transport provision: global, national and local issues

●●●● Introduction

This book aims to raise awareness of the relationship between tourism and transport by developing the concept of a tourist transport system as a means of analysing the processes shaping the provision and consumption of transport services by tourists. Throughout the book, transport is emphasised as a dynamic and active element in the tourist's experience of travelling because it is a vital part of the process of tourism. Some of the first-generation tourism textbooks (e.g. Mathieson and Wall 1982) regarded tourist transport as an essential part of tourism but not worthy of study in its own right. In fact, a number of subsequent texts continue to view transport as a passive element in the tourist experience (Ryan 1996) and it remains a descriptive feature of most texts. It is a dynamic element in every aspect of the tourist experience – without it, the mobility of the tourist would not occur, and it also offers an attraction in its own right (see Plates 10.1 and 10.2).

In Chapter 2 research on contemporary issues in tourism and transport was reviewed in terms of the concepts and methods each discipline (economics, geography, marketing and management) uses to analyse tourist transport. However, the different philosophical backgrounds of researchers from these disciplines mean that their approach to tourist transport is not easy to synthesise into a holistic framework. But at an operational level, these perspectives are integrated into the everyday provision of tourist transport. Moreover, the tendency for researchers to retain their disciplinary training – whether in economics, geography, marketing or management – has simply contributed to the growing body of knowledge on transport and tourism. For our understanding of tourist transport systems and the tourist's experience of travel to grow, a greater degree of coherence and a theoretical basis needs to be developed. This means that research will need to be interdisciplinary in nature. Interdisciplinary research requires people from different disciplines to collaborate and focus on a specific research problem, where different questions are asked about the topic without each researcher losing sight of the problem under consideration. This may help to integrate the contributions that different disciplines can make to the analysis of tourist transport systems in order to achieve a more holistic understanding of the operation, management and use of transport services by tourists.

Although there is not space within this introductory book to undertake a comprehensive review of transport and tourism, it has sought to focus on how the consumer, provider and other agencies (e.g. national governments) interact in different

Plates 10.1 and 10.2 Vintage buses can be an attraction in their own right – see the relaunch of Firstbus, Glasgow's refurbished fleet of vintage buses in the orange and green colours of their original owner, Glasgow Corporation (or Glasgow City Corporation, as it was then) in the 1950s, when they were a familiar sight on the city's streets. Their relaunch was expected to offer visitors and those staying with friends and relatives a memorable trip on transport many Glaswegians had once used daily to commute to work

transport systems. The concept of a tourist transport system was developed as a framework in which to understand the interrelationships between different elements in such systems. Using a systems approach to the analysis of tourist transport also highlighted the importance of *inputs* to the system (e.g. the demand and supply) as well as *controlling influences* (e.g. government policy) and *outputs* (the tourist travel experience) and the effect on the environment. The book has also sought to identify a number of processes that characterise the tourist transport system. For example, deregulation and privatisation is a process now affecting tourist transport systems in North America, Western Europe and Australasia (Button and Gillingwater 1991) and other parts of Asia.

Within the existing literature, the discussion of tourist transport systems has remained fragmented and dependent upon generalised and empirical studies or extremely specialised studies of both tourism and transport. The interface between tourism and transport has still not been integrated into a holistic framework. Whilst tourism is now regarded as a complex phenomenon by educators and researchers, its frequent association with transport has meant that social science researchers have failed to integrate these issues in a framework where the complementarity between tourism and transport could be explored further.

Preston and O'Connor (2008) point to a need for pluralistic methodologies (i.e. those from the subject area one is based in, such as Tourism or Geography) and those from other subject areas to approach the subject in a more holistic manner. For example, they point to the work of Urry (2004) and the research agenda in social science based on mobility (see Hall 2005) where the relationship between travel, mobility and other research agendas can be used to provide a better interdisciplinary perspective on tourism and transport.

In simple terms, transport researchers focus on transport issues whilst tourism researchers focus on tourism and never the twain shall meet in most cases (e.g. Lumsdon and Page 2004a; Lumsdon 2006). The tendency within tourism research to focus on typologies of tourism and tourists has led to a critical separation of the tourist from the mode of transport they use. This has the effect of contributing to the separation of tourism and transport research, with tourist motivation to travel viewed in isolation from the process of travelling. The result is that tourist travel is divided into two discrete elements (transport and the tourist) rather than being conceptualised as a continuous process using a systems approach. But what are the processes shaping tourist transport in the new millennium?

Tourist transport provision in the new millennium: the challenge of globalisation

The last five years have seen a dramatic change in the world economic order, not least the challenge posed by the new processes of production (especially the globalisation of brands and the role of MNCs in seeking cheap locations for producing goods in Asia), which has created a demand for business travel to and from such locations. As Figure 10.1 shows, a number of simultaneously occurring processes of change are happening in terms of the world economy, transport and tourism that affect the production and consumption of tourism services. Amongst these are the growing e-travel revolution, social processes (i.e. demographic shifts in society such

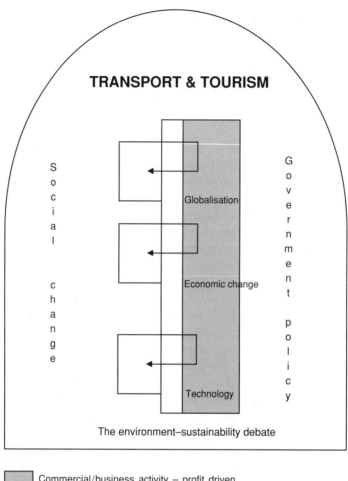

Figure 10.1 **Processes of change in tourist-transport provision**

as an ageing population and growing middle class in many Asian travel markets), the increasingly grey consumer who is much older and more travel experienced and is shaping the demand for tourist travel. Whilst these processes of change are occurring at different times and at different rates across the world, the mediating force of government in seeking to balance the commercial interests of companies and businesses with the interests of consumers has to be set against these wider processes of change in transport and tourism provision.

What Figure 10.1 highlights is the global processes at work that are both interconnected at an international level but also lead to national and local differences in the way global forces interact to form different outcomes in tourist and transport activity. As Derudder and Wilcox (2008) suggest, the impact of globalisation is transforming an international economy based on a shift from territoriality to networks based on world cities as the command points in these networks. Therefore, interconnectivity between these world cities is shaping tourist travel, given the provision of airline networks and airport infrastructure in these locations as the world also becomes more urbanised (see Hjalager 2007 on the economic stages of globalisation and tourism). What seems to be underlying many of the debates on globalisation in tourism and transport (aside from economic arguments on competition) is the environmental – sustainability lobby that also seeks to control the global spread of transport and tourism. Interestingly, some researchers still conceptualise the tourist travel encounter as a social experience (Petit 2002; Lumsdon 2006) although its dominant global impact is profound (Chan 2000). However, cultural differences also affect the global consequences of such activity (Sultan and Simpson 2000), which contribute to the local outcomes of these processes of change. One obvious manifestation of the globalisation in service delivery is the increasingly sophisticated marketing activity undertaken by transport providers seeking to nurture tourist markets, especially through the use of branding (see Driver 1999, 2001; Gustafasson et al. 1999; Gittell 2003; Graham 2009).

Globalisation is also very marked in those sectors that deal with the management and logistics of international travel (Lovelock and Yip 1996), reflected in the business strategies used by transport operators. The earlier work of Porter (1979) on strategy shows how competitive forces shape business strategy, and the research by Kangis and O'Reilly (2003) rightly depicts the dynamic marketplace affecting tourism and the need for appropriate strategies to address these needs. In particular, there is a powerful global trend towards greater cooperation and collaboration between different elements in the supply chain (Sigala 2008). This has not replaced the hard-nosed, head-to-head competition that also prevails in the transport and tourism sector but with profit margins often low in this sector a sharing of expertise and knowledge as well as resources proves to be a smarter way of working, to achieve win–win situations.

Globalisation inevitably produces 'winners and losers' in the pursuit of business, and a number of distinct processes are associated with it:

- *Deregulation*, where the entry barriers to many sectors of the tourist transport business have been removed and large oligopolies are challenged by new entrants (Pearce 1995b). As the example of the US domestic airline industry illustrates, in newly deregulated industries competition increased at a rapid pace. However, there is debate within the American domestic airline industry as to whether consumers have been the main beneficiaries, with lower prices. Goetz and Sutton (1997) explain that the benefits of deregulation have accrued to those passengers travelling on trunk routes, whilst business travellers and passengers travelling to/from more peripheral locations have experienced higher fares. In the UK rail system, a monopoly under British Rail was replaced by franchises that still act as more localised monopolies in most cases, with performance theoretically evaluated and poor service and provision penalised by terminating franchises or non-renewal.
- *Technological change*, which has revolutionised the organisation, management and day-to-day running of tourist transport businesses with the introduction of information technology (IT). IT has also helped reduce some of the costs of business operations. The introduction of CRSs and GDSs certainly assisted with the globalisation of the supply of tourist transport services. The introduction of the Internet has also had a major impact on the supply of transport services (Macdonald-Wallace 1997). In fact many of the world's airlines now have websites and, as Whitaker and Levere (1997) show, some are being used for bookings,

but 'the scope and standard of airline-related material on the Internet varies dramatically'.

In fact the evolution of websites and their use in marketing have now moved beyond a tool simply to advertise and sell tourist transport services. This traditional use, based on sales and marketing, is reflected in the UK express coach network site (*www.nationalexpress.co.uk*). However, there is evidence that some companies (e.g. Red Funnel Ferries in Southampton) developed a more holistic approach to transport and tourism and are using the Internet to address the impact of competitive forces such as rival carriers. The company's website (*www.redfunnel.co.uk*) contains the traditional sales and marketing function. But it also moves into a tactical marketing role where bookings can be actioned and place marketing is undertaken in relation to the main destination it serves – the Isle of White. The website provides ideas for themed itineraries and the main attractions to visit that complement the tourism marketing activities of the public sector.

This is certainly leading the way in providing a seamless tourism experience facilitated by technology and the activities of the transport operator. Some airlines also offer sophisticated systems allowing passengers to plan, book and pay for their flights; others can master little more than sketchy corporate information (Whitaker and Levere 1997: 27).

- *E-travel: the global marketplace* has seen the nature of transport and tourism retailing and the traditional method of selling products transformed not only by the e-mediaries and airlines (Harison and Boonstra 2008) but also through the greater use of *dynamic packaging*, where customers can package their own trip online in much the same way that tour operators or travel agents would have done for clients. This new technology also allows the online agencies to offer progressive discounts for multiple purchases as part of the dynamic package.
- *The wider impact of telecommunications* on travel as the two elements fuse to enable people to travel and work on the move. In fact Lyons and Loo (2008) point to four trends in the information age which are shaping the future of transport:
  - *Substitution*, where telecommunications may decrease demand for travel due to the use of technology such as video conferencing and Skype.
  - *Enhancement*, where telecommunications may create a demand for travel, such as induced demand through the low-cost air travel boom and ease of booking online.
  - *Improvements* it brings to operational efficiency.
  - *Indirect impacts*, through long-term land use changes.
- *Increasing regional and international mobility*, creating a more interconnected world where technology has made travel products accessible to a global online market so that the products can be purchased and consumed more widely.
- *Regional change*: the highest costs for air travel remain in Europe and North America (despite the impact of low-cost carriers) whereas in other trading blocs such as ASEAN lower costs exist. For tourist transport providers in the global economy it can mean airlines are competing on a different cost basis, as Hanlon (2004) observed in terms of regional wage rates and remuneration of airline employees.
- *Hypercompetition*: within the global marketplace, tourist transport providers are facing pressures continually to improve products and to remain competitive. In some cases, organisations are constantly struggling to remain in business as

experience in the international airline industry suggests. As the privatisation characteristics of the 1990s and deregulation (see Meersam and van de Voorde 1996) continues into the new millennium industry leaders and oligopolies find their position challenged or destroyed by fierce competition. According to D'Aveni (1998), this hypercompetition is typified by:

– rapid product innovation;
– aggressive competition;
– shorter product life cycles;
– businesses experimenting with meeting customers' needs;
– the rising importance of alliances;
– the destruction of norms and rules of national oligopolies.

D'Aveni (1998) identifies four processes that are fuelling hypercompetition:

– Customers requiring better quality at lower prices. One of the innovations airlines have pursued to develop improved quality at lower prices is inflight catering (Jones 1995).
– Rapid technological change, especially in the use of IT.
– The rise of aggressive large companies willing to enter markets for a number of years with a loss-leader product in the hope of destroying the competition and capturing the market in the long term, although in the case of BA and the ill-fated GO low-cost carrier, one of the rivals it set out to compete with ultimately purchased it and incorporated it into easyJet.
– Government policies towards barriers to competition are being progressively removed. This is evident in the tourist transport sector throughout the world, albeit to differing degrees depending on the political persuasion and commitment to deregulation. Even where regulation is removed, political will to enforce real competition will depend upon the availability of companies willing to risk entering highly competitive markets.

At first sight D'Aveni's (1998) processes are not particularly different from those listed under globalisation (i.e. deregulation, technological change, consumer preferences and regional change). But the fundamental difference lies in the business strategy of hypercompetitors. As D'Aveni (1998) argues, hypercompetitors tend to destroy the existing competencies of businesses and Forsyth et al. (2005) point to the notion of predation. Predation has occurred post-deregulation in aviation markets and is a symptom of hypercompetition. Those affected by such change are often trapped by an inability to think laterally and adopt new competencies. Even when new competencies are introduced, businesses often have difficulty in diffusing them throughout their organisation. As Akhter (2003: 20) argues, hypercompetition has meant that

> Consumers expect and demand more; competitors aggressively introduce new products, change distribution channels, implement cost cutting programmes, and imitate each other's innovations; and companies regularly redraw the traditional boundaries of markets as they globalise their operations in response to the changing regulatory and competitive climate. Change – or more appropriately, accelerated change – is the watchword for understanding this landscape.

In the case of innovation, much of the existing business and management literature shows that within companies some people will hold back from adopting innovation (laggards). One useful approach that transport and tourism organisations working in the dynamic area of service provision have developed is the idea of champions within the organisation to drive forward innovation to remove barriers. In addition, to promote the value of innovations to customers, organisations use ambassadors to champion these ideas and products to the traveller. One interesting innovation developed in 2003 by Virgin Trains on their long-distance cross-country services (prior to the franchise being awarded to Arriva trains) was the Windowgazer booklet that describes the route taken and sites of interest, with some history and interpretation of the sites. The company has redeveloped its services with new trains to model them on airline-style service, with a club or first-class service with airline-style snacks in plastic containers on cross-country and buffet at seat service on West Coast Mainline services for premium class passengers. At the same time, many non-privatised transport operators still have a legacy of over-staffing, which can impede innovation, as is the case with some operators in the Indian airline sector. Some belatedly look towards the concept of 'change management', but this can sometimes be too little action too late. Often firms are so severely affected by hypercompetitors and their actions that their responses are bound by age-old reactions based on previous rules of competition. However, the hypercompetitor can only remain in a competitive position whilst it retains the advantage.

According to D'Aveni (1998), hypercompetitors enter the market by disrupting the competition in some of the following ways:

- By redefining the product market, thereby redefining the meaning of the quality whilst offering it at a lower price. This was the strategy adopted by easyJet in the UK, which entered the market with low-cost air travel from Luton airport to challenge the market leaders (e.g. BA, British Midland and KLM UK).
- By modifying the industry's purpose and focus by bundling and splitting industries. BA's response to easyJet was to reduce fares in the short term, but then it provided a splitting action by establishing a similar low-cost operation based at London Stansted, with lower landing fees. This avoided eroding profit margins and using high-cost airline capacity from Heathrow and Gatwick. This also raises an ongoing debate for airlines that develop a low-cost operation: should they choose a different brand to differentiate the low-cost service from their existing airline brand, so as not to dilute the full-cost service and brand values, or should the low-cost airline be a lower-cost copy of the existing operation?
- By disrupting the supply chain by redefining the knowledge and know-how needed to deliver the product to the customer, such as the low-cost airline use of the Internet to reach the consumer at a cheaper cost, removing the travel agent from the process.
- By harnessing the global resources from alliances (see Dresner and Windle 1996) to compete with the non-aligned businesses. This is particularly acute in the airline industry although to date the term 'hypercompetitor' has not been used to describe the business strategy of key players.

As Lahiri et al. (2008: 314) summarised:

Hypercompetition is the extreme rivalry whereby competing firms position themselves aggressively against one and other, and seek to disrupt the competitive advantages of industry leaders . . . while both globalisation and rapid technological change lead to hypercompetition, rising consumer expectations and attacks by competitors also drive this forceful type of business.

The two processes of globalisation and hypercompetition are powerful forces affecting the tourist transport sector and a number of themes emerge that are worthy of further discussion:

- business strategies;
- government policy, integration and the environment;
- the role of the consumer;
- the growing importance of tourist safety and security issues;
- the growing significance of service quality;
- the introduction of total quality management systems.

Business strategies used by tourist transport operators

The previous discussion of hypercompetition and globalisation illustrates the speed of change in both the transport and tourism sectors. Traditional forms of strategic planning that adopt a three- to five-year horizon may have been useful for operators to plan their long-term ambitions, but much more emphasis is now placed on tactical marketing responses to the effects of hypercompetition, since without competent marketing strategies many operators will see their market share dwindle or disappear. The most challenging situations have arisen through recent crises such as 9/11, and the development of academic and professional expertise in the area of crisis management (see Glaesser 2003) has highlighted the need for greater attention to responsive solutions where the demand for services can be cut overnight after a catastrophic event. Equally important, as the global profitability of world airlines suggests, is the ability of businesses to manage their finances during crises in profits and trading. This has been most pronounced in the USA with many trading through near-bankruptcy, although European and other airlines have also been faced with similar problems. Strategies in these instances need to be drastic, particularly in cost control, yield management and proficiency in reducing losses in a short timeframe. For example, Orient-Express in 2003 attributed a fall in profits on its flagship European service to the drop in North American visitors due to the Iraqi conflict. However, a very important switch to the domestic market and launch of the Northern Belle aimed at a new UK domestic (and visitor) market helped to restore some of the immediate drop in business.

The business environment is very volatile and highly changeable in the early twenty-first century due to global uncertainty about terrorism, which has meant that business strategies have to be able to adapt to these new conditions quickly if markets and business performance are to be maintained. In some cases acquisitions and mergers have been necessary for companies to continue to operate, where the market has become crowded by too many operators, and in other cases privatisation has been followed by management buy-outs (especially in the land transport sector) to establish new private sector operators. Some of these newly formed companies are now moving back to re-establish virtual monopolies in service provision, after a short period of intense competition (see the UK bus market for an example). What has occurred within the airline industry has also affected the bus/coach market and, to a lesser degree, the cruise ship market with transnational operators, some of whom have integrated transport concerns. The issues this raises for the consumer relate to choice, pricing and control of the supply chain and market. This has been one consequence of both globalisation and privatisation in the tourist transport sector as travellers demand better quality. According to Bootle (2003: 273) even though the low-cost airlines have revolutionised travel, once the scope for cost-cutting has passed, there will be trend towards greater comfort in the travel experience.

Government policy, integration and the environment

Underpinning the provision of services is the process of globalisation and the effect of trading blocs and economic groupings. For governments and NGOs, policy has sought to achieve a delicate balance between the needs of the consumer and ensuring a healthy business environment for companies. For example, in May 2004 the EU admitted a further 10 member states to its ranks and this expanded its borders to the east and south. The result is that the EU expects that transport demand will double by 2020 and that infrastructure provision will need to meet or at least manage demand. But the pace and scale of integrated transport provision in Europe along with other regions of the world is highly variable, despite the needs of more sophisticated travellers, who need well-integrated systems if they are to choose alternative modes of travel on short-haul routes over and above air and car.

At the national level, the efforts of countries such as The Netherlands to ensure a fully integrated public transport system provides a model of how seamless provision can be planned and developed (despite the massive problems during the experimentation with rail privatisation). In the UK, information provision to encourage modal switching from car to public transport has seen the launch of Traveline (*www.traveline.org.uk*) to allow you to pre-plan your journey across all modes of travel in order to achieve a perception of a seamless travel experience.

The tourist use of transport in urban areas is certainly one area in which policymakers and planners are seeking to make inroads in reducing car-based congestion in the next decade (see Page and Richards 2002), which will require better understanding of consumer needs (Beirão and Cabrol 2007). In scenic areas such as National Parks, which by their very nature have been like magnets for the car user due to their perceived remoteness and inaccessibility (Bernier 2003), there will be a need for more sustainable travel options to accommodate visitor numbers and to maintain the visitor experience (Lumsdon 2006; Connell and Page 2008). Whilst the introduction of park-and-ride schemes in urban and rural areas (see Cairns 1998) is a starting point in managing the car, a culture shift in fostering sustainable transport options (see Lumsdon 2000) as an integrated solution to tourist transport will need significant investment in infrastructure and advertising to promote use as well as management tools to implement such policies. Much of the existing action by organisations has focused on redressing the imbalance caused by car use. One of the most innovative schemes is the partnership of the Transport 2000 lobby group and 18 local authorities (*www.transport2000.org.uk*) with its Car Free Leisure Network, where its scheme seeks to facilitate tourists arriving in each of the 18 council areas without their cars to enhance the quality of the tourist experience. Over the next decade, many transport planners will be forced to seriously consider such policies and plans to facilitate such schemes if destinations are not to be choked by cars and begin to resemble massive car parks surrounding the destination.

Positive steps to address air pollution from road-based tourist traffic have also been examined with reference to alternatives to the car's combustion engine. Whilst this will not remove the car from the tourism and leisure transport continuum, it does raise policy issues for government if it is to incentivise alternatives to the petrol and diesel car engine, given the major advances in battery-powered, fuel cell vehicles and hybrid fuel vehicles (see Johansson and Ahman 2002). These vehicles have the potential to reduce the environmental cost of the conventional car by 50 per cent and to cut CO_2 by 40 per cent to tackle global warming and the polluting effects of petrol car engines, since Johansson and Ahman (2002) show that in 1998 in Sweden, the combustion engine generated 37 per cent of NO_x emissions and 27 per cent of CO_2 emissions. This also highlights the potential of alternative transport corridors such as rivers and waterways (Damien 1999) for leisure and tourism traffic, whilst the EU has also proposed examining the concept of a European Motorway of the Sea. Various studies (e.g. Smith 2008; Wietschel 2008) have pointed to the potential of hydrogen to address the concerns regarding the demise of oil (Roberts 2005) as one solution to the mounting demand for non-polluting road transport which is motorised and can help reduce climate change gases, although numerous technical issues still have to be addressed before hydrogen can be considered as a serious alternative fuel source.

One other very positive policy development that will certainly help the tourist and leisure traveller in the next decade if it is embraced as an innovation and implemented is the research at the University of Queensland, Australia (*www.maths.uq.edu.au*) on route optimisation techniques. The idea focuses on registering the demand for a journey and the computer simulation shows how it can be accommodated in real time along with other passenger needs as opposed to set routes and timetables. A more flexible approach to public transport needs would allow visitors to share taxis, combining supply and demand more effectively. Being able to think more creatively and flexibly is critical for the development of public transport use, especially as a leisure and tourist option.

Remaining with the theme of integration, which is a key theme for policy-makers in the new millennium to seek more sustainable use of transport modes, there are numerous examples of private sector operators innovating in this area by connecting the visitor attraction with the transport mode to create a seamless leisure day trip to different destinations, especially where they have some spare capacity (see *www.scotent.co.uk* for some examples of innovation in tourism and good practice in the Scottish transport/tourism sector). For example, in Scotland, Scotrail (*www.scotrail.co.uk*) has developed Days Out by Rail, which is outlined in Figure 10.2 and links Glasgow (Lowlands of Scotland) with the West Highlands and the tourist destinations of Oban, Fort William and Mallaig on the historic West Highland line developed in the late Victorian period and that has one of the most scenic journeys of any UK rail route. The rail operator has traded on the recent success of two massive media events:

● the filming of the Harry Potter films using a vintage steam train on the Mallaig line featuring the Glenfinnan viaduct (see Figure 10.2);

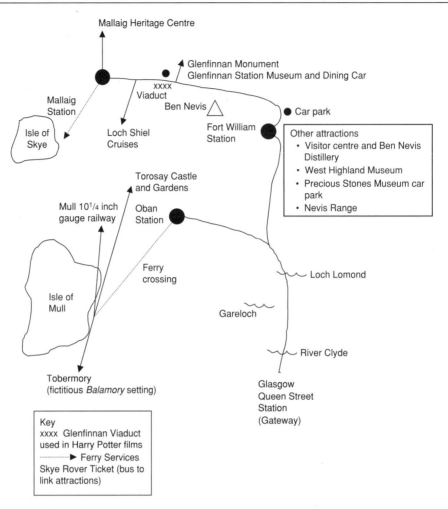

Figure 10.2 Schematic diagram of West Highlands ScotRail product – Days Out by Rail, 2004

Source: Author diagram based on ScotRail leaflet – Days Out by Rail (*www.scotrail.co.uk*).

- the BBC children's series – *Balamory* – set on the Isle of Mull and featuring Tobermory, which experienced a saturation of the local transport infrastructure in the summer season due to tourist demand (see Connell 2005 for more detail on this).

The rail operator shows what collaborative marketing and planning can do to offer an integrated tourist product where discount vouchers to visitor attractions promote leisure use and highlighting other travel options and attractions provides ideas for leisure use (see Figure 10.2). A similar scheme exists in England's Lake District (*www.lake-district.gov.uk*) – the Cross Lakes Shuttle uses bus–boat–bus to move visitors around the Park between Bowness, Hawkshead and Grizedale with provision for carrying cycles. The collaboration with transport operators, Mountain Goat, Windermere Lake Cruises and Coniston Launch has created a new product and a novel way to travel around.

Visitor safety and security

In Chapters 7 and 8 safety (see an interesting statistical recording of air travel accidents for the period 1969–2001 at *www.airdisaster.com*) and security issues were highlighted in relation to their overriding influence on global tourism and the use of different modes of tourist travel. Many governments have faced pressure to implement legislation and policies to increase surveillance for global terrorism and to improve border controls, as the USA has begun to do with the use of biometrics to scan a visitor's pupil and fingerprint to verify identity. Yet these high-profile schemes using technology obscure a much more profound and worrying problem that faces the users of public transport – that of crime and perception of safety whilst travelling. As Page (2003b) highlighted at a pan-European level, rail operators (and bus and coach operators, see Page 2003c) have had to take significant steps to improve safety for their staff, due to a rise in attacks and abuse towards staff, who often work in difficult and trying situations, especially when a crisis occurs. But more profound is the global concern with visitor safety using different forms of public transport (aside from tourist use of hire cars and robberies when straying into no-go areas of cities).

In the case of visitor safety, government investment has been targeted at the use of technology, such as CCTV (see Hall and Page 2005 for more detail on the debate over the use of CCTV in tourism and leisure settings), to increase visitor confidence that safety is being monitored. In 2004, ScotRail received a £2 million grant from the Scottish Executive to improve passenger safety, with additional help points and new CCTV cameras being installed at non-mainline stations, over railway bridges and around station premises. This technology is now becoming widely used (see Plate 10.3 of its installation at Lomond Shores, a leisure shopping environment and the western gateway to the new Loch Lomond and Trossachs National Park). This is seen as helping to reduce car theft and opportunist crime, and highlights the importance of what Barker and Page (2002) suggested was the need to design crime out of tourist environments. Whilst CCTV and surveillance is seen as improving security, it still does not remain a substitute for suitable levels of staffing on tourist transport.

The tourist as a consumer

Much of the rhetoric and hype associated with the rapid expansion of popular business books and the elevation of individuals to 'guru' status since the 1980s is characterised by one consistent theme: that businesses need to understand the customer and to get near to them as 'end users', as is evident with the sophistication of large operators such as the cruise ship industry with careful segmentation of markets and matching of products and vessels accordingly (see Plate 10.4), with massive levels of investment in new capacity. Clearly, the cruise ship industry has seen a new lease of life since the decline of cruising in the 1960s with the advent of cheaper air travel.

Swarbrooke and Horner (2007) reiterate the importance of consumer behaviour research in tourism, since from a tourist transport perspective it allows businesses to plan infrastructure developments, identify product opportunities, set price levels for products and identify market segments and the best marketing medium to promote the product. The cruise ship industry is very sophisticated in this respect and is mirrored by many other operators in the transport sector, such as low-cost airlines and larger airlines. Consumer behaviour research also allows businesses to

Plate 10.3 CCTV monitoring car parking at Lomond Shores, with anti-crime design to reduce car thefts
Source: S.J. Page

modify their product and its delivery to align it more closely with consumer expectations. For the tourist transport business, understanding how tourists make their purchasing decisions and the factors affecting their choice of product is critical. In particular, the travellers' predisposition towards certain forms of transport will obviously affect their overall satisfaction with the product. For the tourism sector in general, Swarbrooke (1997) identifies a number of weaknesses in consumer behaviour research in the UK which are particularly relevant to the transport sector (although the exception may be the major airlines that commission in-house research which remains confidential and commercially sensitive). The main weaknesses are:

- An absence of reliable and up-to-date data (a feature emphasised in Chapter 4 and by Lumsdon 2006).
- A lack of longitudinal studies to trace the evolution of consumer behaviour in tourism through time (although the case of the Malta Tourism Authority – discussed in Chapter 6 – and its monitoring of tourist use of transport is certainly an exception to the rule).

Plate 10.4 One of the trends in the cruise ship industry is towards larger and more luxurious provision, with value adding to the experience as exemplified with P&O Cruises vessel, the *Oriana*

Source: P&O Cruises

- The methodologies and techniques used to collect data on consumer behaviour in tourism remain relatively crude and unsophisticated.
- The most robust data collated by private sector companies remains inaccessible to researchers.
- Methods of segmenting the market remain outdated due to a reliance on the life-cycle concepts and age, despite major societal and value changes that have questioned their validity since the late 1990s, as new terminology, groups and methods of segmentation are used.
- Cross-cultural differences in tourism markets and a predisposition towards using specific tourist transport modes remain poorly understood, despite the significance in fundamental issues related to communication and on-board safety when flying and using transport modes. The research identified by Lumsdon (1997a and b), in part addresses some of these issues in relation to cycling.
- There are few media available to disseminate results to the practitioner audience, since much of the focus is on specific solutions to research problems they identify.

As a result, consumer behaviour is one area that tourist transport operators will need to focus on if they seek to understand what motivates tourists to travel, and to select specific modes of transport.

Tourist transport systems are likely to be affected by various opportunities and constraints on tourist travel. For example, congestion of airspace and availability of airport slots at hubs in developed countries such as North America and Western Europe (French 1994, 1997b) will remain a persistent problem for policy-makers and transport planners, as the recent investigation by the EU into slot allocation at

UK airports shows. At the same time the demand for long-haul travel is set to expand if the forecasts by Airbus and Boeing reach fruition.

Environmental issues do remain prominent in tourist transport systems as a new generation of travellers, having become familiar with green issues in the 1980s, emerge as consumers of tourist transport services; and companies such as Virgin Trains and its new Pendolino train have identified how a new braking method will allow the generation of surplus power to be reused in the national grid (see *www. virgintrains.co.uk*). Understanding the relative importance of these environmental factors in shaping the tourist's desire to travel on different modes of transport will be a major challenge for service providers, as the sustainability debate (see Weiler 1993) focuses on more environmentally sensitive and novel modes of transport.

Increasingly, the patronage of tourist transport services is going to depend upon the ability of providers to differentiate their services on the basis of image, brand (Chang and Yang 2008) market positioning and reputation for service quality. The 1990s were the *decade of the consumer* in relation to tourist travel, with providers responding to legitimate requests for higher standards of comfort, reliability and courtesy as part of the travel experience. The new millennium is seeing a continuity and intensity of these processes of change, whilst the discussion of globalisation and hypercompetition indicates that the pressure on transport providers will intensify. One outcome was the desire of travellers to embrace low-cost experiences by trading price for quality. Passengers are now recognised as customers and their rights and needs are beginning to gain a higher profile in the provision, quality and management of tourist transport services. Taneja's (2005) book *Fasten Your Seatbelt: The Passenger is Flying the Plane* pretty well describes this process, highlighted by the performance of new airline entrants in the USA market (e.g. JetBlue – see Table 10.1) which achieved good scores in customer ratings and achieved major

Table 10.1 JetBlue as a new entrant and expansion into the airline market in the USA

- Founded in 1999 and began operation in 2000 based at New York's JFK with an investment cost of US$128 million
- One of the few US airlines to remain profitable after 9/11
- Legacy carriers responded to its development with rival carriers: Delta started Song; United started Ted (see Chapter 5)
- In 2004 it commenced international flights to the Dominican Republic followed by the Bahamas in 2004, Bermuda in 2006 and Aruba in 2006
- In 2005, the airline profits dropped from US$8.1 million to US$2.7 million due to rising fuel costs
- In February, the company announced its first quarterly loss and the company introduced a Return to Profitability plan to make US$50 million annual cost savings and to boost revenue by US$30 million; in October 2006, the company announced a net loss of US$500,000 for the third quarter and in December 2006 lightened its Airbus A320 fleet by 904lb by removing seats and reducing the number of cabin crew required to staff a flight resulting in less fuel burn
- In January 2007, the company retuned to profitability in the fourth quarter if 2006, meanings its full year loss for 2006 was only US$1 million compared to US$20 million in 2005
- In December 2007, Lufthansa bought a 19 per cent stake in the company
- In April 2008, a Happy Jetting Campaign was launched to focus on value for every customer and award winning on-board service and amenities for all passengers including free DIRECTTV and XN Satellite Radio
- In October 2008, the company moved into its new Terminal 5 at JFK
- In 2008, the company served 52 destinations in 7 countries and was the largest operator of the A320 with 106 aircraft and 35 Embraer 190 jets

Source: JetBlue Airways, *www.jetblue.com*

revenue growth at the expense of the legacy carriers. But the low-cost airlines' strategy in the area of customer quality may best be summarised as trading customer loyalty on the basis of price rather than quality (with the exception of Southwest in the USA), since the fundamental principle of a large untapped market of first-time users will more than compensate for lost business through poor experiences. That said, even poor service at low prices, where complaints are raised over service breakdowns and popularised in the media and press, has not dampened the insatiable appetite for low-cost travel.

Other notable developments shaping the tourist trends include the rise of slow travel with its focus on slowing down from the fast pace of life being experienced by many in westernised economies. This may be seen as one additional component of Poon's (1993) new tourism, as niches which focus on independent travel to do different things and to enjoy destinations in more depth highlight changing consumer tastes in some segments of the market. As the Slow Planet website (*www. slowplanet.com*) states, 'slow travel is about savouring the journey. Travelling to your destination by train or boat or bicycle, or even on foot, rather than crammed into an airplane . . . Slow travel is about taking the time to engage with local people and learn about their culture'. Above all it is a movement dedicated to slowing down one's life based on the principles popularised in Honore (2005) *In Praise of Slowness*.

● ● ● ● Service quality issues in tourist transport

In Chapter 2 the concept of service was introduced in the context of marketing. Whilst that discussion provided a broad overview of the importance of service issues in tourist transport, it is evident from the processes affecting the tourist as a consumer that service quality is assuming a greater role in their purchasing decisions and travel behaviour. Irons (1994) argues that services are relationships, and that whether that relationship is a transient one or a longer-term proposition it needs to be conducted in a professional and consistent manner. As Irons (1994: 13) shows,

> Such a relationship will be based on a series of contacts or interactions. It is from these interactions with the organisation that consumers form their perceptions . . . to assess value, decide to buy, repeat purchase or recommend to others.

Such interactions are also repeated within the organisation and Irons (1994) expresses this process as a triangle (Figure 10.3). Irons explains the triangle in the following way:

- An organisation needs to associate its internal culture with the one it portrays externally and this underpins the relationships evident in Figure 10.3.
- Within the organisation, power needs to be devolved so that the relationships can be developed and the appropriate skill and know-how provided at the point where customer satisfaction is met.
- The organisational values and culture need to be clearly understood by all employees so that they affect their actions and activities in relation to customers.
- Managers need to lead the process, empowering people at the various levels in the organisation to achieve customer-related targets. In other words, managers need not only to exercise a degree of control in the management function, but

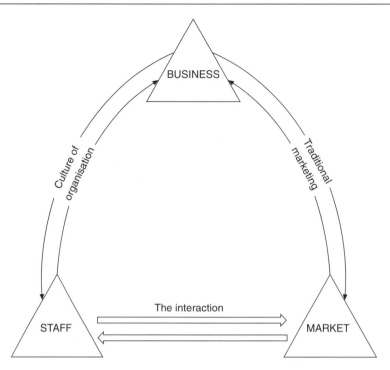

Figure 10.3 Irons' service quality triangle

Source: Based on Irons 1994.

also to lead the organisation in this era of the consumer, as epitomised by Southwest Airlines.

● A customer focus is critical, rather than a focus first on the product and then on its purchasers.

To create a services culture in an organisation, Irons (1997) identified the following key points:

● Service businesses need to identify what the priorities are for the customer. Irons (1997) cites the example of Southwest Airlines in the USA that saw a set of priorities – reliability, low fares, personal treatment – and set about 'rigorously building the airline around meeting these needs and cutting out those things the customer did not want' (Irons 1997: 8), a feature reiterated in many subsequent studies. An examination of its website (*www.southwest.com*) is very interesting reading to explore its formula for success.

● Organisations need to develop a clear vision of 'what they stand for and where they aspire to go . . . This vision should be for the customer, for the staff and for the owners' (Irons 1997: 9).

● Organisations and employees need to communicate so that they understand what is to be achieved, why, how, and the role of employees in the corporate vision.

● The organisation needs to learn from its experience through problem solving and how this can benefit its vision.

● The service culture needs to be led from the top in the organisation rather than through passive forms of managerialism. Success stories in the transport and tourism sector exemplify these forms of leadership as being critical to success as shown in the case of low-cost airlines as new ventures.

● It is at the point of interaction between the market and the consumer that value can be created, and many operators saw how they could add this value through small innovations and developments in customer service.

● Service delivery is an integral part of the process for service organisations and it should drive the business.

Whilst the principles outlined by Irons (1994, 1997) may be useful in outlining how businesses may create a service culture, at a practical level the service requirements of the tourist transport sector need to be examined in more detail. This is because in certain sectors of the tourist transport business, service qualities offer particular challenges to operators because of the nature of the service interaction. It should also be emphasised that in some cases tourists' expectations are rising beyond the reach of mass transport providers and their ability to meet these needs.

Within the literature on tourism and transport there are comparatively few systematic reviews of service quality. Whilst studies reviewed in Chapter 3 on rail travel highlighted the experience of InterCity prior to privatisation, few other reviews exist. Those studies that have been undertaken have largely focused on the airline sector (e.g. Van Borrendam 1989; Ostrowski et al. 1993, 1994). Probably one of the most influential publications to date is that by Witt and Muhlemann (1995), which not only reviews the previous research in the area but also identifies the idiosyncrasies and conditions that influence service quality in airlines.

Service quality: conceptual issues

Ostrowski et al. (1993) argued that service quality issues were comparatively poorly developed in the airline industry, based on a survey of 6000 travellers using two US airlines. They concluded that there was considerable scope for improvement. Hamill (1993) places this in the context of changes in the aviation sector in the 1990s, with deregulation and privatisation forcing companies to become more customer oriented (Kossmann 2006).

Hamill (1993) also points to the strategies pursued by some airlines, where the use of computer reservation systems was seen as improving service. Yet this development had no direct impact on the actual service encounter until it was superseded by the e-revolution and the rise of dynamic packaging where value could be added.

Witt and Muhlemann (1995) explore the problem of establishing a working definition of service quality. Gronroos (1984) introduced the idea of a *technical quality* dimension (the customer interaction with the service organisation) and a *functional quality* dimension (the process through which the technical quality is delivered). As a result, the consumer's perception of service is a result of the service dimensions combining technical and functional aspects. In contrast, Gummesson (1993) argued that four qualities affected customer perceived satisfaction. These were:

● design quality;
● delivery quality;
● relational quality;
● production quality.

A further model of quality was developed by Zeithmal et al. (1990), which was based on gap analysis and focused on four dimensions:

- customers not knowing what to expect;
- inappropriate service quality standards;
- a service–performance gap;
- company promises not matched by delivery.

To evaluate quality, Zeithmal et al. (1990) used 10 dimensions that were reduced to five elements:

- tangibles;
- reliability;
- responsiveness;
- assurance;
- empathy,

which are combined in the SERQUAL model used to evaluate customers' perceptions of quality. Whilst SERQUAL and measures of perceived quality were certainly dominant elements in the research agenda in the late 1980s and early 1990s, Witt and Muhlemann (1995: 34) argue that 'the successful organisation will be one which establishes a total quality culture' based on total quality management (TQM). What has also become evident from the literature on the way that airlines use their staff to deliver service is the pressure upon them to add a significant element of human feeling. A pioneering study by Hochschild (1983) coined the phrase 'emotional labour' to highlight how frontline service staff, in this case airline attendants, were trained to provide customers with a particular form of emotional experience. Here ideas surrounding projecting warmth, always seeming fresh and interactive with each customer highlight the need for empathy, which can have conflicting demands between the organisational need for efficiency and the need to meet the consumer's quest for satisfaction. In some respects this was seen as the commodification of human emotion and many of the newer service organisations in transport and tourism (e.g. Virgin Trains and its airline, Virgin Atlantic) have chosen a different, more quirky and often entertaining approach to customer service as opposed to a stock response such as used by call centres. For the service staff, the emotional responses and impact upon them have seen burn-out become a problem. This has been described as a more relationship-based economy where customer interaction is part of relationship building and customer relationship management (CRM) to maintain consumers given the cost of capturing new consumers in any business sector. The result is that the pressures posed by service quality for staff is significant, including high levels of stress, particularly given the dominance of female labour in this front-line role (Bunting 2004).

But what is TQM, where does it originate and how will it affect tourist transport providers?

Total quality management

It is widely acknowledged that the 1980s saw many service providers in North America respond to a perceived 'quality' crisis posed by products and services offered by rivals in the Pacific Rim (Deming 1982). Many service providers responded with corporate strategies focused on quality issues as a method of retaining market share. Yet if the late 1980s were characterised by a business environment committed to quality, the 1990s were dominated by total quality management as a more sophisticated form of recognising customers' needs as an integral part of an organisation's goals, and now it has been incorporated into new notions of relationship building as part of maintaining relationships, although the basic tenets of TQM are evident throughout the various iterations of service quality that exist in the new millennium. TQM developed as a corporate business management philosophy and it even has an academic journal – *TQM* – devoted to research in this area. Why should this be of interest to the tourist transport system? The growing concern for consumers, quality and total supply management in the tourist transport system is part of the move towards TQM amongst service providers. Furthermore, TQM is likely to assume a greater role in academic and commercial research on tourist transport in the 2000s.

TQM is an all-embracing approach that enables an organisation to develop a more holistic view of consumers, quality issues and service provision as an ongoing process. Yet one of the principles of TQM – the concern for quality – is explicitly dealt with in detail in this book. One difficulty is in establishing a universal definition of quality that could be applied to tourist transport systems. Dotchin and Oakland (1992) provide an excellent review of this issue, citing the work by Townsend and Gebhart (1986) that distinguishes between the subjective evaluation of quality by the customer (quality of perception) and the provider's more objective assessment (quality of fact). Clearly the meaning of quality will vary according to the context and the perception of who is establishing what can be deemed as quality, as the discussion of conceptual issues of quality showed. Whilst the journal *TQM* contains many interesting discussions of this issue, operationalising TQM in a tourist transport context requires organisations to work towards specific goals focused on an agreed concept of quality. Corporate commitment is required so that TQM permeates all areas of the company's business. TQM also provides an organisation with the opportunity to monitor and implement internal procedures and to control suppliers using established quality standards such as BS 5750, as discussed in Chapter 6 in relation to the use of logistics solutions, and supply chain management, as discussed in Chapter 5.

One of the real challenges for TQM in tourist transport systems is to establish what the customer considers as excellence in service provision and the design of service delivery systems to deal with individual tourists' requests, requirements and needs. Gursoy et al. (2004) examined the service quality attributes that affect airline services (i.e. price, safety, timeliness, luggage delivery, on-board service quality, check-in processes, seat pitch, along with the issues identified in Chapter 5 with reference to airline complaints in the USA). But operationalising that into a relative measure of airline quality has seen various studies seek to provide a complex composite measure – the Airline Quality Rating (AQR) (Bowen and Headley 2001) – using multiple performance criteria from some of the above indicators. Gursoy et al. (2004) examined similar data using a statistical technique – correspondence analysis to show the relative positioning of 10 major US airlines. This was useful in showing how airlines could improve their market positioning as well as illustrating what the relative strengths and weaknesses of the airlines are, based on the criteria selected in the analysis. The implications are that such research can help airlines select which strategy to pursue in order to position themselves in relation to their competitors.

It is at the strategic policy and planning stage that organisations may need to agree on how to improve continuously and strive for quality in service provision so that the tourist's travel experience is enhanced. One challenge is to ensure that the process of travel is not perceived as such a mundane and stressful experience for some tourists. Implementing a strategy based on notions of quality is no easy task for organisations where it may involve a change in corporate culture. Nevertheless, a number of critical factors characterise success in TQM in service provision. As Table 10.2 shows, senior management set on developing a policy for TQM will need to follow certain principles and management strategies. Many of the principles

Table 10.2 Implementing a total quality management programme

In developing a TQM in any tourist transport organisation, senior managers will need to consider that:

- an organisation needs long-term commitment to constant improvement, particularly beyond the initial hiatus and impetus around initiatives to re-image, re-brand and redevelop the product offering
- a culture of 'right first time' is critical to developing an outwardly facing organisation that strives for excellence rather than a mundane preoccupation with bland statements on quality
- employees need training and ongoing training to understand customer–supplier relationships and the importance of CRM as well as innovations within the area
- purchasing practices need to consider more than just the price – they must also consider the total cost, particularly the cost of losing customers and the price of recruiting new customers
- improvements in delivery systems need to be managed, so that they are not simply parachuted in and staff left struggling with new changes with little or no knowledge of what to do, especially with the pace of change in technology
- the introduction of methods of supervision and training needs to be explained to avoid fear and intransigence, so that barriers to innovation are removed
- interdepartmental barriers need to be broken down by managing the service process to improve communications and teamwork, particularly the use of virtual teams (i.e. managing people at a distance) to reduce organisation travel costs and staff time tied up with travel, where operations are geographically dispersed
- eliminating
  - goals without methods
  - standards based only on numbers
  - fiction, get facts by using the correct tools (e.g. by using appropriate research techniques)
- forming an ongoing human resource management strategy to develop experts and 'gurus'
- developing a systematic approach to managing the implementation of TQM.

The implementation of a TQM programme can be shaped using these principles to achieve *outcomes* that involve:

- the identification of customer–supplier relationships, so that staff understand the functional linkages, relationships and value that exist in these relationships
- managing processes of change where quality improvements require a new approach
- cultural changes, especially in relation to staff attitudes and the values that staff hold towards the organisation, as exemplified by the case of Southwest Airlines and the team spirit of making sure the job gets done well
- commitment, with rewards for staff loyalty so that staff feel valued, are able to translate corporate objectives into action including:
  - systems based on international standards, using best practice, case studies of excellence and similar organisational learning tools
  - teams to monitor and improve quality throughout the systems
  - tools to analyse and predict what type of corrective action is needed to improve quality, With staff empowered to address service quality issues

Source: Adapted from Dotchin and Oakland (1992: 142); author.

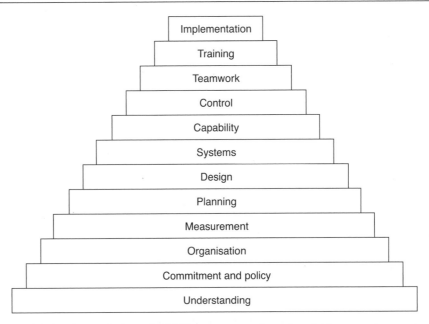

Figure 10.4 Implementation of a TQM programme for a tourist transport operator

discussed in Table 10.2 expand the ideas developed by Irons (1994, 1997) on developing a service culture, whilst TQM is a more systematic attempt to ensure quality is dealt with in a consistent manner. Witt (1995) cites Oakland's (1989) route to implementation as a series of steps that are outlined in Figure 10.4. Oakland (1989) explains that the CEO of any organisation must begin by *understanding* the concepts of TQM and the route to implementation. This then needs to be followed by *commitment and policy* to set out what the organisation hopes to achieve from its quality strategy. Following this, it may be necessary to alter the *organisational structure* to fit with the new ethos. In terms of *measurement*, the inputs (raw materials), output (product), performance of employees and any costs of failure need to be quantified. Even though it is often hard to measure intangible elements in a service, the SERVQUAL survey tool might be used. The process of *planning* is the next step, to assess the nature of the service process, who it serves, when and where. This is a good point to use the results of the SERVQUAL survey to plan changes to the delivery of the service. The next stage is called *systems,* where a quality manual is produced to explain how the company undertakes its quality policies, with the management systems in place. This is also an opportunity to specify the nature of the product being delivered and how it is produced. The term *capability* refers to the next stage where the organisation can assess whether it has the ability to meet each customer's set of requirements or if modifications are needed. This is followed by a *control* function to ensure the service is delivered in a consistent manner, within acceptable tolerance levels, on each occasion.

Since service delivery often involves more than one person, the role of *teamwork* needs to be considered. This may also involve the use of quality circles in the organisation, where employees work in teams to solve problems and promote a commitment to quality. To ensure a continuous improvement in quality, *training* is essential. At the top of the steps is TQM *implementation*. Porter and Parker (1992) note that management behaviour and their willingness to carry through such programmes is often the key to the successful implementation of TQM.

However, interest in TQM is no substitute for the organisational and logistical skills involved in coordinating and managing tourist transport systems (de Barros et al. 2007). Conveying large numbers of people over short and long distances for pleasure and business is a complex process requiring a great deal of planning and organisation on a day-to-day basis as well as in the longer term. Adding a concern for quality provision to this process makes the delivery of services a more complex undertaking and it is not surprising that service interruptions occur due to the sheer volume and scale of people handled in tourist transport systems. But when things do go wrong, companies and their front-line staff must be empowered to deal with incidents, or systems must be in place to deal with crises when they occur. Whether a tourist transport provider prefers a gradual improvement approach to quality or a TQM approach, it is worth considering some of the impediments to quality improvements in relation to the airline sector.

Quality issues in the airline industry

Witt and Muhlemann (1995) identify two persistent problems in meeting travellers' requirements:

- How may a quality service be defined, what factors influence the customer's experience and how may these factors be identified?
- How may performance or delivery of the product be measured or monitored, given the intangible nature of services (Witt and Muhlemann 1995: 35)?

Witt and Muhlemann (1995: 35) identify the following five factors that may pose particular problems:

- the mixed nature of airline markets, where leisure and business travellers may be mixed on any flight, each with different requirements, and this is further complicated on low-cost airlines with business travellers breaking the conventional model of seeking full-service provision;
- lack of direct control over factors contributing to the traveller's experience, including:
  - ticket purchases from travel agents, which can involve mistakes in ticketing (although this has been overtaken by the rise of e-mediaries and online ticketing these systems can cause different problems);
  - experiences at the airport (e.g. air traffic control problems and weather conditions);
  - the impact of airline alliances, where partner airlines may not have harmonised standards of service to ensure a consistent quality throughout the journey regardless of the carrier;
- congestion and slot availability, where large carriers dominate the main slots at a time when air travel in Europe and North America is becoming more congested;
- restrictions versus deregulation, where spatial inequalities occur in service provision depending upon the traveller's location in the system and choice of route, as Goetz and Sutton (1997) observe in the USA;

- differentiation in the product, where the airlines seek to segment the market and attract more travellers through the use of marketing tools such as frequent-flyer programmes or online booking incentives (Barker 1996; Buhalis 2003).

Some airlines, such as SAS, have implemented quality management systems moving near to TQM, and BA is a further example of an airline that has attracted a great deal of attention in the research literature for its focus on quality (see Hamill 1993 for example) despite facing financial problems subsequently. KLM also implemented a full TQM scheme (Van Borrendam 1989), retaining a high-profile role in global aviation. The success of many Asian airlines in the service quality arena, as measured by customer awards, also helps to illustrate how different measures are used to evaluate comparable airline service (see *www.SKYTRAX.com*) and even nine years on the comments of Witt and Muhlemann (1995: 39) remain true: 'Singapore Airlines is probably the best known for customer focus', as confirmed in Chapter 5. Numerous studies in the air transport literature continue to focus on this theme as a key element in airline performance (see Chen and Chang 2005; Pakdil and Aydin 2007; Park 2007; Liou and Tzeng 2007). Aside from quality issues, there is a range of other themes likely to affect tourist transport.

As already discussed, government policy, planning and investment in infrastructure is assuming a significant role in facilitating the efficient movement of people for the purpose of tourism, as highlighted in Chapter 8 with reference to the London Olympic Games in 2012. In this context, the London Tourist Board's (1990) *At the Crossroads: The Future of London's Transport* reaffirms the essential relationship between transport and tourism dealt with in Chapter 1. The London Tourist Board study is unique in this respect since it recognised that:

- An efficient transport network is necessary for tourists to gain access to a destination such as London; tourism would not exist without a transport network as it is part of the tourism infrastructure.
- An integrated transport network with convenient transfers between different modes of transport is essential, with reasonably priced travel options.
- Within the destination, tourists need a choice of transport to transfer between the port of arrival and their final destination.
- Investment in public transport provides social, economic and environmental benefits for both residents and tourists alike. Investment in transport infrastructure is a long-term proposition and is unlikely to yield tangible benefits in market-led economies in relation to tourism. Yet without it tourism would not be able to develop.

As the London Tourist Board study notes, the development and long-term prosperity of tourism depends on transport both to make destinations accessible and to facilitate tourist travel within the destination area, particularly on public transport to reduce their carbon footprint and to address concerns over sustainability. But achieving such use may also require action to address concerns which manifest themselves through the tourist's perception and actual use of public transport for tourism, as illustrated in Insight 10.1. This Insight helps to show, from a research base, what types of concerns planners and policy-makers need to target to achieve long-term transport ambitions of greater use of the existing transport infrastructure. This remains a largely under-researched area and one which deserves more attention as a future issue in building transport infrastructure and services which are more tourist oriented.

Measuring visitor experiences and perceptions of public transport supply in Scotland

Karen Thompson, Strathclyde University

A frequent criticism of destination transport policy is that there is a lack of joined up policy-making between transport and tourism planners. Given the importance of transport as a means of providing access to the remaining elements of the tourism product, there is a strong argument for much closer cooperation between the transport and tourism planners. In practice, however, transport planning does not always explicitly take into account demand created by tourists. Nor is there recognition of the differences in expectations of tourists and local users from a quality perspective. However, within a competitive market, demand for tourist-friendly local transport systems may be an important factor in influencing destination satisfaction and repeat visitation (Thompson and Schofield 2007). Thus, transport and tourism planners alike should be concerned with uncovering barriers to public transport for tourist travel, and Destination Management Organisations (DMOs) would do well to measure the extent to which local destination transport confirms or exceeds visitors' expectations of quality and performance as part of the visitor experience.

The Scottish Government has set an ambitious target of 50 per cent growth in revenue from tourism by 2015. As part of the ongoing strategy to increase tourism's contribution to the Scottish economy, increasingly joined up policy-making is in evidence between transport and tourism decision-makers within Scotland. The National Transport Strategy for Scotland (also see Chapter 3) explicitly acknowledges the importance of transport to achieving the abovementioned objective, stressing that:

> Improved quality, accessibility and affordability will also have a significant broader benefit to the tourism industry who will benefit from both attracting visitors and getting repeat visitors by having improved access and a better journey experience getting to and travelling within Scotland (Scottish Government 2006).

Since 2007, two reports have been commissioned on the role of transport in visitor movements in Scotland. The first report highlighted barriers to public transport use for overseas visitors to Scotland, reviewing experiences and perceptions of public transport supply by overseas visitors (Ferguson and Thompson 2007). The second focused solely on the accessibility of Scotland's cultural product, focusing on cultural sites and events around the country, with the objective of overcoming limitations in public transport provision (Steer Davis Gleave 2008). This latter study considered both domestic and overseas users' access to transport in Scotland for leisure purposes. Whilst neither of the reports was based on empirical research, they collated data from a range of sources to build up a picture of visitor use of public transport in Scotland. A number of interesting findings emerged from the studies which help illustrate visitors' experiences and perceptions of public transport supply in Scotland. Examples are provided below illustrating the visitor experience of public transport in Scotland as measured by three different stakeholders: the DMO, a tourism provider and a transport operator.

Between 1999 and 2005, VisitScotland, the destination management organisation for Scotland, commissioned four Tourism Attitudes Surveys (TAS) with the aims of analysing the visitor experience, identifying their likes, dislikes and their intentions to return to Scotland in the future. The most recent TAS survey in 2005 asked a sample of 651 visitors to Scotland (domestic and international) about their expectations and experiences of Scotland. A key question included in the TAS asked for visitors' ratings of ease of travel around Scotland during their holiday. Figure 10.5 depicts tourist ratings on the question 'How easy was it to travel around during your recent holiday?' Responses are rated on a scale of 1 to 5 with 5 signifying 'very easy'. The average scores, on the right side of the figure, indicate that, on average, visitors from all countries consider Scotland relatively easy to get

▶

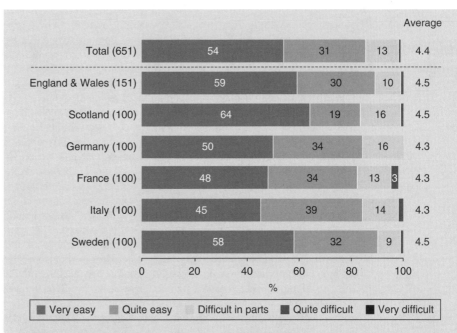

Figure 10.5 Rating of ease of travel around Scotland
Source: VisitScotland 2005.

around. Scottish domestic tourists are the most likely to consider Scotland very easy to get around, perhaps as a result of the local knowledge they hold but also potentially due to the fact that they are less likely to be public transport users, having their car to hand. What was measured by the TAS is clearly the final outcome of the transport service, i.e. visitors actually getting to where they want to go. No attempt was made to measure satisfaction with different attributes of public transport quality or to compare Scotland with other countries; nor is the role of cost clear in the ratings. However, a generally favourable picture appears to be presented as regards the accessibility of the tourism product from the visitor perspective.

As regards visitor perceptions and experiences of public transport, a report by Lowland Market Research on behalf of Cairngorms National Park provides an indication of satisfaction with the transport network serving the national park as reported by visitors. As can be seen from Table 10.3, of the facilities which visitors and residents were asked to rate within the Cairngorms National Park, public transport accounted for the highest percentage of

Table 10.3 How would you rate the following facilities in the Cairngorms area?(%)

	Very good	Good	Average	Poor	Very poor	Not visited/ applicable
Signposts	27	49	9	4	1	11
Provision of car parks	21	58	5	2	0	13
Condition of paths and tracks	20	52	7	2	0	20
Numbers of public toilets	9	36	19	11	2	23
Cleanliness of public toilets	13	40	16	6	1	24
Picnic areas	15	42	8	2	0	32
Public transport	2	5	4	7	9	74
Information boards	18	53	8	2	0	19

Source: Lowland Market Research 2004

▶

ratings at the lowest end of the scale 'very poor'. However, average ratings have not been calculated for each of the facilities. It is also clear from the data that a much higher proportion of visitors are using the car parks in the national park than are travelling by public transport. From this basic snapshot of data, it appears that public transport may be the weakest link in the tourist infrastructure of the Cairngorms National Park.

Whereas transport is only one of a number of elements of the tourist experience measured by tourism providers, greater detail can be obtained from passenger satisfaction surveys undertaken by public transport operators. A customer satisfaction survey, conducted on-board Virgin Trains in 2006, sheds additional light on experiences of passengers travelling by intercity train to Scotland for leisure purposes, with satisfaction ratings measured for a total of 51 different attributes of the journey experience. These attributes include some of the key indicators of public transport satisfaction, such as reliability, speed and customer service. The survey is one of few which permit the disaggregation of tourists' experiences from those of local users. Key differences between leisure/business and overseas/domestic visitors can be identified from the survey as regards satisfaction ratings.

As with the TAS survey (VisitScotland 2005), overall satisfaction levels with the transport mode were found to be relatively positive. Leisure users expressed higher levels of satisfaction than business travellers and, interestingly, the survey established that overseas visitors were, on average, better satisfied than domestic visitors to Scotland with regard to overall satisfaction with the journey experience. By contrast, aspects of the service which overseas visitors rated significantly lower than domestic visitors included the following:

- being able to rely on timetabled services not being cancelled;
- the helpfulness and knowledge of the staff;
- the ticket bought meeting requirements (e.g. best value/fastest route).

Overseas visitors were particularly satisfied with railway station facilities, including hard and soft quality measures: the helpfulness of station staff, accessibility and cleanliness of the station and personal safety within the station. Equally, they expressed a higher level of satisfaction with comfort and cleanliness on-board as well as with luggage storage facilities.

As regards the distinction between leisure and business travellers, significant differences can be observed on a number of attributes of public transport quality, with leisure travellers showing considerably higher levels of satisfaction with the responsiveness of staff, cleanliness of the station and train facilities, and the waiting time to purchase their ticket. However, leisure travellers did tend to be less satisfied with luggage storage facilities on the train.

As regards transport as a barrier to participation in tourist activity, Steer Davis Gleave (2008) investigated the case of transport as a barrier to participation in cultural activities. Their research uncovered mixed messages. For example, tourism industry representatives do not appear to view transport as a major barrier to visitor numbers. However, this bias may be due to the fact that the majority of existing visitors arrive by car and therefore do not communicate problems with public transport to the attractions operators. In contrast, the view among individuals who demonstrate infrequent participation in cultural activities is that a lack of good access by public transport is indeed a barrier, but one of several, including time and cost. The study, however, does not provide further detail on whether any particular aspects of transport other than limited frequency and route density act as barriers to participation.

This Insight illustrates how data providing an overview of visitors' experiences and perceptions of transport supply in Scotland is collected at a number of levels by different stakeholders. However, a lack of detailed research within this area persists, existing research taking place is at a fairly general level and scarcely attempts to investigate in detail the specific attributes and dimensions of public transport performance that influence visitor experiences, perceptions and levels of satisfaction. Moreover, the studies tend to be confined to a specific mode of transport, or a distinct area of tourist activity. It is not therefore possible to distinguish whether experiences and perceptions of transport diverge across modes or within different regions of Scotland. In the case of Scotland, there is no hard evidence to suggest that tourists and others travelling for leisure purposes have lower levels of satisfaction with public transport than local users. However, some key themes do emerge from the above reports. Cost, information and helpfulness of staff have been shown to suffer lower levels of satisfaction among visitors than among locals, illustrating the increased importance of a service-driven public transport system which caters for the needs of all users, including those who are tourists to the area.

Within the airline sector, concerns with dropping yields and low-cost operations along with the reduction in full-service market segments has led some companies to intensify their desire to secure the loyalty of economy travellers. In terms of consumer behaviour, economy class travellers tend to seek the cheapest fare, which means a greater emphasis on securing the loyalty of commercial passengers, regardless of whether they travel economy or business class. It is their repeat business function that is critical. Even some of the privatised airlines have recognised this, with frequent traveller value-added benefits. Their introduction of a premium business service follows the same principle for securing the commercial traveller. Many of the world's airlines have turned to the creative flair of advertising agencies to appeal to their prestige markets such as the business traveller as well as airline alliances to build brand loyalty.

What marketing campaigns show is that the marketing activities are selective and based on the concept of hand-picking. Whilst national airlines continue to use powerful national icons, such as the Koru image with Air New Zealand and the kangaroo with Qantas (displayed on the tail of every aircraft), it is apparent that the targeting of high-yield travellers is now becoming the key focus for airlines. Such activities are likely to continue in the transport sector, as businesses seek to improve yields.

Business cost reduction strategies to remain competitive

Transport operators are also turning to new solutions to reduce other components of their operational costs (Pilarski 2007). For example, in May 1997 Cathay Pacific launched new Airbus A340 services on its Auckland–Hong Kong route – Airbus Industries claims that the fuel cost per seat of the A340 is 40 per cent of that for a Boeing 747. This was part of a \$US9 billion fleet replacement programme for Cathay Pacific. Likewise, the Singapore Airlines role as a market leader with technology led it to be the first in service with the A345 Leadership and A380, making long-haul travel more cost efficient. Fleet replacement costs represent a perennial problem for many airlines. The capital cost of fleet replacement means more innovative solutions need to be sought, such as lease–buy schemes, manufacturer funding and straight lease schemes. This frees airlines from major sunk capital costs over and above those needed to service debt repayments on leases.

Seristö and Vepsäläinen (1997) offer a number of insights into the actual cost and revenue factors associated with airline operations and this study, combined with those by Doganis (2001, 2002), are amongst the best at explaining where the major

Plate 10.5 Many low-cost airlines use a standardised fleet, such as the Boeing 737–300 used by easyJet to reduce maintenance and repair costs
Source: easyJet

operational costs occur, and perhaps where airlines can begin to look at innovative ways of making savings (see also the U.S. Air Transport Association (ATA) website *www.airlines.org* which produces a quarterly Cost Index for passenger airlines based on data supplied by the US Department of Transportation). This is important in an age of cost competitiveness, especially when airlines have been trimming staffing levels (Alamdari and Morrell 1997b) and salaries. Yet as Seristö and Vepsäläinen (1997: 11) argue, 'for many a carrier ever more critical measures will be needed to achieve sustainable profitability', which is also relevant to the wider tourist transport sector. In the analysis of cost drivers in 42 of the world's airlines, a number of variables were examined:

● the fleet composition of airlines (see Plate 10.5);
● the flying personnel used, particularly the number of flight crew per aircraft;
● the route network;
● cost drivers, operating expenses and profitability in terms of:
  – the composition of traffic;
  – route structure;
  – salaries/remuneration levels.

As Table 10.4 shows, airlines can identify three areas for cost drivers to effect changes in operational costs in terms of route network, fleet composition and company policies. This is interesting in light of the ATA (Air Transport Association of America) Cost Index for the first quarter of 2008, where fuel was the main cost (29 per cent) followed by labour (21 per cent).

Table 10.4 The potential for cost reductions amongst airlines

Cost items	Cost drivers		
	Route network	Fleet composition	Company policies
Aircraft crew costs	XXX	XXX	XXX
Engineering overheads	X	XXX	
Direct engineering costs	X	XXX	X
Marketing	XXX		X
Aircraft standing	XXX	X	
Station and ground services	X		X
Passenger services	X		X
General and administrative costs	X		X
Fuel		X	
Airport and en-route costs	X		
Direct passenger service			X

XXX Significant cost reduction potential
X Some cost implications
Source: Adapted from Seristö and Vepsäläinen 1997: 21.

Using quantitative research methods (e.g. factor analysis), the variables were analysed and a model was built (Figure 10.6). This model highlights how various factors and variables were interrelated and, as a result, it identifies the cost items and the factors where cost reductions were possible. Such analyses highlight that transport operators will need to focus on systematic appraisals of costs in a climate of increasing customer expectations, competitiveness amongst providers and a declining yield per passenger through time. One strategy that airlines have followed is the pursuit of cost savings by divesting themselves of non-core activities such as in-flight catering operations. In June 1997, for example, Air New Zealand sold its catering business and planned to involve IBM in running its computer centre in a contracting-out of specialist non-core activities. These changes were identified in the company's 'Project Save' in the 1997/8 financial year.

More recently, BA introduced its two-year *Future Size and Shape Strategy* to restructure the company (*www.ba.com*), seeking to reduce staffing levels by 13,000 on 2001 levels for a company that employed over 50,000 people worldwide. Such savings by airlines are also expected to liberate capital to be reinvested in core business activities (Hanning 1997) and, in the case of BA, its 2003/4 Annual Report noted that it made savings of £869 million against a target of £650 million with the target of 13,000 staff cuts exceeded at 13,082. It also made savings on distribution costs in 2003/4 of £257 million against a £100 million target through greater use of technology and restructuring of travel agent commissions. The ultimate aim was to reach a 10 per cent operating margin, which it did in 2007/8. Other features in the *Future Size and Shape* strategy that were used to cut costs was a reduction in fleet types, reducing costs on procurement and IT and a low-cost fares strategy on its 180 short-haul routes to compete with the low-cost airlines. One sign of the e-travel revolution for a large airline such as BA is that in 2003/4 two-thirds of its passengers now travel with e-tickets and 10,000 customers a day manage their travel online. Thus, whilst repositioning the airline and restructuring costs, BA has also managed to set benchmarks for customer comfort with its Club World flat beds and a sleeper service, at the same time undertaking a

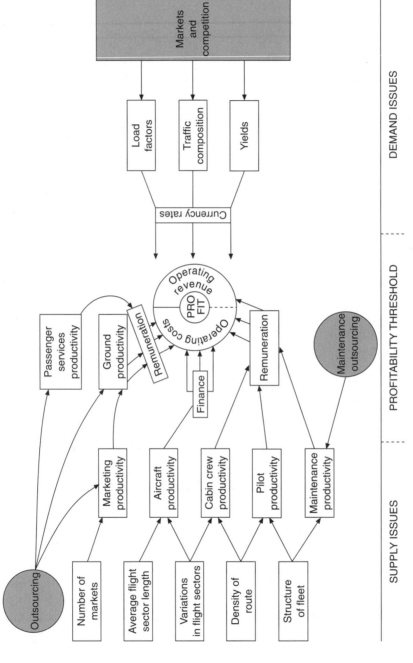

Figure 10.6 Interdependencies in the factors and variables affecting airline costs

Source: Adapted from Seristö and Vepsäläinen 1997.

major advertising campaign to showcase the airline on television in order to re-establish the airline's brand and values.

Adding value in destination and consumer rights

Public transport certainly has a valid role to play in achieving sustainable tourism objectives in local areas. Such initiatives not only make a contribution to the reduction of congestion and environmental pollution in areas of natural beauty as discussed in Chapter 8, but also offer access opportunities for disabled people, cyclists and casual travellers in place of the car. Even in urban areas the development of public transport systems may offer the tourist more opportunities to enjoy the urban environment without the stress of parking and driving a car in congested cities. Brooks (1995) documented the reintroduction of historic Victorian trams in Christchurch, New Zealand, where the five vintage trams cover a 2.5 km inner-city track. By 1997 it was obvious that they were not profitable. Whilst the trams undoubtedly offer an attraction for the tourist, such as those used in Blackpool and Fylde in Lancashire, UK and San Francisco (see Plate 10.6) in California, it is evident that transport systems may sometimes need to be subsidised to generate tourist business for other sectors of the urban economy (as is the case with the tourist tram service in Melbourne) (Page 1993a, 1995b). Yet this seems to run somewhat contrary to the political policy-making environment in some countries where transport users, particularly tourists, need to pay the economic cost of transport.

Within an international context, there is also evidence to suggest that with the globalisation of the airline industry and other transport sectors there is a growing need for an agency to ensure fair competition. According to Downes and Tunney

Plate 10.6 Innovation in transport for tourism can take many forms, as this world-famous fire engine tour, which crosses San Francisco's Golden Gate bridge, shows

Source: Dr Joanne Connell

(1997), European competition law for the air transport industry may 'become the foundation stone for global competition rules for aviation' (Downes and Tunney 1997: 76). The World Trade Organization is seen as the most likely body to ensure competition rules are upheld. At the same time tourist transport providers are facing an operating environment where increased health and safety regulations (see Caves 1996) and airport risk controls as well as measures such as the EU's *Protection of Tourists* (European Parliament 1995) place a greater onus on the operator and packager to provide accurate information to travellers. More recent steps towards Customer Charters for tourist travel by other modes of transport in the EU (see Page 2003 for more detail) may also begin to harmonise these issues. These types of measure are likely to encourage transport operators to consider the tourist experience within the context of ever-increasing demands for quality improvements.

Air rage and passenger behaviour: a worrying trend?

One worrying trend in the airline sector is the rise in 'on-board incidents' where unruly passengers disrupt the flight, and in extreme cases can cause severe problems for in-flight staff and pose safety threats. This has been termed *air rage* (Anon and Thomas 2001). Skapinker (1998b) reports that whilst BA only encountered 10–15 such incidents a year in the mid to late 1990s, a recent debate in the House of Commons over new legislation – the Aviation (Offense) Bill *www.publications. parliament.uk*) updates these statistics. The debate noted a 400 per cent increase in such incidents globally since 1995 with 1055 incidents logged in the UK in the year ending March 2002. The UK CAA classified these incidents, with 50 per cent significant and 5 per cent serious (which is where there is potential to threaten personal safety and in-flight safety). These incidents can endanger the lives of hundreds of people, and air rage has become a newsworthy item. Since Skapinker's study the literature on this subject and the scale of the problem has expanded (see the US website *www.skyrage.org* for current research and links to statistics). It is likely that this is only the tip of the iceberg, but it is certainly a concern for both airline employees and passengers alike, as the author found when observing such an incident that was not reported. One of the contributory factors is alcohol consumption, and BA now empowers its staff to prevent drunker passengers from boarding and to stop serving passengers who appear drunk on board, a feature that the skyrage.org lobby group is also advocating to prevent in-flight incidents. New legislation in 2003 sought to deal with unruly passengers in addition to the 2000 Air Navigation Order. One useful study on *www.skyrage.org* by psychologists at London Metropolitan University (Bor et al nd) expanded upon earlier research by the author (Bor 1999) to illustrate that in the USA the Federal Aviation Administration defines passenger misconduct in three ways, related to refusal to comply with flight attendant requests through to continuous disturbance and interference leading to the possibility of injury, an unscheduled diversion or the use of restraints such as flexcuffs. In the UK the scale of these incidents has grown in recent years from 648 cases in 2002/3 (of which 35 were serious) to 2219 cases in 2006/7 (of which 58 were serious) and typical explanations offered include the rise in binge drinking and nicotine deprivation from non-smoking flights. As Abeyratne (2008) observed, existing aviation conventions do not provide a legal basis for dealing with these incidents unless States make provision in their own laws as the UK has done. In the USA, the FAA regulations prohibit assaults, threats, intimidation or interfering with crew members' duties whilst an aircraft is being operated. Reporting of incidents which fall under this classification (and excluding security violations) are voluntarily reported to the FAA. There were only 147 such reports in 2007, although FAA fines can be up to US$25,000 per violation for an unruly passenger, with one incident potentially leading to several violations.

Airport delays and inadequate information may lead to increased alcohol consumption, and at least one Asian airline has issued cabin staff with restraints to prevent disorderly conduct. Amongst the likely causes of air rage according to Bor et al (nd) are: too much alcohol, passenger personality, timetable delays, stress of air travel, smoking ban, cramped conditions, denial to carry on luggage and poor air quality. What was interesting in the House of Commons discussion of air rage was the qualitative correlation between its increase, the growth of low-cost airlines and a growth in antisocial behaviour, a feature that has seen significant government legislation and attention in the last five years. Whether this commentary is rhetoric or based on empirical data it is clear that the airlines and their staff recognise the rise in such behaviour, which poses problems for management (Bor 1999). Although such events usually occur on long-haul flights, all airlines are imposing heavy fines on unruly passengers, especially where pilots divert to eject them. It is just one additional issue with which airlines now have to deal. Managing such situations in an appropriate manner can also result in commitment and customer loyalty if the emphasis is on the enhancement of a quality experience for all passengers. The issue is therefore certainly a problematic and worrying trend for airlines, especially those that serve alcohol in-flight, and it highlights one further security and safety concern now affecting tourist travel in the new millennium (Sweet 2003).

Questions

1 What is globalisation and how are transport operators responding to operating in a global tourism economy?

2 What types of problem can affect service quality in tourist transport systems?

3 What is hypercompetition? How are transport operators responding to such issues?

4 Are travellers developing unrealistic expectations of tourist transport providers? What can transport operators do to avoid a continued gap between expectation and delivery in the tourist travel experience?

Further reading

There is an enormous business literature on quality issues, quality management and the challenges facing service organisations involved in service delivery. However, the following offer a good starting point for a literature that is laden with acronyms, hype, jargon and repetitive messages focused on a simple set of principles.

Abeyratne, R. (2008) 'The fear of flying and air rage – some legal issues', *Journal of Transportation Security*, 1(1): 45–66.

Berry, L.L. and Parasuraman, A. (1991) *Marketing Services: Competing Through Quality*, New York: Free Press.

Bor, R. (1999) 'Unruly passenger behaviour and in-flight violence: A psychological perspective', *Travel Medicine International*, 17(1): 5–10.

Bunting, M. (2004) *Willing Slaves: The Overwork Culture is Ruling Our Lives*, Harper-Collins: London. This is a good overview of the new emotional labour debate along with the role of working in the service economy in the new millennium.

Fitzsimmons, J.A. and Sullivan, R.S. (1982) *Service Operations Management*, New York: McGraw-Hill.

Hochschild, A. (1983) *The Managed Heart: Commercialization of Human Feeling*, University of California Press: Berkeley. This is a classic study that introduced the emotional labour debate and examines many of the service issues from the point of view of how they impact upon employees.

Ilinitch, A., Lewin, A. and D'Aveni, R. (eds) (1998) *Managing in Times of Disorder: Hyper competition Organisational Responses*, London: Sage.

Sultan, F. and Simpson, M. (2000) 'International service variants: Airline passenger expectations and perceptions of service quality', *Journal of Services Marketing*, 14(3): 188–216. This provides a good analysis of cultural differences in service quality.

Townsend, P.L. and Gebhart, J.E. (1986) *Commit to Quality*, New York: John Wiley.

Zeithmal, A. and Berry, L.L. (1985) 'A conceptual model of service quality and its implications for future research', *Journal of Marketing*, Fall: 41–50.

Zins, A. (2001) 'Relative attitudes and commitment in customer loyalty models: Experiences in the commercial airline industry', *International Journal of Service Industry Management*, 12(3): 269–94. This is a good analysis of service encounters in tourism with reference to the airline industry.

The following popular books are worth consulting for more up-to-date discussion of the key issues:

Anon and Thomas, A.R. (2001) *Air Rage: Crisis in the Skies*, New Jersey: Prometheus Books.

Sweet, K. (2003) *Aviation and Airport Security: Terrorism and Safety Concerns*, Englewood Cliffs, NJ: Pearson Education.

Thomas, A.R. (2003) *Aviation Insecurity*, New York: Prometheus Books.

A good example of an innovative green transport scheme can be found in:

Hjalager, A. (2007) 'Stages in the economic globalization of tourism', *Annals of Tourism Research*, 34(2): 437–57.

Lumsdon, L. and Owen, E. (2004) 'Tourism Transport: the green key initiative', in L. Lumsdon and S.J. Page (eds) *Tourism and Transport: Issues and Agenda for the New Millennium*, Oxford: Elsevier, 157–76.

In terms of visitor safety see:

Cozens, P., Neale, R., Whitaker, J. and Hillier, D. (2003) 'Managing crime and the fear of crime at railway stations – a case study in South Wales (UK)', *International Journal of Transport Management*, 1(3): 121–32.

Bibliography

Abeyratne, R. (1993) 'Air transport tax and its consequences on tourism', *Annals of Tourism Research*, 20(3): 450–60.

Abeyratne, R. (1995) 'Proposals and guidelines for the carriage of elderly and disabled persons by air', *Journal of Travel Research*, 33(3): 52–9.

Abeyratne, R. (1998) 'The regulatory management in air transport', *Journal of Air Transport Management*, 4(1): 25–37.

Abeyratne, R. (2008) 'The fear of flying and air rage – Some legal issues', *Journal of Transportation Security*, 1(1): 45–66.

Adams, J. (1981) *Transport Planning: Vision and Practice*, London: Routledge & Kegan Paul.

Adamson, M., Jones, W. and Platt, R. (1991) 'Competition issues in privatisation: lessons for the railways', in D. Banister and K.J. Button (eds) *Transport in a Free Market Economy*, Basingstoke, Macmillan, 49–78.

Addley, E. (2006) 'Boom in green holidays as ethical travel takes off', *The Guardian*, 17 July (www.guardian.co.uk/uk_news/story/0,1822040,00.html), accessed 13 July 2008.

Agriculture Western Australia (2000a) *Grape Phylloxera: Exotic Threat to Western Australia, Factsheet no. 0002–2000*, Perth: Department of Agriculture.

Agriculture Western Australia (2000b) *Viticulture Industry Protection Plan*, Perth: Department of Agriculture.

Airbus (2003) *Global Market Forecasts 2003–2022*, Lyon: Airbus.

Airbus (2007) *Global Market Forecast 2007–2026*, Toulouse: Airbus.

Air Transport Action Group (ATAG) (1993) *Surface Transportation and Airports*, Geneva: ATAG.

Air Transport Action Group (ATAG) (1994) *North American Traffic Forecasts 1984–2010*, Geneva: ATAG. (www.atag.org/NATF/Index.htm).

Air Transport Action Group (ATAG) (1997a) *The Economic Benefits of Air Transport*, Geneva: ATAG. (www.atag.org/ECO/Index.htm).

Air Transport Action Group (ATAG) (1997b) *Asia Pacific Air Traffic Growth and Constraints*, Geneva: ATAG. (www.atag.org/ASIA/Index.htm).

Air Transport Action Group (ATAG) (2000) *The Economic Benefits of Air Transport*, Brussels: ATAG.

Air Transport Action Group (ATAG) (2001) *Asia-Pacific Air Traffic: Growth and Constraints*, Brussels: ATAG.

Air Transport Action Group (ATAG) (2005) *Aviation and Environment Summit Discussion Paper*, Geneva: Air Transport Action Group.

Air Transport Action Group (ATAG) (2008) *The Economic and Social Benefits of Air Transport 2008*, Geneva: ATAG.

Airey, D. and Tribe, J. (eds) (2005) *Tourism Education Handbook*, Oxford: Pergamon.

Akhter, S. (2003) 'Strategic planning, hypercompetition, and knowledge management', *Business Horizons*, 36(1): 19–24.

Alamdari, F. and Morrell, P. (1997a) 'Airline alliances: A catalyst for regulatory change in key markets', *Journal of Air Transport Management*, 3(1): 1–2.

Alamdari, F. and Morrell, P. (1997b) 'Airline labour cost reduction: Post-liberalisation experience in the USA and Europe', *Journal of Air Transport Management*, 3(2): 53–66.

Allen, D. and Williams, G. (1985) 'The development of management information to meet the needs of a new management structure', in K.J. Button and D. Pitfield (eds) *International Railway Economics: Studies in Management and Efficiency*, Aldershot, Gower, 85–100.

Anderson, R., Correia, S. and Wirasinghe, C. (2007) 'Development of level of service standards for airport facilities: Application to São Paulo International Airport', *Journal of Air Transport Management*, 13(2): 97–103.

Anon (1992) 'Japan', *International Tourism Reports*, 4: 5–35.

Anon (1997) *The Europa World Yearbook 1997*, Woking: Gresham Press.

Anon (1998) 'Scenic wonder pays price of popularity', *New Zealand Herald*, 26 February: A24.

Anon and Thomas, A.R. (2001) *Air Rage: Crisis in the Skies*, Amherst, NY: Prometheus Books.

Annals of Tourism Research (1991) 'Special issue: Tourism social science', *Annals of Tourism Research*, 18(1).

APEC (2003) *2003 APEC Economic Outlook*, Singapore: APEC.

Archdale, G. (1991) 'Computer reservation systems: The international scene', *INSIGHTS*, November: D15–20.

Archer, B.H. (1987) 'Demand forecasting and estimation', in J.R.B. Ritchie and C.R. Goeldner (eds) *Travel, Tourism and Hospitality Research*, New York: Wiley, 77–85.

Archer, B.H. (1989) 'Tourism and small island economies', in C.P. Cooper (ed.) *Progress in Tourism, Recreation and Hospitality Management*, Volume 1, London: Belhaven, 125–35.

Archer, B. (1995) 'The impact of international tourism on the economy of Bermuda', *Journal of Travel Research*, 34(2): 27–30.

Archway (2008) *Good Practice Guide: Transport*, Bristol: Archway.

Ardill, J. (1987) 'The environmental impact', in B. Jones (ed.) *The Tunnel: The Channel Tunnel and Beyond*, Chichester: Ellis Harwood, 177–212.

Areeda, P. and Turner, D. (1975) 'Predatory prices and related practices under Section 2 of the Sherman Act', *Harvard Law Review* 88(4): 697–783.

Ashford, H. and Moore, C. (1992) *Airport Finance*, New York: Van Nostrand Reinhold.

Ashford, H., Stanton, H. and Moore, C. (1991) *Airport Operations*, London: Pitman.

Association of German Chambers of Industry and Commerce, DIHK. (www.dihk. de/english/).

Attard, M. (2005) 'Land transport policy in a small island state – The case of Malta', *Transport Policy*, 12(1): 23–33.

Attard, M. and Hall, D.R. (2003) 'Public transport modernisation and adjustment to EU accession requirements: The case of Malta's buses', *Journal of Transport Geography*, 11(1): 13–24.

Auger, R.R. and Morgenthaler T.I. (2009) 'Jet lag and other sleep disorders relevant to the traveller', *Travel Medicine and Infectious Disease*, 7(2): 60–68.

Australian National Audit Office (ANAO) (2001) *Managing for Quarantine Effectiveness: Department of Agriculture, Fisheries and Forestry: Australia*, The Auditor-General Audit Report No. 47 2000–2001 Performance Audit, Canberra: Commonwealth of Australia.

Backx, M. and Gedajlovic, E. (2002) 'Public, private and mixed ownership and the performance of international airlines', *Journal of Air Transport Management*, 8: 213–20.

Bailey, E. and Baumol, W. (1984) 'Deregulation and the theory of contestable markets', *Yale Journal of Regulation,* 2: 111–37.

Ballantyne, T. (1996) 'Airlines in China', *Travel and Tourism Analyst*, 2: 4–20.

Baloglu, S. and Shoemaker, S. (2001) 'Prediction of senior travelers' motorcoach use from demographic, psychological, and psychographic characteristics', *Journal of Travel Research*, 40(1): 12–18.

Bania, N., Bauer, P. and Zlatoper, T. (1998) 'US air passenger service: A taxonomy of route networks, hub locations and competition', *Transportation Research E*, 34(1): 53–74.

Banister, D. (1992) 'Policy responses in the UK', in D. Banister and K.J. Button (eds) *Transport, the Environment and Sustainable Development*, London: E & FN Spon, 53–78.

Banister, D. (1994) *Transport Planning in the UK, USA and Europe*, London: E & FN Spon.

Banister, D. (ed.) (1998) *Transport Policy and the Environment*, London: E & FN Spon.

Banister, D. and Button, K.J. (eds) (1991) *Transport in a Free Market Economy*, Basingstoke: Macmillan.

Banister, D. and Button, K.J. (eds) (1992) *Transport, the Environment and Sustainable Development*, London: E & FN Spon.

Banister, D. and Hall, P. (eds) (1981) *Transport and Public Policy Planning*, London: Mansell.

Baranowski, S. (2007) 'Common ground: linking transport and tourism history', *Journal of Transport History*, 28(1): 120–24.

Barbier, E.B. (1988) *New Approaches in Environmental and Resource Economics: Towards an Economics of Sustainable Development*, London: International Institute for Environment and Development.

Barker, M. (1986) *Transport and Trade*, Edinburgh: Oliver & Boyd.

Barker, M. and Page, S.J. (2002) 'Visitor safety in urban environments', *Cities: The International Journal of Urban Policy and Planning*, 19(4): 273–82.

Barlay, S. (1995) *Cleared for Take-off: Behind the Scenes of Air Travel*, London: Kyle Cathie Limited.

Barnes, C. (1989) *Successful Marketing for the Transport Operator: A Practical Guide*, London: Kogan Page.

BaRon, R. (1997) 'Global tourism trends to 1996', *Tourism Economics*, 3(3): 289–300.

Barrett, S. (2004) 'How do the demands for airport services differ between full-service carriers and low-cost carriers?', *Journal of Air Transport Management*, 10(1): 33–9.

Barrett, S. (2008) 'The emergence of a low cost carrier sector', in A. Graham, A. Papatheodorou and P. Forsyth (eds) *Aviation and Tourism: Implications for Leisure Travel*, Aldershot: Ashgate, 103–18.

Basso, L. and Zhang, A. (2008) 'On the relationship between airport pricing models', *Transportation Research*, B42(9): 725–35.

Baum, T. (ed.) (1993) *Human Resource Issues in International Tourism*, Oxford: Butterworth-Heinemann.

Beaver, A. (1996) 'Frequent flyer programmes: the beginning of the end?', *Tourism Economics*, 21: 43–60.

Becken, S. (2007) Tourists' perception of international air travel's impact on the global climate and potential climate change policies', *Journal of Sustainable Tourism*, 15(4): 351–68.

Becken, S. (2008a) 'Carbon footprint of New Zealand tourism – Overview', Lincoln University (www.leap.ac.nz/site/section.asp?bid=24&SectionID=1075), accessed 15 October 2008.

Becken, S. (2008b) 'Indicators for managing tourism in the face of peak oil', *Tourism Management*, 29: 695–705.

Becken, S. and Hay, J. (2007) *Tourism and Climate Change – Risks and Opportunities*, Cleveland: Channel View Publications.

Becken, S. and Simmons, D. (2008) 'Using the concept of yield to assess sustainability of different tourist types', *Ecological Economics*, 67: 420–29.

Becken, S., Vuletich, I. and Campbell, S. (2007) 'Developing a GIS-supported tourist flow model for New Zealand', in D. Airey and J. Tribe (eds) *Developments in Tourism Research*, Elsevier: Oxford, 107–22.

Beesley, M.E. (1989) 'Transport research and economics', *Journal of Transport Economics and Policy*, 23: 17–28.

Beioley, S. (1995) 'On yer bike – cycling and tourism', *INSIGHTS*: A17–A31.

Beioley, S. (1997) 'Four weddings, a funeral and the visiting friends and relatives market', *INSIGHTS*: B1–B6.

Beirão, G. and Cabrol, S. (2007) 'Understanding attitudes towards public transport and private car: A qualitative study', *Transport Policy*, 14(6): 478–89.

Bel, G. (2009) 'How to compete for a place in the world with a hand tied behind your back: The case of air transport services in Girona', *Tourism Management*, 30.

Bell, D., Dunlop, I. and Glazebrook, D. (2008) 'Peak oil, risk and opportunity', *Risk Management*, April (www.greencrossaustralia.org/media/84722/csa20po20&20risk_mgmnt.pdf), accessed 10 October 2008.

Bell, G., Blackledge, D. and Bowen, P. (1983) *The Economics of Transport and Planning*, London: Heinemann.

Belobaba, P. (1987) *Air Travel Demand and Airline Seat Inventory Management*, Cambridge, MA.: MIT Flight Transportation Laboratory Report R87–7.

Belobaba, P. and Wilson, J. (1997) 'Impacts of yield management in competitive airline markets', *Journal of Air Transport Management*, 3(1): 3–10.

Bennett, M. (1997) 'Strategic alliances in the world airline industry', *Progress in Tourism and Hospitality Research*, 3: 213–23.

Bentley, R.W. (2002) 'Global oil and gas depletion: an overview. Viewpoint', *Energy Policy*, 30: 189–205.

Berkelman, R.L., Bryan, R.T., Osterholm, M.T., LeDuc, J.W. and Hughes, J.M. (1994) 'Infectious disease surveillance: A crumbling foundation', *Science*, 264: 368–70.

Bernard, D.T. and Scott, V.N. (1995) 'Risk assessment and foodborne micro-organisms: The difficulties of biological diversity', *Food Control*, 6: 329–33.

Bernier, X. (2003) 'Traffic, national parks, and regional natural parks in the French Alps: Interaction between the objectives of accessibility, protection and development', *Revue de Géographie Alpine*, 91(2): 27–40.

Berry, L.L. and Parasuraman, A. (1991) *Marketing Services: Competing Through Quality*, New York: Free Press.

Bertolini, L. and Spit, T. (1998) *Cities on Rails: The Redevelopment of Station Areas*, London: E & FN Spon.

Bertrand, I. (1997) 'Airlines in the Caribbean', *Travel and Tourism Analyst*, 6: 4–24.

Biosecurity Strategy Development Team (2001a) *A Biosecurity Strategy for New Zealand: Strategy Vision Framework Background Paper for Stakeholder Working Groups*, Wellington: Biosecurity Strategy Development Team.

Biosecurity Strategy Development Team (2001b) *Issues Paper: Developing a Biosecurity Strategy for New Zealand: A Public Consultation Paper*, Wellington: Biosecurity Strategy Development Team.

Biosecurity Strategy Development Team (2002) *Developing a Biosecurity Strategy for New Zealand: Submissions on the 'Issues Paper': A Summary Report*, Wellington: Biosecurity Strategy Development Team.

Bird, P. and Rutherford, B.A. (1989) *Understanding Company Accounts*, London: Pitman.

Bishop and Gimblett (2000) 'Management of recreational areas: Geographic information systems, autonomous agents and virtual reality', *Environmental and Planning B: Planning and Design*, 27: 423–35.

Bitner, M.J. (1992) 'Servicescapes: The impact of physical surroundings on customers and employees', *Journal of Marketing*, 56(2): 57–71.

Bitner, M.J., Booms, B.H. and Tetreanit, M.S. (1990) 'The service encounter: Diagnosing favourable and unfavourable incidents', *Journal of Marketing*, 1: 71–84.

Black, N. and Clark, A. (1998) *Tourism in North West Queensland: 1996, Tourist Characteristics, Numbers and Travel Flows*, Townsville, Australia: Tropical Savannas CRC.

Black, N. and Rutledge, J. (1995) *The Outback: The Authentic Australian Adventure*, Townsville, Australia: James Cook University Press.

Boeing (2005) *Current Market Outlook 2005*, Seattle: Boeing Commercial Airplanes Marketing.

Boeing Commercial Airplane Group (1994) *1994 Current Market Outlook*, Seattle: Boeing Commercial Airplane Group.

Boeing Commercial Airplane Group (1996) *1996 Current Market Outlook*, Seattle: Boeing Commercial Airplane Group.

Boeing Commercial Airline Group (2003) *2002 Current Market Outlook*, Seattle: Boeing Commercial Airline Group.

Beunen, R., Jaarsma, C. and Regnerus, H. (2006) 'Evaluating the effects of parking policy measures in nature areas', *Journal of Transport Geography*, 14(3): 376–83.

Beunen, R., Regnerus, H. and Jaarsma, C. (2007) 'Gateways as a means of visitor management in national parks and protected areas', *Tourism Management*, 29(1): 138–14.

Böhler, S., Grischkat, S., Haustein, S. and Hunecke, M. (2006) 'Encouraging environmentally sustainable holiday travel', *Transportation Research Part A*, 40: 652–70.

Borgdorff, M.W and Motarjemi, Y. (1997) 'Foodborne disease surveillance: What are the options?', *World Health Statistics Quarterly*, 50(1/2): 12–23.

Bor, R. (1999) 'Unruly passenger behaviour and in-flight violence: A psychological perspective', *Travel Medicine International*, 17(1): 5–10.

Bor, R. (2003) 'Trends in disruptive passenger behaviour on board UK registered aircraft: 1999–2003', *Travel Medicine and Infectious Disease*, 1(3): 153–7.

Bóte Gomez, V. and Sinclair, M.T. (1991) 'Integration in the tourism industry: A case study approach', in M.T. Sinclair and M.J. Stabler (eds) *The Tourism Industry: An International Analysis*, Oxford: CAB International, 67–90.

Bootle, R. (2003) *Money for Nothing: Real Wealth, Financial Fantasies and the Economy of the Future*, London: Nicholas Brealey Publishing.

Bowen, J. (1997) 'The Asia Pacific airline industry: Prospects for multilateral liberalisation', in C. Findlay, L. Chia and K. Singh (eds) *Asia Pacific Air Transport: Challenges and Policy Reforms*, Singapore: Institute of South East Asian Studies, 123–53.

Bowen, B. and Headley, D. (2001) *The Airline Quality Rating 2001* (www.unomaha.edu), accessed 24 June 2003.

Bradfield, R., Wright, G., Burt, G., Cairns, G. and van der Heijden, K. (2005) 'The origins and evolution of scenario techniques in long range business planning', *Futures*, 37: 795–812.

Braithwaite, G., Caves, R. and Faulkner, J. (1998) 'Australian aviation safety: Observations from the lucky country', *Journal of Air Transport Management*, 4(1): 55–62.

Bray, R. and Raitz, V. (2001) *Flight to the Sun*, London: Continuum.

Briggs, S. (1997) 'Marketing on the Internet: Tangled webs or powerful network?', *INSIGHTS*, A27–A34.

Brihla, N. (2008) 'Airport requirements for leisure travellers', in A. Graham, A. Papatheodorou and P. Forsyth (eds) *Aviation and Tourism: Implications for Leisure Travel*, Aldershot: Ashgate, 167–76.

Bristow, A.L., Tight, M., Pridmore, A. and May, A.D. (2008) 'Developing pathways to low carbon land-based passenger transport in Great Britain by 2050', *Energy Policy*, 36: 3427–35.

British Airports Authority (1997) *Investing for Growth: BAA Annual Report 1996/97*, London: British Airports Authority.

British Airports Authority (2004) *Annual Report*, London: British Airports Authority.

British Airways (BA) (1992) *Annual Environmental Report*, Hounslow: British Airways.

British Airways (BA) (1997) *Annual Environmental Report*, Hounslow: British Airways (http://www.british-airways.com).

British Airways (BA) (2003) *2002/2003 Social and Environmental Report*, Harmondsworth: British Airways.

British Airways (BA) (2004) *Social and Environmental Report* 2003/2004, Harmandsworth: British Airways.

British Railways Board (1992) *The British Rail Passenger's Charter*, London: British Railways Board.

British Railways Board (1996) *National Conditions of Carriage*, London: British Railways Board.

British Tourist Authority (1991) *1993 Cross-Channel Marketing Strategy*, London: British Tourist Authority.

British Travel Association and the University of Keele (1967 and 1969) *Pilot National Recreation Survey*, Keele: British Travel Association and the University of Keele.

Britton, S. (1982) 'The political economy of tourism in the Third World', *Annals of Tourism Research*, 9(3): 331–58.

Broads Authority (1997) *Broads Plan*, Norwich: Broads Authority.

Broads Authority (2004) *Broads Plan*, Norwich: Broads Authority.

Brooks, K. (1995) 'Old trams creak back to streets', *New Zealand Herald*, 16 January: 9.

Brons, M., Pels, E., Nijkamp, P. and Rietveld, P. (2002) 'Price elasticities of demand for air travel: a meta-analysis', *Journal of Air Transport Management*, 8: 165–75.

Brown, G.M., Pandi-Perumal, S.R., Trakht, I., Cardinali, D.P. (2009) 'Melatonin and its relevance to jet lag', *Travel Medicine and Infectious Disease*, 7(2): 69–81.

Broughton, P. and Walker, L. (2009) *Motorcycling and Leisure: Understanding the Recreational PTW Rider*, Aldershot: Ashgate.

Buckley, P.J. (1987) 'Tourism: an economic transaction analysis', *Tourism Management*, 8(3): 190–4.

Buckley, P.J. and Casson, M. (1987) *The Economic Theory of the Multinational Enterprise: Selected Papers*, London: Macmillan.

Buhalis, D. (2003) *e-Tourism: Information Technology for Strategic Tourism Management*, Harlow: Pearson Education.

Buhalis, D. and Licata, M. (2002) 'The future of eTourism intermediaries', *Tourism Management*, 23(3): 207–20.

Bull, A. (1991) *The Economics of Travel and Tourism*, London: Pitman.

Bull, A. (1996) 'The economics of cruising: An application to the short ocean cruise market', *Journal of Tourism Studies*, 7(2): 28–35.

Bunn, D. (1993) 'Forecasting with scenarios', *European Journal of Operational Research*, 68(3): 291–303.

Bunting, M. (2004) *Willing Slaves: The Overwork Culture is Ruling Our Lives*, London: HarperCollins.

Burkart, A. and Medlik, S. (1974) *Tourism, Past, Present and Future*, Oxford: Heinemann.

Burkart, A. and Medlik, S. (eds) (1975) *The Management of Tourism*, Oxford: Heinemann.

Burns, P. (1996) 'Japan's Ten Million programme: The paradox of statistical success', *Progress in Tourism and Hospitality Research*, 2: 181–92.

Burt, T. (1998) 'Europeans cruise to luxury contracts', *Financial Times*, 5 February: 4.

Burton, J. and Hanlon, P. (1994) 'Airline alliances: cooperating to compete?', *Journal of Air Transport Management*, 1(4): 209–28.

Burton, T. (1966) 'A day in the country: A survey of leisure activity at Box Hill in Surrey', *Journal of the Royal Institute of Chartered Surveyors*, 98: 378–80.

Bus and Coach Council (1991) *Buses and Coaches: The Way Forward*, London: Bus and Coach Council.

Button, K.J. (1982) *Transport Economics*, London: Heinemann.

Button, K.J. (1990) 'The Channel Tunnel: Economic implications for the South East', *Geographical Journal*, 156(2): 87–99.

Button, K.J. (1996) 'Aviation deregulation in the European Union: Do actors learn in the regulation game?', *Contemporary Economic Policy*, 14: 70–80.

Button, K.J. (1997) 'Developments in the European Union: Lessons for the Pacific Asia region', in C. Findlay, L. Chia and K. Singh (eds) *Asia Pacific Air Transport: Challenges and Reforms*, Singapore: Institute of South East Asian Studies, 170–80.

Button, K.J. and Gillingwater, K. (eds) (1983) *Future Transport Policy*, London: Routledge.

Button, K.J. and Gillingwater, K. (eds) (1991) *Airline Deregulation: International Experiences*, London: Fulton.

Button, K.J. and Rothengatter, W. (1992) 'Global environmental degradation: The role of transport', in D. Banister and K.J. Button (eds) *Transport, the Environment and Sustainable Development*, London: E & FN Spon, 19–52.

Button, K.J., Haynes, K. and Stough, R. (1998) *Flying into the Future: Air Transport Policy in the European Union*, Cheltenham: Edward Elgar.

Bywater, M. (1990) 'Japanese investment in South Pacific tourism', *Travel and Tourism Analyst*, 3: 51–64.

CAA (2006) *No Frills Carriers: Revolution or Evolution?*, London: CAA.

Cairns, M. (1998) 'The development of park and ride in Scotland', *Journal of Transport Geography*, 6(4): 295–307.

Calder, S. (2002) *No Frills: the Truth Behind the Low-cost Revolution in the Skies*, London: Virgin.

Calentone, R., Benedetto, A. and Bojanic, D. (1987) 'A comprehensive review of tourism forecasting literature', *Journal of Travel Research*; 36(3): 79–84.

Campbell, C. (1966) *An Approach to Recreational Geography*, BC Occasional Papers No. 7.

Campbell, C.J. and Laherrère, J.H. (1998) 'The end of cheap oil', *Scientific American*, March: 60–65.

Canina, L., Walsh, K. and Enz, C. (2003) 'The effects of gasoline-price changes on room demand: a study of branded hotels from 1988 through 2000', *Cornell Hotel and Restaurant Administration Quarterly*, 44(4), 29–37.

Cannon, T. (1989) *Basic Marketing Principles and Practice*, 3rd edn, London: Holt, Rinehart & Winston.

Carlsson, F. (2002) 'Environmental charges in airline markets', *Transportation Research D*, 7(2): 137–53.

Carlton, J.T. and Geller, J.B. (1993) 'Ecological roulette: The global transport of non-indigenous marine organisms', *Science*, 261: 78–82.

Carpenter, T. (1994) *The Environmental Impact of Railways*, Chichester: Wiley.

Carter, D. (1996) 'Broader horizons beckon', *Financial Times'*, 18 November (World Airports Survey), II.

Casson, M. (2004) 'The future of the UK railway system: Michael Brooke's vision', *International Business Review*, 13(2): 181–214.

Caves, R. (1994) 'A search for more apron capacity', *Journal of Air Transport Management*, 1(2): 109–20.

Caves, R. (1996) 'Control of risk near airports', *Built Environment*, 22(3): 223–33.

Caves, R. and Gosling, D. (1999) *Strategic Airport Planning*, Oxford: Pergamon.

CEDRE (1990) *Transports a grande vitesse: développement régional et ménagement du territoire, rapport de synthesè*, Strasburg: Centre Europeen du Développement Regional.

Central Otago Winegrowers Association (COWA) (2002) *Winegrowers Respond to Phylloxera*, COWA Press Release, 4 February.

Chalk, J., Chalk, A., Steiber, J.A. and Hopkins, A.W (1987) 'Managing the airlines in the 1990s', *Journal of Business Strategy*, 7(3): 87–91.

Chan, D. (2000) 'The development of the airline industry from 1978–1998: A strategic global overview', *Journal of Management Development*, 19(6): 489–514.

Chang, H. and Yang, C. (2008) 'Do airline self-service check-in kiosks meet the needs of passengers?', *Tourism Management*, 29(5): 980–93.

Chang, H.-L. and Yang, C.-H. (2008) 'Explore airlines' brand niches through measuring passengers' repurchase motivation and an application of Rasch measurement', *Journal of Air Transport Management*, 14(3): 105–12.

Channel Tunnel Group (1985) *The Channel Tunnel Project: Environmental Effects in the UK*, London: Channel Tunnel Group.

Channel Tunnel Joint Consultative Committee (1986) *Kent Impact Study*, London: Department of Transport.

Charlton, C. (1998) 'Public transport and sustainability: the case of the Devon and Cornwall Rail Partnership', in C.M. Hall and A. Lew (eds) *The Geography of Sustainable Tourism*, Harlow: Addison-Wesley Longman.

Charlton, C., Gibb, R. and Shaw, J. (1997) 'Regulation and continuing monopoly on Britain's railways', *Journal of Transport Geography*, 5(2): 147–53.

Charlton, C. and Gibb, R. (1998) 'Transport deregulation and privatisation', *Journal of Transport Geography*, 6(2): 85.

Chartered Institute of Public Finance and Accountancy (CIPFA) (1996) *The UK Airports Industry: Airport Statistics 1994/95*, London: CIPFA.

Chase, G. and McKee, D. (2003) 'The economic impact of cruise tourism on Jamaica', *Journal of Tourism Studies*, 14(2): 16–22.

Chatterjee, K. and Gordon, A. (2006) 'Planning for an unpredictable future: Transport in Great Britain to 2030', *Transport Policy*, 13(3): 254–64.

Chen, F. and Chang, Y. (2005) 'Examining airline service quality from a process perspective', *Journal of Air Transport Management*, 11(2): 79–87.

Chermack, T., Lynham, S. and Ruona, W. (2001) 'A review of scenario planning literature', *Futures Research Quarterly*, Summer: 7–31.

Chew, S. (1997) 'SIA eyes more ventures overseas to raise bottom line', *Straits Times* (Singapore), 17 February.

Childs, D. (2000) 'The emergence of no-frills airlines in Europe: An example of successful marketing strategy', *Travel and Tourism Analyst*, 1: 87–121.

Chimonas, M., Vaughan, G., Widdowson, M. and Cramer, E. (2008) 'Passenger behaviours associated with norovirus infection on board a cruise ship – Alaska', *Journal of Travel Medicine*, 15(3): 177–83.

Chin, A. (2005) 'Transport policies in ASEAN countries', in K. Button and D. Hensher (eds) *Handbook of Transport Strategy, Policy and Institutions*, Oxford: Elsevier, 745–62.

Chin, A. and Tay, J. (2001) 'Developments in air transport: implications for investment decisions, profitability and the survival of Asian airlines', *Journal of Air Transport Management*, 7(5): 319–30.

Chin, B. (2008) *Cruising in the Global Economy*, Aldershot: Ashgate.

Chou, Y.H. (1993) 'Airline deregulation and nodal accessibility', *Journal of Transport Geography*, 1(1): 36–46.

Christopher, M. (1994) *Logistics and Supply Chain Management*, New York: Irwin.

Chubb, M. (1989) 'Tourism patterns and determinants in the Great Lakes region: Population, resources and perceptions', *GeoJournal*, 19(3): 291–6.

Cidell, J. (2003) 'The conversion of military bases to commercial airports: Existing conversions and future possibilities', *Journal of Transport Geography*, 11(2): 93–102.

Civil Aviation Authority (CAA) (1997) *Reports and Accounts 1997*, London: Civil Aviation Authority.

Clift, S. and Page, S.J. (eds) (1996) *Health and the International Tourist*, London: Routledge.

Cline, R., Ruhl, T., Gosling, G. and Gillen, D. (1998) 'Air transportation demand forecasts in emerging market economies: A case study of the Kyrgyz Republic in the former Soviet Union', *Journal of Air Transport Management*, 4(1): 11–23.

Coase, R. (1937) 'The nature of the firm', *Economica*, 4: 386–405.

Cockerell, N. (1994) 'Europe to the Asia Pacific region', *Travel and Tourism Analyst*, 1: 65–82.

Cockerell, N. (1997) 'Growth of river cruising', *Travel Industry Monitor*, October: 7–8.

Cohen, E. (1972) 'Towards a sociology of international tourism', *Social Research*, 39: 164–82.

Cohen, A. and Harris, N. (1998) 'Mode choice for VFR journeys', *Journal of Transport Geography*, 6(1): 43–51.

Cole, S. (1994) 'Rail privatisation and its impact on the local authority's transport role', *INSIGHTS*: A73–A77.

Collier, A. (1989) *Principles of Tourism*, Auckland, Longman Paul.

Collier, A. (1994) *Principles of Tourism*, 3rd edn, Auckland, Longman Paul.

Commonwealth of Australia (1999) *Incoming Passenger Card*, Canberra: Commonwealth of Australia.

Competition Commission (2008) *BAA Airports Markets Investigation: Provisional Report*, London: Competition Commission.

Confederation of Passenger Transport (2002) *The Bus and Coach Industry in Scotland*, London: CPT.

Conlin, M. (1995) 'Rejuvenation planning for island tourism: The Bermuda example', in M. Conlin and T. Baum (eds) *Island Tourism*, Chichester: Wiley, 181–202.

Connell, J. (2004) *Visitor Destination and Infrastructure Study: Phase 1, Balloch*, Scotland: Loch Lomond and Trossachs National Park Authority.

Connell, J. (2005) 'Toddlers, tourism and Tobermory: Destination marketing issues and television induced tourism', *Tourism Management*, 26(5): 763–76.

Connell, J. and Page, S.J. (2008) 'Exploring the spatial patterns of car-based tourist travel in Loch Lomond and Trossachs National Park, Scotland', *Tourism Management*, 29(3): 561–80.

Cookson, S.T., Carballo, M., Nolan, C.M., Keystone, J.S. and Jong, E.C. (2001) 'Migrating populations: A closer view of who, why, and so what', *Journal of Emerging Infectious Diseases*, 7(3) (Supplement, June): 551.

Cooley, C. (1894) 'The theory of transportation', *Publications of the American Economic Association*, 9(3): 13–148.

Cooper, C., Fletcher, J., Gilbert, D. and Wanhill, S. (1993) *Tourism, Principles and Practice*, London: Pitman.

Cooper, C., Fletcher, J., Gilbert, D. and Wanhill, S. (1998) *Tourism, Principles and Practice*, 2nd edn, Harlow: Addison-Wesley Longman.

Cooper, J. (ed.) (1988) *Logistics and Distribution Planning: Strategies for Management*, London: Kogan Page.

Coppock, J.T. (ed.) (1977) *Second Homes: Curse or Blessing*, Oxford: Pergamon.

Coppock, J.T. and Duffield, B. (1975) *Recreation in the Countryside*, London: Macmillan.

Cornish, E. (2004) *Futuring: The Exploration of the Future*, Bethesda, MD: World Future Society.

Correia, A.R., Wirasinghe, S.C., de Barros, A.G. (2008) 'A global index for level of service evaluation at airport passenger terminals', *Transportation Research Part E: Logistics and Transportation Review*, 44(4): 607–20.

Cossar, J. (1993) 'Travellers' health: a review', *Travel Medicine International*, 17: 2–6.

Cossar, J., Reid, D., Fallon, R., Bell, E., Riding, M., Follett, E., Dow, B., Mitchell, S. and Grist, N. (1990) 'A cumulative review of studies of travellers, their experience of illness and the implications of these findings', *Journal of Infection*, 21: 27–42.

Coste, O. and Lagarde, D. (2009) 'Clinical management of jet lag: What can be proposed when performance is critical?', *Travel Medicine and Infectious Disease*, 7(2): 82–7.

Countryside Commission (1992) *Trends in Transport and the Countryside*, Cheltenham: Countryside Commission.

Countryside Commission (1995) *The Market for Recreational Cycling in the Countryside*, Cheltenham: Countryside Commission.

Cowell, D.W. (1986) *The Marketing of Services*, London: Heinemann.

Craven, J. (1990) *Introduction to Economics*, 2nd edn, Oxford: Blackwell.

Creaton, S. (2005) *Ryanair: How a Small Irish Airline Conquered the World*, London: Aurum Press.

Cullinane, S. (1992) 'Attitudes towards the car in the U.K.: Some implications for policies on congestion and the environment', *Transportation Research A*, 26(4): 291–301.

Cullinane, S. and Cullinane, K. (1999) 'Attitudes towards traffic problems and public transport in the Dartmoor and Lake District National Parks', *Journal of Transport Geography*, 7(1): 79–87.

D'Aveni, R. (1998) 'Hypercompetition closes in', *Financial Times*, 4 February (Global Business Series: Part 2, 12–13).

Dallen, J. (2007) 'The challenges of diverse visitor perceptions: Rail policy and sustainable transport at the resort destination', *Journal of Transport Geography*, 15(2): 104–15.

Damien, M. (1999) 'Waterways: A device for the development of regional tourism and recreation', *Hommes et Terres du Nord*, 4: 261–70.

Dann, G. (1994) 'Travel by train: Keeping nostalgia on track', in A. Seaton (ed.) *Tourism: State of the Art*, Chichester: Wiley.

Darcy, S. (2007) 'Flying with impairments: Improving airline practices by understanding the experiences of people with disabilities', in N.R. Moisey and W.C. Norman (eds) *Beating the Odds with Tourism Research!*, Las Vegas, Nevada: The Travel and Tourism Research Association, 61–70. (www.ttra.com/).

Davenport, J. and Davenport, J. (2006) 'The impact of tourism and personal leisure transport on coastal environments: a review', *Estuarine, Coastal and Shelf Science*, 67(1–2): 280–92.

David, F.R. (1989) 'How companies define their mission statements', *Long Range Planning*, 22(1): 90–7.

Dean, C. (1993) 'Travel by excursion coach in the United Kingdom', *Service Industries Journal*, 31(4): 59–64.

de Barros, A.G., Somasundaraswaran, A.K. and Wirasinghe, S.C. (2007) 'Evaluation of level of service for transfer passengers at airports', *Journal of Air Transport Management*, 13(5): 293–98.

Debbage, K. (2005) 'Airlines, airports and international aviation', in L. Pender and R. Sharpley (eds) *The Management of Tourism*, London: Sage.

Debbage, K. and Alkaabi, K. (2008) 'Market power and vertical (dis)integration? Airline networks and destination development in the United States and Dubai', in A. Graham, A. Papatheodorou and P. Forsyth (eds) *Aviation and Tourism: Implications for Leisure Travel*, Aldershot: Ashgate, 147–63.

DEFRA (2007) 'Public understanding of sustainable leisure and tourism', A research report completed for the Department for Environment, Food and Rural Affairs by the University of Surrey (www.defra.gov.uk), accessed 20 March 2008.

Deitch, R. and Ladany, S. (2000) 'The bus touring problem: Cluster – first, route – second heuristic', *Tourism Economics*, 6(3): 263–79.

De Kadt, E. (ed.) (1979) *Tourism: Passport to Development?*, New York: Oxford University Press.

Deming, W.E. (1982) *Quality Productivity and Competitive Position*, Cambridge, MA: Massachusetts Institute of Technology Press.

Dempsey, P., Goetz, A. and Szyliowicz, J. (1997) *Denver International Airport: Lessons Learned*, New York: McGraw-Hill,

de Neufville, R. (1991) 'Strategic planning for airport capacity: an appreciation for Australia's process for Sydney', *Australian Planner*, 29: 174–80.

de Neufville, R. (1994) 'The baggage system at Denver: Prospects and lessons', *Journal of Air Transport Management*, 1(4): 229–36.

Department of Employment/English Tourist Board (1991) *Tourism and the Environment: Maintaining the Balance*, London: HMSO.

Department of the Environment (1989) *Environmental Assessment: A Guide to the Procedures*, London: HMSO.

Department of the Environment (1991) *This Common Inheritance*, London: HMSO.

Department of the Environment, Transport and the Regions (1997) *Transport Statistics Great Britain 1997*, London: HMSO.

Department of Transport (1987), *Tourism, Leisure and Roads*, London: HMSO.

Department of Transport (1992a) *New Opportunities for the Railways*, Cmnd. 2012, London: HMSO.

Department of Transport (1992b) *The Franchising of Passenger Rail Services: A Consultative Document*, London: Department of Transport.

Department of Transport (1993) *Railways Bill 1993*, Bill 117, London: HMSO.

Department of Transport (1994) *Britain's Railways: A New Era*, London: Department of Transport.

Department of Transport (1996) *Transport Statistics Report: Cycling in Great Britain*, London: HMSO.

Department for Transport (2006a) *The Future of Air Transport: Progress Report*, London: Department for Transport.

Department for Transport (2006b) *Attitudes of, and Experiences towards Air Travel*, London: Department for Transport.

Department for Transport, Local Government and The Regions (2001) *Transport Statistics Bulletin, National Travel Survey*, Norwich: The Stationery Office.

Department for Transport (DfT) (2003) *Car use in GB: Personal travel factsheet 7*, Department for Transport/National Statistics, January.

Department of the Treasury (n.d.) *United States Customs Declaration*, Customs Form 6059B (101695), Washington, DC: Department of the Treasury.

Derudder, B., Devriendt, L. and Witlox, F. (2005) *Flying where you don't want to go: An Empirical Analysis of Hubs in the Global Airline Network*, Gent: Ghent University.

Derudder, B. and Wilcox, F. (2008) 'Mapping world city networks through airline flows: Context, relevance, and problems', *Journal of Transport Geography*, 16(5): 305–12.

DETR (2000) *Air Traffic Forecasts for the United Kingdom 2000*, London: HMSO.

Dickinson, J., Calver, S., Watters, K. and Wilks, K. (2004) 'Journeys to heritage attractions in the UK: A case study of National Trust visitors in the south west', *Journal of Transport Geography*, 12: 103–13.

Dickinson, R. (1993) 'Cruise industry outlook in the Caribbean', in D.J. Gayle and J.N. Goodrich (eds) *Tourism Marketing and Management in the Caribbean*, London: Routledge, 113–21.

Dickinson, R. and Vladimir, A. (1997) *Selling the Sea: An Inside Look at the Cruise Industry*, Chichester: Wiley.

Dickinson, J. and Robbins, D. (2008) 'Representations of tourism transport problems in a rural destination', *Tourism Management*, 29(6): 1110–21.

Docherty, I. and Shaw, J. (2003) *A New Deal for Transport? The UK's Struggle with the Sustainable Transport Agenda*, Oxford: Blackwell.

Doganis, R. (1991) *Flying Off Course: The Economics of International Airlines*, London: Routledge.

Doganis, R. (1992) *The Airport Business*, London: Routledge.

Doganis, R. (2001) *The Airline Business in the Twenty-first Century*, London: Routledge.

Doganis, R. (2002) *Flying Off Course*, 3rd edn, London: Routledge.

Doganis, R. (2003) *Flying Off Course*, 2nd edn, London: Routledge.

Doll, C. and Wietschel, M. (2008) 'Externalities of the transport sector and the role of hydrogen in a sustainable transport vision', *Energy Policy*, 36(11): 4069–78.

Donne, M. (2002) 'Deep vein thrombosis and the future of air travel', *Travel and Tourism Analyst*, 4.

Doganis, R. and Graham, A. (1987) *Airport Management: The Role of Performance Indicators*, London: Polytechnic of Central London.

Dotchin, J.A. and Oakland, J.S. (1992) 'Theories and concepts in Total Quality Management', *Total Quality Management*, 3(2): 133–45.

Douglas, N. and Douglas, N. (1996) 'P&O's Pacific', *The Journal of Tourism Studies*, 7(2): 2–14.

Douglas, N. and Douglas, N. (2000) 'Tourism in South and Southeast Asia, historical dimensions', in C.M. Hall and S.J. Page (eds) *Tourism in South and Southeast Asia: Issues and Cases*, Oxford: Butterworth Heinemann, 29–44.

Downes, J. and Tunney, J. (1997) 'The legal framework for airline competition', *Travel and Tourism Analyst*, 3: 76–92.

Downward, P. and Lumsdon, L. (1999) 'The determinants of day excursion coach travel: A qualitative marketing analysis', *Service Industries Journal*, 19(4): 158–68.

Downward, P. and Lumsdon, L. (2004) 'Tourism, transport and visitor spending: A study in the North York Moors National *Park*', *Journal of Travel Research*, 42(4): 415–20.

Downward, P.M., Lumsdon, L. and Rhoden, S. (2006) 'Transport and tourism: Can public transport encourage a modal shift in the day-travel market?', *Journal of Sustainable Tourism*, 14(2): 139–56.

Dresner, M. and Windle, R. (1995) 'Are US air carriers to be feared? Implications of hubbing to North Atlantic competition', *Transport Policy*, 2(3): 195–202.

Dresner, M. and Windle, R. (1996) 'Alliances and code sharing in the international airline industry', *Built Environment*, 22(3): 201–11.

Driver, J. (1999) 'Development in airline practice', *Journal of Marketing Practice*, 5: 134–51.

Driver, J. (2001) 'Airline marketing in regulatory context', *Marketing Intelligence and Planning*, 19(2): 125–35.

DTLR (2001) *Transport Local Government Regions: Focus on personal travel*, London: The Stationery Office, December.

Duffell, R. and Harman, R. (1992) 'Rail travel and the leisure market', *Transport, Planning and Technology*, 16: 291–304.

Duinker, P. and Greig, L. (2007) 'Scenario analysis in environmental impact assessment: Improving explorations of the future', *Environmental Impact Assessment Review*, 27(3): 206–19.

Duncan, R.C. and Youngquist, W. (1999) 'Encircling the peak of world oil production', *Natural Resources Research*, 8(3), 219–32.

Dunning, J. (1977) 'Trade, location of economic activity and the MNE: a search for an eclectic approach', in B. Ohlin, P. Hesselborn and P. Wijkman (eds) *The Internationaln Allocation of Economic Activity*, London: Macmillan.

Dwyer, L. and Forsyth, P. (1996) 'Economic impacts of cruise tourism in Australia', *Journal of Tourism Studies*, 7(2): 36–45.

Eadington, W.R. and Redman, M. (1991) 'Economics and tourism', *Annals of Tourism Research*, 18(1): 41–56.

Eaton, A. (1996) *Globalization and Human Resource Management in the Airline Industry*, Aldershot: Avebury Aviation.

Eaton, B. and Holding, D. (1996) 'The evaluation of public transport alternatives to the car in British national parks', *Journal of Transport Geography*, 4(1): 55–65.

Eby, D. and Molnar, L. (2000) 'Importance of scenic byways in route choice: A survey of driving in the United States', *Transportation Research A*: 95–106.

Echevarne, R. (2008) 'The impact of attracting low-cost carriers to airports', in A. Graham, A. Papatheodorou and P. Forsyth (eds) *Aviation and Tourism: Implications for Leisure Travel*, Aldershot: Ashgate, 177–92.

Eckton, G. (2003) 'Road-user charging and the Lake District National *Park*', *Journal of Transport Geography*, 11: 307–17.

Edwards, A. (1991) *European Long Haul Travel Market: Forecasts to 2000*, London: Economist Intelligence Unit.

Edwards, A. (1992) *Long Term Tourism Forecasts to 2005*, London: Economist Intelligence Unit.

Edwards, A. and Graham, A. (2000) *International Tourism Forecasts to 2005*, London: Travel and Tourism Intelligence.

Energy Watch Group (2007) 'Crude oil. The supply outlook', EWG Series No 3/2007. Ottobrunn.

English Historic Towns Forum (1997) *Code of Practice for Coach Tourism*, Bristol: EHTF.

English Historic Towns Forum (1994) *Getting It Right: A Guide to Visitor Management in Historic Towns*, Bath: EHTF.

English Tourist Board/Employment Department (1991) *Tourism and Environment: Maintaining the Balance*, London: English Tourist Board.

Enoch, M. (2003) 'Transport practice and policy in Mauritius', *Journal of Transport Geography*, 11(4): 297–306.

Enoch, M. and Potter, S. (2003) 'Encouraging the commercial sector to help employees to change their travel behaviour', *Transport Policy*, 10(1): 51–8.

Europa (2008) *Energy and Transport Statistics*, Brussels: European Commission.

European Conference of Ministers of Transport (1992) *Privatisation of Railways*, Brussels: European Conference of Ministers of Transport.

European Low Fares Airline Association (ELFAA) (2002) *Liberalisation of European Air Transport: the benefits of low fare airlines to consumers. Airports, Regions and the Environment*, Brussels: ELFAA.

European Parliament (1995) *Protection of Tourists*, Luxembourg: European Parliament.

EuroRAP (2002) 'Comparison of European fatality rates', *European Road Assessment Programme*, February (now included as part of the EuroRap Pilot Phase Report, see Lynam et al. (2003).

Eurostat (1987) *Transport, Communications, Tourism*, Luxembourg: Office for Official Publications of the European Communities.

Eurostat (2003) *European Energy and Transport in Figures*, Brussels: European Union.

Evans, G. and Shaw, S. (2001) 'Urban leisure and transport: Regeneration effects', *Journal of Leisure Property*, 1(4): 350–72.

Evans, N. (2001) 'Collaborative strategy: An analysis of the changing world of international airline alliances', *Tourism Management*, 22(3): 229–43.

Evans, N., Campbell, D. and Stonehouse, G. (2003) *Strategic Management for Travel and Tourism*, Oxford: Butterworth-Heinemann.

Evening Times (2001) 'Tourist caused crash', *Evening Times*, 13 October: 6.

Fageda, X. and Fernández-Villadangos, L. (2009) 'Triggering competition in the Spanish airline market: The role of airport capacity and low-cost carriers', *Journal of Air Transport Management*, 15(1): 36–40.

Fahey, L. and Randall, R. (1997) *Learning from the Future: Competitive Foresight Scenarios*, Chichester: John Wiley.

Farrell, A.E. and Brandt, A.R. (2006) 'Risks of the oil transition', *Environmental Research Letters*, 1: 1–6.

Farrington, J.H. (1985) 'Transport geography and policy: Deregulation and privatisation', *Transactions of the Institute of British Geographers*, 10(1): 109–19.

Farrington, J.H. (1995) 'Transport, environment and energy', in B.S. Hoyle and R.D. Knowles (eds) *Modern Transport Geography*, London: Belhaven, 51–66.

Farrington, J. and Ord, D. (1998) 'Bure Valley Railway: an EIA', *Project Appraisal*, 3(4): 210–18.

Fasari, Y. and Prastacos, P. (2004) 'GIS applications in the planning and management of tourism', in A. Lew, C.M. Hall and A. Williams (eds) *A Companion of Tourism*, Oxford: Blackwell, 596–605.

Faulks, R. (1990) *Principles of Transport*, 4th edn, Maidenhead: McGraw-Hill.

Federal Aviation Administration (FAA) (2003) *Airport Activity Statistics*, Washington, DC: US Government Printing Office.

Feiler, G. and Goodovitch, T. (1994) 'Decline and growth, privatisation and protectionism in the Middle-East airline industry', *Journal of Transport Geography*, 2(1): 55–64.

Feldhoff, T. (2003) 'Japan's capital city and its airports: Problems and prospects from sub national and supranational perspectives', *Journal of Air Transport Management*, 9(4): 241–54.

Ferguson, N. and Thompson, K. (2007) *An Investigation of Visitor Travel Behaviour in Scotland*, A review of existing data and literature commissioned by the Scottish Executive, Transport Department. (www.scotland.gov.uk/Publications/2007/04/30170641/0).

Fidler, D.P. (1996) 'ABA sponsors program on law and emerging infectious diseases', *Journal of Emerging Infectious Diseases*, 2(4): 364.

Findlay, C. and Forsyth, P. (1984) 'Competitiveness in internationally traded services: The case of air transport', *Working Paper No. 10*, ASEAN-Australian Joint Research Project, Kuala Lumpur and Canberra.

Findlay, C., Sieh, L. and Singh, K. (eds) (1997) *Asia Pacific Air Transport: Challenges and Policy Reforms*, Singapore: Institute of South East Asian Studies.

Fitzsimmons, J.A. and Sullivan, R.S. (1982) *Service Operations Management*, New York: McGraw-Hill.

Flipo, J. (1988) 'On the intangibility of services', *Service Industries Journal*, 8(3): 286–98.

Forer, P. and Page, S.J. (1998) 'Spatial modelling of tourist flows in Northland', Paper presented at the Tourism Down Under Conference, Akaroa, New Zealand, 3–5 December.

Forer, P.C. and Pearce, D.G. (1984) 'Spatial patterns of package tourism in New Zealand', *New Zealand Geographer*, 40(1): 34–42.

Forer, P. and Simmons, D. (2002) 'Serial experiences: Monitoring, modelling and visualising the free independent traveller in New Zealand at multiple scales with GIS', in A. Arnberger, C. Brandenberg and A. Muhar (eds) *Monitoring and Management of Visitor Flows in Recreational and Protected Areas*, Vienna: Institute of Landscape Architecture and Landscape Management, Bodenkulture University, 173–80.

Forsyth, P. (1997a) 'Privatisation in Asia Pacific aviation', in C. Findlay, L. Chia and K. Singh (eds) *Asia Pacific Air Transport: Challenges and Policy Reforms*, Singapore: Institute of South East Asian Studies, 48–64.

Forsyth, P. (1997b) 'Price regulation of airports: Principles with Australian applications', *Transportation Research E*, 33(4): 297–309.

Forsyth, P. (2003) 'Regulation under stress: Developments in Australian airport policy', *Journal of Air Transport Management*, 9: 25–35.

Forsyth, P. (2008) 'Tourism and aviation: Exploring the links', in A. Graham, A. Papatheodorou and P. Forsyth (eds) *Aviation and Tourism: Implications for Leisure Travel*, Aldershot: Ashgate, 73–84.

Forsyth, P. and King, J. (1996) 'Competition, cooperation and financial performance in South Pacific aviation', in G. Hufbaner and C. Findlay (eds) *Flying High: Liberalising Aviation in the Asia Pacific*, Washington and Canberra: Institute for International Economics and Australia–Japan Research Centre, 99–176.

Forsyth, P., Gillen, D.W., Mayer, O.G. and Niemeier, H.-M. (eds) (2005) *Competition versus Predation in Aviation Markets: A Survey of Experience in North America, Europe and Australia*, Aldershot: Ashgate.

Forsyth, P., Hoque, S., Dwyer, L., Spurr, R., Van Ho, T. and Pambudi D. (2008) 'The carbon footprint of Australian tourism', *Sustainable Tourism CRC* (www.crctourism.com.au/bookshop/BookDetail.aspx?d=599), accessed 15 October 2008.

Forsyth, T. (1997) 'Environmental responsibility and business regulation: The case of sustainable tourism', *Geographical Journal*, 163(3): 270–80.

Foster, D. (1985) *Travel and Tourism Management*, London: Macmillan.

Francis, G., Fidato, A. and Humphreys, I. (2003) 'Airport-airline interaction: The impact of low-cost carriers on two European airports', *Journal of Air Transport Management*, 9(4): 267–73.

Francis, G., Humphreys, J. and Fry, J. (2002) 'The benchmarking of airport performance', *Journal of Air Transport Management*, 8: 239–47.

Francis, G., Humphreys, I. and Ison, S. (2004) 'Airports' perspectives on the growth of low-cost airlines and the remodelling of the airport-airline relationship', *Tourism Management*, 25(4): 507–14.

Franke, M. (2004) 'Competition between network carriers and low-cost carriers: Retreat, battle or breakthrough to a new level of efficiency?', *Journal of Air Transport Management*, 10(1): 15–21.

Frapin-Beange, A., Bennett, M. and Wood, R. (1994) 'Some current issues in airline catering', *Tourism Management*, 15(4): 295–305.

Freathy, P. (2004) 'The commercialisation of European airports: Successful strategies in a decade of turbulence?', *Journal of Air Transport Management*, 10(3): 191–97.

Frechtling, D. (1996) *Practical Tourism Forecasting*, Oxford: Butterworth-Heinemann.

French, T. (1994) 'European airport capacities and airport congestion', *Travel and Tourism Analyst*, 5: 4–19.

French, T. (1995) *Regional Airlines in Europe: Strategies for Survival*, London: Economist Intelligence Unit.

French, T. (1996a) 'World airport development plans and constraints', *Travel and Tourism Analyst*, 1: 4–16.

French, T. (1996b) 'No frills airlines in Europe', *Travel and Tourism Analyst*, 3: 4–19.

French, T. (1997a) *Airports in Europe: Meeting the Market Challenge*, London: Travel and Tourism Intelligence.

French, T. (1997b) 'Global trends in airline alliances', *Travel and Tourism Analyst*, 4: 81–101.

Fridgen, J.D. (1984) 'Environmental psychology and tourism', *Annals of Tourism Research*, 11: 19–40.

Friedman, T. (2005) *The World is Flat: A Brief History of the Globalised World in the 21st Century*, London: Allen Lane.

Galeana, O. (2008) 'The privatisation of Mexican airports', *Journal of Air Transport Management*, 14(6): 320–23.

Gallacher, J. and Odell, M. (1994) 'Airline alliances, tagging along', *Airline Business*, July.

Gant, R. and Smith, J. (1992) 'Tourism and national development planning in Tunisia', *Tourism Management*, 13(3): 331–6.

Gayle, D.J. and Goodrich, J.N. (eds) (1993) *Tourism Marketing and Management in the Caribbean*, London: Routledge.

German Advisory Council on Global Change (2002) *Charging the Use of Global Commons*, Berlin (www.wbgu.de/wbgu_sn2002_engl.html), accessed 20 November 2004.

Getz, D. and Page, S.J. (eds) (1997) *The Business of Rural Tourism: International Perspectives*, London: International Thomson Publishing.

Geuens, M., Vantomme, D. and Brengman, M. (2004) 'Developing a typology of airport shoppers', *Tourism Management*, 25: 615–22.

Gibb, R. (ed.) (1996) *The Channel Tunnel*, Chichester: Wiley.

Gibb, R. and Charlton, C. (1992) 'International surface passenger transport: Prospects and potential', in B.S. Hoyle and R.D. Knowles (eds) *Modern Transport Geography*, London: Belhaven, 215–32.

Gibb, R., Lowndes, T. and Charlton, C. (1996) 'The privatisation of British Rail', *Applied Geography*, 16(1): 35–51.

Gibb, R., Shaw, J. and Charlton, C. (1998) 'Competition, regulation and the privatisation of British Rail', *Environment and Planning C: Government and Policy* 16(6): 757–68.

Gibson, P. (2006) *Cruise Operations Management*, Oxford: Butterworth Heinemann.

Giddens, A. (2000) *The Third Way and Its Critics*, London: Polity Press.

Gilbert, D.C. (1989) 'Tourism marketing: Its emergence and establishment', in C.P. Cooper (ed.) *Progress in Tourism, Recreation and Hospitality Management*, Volume 1, London: Belhaven, 77–90.

Gilbert, D.C. (1990) 'Conceptual issues in the meaning of tourism', in C.P. Cooper (ed.) *Progress in Tourism, Recreation and Hospitality Management*, Volume 2, London: Belhaven, 4–27.

Gilbert, D.C. and Joshi, I. (1992) 'Quality management and the tourism and hospitality industry', in C.P. Cooper and A. Lockwood (eds) *Progress in Tourism, Recreation and Hospitality Management*, Volume 4, London: Belhaven, 149–68.

Gilbert, D. and Wong, R. (2003) 'Passenger expectations and airline services: A Hong Kong based study', *Tourism Management*, 24(5): 519–32.

Gilbert, E.W. (1939) 'The growth of inland and seaside health resorts in England', *Scottish Geographical Magazine*, 55(1): 16–35.

Gillen, D. and Lall, A. (2004) 'Competitive advantage of low-cost carriers: Some implications for airports', *Journal of Air Transport Management*, 10(1): 41–50.

Gillen, D. and Morrison, W (2003) 'Bundling, integration and the delivered price of air travel: Are low-cost carriers full-service competitors?', *Journal of Air Transport Management*, 9(1): 15–23.

Gillen, D. and Waters, W (1997) 'Introduction: Airport performance measurement and airport pricing', *Transportation Research E*, 33(4): 245–7.

Gillen, D., Morrison, W. and Stewart, C. (2004) *Air Travel Demand Elasticities: Concepts, Issues and Measurement*. Final report. Department of Finance Canada (www.fin.gc.ca/consultresp/Airtravel/airtravStdy_e.html), accessed 20 November 2006.

Ginzburg, H.M. (1996) 'Commentary needed: Comprehensive response to the spread of infectious diseases', *Journal of Emerging Infectious Diseases*, 2(2): 151.

Gittell, J. (2003) *The Southwest Airlines Way*, New York: McGraw Hill.

Glaesser, D. (2003) *Crisis Management in the Tourism Industry*, Oxford: Butterworth-Heinemann.

Glaister, S. (1981) *Fundamentals of Transport Economics*, Oxford: Blackwell.

Glaister, S. and Mulley, C.M. (1983) *Public Control of the Bus Industry*, Aldershot: Gower.

Glyptis, S. (1981) 'People at play in the countryside', *Geography*, 66(4): 277–85.

Glyptis, S. (1991) *Countryside Recreation*, Harlow: Longman.

Gnoth, J. (1995) 'Quality of service and tourist satisfaction', in S. Witt and L. Moutinho (eds) *Tourism Marketing and Management Handbook: Student Edition*, Hemel Hempstead: Prentice Hall, 243–54.

Go, F. (1993) 'International airline trends', in F. Go and D. Frechtling (eds) *World Travel and Tourism Review: Indicators, Trends and Issues*, Volume 3, Oxford: CAB International, 178–83.

Go, F. and Murakami, M. (1990) 'Transnational corporations capture Japanese travel market', *Tourism Management*, 11(4): 348–58.

Goetz, A. and Sutton, C. (1997) 'The geography of deregulation in the US airline industry', *Annals of the Association of American Geographers*, 87(2): 238–63.

Goetz, A. and Szyliowicz, J. (1997) 'Revisiting transportation planning and decision making theory: The case of Denver International Airport', *Transportation Research A*, 31(4): 263–80.

Goh, K. and Uncles, M. (2003) 'The benefits of airline global alliances: An empirical assessment of the perceptions of business travellers', *Transportation Research Part A: Policy and Practice*, 37(6): 479–97.

Golich, V.L. (1988) 'Airline deregulation: Economic boom or safety bust', *Transportation Quarterly*, 42: 159–79.

Goodall, B. (1991) 'Understanding holiday choice', in C.P. Cooper (ed.) *Progress in Tourism, Recreation and Hospitality Management*, Volume 3, London: Belhaven, 58–79.

Goodall, B. (1992) 'Environmental auditing for tourism', in C.P. Cooper and A. Lockwood (eds) *Progress in Tourism, Recreation and Hospitality Management*, Volume 4, London: Belhaven, 60–74.

Goodall, B. and Stabler, M. (1997) 'Environmental awareness, action and performance in the Guernsey hospitality sector', *Tourism Management*, 18(1): 19–34.

Goodenough, R. and Page, S.J. (1993) 'Tourism training and education in the 1990s', *Journal of Geography in Higher Education*, 17(1): 57–75.

Goodenough, R. and Page, S.J. (1994) 'Evaluating the environmental impact of the Channel Tunnel rail-link', *Applied Geography*, 14(1): 26–50.

Gormsen, E. (1995) 'International tourism in China: Its organisation and socio-economic impact', in A. Lew and L. Yu (eds) *Tourism in China: Geographical, Political and Economic Perspectives*, Boulder, COL: Westview Press, 63–88.

Gössling, S. (2003) 'Global environmental consequences of tourism', *Global Environmental Change*, 2(4): 283–302.

Gössling, S., Peeters, P., Ceron, J.P., Dubois, G., Patterson., T. and Richardson, R. (2005) 'The eco-efficiency of tourism', *Ecological Economics*, 54(4): 417–34.

Government of Ireland (1990) *Operational Programme on Peripherality: Roads and Other Transport Infrastructure 1989–1993*, Dublin: Stationery Office.

Graham, A. (1992) 'Airports in the United States', in R. Doganis, *The Airport Business*, London: Routledge, 188–206.

Graham, A. (2001) *Managing Airports*, Oxford: Butterworth-Heinemann.

Graham, A. (2003) *Managing Airports*, 2nd edn, Oxford: Butterworth-Heinemann.

Graham, A. (2009) *Managing Airports*, 3rd edn, Oxford: Butterworth-Heinemann.

Graham, A., Papatheodorou, A. and Forsyth, P. (eds) (2008) *Aviation and Tourism: Implications for Leisure Travel*, Aldershot: Ashgate.

Graham, B. (1995) *Geography and Air Transport*, Chichester: Wiley.

Graham, B. (1997a) 'Air transport liberalisation in the European Union: An assessment', *Regional Studies*, 31: 807–12.

Graham, B. (1997b) 'Regional airline services in the liberalised European Union Single Aviation Market', *Journal of Air Transport Management*.

Graham, B. (1998) 'Liberalisation, regional economic development and the geography of demand for air transport in the European Union', *Journal of Transport Geography*, 6(2): 87–104.

Graham, B. (2008) 'New air services: Tourism and economic development', in A. Graham, A. Papatheodorou and P. Forsyth (eds) *Aviation and Tourism: Implications for Leisure Travel*, Aldershot: Ashgate, 227–38.

Graham, B. and Goetz, A. (2008) 'Global air transport', in R. Knowles, J. Shaw and I. Docherty (eds) *Transport Geographies: Mobilities, Flows and Spaces*, Oxford: Blackwell, 137–55.

Graham, B. and Vowles, T. (2006) 'Carriers within carriers: A strategic response to low-cost airlien competition', *Transport Reviews*, 26: 105–26.

Graham, D.J. and Glaister, S. (2002) 'The demand for automobile fuel. A survey of elasticities', *Journal of Transport Economics and Policy*, 36(1), 1–26.

Grant, M., Human, B. and Le Pelley, B. (1997) 'More than getting from A to B: Transport strategies and tourism', *INSIGHTS*: A43–A48.

Gray, H. (1982) 'The contribution of economics to tourism', *Annals of Tourism Research*, 9: 105–25.

Great Eastern Railways Ltd. (1997) *Passenger's Charter*, London: Great Eastern Railways Ltd.

Green, C. (1994) 'The future for InterCity: 1994 and beyond', in M. Vincent (ed.) *The InterCity Story*, Somerset: Oxford Publishing Company, 142–52.

Green, W. (2001) *Review of Current Biosecurity Research in New Zealand*, Wellington: Biosecurity Strategy Development Team.

Greene, D.L., Hopson, J.L. and Li, J. (2006) 'Have we run out of oil, yet? Oil peaking analysis from an optimist's perspective', *Energy Policy*, 34: 515–31.

Griffith, L. (1989) 'Airways sanctions against South Africa', *Area*, 21(3): 249–59.

Groß, S. and Schröder, A. (eds) (2007) *Handbook of Low Cost Airlines: Strategies, Business Processes and Market Environment*, Berlin: Erich Schmidt Verlag.

Gronau, W. and Kagermeier, A. (2007) 'Key factors for successful leisure and tourism public transport provision', Journal of Transport Geography, 15(2): 127–35.

Gronroos, C. (1980) *An Applied Service Marketing Theory*, Helsinki: Working Paper No. 57, Swedish School of Economics and Business Administration.

Gronroos, C. (1984) 'A service quality model and its marketing implications', *European Management Journal*, 11(3): 332–41.

Gudmuudsson, S.V. and Rhoades, D. (2001) 'Airline alliance survival analysis: Typology, strategy and duration', *Transport Policy*, 8: 209–18.

Guiver, J., Lumsdon, L. and Weston, R. (2007) 'Traffic reduction at visitor attractions: The case of Hadrian's Wall', *Journal of Transport Geography*, 16(2): 142–50.

Guiver, J., Lumsdon, L., Weston, R. and Ferguson, M. (2006) 'Do buses help meet tourism objectives? The contribution and potential of scheduled buses in rural destination areas', *Transport Policy*, 14(4): 275–82.

Gummesson, E. (1993) *Quality Management in Service Organisations*, Stockholm: International Service Quality Organisation.

Gunn, C.A. (1988) *Tourism Planning*, 2nd edn, New York: Taylor & Francis.

Gunn, C.A. (1994) *Tourism Planning*, London: Taylor & Francis.

Gursoy, D., Chen, M. and Kim, H. (2004) 'The US airlines relative positioning based on attributes of service quality', *Tourism Management*, 26(1): 57–67.

Gustafasson, A., Ekdahl, F. and Edvardsson, B. (1999) 'Customer focused service development in practice: A case study at Scandinavian Airlines System (SAS)', *International Journal of Service Industry Management*, 10(4): 344–58.

Gutiérrez, J., Condeço-Melhorado, A. and Martín, J.C. (2005) 'Using accessibility indicators and GIS to assess spatial spillovers of transport infrastructure investment', *Journal of Transport Geography*, in press, corrected proof. Available online 23 February 2009.

Haghani, A. and Chen, M. (1998) 'Optimization gave assignments at airport terminals', *Transportation Research A*, 32(6): 427–54.

Hall, C.M. (1991) *Introduction to Tourism in Australia: Impacts, Planning and Development*, Melbourne: Longman Cheshire.

Hall, C.M. (1992) 'Tourism in Antarctica: Activities, impacts, and management', *Journal of Travel Research*, 30(4): 2–9.

Hall, C.M. (1997) *Tourism in the Pacific Rim*, 2nd edn, Melbourne: Addison-Wesley Longman.

Hall, C.M. (2004) *Tourism*, Harlow: Prentice Hall.

Hall, C.M. (2005) *Tourism: Rethinking the Social Science of Mobility*, Harlow: Pearson Education.

Hall, C.M. and Jenkins, J. (1995) *Tourism and Public Policy*, London: Routledge.

Hall, C.M. and Johnson, G. (1998) 'Wine tourism: An imbalanced partnership', in R. Dowling and J. Carlsen (eds), *Wine Tourism Perfect Partners: Proceedings of the First Australian Wine Tourism Conference*, Margaret River, Western Australia, May 1998, Canberra: Bureau of Tourism Research, 51–72.

Hall, C.M. and Lew, A. (eds) (1998) *The Geography of Sustainable Tourism*, Harlow: Addison-Wesley Longman.

Hall, C.M. and Page, S.J. (eds) (1996) *Tourism in the Pacific: Issues and Cases*, London: International Thomson Business Press.

Hall, C.M. and Page, S.J. (1999) *The Geography of Tourism and Recreation: Environment, Place and Space*, London: Routledge.

Hall, C.M. and Page, S.J. (eds) (2000) *Tourism in South and South East Asia*, Oxford: Butterworth-Heinemann.

Hall, C.M. and Page, S.J. (2002) *The Geography of Tourism and Recreation: Environment, Place and Space*, 2nd edn, London: Routledge.

Hall, C.M. and Page, S.J. (2006) *The Geography of Tourism and Recreation: Environment, Place and Space*, 3rd edn, London: Routledge.

Hall, C.M., Sharples, E. and Smith, A. (2003) 'The experience of consumption or the consumption of experiences?: Challenges and issues in food tourism', in C.M. Hall, E. Sharples, R. Mitchell, B. Cambourne and N. Macionis (eds) *Food Tourism Around the World: Development, Management and Markets*, Oxford: Butterworth-Heinemann, 314–35.

Hall, C.M., Sharples, E., Cambourne, B. and Macionis, N. (eds) (2000) *Wine Tourism Around the World: Development, Management and Markets*, Oxford: Butterworth-Heinemann.

Hall, D. (1993) 'Getting around: Transport and sustainability', *Town and Country Planning*, 62(1/2): 8–12.

Hall, D.R. (1993a) 'Transport implications of tourism development', in D.R. Hall (ed.) *Transport and Economic Development in the new Central and Eastern Europe*, London: Belhaven, 206–25.

Hall, D.R. (1993b) 'Key themes and agendas', in D.R. Hall (ed.) *Transport and Economic Development in the new Central and Eastern Europe*, London: Belhaven, 226–36.

Hall, D.R. (1997) personal communication.

Hall, D.R. (1999) 'Conceptualising tourism transport: Inequality and externality issues', *Journal of Transport Geography*, 7(3): 181–8.

Hall, D.R. (2008) 'Transport, tourism and leisure', in R. Knowles, J. Shaw and I. Docherty (eds) *Transport Geographies: Mobilities, Flows and Spaces*, Oxford: Blackwell, 196–212.

Halpern, N. and Niskala, J. (2008) 'Airport marketing and tourism in remote destinations: Exploring the potential in Europe's northern periphery', in A. Graham, A. Papatheodorou and P. Forsyth (eds) *Aviation and Tourism: Implications for Leisure Travel*, Aldershot: Ashgate, 193–208.

Halsall, D. (1982) *Transport for Recreation*, Lancaster: Institute of British Geographers Transport Study Group.

Halsall, D. (1992) 'Transport for tourism and recreation', in B.S. Hoyle and R.D. Knowles (eds) *Modern Transport Geography*, London: Belhaven, 155–77.

Hamill, J. (1993) 'Competitive strategies in the world airline industry', *European Management Journal*, 11(3): 332–41.

Hamilton, J. (1988) 'Trends in tourism demand patterns in New Zealand', *International Journal of Hospitality Management*, 7(4): 299–320.

Han, J. and Hayashi, Y. (2008) 'Assessment of private car stock and its environmental impacts in China from 2000 to 2020', *Transportation Research Part D: Transport and Environment*, 13(7): 471–8.

Handy, C. (1989) *The Age of Unreason*, London: Business Books Ltd.

Hanghani, A. and Chen, M. (1998) 'Optimising gate assignments at airport terminals', *Transportation Research A*, 32(6): 437–54.

Hanks K.P. (2006) 'How should airports be regulated?', *Journal of Airport Management*, 1(1): 17–24.

Hanlon, P. (1996) *Global Airlines: Competition in a Transnational Industry*, Oxford: Butterworth-Heinemann.

Hanlon, P. (2004) *Global Airlines,* 2nd edn, Oxford: Butterworth-Heinemann.

Hanlon, P. (2007) *Global Airlines*, 3rd edn, Oxford: Butterworth-Heinemann.

Hannegan, T. and Mulvey, F. (1995) 'International airline alliances: An analysis of code-sharing's impact on airlines and consumers', *Journal of Air Transport Management*, 2(2): 131–7.

Hanning, P. (1997) 'Caterers cut as airline goes leaner', *New Zealand Herald*, 14 June: A15.

Hansen, H. (2008) 'German tourism sector suffers as energy costs rise', Reuters UK (www.uk.reuters.com/articlePrint?articleID=UKL361416720080803), accessed 18 August 2008.

Harding, R. (1994) 'Aeromedical aspects of commercial air travel', *Journal of Travel Medicine*, 1(4): 211–15.

Hargarten, S. (1995) 'Injury prevention: A crucial aspect of travel medicine', *Journal of Travel Medicine*' 1(1): 48–50.

Hargaten, S., Baker, T. and Guptil, K. (1991) 'Overseas fatalities of United States citizen travelers: An analysis of death related to international travel', *Annals of Emergency Medicine*, 20: 622–6.

Harper, K. (1998a) 'Channel rail link collapses', *The Guardian*, 29 January: 1.

Harper, K. (1998b) 'BA to suffer £200 m hit from strong pound', *The Guardian*, 10 February: 16.

Harris, R., Griffin, T. and Williams, P. (2002) *Sustainable Tourism*, 2nd edn, Oxford: Butterworth Heinemann.

Harris, R. and Masberg, B. (1997) 'Factors critical to the success of implementing vintage trolley operations', *Journal of Travel Research*, 35(3): 41–5.

Harrison, C. (1991) *The Countryside in a Changing Society*, London: TML Partnership.

Harison, E. and Boonstra, A. (2008) 'Reaching new altitudes in e-commerce: Assessing the performance of airline websites', *Journal of Air Transport Management*, 14(2): 92–8.

Hastings, M. (2007) 'Addressing binge flying is vital for the climate', *The Guardian Weekly*, 11 May: 19.

Hay, A. (1973) *Transport for the Space Economy: A Geographical Study*, London: Macmillan.

Hayashi, Y., Yang, Z. and Osman, O. (1998) 'The effects of economic restructuring on China's system for financing transport infrastructure', *Transportation Research A*, 32(3): 183–95.

Henshall, D., Roberts, R. and Leighton, A. (1985) 'Fly-drive tourists: Motivation and destination choice factors', *Journal of Travel Research*, 23(3): 23–7.

Hensher, D., King, J. and Oum, T. (eds) (1996) *Transport Policy*, Proceedings of the 7th World Conference on Transport Research, Oxford: Pergamon.

Hensher, D. and Button, K. (eds) (2003) *Handbook of Transport and the Environment*, Oxford: Elsevier.

Hepworth, M. and Ducatel, K. (1992) *Transport in the Information Age: Wheels and Wires*, London: Belhaven.

Heraty, M.J. (1989) 'Tourism transport: Implications for developing countries', *Tourism Management*, 10(4): 288–92.

Hibbs, J. (2003) *Transport Economics and Policy: A Practical Analysis of Performance, Efficiency and Marketing Objectives*, London: Kogan Page.

Hickman, R. and Bannister, D. (2007) 'Looking over the horizon: Transport and reduced CO_2 emissions in the UK by 2030', *Transport Policy*, 14(5): 377–87.

Hilling, D. (1996) *Transport and Developing Countries*, London: Routledge.

Hine, J. and Mitchell, F. (2003) *Transport Disadvantage and Social Exclusion: Exclusionary Mechanisms in Transport in Urban Scotland*, Aldershot: Ashgate.

Hirsch, R. (2005) 'The inevitable peaking of world oil production', *Bulletin of the Atlantic Council of the United States*, XVI(5): 1–9.

Hirsch, R., Bezdek, R. and Wendling, R. (2005) 'Peaking of world oil production: Impacts, mitigation and risk management', Prepared for US Department of Energy.

Hjalager, A. (2007) 'Stages in the economic globalization of tourism', *Annals of Tourism Research*, 34(2): 437–57.

HMSO (1978) *Airports Policy*, London: HMSO.

HMSO (1985) *Airports Policy*, Cmnd. 9542, London: HMSO.

HMSO. HMSO (1990) *International Passenger Survey*, London: HMSO.

HMSO (1994) *Royal Commission on Environmental Pollution. Eighteenth Report, Transport and the Environment*, Cmnd. 2674, London: HMSO.

HMSO (1997a) *Social Trends 1997*, London: HMSO.

HMSO (1997b) *Royal Commission on the Environment*, London: HMSO.

HM Treasury (2006) *The Eddington Transport Study*, London: HMSO.

Hoare, A. (1974) 'International airports as growth poles: A case study of Heathrow Airport', *Transactions of the Institute of British Geographers*, 63(1): 75–96.

Hobson, J.S.P. and Uysal, M. (1992) 'Infrastructure: The silent crisis facing the future of tourism', *Hospitality Research Journal*, 17(1): 209–15.

Hochschild, A. (1983) *The Managed Heart: Commercialization of Human Feeling*, Berkeley: University of California Press.

Hodgson, P. (1991) 'Market research in tourism: How important is it?', *Tourism Management*, 11(4): 274–7.

Hofer, C., Dresner, M.E., Windle, R.J. (2009) 'The impact of airline financial distress on US air fares: A contingency approach', *Transportation Research Part E: Logistics and Transportation Review*, 45(1): 238–49.

Hoivik, T. and Heiberg, T. (1980) 'Centre–periphery tourism and self reliance', *International Social Science Journal*, 32(1): 69–98.

Holder, J. (1988) 'Pattern and impact of tourism on the environment of the Caribbean', *Tourism Management*, 9(2): 119–27.

Holden, A. (2007) *Tourism and the Environment*, 2nd edn, London: Routledge.

Holding, D. (2001) 'The Sanfte Mobilitaet project: Achieving reduced car-dependence in European resort areas', *Tourism Management*, 22(4): 411–17.

Holliday, I., Marcou, G. and Vickerman, R. (1991) *The Channel Tunnel: Public Policy, Regional Development and European Integration*, London: Belhaven.

Hollings, D. (1997) 'Europe's railway in the 21st century', *Travel and Tourism Analyst*, 4: 4–24.

Holloway, J.C. (1989) *The Business of Tourism*, 3rd edn, London: Pitman.

Holloway, J.C. (1995) *Marketing for Tourism*, London: Pitman.

Holloway, J.C. (1998) *The Business of Tourism*, 5th edn, Harlow: Addison-Wesley Longman.

Holloway, J.C. and Plant, R. (1988) *Marketing for Tourism*, Pitman: London.

Holloway, J.C. and Robinson, C. (1995) *Marketing for Tourism*, 3rd edn, Harlow: Longman.

Holloway, S. (2003) *Straight and Level: Practical Airline Economics*, Aldershot: Ashgate.

Holtbrügge, D., Wilson, S. and Berg, N. (2006) 'Human resource management at Star Alliance: Pressures for standardisation and differentiation', *Journal of Air Transport Management*, 12(6): 306–12.

Honore, C. (2005) *In Praise of Slowness*, New York: Harper Collins.

Hooper, P. (1998) 'Airline competition and deregulation in developed and developing country contexts: Australia and India', *Journal of Transport Geography*, 6(2): 105–16.

Hooper, P. (2002) 'Privatization of airports in Asia', *Journal of Air Transport Management*, 8(5): 289–300.

Hooper, P. and Hensher, D. (1997) 'Measuring total factor productivity of airports: An index number approach', *Transportation Research E*, 33(4): 249–59.

Horner, A. (1991) 'Geographical aspects of airport and air-route development in Ireland', *Irish Geography*, 24(1): 35–47.

Horner, S. and Swarbrooke, J. (1996) *Marketing Tourism, Hospitality and Leisure in Europe*, London: International Thomson Business Press.

Horonjeft, R. and McKelvey, F. (1983) *Planning and Design of Airports*, New York: McGraw-Hill.

House of Commons (2004) Environmental Audit Committee, *Aviation: Sustainability and the Government Response*, London: House of Commons (http://www.publications.parliament.uk).

House of Commons Transport Committee (2006) *Going for Gold: Transport for London's 2012 Olympic Games*, London: House of Commons (http://www.publications.parliament.uk).

Hoyle, B.S. and Knowles, R.D. (eds) (1992) *Modern Transport Geography*, London: Belhaven.

Hoyle, B. and Knowles, R. (eds) (1998) *Modern Transport Geography*, 2nd edn, Chichester: Wiley.

Hsu, C. and Chao, C. (2004) 'Space allocation for commercial activities at international passenger terminals', *Transportation Research E*, 41(1): 29–51.

Hsu, C. and Shih, H. (2008) 'Small world network theory in the study of network connectivity and efficiency of complementary international airline alliances', *Journal of Air Transport Management*, 14(3): 123–9.

Humberto F.A.J., Bettini, A. and Oliveira, V.M. (2008) 'Airline capacity setting after re-regulation: The Brazilian case in the early 2000s', *Journal of Air Transport Management*, 14(6): 289–92.

Humphries, B. (1992) 'The air transport market', *INSIGHTS*, September: A37–A42.

Humphries, B. (1994) 'The implications of international code-sharing', *Journal of Air Transport Management*, 1(4): 195–208.

Huang, B., Yao, L. and Raguraman, K. (2006) 'Bi-level GA and GIS for multi-object TSP route planning', *Transport Planning and Technology*, 29(2): 105–24.

Hunt, J. (1988) 'Airlines in Asia', *Travel and Tourism Analyst*, 5: 5–25.

Hyde, K. and Laesser, C. (2008) 'A structural theory of the vacation', *Tourism Management*, in press.

IATA (2008a) 'IATA economic briefing. Outlook for oil and jet fuel prices', September (www.iata.org/economics), accessed 10 October 2008.

IATA (2008b) 'Fact sheet – fuel' (www.iata.org/pressroom/facts_figures/fact_sheets/fuel.htm), accessed 8 October 2008.

IATA (2008c) 'Traffic slowdown continues – Asia leads August decline', Press Release, September (www.iata.org/pressroom/pr/2008-09-30-01.html), accessed 10 October 2008.

ICAO (2007) *Annual Report*, Geneva: ICAO.

Iatrou, K. and Oretti, M. (2007) *Airline Choices for the Future: From Alliances to Mergers*, Aldershot: Ashgate.

IHS (2006) *Petroleum Exploration and Production Statistics (PEPS)*, Geneva and London: HIS Energy.

Ingold, A., McMahon, Beattie, V. and Yeoman, I. (eds) (2000) *Yield Management: Strategies for the Service Industries*, London: Continuum.

Inkson, K. and Kolb, D. (1995) *Management: A New Zealand Perspective*, Auckland: Longman Paul.

Instinct and Reason (2008) 'Propensity for UK and German travelers to adapt travel intentions due to rising awareness of climate change issues', Prepared for Department of Resources, Energy and Tourism, 2 May 2008. Surrey Hills, NSW, Australia.

International Energy Agency (2006) *World Energy Outlook*, Paris: OECD.

International Energy Agency (2008) 'Oil market reports' (www.oilmarketreport.org/), accessed 10 October 2008.

IPCC (1999) Intergovernmental Panel on Climate Change (ipcc.ch).

IPCC (2007) 'Climate change 2007. Mitigation of climate change', Working Group II Contribution to the Fourth Assessment. Summary for Policymakers and Technical Summary.

Irons, K. (1994) *Managing Service Companies: Strategies for Success*, London: Economist Intelligence Unit and Addison-Wesley Publishing Company.

Irons, K. (1997) *The World of Superservice: Creating Profit through a Passion for Customer Service*, Harlow: Addison-Wesley.

ISD Scotland (2003) 'Morbidity in Scotland: General morbidity involving hospital care', *Information and Statistics Division of National Statistics*, No 03/05, April.

Jagger, S. (2008) 'Soaring oil price sets airlines on course to recession, expert says', *Times Online*, 31 May (http://business.timesonline.co.uk), 2 August 2008.

Jahanshahi, M. (1998) 'The US railroad industry and open access', *Transport Policy*, 5(2): 73–81.

Janelle, D. and Beuthe, M. (1997) 'Globalization and research issues in transportation', *Journal of Transport Geography*, 5(3): 199–206.

Janic, M. (2007) *The Sustainability of Air Transportation*, Aldershot: Ashgate.

Jarach, D. (2005) *Airport Marketing: Strategies to Cope with the New Millennium Environment*, Aldershot: Ashgate.

Javalgi, R.G., Thomas, E.G. and Rao, S.R. (1992) 'US pleasure travellers' perceptions of selected European destinations', *European Journal of Marketing*, 26(1): 46–64.

Jefferson, A. and Lickorish, L. (1991) *Marketing Tourism: A Practical Guide*, Harlow: Longman.

Jeffries, D. (2001) *Governments and Tourism*, Oxford: Butterworth-Heinemann.

Jemiolo, J. and Oster, C.V. (1981) 'Regional changes in airline service since deregulation', *Transportation Quarterly*, 41: 569–86.

Jennings, G. (ed.) (2007) *Water-based Tourism, Leisure, Sport and Recreation*, Oxford: Butterworth Heinemann.

Jensen, T.C. (1998) 'Income and price elasticities by nationality for tourists in Denmark', *Tourism Economics*, 4: 101–30.

Johansson, B. and Ahman, M. (2002) 'A comparison of technologies for carbon-neutral passenger transport', *Transportation Research D*, 7(3): 175–96.

Johnson, P. (1988) 'The impact of a new entry on UK domestic air transport: A case study of the London–Glasgow route', *Service Industries Journal*, 8(3): 299–316.

Johnson, V. and Cottingham, M. (2008) 'Plane truths: Do the economic arguments for aviation growth really fly?', Nef (the New Economics Foundation) Report. London (www.neweconomics.org), accessed 10 October 2008.

Jones, D. and White, P. (1994) 'Modelling of cross-country rail services', *Journal of Transport Geography*, 2(2): 111–21.

Jones, P. (1995) 'Developing new products and services in flight catering', *International Journal of Contemporary Hospitality Management*, 7(2/3): 24–8.

Käferstein, F., Motarjemi, Y. and Bettcher, D. (1997), 'Foodborne disease control: A transnational challenge', *Journal of Emerging Infectious Diseases*, 3(4): 503–10.

Kandampully, J., Mok, C. and Sparks, B. (2001) *Service Quality Management in Hospitality, Tourism and Leisure*, New York: Haworth Press.

Kangis, P. and O'Reilly, M. (2003) 'Strategies in a dynamic marketplace: A case study in the airline industry', *Journal of Business Research*, 56(2): 105–11.

Kaul, R.N. (1985) *Dynamics of Tourism: A Trilogy* (Volume III) *Transportation and Marketing*, New Delhi: Sterling Publishers.

Khadaroo, J. and Seetanah, B. (2006) 'Transport infrastructure and tourism development', *Annals of Tourism Research*, 34(4): 1021–32.

Khadaroo, J. and Seetanah, B. (2007) 'The role of transport infrastructure in international tourism development: a gravity model approach', *Tourism Management*, 29(5): 831–40.

Kihl, M. (1988) 'The impacts of deregulation on passenger transportation in small towns', *Transportation Quarterly*, 42: 27–43.

Killen, J. and Smith, A. (1989) 'Transportation', in R.W.G. Carter and A.J. Parker (eds) *Ireland: A Contemporary Geographical Perspective*, London: Routledge, 271–300.

King, B. (2004) 'Using demand simulation to create mass tourism: The implementation of China's "Golden Week" holiday policy', Paper presented at the Tourism: State of the Art II conference, University of Strathclyde, Glasgow, 27–30 June.

Kirkcaldy, A. and Dudley Evans, A. (1913) *History and Economics of Transport*, Pitman: London.

Knowles, R.D. (ed.) (1985) *Implications of the 1985 Transport Bill*, Salford: Transport Geography Study Group, Institute of British Geographers.

Knowles, R.D. (1989) 'Urban public transport in Thatcher's Britain', in R.D. Knowles (ed.) *Transport Policy and Urban Development: Methodology and Evaluation*, Salford: Transport Geography Study Group, Institute of British Geographers.

Knowles, R.D. (1993) 'Research agendas in transport geography for the 1990s', *Journal of Transport Geography*, 1(1): 3–12.

Knowles, R.D. (1998) 'Passenger rail privatisation in Great Britain and its implications, especially for urban areas', *Journal of Transport Geography*, 6(2): 117–33.

Knowles, R.D. and Hall, D.R. (1992) 'Transport policy and control', in B. Hoyle and R.D. Knowles (eds) *Modern Transport Geography*, London: Belhaven, 11–32.

Knowles, R.D., Shaw, J. and Docherty, I. (eds) (2008) *Transport Geographies: Mobilities, Flows and Spaces*, Oxford: Blackwell.

Knowles, S.T. and Garland, M. (1994) 'The strategic importance of CRSs in the airline industry', *Travel and Tourism Analyst*, 4: 4–16.

Knowles, T., Diamantis, D. and El-Mourhabi, J. (2001) *The Globalization of Tourism and Hospitality: A Strategic Perspective*, 1st edn, London: Continuum.

Kosters, M. (1992) 'Tourism by train: Its role in alternative tourism', in V. Smith and W. Eadington (eds) *Tourism Alternatives: Potential and Problems in the Development of Tourism*, Philadelphia, PA: University of Pennsylvania Press.

Kotler, P. and Armstrong, G. (1991) *Principles of Marketing*, 5th edn, Englewood Cliffs, NJ: Prentice-Hall.

Kotler, P., Wong, V., Saunders, J. and Armstrong, G. (2005) *Principles of Marketing*, 4th edn, Harlow: Prentice Hall.

Kotter, J.P. and Schlesinger, L.A. (1979) 'Choosing strategies for change' *Harvard Business Review*, Harvard Business School of Publishing, March-April: 67–76.

Kozak, M. (2004) *Destination Benchmarking: Concepts, Practices and Operations*, Wallingford: CABI.

Krippendorf, J. (1987) *The Holidaymakers*, Oxford: Butterworth Heinemann.

Kwon, T.H. (2005) 'A scenario analysis of CO_2 emission trends from car gravel: Great Britain 2000–2003', *Transport Policy*, 12(2): 175–84.

Ladany, S. (1999) 'Optimal tourist bus tours', *Tourism Economics*, 5(2): 175–90.

Lahiri, S., Pérez-Nordtvedt, L. and Renn, R. (2008) 'Will the new competitive landscape cause your firm's decline? It depends on your mindset', *Business Horizons*, 51(4): 311–20.

Lamb, B. and Davidson, S. (1996) 'Tourism and transportation in Ontario, Canada', in L. Harrison and W. Husbands (eds) *Practising Responsible Tourism: International Case Studies in Tourism Planning, Policy and Development*, Chichester: Wiley, 261–76.

Land Use Consultants (1986) *The Channel Fixed Link: Environmental Appraisal of Alternative Proposals: A Report Prepared for the Department of Transport*, London: HMSO.

Lang, T. (1998) 'An overview of four futures methodologies'. (www.futures.hawaii. edu/j7/LANG.html).

Langley, R. (1997) *Airports*, London: Keynote Publications.

Latham, J. (1989) 'The statistical measurement of tourism', in C.P. Cooper (ed.) *Progress in Tourism, Recreation and Hospitality Management*, Volume 1, London: Belhaven, 55–76.

Latham, J. (1992) 'International tourism statistics', in C.P. Cooper and A. Lockwood (eds) *Progress in Tourism, Recreation and Hospitality Management*, Volume 4, London: Belhaven, 267–73.

Latham, J. and Edwards, C. (2003) 'The statistical measurement of tourism', in C. Cooper (ed.) *Classic Reviews in Tourism*, Clevedon: Channel View, 22–54.

Lavery, P. (1989) *Travel and Tourism*, 1st edn, Huntingdon: Elm.

Laws, E. (1991) *Tourism Marketing: Service Quality and Management Perspectives*, Cheltenham: Stanley Thornes.

Laws, E. (1995) *Managing Packaged Tourism*, London: International Thomson Business Press.

Laws, E. and Ryan, C. (1992) 'Service on flights: Issues and analysis by the use of diaries', *Journal of Travel and Tourism Marketing*, 1(3): 61–71.

Lawton, L.J. and Butler, R.W. (1987) 'Cruise ship industry: Patterns in the Caribbean 1880–1986', *Tourism Management*, 8(4): 329–43.

Lawton, T. (1999) 'The limits of price leadership: Needs-based positioning strategy and the long-term competitiveness of Europe's low fare airlines', *Long Range Planning*, 32(6): 573–86.

Lay, M. (2005) 'The history of transport planning', in K. Button and D. Hensher (eds) *Handbook of Transport Strategy, Policy and Institutions*, Oxford: Elsevier, 157–74.

Lee, D. (2003) 'Concentration and price trends in the US domestic airline industry: 1990–2000', *Journal of Air Transport Management*, 9: 91–101.

Lee, D., Lim, L. and Raper, S. (2005) 'The role of aviation emissions in climate stabilization scenarios', Poster at *Avoiding Dangerous Climate Change*, Conference, 1–3 February, Exeter, UK.

Lee, M., Fayed, H. and Fletcher, J. (2002) 'GATS and tourism', *Tourism Analysis*, 7(2): 125–37.

Lee, N. and Wood, C. (1988) 'The European Directive on environmental assessment: Implementation at last?', *The Environmentalist*, 9(3): 177–86.

Leggat, P. (1997) 'Travel health advice provided by in-flight magazines of international airlines in Australia', *Journal of Travel Medicine*, 4(2): 102–3.

Leggat, P. and Nowak, M. (1997) 'Dietary advice for airline travel', *Journal of Travel Medicine*, 4(1): 14–16.

Legors, F, and Danis, M. (1998) 'Surveillance of malaria in European Union countries', *Eurosurveillance*, 3: 45–7.

Leinbach, T. (1995) 'Transport and third world development: Review, issues and prescription', *Transportation Research A*, 29(5): 337–44.

Leiper, N. (1990) *Tourism Systems: An Interdisciplinary Perspective*, Palmerston North, NZ: Massey University, Department of Management Systems, Occasional Paper 2.

Leiper, N. (2008) 'Why "the tourism industry" is misleading as a generic expression: The case for the plural variation, "tourism industries"', *Tourism Management*, 29(2): 237–51.

Leiper, N. and Simmons, D. (1993) 'Tourism: A social science perspective', in H. Perkins and G. Cushman (eds) *Leisure, Recreation and Tourism*, Auckland: Longman Paul, 204–20.

Lennon, J. (ed.) (2002) *Tourist Statistics*, London: Continuum.

Lennon, J., Cockerell, N. and Trew, J. (2006) *Benchmarking National Tourism Organisations and Agencies: Understanding Best Practice*, Oxford: Elsevier.

Lew, A. (1991) 'Scenic roads and rural development in the US', *Tourism Recreation Research*, 16(2): 23–30.

Lew, A. and Yu, L. (eds) (1995) *Tourism in China: Geographic, Political and Economic Perspectives*, Boulder, CO: Westview Press.

Lew, A., Hall, C.M. and Williams, A. (eds) (2004) *A Companion of Tourism*, Oxford: Blackwell.

Lew, A. and McKercher, B. (2002) 'Trip destinations, gateways and itineraries: The example of Hong Kong', *Tourism Management*, 23(6): 609–21.

Li, G. (2008) 'The nature of leisure travel demand', in A. Graham, A. Papatheodorou and P. Forsyth (eds) *Aviation and Tourism: Implications for Leisure Travel*, Aldershot: Ashgate, 7–20.

Li, X., Poon, C., Lee, S., Chung, S. and Luk, F. (2003) 'Waste reduction and recycling strategies for the in-flight services in the airline industry' *Resources, Conservation and Recycling*, 37(2): 87–99.

Lickorish, L.J. in association with Jefferson, A., Bodlender, J. and Jenkins, C.L. (1991) *Developing Tourism Destinations: Policies and Perspectives*, Harlow: Longman.

Lindgren, M. and Bandhold, H. (2003) *Scenario Planning: The Link between Future and Strategy*, Aldershot: Palgrave.

Liou, J. and Tzeng, G. (2007) 'A non-additive model for evaluating airline service quality', *Journal of Air Transport Management*, 13(3): 131–8.

Lipsey, R.G. (1989) *An Introduction to Positive Economics*, London: Weidenfeld & Nicolson.

Lockhart, D. and Ashton, S. (1987) 'Recent trends in Maltese tourism', *Geography*, 72: 255–8.

Lockhart, D., Drakakis-Smith, D. and Schembri, J. (1993) *The Development Process in Small Island States*, London: Routledge.

Lohmann, G., Albers, S., Koch, B. and Pavlovich, K. (2009) 'From hub to tourist destination – An explorative study of Singapore and Dubai's aviation-based transformation', *Journal of Air Transport Management*, 15(3).

London Tourist Board (1987) *The Tourism Strategy for London*, London: London Tourist Board.

London Tourist Board (1990) *At the Crossroads: The Future of London's Transport*, London: London Tourist Board.

Lonely Planet (2007) 'Annual travellers pulse survey' (www.lonelyplanet.com/pressroom/news/press_release.cfm?press_release_id=313), 20 May 2008.

Lovelock, C. (1992a) 'Seeking synergy in service operations: Seven things marketers need to know about service operations', *European Management Journal*, 10(1): 22–9.

Lovelock, C. (1992b) *Managing Services: Marketing, Operations and Human Resources*, 2nd edn, Englewood Cliffs, NJ: Prentice-Hall.

Lovelock, C. and Yip, G. (1996) 'Global strategies for service businesses', *California Management Review*, 38(2): 64–86.

Loverseed, H. (1996) 'Car rental in the USA', *Travel and Tourism Analyst*, 4: 4–19.

Lowe, J.C. and Morydas, S. (1975) *The Geography of Movement*, Boston, MA: Houghton Mifflin.

Lowland Market Research (2004) *Cairngorms National Park Visitor Survey Final Report*, Granton on Spey: Lowlands Market Research/Cairngorms National Park.

Lue, C., Vrompton, J. and Fesenmaier, D. (1993) 'Conceptualisation of multi-destination pleasure trips', *Annals of Tourism Research*, 20(2): 289–301.

Lumpé, M. (2008) *Leadership and Organisation in the Aviation Industry*, Aldershot: Ashgate.

Lumsdon, L. (1996a) 'Future for cycle tourism in Britain', *INSIGHTS*: A27–A32.

Lumsdon, L. (1996b) *Cycling Opportunities: Making the Most of the National Cycling Network*, Stockport: Simon Holt Marketing Services.

Lumsdon, L. (1997a) *Tourism Marketing*, London: International Thomson Business Press.

Lumsdon, L. (1997b) 'Recreational cycling: Is this the way to stimulate interest in everyday urban cycling?', in R. Tolley (ed.) *The Greening of Urban Transport Planning for Walking and Cycling in Western Cities*, Chichester: Wiley, 113–27.

Lumsdon, L. (2000) 'Transport and tourism: Cycle tourism: a model for sustainable development', *Journal of Sustainable Tourism*, 8(5): 361–77.

Lumsdon, L. (2006) 'Factors affecting the design of tourism bus services', *Annals of Tourism Research*, 33(3): 748–66.

Lumsdon, L., Downward, P. and Cope, A. (2004) 'Monitoring of cycle tourism on long distance trails: The North Sea cycle route', *Journal of Transport Geography*, 12(1): 13–22.

Lumsdon, L. and Page, S.J. (eds) (2004a) *Tourism and Transport: Issues and Agenda for the New Millennium*, Oxford: Elsevier.

Lumsdon, L. and Page, S.J. (2004b) 'Progress in transport and tourism research: Reformulating the transport–tourism interface and future research agendas', in L. Lumsdon and S.J. Page (eds) *Tourism and Transport: Issues and Agenda for the New Millennium*, Oxford: Elsevier, 1–28.

Lumsdon, L. and Speakman, C. (1995) *Railways to Cycleways in the Forest of Dean and the Wye Valley*, Ilkley: Transport for Leisure.

Lumsdon, L. and Tolley, R. (2004) 'Non-motorised transport and tourism: A case study: Cycle tourism', in L. Lumsdon and S.J. Page (eds) *Tourism and Transport: Issues and Agenda for the New Millennium*, Oxford: Elsevier, 157–70.

Lundberg, D.E. (1980) *The Tourist Business*, New York: Van Nostrand Reinhold.

Lynam, D., Sutch, T., Broughton, J. and Lawson, S. (2003) 'The European Road Assessment Programme: Completing the pilot phase – 2001 & 2002. *Traffic Engineering and Control*, 44(5): 168–72.

Lynn Jones Research Ltd (2003) *The Significance of the Coach Tour Market for Tourism in Scotland*, Edinburgh: Lynn Jones Research Ltd.

Lyons, G., Chatterjee, K., Beecroft, M. and Marsden, G. (2002) 'Determinants of travel demand: exploring the future of society and lifestyles in the UK', *Transport Policy*, 9(1), 17–27.

Lyons, G. and Loo, B. (2008) 'Transport directions to the future', in R.D. Knowles, J. Shaw and I. Docherty (eds) *Transport Geographies: Mobilities, Flows and Spaces*, Oxford: Blackwell, 215–26.

Marsh, G. (2008) 'Biofuels: aviation alternative?', Feature Article, *Renewable Energy Focus*, July/August.

Maldonado, J. (1990) 'Strategic planning: An approach to improving airport planning under uncertainty', in: *Technology and Policy Program*, MSc Thesis, Massachusetts Institute of Technology, Cambridge, MA.

May, A., Shepherd, S. and Emberger, G. (2005) 'Optimisation of transport strategies', in K. Button and D. Hensher (eds) *Handbook of Transport Strategy, Policy and Institutions*, Oxford: Elsevier, 665–86.

McClintock, H. and Cleary, J. (1996) 'Cycle fatalities and cyclists' safety: Experience from Greater Nottingham and lessons for future cycling provision', *Transport Policy*, 3(1/2): 67–77.

McHale, J. (1969) *The Future of the Future*, New York: George Braziller.

McIntosh, I.B. (1989) 'Travel considerations in the elderly', *Travel Medicine International*: 69–72.

McIntosh, I.B. (1990a) 'The stress of modern travel', *Travel Medicine International*: 118–21.

McIntosh, I.B. (1990b) 'Travel sickness', *Travel Medicine International*: 80–3.

McIntosh, I.B. (1995) 'Travel phobias', *Journal of Travel Medicine*, 2(2): 99–100.

McIntosh, I.B. (1998) 'Health hazards and the elderly traveller', *Journal of Travel Medicine*, 5(1): 27–9.

McIntosh, R.W. (1973) *Tourism: Principles, Practices and Philosophies*, Columbus, OH: Grid.

McIntosh, R.W. and Goeldner, C.R. (1990) *Tourism: Principles, Practices and Philosophies*, Columbus, OH: Grid.

McKercher, B. and Lew, A. (2004) 'Tourist flows and the spatial distribution of tourists', in A. Lew, C.M. Hall and A. Williams (eds) *A Companion of Tourism*, Oxford: Blackwell, 36–48.

McLennan, R., Inkson, K., Dakin, S., Dewe, P. and Elkin, G. (1987) *People and Enterprises: Human Behaviour in New Zealand Organisations*, Auckland: Rinehart Winston.

MacCannel, D. (1976) *The Tourist: A New Theory of the Leisure Class*, New York: Schocken Books.

Macdonald-Wallace, D. (1997) 'Internet: Worldwide road to success', *INSIGHTS*: A1–A4.

Mackie, P. and Nellthorp, J. (2003) 'Transport appraisal in a policy context', in A. Pearman, P. Mackie and J. Nellthorp (eds) *Transport Projects, Programmes and Policies: Evaluation Needs and Capabilities*, Aldershot, Ashgate, 3–16.

Maldonado, J. (1990) 'Strategic planning: An approach to improving airport planning under uncertainty', Master's thesis, Massachusetts Institute of Technology, Cambridge, MA.

Maldonado, J. (1990) 'Strategic planning: An approach to improving airport planning under uncertainty', in: *Technology and Policy Program,* Msc Thesis, Massachusetts Institute of Technology, Cambridge, MA.

Majumdar, A. (1994) 'Air traffic control problems in Europe: Their consequences and proposed solutions', *Journal of Air Transport Management*, 1(3): 165–78.

Majumdar, A. (1995) 'Commercialising and restructuring air traffic control: A review of the experience and issues involved', *Journal of Air Transport Management*, 2(2): 111–22.

Manete, H. et al. (2000) 'Artist Work Package 2: Final Report', Venice CISET, University Ca' Foscari of Venice (unpublished) 27 January.

Mann, J.M. and Mantel, C.F. (1992) 'Travel and health: A global agenda', *Travel Medicine Two*, Proceedings of the Second International Conference on Travel Medicine, Paris, 1–4.

Mansfeld, Y. (1990) 'Spatial patterns of international tourist flows: Towards a theoretical approach', *Progress in Human Geography*, 14(3): 372–90.

Mansfeld, Y. (1992) 'Tourism: Towards a behavioural approach', *Progress in Planning*, 38(1): 1–92.

Marsh, J. and Staple, S. (1995) 'Cruise tourism in the Canadian Arctic and its implications', in C.M. Hall and M. Johnston (eds) *Polar Tourism: Tourism in Arctic and Antarctic Regions*, Chichester: Wiley, 63–72.

Martin, J. and Roman, C. (2003) 'New potential hubs in the South-Atlantic market: A problem', *Journal of Transport Geography*, 11(3): 139–49.

Martin-Cejas, R. and Sánchez, P. (2009) 'Ecological footprint analysis of road transport related to tourism', *Tourism Management*, 30.

Mason, G. and Barker, N. (1996) 'Buy now fly later: An investigation of airline frequent flyer programmes', *Tourism Management*, 17(3): 219–23.

Mason, K. (2000) 'The propensity of business travellers to use low-cost airlines', *Journal of Transport Geography*, 8(2): 107–19.

Mason, K. (2001) 'Marketing low-cost airline services to business travellers', *Journal of Air Transport Management*, 7(2): 103–9.

Mason, P. (1994) 'A visitor code for the Arctic', *Tourism Managememt*, 15(2): 93–7.

Mathieson, A. and Wall, G. (1982) *Tourism: Economic, Physical and Social Impacts*, Harlow: Longman.

Matthews, L. (1995) 'Forecasting peak passenger flows at airports', *Transportation*, 22(1): 55–72.

Maunder, D. and Mbara, T. (1995) *The Initial Effects of Introducing Commuter Omnibus Services in Harare*, Zimbabwe: Crowthorne, Transport Research Laboratory Report 123.

May, A. and Roberts, M. (1995) 'The design of integrated transport strategies', *Transport Policy*, 2(2): 97–106.

Meersam, H. and van de Voorde, E. (1996) 'The privatisation of air transport in Europe: Interaction between policy, economic power and market performance', *Built Environment*, 22(3): 177–91.

Meethan, K. (2004) 'Transnational corporations, globalisation and tourism', in A. Lew, C.M. Hall and A. Williams (eds) *A Companion of Tourism*, Oxford: Blackwell, 110–21.

Meredith, J. (1994) 'Air traffic management in Europe: Can it cope with future growth?', *Journal of Air Transport Management* 1(3): 179–80.

Middleton, V.T.C (1988) *Marketing in Travel and Tourism*, London: Heinemann.

Middleton, V. (1998) *Sustainable Tourism: A Marketing Perspective*, Oxford: Butterworth-Heinemann.

Middleton, V. and Clarke, J. (2001) *Marketing in Travel and Tourism*, Oxford: Butterworth-Heinemann.

Middleton, V. and Hawkins, R. (1998) *Sustainable Tourism: A Marketing Perspective*, Oxford: Butterworth Heinemann.

Mill, R.C (1992) *Tourism: The International Business*, 2nd edn, Englewood Cliffs, NJ: Prentice-Hall.

Mill, R.C. and Morrison, A.M. (1985) *The Tourism System: An Introductory Text*, Englewood Cliffs, NJ: Prentice-Hall.

Milman, A. and Pope, D. (1997) 'The US airline industry', *Travel and Tourism Analyst*, 3: 4–21.

Mings, R. and Hughs, K. (1992) 'The spatial configuration of travel to Yellowstone National Park', *Journal of Travel Research*, 30: 38–46.

Mitchell, M. (ed.) (1997) *The Aftermath of Road Accidents*, London: Routledge.

Mitchell, R. and Hall, C.M. (2001) 'The winery consumer: A New Zealand perspective', *Tourism Recreation Research*, 26(2): 63–75.

Monopolies and Mergers Commission (1989) *Cross-Channel Car Ferries*, Cmnd. 584, London: HMSO.

Moore, A. (1985) 'Japanese tourists', *Annals of Tourism Research*, 12(4): 619–43.

Morean, B. (1983) 'The language of Japanese tourism', *Annals of Tourism Research*, 10(2): 93–109.

Moriarty, P. and Honnery, D. (2008) 'The prospects for global green car mobility', *Journal of Cleaner Production*, 16: 1717–26.

Moriarty, P. and Honnery, D. (2008) 'Low-mobility: the future of transport', *Futures*, 40(10): 865–72.

Morley, C. (2006) 'Airline alliances', in L. Dwyer and P. Forsyth (eds) *International Handbook on the Economics of Tourism*, Cheltenham: Edward Elgar, 209–23.

Morrell, P. (2005) 'Airlines within airlines: an analysis of US network airline responses to low cost carriers, *Journal of Air Transport Management*, 11(5): 303–12.

Morris, S. (1990) *Japanese Outbound Travel Market in the 1990s*, London: Economist Intelligence Unit.

Morris, S. (1994) 'Japan outbound', *Travel and Tourism Analyst*, 1: 40–64.

Morrison, A., Yang, C., O'Leary, J. and Nadkarni, N. (1996) 'Comparative profiles of travellers on cruises and land-based resort vacations', *Journal of Tourism Studies*, 7(2): 15–27.

Morrison, S. and Winston, C. (1986) *The Economic Effects of Airline Deregulation*, Washington, DC: Brookings Institution.

Morrison, W (2004) 'Dimensions of predatory pricing in air travel markets', *Journal of Air Transport Management*, 10: 87–95.

Moscardo, G. and Pearce, P. (2004) 'Life cycle, tourist motivation and transport: Some consequences for the tourist experience', in L. Lumsdon and S. J. Page. (eds) *Tourism and Transport: Issues and Agenda for the New Millennium*, Oxford: Elsevier, 29–44.

Moscardo, G., Morrison, A., Cai, L., Nadkarni, N. and O'Leary, J. (1996) 'Tourist perspectives on cruising: Multidimensional scaling analyses of cruising and other holiday types', *Journal of Tourism Studies*, 7(2): 54–64.

Moses, L.N. and Savage, I. (1990) 'Aviation deregulation and safety: Theory and evidence', *Journal of Transport Economics and Policy*, 14: 171–88.

Mulligan, C. (1979) 'The Snowdon sherpa: Public transport and national park management experiment', in D. Halsall and B. Turton (eds) *Rural Transport Problems in Britain, Papers and Discussion*, Keele: Institute of British Geographers Transport Study Group.

Murphy, P.E. (1985) *Tourism: A Community Approach*, London: Routledge.

Murray, A. (2001) *Off the Rails: Britain's Great Railway Crisis: Cause, Consequences and Cure*, London: Verso.

Murray, M. and Graham, B. (1997) 'Exploring the dialectics of route-based tourism: The Camino de Santiago', *Tourism Management*, 18(8): 513–24.

National Air Traffic Services Ltd (1997) *Reports and Accounts 1997*, London: Civil Aviation Authority.

National Consumer Council (1991) *Consumer Concerns 1990*, London: National Consumer Council.

National Consumer Council (1992) *British Rail Privatisation*, London: National Consumer Council.

National Tours Association (1992) *Tourism Traveller Index. The Benchmark Study*, USA: National Tours Association.

Neri, J., Cramer, E., Vaughan, H., Vinjé, V. and Mainzer, H. (2008) 'Passenger behaviours during norovirus outbreaks on cruise ships', *Journal of Travel Medicine*, 15(3): 172–6.

Newson, M. (1992) 'Environmental economics, resources and commerce', in M. Newson (ed.) *Managing the Human Impact on the National Environment: Patterns and Processes*, London: Belhaven, 80–106.

Newman, P. and Kenworthy, J. (1999) *Sustainability and Cities: Overcoming Automobile Dependence*, Washington, DC: Island Press.

New Zealand Customs Service (2001) *New Zealand Passenger Arrival Card – and Notes*, Wellington: New Zealand Customs Service.

New Zealand Ministry of Tourism (2008) 'New Zealand tourism forecast 2008 to 2014', Wellington (www.tourismresearch.govt.nz/Data–Analysis/Forecasts/2008—2014-Forecasts-National/), accessed 12 October 2008.

New Zealand Winegrowers (2002) (www.nzwine.com/statistics/).

Nie, X., Batta, R., Drury, C. and Lin, L. (2009) 'Passenger grouping with risk levels in an airport security system', *European Journal of Operational Research*, 194(2): 574–84.

Njegovan, N. (2006) 'Elasticities of demand for leisure air travel: A system modelling approach', *Journal of Air Transport Management*, 12: 33–9.

Noe, F. (1999) *Tourism Service Satisfaction*, Champaign, IL: Sagamore.

Nozawa, H. (1992) 'A marketing analysis of Japanese outbound travel', *Tourism Management*, 13(2): 226–34.

Nykvist, B. and Whitmarsh, L. (2008) 'A multi-level analysis of sustainable mobility transitions: niche development in the UK and Sweden', *Technological Forecasting and Social Change*, 75(9): 1373–87.

Oakland, J. (1989) *Total Quality Management*, Oxford: Heinemann.

O'Brien, J. (1996) 'Smile – you are on the web', *Sunday Times*, Culture Section, 9 January: 51.

O'Connor, K. (1995) 'Airport development in South East Asia', *Journal of Transport Geography*, 3(4): 269–79.

O'Connor, K. (1996) 'Airport development: A Pacific Asian perspective', *Built Environment*, 22(3): 212–22.

OECD (1992) *Torurism Policy and International Tourism in OECD Countries*, Paris: OECD.

OECD (2001) *Environmental Outlook*, Paris: OECD.

OECD (2002) *Trends in the Transport Sector 1970–2000*, Paris: OECD.

OECD (2005) *OECD in Figures 2005 – Transport*, Paris: OECD.

OECD (2008a) *Tourism in OECD Countries 2008: Trends and Policies*, Paris: OECD.

OECD (2008b) 'The tourism economy and globalisation: strategic issues and policies', Background Report, High level meeting of the Tourism Committee, CFE/TOU (2008) 9, Paris: OECD.

Office for Science and Technology (OfST) (2006) *Transport—Intelligent Futures Project*, London: OfST.

OGM (2002) *The Development of International Passenger Markets and Policy*, Brussels: European Union.

O'Hare, G. and Barrett, H. (1997) 'The destination life cycle: International tourism in Peru', *Scottish Geographical Magazine*, 113(2): 66–73.

O'Kelly, M.E. (1986) 'The location of interacting hub facilities', *Transportation Science*, 20(2): 92–106.

Oliver, T. (2001) 'The consumption of tour routes in cultural landscapes', in J. Mazanec, G. Crouch, J.B. Ritchie and A. Woodside (eds) *Consumer Psychology of Tourism, Hospitality and Leisure*, Wallingford: CABI, 273–84.

Ontario Ministry of Culture, Tourism and Recreation (1994) *Ontario's Tourism Industry: Opportunity, Progress, Innovation*, Toronto: Ontario Ministry of Culture, Tourism and Recreation.

Ontario Ministry of Transportation (1993) *Strategic Directions: Draft*, Ontario: Ontario Ministry of Transportation.

Oosterveld, W. (1995) 'Motion sickness', *Journal of Travel Medicine*, 2(3): 182–7.

Oppermann, M. (1995) 'A model of travel itineraries', *Journal of Travel Research*, 33(4): 57–61.

Orams, M. (1998) *Marine Tourism*, London: Routledge.

Orbasli, A. (2000) *Tourists in Historic Towns: Urban Conservation and Heritage Management*, London: Spon Press.

Orbasli, A. and Shaw, S. (2004) 'Transport and visitors in historic cities', in L. Lumsdon and S.J. Page (eds) *Tourism and Transport Issues and Agenda for the New Millennium*, Oxford: Elsevier, 93–104.

O'Rourke, V. (1996) 'Queensland rail: A sleeper awakes', *Chartered Institute of Transport* (Queensland section), September.

Orient-Express (2004) *A World of Distinction*, London: Orient-Express.

Ortuzar, J. de D. and Willumsen, L.E. (1990) *Modelling Transport*, Chichester: John Wiley.

Ortuzar, J., Hensher, D. and Jara-Diaz, S. (1998) *Travel Behaviour Research: Updating the State of Play*, Oxford: Pergamon.

Ostrowski, P., O'Brien, T. and Gordon, G. (1993) 'Service quality and customer loyalty in the commercial airline industry', *Journal of Travel Research*, 32(2): 16–24.

Ostrowski, P., O'Brien, T. and Gordon, G. (1994) 'Determinants of service quality in the commercial airline industry: Differences between business and leisure travellers', *Journal of Travel and Tourism Marketing*, 3(1): 19–47.

Oum, T. (1995) 'A comparative study of productivity and cost competitiveness of the world's major airlines', *Discussion Paper No. 363*, Osaka: Institute of Social and Economic Research, Osaka University.

Oum, T. (1997) 'Challenges and opportunities for Asian airlines and governments', in C. Findlay, L. Chia and K. Singh (eds) *Asia Pacific Air Transport: Challenges and Policy Reforms*, Singapore: Institute for South East Asian Studies, 1–22.

Oum, T. and Park, J. (1997) 'Airline alliances: Current status', *Journal of Air Transport Management*, 3(3): 133–44.

Oum, T. and Yu, C. (1995) 'A productivity comparison of the world's major airlines', *Journal of Air Transport Management*, 2(3/4): 181–95.

Oum, T. and Yu, C. (1998) 'Cost competitiveness of major airlines: An international comparison', *Transportation research A*, 32(6): 407–22.

Oum, T. and Yu, C. (2000) *Shaping Air Transport in Asia Pacific*, Aldershot: Ashgate.

Oum, T., Yu, C. and Fu, X. (2003) 'A comparative analysis of productivity performance of the world's major airports: Summary report of the ATRS global airport benchmarking research report – 2002', *Journal of Air Transport Management*, 9(5): 285–97.

Oum, T., Fu, X. and Yu, C. (2005) 'New evidence on airline efficiency and yields: A comparative analysis of major North American air carriers and its implications', *Transport Policy*, 12(2): 153–64.

Oum, T., Yan, J. and Yu, C. (2008) 'Ownership forms matter for airport efficiency: A stochastic frontier investigation of worldwide airports', *Journal of Urban Economics*, 64(2): 422–35.

Oxley, P. and Richards, M. (1995) 'Disability and transport: A review of the personal costs of disability in relation to transport', *Transport Policy*, 2(1): 57–66.

Page, C., Wilson, M. and Kolb, D. (1994) *On the Inside Looking In: Management Competencies in New Zealand*, Wellington: Ministry of Commerce.

Page, M. (2005) 'Non-motorised transportation policy', in K. Button and D. Hensher (eds) *Handbook of Transport Strategy, Policy and Institutions*, Oxford: Elsevier, 581–96.

Page, S.J. (1987) 'London Docklands: Redevelopment schemes in the 1980s', *Geography*, 72(1): 59–63.

Page, S.J. (1989a) 'Changing patterns of international tourism in New Zealand', *Tourism Management*, 10(4): 337–41.

Page, S.J. (1989b) 'Tourist development in London Docklands in the 1980s and 1990s', *GeoJournal*, 19(3): 291–5.

Page, S.J. (1989c) 'Tourism planning in London', *Town and Country Planning*, 58(3): 334–5.

Page, S.J. (1991) 'Tourism in London: The Docklands connection', *Geography Review*, 4(3): 3–7.

Page, S.J. (1992a) 'Managing tourism in a small historic city', *Town and Country Planning*, 61(7/8): 208–11.

Page, S.J. (1992c) 'Perspectives on the environmental impact of the Channel Tunnel on tourism', in C.P. Cooper and A. Lockwood (eds) *Progress in Tourism, Recreation and Hospitality Management*, Volume 4, London: Belhaven, 82–102.

Page, S.J. (1993a) 'Regenerating Wellington's waterfront', *Town and Country Planning*, 63(1/2): 29–31.

Page, S.J. (1993b) 'Tourism and peripherality: A review of tourism in the Republic of Ireland', in C.P. Cooper (ed.) *Progress in Tourism, Recreation and Hospitality Management*, Volume 5, London: Belhaven, 26–53.

Page, S.J. (1993c) 'European rail travel', *Travel and Tourism Analyst*, 1: 5–30.

Page, S.J. (1993d) 'Editorial', *Tourism Management*, 14(6): 419–23.

Page, S.J. (1994a) 'Editorial: The spatial implications of the Channel Tunnel', *Applied Geography*, 14(1): 3–8.

Page, S.J. (1994b) 'European bus and coach travel', *Travel and Tourism Analyst*, 1: 19–39.

Page, S.J. (1995a) 'Waterfront revitalisation in London: Market-led planning and tourism in London Docklands', in S. Craig-Smith and M. Fagence (eds) *Urban Waterfront Development: An International Survey*, New York: Praeger, 53–70.

Page, S.J. (1995b) *Urban Tourism*, London: Routledge.

Page, S.J. (1996) 'Pacific Islands', *International Tourism Reports*, 1: 67–102.

Page, S.J. (1997) *The Costs of Adventure Tourism Accidents for the New Zealand Tourism Industry: Final Report*, Wellington: The Tourism Policy Group, Ministry of Commerce.

Page, S.J. (1998) 'Transport for tourism and recreation', in B. Hoyle and R.D. Knowles (eds) *Modern Transport Geography*, 2nd edn, Chichester: John Wiley.

Page, S.J. (1999) *Transport and Tourism*, 1st edn, Harlow: Addison-Wesley Longman.

Page, S.J. (2002a) 'Tourist health and safety: Issues for the new millennium', *Traveland Tourism Analyst*, 4.

Page, S.J. (2002b) 'Tourist health and safety', *Travel and Tourism Analyst*, 10: 1–32.

Page, S.J. (2003) *Tourism Management: Managing for Change*, Oxford: Butterworth-Heinemann.

Page, S.J. (2009) *Tourism Management: Managing for Change*, 3rd edn, Oxford: Butterworth-Heinemann.

Page, S.J. Bentley, T., Meyer, D. and Chalmers, D.J. (2001) 'Scoping the extent of tourist road traffic accidents in New Zealand', *Current Issues in Tourism*, 4(6): 503–26.

Page, S.J. and Connell, J. (eds) (2008) *Sustainable Tourism Management*, London: Routledge.

Page, S.J. and Dowling, R. (2002) *Ecotourism*, Harlow: Prentice Hall.

Page, S.J. and Fidgeon, P. (1989) 'London Docklands: A tourism perspective', *Geography*, 74(1): 66–8.

Page, S.J. and Hall, C.M. (2002) *Managing Urban Tourism*, Harlow: Prentice Hall.

Page, S.J. and Hardyman, R. (1996) 'Place-marketing and town centre management in the UK', *Cities: The International Journal of Urban Policy and Planning*, 13(3):153–64.

Page, S.J. and Meyer, D. (1996) 'Tourist accidents: An exploratory analysis', *Annals of Tourism Research*, 23(3): 666–90.

Page, S.J. and Sinclair, M.T. (1992a) 'The Channel Tunnel: An opportunity for London's tourism industry', *Tourism Recreation Research*, 17(2): 57–70.

Page, S.J. and Sinclair, M.T. (1992b) 'The Channel Tunnel and tourism markets', *Travel and Tourism Analyst*, 1: 8–32.

Page, S.J. and Thorn, K. (1997) 'Towards sustainable tourism planning in New Zealand: Public sector planning responses', *Journal of Sustainable Tourism*, 5(1): 59–77.

Page, S.J. and Thorn, K. (2002) 'Towards sustainable tourism development and planning in New Zealand: The public sector response revisited', *Journal of Sustainable Tourism*, 10(3): 222–39.

Page, S.J., Yeoman, I., Greenwood, C. and Connell, J. (2010) 'Scenario planning as a tool to understand uncertainty in tourism: The example of transport and tourism in Scotland in 2025', *Current Issues in Tourism*.

Pagliari, R. (2003) 'The impact of airline franchising on air service provision in the Highlands and Islands of Scotland', *Journal of Transport Geography*, 11: 117–29.

Paixao, M., Dewar, R.D., Cossar, J.H., Covell, R.G. and Reid, D. (1991)'What do Scots die of when abroad?', *Scottish Medical Journal*, 36(4): 114–16.

Pakdil, F. and Aydin, O. (2007) 'Expectations and perceptions in airline services: An analysis using weighted SERVQUAL scores', *Journal of Air Transport Management*, 13(4): 229–37.

Palhares, G. (2003) 'The role of transport in tourism development: Nodal functions and management practices', *International Journal of Tourism Research*, 5(5): 403–7.

Palmer-Tous, T., Riera-Font, A. and Rosello-Nadal, J. (2007) 'Taxing tourism: The case of rental cars in Mallorca', *Tourism Management*, 28: 271–9.

Papatheodorou, A. (2002) 'Civil aviation regimes and leisure tourism in Europe', *Journal of Air Transport Management*, 8(6): 381–8.

Park, J. (2007) 'Passenger perceptions of service quality: Korean and Australian case studies', *Journal of Air Transport Management*, 13(4): 238–42.

Patmore, J.A. (1983) *Recreation and Resources*, Oxford: Blackwell.

Patzek, T.W. (2007) 'How can we outlive our way of life?', Paper prepared for the 20th Round Table on sustainable Development of Biofuels: Is the Cure worse than the Disease?, Paris: OECD.

Pearce, D.G. (1979) 'Towards a geography of tourism', *Annals of Tourism Research*, 6(3): 245–72.

Pearce, D.G. (1985) 'Tourism and environmental research: A review', *International Journal of Environmental Studies*, 25(4): 247–55.

Pearce, D.G. (1987) *Tourism Today: A Geographical Analysis*, Harlow: Longman.

Pearce, D.G. (1990) *Tourist Development*, 2nd edn, Harlow: Longman.

Pearce, D.G. (1992) *Tourism Organisations*, Harlow: Longman.

Pearce, D.G. (1995a) *Tourism Today: A Geographical Analysis*, 2nd edn, Harlow: Longman.

Pearce, D.G. (1995b) 'CER, Trans-Tasman tourism and a single aviation market', *Tourism Management*, 16(2): 111–20.

Pearce, D.G. and Butler, R.W. (eds) (1992) *Tourism Research: Critiques and Challenges*, London: Routledge.

Pearce, D.G. and Elliot, J.M. (1983) 'The Trip Index', *Journal of Travel Research*, 22(1): 6–9.

Pearce, P.L. (1982) *The Social Psychology of Tourist Behaviour*, Oxford: Pergamon.

Pearce, P.L. (1992) 'Fundamentals of tourist motivation', in D.G. Pearce and R. Butler (eds) *Tourism Research: Critiques and Challenges*, London: Routledge, 113–34.

Pearson, R.C. and Goheen, A.C. (eds) (1998) *Compendium of Grape Diseases*, Saint Paul, MN: The American Phytopathological Society.

Peeters, P.M., van Egmond, T. and Visser, N. (2004) *European Tourism, Transport and Environment, Final version*, Breda: NHTV CSTT.

Peeters, P., Gössling, S. and Becken, S. (2006) 'Innovation towards tourism sustainability: Climate change and aviation', *Special Issue International Journal of Innovation and Sustainable Development* (edited by M. Hall), 1(3), 184–200.

Peeters, P., Szimba, E. and Duinjnisveld, M. (2007) 'Major environmental impacts of European tourist transport', *Journal of Transport Geography*, 15(2): 83–93.

Peisley, T. (2006) *The Future of Cruising – Boom or Bust?*, Colchester: Seatrade Communications Limited.

Penner, J., Lister, D.H., Griggs, D.J., Dokken, D.J. and McFarland, M. (eds) (1999) *Aviation and the Global Atmosphere; A Special Report of IPCC Working Groups I and III*, Cambridge: Cambridge University Press.

Perkins, H.C. and Cushman, G. (eds) (1993) *Leisure, Recreation and Tourism*, Auckland: Longman Paul.

Perks, A. (1993) 'Tourism and transport issues for the Channel Islands of Guernsey and Alderney', MSc thesis, Department of Management Studies, University of Surrey, Guildford.

Perl, A., Patterson, J. and Perez, M. (1997) 'Pricing aircraft emissions at Lyon-Satolas airport', *Transportation Research D*, 2(2): 89–105.

Peters, T.J. and Waterman, R.H. (1982) *In Search of Excellence*, London: Harper & Row.

Peterson, B.S. (2004) *Bluestreak: Inside JetBlue, the Upstart that Rocked an Industry*, New York: Portfolio.

Petit, J. (2002) 'Transport planning and tourism: Specific constraints and innovations in an alpine tourist context', *Revue de Geographie Alpiné*, 90(1): 49–66.

Petrick, J. (2004) 'The roles of quality, value and satisfaction in predicting cruise ship behavioural intentions', *Journal of Travel Research*, 42(4): 397–407.

Petrie, J. and Dawson, A. (1994) 'Recent developments in the treatment of jet-lag', *Journal of Travel Medicine*, 1(2): 19–83.

Phang, S. (2003) 'Strategic development of airport and rail infrastructure: The case of Singapore', *Transport Policy*, 10(1): 27–33.

Pigram, J.J. (1992) 'Planning for tourism in rural areas: Bridging the policy implementation gap', in D.G. Pearce and R.W. Butler (eds) *Tourism Research: Critiques and Challenges*, London: Routledge, 156–74.

Pilarski, A.M. (2007) *Why Can't We Make Money in Aviation?*, Aldershot: Ashgate.

Pitfield, D. (2007) 'The impact of traffic, market shares and concentration of airline alliances on selected European–US routes', *Journal of Air Transport Management*, 13(4): 192–202.

Planning Department Study (2003) Information Note No 15: Technical Note on Tourism Transport Planning (www.pland.gov.hk).

Polunin, I. (1989) 'Japanese travel boom', *Tourism Management*, 10(1): 4–8.

Poon, A. (1989) 'Competitive strategies for a new tourism', in C.P. Cooper (ed.) *Progress in Tourism, Recreation and Hospitality Management*, Volume 4, London: Belhaven, 91–102.

Poon, A. (1993) *Tourism, Technology and Competitive Strategies*, Wallingford: CAB International.

Porter, L.J. and Parker, A.J. (1992) 'Total Quality Management: The critical success factors', *Total Quality Management*, 4(1): 13–22.

Porter, M. (1979) 'How competitive forces shape strategy', *Harvard Business Review*, March/April, 137–45.

Porter, M.E. (1990) *The Competitive Advantage of Nations*, New York: Free Press.

Potter, S. (1987) *On the Right Lines: The Limits of Technological Innovation*, London: Pinter.

Potter, S. (1997) *Vital Travel Statistics*, London: Landor Publishing Limited.

Potter, S. and Bailey, I. (2008) 'Transport and the environment', in R.D. Knowles, J. Shaw and I. Docherty (eds) *Transport Geographies: Mobilities, Flows and Spaces*, Oxford: Blackwell, 49–61.

Prentice, R. (2005) 'Tourism motivations and typologies', in A. Lew, C.M. Hall and A. Williams (eds) *A Companion to Tourism*, Oxford: Blackwell, 261–79.

Preston, J. and O'Connor, K. (2008) 'Revitalised transport geographies', in R.D. Knowles, J. Shaw and I. Docherty (eds) *Transport Geographies: Mobilities, Flows and Spaces*, Oxford: Blackwell, 227–37.

Prideaux, J. (1990) 'InterCity: Passenger railway without subsidy', *Royal Society of Arts Journal*, March: 244–54.

Prideaux, B. (1999) 'Tracks to tourism: Queensland rail joins the tourism industry', *International Journal of Tourism Research*, 1(2): 73–86.

Prideaux, B. (2000a) 'The role of the transport system in destination development', *Tourism Management*, 21(1): 53–64.

Prideaux, B. (2000b) 'The resort development spectrum', *Tourism Management*, 21(3): 225–41.

Prideaux, B. (2004) 'Transport and destination development', in L. Lumsdon and S.J. Page (eds) *Tourism and Transport: Issues and Agenda for the New Millennium*, Oxford: Elsevier, 79–92.

Prideaux, B. and Carson, D. (eds) (2009) *Drive Tourism: Trends and Emerging Markets*, London: Routledge.

Prideaux, B., Laws, E. and Faulkner, W. (2003) 'Events in Indonesia: Exploring the limits to formal tourism trends forecasting methods in complex crisis situations', *Tourism Management*, 24(4): 475–87.

Prins, V. and Lombard, P. (1995) 'Regulation of commercialised state-owned enterprises: Case study of South African airports and air traffic and navigation services', *Journal of Air Transport Management*, 2(3–4): 163–71.

Pucher, J. and Buehler, R. (2006) 'Why Canadians cycle more than Americans: A comparative analysis of bicycling trends and policies', *Transport Policy*, 13: 265–79.

Qaiters, C.G. and Bergiel, B.J. (1989) *Consumer Behaviour: A Decision-Making Approach*, Ohio: South Western Publishing.

Quayle, M. (1993) *Logistics: An Integrated Approach*, Kent: Hodder & Stoughton.

Raguraman, K. (1986) 'Capacity and route regulation in international scheduled air transportation: A case study of Singapore', *Singapore Journal of Tropical Geography*, 7(1): 53–69.

Raguraman, K. (1997)'Airlines as instruments for nation building and national identity: Case study of Malaysia and Singapore', *Journal of Transport Geography*, 5(4): 239–56.

Regnerus, H., Beunen, R. and Jaarsma, F. (2007) 'Recreational traffic management: The relations between research and implementation', *Transport Policy*, 14(3): 258–67.

Reynolds-Feighan, A. (2001) 'Traffic distribution in low-cost and full-service carrier networks in the US air transportation market', *Journal of Air Transport Management*, 7(5): 265–75.

Reynolds-Feighan, A. and Feighan, K. (1997) 'Airport services and airport charging systems: A critical review of the EU common framework', *Transportation Research E*, 33(4): 311–20.

Richards, B. (2001) *Future Transport in Cities*, London: Routledge.

Rigas, K. (2009) 'Boat or airplane? Passengers' perceptions of transport services to islands. The example of the Greek domestic leisure market', *Journal of Transport Geography*.

Ringland, G. (2002) *Scenarios in Public Policy*, Chichester: John Wiley.

Ritchie, B. (1997) 'Cycle tourism in the South Island of New Zealand: Infrastructure considerations for the twenty-first century', Paper presented at *Trails in the Third Millennium*, Cromwell, NZ, 2–5 December, 325–34.

Ritchie, B. (2004) 'Chaos, crises and disaster: A strategic approach to crisis management in the tourism industry', *Tourism Management*, 25(4): 669–83.

Ritchie, J.B.R. and Crouch, G. (2003) *The Competitive Destination*, Wallingford: CABI.

Robson, W. (1997) *Strategic Management and Information Systems: An Integrated Approach*, 2nd edn, London: Pitman.

Robbins, D. and Dickinson, J. (2007) 'Can domestic tourism growth and reduced car dependency be achieved simultaneously in the UK?', In P. Peeters (ed.) *Tourism and Climate Change Mitigation. Methods, Greenhouse Gas Reductions and Policies*, NHTV Academic Studies 6, Breda: NHTV.

Robbins, D. and Thompson, K. (2007) 'Special issue on transport at tourist destinations', *Journal of Transport Geography*, 15(2): 80–82.

Roberts, P. (2005) *The End of Oil*, London: Bloomsbury Books.

Român, C., Espino, R. and Martin, J. (2007) 'Competition of high-speed train with air transport: the case of Madrid–Barcelona', *Journal of Air Transport Management*, 13(5): 277–84.

Romeril, M. (1985) 'Tourism and the environment: Towards a symbiotic relationship', *Journal of Environmental Studies*, 25: 215–18.

Romeril, M. (1989) 'Tourism and the environment: Accord or discord?', *Tourism Management*, 10(3): 204–8.

Root, A. (ed.) (2003) *Delivering Sustainable Transport*, Oxford: Pergamon.

Ross, G. (1994) *The Psychology of Tourism*, Melbourne: Hospitality Press.

Ross, W.A. (1987) 'Evaluating environmental impact statements', *Journal of Environmental Management*, 25: 137–47.

Rowe, V. (1994) *International Business Travel: A Changing Profile*, London: Economist Intelligence Unit.

Rudkin, B. and Hall, C.M. (1996) 'Off the beaten track: The health implications of the development of special-interest tourism services in South-East Asia and the South Pacific', in S. Clift and S.J. Page (eds), *Health and the International Tourist*, London: Routledge, 89–107.

Russell, R.C. (1987) 'Survival of insects in the wheel bays of a Boeing 747B aircraft on flights between tropical and temperate airports', *Bulletin of the World Health Organization*, 65: 659–62.

Ryan, C. (1991) *Recreational Tourism: A Social Science Perspective*, London: Routledge.

Ryan, C. (ed.) (1996) *The Tourist Experience*, London: Cassell.

Ryan, C. (2003) *Recreational Tourism*, Channel View: Clevedon.

Ryan, C. and Huimin, G. (eds) (2009) *Tourism in China: Destination, Cultures and Communities*, London: Routledge.

Rycroft, R. and Szylowicz, J. (1980) 'The technological dimension of decision-making: The case of the Aswan high dam', *World Politics*, 32: 36–61.

Sakai, M. (2006) 'public sector investment in tourism infrastructure', in L. Dwyer and P. Forsyth (eds) *International Handbook on the Economics of Tourism*, Cheltenham: Edward Elgar, 266–79.

Sarkis, J. and Talluri, S. (2004) 'Performance based clustering for benchmarking of US airports', *Transportation Research*, A38: 329–46.

Scheyvens, R. (2002) *Tourism for Development*, Harlow: Prentice Hall.

Schiefelbusch, M., Jain, A., Schäfer, T. and Müller, D. (2007) 'Transport and tourism: Roadmap to integrated planning developing and assessing integrated travel chains', *Journal of Transport Geography*, 15(2): 94–103.

Schieven, A. (1988) *A Study of Cycle Tourists on Prince Edward Island*, unpublished Master's thesis, University of Waterloo, Canada.

Schiffman, L.G. and Kanuk, L.L. (1991) *Consumer Behaviour*, 2nd edn, Englewood Cliffs, NJ: Prentice-Hall.

Schmidberger, S., Bals, L., Hartmann, E. and Jahns, C. (2009) 'Ground handling services at European hub airports: Development of a performance measurement system for benchmarking', *International Journal of Production Economics*, 117(1): 104–16.

Schnaars, S. (1987) 'How to develop scenarios', *Long Range Planning*, 20(1): 105–14.

Schoemaker, P. (1995) 'Scenario planning: A tool for strategic thinking', *Sloan Management Review*, Winter: 25–40.

Schoemaker, P.J.H. (1993) 'Multiple scenario development: Its conceptual and behavioral foundation', *Strategic Management Journal*, 14: 193–213.

Schumpeter, J. (1952) *Can Capitalism Survive?*, New York: Harper & Row.

Schwartz, P. (1996) *The Art of the Long View: Planning for the Future in an Uncertain World*, New York: Currency Doubleday.

Scott, D., Amelung, B., Becken, S., Ceron, J.P., Dubois, G., Goessling, S., Peeters, P. and Simpson, M. (2007) *Climate Change and Tourism: Responding to Global Challenges*, Madrid/Paris: United Nations World Tourism Organisation and United Nations Environment Programme.

Scotsman (2001) 'Tourist road hazard', *Scotsman*, 10 November: 11.

Scottish Executive (2000) *Scottish Transport Statistics*, Edinburgh: Scottish Executive.

Scottish Executive (2002) *Proposals for a Highlands and Islands Integrated Transport Authority:* Volume 1, *Main Report*, Edinburgh: Scottish Executive.

Scottish Executive (2002) *Scottish Statistics*, Edinburgh: Scottish Executive National Statistics Publications, 23 June.

Scottish Tourist Board (1991) *Tourism Potential of Cycling and Cycle Routes in Scotland*, Edinburgh: Scottish Tourist Board.

Scottish Government (2006) *National Transport Strategy*, Edinburgh: Scottish Government. (www.scotland.gov.uk/Publications/2006/12/04104414/0).

Scottish Executive (2006a) *Scotland's National Transport Strategy: A Consultative Summary*, Edinburgh: Scottish Executive.

Scottish Executive (2006b) *Scotland's National Transport Strategy*, Edinburgh: Scottish Executive.

Sealy, K. (1976) *Airport Strategy and Planning*, Oxford: Oxford University Press.

Sealy, K. (1992) 'International air transport', in B.S. Hoyle and R.D. Knowles (eds) *Modern Transport Geography*, London: Belhaven, 233–56.

Seaton, A. and Bennett, M. (1996) *Marketing Tourism Products: Concepts, Issues, Cases*, London: International Thomson Business Press.

Seaton, A. and Palmer, C. (1997) 'Understanding VFR tourism behaviour: The first five years of the United Kingdom Survey', *Tourism Management*, 18(6): 345–55.

Seibert, J.C. (1973) *Concepts of Marketing Management*, New York: Harper & Row.

Selman, P. (1992) *Environmental Planning: The Conservation and Development of Biophysical Resources*, London: Paul Chapman.

Seristö, H. and Vepsäläinen, A (1997) 'Airline cost drivers: Cost implications of fleet, routes, and personnel policies', *Journal of Air Transport Management*, 3(1): 11–22.

SERPLAN (1989) *The Channel Tunnel: Impact on the South East*, London: SERPLAN.

SETEC/Wilbur Smith Associates (1989) *Review of Market Trends and Forecasts*, Paris: Eurotunnel.

Seys, S.A. and Bender, J.B. (2001) 'The changing epidemiology of malaria in Minnesota', *Journal of Emerging Infectious Diseases*, 7(6): 993–5.

Shailes, A., Senior, M. and Andrew, B. (2001) 'Tourist travel behaviour in response to congestion: The case of car trips to Cornwall', *Journal of Transport Geography*, 9: 49–60.

Sharples, J.M. and Fletcher, J.P. (2001) *Tourist Road Accidents in Rural Scotland*, Edinburgh: Scottish Executive Central Research Unit.

Sharpley, R. (1993) *Tourism and Leisure in the Countryside*, Huntingdon: Elm.

Sharpley, R. and Craven, B. (2001) 'The 2001 foot and mouth crisis: Rural economy and tourism policy implications: a comment', *Current Issues in Tourism*, 4(6), 527–37.

Shaw, G. and Coles, T. (2004) 'Disability, holiday making and the tourism industry in the UK: A preliminary survey', *Tourism Management*, 25(3): 397–403.

Shaw, G. and Williams, A. (2004) *Tourism and Tourism Spaces*, London: Sage.

Shaw, J. (2000) *Competition, Regulation and the Privatisation of British Rail*, Aldershot: Ashgate.

Shaw, J., Walton, W and Farrington, J. (2003) 'Assessing the potential for a "rail renaissance" in Great Britain', *Geoforum*, 34: 141–56.

Shaw, S. (1982) *Airline Marketing and Management*, London: Pitman.

Shaw, S. (2003) *Airline Marketing and Management*, Aldershot: Ashgate.

Shaw, S. (2004) *Airline Marketing and Management*, 5th edn, Aldershot: Ashgate.

Shaw, S. (2007) *Airline Marketing and Management*, 6th edn, Aldershot: Ashgate.

Shaw, S. (2008) 'Aviation marketing and the leisure market', in A. Graham, A. Papatheodorou and P. Forsyth (eds) *Aviation and Tourism: Implications for Leisure Travel*, Aldershot: Ashgate, 35–48.

Shaw, S.L. (1993) 'Hub structures of major US passenger airlines', *Journal of Transport Geography*, 1(1): 47–58.

Shaw, J., Knowles, R.D. and Docherty, I. (2008) 'Transport, governance and ownership', in R.D. Knowles, J. Shaw and I. Docherty (eds) *Transport Geographies: Mobilities, Flows and Spaces*, Oxford: Blackwell, 62–80.

Sheldon, P. (1997) *Tourism Information Technology*, Wallingford: CAB International.

Shen, Q. (1997) 'Urban transportation in Shanghai, China: Problems and planning implications', *International Journal of Urban and Regional Research*, 21(4): 589–606.

Sherman, C. (2002) 'Motion sickness: Review of causes and preventive strategies', *Journal of Travel Medicine*, 9(5): 251–6.

Shilton, D. (1982) 'Modelling the demand for high speed train services', *Journal of the Operational Research Society*, 33: 713–22.

Shon, Z., Chen, F. and Chang, Y. (2003) 'Airline e-commerce: The revolution of ticketing channels', *Journal of Air Transportation*, 9: 325–31.

Sigala, M. (2008) 'Applications and implications of information and communication technology for airports and leisure travellers', in A. Graham, A. Papatheodorou and P. Forsyth (eds) *Aviation and Tourism: Implications for Leisure Travel*, Aldershot: Ashgate, 209–26.

Sikorski, D. (1990) 'A comparative evaluation of the government's role in national airlines', *Asia Pacific Journal of Management*, 7(1): 97–120.

Simmons, D. and Leiper, N. (1993) 'Tourism: A social science perspective', in H.C. Perkins and G. Cushman (eds) *Leisure, Recreation and Tourism*, Auckland: LongmanPaul, 204–20.

Simon, D. (1996) *Transport and Development in the Third World*, London: Routledge.

Sinclair, M.T. (1991) 'The economics of tourism', in C.P. Cooper (ed.) *Progress in Tourism, Recreation and Hospitality Management*, Volume 3, London: Belhaven, 1–27.

Sinclair, M.T. and Page, S.J. (1993) 'The Euroregion: A new framework for regional development', *Regional Studies*, 27(5): 475–83.

Sinclair, M.T. and Stabler, M. (1991) 'New perspectives on the tourism industry', in M.T. Sinclair and M.J. Stabler (eds) *The Tourism Industry: An International Analysis*, Oxford: CAB International, 1–14.

Sinclair, M.T. and Stabler, M. (1997) *The Economics of Tourism*, London: Routledge.

Singapore Airlines (1991) *Singapore Airlines Annual Report 1991–92*, Singapore: Singapore Airlines.

Singapore Airlines (1997) *Singapore Airlines Annual Report 1996–97*, Singapore: Singapore Airlines.

Singapore Mass Rapid Transit (SMRT) (1997) *At Your Service: SMRT's Commitment to Passengers*, Singapore: SMRT.

Skapinker, M. (1996) 'Airports are poised and ready for takeoff', *Financial Times*, 18 November (World Airports Survey): I.

Skapinker, M. (1998a) 'Shopping while you wait', *Financial Times*, 5 February (Special Report: The Business of Travel): VI.

Skapinker, M. (1998b) 'When passenger trouble strikes', *Financial Times*, 5 February (Business of Travel Supplement: VI).

Smith, A. and Hall, C.M. (2001) 'A stakeholder generated SWOT analysis of the New Zealand food and wine tourism industry', Paper presented at the New Zealand Wine and Food Tourism Conference, Hawkes Bay, November.

Smith, C. and Jenner, P. (1997) 'The seniors' travel market', *Travel and Tourism Analyst*, 5: 43–62.

Smith, D., Odegard, J. and Shea, W. (1984) *Airport Planning*, Belmont, CA: Wadsworth Inc.

Smith, M.J.T. (1989) *Aircraft Noise*, Cambridge: Cambridge University Press.

Smith, R. (2008) 'Enabling technologies for demand management: Transport', *Energy Policy*, 36(12): 4444–8.

Smith, S.L.J. (1989) *Tourism Analysis*, Harlow: Longman.

Smith, V.L. (1992) 'Boracay, Philippines: A case study in alternative tourism', in V.L. Smith and W.R. Eadington (eds) *Tourism Alternatives: Potential and Problems in the Development of Tourism*, Philadelphia, PA: University of Pennsylvania Press, 133–57.

Smith, V.L. and Eadington W.R. (eds) (1992) *Tourism Alternatives: Potential and Problems in the Development of Tourism*, Philadelphia, PA: University of Pennsylvania Press.

Soames, T. (1997) 'Ground handling liberalisation', *Journal of Air Transport Management*, 3(2): 83–94.

Sofield, T. and Li, F. (1997) 'Rural tourism in China: Development issues in perspective', in D. Getz and S.J. Page (eds) *The Business of Rural Tourism: International Perspectives*, London: International Thomson Business Press, 120–37.

Somerville, H. (1992) 'The airline industry's perspective', in D. Banister and K.J. Button (eds) *Transport, the Environment and Sustainable Development*, London: E & FN Spon: 161–74.

Song, H. and Witt, S. (2000) *Tourism Demand Modelling and Forecasting: Modern Econometric Approaches*, Oxford: Pergamon.

Song, H. and Li, G. (2008) 'Tourism demand modelling and forecasting – A review of recent research', *Tourism Management*, 29(2): 203–20.

Speak, C. (1997) 'The new airport: Kai Tak airport', *Geography*, 82(3): 266–8.

Speakman, C. (1996) 'Britain's changing railways and the tourist package', *INSIGHTS*: A45–A48.

Starkie, D.N. (1976) *Transportation Planning, Policy and Analysis*, Oxford: Pergamon Press.

Stasinopoulos, D. (1992) 'The second aviation package of the European Community', *Journal of Transport Economics and Policy*, 26: 83–7.

Stasinopoulos, D. (1993) 'The third phase of liberalisation in community aviation and the need for supplementary measures', *Journal of Transport Economics and Policy*, 27: 323–8.

Steer Davies Gleave (2008) 'Exploring the links between transport and culture', A review of the role of transport as a barrier to participation in cultural activities in Scotland commissioned by the Scottish Executive, Transport Department. (www.scotland.gov.uk/Publications/2008/08/08123433/0).

Stern, N. (2006) *Stern Review on the Economics of Climate Change*, London: HM Treasury (www.hm-treasury.gov.uk/independent_reviews/stern_review_economics_climate_change/sternreview_index.cfm), accessed 14 November 2006.

Steiner, T. and Bristow, A. (2000) 'Road pricing in National Parks: A case study in the Yorkshire Dales National Park', *Transport Policy*, 7(2): 93–103.

Steward, S. (1986) *Air Disasters*, London: Arrow.

Stirland, R. (2004) Personal communication, May 2004.

Stopher, P. (2004) 'Reducing road congestion', *Transport Policy*, 11: 117–31.

Stradling, S. and Anable, J. (2008) 'Individual transport patterns', in R.D. Knowles, J. Shaw and I. Docherty (eds) *Transport Geographies: Mobilities, Flows and Spaces*, Oxford: Blackwell, 179–95.

Stubbs, J. and Jegede, F. (1998) 'The integration of rail and air transport in Britain', *Journal of Transport Geography*, 6(1): 53–67.

Stubbs, P.C., Tyson, W.J. and Dalvi, M. (1980) *Transport Economics*, London: Allen & Unwin.

Su, M. and Wall, G. (2009) 'The Qinghai-Tibet railway and Tibetan tourism: Traveller's perspectives', *Tourism Management*, 30.

Sull, D. (1999) 'EasyJet's $500 million gamble', *European Management Journal*, 17(1): 20–38.

Sultan, F. and Simpson, M. (2000) 'International service variants: Airline passenger expectations and perception of service', *Journal of Services Marketing*, 14(3): 188–216.

Suna, Y. and Lyndon, L. (2004) 'Agent-based personalised tourist route advice system', in XXth ISPRS Congress, Geo-Imagery Bridging Continents, 12–13 July, Istanbul, Turkey.

Sustrans (1995) *The National Cycle Network: Bidding Document to the Millennium Commission*, Bristol: Sustrans.

Sustrans (1996) *Local Agenda 21 and the National Cycle Network: Routes to Local Sustainability*, Bristol: Sustrans.

Sustrans (1997) *The Tourism Potential of National Cycle Routes*, London: The Tourism Society.

Sustrans (2002) *National Cycle Network: Route Usage Monitoring Programme*, Bristol: Sustrans.

Swarbrooke, J. (1994) 'The future of the past: Heritage tourism in the twenty-first century', in A. Seaton (ed.) *Tourism: State of the Art*, Chichester: John Wiley.

Swarbrooke, J. (1997) 'Understanding the tourist: Some thoughts on consumer behaviour research in tourism', *INSIGHTS*: A67–A76.

Swarbrooke, J. and Horner, S. (2007) *Consumer Behaviour in Tourism*, 2nd edn, Oxford: Butterworth Heinemann.

Szyliowicz, J. and Goetz, A. (1995) 'Getting realistic about megaproject planning: The case of the new Denver International Airport', *Policy Sciences*, 28: 347–67.

Taaffe, E.J. and Gauthier, H.L. (1973) *Geography of Transportation*, Englewood Cliffs, NJ: Prentice-Hall.

Taneja, N. (1988) *The International Airline Industry: Issues and Challenges*, Lexington, MA: Lexington Books.

Taneja, N. (2005) *Fasten Your Seatbelt: The Passenger is Flying the Plane*, Aldershot: Ashgate.

Tang, S. and Lo, H. (2008) 'The impact of public transport policy on the viability and sustainability of mass railway transit – The Hong Kong experience', *Transportation Research Part A: Policy and Practice*, 42(4): 563–76.

Taplin, J.H.E. (1993) 'Economic reform and transport policy in China', *Journal of Transport Economics and Policy*, 27(1): 75–86.

Taplin, J. and McGinley, C. (2000) 'A linear programme to model daily car touring choices', *Annals of Tourism Research*, 27(2): 431–67.

Taplin, J. and Qiu, M. (1997) 'Car trip attraction and route choice in Australia', *Annals of Tourism Research*, 24(3): 624–37.

Tapper, R. and Font, X. (2004) *Tourism Supply Chains*, Final report of a desk research project for the Travel Foundation, Leeds Metropolitan University. (www.icrtourism.org/documents/TourismSupplyChainsfinalreport31January 2004.pdf).

Taylor, C. (1983) 'Rail passenger transport in Australia: A critical analysis of the network and services', unpublished PhD thesis, Department of Regional and Town Planning, University of Queensland.

TEST (1991) *The Wrong Side of the Tracks*, London: TEST.

Teye, W.B. (1992) 'Land transportation and tourism in Bermuda', *Tourism Management*, 13(4): 395–405.

Teye, V.B. and Leclerc, D. (1998) 'Product and service delivery satisfaction among North American cruise passengers', *Tourism Management*, 19(2): 153–60.

Therivel, R.B. and Barret, B.F.D. (1990) 'Airport development and E.I.A.: Kansai International Airport, Japan', *Land Use Policy*, 7(1): 80–6.

Thompson, I. (2002) 'Air transport liberalisation and the development of third level airports in France', *Journal of Transport Geography*, 10: 73–285.

Thompson, K. and Schofield, P. (2007) 'An investigation of the relationship between public transport performance and destination satisfaction', *Journal of Transport Geography*, 15(2): 136–44.

Thornberry, N. and Hennessey, H. (1992) 'Customer care, much more than a smile: Developing a customer service infrastructure', *European Management Journal*, 10(4): 460–4.

Tieran, S., Rhoades, D. and Waguespack, B. (2008) 'Airline alliance service quality performance – An analysis of US and EU member airlines', *Journal of Air Transport Management*, 14(2): 99–102.

Todd, G. and Mather, S. (1993) *Tourism in the Caribbean*, London: Economist Intelligence Unit.

Tokuhisa, T. (1980) 'Tourism within, from and to Japan', *International Social Science Journal*, 32(1): 128–50.

Tol, R. (2007) 'The impact of a carbon tax on international tourism', *Transportation Research D*, 12(2): 129–42.

Tolley, R. (ed.) (1990) *The Greening of Urban Transport: Planning for Walking and Cycling in Western Cities*, London: Belhaven.

Tolley, R. (ed.) (2003) *Creating Sustainable Transport: Planning for Walking and Cycling*, Cambridge: Woodhead.

Tolley, R. and Turton, B. (eds) (1987) *Short Sea Crossings and the Channel Tunnel*, Keele: Institute of British Geographers Transport Study Group.

Tolley, R. and Turton, B. (eds) (1995) *Transport Systems, Policy and Planning: A Geographical Approach*, Harlow: Longman.

Toms, M. (1994) 'Charging for airports: The new BAA approach', *Journal of Ai Transport Management*, 1(2): 77–82.

Tourism Society (1990) *Tourism and the Environment: A Memorandum to the Department of Employment Task Force*, London: The UK Tourism Society.

Tourism Industry Association of Canada (2008) *The Report on Tourism Competitiveness: A Call for Action*, Ontario: TIAC.

Tourism New Zealand (2008) 'Environment: Attitudes and behaviour. Key Messages from the Campaign Tracking Research 06/07', Auckland.

Tourism and Transport Forum (2007) *Assessing the Impact of Airport Privatisation*, Sydney: STTF.

Tovar, B. and Martín-Cejas, R.R. (2009) 'Are outsourcing and non-aeronautical revenues important drivers in the efficiency of Spanish airports?', *Journal of Air Transport Management*, 15(3).

Townsend, P.L. and Gebhart, J.E. (1986) *Commit to Quality*, New York: John Wiley.

TPR Associates (1999) *The European Tourist: A Market Profile*, 9th edn, London: TPR Associates.

Travelmole (2008) Jetstar's carbon-offset program soars ahead, 29 January. (http://www.travelmole.com/stories/1125905.php#).

Trew, J. and Cockerell, N. (2004) 'The French market', *INSIGHTS*, March: B77–100.

Tribe, J. (1996) *Corporate Strategy for Tourism*, London: International Thomson Business Press.

Turner, J. (1997) 'The policy process', in B. Axford, G. Browning, R. Huggins, B. Rosamond and J. Turner, *Politics: An Introduction*, London: Routledge, 409–39.

Turton, B. (1991) 'The changing transport pattern', in R.J. Johnston and V. Gardiner (eds) *The Changing Geography of the British Isles*, 2nd edn, London: Routledge, 171–97.

Turton, B. (1992a) 'British Rail passenger policies', *Geography*, 77(1): 64–7.

Turton, B. (1992b) 'Inter-urban transport', in B. Hoyle and R. Knowles (eds) *Modern Transport Geography*, London: Belhaven, 105–24.

Turton, B. (2004) 'Airlines and tourism development: The case of Zimbabwe', in L. Lumsdon and S.J. Page (eds) *Tourism and Transport: Issues and Agenda for the New Millennium*, Oxford: Elsevier, 69–78.

Turton, B. and Mutambirwa, C. (1996) 'Air transport services and the expansion of international tourism in Zimbabwe', *Tourism Management*, 17(6): 453–62.

UK Cabinet Office Performance and Innovation Unit (2001) *A Futurist's Toolbox: Methodologies in Futures Work*, Strategic Futures Team, UK Cabinet Office Performance and Innovation Unit, London.

United Nations World Tourism Organization (2001) *Tourism 2020 Vision*. Madrid: World Tourism Organization.

United Nations (2003) Economic and Social Committee for Asia, *Statistical Abstract of Transport in Asia 1990–2001*, *New* York: United Nations.

UN (2007) *Statistical Yearbook of Asia and the Pacific*, New York: UN.

Upham, P., Thomas, C., Gillingwater, D. and Raper, D. (2004) 'Environmental capacity and airport operations: Current issues and future prospects', *Journal of Air Transport Management*, 9(3): 145–51.

Urry, J. (1990) *The Tourist Gaze*, London: Sage.

Urry, J. (2001) 'Transports of delight', *Leisure Studies*, 20(4): 237–45.

Urry, J. (2004) 'The new mobilities paradigm', Paper presented at a workshop on mobility and the cosmopolitan perspective, Reflexive Modernisation Research Centre, Munich.

US Bureau of the Census (1996) *Statistical Abstract of the United States 1995*, Washington: Reference Press Inc.

US Department of Transportation (2003) *Aviation Consumer Complaints* (www.dot.gov).

US Department of Transportation (2008) *Air Travel Consumer Reports for 2008*. (http://airconsumer.ost.dot.gov/reports/atcr08.htm).

Usyal, M. and Crompton, V.L. (1985) 'An overview of approaches used to forecast tourism demand', *Journal of Travel Research*, 23(4): 7–15.

Vahrenkamp, R. (2006) 'Automobile tourism and Nazi propaganda: Constructing the Munich–Saltzburg Autobahn 1933–1945', *Journal of Transport History*, 27(2): 21–38.

Van Borrendam, A. (1989) 'KLM strives for customer satisfaction', *TQM Magazine*, 1(2): 105–9.

Van Dierdonck, R. (1992) 'Success strategies in a service economy', *European Marketing Journal*, 10(3): 365–73.

van der Heijden, K., Bradfield, R., Burt, G., Cairns, G. and Wright, G. (2002) *The Sixth Sense, Accelerating Organisational Learning with Scenarios*. Chichester: John Wiley & Sons.

Van Excel, J., Rienstra, S., Gommers, M., Pearman, A. and Tsamboulas, D. (2002) 'EU involvement in TENS development: Network effects and European value added', *Transport Policy*, 9: 299–311.

Van Excel, J., Rienstra, S., Gommers, M., Pearman, A. and Tsmaboulas, D. (2002) 'EU involvement in TEN development: Network effects and European value added', *Transport Policy*, 9(3): 299–311.

Van Middelkoop, M., Borgers A. and Timmermans, H. (2003) 'Inducing heuristic principles of tourist choice of travel mode: A rule-based approach', *Journal of Travel Research*, 42(1): 75–83.

Van Mierlo, J., Maggetto, G. and Lataire, P. (2006) 'Which energy source for road transport in the future? A comparison of battery, hybrid and fuel cell vehicles', *Energy Conversion and Management*, 47: 2748–60.

Van Reeven, P. (2005) 'Transport policy in the European Union', in K. Button and D. Hensher (eds) *Handbook of Transport Strategy, Policy and Institutions*, Oxford: Elsevier, 705–24.

Van Wee, B., van den Brink, R. and Nijland, H. (2003) 'Environmental impacts of high speed rail links in cost-benefit analyses: A case study of the Zuider Zee line', *Transportation Research D*, 8(4): 299–314.

Vasigh, B., Fleming, K. and Tacker, T. (2008) *Introduction to Air Transport Economics*, Aldershot: Ashgate.

Veal, A. (1992) *Research Methods in Leisure and Tourism*, Harlow: Longman.

Verchere, I. (1994) *The Air Transport Industry in Crisis*, London: Economist Intelligence Unit.

Véronneau, S. and Roy, J. (2009) 'Global service supply chains: An empirical study of current practices and challenges of a cruise line corporation', *Tourism Management*, 30(1): 128–39.

Vespermann, J., Wald, A. and Vesepermann, R.G. (2008) 'Aviation growth in the Middle East – Impacts on incumbent players and potential strategic reactions', *Journal of Transport Geography*, 16(6): 388–94.

Viant, A. (1993) 'Enticing the elderly to travel: An exercise in Euro-management', *Tourism Management*, 14(1): 52–60.

Vickerman, R. (1995) 'The Channel Tunnel: A progress report', *Travel and Tourism Analyst*, 3: 4–20.

Vickerman, R. (2000) 'Channel Tunnel', *Travel and Tourism Analyst*, 1.

Vincent, M. and Burley, S. (1994) 'Delighting the customer', in M. Vincent and C. Green (eds) *The InterCity Story*, Somerset: Oxford Publishing Company, 107–18.

VisitScotland (2002) *Know Your Market*, (www.scotexchange.net), accessed 6 June 2004.

VisitScotland (2003) *Tourism in Scotland 2002*, VisitScotland.

VisitScotland (2005) *Tourism Attitudes Survey 2005*. Stockport: Harris Interactive.

VisitScotland (2007) *Tourism Prospectus*, Edinburgh: VisitScotland.

Wackermann, G. (1997) 'Transport, trade, tourism and the world economic system', *International Social Science Journal*, 151(1): 23–40.

Wade, D., Mwsaqa, B. and Eagles, P. (2001) 'A history and market analysis of tourism in Tanzania', *Tourism Management*, 22(1): 93–101.

Wager, J. (1967) 'Outdoor recreation on common land', *Journal of the Town Planning Institute*, 53: 398–403.

Wahab, S. andPigram, J. (eds) (1997) *Tourism Development and Growth: The Growth of Sustainability*, London: Routledge.

Wales Tourist Board (1992) *Infrastructure Services for Tourism: A Paper for Discussion*, Cardiff: Wales Tourist Board.

Wall, G. (1971) 'Car owners and holiday activities', in P. Lavery (ed.) *Recreational Geography*, Newton Abbot: David & Charles.

Wall, G. (1972) 'Socioeconomic variations in pleasure trip patterns: The case of Hull car owners', *Transactions of the Institute of British Geographers*, 57: 45–58.

Walker, L. and Page, S.J. (2004) 'The contribution of tourists and visitors to road traffic accidents: A preliminary analysis of trends and issues for Central Scotland', *Current Issues in Tourism*, 7(3): 217–42.

Wang, Z. and Horsburgh, S. (2007) 'Linking network coherence to service performance: Modelling airline strategic alliances', *Journal of Marketing Channels*, 14(3): 51–81.

Wansink, B. and Ittersum, K. (2004) 'Stopping decisions of travellers', *Tourism Management*, 25(3): 319–30.

Wardle, D.A. (2003) 'Global sale of green air travel supported using biodiesel', *Renewable and Sustainable Energy Reviews*, 7: 1–64.

Wardman, M., Hatfield, R. and Page, M. (1997) 'The UK national cycling strategy: Can improved facilities meet the targets?', *Transport Policy*, 4(2): 123–33.

Warnock-Smith, D. and Morrell, P. (2008) 'Air transport liberalisation and traffic growth in tourism-dependent economies: A case-history of some US-Caribbean markets', *Journal of Air Transport Management*, 14(2): 82–91.

Wathern, P. (1990) *Environmental Impact Assessment: Theory and Practice*, London: Unwin Hyman.

Weatherford, L. and Bodily, S. (1992) 'A taxonomy and research overview of perishable asset revenue management: Yield management, overbooking and pricing', *Operations Research*, 40: 831–4.

Weaver, D. (2006) *Sustainable Tourism*, Oxford: Butterworth Heinemann.

Weaver, D. and Elliot, K. (1996) 'Spatial patterns and problems in Namibian tourism', *The Geographical Journal*, 162(2): 205–17.

Weiler, B. (1993) 'Guest Editor's Introduction', *Tourism Management*, 14(2): 83–4.

Wells, A. (1989) *Air Transportation: A Management Perspective*, 2nd edn, Wadsworth Inc.

Wen, Z. (1997) 'China's domestic tourism: Impetus, development and trends', *Tourism Management*, 18(8): 565–71.

Wensveen, J. (2007) *Air Transportation: A Management Perspective*, 6th edn, Aldershot: Ashgate.

Wheatcroft, S. (1978) 'Transport, tourism and the service industry', *Chartered Institute of Transport Journal*, 38(7): 197–206.

Wheatcroft, S. (1994) *Aviation and Tourism Policies*, London: Routledge/World Tourism Organization.

Wheeler, B. (1991) 'Tourism: Troubled times', *Tourism Management*, 12(2): 91–6.

Wheeler, B. (1992a) 'Is progressive tourism appropriate?', *Tourism Management*, 13(1): 104–5.

Wheeler, B. (1992b) 'Alternative tourism: A deceptive ploy', in C.P. Cooper and A. Lockwood (eds) *Progress in Tourism, Recreation and Hospitality Management*, Volume 4, London: Belhaven, 140–6.

Wheeler, B. (1994) 'Egotourism, sustainable tourism and the environment: A symbiotic, symbolic or shambolic relationship', in A. Seaton (ed.) *Tourism: The State of the Art*, Chichester: John Wiley, 647–54.

Whitaker, R. and Levere, J. (1997) 'Web fever', *Airline Business*, February: 26–33.

White, H.P. and Senior, M.L. (1983) *Transport Geography*, Harlow: Longman.

White, P. and Farrington, J. (1998) 'Bus and coach deregulation and privatisation in Great Britain, with particular reference to Scotland', *Journal of Transport Geography*, 6(2): 135–41.

Whitelegg, J. (1987) 'Rural railways and disinvestment in rural areas', *Regional Studies*, 21(1): 55–64.

Whitelegg, J. (1993) *Transport for a Sustainable Future: The Case for Europe*, Belhaven: London.

Whitelegg, J. (1998) 'Down the tube', *The Guardian*, 29 January: 21.

Wie, B. and Choy, D. (1993) 'Traffic impact analysis of tourism development', *Annals of Tourism Research*, 20(3): 505–18.

Wilkins, M. and Hall, C.M. (2001) 'An industry stakeholder SWOT analysis of wine tourism in the Okanagan Valley, British Columbia', *International Journal of Wine Marketing*, 13(3): 77–81.

Wilkinson, P.F. (1989) 'Strategies for tourism in island microstates', *Annals of Tourism Research*, 16(2): 153–77.

Wilkinson, J. (2007) 'Peak oil: a few facts and figures', ASPO South Australia. (www.ASPO-Australia.org.au).

Wilks, J. (1999) 'International tourists, motor vehicles and road safety: A review of the literature leading up to the Sydney 2000 Olympics', *Journal of Travel Medicine*, 6, 115–21.

Wilks, J. and Page, S.J. (eds) (2003) *Managing Tourist Health and Safety*, Oxford: Elsevier.

Williams, A. (1995) 'Capital and the transnationalisation of tourism', in A. Montanari and A. Williams (eds) *European Tourism: Regions, Spaces and Restructuring*, Chichester: John Wiley, 163–85.

Williams, G. (1993) *The Airline Industry and the Impact of Deregulation*, Brookfield, VT: Ashgate.

Williams, G. (2001) 'Will Europe's charter carriers be replaced by "no-frills" scheduled airlines?', *Journal of Air Transport Management*, 7(5): 277–86.

Williams, G. (2008) 'The future of charter operations', in A. Graham, A. Papatheodorou and P. Forsyth (eds) *Aviation and Tourism: Implications for Leisure Travel*, Aldershot: Ashgate, 85–102.

Williams, G. and Pagliari, R. (2004) 'A comparative analysis of the application and use of public service obligations in air transport in the EU', *Transport Policy*, 11: 55–66.

Williams, P.W. (1987) 'Evaluating environmental impact on physical capacity in tourism', in J.R.B. Ritchie and C.R. Goeldner (eds) *Travel, Tourism and Hospitality Research*, New York: John Wiley, 385–97.

Williams, V., Noland, R. and Toumi, R. (2002) 'Reducing the climate change impacts of aviation by restricting cruise altitudes', *Transportation Research D*, 7: 451–64.

Williams, V., Noland, R.B. and Toumi, R. (2003) 'Air transport cruise altitude restrictions to minimise contrail formation', *Climate Policy*, 3, 207–19.

Wilson, I. and Ralston, B. (2006) *Scenario Planning Handbook: Developing Strategies in Uncertain Times*, Southwestern.

Wilson, M.E. (1995) 'Travel and the emergence of infectious diseases', *Journal of Emerging Infectious Diseases*, 1(2): 39–46.

Wine Institute of California (2002) *Pierce's Disease Update*, San Francisco, CA: Wine Institute of California.

Wit, R.C.N., Boon, B.H., van Velzen, A., Cames, M., Deuber, O. and Lee, D.S. (2005) *Giving Wings to Emission Trading. Inclusion of Aviation under the European Emission Trading System (ETS): Design and Impacts*, 05.7789.20, Delft: CE.

Withyman, W. (1985) 'The ins and outs of international travel and tourism data', *International Tourism Quarterly*, Special Report No. 55.

Witt, C. (1995) 'Total quality management', in S. Witt and L. Moutinho (eds) *Tourism, Marketing and Management Handbook: Student Edition*, Hemel Hempstead: Prentice Hall, 229–42.

Witt, C. and Muhlemann, A. (1995) 'Service quality in airlines', *Tourism Economics*, (1): 33–49.

Witt, S.F., Brooke, M.Z. and Buckley, P.J. (1991) *The Management of International Tourism*, London: Routledge.

Witt, S.F. and Martin, C. (1989) 'Demand forecasting in tourism and recreation', in C.P. Cooper (ed.) *Progress in Tourism, Recreation and Hospitality Management*, Volume 1, London: Belhaven, 4–32.

Witt, S.F. and Martin, C. (1992) *Modelling and Forecasting Demand in Tourism*, London: Academic Press.

Witt, S.F. and Moutinho, L. (eds) (1989) *Tourism Marketing and Management Handbook*, Hemel Hempstead: Prentice Hall.

Witt, S. and Witt, C. (1995) 'Forecasting tourism demand: A review of empirical research', *International Journal of Forecasting*, 11: 447–75.

Wolmar, C. (1996) *The Great British Railway Disaster*, London: Ian Allen Publishing.

Wolmar, C. (2001) *Broken Rails: How Privatisation Wrecked Britain's Railways*, London: Aurum Press.

Wong, D., Pitfield, D. and Humphreys, I. (2004) 'The impact of regional jets on air services at selected US airports and markets', *Journal of Transport Geography*, available online June 2004.

Wood, R. (2000) 'Caribbean cruise tourism: Globalisation at sea', *Annals of Tourism Research*, 27(2): 345–70.

Wood, R. (2004) 'Cruise ships: Deterritorialised zones', in L. Lumsdon and S.J. Page (eds) *Tourism and Transport: Issues and Agenda for the New Millennium*, Oxford: Elsevier, 133–46.

Wood, K. and House, S. (1991) *The Good Tourist*, London: Mandarin.

Wood, K. and House, S. (1992) *The Good Tourist in France*, London: Mandarin.

World Commission on the Environment and Development (1987) *Our Common Future* (Brundtland Commission's Report), Oxford: Oxford University Press.

World Economic Forum (2008) *Travel and Tourism Competitiveness Report*, Geneva: WEF.

World Tourism Organization (1992) *Yearbook of Tourism Statistics*, Madrid: World Tourism Organization.

World Tourism Organization (1994) *Global Distribution Systems (GDSs) in the Tourism Industry*, A study prepared for the World Tourism Organization by O. Vialle, Madrid: World Tourism Organization.

World Tourism Organization (1997) *Yearbook of Tourism Statistics*, Madrid: World Tourism Organization.

World Tourism Organization (2004) *World Tourism Barometer*, Madrid: World Tourism Organization.

World Travel and Tourism Council, World Tourism Organization and Earth Council (1997) *Agenda 21 for the Travel and Tourism Industry: Towards Environmentally Sustainable Development*, London: Intercontinental.

Worldwatch Institute (2008) 'Chinese airlines report losses as high oil prices eat up margins', News Updates (www.worldwatch.org/node/4422), accessed 10 October 2008.

Wright, C. and Egan, J. (2000) 'De-Marketing the car', *Transport Policy*, 7(4): 287–94.

Xiuyun Yang, X., Tok, S. and Su, F. (2008) 'The privatization and commercialization of China's airports', *Journal of Air Transport Management*, 14(5): 243–251.

Yamauchi, H. (1997) 'Air transport policy in Japan: Limited competition under regulation', in C. Findlay, C. Sien and K. Singh (eds) *Asia Pacific Air Transport: Challenges and Policy Reforms*, Singapore: Institute of South East Asian Studies, 106–22.

Yang, X., Tok, S. K., Su, F. (2008) 'The privatization and commercialization of China's airports', *Journal of Air Transport Management*, 14(5): 243–51.

Yardley, L. (1992) 'Motion sickness and perception: A reappraisal of the sensory conflict approach', *British Journal of Psychology*, 82: 449–71.

Yeoman, I., Lennon. J., Blake, A., Galt, M., Greenwood, C. and McMahon-Beattie, U. (2007) 'Oil depletion: What does this mean for Scottish tourism?', *Tourism Management*, 28(5): 1354–65.

Yolonda, L., Youngs, A., White, D. and Wodrich. J. (2008) 'Transportation systems as cultural landscapes in National Parks: The case of Yosemite', *Society and Natural Resources*, 21(9): 797–811.

Youssef, W and Hansen, M. (1994) 'Consequences of strategic alliances between international airlines: The case of Swissair', *Transportation Research A*, 28(5): 415–31.

Yu, L. and Goulden, M. (2006) 'A comparative analysis of international tourists' satisfaction in Mongolia', *Tourism Management*, 27(6): 1331–42.

Yuen Chi-Lok, A. and Zhang, A. (in press) 'Effects of competition and policy changes on Chinese airport productivity: An empirical investigation', *Journal for Air Transport Management*.

Zachiaras, J. (2006) 'Exploratory spatial behaviour in real and virtual environments', *Landscape and Urban Planning*, 78(1/2): 1–13.

Zeithmal, A. and Berry, L.L. (1985) 'A conceptual model of service quality and its implications for future research', *Journal of Marketing*, Fall: 41–50.

Zeithmal, V., Parasuraman, A. and Berry, L. (1990) *Delivering Service Quality*, New York: Free Press.

Zhang, A. and Zhang, Y. (1997) 'Concession revenue and optimal airport pricing', *Transportation Research E*, 33(4): 287–96.

Zhang, W. (1997) 'China's domestic tourism: Impetus, development and trends', *Tourism Management*, 18(8): 565–72.

Zhang, Y. and Round, D. (2008) 'China's airline deregulation since 1997 and the driving forces behind the 2002 airline consolidations', *Journal of Air Transport Management*, 14(3): 130–42.

Zins, A. (2001) 'Relative attitudes and commitment in customer loyalty models: Some experiences in the commercial airline industry', *International Journal of Service Industry Management*, 12(3): 269–94.

Zinyama, L. (1989) 'Some recent trends in tourist arrivals in Zimbabwe', *Geography*, 74(1): 62–5.

Index